CHILTON

STARK COUNTY DISTRICT LIBRARY

3 1333 01105 7898

Small Engine R

W9-ALM-968

2 Hp to 12 Hp

JAC 621.434 C538sen

Chilton small engine repair

STARK COUNTY
DISTRICT LIBRARY
CANTON, OHIO 44702

DEMCO

Small Engine Repair

2 Hp to 12 Hp

Edited by
Richard J. Rivele

Chilton Book Company
Radnor, Pennsylvania

Copyright © 1993 by Chilton Book Company
All Rights Reserved
Published in Radnor, Pennsylvania 19089, by Chilton Book Company

No part of this book may be reproduced, transmitted, or stored
in any form or by any means, electronic or mechanical,
without prior written permission from the publisher

ISBN 0-8019-8323-1
Manufactured in the United States of America

1 2 3 4 5 6 7 8 9 0   2 1 0 9 8 7 6 5 4 3

SAFETY NOTICE

Proper service and repair procedures are vital to the safe, reliable operation of all motor vehicles, as well as the personal safety of those performing repairs. This manual outlines procedures for servicing and repairing vehicles using safe, effective methods. The procedures contain many NOTES, CAUTIONS and WARNINGS which should be followed along with standard safety procedures to eliminate the possibility of personal injury or improper service which could damage the vehicle or compromise its safety.

It is important to note that the repair procedures, techniques, tools and parts for servicing motor vehicles, as well as the skill and experience of the individual performing the work, vary widely. It is not possible to anticipate all of the conceivable ways or conditions under which vehicles may be serviced, or to provide cautions as to all of the possible hazards that may result. Standard and accepted safety precautions and equipment should be used when handling toxic or flammable fluids, and safety goggles or other protection should be used during cutting, grinding, chiseling, prying, or any other process that can cause material removal or projectiles.

Some procedures require the use of tools specially designed for a specific purpose. Before substituting another tool or procedure, you must be completely satisfied that neither your personal safety nor the performance of the vehicle will be endangered.

PART NUMBERS

Part numbers listed in this reference are not recommendations by Chilton for any product by brand name. They are references that can be used with interchange manuals and aftermarket supplier catalogs to locate each brand supplier's discrete part number.

ACKNOWLEDGMENTS

Chilton Book Company expresses appreciation to Briggs & Stratton Corp., Milwaukee, Wis.; Kohler Co., Kohler, Wisc.; Wisconsin Engines, Teledyne Wisconsin Motor Co., Milwaukee, Wisc.; Clinton Engines Corp., Maquoketa, Iowa; and Tecumseh Products Co., Grafton, Wis., for their generous assistance in the preparation of this book.

Contents

Chapter 11   KOHLER COMMAND 11 and 12.5 Hp

Chapter 12   KOHLER MAGNUM

Chapter 13   TECUMSEH 4-STROKE 2 THROUGH 5 Hp

Chapter 14   TECUMSEH 4-STROKE 6 THROUGH 12 Hp

1
How to Use This Book

HOW TO USE THIS BOOK

This book covers popular small, air-cooled engines of 2-12 hp.

Each Chapter contains maintenance, tune-up, repair and overhaul information procedures. Studies have shown that a properly tuned and maintained engine translates into lower operating costs, and periodic maintenance will catch minor problems before they turn into major repair bills.

A secondary purpose of this book is a reference guide for owners who want to understand their engine and/or their repair shop better. In this case, no tools at all are required. Knowing just what a particular repair job requires in parts and labor time will allow you to evaluate whether or not you're getting a fair price quote and help decipher itemized bills from a repair shop.

Before attempting any repairs or service on your engine, read through the entire procedure outlined in the appropriate Chapter. This will give you the overall view of what tools and supplies will be required.

Each operation should be approached logically and all procedures thoroughly understood before attempting any work. Some special tools that may be required can often be rented from local automotive or power equipment jobbers, or places specializing in renting tools and equipment. Check the yellow pages of your phone book.

All Chapters contain adjustments, maintenance, removal and installation procedures, and overhaul procedures. When overhaul is not considered practical, we tell you how to remove the failed part and then how to install the new or rebuilt replacement. In this way, you at least save the labor costs. Backyard overhaul of some components is just not practical, but the removal and installation procedure is often simple and well within the capabilities of the average do-it-yourselfer.

A basic mechanic's rule should be followed: all threaded fasteners (screws, nuts, and bolts) are removed by turning counterclockwise, and tightened by turning clockwise, unless otherwise noted.

Safety is always the most important rule. Constantly be aware of the dangers involved in working on or around an automobile and take proper precautions to avoid the risk of personal injury or damage to the equipment. See the section in this Chapter, Servicing Your Engine Safely, and the SAFETY NOTICE on the acknowledgment page before attempting any service procedures and pay attention to the instructions provided. There are 3 common mistakes in mechanical work:

1. Incorrect order of assembly, disassembly or adjustment. When taking something apart or putting it together, doing things in the wrong order usually just costs you extra time; however it CAN break something. Read the entire procedure before beginning disassembly. Do everything in the order in which the instructions say you should do it, even if you can't immediately see a reason for it. When you're taking apart something that is very intricate (for example, a carburetor), you might want to draw a picture of how it looks when assembled at one point in order to make sure you get everything back in its proper position. We will supply exploded views whenever possible, but sometimes the job requires more attention to detail than an illustration provides. When making adjustments (especially tune-up adjustments), do them in order. One adjustment often affects another and you cannot expect satisfactory results unless each adjustment is made only when it cannot be changed by any other.

2. Overtorquing (or undertorquing) nuts and bolts. While it is more common for

overtorquing to cause damage, undertorquing can cause a fastener to vibrate loose and cause serious damage, especially when dealing with aluminum parts. Pay attention to torque specifications and utilize a torque wrench in assembly. If a torque figure is not available, remember that, if you are using the right tool to do the job, you will probably not have to strain yourself to get a fastener tight enough. The pitch of most threads is so slight that the tension you put on the wrench will be multiplied many times in actual force on what you are tightening. A good example of how critical torque is can be seen in the case of spark plug installation, especially where you are putting the plug into an aluminum cylinder head. Too little torque can fail to crush the gasket, causing leakage of combustion gases and consequent overheating of the plug and engine parts. Too much torque can damage the threads or distort the plug, which changes the spark gap at the electrode. Since more and more manufacturers are using aluminum in their engine and chassis parts to save weight, a torque wrench should be in any serious do-it-yourselfer's tool box.

There are many commercial chemical products available for ensuring that fasteners won't come loose, even if they are not torqued just right (a very common brand is Loctite®). If you're worried about getting something together tight enough to hold, but loose enough to avoid mechanical damage during assembly, one of these products might offer substantial insurance. Read the label on the package and make sure the product is compatible with the materials, fluids, etc. involved before choosing one.

3. Crossthreading. This occurs when a part such as a bolt is screwed into a nut or casting at the wrong angle and forced, causing the threads to become damaged. Crossthreading is more likely to occur if access is difficult. It helps to clean and lubricate fasteners, and to start threading with the part to be installed going straight in, using your fingers. If you encounter resistance, unscrew the part and start over again at a different angle until it can be inserted and turned several times without much effort. Keep in mind that many parts, especially spark plugs, use tapered threads so that gentle turning will automatically bring the part you're threading to the proper angle if you don't force it or resist a change in angle. Don't put a wrench on the part until it's been turned in a couple of times by hand. If you suddenly encounter resistance and the part has not seated fully, don't force it. Pull it back out and make sure it's clean and threading properly.

Always take your time and be patient; once you have some experience, working on your piece of equipment will become an enjoyable hobby.

TOOLS AND EQUIPMENT

Naturally, without the proper tools and equipment it is impossible to properly service your engine. It would be impossible to catalog each tool that you would need to perform each or every operation in this book. It would also be unwise for the amateur to rush out and buy an expensive set of tools an the theory that he or she may need one or more of them at sometime.

The best approach is to proceed slowly, gathering together a good quality set of those tools that are used most frequently. Don't be misled by the low cost of bargain tools. It is far better to spend a little more for better quality. Forged wrenches, 6- or 12-point sockets and fine tooth ratchets are by far preferable to their less expensive counterparts. As any good mechanic can tell you, there are few worse experiences than trying to work on an engine with bad tools. Your monetary savings will be far outweighed by frustration and mangled knuckles.

Certain tools, plus a basic ability to handle tools, are required to get started.

Begin accumulating those tools that are used most frequently; those associated with routine maintenance and tune-up.

In addition to the normal assortment of screwdrivers and pliers you should have the following tools for routine maintenance jobs:

1. U.S. and metric wrenches, sockets and combination open end/box end wrenches in sizes from ¼ in. to ⅞ in. and 3mm to 22mm; and a spark plug socket ($^{13}/_{16}$ in. and/or ⅝ in.) If possible, buy various length socket drive extensions.

2. Wire spark plug gauge/adjusting tools

3. Set of feeler blades.

4. Hydrometer for checking the battery

5. A container for draining oil

6. Many rags for wiping up the inevitable mess.

In addition to the above items there are several others that are not absolutely necessary, but handy to have around. These include oil-dry (cat box litter works just as well and may be cheaper), a funnel, and the usual supply of lubricants and fluids, although these can be purchased as needed. This is a basic list for routine maintenance, but only your personal needs and desires can accurately determine your list of necessary tools.

In addition to these basic tools, there are several other tools and gauges you may find useful. These include:

1. A compression gauge. The screw-in type is slower to use, but eliminates the possibility of a faulty reading due to escaping pressure

2. A test light

3. An induction meter. This is used for determining whether or not there is current in a wire.

As a final note, you will probably find a torque wrench necessary for all but the most basic work. The beam type models are perfectly adequate, although the click (breakaway) type are more precise, and you don't have to crane your neck to see a torque reading in awkward situations. The breakaway torque wrenches are more expensive and should be recalibrated periodically.

Torque specification for each fastener will be given in the procedure in any case that a specific torque value is required. If no torque specifications are given, use the following values as a guide, based upon fastener size:

Bolts marked 6T
  6mm bolt/nut — 5-7 ft. lbs.
  8mm bolt/nut — 12-17 ft. lbs.
  10mm bolt/nut — 23-34 ft. lbs.
  12mm bolt/nut — 41-59 ft. lbs.
  14mm bolt/nut — 56-76 ft. lbs.

Bolts marked 8T
  6mm bolt/nut — 6-9 ft. lbs.
  8mm bolt/nut — 13-20 ft. lbs.
  10mm bolt/nut — 27-40 ft. lbs.
  12mm bolt/nut — 46-69 ft. lbs.
  14mm bolt/nut — 75-101 ft. lbs.

SERVICING YOUR ENGINE SAFELY

It is virtually impossible to anticipate all of the hazards involved with equipment maintenance and service but care and common sense will prevent most accidents.

The rules of safety for mechanics range from DON'T smoke around gasoline, to use the proper tool for the job. The trick to avoiding injuries is to develop safe work habits and take every possible precaution.

Do's

• Do keep a fire extinguisher and first aid kit within easy reach.

• Do wear safety glasses or goggles when cutting, drilling, grinding or prying. If you wear glasses for the sake of vision, then they should be made of hardened glass that can serve also as safety glasses, or wear safety goggles over your regular glasses.

• Do shield your eyes whenever you work around the battery. Batteries contain sulphuric acid; in case of contact with the eyes or skin, flush the area with water or a mixture of water and baking soda and get medical attention immediately.

• Do use adequate ventilation when working with any chemicals.

• Do disconnect the negative battery cable when working on anything electrical, or when work around or near the electrical system.

• Do follow manufacturer's directions whenever working with potentially hazardous materials.

• Do properly maintain your tools. Loose hammerheads, mushroomed punches and chisels, frayed or poorly grounded electrical cords, excessively worn screwdrivers, spread wrenches (open end), cracked sockets, slipping ratchets, or faulty droplight sockets can cause accidents.

• Do use the proper size and type of tool for the job being done.

• Do when possible, pull on a wrench handle rather than push on it, and adjust your stance to prevent a fall.

• Do be sure that adjustable wrenches are tightly adjusted on the nut or bolt and pulled so that the face is on the side of the fixed jaw.

• Do select a wrench or socket that fits the nut or bolt. The wrench or socket should sit straight, not cocked.

• Do strike squarely with a hammer to avoid glancing blows.

Don'ts

• Don't run an engine in a garage or anywhere else without proper ventilation--EVER! Carbon monoxide is poisonous; it is absorbed by the body 400 times faster than oxygen; it takes a long time to leave the human body and you can build up a deadly supply of it in your system by simply breathing in a little every day. You may not realize you are slowly poisoning yourself. Always use power vents, windows, fans or open the garage doors.

• Don't work around moving parts while wearing a necktie or other loose clothing. Short sleeves are much safer than long, loose sleeves. Hard-toed shoes with neoprene soles protect your toes and give a better grip on slippery surfaces. Jewelry such as watches, fancy belt buckles, beads or body adornment of any kind is not safe working around moving parts. Long hair should be hidden under a hat or cap

• Don't use pockets for toolboxes. A fall or bump can drive a screwdriver deep into your body. Even a wiping cloth hanging from the back pocket can wrap around a spinning shaft.

• Don't smoke when working around gasoline, cleaning solvent or other flammable material.

• Don't smoke when working around the battery. When the battery is being charged, it gives off explosive hydrogen gas.

• Don't use gasoline to wash your hands; there are excellent soaps available. Aside from being flammable, gasoline also removes all the natural oils from the skin so that bone dry hands will suck up oil and grease.

ENGINE OPERATION AND GENERAL INFORMATION

How an Internal Combustion Engine Develops Power

The energy source that runs an internal combustion engine is heat created by the combustion of an air/fuel mixture. The combustion process takes place within a sealed cylinder containing a piston which is able to move up and down in the cylinder. The piston is connected to a crankshaft by a connecting rod. The lower end of the rod is connected to the crankshaft at a point which is offset from the centerline of the crankshaft, allowing it to turn a large circle. This is why the piston moves up and down, and why pressure on the top of the piston eventually becomes torque, or turning force, on the crankshaft.

The sealed cylinder, or "combustion chamber" traps the air/fuel mixture. When burning takes place in a confined space such as this, the heat it produces becomes pressure which can be used mechanically to produce power. As the fuel burns and the piston goes down, the chamber becomes larger and larger, allowing for continued use of this pressure. The fact that the size of the chamber changes with the position of the piston also allows the air/fuel to be compressed, or packed into a confined space before it is burned, which has the effect of greatly increasing the amount of pressure made by the heat of burning, and makes the engine produce more power on less fuel. The variable size of the chamber also permits the engine to do its own breathing-to ex

pel burnt gases and pull in fuel and fresh air (see the description of the four events in the operating cycle of a four-stroke engine below).

As you can see from how the engine produces power, leakage from the combustion chamber will have a tremendous effect on operating efficiency. One of the most important aspects of engine overhaul work involves repair or replacement of parts so that the combustion chamber will be as tightly sealed as possible.

Four-Stroke Engines

The entire series of four events that occur in order for an engine to operate may take place in one revolution of the crankshaft or it may take two revolutions of the crankshaft. The former is termed a two-cycle engine and the latter a four-cycle engine.

The four events that must occur in order for any internal combustion engine to operate are:

Intake stroke of a four-stroke engine

Compression stroke of a four-stroke engine

Power stroke of a four-stroke engine

Exhaust stroke of a four-stroke engine

intake, compression, expansion or power, and exhaust. When all of these take place in succession, this is considered one cycle.

In a four-cycle engine, the intake portion of the cycle takes place when the piston is traveling downward, creating a vacuum within the cylinder. Just as the piston starts to travel downward, a mechanically operated valve opens, allowing the fuel/air mixture to be drawn into the cylinder.

As the piston begins to travel upward, the valve closes and the fuel/air mixture becomes trapped in the cylinder. The piston travels upward and compresses the air/fuel mixture. This is the compression part of the cycle.

Just as the piston reaches the top of its stroke and starts back down the cylinder, an electric spark ignites the air/fuel mixture and the resulting explosion and rapid expansion of the gases forces the piston downward in the cylinder. This is the expansion or power stroke of the cycle.

Just as the piston reaches the end of its downward travel on the compression stroke, another mechanically operated valve is opened. The next upward stroke of the piston forces the burned gases out the opened valve. This is the exhaust stroke.

When the piston reaches the top of the cylinder, thus ending the exhaust stroke, the exhaust valve is closed and the intake valve opened. The next downward stroke of the piston is the intake stroke that the whole series of events began with.

Two-Stroke Engines

In a two-stroke engine, intake, compression, power, and exhaust take place in one downward stroke and one upward stroke of the piston. The spark plug fires every time the piston reaches the top of each stroke, not every other stroke as in a four-stroke engine. (On some four-stroke engines, the magneto is operated by the crankshaft so that the spark plug actually fires once in every engine revolution. However, since the plug fires only into already burnt gases, this has no appreciable effect on engine operation.)

The piston in a two-cycle engine is used as a sliding valve for the cylinder intake and exhaust ports. The crankcase is used as a pump in order to slightly compress new fuel/air mixture and force it through the cylinder. In some designs, the piston also opens and closes a third port connecting the intake tube and carburetor to the crankcase. The intake and exhaust ports are both open when the piston is at the end of its downward stroke, which is called bottom dead center or BDC. Since the exhaust port is opened to the outside atmospheric pressure,

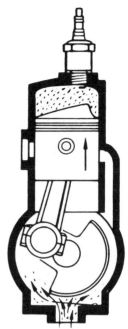

The compression stroke of a two-stroke engine; the intake port is open and the air/fuel mixture is entering the crankcase

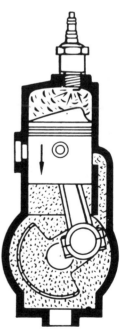

The power stroke of a two-stroke engine; the intake port is closed and, as the piston is being forced down by the expanding gases above, the air/fuel mixture in the crankcase is being compressed

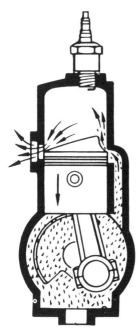

The exhaust stroke of a two-stroke engine; the piston travels past the exhaust port, thus opening it, then past the intake port, opening that. As the exhaust gases flow out, the air/fuel mixture flows in due to being under pressure in the crankcase. The next stroke of the piston is the compression stroke and the series of events starts over again

the exhaust gases, which are under a much higher pressure due to combustion, will escape to the outside through the exhaust port. After the pressure of the exhaust gases has been somewhat relieved, the piston uncovers the intake port, and a fresh charge of air/fuel is pumped through the intake port, forcing the exhaust gases out in front of it. We say that the air/fuel mixture is being pumped into the cylinder because it is under pressure caused by the downward movement of the piston. In the most common type of two-stroke engine, the air/fuel mixture is drawn through a one-way valve, known as a reed valve, and into the crankcase

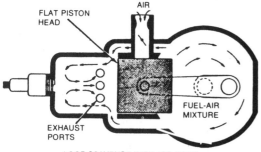

LOOP SCAVENGE WITH 3RD PORT

Some engines use a third port, which is opened and closed by the bottom of the piston, to control the admission of air/fuel mixture into the crankcase

by the vacuum caused by upward movement of the piston. When the piston reaches top dead center or TDC and starts back down, the one-way valve in the crankcase is closed by its natural spring action and the building pressure caused by the downward movement of the piston. In the three port type of engine, the upward movement of the piston creates a vacuum in the crankcase. When the skirt (bottom) of the piston uncovers the third port as the piston nears the top of its travel, the vacuum in the crankcase draws in air/fuel mixture. As the piston descends, the third port is again covered by the piston skirt, and the crankcase is sealed for compression of the mixture. The air/fuel mixture is compressed until the piston moves past the intake port, thus allowing the compressed mixture to enter the cylinder. The piston starts its upward stroke, closing off the intake port and then the exhaust port, thus sealing the cylinder. The air/fuel mixture in the cylinder is compressed and at the same time, a fresh charge of air/fuel mixture is being drawn into the crankcase. When the piston reaches TDC, a spark ignites the compressed air/fuel mixture and the resulting expansion of the gases forces the piston back down the cylinder. The piston passes the exhaust port first, allowing the exhaust gases to begin to escape. The piston travels down the cylinder a little farther and past the intake port. The fresh air/fuel mixture in the crankcase, which was compressed by the downward stroke of the piston, is forced through the intake port and the whole cycle starts over.

Fuel Systems

The fuel system in a small engine consists of a fuel supply or storage vessel, a fuel pump, various fuel lines, and the carburetor. Fuel is stored in the fuel tank and pumped from the tank into the carburetor. Most small engines do not have an actual fuel pump. The carburetor receives gasoline by gravity feed or the fuel is drawn into the carburetor by venturi vacuum. The function of the carburetor is to mix the fuel with air in the proper proportions.

TYPES OF CARBURETORS

Small engine carburetors are categorized by the way in which the fuel is delivered to the carburetor fuel inlet passage in the venturi (fuel nozzle).

Plain Tube Carburetors

Carburetors used on engines that run at a constant speed, carrying the same load all of the time, can be relatively simple in design because they are only required to mix fuel and air at a

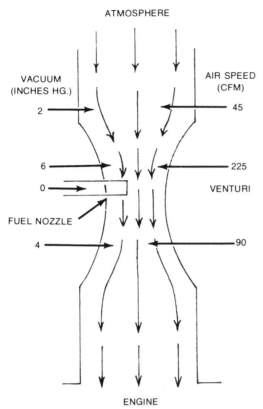

All carburetors operate on the venturi principle. The numbers represent hypothetical ratios of air speed and vacuum in relation to the venturi. Zero vacuum at the fuel nozzle is atmospheric pressure

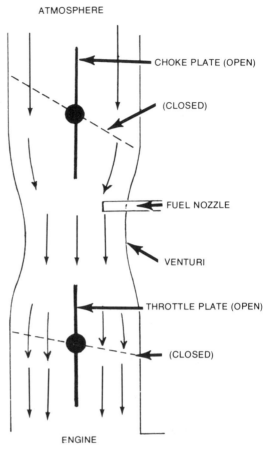

The positioning of the choke and throttle plates in relation to the position of the venturi

constant ratio. Such is the case with plain tube carburetors.

All carburetors operate on the principle that a gas will flow from a large or wide volume passage through a smaller or narrower volume passage at an increased speed and a decreased pressure over that of the larger passage. This is called the venturi principle. The narrower passage in the carburetor where this acceleration takes place is therefore called the venturi.

A fuel inlet passage is placed at the carburetor venturi. Because of the reduced pressure (vacuum) and the high speed of the air rushing past at that point in the carburetor, the fuel is drawn out of the passage and atomized with the air.

The fuel inlet passage, in most carburetors, can regulate how much fuel is allowed to pass. This is done by a needle valve which consists of a tapered rod (needle) inserted in the opening (seat), partially blocking the flow of fuel out of the opening. The needle is movable in and out of the opening and, since it is tapered at that end, it can regulate the flow of fuel.

The choke of a plain tube carburetor is locat-

ed before the venturi or on the atmospheric side. The purpose of the choke is to increase the vacuum within the carburetor during low cranking or starting speeds of the engine. During cranking speeds, there is not enough vacuum present to draw the fuel out through the inlet and into the carburetor to become mixed with the air. When the choke plate closes off the end of the carburetor open to the atmosphere, the vacuum condition in the venturi increases greatly, thus enabling the fuel to be drawn out of the opening.

In most cases the choke is manufactured with a small hole in it so that not all air is blocked off. When the engine starts, the choke is opened slightly to allow more air to pass. The choke usually is not opened all the way until the engine is warmed up and can operate on the leaner fuel/air mixture that comes into the engine when the choke is completely opened and not restricting the air flow at all. Thus, the choke also provides the richer mixtures (more fuel for the amount of air) required when the engine is cold.

Many of the chokes used on small engine carburetors are entirely automatic. In many cases, the choke is required to provide just sufficient vacuum to get the fuel moving and give rich mixture during cranking. Once the engine is running, the choke can be opened in just a few seconds without causing it to stall. It will run fairly well on a normal, lean mixture because the carburetor is close to the engine and puddling of fuel that occurs in engines with long manifolds while they are cold is no problem.

This type of choke is held shut by the pressure of a spring, and opened by the action of a diaphragm. Manifold vacuum is fed to the side of the diaphragm on which the spring is located through a small orifice. There is no vacuum when the engine is stopped, but upon starting, manifold vacuum gradually draws air out of the diaphragm chamber, and draws the diaphragm downward, against spring pressure. A rod linking the diaphragm to the choke then pulls it open.

This type of choke is also capable of keeping the mixture adequately rich during sudden increases in throttle opening; vacuum normally gets very low under these circumstances, and the choke tends to close slightly as the throttle opens, thus aiding fuel flow.

The throttle plate in a carburetor is installed on the engine side of the venturi. The purpose of the throttle plate is to regulate the flow of air/fuel mixture going into the engine. Thus the throttle plate regulates the speed and power output of an engine. By restricting the flow of air/fuel mixture going into the engine, the throttle plate is also restricting the combustion explosion and the energy created by the explosion.

These are the basic components required for any carburetor to operate on an engine. It is possible for such a carburetor to be installed on an engine and work. However, most engines operate at various speeds, under various load conditions, at different altitudes, and in a variety of temperatures. All of these variations require that the fuel/air mixture can be changed on command. In other words, the simple plain tube carburetor is not sufficient in most cases.

Suction Carburetor

Next to the plain tube carburetor, this is the simplest in design. With this type of carburetor, the fuel supply is located directly below the carburetor in a fuel tank. In fact, the carburetor and fuel tank are considered one assembly in most cases because a pipe extends from the carburetor venturi down into the fuel tank. When the engine is running, the partial vacuum in the venturi, and the relatively higher atmospheric pressure in the fuel tank, force the fuel up through the fuel pipe and into the carburetor venturi. There is a check ball located in the bottom of the pipe that prevents the fuel in the pipe from draining back into the fuel tank when the engine is shut down. In most engines there is a screen located at the end of the pipe to prevent dirt from entering and blocking the fuel nozzle.

Some suction carburetors are designed with an extra fuel inlet passage for when the engine is idling. This extra passage would be located on the engine side of the throttle plate. Since the vacuum condition in front of an idling engine might not be enough for the fuel to be drawn out at that point, the extra passage is installed

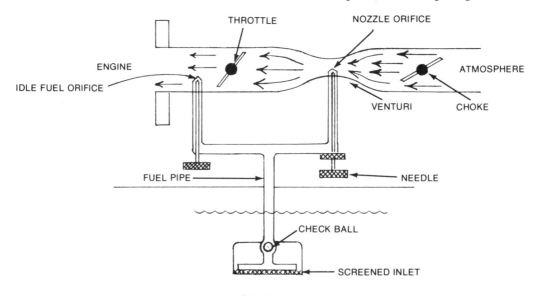

Diagram of a suction type carburetor

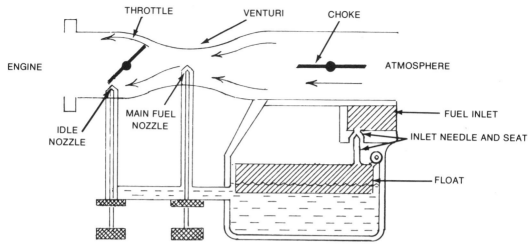

Diagram of a float type carburetor

behind the throttle plate where the vacuum is great enough to draw the fuel out. This extra fuel inlet passage would also have a regulating needle as does the main inlet.

Float Type Carburetors

The fuel tank used with float type carburetors is usually located on top of, or at least above, the level of the carburetor. Fuel is fed to the carburetor by gravity. If the fuel tank is located below the level of the carburetor, a fuel pump is employed to pump fuel to the carburetor. Fuel enters the carburetor through a valve and into a float bowl and, as it fills the bowl, a float rises on the surface of the fuel. The float is connected to the inlet valve and, as the level rises, a needle is inserted into the inlet valve and the flow coming into the float bowl is checked. As the fuel is drawn into the main fuel nozzle in the venturi and the level in the bowl drops, the float drops and the needle opens the valve allowing more fuel to run into the bowl.

Although there are many different float carburetors, all operate in this manner.

Diaphragm Type Carburetors

Fuel is delivered to the diaphragm type carburetor in the same manner as to the float type carburetor.

A flexible diaphragm operates the fuel inlet

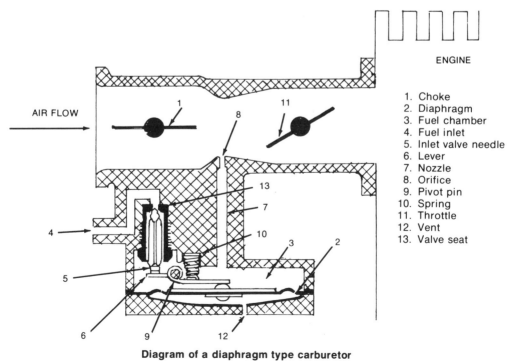

1. Choke
2. Diaphragm
3. Fuel chamber
4. Fuel inlet
5. Inlet valve needle
6. Lever
7. Nozzle
8. Orifice
9. Pivot pin
10. Spring
11. Throttle
12. Vent
13. Valve seat

Diagram of a diaphragm type carburetor

valve, hence the description "diaphragm carburetor."

Atmospheric pressure is maintained on the under side of the diaphragm by a vent hole in the bottom of the carburetor. The other side of the diaphragm is acted upon by the varying vacuum conditions in the carburetor.

When the vacuum condition in the carburetor is increased by the opening of the throttle plate, and the demand for an increased flow of fuel, the center diaphragm is bellowed upward by the increased vacuum. The center of the diaphragm is connected by a lever to the fuel inlet valve needle. The needle is dropped down away from the inlet valve and fuel is allowed to drop in. When the throttle plate is closed and the need for fuel is reduced, the vacuum condition also decreases and the diaphragm is returned by a spring located on the atmospheric side to its normal flattened position. This closes the fuel inlet valve by raising the needle up into position against its seat.

This type of carburetor also has an idle orifice positioned behind the throttle plate to compensate for the low vacuum condition in front of the throttle plate during idle speeds.

Some diaphragm type carburetors incorporate an integral fuel pump. It consists of a second diaphragm having fuel on one side, and exposed to the pressure fluctuations of the crankcase or the intake manifold on the other side. The vibration of this diaphragm, in conjunction with the action of check valves in the passages leading to and from the fuel side of the diaphragm chamber work together to pump fuel, under pressure, to the fuel inlet valve.

REED VALVES

Reed valves are used on those two stroke engines in which the intake tube leading from the

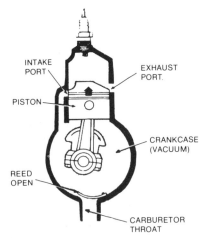

INTAKE PORT

EXHAUST PORT.

PISTON

CRANKCASE (VACUUM)

REED OPEN

CARBURETOR THROAT

The reed valve in the open position (piston moving upward)

carburetor empties right into the crankcase. The reed serves as a kind of check valve, so that air/fuel cannot be forced back out of the crankcase. When the piston begins to rise, a slight vacuum is created under it, sucking the reed open against its spring pressure, as shown in the illustration. When the piston reaches the top of its travel, and the pressure in the crankcase gets near to outside (atmospheric) pressure, the valve's spring action pulls it flat against the intake opening (the reed is really a kind of flat spring). Then, as the piston descends, the build-up in pressure in the crankcase, in combination with the slight amount of oil that gets onto the reed, seals the intake very tightly, forcing practically the full charge into the cylinder.

Ignition Systems

The function of an ignition system is to provide the electrical spark that ignites the air/fuel mixture in the cylinder at precisely the correct time.

There are three types of ignition systems used on small engines: either a battery ignition, a magneto ignition or a breakerless ignition system.

The battery ignition, as the name implies, gets its initial electrical charge from a storage battery. The magneto ignition actually generates its own electricity, thus eliminating the need for a battery as far as ignition is concerned.

Battery and magneto ignition systems are similar in one respect. Both systems take a relatively small amount of voltage, such as 12 volts in the case of a battery ignition, then step up that to an extremely high voltage, in some systems as high as 20,000 volts.

The breakerless ignition system operates on the same general principle as the magneto system but does not use breaker points and conventional ignition condenser to time the spark. A trigger module containing solid state electronics performs the same function as the breaker points.

BASIC BATTERY IGNITION SYSTEM

Battery ignition systems are found mostly on larger one cylinder engines, such as those installed on lawn tractors, larger pumps and generators.

As previously stated, the initial electrical charge comes from a storage battery. The entire ignition system is grounded so that current will flow from the battery throughout the primary circuit.

The ignition system is composed of two segments, the primary circuit and the secondary circuit. Current from the battery flows through

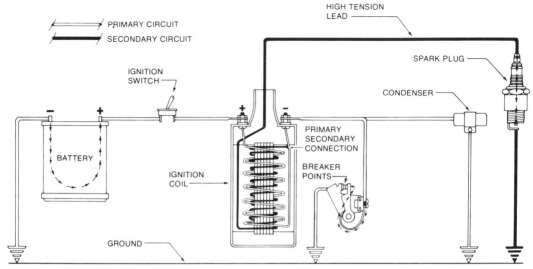

PRIMARY CIRCUIT
SECONDARY CIRCUIT

HIGH TENSION LEAD
SPARK PLUG
IGNITION SWITCH
CONDENSER
BATTERY
IGNITION COIL
PRIMARY SECONDARY CONNECTION
BREAKER POINTS
GROUND

Diagram of a battery type ignition for a single cylinder engine

the primary circuit and the current that fires the spark plug flows through the secondary circuit. The current in the primary circuit actually creates the secondary current magnetically.

When the engine is running, current flows from the battery, through the breaker points, and on to the ignition coil. The current then flows through the primary windings of the coil which are wrapped around a soft iron core and grounded. The primary current flowing through these primary windings causes a magnetic field to be created around the soft iron core of the coil. At precisely the right time, the breaker points open and break the primary circuit, cutting off the flow of current coming from the battery. This causes the magnetic field in the coil to collapse toward the center of the soft iron core. As the field collapses, the lines of force of the magnetic field must pass through the secondary windings of the coil. These windings are also wrapped around the soft iron core of the coil, except that there are many more windings and the wire is thinner than those of the primary windings. When the magnetic field collapses and passes through the secondary windings, current flow is induced in the secondary circuit which is grounded at the spark plug. Because the wire of the secondary windings is smaller and there are many more coils around the soft iron core, the current created or induced in the secondary side of the ignition is of much greater voltage than the primary side. This current in the secondary circuit flows toward the grounded end of the circuit which is the spark plug. The current flows down the center of the spark plug to the center electrode. In order to reach the ground, it must jump across a gap to the grounded electrode. When it does, a spark is created and it is this spark that ignites the air/fuel mixture in the cylinder.

MAGNETO TYPE IGNITION SYSTEMS

Magneto ignition systems create the initial primary circuit current, thereby eliminating the need for ignition batteries.

Flywheel Type Magnetos

On this type of magneto, the flywheel of the engine carries the permanent magnets that are used to create the primary current.

The magnets are arranged so that about $\frac{1}{3}$ of the area enclosed by the flywheel is a magnetic field. In the center of the flywheel is a three pronged coil, the three prongs representing the core. The center prong has the primary and secondary windings and is set up just like a battery ignition coil.

As the magnets in the flywheel pass the two outside prongs, the primary current is induced in the coil and a magnetic field is set up around the center prong. At the point when the primary current is at its strongest which is also the time when the secondary current is needed at the spark plug, the breaker points interrupt the primary current, causing the magnetic field to collapse through the secondary windings. This induces the secondary current which flows to the grounded spark plug.

Unit Type Magnetos

Unit type magnetos operate in the same way as flywheel magnetos.

Permanent magnets are rotated through a mechanical connection to the crankshaft of the engine. The rotating magnets create the primary current which is routed through the breaker

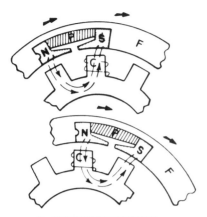

P—PERMANENT MAGNET
N—NORTH POLE SHOE
S—SOUTH POLE SHOE
F—FLYWHEEL
C—LAMINATED COIL CORE

A cutaway view of a flywheel used in a flywheel magneto. The magnets are arranged so that there is a magnetic field covering about ⅓ of the area enclosed by the flywheel. On flywheel magnetos where the coil and core are mounted on the outside of the flywheel, the magnets would be arranged on the outside of the flywheel

points and on to windings around a soft iron core which is also wrapped by the secondary windings. At precisely the right moment, the points interrupt the primary current, causing the magnetic field to collapse through the sec-

ondary windings and inducing the secondary current to the spark plug.

Because the magnets in the unit magneto are driven by the crankshaft of the engine through a gear mechanism, starting is a problem. At starting speeds, the magnets in the magneto cannot be rotated fast enough to create a primary current. To overcome this difficulty, unit magnetos have an impulse coupling on their shaft which drives the magnets. When the engine is turned over at starting speed, a catch engages a coil spring that is wound up in much the same manner as those that propel wind-up toys. As the shaft rotates further, it releases the spring. The spring unwinds rapidly, spinning the magnets fast enough to cause the primary current to be induced in the primary circuit. When the engine starts to run, centrifugal force keeps the catch in the impulse coupling from engaging the wind-up spring.

BREAKERLESS IGNITION

The breakerless system consists of four major components:

- Ignition winding on alternator stator
- Trigger module
- Ignition coil assembly
- Flywheel-mounted trigger

The ignition winding is separate from other windings on the alternator stator. It functions like the magneto winding. The trigger module contains three diodes, a resistor, a sensing coil

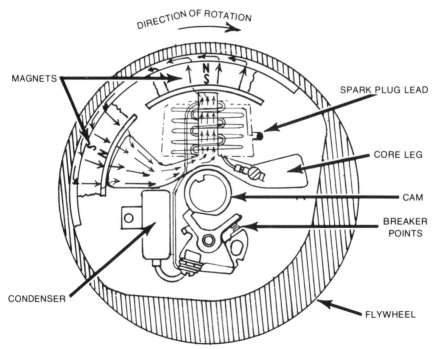

The three legs of the core pass through the magnetic field created by the rotating magnets. In this position, the lines of force are concentrated in the left and center core legs and are interlocking the coil windings

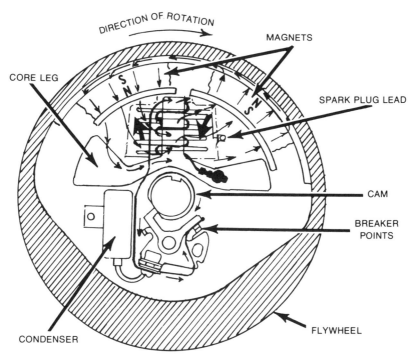

The flywheel has turned to the point where the lines of force of the permanent magnets are being withdrawn from the left and center cores and are being attracted by the center and right cores. Since the center core is both drawing and attracting the lines of force, the lines are cutting up one side and down the other (indicated by the heavy black arrows). The breaker points are now closed and a current is now induced in the primary circuit by the lines of force cutting up and down the center core leg

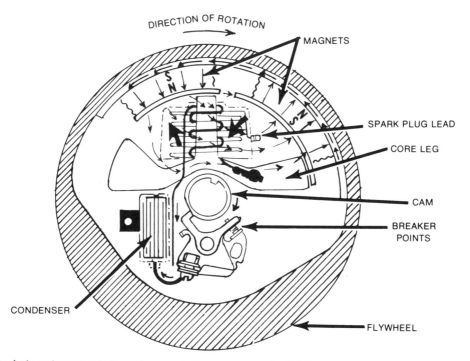

With the induced current in the primary windings, a magnetic field is created around the center core leg (coil). When the field is created around the center leg, the points are opened and the condenser begins to absorb the reverse flow of current

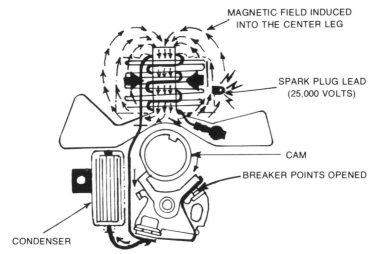

MAGNETIC FIELD INDUCED
INTO THE CENTER LEG

SPARK PLUG LEAD
(25,000 VOLTS)

CAM

BREAKER POINTS OPENED

CONDENSER

When the breaker points are opened, the induced magnetic field collapses. The collapsing of the magnetic field induces the secondary current into secondary windings leading to the spark plug

and magnet and an SCR, a sort of electronic switch. The ignition coil assembly includes a capacitor and a pulse transformer that serves the same purpose as the ignition coil in other systems. The flywheel has a projection that triggers ignition.

In some applications a 22 ohm, ½ watt resistor has been placed between the key switch and the ignition coil. This has been added to prevent current feedback through a dirty or wet switch. This feedback, if not held in check by a resistor, can damage the trigger unit.

Lubrication Systems
FOUR-STROKE ENGINES

Most small four stroke engines are lubricated by the splash system. All vital moving parts are splashed with lubricating oil that is stored in the crankcase. The connecting rod bearing gap usually has an arm extending down into the area in which the oil lies. As the crankshaft turns, the arm, commonly called a dipper, splashes oil up onto the cylinder walls, crankshaft bearings and camshaft bearings. In some

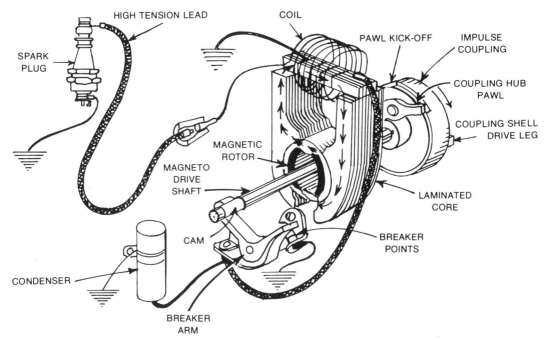

HIGH TENSION LEAD

COIL

PAWL KICK-OFF

IMPULSE
COUPLING

SPARK
PLUG

COUPLING HUB
PAWL

COUPLING SHELL
DRIVE LEG

MAGNETIC
ROTOR

MAGNETO
DRIVE
SHAFT

LAMINATED
CORE

CAM

BREAKER
POINTS

CONDENSER

BREAKER
ARM

Diagram for a unit type magneto for a single cylinder engine

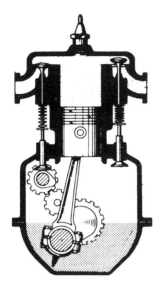

Lubrication of a four-stroke engine

cases, the connecting rod bearing cap screws are locked in place by lock plates which double as oil dippers. When the lock plate's tabs are bent up beside the cap screws, they extend a little past the tops of the screws and, when they enter the oil, they provide a sufficient splash to lubricate the engine.

In larger four stroke engines, a pressure system is used to lubricate the engine. This type of lubrication system pumps the oil through special passages in the block and to the components to be lubricated. In some cases, the camshaft and crankshaft have their center drilled so that oil can be pumped through the center and to the bearing journals. Most oil pumps in small engines are gear types.

In addition to lubricating the engine, oil in four stroke engines has other important functions. One of those additional functions is to help cool the engine. The oil actually absorbs heat from high temperature areas and dissipates it throughout other parts of the engine that are not directly exposed to the very high temperatures of combustion.

Oil in the crankcase also functions as a sealer. It helps to seal off the combustion chamber (top of the piston) from the crankcase, thus maintaining compression which is vital to satisfactory engine operation, while at the same time lubricating the cylinder walls and piston rings.

Engine oil also keeps harmful bits of dust, metal, carbon, or any other material that might be present in the crankcase, in suspension. This keeps potentially harmful abrasives away from vital moving parts.

Most manufacturers recommend a good grade, medium weight detergent oil for their

engines. The detergent properties of engine oil do not mean that the oil is capable of cleaning away dirt or sludge deposits already present in the engine. It means that the oil will help fight the formation of such deposits. In other words, the oil keeps the dirt in suspension.

A certain amount of combustion leaks past the piston rings and into the crankcase. Raw gas, carbon, products of combustion, and other undesirable material still manage to make their way into the lubricating oil. The oil becomes diluted by the gas and loses its cooling properties. When it is filled with abrasives, it loses its detergent properties due to chemical reactions, constant heat, and pollutants. The oil can then actually become harmful to the engine. Thus, one can see the need for keeping oil as clean as possible by changing it frequently.

TWO-STROKE ENGINES

Since the two-stroke engine uses its crankcase to compress the air/fuel mixture so that it can be forced up into the combustion chamber, it cannot also be used as an oil sump. The oil would be splashed around and forced up into the combustion chamber, resulting in the loss of great amounts of lubricating oil while at the same time "contaminating" the air/fuel mixture. In fact the air/fuel mixture would be so filled with oil that it would not ignite.

A two stroke engine is lubricated by mixing the lubricating oil in with the fuel. A mixture of fuel and lubricating oil is sucked into the crankcase and, while it is being compressed by the downward movement of the piston, enough oil attaches itself to the moving parts of the engine to sufficiently lubricate the engine. The rest of the oil is burned along with the fuel/air mixture. As can well be imagined, the mixture ratio of fuel and oil is critical to a two stroke engine. Too much oil will foul the spark plug and too little oil will not lubricate the engine sufficiently, causing excessive wear and possibly engine seizure. Follow the manufacturer's recommenda-

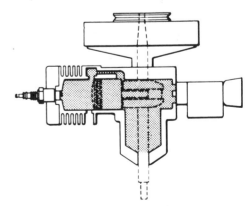

Lubrication of a two-stroke engine

tions closely. Most recommend that detergent oils not be used in two-stroke engines.

Governors

The governor is a control that opens and closes the engine throttle to maintain its speed when the load on the engine changes. Consider an engine which is operating a generator. The generator must operate within a very narrow speed range in order to provide the stable output current electrical appliances require. Yet, as appliances in the circuit are turned on and off, the load on the generator changes, which tends to either allow the engine to speed up or force it to slow down.

The governor measures engine speed and responds accordingly. As the speed drops, the throttle is opened. As speed increases the throttle is closed. The governor has a "speed droop," which means that it does not try to keep the engine at exactly the same speed, but allows a gradual drop in speed as load increases. If a governor has a speed droop of 100 rpm, and is set so that the engine runs at 3650 rpm with no load, loading the engine will cause the throttle to be opened to about the half-way point at 3600 rpm, and all the way at 3550 rpm.

The governor is basically just a spring that pulls the throttle open while some other force, which varies with engine speed, tries to close it. The simplest method of providing the closing force is the air vane. The vane is hinged at the leading edge. When it turns on the hinge, it closes the throttle through a simple wire link. The vane is housed inside the cooling system, directly in the path of cooling air. When engine speed increases, air pressure on the vane increases. At a certain speed, the force on the vane is great enough to overcome the tension of the spring and begin stretching the spring, closing the throttle. The point at which the spring has stretched enough to nearly close the throttle, and keep the engine speed steady without any load, is somewhat above the point where the vane just begins to stretch the spring. This range is the speed droop. It accounts for the fact that as load is applied to an engine, it finds a slightly lower speed at which it operates.

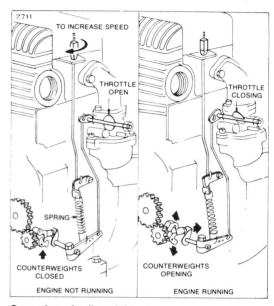

Operation of a flyweight governor

The flyweight type governor works very similarly. Here, the increasing closing force comes from hinged weights which spin in a circle, driven through gearing from the engine's crankshaft. As engine speed increases, centrifugal force makes the weights turn outward on their hinges and force the throttle closed via a collar which the bottoms of the weights work against.

The spring and flyweights or wind vane are connected via a lever which contains various holes in which the end of the spring can be installed. If the governor is too sensitive (speed droop too small), it will hunt back and forth, causing the throttle to jump violently from full open to idle position and back. If the governor is not sensitive enough (speed drop too great), the engine will slow excessively before it adjusts to the load. The spring is moved from hole to hole in order to change this sensitivity. If the spring is hooked near the shaft the lever turns on, a small change in force from the flyweights or air vane will stretch the spring a great deal, making the governor very sensitive. If the spring is hooked to a hole farther away from the pivot point of the lever, a large change in engine speed will be required to stretch it, making the governor slow to respond. The governor speed setting is changed by simply stretching the spring — pulling the end opposite the point where it fits into the lever away from the lever, utilizing any of various kinds of mechanical linkages.

Cooling Systems

Most small engines are cooled directly by the outside air because this type of system is much

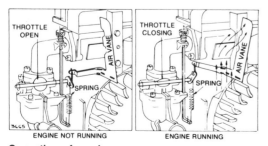

Operation of an air vane governor

less expensive to manufacture, is more easily maintained and repaired, and; if the engine is operating correctly, is more reliable. This type of cooling also saves engine weight, and this is an important side benefit, as many small engines are used to operate hand carried or hand propelled machinery.

Air is a much less efficient coolant than water. It carries much less heat, so that a given volume of air will rise to a very high temperature without actually carrying away very much heat. And, it readily forms stagnant areas around solid objects. Water carries a lot of heat without much temperature rise; it grips tightly to whatever metal object it is cooling, and can easily be kept in uniform motion. For these reasons, air cooled engines are not as tolerant of inefficient, heat producing operation. They must be kept running at peak efficiency if maximum component life is to be realized.

The biggest key to making air cooling work is finning. The parts of the cylinder and cylinder head which are exposed to burning gases inside are cast in such a way as to very greatly increase the metal surface exposed to air. At a number of points, the metal of a cylinder, for example, is forced outward from the main structure into a thin sheet or fin that may increase the surface available to air for cooling as much as ten times. While the fins at first might seem to represent excess weight, they actually form an integral portion of the structure of the engine, increasing its rigidity, and decreasing the thickness required in the main structure. While the outer ends of the fins seem to be very far from the source of the heat they in fact carry lots of heat to the cooling air because metal parts are excellent heat conductors, moving energy from hot to cool portions in a process that is a little like the flow of electricity.

Since the air heats fast and can easily become

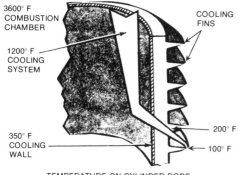

TEMPERATURE ON CYLINDER BORE

3600° F COMBUSTION CHAMBER
1200° F COOLING SYSTEM
350° F COOLING WALL
COOLING FINS
200° F
100° F

The illustration shows how, as the one-third of energy handled by the engine passes through the cylinder walls and fins, the temperature of the metal drops from 350°F on the cylinder wall to only 100°F at the tips of the fins

stagnant, forming a blanket near the metal, the second secret of air cooling is high velocity. The air must be guided in a precise manner around every part of the engine coming into contact with the burning fuel. This is done by shrouding the outer edges of the fins where necessary with light metal ducts. Use of a very powerful, centrifugal fan which slings the air outward and through the engine (or draws the air through the engine at high speed) ensures that there will be enough air moving along all the hot parts to break up any stagnant pockets and prevent any of the air from being there long enough to reach excessively high temperatures.

Since air cooling is more sensitive than conventional water cooling systems, always observe the following precautions when operating any air-cooled engine:

1. You have to have a sharper eye with air cooled engines. Watch for sluggish operation and excessive oil consumption that may mean things are getting too hot.

2. Never overload the engine. If the engine runs full throttle below governed rpm, it will be running short of cooling air, and will usually overheat.

3. Use oil of the proper viscosity. Too low a viscosity (or even very dirty oil) will cause excess friction and overheating.

4. Keep all cooling system ducts, shrouds, or seals in top shape — replace any that become loose or even dented. Replace parts whose fins are broken off.

5. Keep fins clean of dust, oil and debris.

6. Keep the cooling air blower clean, and watch carefully for even partial clogging of the air intake screen. If any of the blower's blades break off, replace the blower or flywheel.

7. Some air cooled engines use thermostatically or throttle controlled air vane to restrict cooling air at low temperatures or under light loads; make sure it works freely and opens when it's supposed to.

8. Keep the engine in good tune. Lean fuel mixtures, late ignition timing, engine knock, or any other combustion problem will severely overheat the engine.

Battery

FLUID LEVEL (EXCEPT MAINTENANCE FREE BATTERIES)

Check the battery electrolyte level at least once a month, or more often in hot weather or during periods of extended operation. The level can be checked through the case on translucent polypropylene batteries; the cell caps must be removed on other models. The electrolyte level in each cell should be kept filled to the split ring inside, or the line marked on the outside of the case.

If the level is low, add only distilled water, or colorless, odorless drinking water, through the opening until the level is correct. Each cell is completely separate from the others, so each must be checked and filled individually.

If water is added in freezing weather, the engine should be operated to allow the water to mix with the electrolyte. Otherwise, the battery could freeze.

SPECIFIC GRAVITY (EXCEPT MAINTENANCE FREE BATTERIES)

At least once a year, check the specific gravity of the battery. It should be between 1.20 and 1.26 at room temperature.

The specific gravity can be checked with the use of an hydrometer, an inexpensive instrument available from many sources, including auto parts stores. The hydrometer has a squeeze bulb at one end and nozzle at the other. Battery electrolyte is sucked into the hydrometer until the float is lifted from its seat. The specific gravity is then read by noting the position of the float. Generally, if after charging, the specific gravity between any two cells varies more than 50 points (0.050), the battery is bad and should be replaced.

It is not possible to check the specific gravity in this manner on sealed (maintenance free) batteries. Instead, the indicator built into the top of the case must be relied on to display any signs of battery deterioration.

Cables and Clamps

Once a year, the battery terminals and the cable clamps should be cleaned.

1. Loosen the clamps and remove the cables, negative cable first. On batteries with posts on top, the use of a puller specially made for the purpose is recommended. These are inexpensive, and available in auto parts stores.

2. Clean the cable clamps and the battery terminal with a wire brush, until all corrosion, grease, etc. is removed and the metal is shiny. It is especially important to clean the inside of the clamp thoroughly, since a small deposit of foreign material or oxidation there will prevent a sound electrical connection and inhibit either starting or charging. Special tools are available for cleaning these parts, one type for conventional batteries and another type for side terminal batteries.

3. Before installing the cables, loosen the battery hold-down clamp or strap, remove the battery and check the battery tray. Clear it of any debris, and check it for soundness. Rust should be wire brushed away, and the metal given a coat of anti-rust paint. Replace the battery and tighten the hold-down clamp or strap securely, but be careful not to overtighten, which will crack the battery case.

4. After the clamps and terminals are clean, install the cables, positive cable first; do not hammer on the clamps to install. Tighten the clamps securely, but do not distort them. Give the clamps and terminals a thin external coat of grease after installation, to retard corrosion.

5. Check the cables at the same time that the terminals are cleaned. If the cable insulation is cracked or broken, or if the ends are frayed, the cable should be replaced with a new cable of the same length and gauge.

Starting Systems
ELECTRIC STARTERS

Many small engines utilize direct current electric motors for starting purposes. These are run off a standard battery, and the entire system is quite similar to ordinary automotive equipment of this type, except for its smaller size. Direct current motors consist of a stationary coil of wire which is mounted on the inside of the housing, and a rotating coil, which is mounted on the shaft, and is surrounded by the "stator," or stationary coil. Direct current from the battery passes through both coils in series, being carried to the "armature" or rotating coil through brushes. The brushes are mounted inside the housing and rub against commutator rings, which spin with the rotor shaft. The brushes are sprung against the rings so they stay in constant contact. The most common problems with these motors occur when the brushes wear and lose their spring tension.

Some starter motors turn the engine over by engaging a pinion — a gear on the end of the shaft — with a toothed flywheel. Some starter pinions are moved forward into mesh with the flywheel through the action of a magnetic solenoid, while others employ the Bendix drive. The Bendix type pinion spins forward, against the tension of a spring, via the action of spiral cut grooves in the armature shaft. When the engine starts, the pinion is spun back toward the starter, and then held by the spring. In the solenoid design, an overrunning clutch allows the pinion

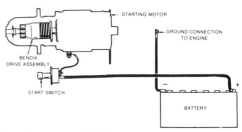

Electric starter with Bendix type engagement

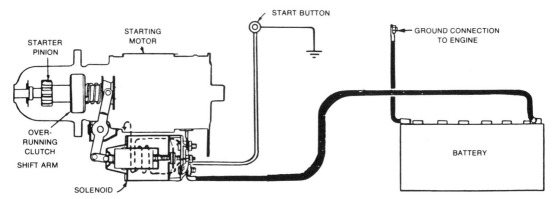

Electric starter with solenoid type engagement

to spin faster than the starter armature, thus keeping the engine from over-speeding it as it starts. When operating engines with this type of drive, allow the starter to disengage as soon as the engine fires to avoid overheating the overrunning clutch. In both types, but especially the Bendix type, poor engagement may result from poor lubrication of the spiral grooves which guide the pinion along the armature shaft.

Some electric starters drive through belts and double as generators when the engine starts. This design incorporates a relay that switches the polarity (direction of current flow) through the unit when the engine comes up to speed. Because of the large amount of torque required to turn the engine over, it is important to keep the drive belt under proper tension, and to replace it if it becomes glazed (which can cause it to slip).

RECOIL STARTERS

Recoil starters employ a rope or cable wound around a pulley, but automatically rewind the rope when it is released. The rewind force is provided by a large clock type spring which connects the pulley to the engine housing. When the rope is pulled, a cam action engages dogs which cause the engine flywheel to turn with the pulley. When the engine starts, its motion disengages the dogs.

When working on recoil starters, it is absolutely necessary to completely release the tension of the spring before disassembling the unit. If spring tension is released suddenly or unexpectedly, the force released is tremendous, and is very likely to cause personal injury.

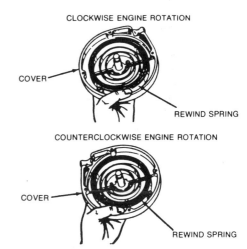

The illustration shows how the rewind spring is mounted inside the cover on one popular type of recoil starter

2

Routine Care, Maintenance, Storage and Operating Precautions

ROUTINE CARE, MAINTENANCE, STORAGE AND OPERATING PRECAUTIONS

Operating Precautions

GENERAL

1. Before starting the engine, make sure it is full of the proper grade of lubricating oil. Some sort of record of the viscosity of the oil in use should be kept so that the proper grade may be added when necessary and the oil may be changed to keep the viscosity in conformance with recommendations for the outside air temperature range that is prevalent. If the engine is run in hot weather with an oil of too low a viscosity in the crankcase, very serious damage can result. The same sort of damage (from overheating) can occur if the oil level is too low. Remember that all engines must consume some oil to run properly and that, even if the engine is in continuous service, it should be stopped every few hours for an oil level check, and the crankcase refilled.

In the case of 2–stroke engines, a recommended 2–stroke oil must be used, and it must be mixed in the proportions recommended for that engine by the manufacturer. If several 2–strokes using different fuel mixes are in use at the same location, each fuel container should be marked so that only the mix recommended for each engine is used in it. Do not simply use a pre-mixed batch of fuel — there is no standard mix. Make sure what you're using is in the exact proportion recommended by the manufacturer. Also, fuel and oil must be uniformly mixed. Usually, this is done by filling the container about 25% of the way with gas, pouring in the oil, and then completing the filling job. After this, the container should be shaken vigorously with the cap applied tightly to complete the mixing process. When using fuel that has been setting for several weeks, shake up the can

before refilling the engine fuel tank to ensure uniform mixing.

2. Check that all cooling system air inlets are clear before starting the engine, and check occasionally to make sure nothing has clogged the air intake, especially if a screen is used. Check the condition of fins, fan blades, and thermostatic airflow controls as described above in the description of air cooling systems, periodically.

3. Watch the engine during operation to ensure it is running smoothly at governed speed. If operation is sluggish, stop it immediately and check for possible overloading, overheating, or lack of oil or two stroke lubrication. If the engine lacks power and overheats, check fuel air mixture adjustments (especially on 2–stroke engines) and ignition timing.

4. Check for exhaust smoke during operation. If the engine smokes, check first for excessive oil consumption. If this is not due to running too hot or with the crankcase too full, the crankcase breather or engine must be repaired. Smoke can also occur due to a very rich mixture. If necessary, service the air cleaner and check for any restrictions in the air intake. Make sure the choke is fully opened if it is a manual design, and that it is opening properly if it is an automatic design. Adjust the carburetor mixture, if necessary. Smoke may also accompany severe engine knock due to very advanced ignition timing. Check the timing if there is knock.

5. Make sure to use only clean, fresh fuel. Fuel can begin deteriorating only a month after it is purchased. Fuel containing water or rust or other dirt should be discarded. Use leaded or unleaded fuel as per manufacturer's recommendations. Make sure the fuel also meets octane requirements.

6. Set the throttle only slightly above idle in starting (unless this conflicts with specific recommendations for starting), and idle the engine for several minutes before putting it to work.

This will allow oil to work. This will allow oil to become thin enough to reach all moving parts of the engine before they begin carrying too much load. It's also a good idea to idle the engine for a minute or two before shutdown, to cool the hottest parts more gradually.

7. Make sure the engine remains tightly mounted, as vibration can severely damage the engine or other parts, or cause potentially dangerous mechanical damage.

SAFETY PRECAUTIONS

1. Never refuel the engine unless it is stopped. Hot exhaust system parts or an electrical spark could ignite the fuel. Also, avoid spillage of fuel, especially when the engine is hot. If fuel spills, make sure it is completely removed before starting the engine. Check the engine occasionally for fuel leaks and repair them immediately. Also, keep ignition high tension wiring in top shape. Brittle insulation can crack, causing a spark which could ignite spilled fuel.

2. Keep all sources of ignition away from batteries, especially when they are being rapidly charged or caps are off. When installing jumper cables between batteries, remove caps and place a rag over open vent holes. Make positive connections first (make sure you connect positive to positive); make negative connections by first connecting the cable to the negative side of the good battery, and making the final connection to a bare spot on the frame of the piece of equipment with the dead battery.

3. Be careful not to come in contact with output terminals on an electric generator, which are often located externally. Remember that metal tools are excellent conductors, and that they too must be kept away from electrical terminals. Even if you do not become exposed to electrical shock via tools, they can serve as a conductor and become hot enough to cause serious burns. This can happen if they touch positive and negative terminals of a battery.

Many electric generators are used only in case of a failure in commercial power. In these cases, they are often connected into a circuit through a transfer switch. Remember that the transfer switch is energized even when the generator is not running. Remember, too, that the output terminals of a generator are hot once the generator is running and electrically excited – it does not need to be carrying a load.

4. Make sure that exhaust gases are properly vented. If you are working near an engine which is enclosed, leaks in the exhaust system can prove dangerous even when the bulk of the exhaust is being carried to the outside air.

5. If your small engine is utilized in a marine engine compartment, remember that the compartment must be thoroughly aired out before starting the engine, or explosion of accumulated fumes may result.

6. Remember that many pieces of equipment driven by small engines are too heavy to be safely carried by a single person. Often, even though the total weight may be within reasonable limits, you may strain yourself because of the difficulty of handling the unit's bulk. Get help!

7. Keep the operating area clean. It should be wiped clean of fluids which could catch fire, and kept free of debris which might be drawn into a fan or blower and thrown out at high speed. This, of course, includes removing debris from a lawn which is to be moved with a rotary mower or blown clean by a rotary blower.

8. When working on any engine driven accessory, disconnect the spark plug wire to avoid possible accidental starting of the motor if it should be turned over.

9. Keep all safety guards tightly in place, and replace them should they become damaged. Always be fully aware of all moving parts and the possibility of coming into contact with them even if guards are in place.

10. Keep governors in good operating condition, and do not reset for a speed higher than the recommendations of the manufacturer of the equipment.

11. Periodically tighten mounting bolts of both the engine and any machinery driven off it, especially that which turns at crankshaft rpm, such as rotary blades.

HOT AND COLD WEATHER OPERATION

There are a few things that must be done when a small engine is to be operated in hot or cold weather, that is, when temperatures are either below 30°F (−1°C), or above 75°F (24°C).

Hot Weather

1. Keep the cooling fins of the engine block clean and free of all obstructions. Remove all dirt, built up oil and grease, flaking paint and grass.

2. Air should be able to flow to and from the engine with no obstructions. Keep all fairing and cover openings free from obstructions.

3. During hot weather service, heavier weight oil should be used in the crankcase. Follow the manufacturer's recommendations as to the heaviest weight oil allowed in the crankcase.

4. Check the oil level each time the fuel tank is filled. An engine will use more oil in extremely hot weather.

5. Check the battery water level more frequently since, in hot weather, the water in the battery will evaporate more quickly.

6. Be on the lookout for vapor lock, which occurs within the carburetor.

7. Use regular grade gasoline rather than premium.

8. Use unleaded gasoline if possible.

9. The most important thing to remember is to keep the engine as clean as possible. Blow it off with compressed air or wash it as often as possible.

WARNING: *Wash the engine only after it has had sufficient time to cool down to ambient temperatures. Avoid getting water in or even near the carburetor intake opening.*

Cold Weather

1. A lightweight oil should be installed in the crankcase when operating in cold weather. Consult the manufacturer's recommendations.

2. If the engine is filled with summer weight oil, the engine should be moved to a warm — above 60°F (16°C) — location and allowed to reach ambient temperature before starting. This is because a heavy summer weight oil will be even thicker at cold temperatures. So thick, in fact, that it will be unable to sufficiently lubricate the engine when it is first started and running. Damage could occur due to lack of lubrication.

3. Change the oil only after the engine has been operated long enough for operating temperatures to have been reached. Change the oil while the engine is still hot.

4. Use fresh gasoline. Fill the gas tank daily to prevent the formation of condensation in the tank and fuel lines.

5. Keep the battery in a fully charged condition, since cold weather infringes upon a battery's maximum current output capabilities.

6. If the engine is run only for short periods of time, have the battery charged every so often to ensure maximum power output when it is needed most.

Routine Maintenance

Care of a small engine is divided into the following five categories: lubrication; filter service; tune-up; carburetor overhaul and fuel pump repair/replacement; combustion chamber deposit removal and valve repair; complete overhaul. Routine maintenance consists of the first three categories. These are described below.

Lubrication

This category includes simple replenishment of lost fluids, and, in part, is the responsibility of the operator. Operators must be aware of not only the need to run the engine only when it is adequately lubricated, but of the need to cease operation and perform required maintenance,

even if the actual work is done by a mechanic.

Before starting the engine, fill the crankcase and the air cleaner with the proper oil and fill the gasoline tank. Never try to fill the fuel tank of an engine that is running, and if the engine is still hot from running, allow it to cool down before refuel ing it.

Use a good grade, clean, fresh, lead free or leaded regular grade automotive gasoline. The use of highly leaded gasoline (high octane) should be avoided, as it causes deposits on the valves and valve seats, spark plugs, and the cylinder head, thus shortening engine life.

Any high quality detergent oil having the American Petroleum Institute classification "For Service SG" can be used. Detergent oils keep the engine cleaner by retarding the formation of gum and varnish deposits. Do not use any oil additives. In the summer — above 40°F (4°C) — use SAE 30 weight oil. If that is not available, use SAE 10W-30 or SAE 10W-40 weight oil. In the winter — under 40°F (4°C) — use SAE 5W-20 or SAE 5W-30 weight oil. If neither of these is available, use SAE 10W or SAE 10W-30 weight oil. If the engine is operated in ambient temperatures that are below 0°F (−18°C), use SAE 10W or SAE 10W-30 weight oil diluted 10% with kerosene.

The oil should be changed after each 25 hours of service or engine operation, and more often under dirty or dusty operating conditions, or as the manufacturer specifies. In normal running of any engine, small particles of metal from the cylinder walls, pistons and bearings will gradually work into the oil. Dust particles from the air also get into the oil. If the oil is not changed regularly, these foreign particles cause increased friction and a grinding action which shorten the life of the engine. Fresh oil also assists in cooling the engine, for old oil gradually becomes thick and cannot dissipate the heat fast enough. Oil oil will also gradually lose its lubrication properties.

In 2–stroke engines, lubrication consists of ensuring the engine runs on a mix of fuel and oil which is in the proper proportion, and that the oil used meets the specifications of the manufacturer. Since running a 2–stroke engine on straight gasoline or an improper mix is very much like operating a four stroke engine without oil, it must be seen that proper preparation of fuel/oil mix is literally a life and death matter for the engine — failure to provide the proper mix may result in immediate engine failure. Always observe the following points:

1. Use an oil specifically designed for 2–stroke engines, and of the viscosity recommended by the manufacturer. The wrong oil may solidify in many different parts of the en-

gine, may leave ash deposits in the combustion chamber, or foul the spark plug. Don't forget that the oil must not only lubricate well, but burn well.

2. Measure the oil accurately into the fuel container in the exact proportion recommended. Mix thoroughly according to the directions on the can (see "2–Stroke Lubrication" above). Do not simply use a standard, pre-mixed fuel unless you can determine that it is in the correct proportion. Where engines requiring different mixes are used at a common site, label fuel cans with the fuel/oil mixture ratio contained.

3. Remember that available lubrication in a 2–stroke also depends on fuel/air ration. Ensure that carburetors are properly adjusted, and that there are no air leaks so that sufficient lubrication will always be available. Watch, too, for clogged air cleaners, partially closed chokes, or too rich an adjustment, as these will lead to plug fouling. Correct immediately any conditions causing 4–cycling or misfire, as gasoline may dilute oil lubing pistons and rings under these conditions.

Filter Service

Air filter service is usually performed at the time of oil change, but may be performed at a longer interval — check specific recommendations. The air cleaner must be serviced much more frequently if the engine is operated in dusty conditions. Check specific recommendations here, also.

Oil type air cleaners require draining of old oil; a thorough cleaning of oil bowl and element with solvent; oiling of the element; and refilling of bowl to the specified level with new oil of the type used in the engine.

Most dry element air cleaners require that the element be replaced — they usually cannot be cleaned with compressed air. Some also employ a swirl chamber to remove large dust particles before they reach the main element. This chamber must be thoroughly cleaned out and, in some cases, a dust catching bowl must be emptied and cleaned.

Other types of dry element type air cleaners may require cleaning in soap and water, thorough drying and, in some cases, oiling.

Fuel sediment bowls and strainers, or filters are used on many engines to ensure that the use of dirty fuel or the entrance of dirt into the gas tank will not cause dirt to get into the carburetor. Since only dirt that enters with the fuel or works its way into the tank reaches the filter, it should be obvious that the first step in fuel filter maintenance is the use of clean gas, and the second, proper maintenance of the tank filler cap and gasket. The filter is usually serviced at the same time the oil is changed or at twice that interval. Fuel tank valves are turned off, and the bowl or filter housing is removed and cleaned. Strainers are cleaned in solvent and dried, and pleated paper type elements are replaced.

Oil filters are replaced at every oil change or every other change — consult specific recommendations. Throw-away type filters usually require the use of a strap wrench for ready removal. Wipe the filter base clean, lubricate the seal on the filter with clean oil, and tighten only by hand, or the amount specified on the filter. In the case of cartridge type filters, clean the housing with solvent and dry. Make sure to replace seals both at the filter base and around the mounting bolt, as applicable.

Filters deserve the same consistency of attention to recommended service intervals as oil changes. Oil change intervals are determined by the ability of the filter to prolong the life of the oil directly in mind. If the filter is allowed to accumulate dirt to the point where it bypasses due to loss of oil pressure, the oil will be subjected to a much greater than normal amount of material to keep in suspension. This shortens the potential life of the oil drastically, greatly increases the changes of clogging engine oil passages, and may allow abrasive particles large enough to be trapped between moving parts to circulate with the oil. Remember, too, that operation in dusty areas can cause a filter to become clogged and by-passed very quickly. Follow manufacturer's recommendations for more frequent changes under these conditions.

Tune-Up

The following list of procedures is rather extensive for a simple tune-up. Normally one would just check the condition of the spark plug, points, condenser, and wiring, make the necessary adjustments to these components and the carburetor, maybe change the oil, and service the carburetor if needed.

However if the following is performed, you will either be sure that the engine is functioning properly or you will know what major repairs should be made. In other words the engine is going to run well or you will find the cause of any problems.

1. Remove the air cleaner and check for the proper servicing.

2. Check the oil level and drain the crankcase. Clean the fuel tank and lines if separate from the carburetor.

3. Remove the blower housing and inspect the rope, rewind assembly and starter clutch of the starter mechanism. Thoroughly clean the cooling fins with compressed air, if possible,

and check that all control flaps operate freely.

4. Spin the flywheel to check compression. It should be spun in the direction opposite to normal rotation, and as rapidly as possible. A sharp rebound indicates good compression. 4–stroke engines may also be checked with a compression gauge in place of the spark plug — consult manufacturer's specifications in the individual repair section.

5. Remove the carburetor and disassemble and inspect it for wear or damage. Wash it in solvent, replace parts as necessary, and assemble. Set the initial adjustments.

6. Inspect the crossover tube or the intake elbow for damaged gaskets.

7. Check the governor blade, linkage, and spring for damage or wear; if it is mechanical, check the linkage adjustment.

8. Remove the flywheel and check for seal leakage, both on the flywheel and power take off sides. Check the flywheel key for wear and damage.

9. Remove the breaker cover and check for proper sealing.

10. Inspect the breaker points and condenser. Replace or clean and adjust them. Check the plunger or the cam. Lubricate the cam follower.

11. Check the coil and inspect all wires for breaks or damaged insulation. Be sure the lead wires do not touch the flywheel. Check the stop switch and the lead.

12. Replace the breaker cover, using sealer where the wires enter.

13. Install the flywheel and time the ignition if necessary. Set the air gap and check for ignition spark.

14. Remove the cylinder head, check the gasket, remove the spark plug, clean off the carbon, and inspect the valves for proper seating.

15. Replace the cylinder head, using a new gasket, torque it to the proper specification, and set the spark plug gap or replace the plug if necessary.

16. Replace the oil and fuel and check the muffler for restrictions or damage.

17. Adjust the remote control linkage and cable, if used, for correct operation.

18. Service the air cleaner and check the gaskets and element for damage.

19. Run the engine and adjust the idle mixture and high speed mixture of the carburetor.

Storage

If an engine is to be out of service for more than 30 days, the following steps should be performed:

1. Run the engine for 5–10 minutes until it is thoroughly warmed up to normal operating temperatures.

2. Turn off the fuel supply while the engine is still running, and continue running it until the engine stops from lack of fuel. This procedure removes all fuel from the carburetor.

3. Drain the oil from the crankcase while the engine is still warm.

4. Fill the crankcase with clean oil and tag the engine to indicate what weight oil was installed.

5. Remove the spark plug and squirt about an ounce of oil into the cylinder. Turn the engine over a few times to coat the cylinder walls, the top of the piston, and the head with a protective coating of oil. Reinstall the spark plug and tighten it to the proper torque.

6. Clean or replace the air cleaner. Refer to the manufacturer's recommendations.

7. Clean the governor linkage, making sure that it is in good working order and oiling all joints.

8. Plug the exhaust outlet and the fuel inlet openings. Use clean, lintless rags.

9. Remove the battery and store it in a cool place where there is no danger of freezing. Do not store any wet cell battery directly in contact with the ground or cement floor, as it will establish a ground and discharge itself. A completely discharged battery can never be brought back to its original output capacity. Store the battery on a work bench or on blocks of wood on the floor.

10. Wipe off or wash the engine. Wash only after the engine has had time to cool down to ambient temperature and avoid getting water in the carburetor intake port.

11. Coat all parts that might rust with a light coating of oil. Paint all non-operating parts with a rust inhibiting paint.

12. Provide the entire unit with a suitable covering. Plastic is good where the application and removal of sunlight will not promote the formation of condensation under the plastic covering. If this is the case, use a covering that is able to "breathe," such as a canvas.

TROUBLESHOOTING THE SMALL ENGINE

How To Go About It

Start with the simplest, most obvious causes first — many engine mechanics and operators have difficulty identifying trouble because they start out assuming everything that is obvious has already been checked. Check to see that there is fuel in the tank, and that it is clean, that the tank is properly vented, and that the fuel filter or sediment bowl is not full of dirt. Check to see that the spark plug wire is connected and that the spark plug is not fouled. If the cause of the trouble is not immediately obvious, use your basic knowledge of how the engine works. For example, if the engine runs fine but is very hard to start, you might conclude that the choke does not close, since its function is confined, mainly, to engine starting.

The guide below will point out many possible causes of the most basic problems. Find the "PROBLEM" which matches the engine's behavior, and then check out the possibilities listed under "CAUSES AND REMEDIES." Refer to the manufacturer's section which pertains to your engine, if necessary, in making repairs.

Troubleshooting Guide

PROBLEM: The engine does not start or is hard to start.
CAUSES AND REMEDIES:
1. The fuel tank is empty.
2. The fuel shut-off valve is closed; open it.
3. The fuel line is clogged. Remove the fuel line and clean it. Clean the carburetor, if necessary.
4. The fuel tank is not vented properly. Check the fuel tank cap vent to see if it is open.
5. There is water in the fuel supply. Drain the tank, clean the fuel lines and the carburetor, and dry the spark plug. Fill the tank with fresh fuel. Check the fuel supply before pouring it into the engine's fuel tank. Chances are it might be the source of the water.
6. The engine is over-choked. Open the choke and throttle wide on manual choke engines. On engines with automatic chokes, close the throttle. Then, turn the engine over with several pulls of the starter rope. If engine does not start, set throttle to just above idle, close choke again, and again attempt to start the engine. If one or two pulls does not make engine fire, try cranking with the choke closed only half way. If engine still fails to start, remove the spark plug and dry it, and spin the engine over several times to clean excess fuel out of the engine. Replace the spark plug and perform the normal starting procedure. Over-choking is most often due to continued cranking with the choke fully shut.
7. The carburetor is improperly adjusted; adjust it to the standard recommended preliminary settings. See the carburetor section.
8. Magneto wiring is loose or defective. Check the magneto wiring for shorts or grounds and repair it, if necessary.
9. No spark. Check for spark, and if there is none, check and, if necessary, replace the contact points, and set contact gap and timing. If there is still no spark, replace further magneto parts (especially coil and high tension wire) as necessary.
10. The spark plug is fouled. Remove, clean, and regap the spark plug.
11. The spark plug is damaged (cracked porcelain, bent electrodes etc.). Replace the spark plug.

12. Compression is poor. The head is loose or the gasket is leaking. Sticking or burned valves or worn piston rings could also be the cause. In any case, the engine will have to be disassembled and the cause of the problem corrected.
PROBLEM: The engine misses under load (if a two-stroke, it may "four-cycle.")
CAUSES AND REMEDIES:
1. The spark plug is fouled. Remove, clean, and regap the spark plug.
2. The spark plug is damaged. Replace the spark plug.
3. The spark plug is improperly gapped. Regap the spark plug to the proper gap.
4. The breaker points are pitted or improperly gapped. Replace the points, or set the gap.
5. The breaker point's breaker arm is sluggish. Clean and lubricate it.
6. The condenser is faulty. Replace it.
7. The carburetor is not adjusted properly. Adjust it.
8. The fuel system is partly clogged, or the fuel shut-off valve is partly closed. Open the valve and check the fuel filter/strainer, tank, lines, and carburetor for dirt. Clean all parts as necessary.
9. If the engine is a two-stroke, the exhaust ports may be clogged. Remove the exhaust manifold and inspect the ports. If they are clogged with carbon, clean them with a soft tool such as a wooden stick. Check also for bad crankshaft seals.
10. The valves are not adjusted properly. Adjust the valve clearance.
11. The valve springs are weak. Replace them.
PROBLEM: The engine knocks.
CAUSES AND REMEDIES:
1. The magneto is not timed correctly. Time the magneto.
2. The carburetor is not properly adjusted (may be too lean). Adjust the carburetor for best mixture.
3. The engine has overheated. Stop the engine and find the cause of overheating.
4. Carbon has built up in the combustion chamber, resulting in retention of excess heat and an increase in compression which causes pre-ignition. Remove the cylinder head, and remove the carbon from the head and the top of the piston.
5. The connecting rod is loose or worn. Replace it.
6. The flywheel is loose. Check the flywheel key and keyway and the end of the crankshaft. Replace any worn parts. Tighten the flywheel nut to the specified torque.
7. The cylinder is worn. Rebuild/replace parts as necessary.
PROBLEM: The engine vibrates excessively.
CAUSES AND REMEDIES:
1. The engine is not mounted securely to the

equipment that it operates. Tighten any loose mounting bolts.

2. The equipment that the engine operates is not balanced. Check the equipment.

3. The crankshaft is bent. Replace the crankshaft.

4. The counter balance shaft is improperly timed (recent re-assembly) or broken. Disassemble the crankcase, inspect, and replace or repair parts as necessary.

PROBLEM: The engine lacks power.

CAUSES AND REMEDIES:

1. The choke is partially closed. Open the choke.

2. The carburetor is not adjusted correctly. Adjust it.

3. The ignition is not timed correctly. Time the ignition.

4. There is a lack of lubrication or not enough oil in the crankcase. Fill the crankcase to the correct level.

5. The air cleaner is fouled. Clean it.

6. The valves are not sealing. Do a valve job.

7. Ring seal is poor. Repair/replace rings, piston, or cylinder/cylinder liner.

8. If the engine is a two stroke, the exhaust ports may be clogged with carbon. Remove the exhaust manifold and inspect. Clean with a soft instrument such as a wooden stick, if dirty. Ports may clog frequently if the carburetor mixture is adjusted too rich, or if there is excessive oil or oil of the wrong type in the fuel.

PROBLEM: The engine operates erratically, surges, and runs unevenly.

CAUSES AND REMEDIES:

1. The fuel line is clogged. Unclog it.

2. The fuel tank cap vent is clogged. Open the vent hole.

3. There is water in the fuel. Drain the tank, the carburetor, and the fuel lines and refill with fresh gasoline.

4. The fuel pump is faulty. Check the operation of the fuel pump if so equipped.

5. The governor is improperly set or parts are sticking or binding. Set the governor and check for binding parts and cor
rect them.

6. The carburetor is not adjusted properly. Adjust it.

PROBLEM: Engine overheats.

CAUSES AND REMEDIES:

1. The ignition is not timed properly. Time the engine's ignition.

2. The fuel mixture is too lean. Adjust the carburetor.

3. The air intake screen or cooling fins are clogged. Clean away any obstructions.

4. The engine is being operated without the

blower housing or shrouds in place. Install the blower housing and shrouds.

5. The engine is operating under an excessive load. Reduce the load and check associated equipment.

6. The oil level is too high. Check the oil level and drain some out if necessary.

7. There is not enough oil in the crankcase. Check the oil level and adjust accordingly.

8. The oil in the crankcase is of too low a viscosity or is excessively contaminated with fuel (four stroke). If the engine is a two-stroke, check for adequate fuel/oil mix — oil must be mixed with the fuel in proper proportions and be fully mixed. Check condition of crankcase oil (four-stroke) and if it appears very dirty, or there is doubt about proper viscosity, replace it.

9. The valve tappet clearance is too close. Adjust the valves to the proper specification.

10. Carbon has built up in the combustion chamber. Remove the cylinder and clean the head and piston of all carbon.

11. An improper amount of oil is mixed with the fuel (two stroke engines only). Drain the fuel tank and fill with correct mixture.

PROBLEM: The crankcase breather is passing oil (four stroke engines only).

CAUSES AND REMEDIES:

1. The crankcase is substantially over-filled with oil. Check oil level several minutes after engine has stopped. Wipe the dipstick clean before checking the level. If the crankcase is too full, drain oil as necessary until oil level is at or slightly below the upper mark.

2. The engine is being operated at two high rpm. Slow it down by adjusting the governor.

3. The oil fill cap or gasket is missing or damaged. Install a new cap and gasket and tighten it securely.

4. The breather mechanism is damaged. Replace the reed plate assembly.

5. The breather mechanism is dirty. Remove, clean, and replace it.

6. The drain hole in the breather is clogged. Clean the breather assembly and open the hole.

7. The piston ring gaps are aligned. Disassemble the engine and offset the ring gaps 90 degrees from each other.

8. The breather is loose or the gaskets are leaking. Tighten the breather to the crankcase.

9. The rings are not seated properly or they are worn. Install new rings.

PROBLEM: The engine backfires.

CAUSES AND REMEDIES:

1. The carburetor is adjusted so the air/fuel mixture is too lean. Adjust the carburetor.

2. The ignition is not timed correctly. Time the engine.

3. The valves are sticking. Do a valve job.

3
Briggs & Stratton
2 to 5 Hp

ENGINE IDENTIFICATION

The Briggs & Stratton model designation system consists of up to a six digit number. It is possible to determine most of the important mechanical features of the engine by merely knowing the model number. An explanation of what each number means is given below.

1. The first one or two digits indicate the cubic inch displacement (cid).

2. The first digit after the displacement indicates the basic design series, relating to cylinder construction, ignition and general configuration.

3. The second digit after the displacement indicates the position of the crankshaft and the type of carburetor the engine has.

4. The third digit after the displacement indicates the type of bearings and whether or not the engine is equipped with a reduction gear or auxiliary drive.

Briggs and Stratton Model Numbering System

Cubic Inch Displacement	First Digit After Displacement Basic Design Series	Second Digit After Displacement Crankshaft, Carburetor Governor	Third Digit After Displacement Bearings, Reduction Gears & Auxiliary Drives	Fourth Digit After Displacement Type of Starter
6	0	0-	0-Plain Bearing	0-Without Starter
8	1	1-Horizontal	1-Flange Mounting	1-Rope Starter
9	2	Vacu-Jet	Plain Bearing	
10	3	2-Horizontal	2-Ball Bearing	2-Rewind Starter
13	4	Pulsa-Jet		
14	5	3-Horizontal (Pneumatic)	3-Flange Mounting	3-Electric-110 Volt,
17	6	Flo-Jet (Governor)	Ball Bearing	Gear Drive
19	7	4-Horizontal (Mechanical)	4-	4-Elec. Starter-
20	8	Flo-Jet (Governor)		Generator-12 Volt,
23	9			Belt Drive
24		5-Vertical	5-Gear Reduction	5-Electric Starter
30		Vacu-Jet	(6 to 1)	Only-12 Volt,
32				Gear Drive
		6-	6-Gear Reduction	6-Wind-up Starter
			(6 to 1)	
			Reverse Rotation	
		7-Vertical	7-	7-Electric Starter,
		Flo-Jet		12 Volt Gear Drive,
				with Alternator
		8-	8-Auxiliary Drive	8-Vertical-pull Starter
			Perpendicular to	
			Crankshaft	
		9-Vertical	9-Auxiliary Drive	
		Pulsa-Jet	Parallel to	
			Crankshaft	

General Engine Specifications

Model	Bore Size (in.)	Horsepower
Aluminum Engines		
6B 60000	2.375	2
8B, 80000, 82000	2.375	3
92000	2.5625	3.5
100000	2.5	4
110000, 111000, 111,200	2.7812	4
130000	2.5625	5
Cast Iron Engines		
5, 6, N	2.000	2
8	2.250	3
9	2.250	3.5
14	2.625	5

5. The last digit indicates the type of starter. The model identification plate is usually located on the air baffle surrounding the cylinder.

MAINTENANCE

Air Cleaners

A properly serviced air cleaner protects the engine from dust particles that are in the air.

When servicing an air cleaner, check the air cleaner mounting and gaskets for worn or damaged mating surfaces. Replace any worn or damaged parts to prevent dirt and dust from entering the engine through openings caused by improper sealing. Straighten or replace any bent mounting studs.

SERVICING

Oil/Foam Air Cleaners

Clean and re-oil the air cleaner element every 25 hours of operation under normal operating conditions. The capacity of the oil/foam air cleaner is adequate for a full season's use without cleaning. Under very dusty conditions, clean the air cleaner every few hours of operation.

The oil/foam air cleaner is serviced in the following manner:

1. Remove the screw that holds the halves of the air cleaner shell together and retains it to the carburetor.

2. Remove the air cleaner carefully to prevent dirt from entering the carburetor.

3. Take the air cleaner apart (split the two halves).

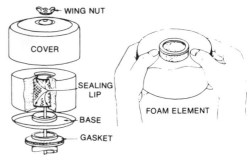

Oil foam air cleaner

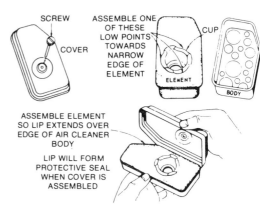

Oil foam air cleaner

4. Wash the foam in kerosene or liquid detergent and water to remove the dirt.

5. Wrap the foam in a clean cloth and squeeze it dry.

6. Saturate the foam in clean engine oil and squeeze it to remove the excess oil.

7. Assemble the air cleaner and fasten it to the carburetor with the attaching screw.

Oil Bath Air Cleaner

Pour the old oil out of the bowl. Wash the element thoroughly in solvent and squeeze it dry. Clean the bowl and refill it with the same type of oil used in the crankcase.

Dry Element Air Cleaner

Remove the element of the air cleaner and tap (top and bottom) it on a flat surface or wash it in non-sudsing detergent and flush it from the inside until the water coming out is clear. After washing, air dry the element thoroughly before reinstalling it on the engine. NEVER OIL A DRY ELEMENT.

Heavy Duty Air Cleaner

Clean and re-oil the foam pre-cleaner at three month intervals or every 25 hours, whichever comes first.

Clean the paper element every year or 100 hours, whichever comes first. Use the dry ele-

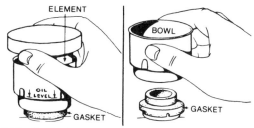

Oil bath air cleaner

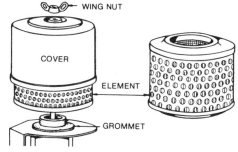

Dry element air cleaner

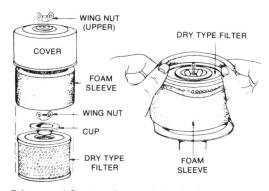

Briggs and Stratton heavy duty air cleaner

Oil Viscosity Recommendations

Winter (under 40°F.)	Summer (above 40°F.)
SAE 5W-20, or SAE 5W-30	SAE 30
If above are not available: SAE 10W or SAE 10W-30 (under 0°F.) Use SAE 10W or SAE 10W-30 in proportions of 90% motor oil/ 10% kerosene	If above is not available: SAE 10W-40 or SAE 10W-30

You should use a high quality detergent oil designated "For Service SG". Detergent oil is recommended because of its important ability to keep gum and varnish from clogging the lubrication system. Briggs & Stratton specifically recommends that no special oil additives be used.

Oil must be changed every 25 hours of operation. If the atmosphere in which the engine is operating is very dirty, oil changes should be made more frequently, as often as every 12 hours, if necessary. Oil should be changed after 5 hours of operation in the case of brand new engines. Drain engine oil when hot.

In hot weather, when under heavy load, or when brand new, engines may consume oil at a rate which will require you to refill the crankcase several times between oil changes. Check the oil level every hour or so until you can accurately estimate how long the engine can go between refills. To check oil level, stop the engine and allow it to sit for a couple of minutes, then re

move the dipstick or filler cap. Fill the crankcase to the top of the filler pipe when there is no dipstick, or wipe the dipstick clean, reinsert it, and add oil as necessary until the level reaches the upper mark.

On cast iron engines with a gear reduction

ment procedure for cleaning the paper element of the heavy duty air cleaner.

Use the oil foam cleaning procedure to clean the foam sleeve of the heavy duty air cleaner.

If the engine is operated under very dusty conditions, clean the air cleaner more often.

Lubrication

OIL AND FUEL RECOMMENDATIONS

Briggs & Stratton recommends unleaded fuel. Premium fuel is not required, as regular will have sufficient knock resistance if the engine is in proper condition. The factory recommends that fuel be purchased in lots small enough to be used up in 30 days or less. When fuel is older than that, it can form gum and varnish, or may be improperly tailored to the prevailing temperature.

Engine Oil Capacity Chart

Basic Model Series	Capacity Pints
Aluminum	
6, 8, 9, 11 Cu. in. Vert. Crankshaft	1¼
6, 8, 9 Cu. in. Horiz. Crankshaft	1¼
10, 13 Cu. in. Vert. Crankshaft	1¾
10, 13 Cu. in. Horiz. Crankshaft	1¼
Cast Iron	
9, 14, 19, 20 Cu. in. Horiz. Crank.	3

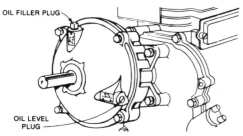

Location of oil fill and level check plugs, 6-1 gear reduction equipped engines

unit, crankcase and reduction gears are lubricated by a common oil supply. When draining crankcase, also remove drain plug in reduction unit.

On aluminum engines with reduction gear, a separate oil supply lubricates the gears, although the same type of oil used in the crankcase is used in the reduction gear cover. On these engines, remove the drain plug every fourth oil change (100 hours), then install the plug and refill. The level in the reduction gear cover must be checked during the refill operation by removing the level plug from the side of the gearcase, removing the filler plug, and then filling the case through the filler plug hole until oil runs out the level plug hole. Then, install both plugs.

On 6–1 gear reduction engines (models 6, 8, 8000, 10000, and 13000), no changes are required for the oil in the reduction gear case, but level must be checked and the case refilled, as described in the paragraph above, every 100 hours. Make sure the oil level plug (with screw-driver slot and no vent) is installed in the hole on the side of the case.

TUNE-UP

Spark Plugs

Remove the spark plug with a ¾ in. (1½ in. plug) or a $^{15}\!/_{16}$ in. (2 in. plug) deep well socket wrench. Clean carbon deposits off the center and side electrodes with a sharp instrument. If possible, you should also attempt to remove deposits from the recess between the insulator and the threaded portion of the plug. If the electrodes are burned away or the insulator is cracked at any point, replace the plug. Using a wire type feeler gauge, adjust the gap by bending the side electrode where it is curved until the gap is 0.030 in. (0.8mm).

When installing the plug, make sure the threads of the plug and the threads in the cylinder head are clean. It is best to oil the plug threads very lightly. Be careful not to overtorque the plug, especially if the engine has

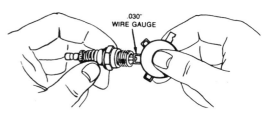

Checking spark plug gap with a wire feeler gauge

Tune-Up Specifications

Model	Plug Type	Plug Gap (in.)	Point Gap (in.)	Armature Gap		Idle Speed
				2 leg	3 leg	
Aluminum Block						
6B, 6000, 8B	①	.030	.020	.006–.010	.012–.016	1750
80000, 82000, 92000, 110900	①	.030	.020	.006–.010	.012–.016	1750
100000, 130000	①	.030	.020	.010–.014	.016–.019	1750
Cast Iron Block						
5, 6, N, 8	①	.030	.020	—	.022–.026	1750
9	①	.030	.020	—	—	1200
14	①	.030	.020	—	—	1200

① Manufacturer's Code		Manufacturer
1½ in. plug	2 in. plug	
CJ-8	J-8	Champion
RCJ-8	RJ-8	Champion (resistor)
A-7NX	A-71	Autolite
AR-7N	AR-80	Autolite (resistor)
CS-45	GC-46	A.C.
—	R-46	A.C. (resistor)

an aluminum head. If you use a torque wrench, torque to about 15 ft. lbs.

Breaker Points

All Briggs & Stratton engines have magneto ignition systems. Three types are used: Flywheel Type — Internal Breaker, Flywheel Type — External Breaker, and Magna-Matic.

REMOVAL AND INSTALLATION

Flywheel Type — Internal Breaker

This ignition system has the magneto located on the flywheel and the breaker points located under the flywheel.

The flywheel is located on the crankshaft with a soft metal key. It is held in place by a nut or starter clutch. The flywheel key must be in good condition to insure proper location of the flywheel for ignition timing. Do not use a steel key under any circumstances. Use only a soft metal key, as originally supplied.

The keyway in both flywheel and crankshaft should not be distorted. Flywheels are made of aluminum, zinc, or cast iron.

1. Place a block of wood under the flywheel fins to prevent the flywheel from turning while you are loosening the nut or starter clutch. Be

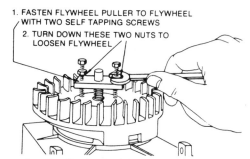

1. FASTEN FLYWHEEL PULLER TO FLYWHEEL WITH TWO SELF TAPPING SCREWS
2. TURN DOWN THESE TWO NUTS TO LOOSEN FLYWHEEL

Removing the flywheel with a puller

careful not to bend the flywheel. lThere are special flywheel holders available for this purpose; Briggs & Stratton recommends their use on flywheels of 6¾ in. 171.45mm) diameter or less.

2. On rope starter engines, the ½ in. flywheel nut has a lefthand thread and the ⅝ in. nut has a righthand thread. The starter clutch used on rewind or wind-up starters has a righthand thread.

Some flywheels have two holes provided for the use of a flywheel puller. Use a small gear puller or automotive steering wheel puller to remove the flywheel if a flywheel puller is not available. Be careful not to bend the flywheel if a gear puller is used. On rope starter engines leave the nut on for the puller to bear against. Small cast iron flywheels do not require a puller.

3. Remove the breaker cover. Care should be taken when removing the cover, to avoid damaging it. If the cover is bent or damaged, it should be replaced to insure a proper seal.

The breaker point gap on all models is 0.020 in. (0.5mm). Check the points for contact and for signs of burning or pitting. Points that are set too wide will advance the spark timing and may cause kickback when starting. Points that are set too close will retard the spark timing and decrease engine power.

On models that have a separate condenser, the point set is removed by first removing the condenser and armature wires from the breaker point clip. Loosen the adjusting lock screw and remove the breaker point assembly.

On models where the condenser is incorpo-

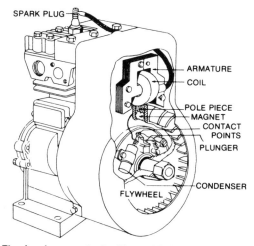

SPARK PLUG

ARMATURE
COIL
POLE PIECE
MAGNET
CONTACT POINTS
PLUNGER

CONDENSER
FLYWHEEL

Flywheel magneto ignition with internal breaker points and external armature

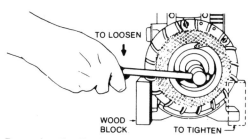

TO LOOSEN

WOOD BLOCK   TO TIGHTEN

Removing the flywheel

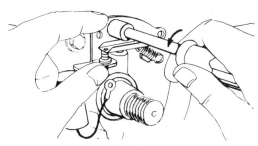

Removing the breaker point assembly

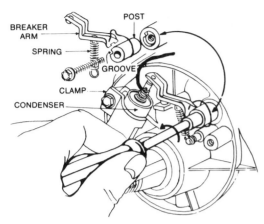

Removing the integral breaker point and condenser assembly

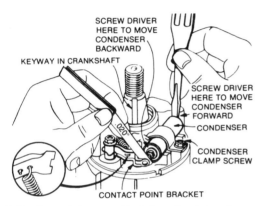

Adjusting point gap on the integral point and condenser assembly

rated with the breaker points, loosen the screw which holds the post. The condenser/point assembly is removed by loosening the screw which holds the condenser clamp.

4. When installing a point set with the separate condenser, be sure that the small boss on the magneto plate enters the hole in the point bracket. Mount the point set to the magneto plate or the cylinder with a lock screw. Fasten the armature lead wire to the breaker points with the clip and screw. If these lead wires do not have terminals, the bare end of the wires can be inserted into the clip and the screw tightened to make a good connection. Do not let the ends of the wire touch either the point bracket or the magneto plate, or the ignition will be grounded.

5. To install the integral condenser/point set, place the mounting post of the breaker arm into the recess in the cylinder so that the groove in the post fits the notch in the recess. Tighten the mounting screw securely. Use a ¼ in. wrench. Slip the open loop of the breaker arm spring through the two holes in the arm, then hook the closed loop of the spring over the small post

protruding from the cylinder. Push the flat end of the breaker arm into the groove in the mounting post. This places tension on the spring and pulls the arm against the plunger. If the condenser post is threaded, attach the soil primary wire and the ground wire (if furnished) with the lock washer and nut. If the primary wire is fastened to the condenser with a spring fastener, compress the spring and slip the primary wire and ground wire into the hole in the condenser post. Release the spring. Lay the condenser in place and tighten the condenser clamp securely. Install the spring in the breaker arm.

POINT GAP ADJUSTMENT

Turn the crankshaft until the points are open to the widest gap. When adjusting a breaker point assembly with an integral condenser, move the condenser forward or backward with a screwdriver until the proper gap is obtained – 0.020 in. (0.5mm). Point sets with a separate condenser are adjusted by moving the contact point bracket up and down after the lock screw has been loosened. The point gap is set to 0.020 in. (0.5mm).

BREAKER POINT PLUNGER

If the breaker point plunger hole becomes excessively worn, oil will leak past the plunger

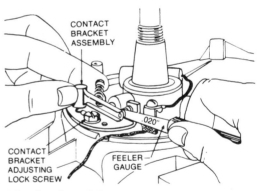

Adjusting the point gap

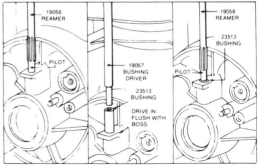

Replacing the breaker plunger bushing

and may get on the points, causing them to burn. To check the hole, loosen the breaker point mounting screw and move the breaker points out of the way. Remove the plunger. If the flat end of the #19055 plug gauge will enter the plunger hole for a distance of ¼ in. (6mm) or more, the hole should be rebushed.

To install the bushing, it is necessary that the breaker points, armature, and crankshaft be removed. Use a #19056 reamer to ream out the old plunger hole. This should be done by hand. The reamer must be in alignment with the plunger hole. Drive the bushing, #23513, into the hole until the upper end of the bushing is flush with the top of the boss. Remove all metal chips and dirt from the engine.

If the breaker point plunger is worn to a length of 0.870 in. (22mm) or less, it should be replaced. Plungers must be inserted with the groove at the top or oil will enter the breaker box. Insert the plunger into the hole in the cylinder.

ARMATURE AIR GAP ADJUSTMENT

Set the air gap between the flywheel and the armature as follows: With the armature up as far as possible and just one screw tightened, slip the proper gauge between the armature and flywheel. Turn the flywheel until the magnets are directly below the armature. Loosen the one mounting screw and the magnets should pull the armature down firmly against the thickness gauge. kTighten the mounting screws.

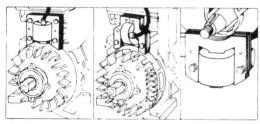

Variations in armature positioning

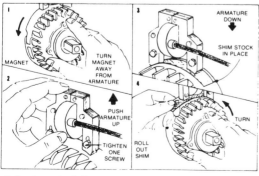

Adjustment of the armature gap

Flywheel Type — External Breaker

1. Turn the crankshaft until the points open to their widest gap. This makes it easier to assemble and adjust the points later if the crankshaft is not removed.

2. Remove the condenser and upper and lower mounting screws.

3. Loosen the lock nut and back off the breaker point screw.

4. Install the points in the reverse order of removal.

To avoid the possibility of oil leaking past the breaker point plunger or moisture entering the crankcase between the plunger and the bushing, a plunger seal is installed on the engine models using this type of ignition system. To install a new seal on the plunger, remove the breaker point assembly and con
denser. Remove the retainer and eyelet, remove the old seal, and install the new one. Use extreme care when installing the seal on the plunger to avoid damaging the seal. Replace the eyelet and retainer and replace the points and condenser.

NOTE: *Apply a small amount of sealer to the threads of both mounting screws and the adjustment screw. The sealer prevents oil from leaking into the breaker point area.*

POINT GAP ADJUSTMENT

Turn the crankshaft until the points open to their widest gap. Turn the breaker point adjusting screw until the points open to 0.020 in. (0.5mm) and tighten the lock nut. When the cover is installed, seal the point where the primary wire passes under the cover. This area must be resealed to prevent the entry of dust and moisture.

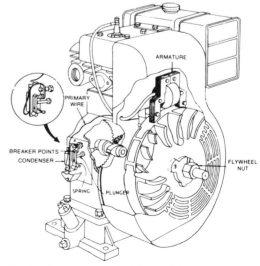

Flywheel magneto ignition with an external breaker assembly

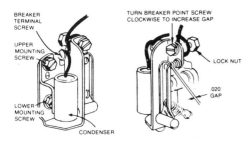

Breaker point gap adjustment

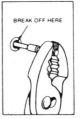

Removing an unthreaded plunger bushing

REPLACING THREADED BREAKER PLUNGER AND BUSHING

Remove the breaker cover and the condenser and breaker point assembly.

Place a thick ⅜ in. (9.5mm) inside diameter washer over the end of the bushing and screw on the ⅜–24 nut. Tighten the nut to pull the bushing out of the hole. After the bushing has been moved about ⅛ in. (3mm), remove the nut and put on a second thick washer and repeat the procedure. A total stack of ⅜ in. (9.5mm) washers will be required to completely remove the bushing. Be sure the plunger does not fall out of the bushing as it is removed.

Place the new plunger in the bushing with the large end of the plunger opposite the threads on the bushing. Screw the ⅜–24 in. nut onto the threads to protect them and insert the bushing into the cylinder. Place a piece of tubing the same diameter as the nut and, using a hammer, drive the bushing into the cylinder until the square shoulder on the bushing is flush with the face of the cylinder. Check to be sure that the plunger operates freely.

REPLACING UNTHREADED BREAKER PLUNGER AND BUSHING

Pull the plunger out as far as possible and use a pair of pliers to break the plunger off as close as possible to the bushing. Use a ¼–20 in. tap or a #93029 self threading screw to thread the hole in the bushing to a depth of about ½–⅝ in. (13–15mm). Use a ¼–20 × ½ in. hex head screw and two spacer washers to pull the bushing out of the cylinder. The bushing will be free when it has been extracted ⁵⁄₁₆ in. (8mm). Carefully remove the bushing and the remainder of

the broken plunger. Do not allow the plunger or metal chips to drop into the crankcase.

Correctly insert the new plunger into the new bushing. Insert the plunger and the bushing into the cylinder. Use a hammer and the old bushing to drive the new bushing into the cylinder until the new bushing is flush with the face of the cylinder. Make sure that the plunger operates freely.

PLUNGER SEAL

Later models with Flywheel Type-External Breaker Ignition feature a plunger seal. This seal keeps both oil and moisture from entering the breaker box. If the points have become contaminated on an engine manufactured without this feature, the seal may be installed. Parts, part numbers, and their locations are shown in the illustration. Install the seal onto the plunger very carefully to avoid fracturing it.

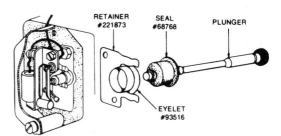

Plunger seal used on later model engines

Magna-Matic Ignition System

1. Using pullers similar to factory designs numbered #19068 and 19203, screw the two bolts into the holes tapped into the flywheel. The bolts are turned until the flywheel is forced off the crankshaft. Only this type of device should be used to pull these flywheels.

2. Loosen the socket head screw in the rotor clamp which will allow the clamp to loosen. It may be necessary to use a puller to remove the rotor from the crankshaft. On older models, loosen the small lock screw, then the set screw.

3. Usually the coil and armature are not separated, but left assembled for convenience. However, if one or both need replacement, proceed as follows: the coil primary wire and the

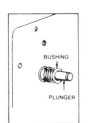
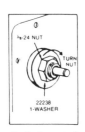

Removing a threaded plunger bushing

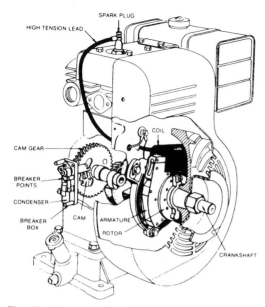

The Magna-Matic ignition system

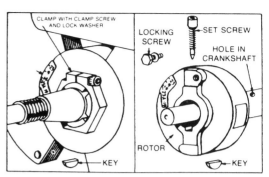

Removing the rotor

coil ground wire must be unfastened. Pry out the clips that hold the coil and coil core to the armature. The coil core is a slip fit in the coil and can be pushed out of the coil.

4. Turn the crankshaft until the points open to the widest gap. This makes it easier to assemble and adjust the points later if the crankshaft is not removed. With the terminal screw out, remove the spring screw. Loosen the breaker shaft nut until the nut is flush with the end of the shaft. Tap the nut to free the breaker arm from the tapered end of the breaker shaft. Remove the nut, lockwasher, and breaker arm. Remove the breaker plate screw, breaker plate, pivot, insulating plate, and eccentric. Pry out the breaker shaft seal with a sharp pointed tool.

5. Remove the two mounting screws, then remove the breaker box, turning it slightly to clean the arm at the inner end of the breaker shaft. The breaker points need not be removed to remove the breaker box.

6. The breaker shaft can be removed, after the breaker points are removed, by turning the shaft one half turn to clear the retaining spur at the inside of the breaker box.

To install:

7. Install the breaker shaft with the arm upward so the arm will clear the retainer boss. Push the shaft all the way in, then turn the arm downward.

8. Pull the primary wire through the hole at the lower left corner of the breaker box. See that the primary wire rests in the groove at the top end of the box, then tighten the two mounting screws to hold the box in place.

9. To install the breaker points, press in the new oil seal with the metal side out. Put the new breaker plate on the top of the insulating plate, making sure that the detent in the breaker plate engages the hole in the insulating plate. Fasten the breaker plate screw enough to put a light tension on the plate. Adjust the eccentric so that the left edge of the insulating plate is parallel to the edge of the box and tighten the screw. This locates the breaker plate so that the proper gap adjustments may be made. Turn the breaker shaft clockwise as far as possible and hold it in this position. Place the new breaker points on the shaft, then the lockwasher, and tighten the nut down on the lockwasher. Replace the spring screw and terminal screw.

10. To adjust the breaker points, turn the crankshaft until the breaker points open to the widest gap. Loosen the breaker point plate screw slightly. Rotate the eccentric to obtain a point gap of 0.020 in. (0.5mm). Tighten the breaker plate screw.

11. Push the coil core into the coil with the

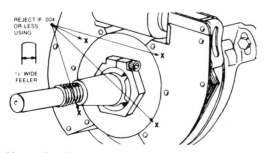

Measuring the armature gap

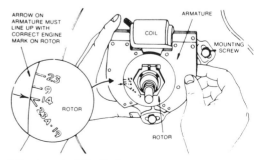

Adjustment of the timing

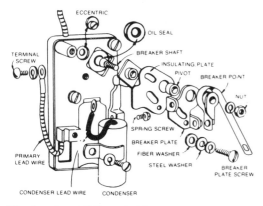

The breaker point assembly

rounded side toward the ignition cable. Place the coil and core on the armature with the coil retainer between the coil and the armature and with the rounded side toward the coil. Hook the lower end of the clips into the armature, then press the upper end onto the coil core.

12. Fasten the coil ground wire (bare double wires) to the armature support. Next, place the assembly against the cylinder and around the rotor and bearing support. Insert the three mounting screws together with the washer and lockwasher into the three long oval holes in the armature. Tighten them enough to hold the armature in place but loose enough so the armature can be moved for adjustment of the timing. Attach the primary wires from the coil and the breaker points to the terminal at the upper side of the backing plate. This terminal is insulated from the backing plate. Push the ignition cable through the louvered hole at the left side of the backing plate.

NOTE: *On Model 9 engines, knot the ignition cable before inserting it through the backing plate. Be sure all wires are clean of the flywheel.*

13. The rotor and armature are correctly timed at the factory and require timing only if the armature has been removed from the en-

gine, or if the cam gear or crankshaft has been replaced.

If it is necessary to adjust the rotor, proceed as follows: with the point gap set at 0.020 in. (0.5mm), turn the crankshaft in the normal direction of rotation until the breaker points close and just start to open. Use a timing light or insert a piece of tissue paper between the breaker points to determine when the points begin to open. With the three armature mounting screws slightly loose, rotate the armature until the arrow on the armature lines up with the arrow on the rotor. Align with the corresponding number of engine models, for example, on Model 9, align with #9. Retighten the armature mounting screws.

14a. To install the set screw type rotor, place the woodruff key in the keyway on the crankshaft, then slide the rotor onto the crankshaft until the set screw hole in the rotor and the crankshaft are aligned. Be sure the key remains in place. Tighten the set screw securely, then tighten the lock screw to prevent the set screw from loosening. The lock screw is self-threading and the hole does not require tapping.

14b. To install the clamp type rotor, place the woodruff key in place in the crankshaft and align the keyway in the rotor with the woodruff key. If necessary, use a short length of pipe and a hammer to drive the rotor onto the shaft until a 0.025 in. (0.6mm) feeler gauge can be inserted between the rotor and the bearing support. The split in the clamp must be between the slots in the rotor. Tighten the clamp screws to 60–70 inch lbs.

15. The armature air gap on engines equipped with Magna-Matic ignition system is fixed and can change only if wear occurs on the crankshaft journal and/or main bearing. Check for wear by inserting a ½ in. (12.7mm) wide feeler gauge at several points between the rotor and armature. Minimum feeler gauge thickness is 0.004 in. (0.1mm). Keep the feeler gauge away from the magnets on the rotor or you will have a false reading.

Mixture Adjustment

920000 Engines w/Automatic Choke

1. Start the engine and run it long enough to reach operating temperature. If the carburetor is so far out of adjustment that it will not start, close the needle valve by turning it clockwise. Then open the needle valve 1½ turns counterclockwise.

2. Move the control so that the engine runs at normal operating speed. Turn the needle valve clockwise until the engine starts to lose

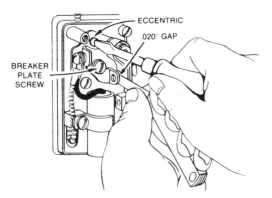

Adjusting the breaker point gap

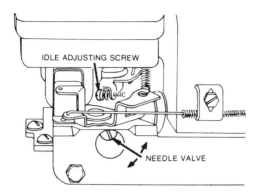

IDLE ADJUSTING SCREW

NEEDLE VALVE

Carburetor adjustment screws

speed because of too lean a mixture. Then slowly turn the needle valve counterclockwise and out past the point of smoothest operation until the engine just begins to run uneven
ly because of too rich a mixture. Turn the needle back clockwise to the midpoint between the rich and lean mixture extremes. This should be where the engine operates smoothest. The final adjustment of the needle valve should be slightly on the rich side (counterclockwise) of the mid-point.

3. Move the engine control to the slow position and turn the idle adjusting screw until a fast idle of about 1750 rpm is obtained. If the engine idles at a speed lower than 1750 rpm, it may not accelerate properly. It is not practical to attempt to obtain acceleration from speeds below 1750 rpm, because the mixture which would be required would be too rich for normal operating speeds.

4. To check the idle adjustment, move the engine control from slow to fast speed. The engine should accelerate smoothly. If the engine tends to stall or die out, increase the idle speed or readjust the carburetor, usually to a slightly richer mixture.

Flooding can occur if the engine is tipped at an angle for a prolonged period of time, if the engine is cranked repeatedly with the spark plug wire disconnected, or if the carburetor mixture is too rich.

In case of flooding, move the governor control to the stop position and pull the starter rope at least six times.

When the control is placed in the stop position, the governor spring holds the throttle in a closed idle position. Cranking the engine with a closed throttle creates a higher vacuum which opens the choke rapidly, permitting the engine to clean itself of excess fuel.

Then move the control to the fast position and start the engine. If the engine continues to flood, lean the carburetor needle valve by about ⅛–¼ of a turn clockwise.

Pulsa-Jet and Vacu-Jet
(Model Series 82000, 92000 Only)

Models 82500 and 92500 have a Vacu-Jet carburetor and Models 82900 and 92900 have a Pulsa-Jet carburetor.

Adjust the carburetor with the air cleaner installed and the fuel tank half full.

Turn the needle valve clockwise to close it. Then open it about 1½ turns. This will permit the engine to be started and warmed up before making the final adjustment.

With the engine running at normal operating speed (about 3000 rpm without a load) turn the needle valve clockwise until the engine starts to lose speed because of a too lean mixture.

Then slowly turn the needle valve counterclockwise past the point of smoothest operation, until the engine just begins to run unevenly. This mixture will give the best performance under a load.

Hold the throttle in the idle position. Turn the idle speed adjusting screw until a fast idle is obtained (about 1750 rpm).

Test the engine under full load. If the engine tends to stall or die out, it usually indicates that the mixture is slightly lean and it may be necessary to open the needle valve slightly to provide a richer mixture. This slightly richer mixture may cause a slight unevenness in idling.

The breather tube and fuel intake tube thread into the cylinder on the model 82500 and 82900 engines. The fuel intake tube is bolted to the cylinder on the model 92500 and 92900 engines. Check for a good fit to prevent any air leaks or dirt entry. The fuel intake tube must not be distorted at the point where the carburetor O-ring fits or air leaks will occur.

Two Piece Flo-Jet

1. Start the engine and run it at 3000 rpm until it warms up.

2. Turn the needle valve (flat handle) to both extremes of operation noting the location of the valve at both points. That is, turn the valve inward until the mixture becomes too lean and the engine starts to slow, then note the position of the valve. Turn it outward slowly until the mixture becomes too rich and the engine begins to slow. Turn the valve back inward to the midpoint between the two extremes.

3. Install a tachometer on the engine. Pull the throttle to the idle position and hold it there through the rest of this step. Adjust the idle speed screw until the engine idles at 1750 rpm if it's an aluminum engine, or 1200 rpm, if it's a cast iron engine. Then, turn the idle valve in and out to adjust mixture, as described in Step 2. If idle valve adjustment changes idle speed, adjust speed to specification.

4. Release the throttle and observe the en-

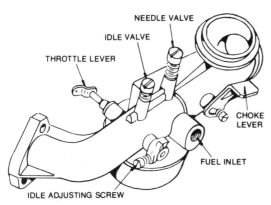

Idle valve and needle valve locations on the One Piece Flo-Jet

Blade Length (in.)	Max. Governed Speed (R.P.M.)
18	4032
19	3820
20	3629
21	3456
22	3299
23	3155
24	3024
25	2903
26	2791

gine's response. The engine should accelerate without hesitation. If response is poor, one of the mixture adjustments is too lean. Readjust either or both as necessary. If idle speed was changed after idle valve was adjusted, readjust the idle valve first.

One Piece Flo-Jet

Follow the instructions for adjusting the Two Piece Flo-Jet carburetor (above). On the large, One Piece Flo-Jet, the needle valve is located under the float bowl, and the idle valve on top of the venturi passage. On the small One Piece Flo-Jet, both valves are adjusted by screws located on top of the venturi passage. The needle valve is located on the air horn side, is centered above the float bowl, and uses a larger screw head.

Governor Adjustments

SETTING MAXIMUM GOVERNED SPEED WITH ROTARY LAWNMOWER BLADES

NOTE: *Strict limits on engine rpm must be observed when setting top governed speed on rotary lawnmowers. This is done so that blade tip speeds will be kept to less than 19,000 feet per minute. Briggs & Stratton suggests setting the governor 200 rpm low to allow for possible error in the tachometer reading. These figures below, based on blade length, must be strictly adhered to, or a serious accident could result!*

Models N, 6 and 8

There is no adjustment between the governor lever and the governor crank on these models. However, governor action can be changed by inserting the governor link or spring in different holes of the governor and throttle levers. In general, the closer to the pivot end of the lever, the smaller the difference between load and no-load engine speed. The engine will begin to

"hunt" if the spring is brought too close to the pivot point. The farther the spring is from the pivot end, the tendency to hunt will decrease, but the speed drop will be greater as the load increases. If the governor speed is lowered, the spring can usually be moved closer to the pivot. The standard setting is the 4th hole from the pivot point.

Models 6B, 8B, 60000 and 80000

Loosen the screw which holds the governor lever to the governor shaft. Turn the governor lever counterclockwise until the carburetor throttle is wide open. With a screwdriver, turn the governor shaft counterclockwise as far as it

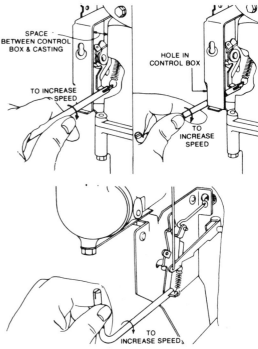

Bending the spring anchor tang to get desired top speed

You can make a tool like the one shown to adjust spring anchor tang

will go. Tighten the screw which holds the governor lever to the governor shaft.

Cast Iron Models 9 and 14

Loosen the screw which holds the governor lever to the governor shaft. Push the lever counterclockwise as far as it will go. Hold it in position and turn the governor shaft counterclockwise as far as it will go. This can be done with a screwdriver. Securely tighten the screw that holds the governor lever to the shaft.

Aluminum Models 100000 and 130000

Vertical and horizontal shaft engine governors are adjusted by setting the control lever in the high speed position. Loosen the nut on the governor lever. Turn the governor shaft clockwise with a screwdriver to the end of its travel. Tighten the nut. The throttle must be wide open. Check to see if the throttle can be moved from idle to wide open without binding.

ADJUSTING TOP NO LOAD SPEED

Set the control lever to the maximum speed position with the engine running. Bend the spring anchor tang to get the desired top speed.

ADJUSTMENT FOR CLOSER GOVERNING (GENERATOR APPLICATIONS ONLY)

1. Snap knob upward to release adjusting nut.
2. Pull knob out against stop.
3. Then, bend the spring anchor tang to get top no-load speed as described below, depending upon the application.

On models 100200 and 130200 with 3600

rpm generator, set the no load speed at 4,600 using the standard governor spring.

On models 100200 and 130200 with 1800 rpm generator, set the no load speed at 2800 rpm, and set throttle stop at 1600 rpm.

4. Snap knob back into its normal position.
5. Adjust the knob for the desired generator speed.

Choke Adjustment

Choke-a-Matic, Pulsa-Jet and Vacu-Jet Carburetors

To check the operation of the choke linkage, move the speed adjustment lever to the choke position. If the choke slide does not fully close, bend the choke link. The speed adjustment lever must make good contact against the top switch.

Install the carburetor and adjust it in the same manner as the Pulsa-Jet carburetor.

Two-piece Flo-Jet w/Automatic Choke

Hold the choke shaft so the thermostat lever is free. At room temperature (68°F [20°C]), the screw in the thermostat collar should be in the center of the stops. If not, loosen the stop screw and adjust the screw.

Loosen the set screw on the lever of the thermostat assembly. Slide the lever to the right or left on the shaft to ensure free movement of the choke link in any position. Rotate the thermostat shaft clockwise until the stop screw strikes the tube. Hold it in position and set the lever on the thermostat shaft so that the choke valve will be held open about ⅛ in. (3mm) from a closed position. Then tighten the set screw in the lever.

Rotate the thermostat shaft counterclockwise until the stop screw strikes the opposite side of the tube. Then open the choke valve manually until it stops against the top of the choke link opening. The choke valve should

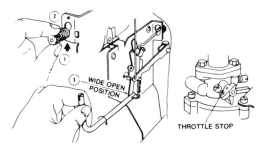

Obtaining closer governing on generator applications

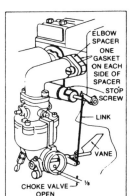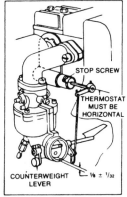

Adjusting automatic choke—Two Piece Flo-Jet

now be open approximately ⅛ in. (3mm) as before.

Check the position of the counterweight lever. With the choke valve in a wide open position (horizontal) the counterweight lever should also be in a horizontal position with the free end toward the right.

Operate the choke manually to be sure that all parts are free to move without binding or rubbing in any position.

Compression Checking

You can check the compression in any Briggs and Stratton engine by performing the following simple procedure: spin the flywheel counterclockwise (flywheel side) against the compression stroke. A sharp rebound indicates that there is satisfactory compression. A slight or no rebound indicates poor compression.

It has been determined that this test is an accurate indication of compression and is recommended by Briggs and Stratton. Briggs and Stratton does not supply compression pressures.

Loss of compression will usually be the result of one or a combination of the following:

1. The cylinder head gasket is blown or leaking.
2. The valves are sticking or not seating properly.
3. The piston rings are not sealing, which would also cause the engine to consume an excessive amount of oil.

Carbon deposits in the combustion chamber should be removed every 100 or 200 hours of use (more often when run at a steady load), or whenever the cylinder head is removed.

CARBURETED FUEL SYSTEM

Operation

Before removing any carburetor for repair, look for signs of air leakage or mounting gaskets that are loose, have deteriorated, or are otherwise damaged.

Note the position of the governor springs, governor link, remote control, or other attachments to facilitate reassembly. Be careful not to bend the links or stretch the springs.

Automatic Choke

All 92000 model engines built since August 1968 have an automatic choke system.

The automatic choke operates in conjunction with engine vacuum, similar to the Pulsa-Jet fuel pump.

A diaphragm under the carburetor is connected to the choke shaft by a link. A calibrated

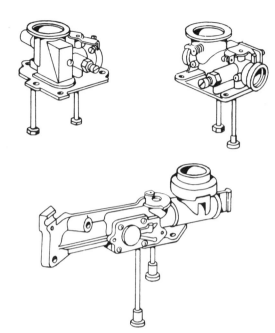

The three types of Pulsa-Jet carburetors

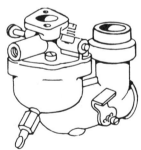

The two types of Flo-Jet carburetors

spring under the diaphragm holds the choke closed when the engine is not running. Upon starting, vacuum created during the intake stroke is routed to the bottom of the diaphragm through a calibrated passage, thereby opening the choke.

This system also has the ability to respond in the same manner as an accelerator pump. As speed decreases during heavy loads, the choke

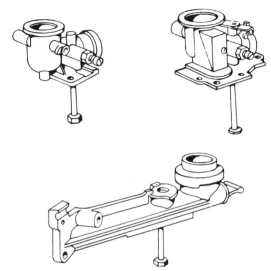

The three types of Vacu-Jet carburetors

valve partially closes, enriching the air/fuel mixture, thereby improving low speed performance and lugging power.

To check the automatic choke, remove the air cleaner and replace the stud. Observe the position of the choke valve; it should be fully closed. Move the speed control to the stop position; the governor spring should be holding the throttle in a closed position. Give the starter rope several quick pulls. The choke valve should alternately open and close.

If the choke valve does not react as stated in the previous paragraph, the carburetor will have to be disassembled to determine the problem. Before doing so, however, check the following items so you know what to look for:

ENGINE IS UNDERCHOKED

1. Carburetor is adjusted too lean.
2. The fuel pipe check valve is inoperative (Vacu-Jet only).
3. The air cleaner stud is bent.
4. The choke shaft is sticking due to dirt.
5. The choke spring is too short or damaged.
6. The diaphragm is not preloaded.

ENGINE IS OVERCHOKED

1. Carburetor is adjusted too rich.
2. The ari cleaner stud is bent.
3. The choke shaft is sticking due to dirt.
4. The diaphragm is ruptured.
5. The vacuum passage is restricted.
6. The choke spring is distorted or stretched.
7. There is gasoline or oil in the vacuum chamber.
8. There is a leak between the link and the diaphragm.
9. The diaphragm was folded during assembly, causing a vacuum leak.
10. The machined surface on the tank top is not flat.

REPLACING THE AUTOMATIC CHOKE

Inspect the automatic choke for free operation. Any sticking problems should be corrected as proper choke operation depends on freedom of the choke to travel as dictated by engine vacuum.

Remove the carburetor and fuel tank assembly from the engine. The choke link cover may now be removed and the choke link disconnected from the choke shaft. Disassemble the carburetor from the tank top, being careful not to damage the diaphragm.

CHECKING THE DIAPHRAGM AND SPRING

The diaphragm can be reused, provided it has not developed wear spots or punctures. On the

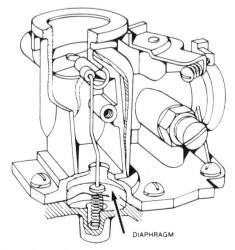

Automatic choke system

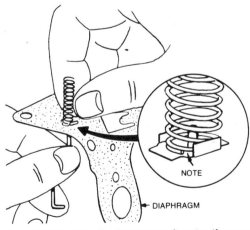

Assembling the diaphragm spring to the new diaphragm

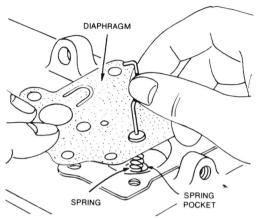

Installing the diaphragm and spring into the spring pocket

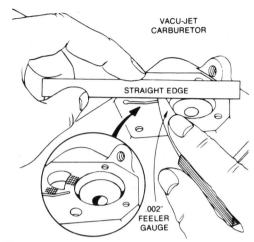

Checking the tank top for warpage

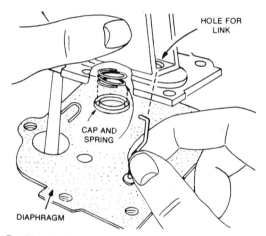

Positioning the diaphragm on top of the fuel tank

Pulsa-Jet models, make sure that the fuel pump valves are not damaged. Also check the choke spring length. The Pulsa-Jet spring minimum length is $1\frac{1}{8}$ in. (28.5mm) and the maximum is $1\frac{7}{32}$ in. (31mm). Vacu-Jet spring length minimum is $\frac{15}{16}$ in., (23.8mm) maximum length 1 in. (25.4mm). If the spring length is shorter or longer than specified, replace the diaphragm and the spring.

CHECKING THE TANK TOP

The machined surface on the top of the tank must be flat in order for the diaphragm to provide an adequate seal between the carburetor and the tank. If the machined surface on the tank is not flat, it is possible for gasoline to enter the vacuum chamber by passing between the machined surface and the diaphragm. Once fuel has entered the vacuum chamber, it can move through the vacuum passage and into the carburetor. The flatness of the machined surface on the tank top can be checked by using a straightedge and a feeler gauge. The surface should not vary more than 0.002 in. (0.05mm). Replace the tank if a 0.002 in. (0.05mm) feeler gauge can be passed under the straightedge.

If a new diaphragm is installed, assemble the spring to the replacement diaphragm, taking care not to bend or distort the spring.

Place the diaphragm on the tank surface, positioning the spring in the spring pocket.

Place the carburetor on the diaphragm ensuring that the choke link and diaphragm are properly aligned between the carburetor and the tank top. On Pulsa-Jet models, place the pump spring and cap on the diaphragm over the recess or pump chamber in the fuel tank. Thread in the carburetor mounting screws to about two threads. Do not tighten them. Close the choke valve and insert the choke link into the choke shaft.

Remove the air cleaner gasket, if it is in place, before continuing. Insert a $\frac{3}{8}$ in. bolt or rod into the carburetor air horn. With the bolt in posi-

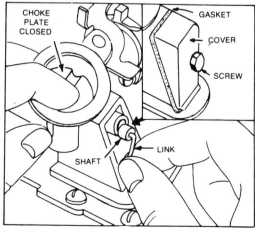

Inserting the choke link into the choke shaft

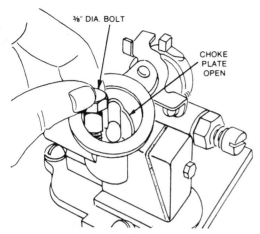

Pre-loading the diaphragm to adjust the choke

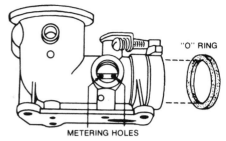

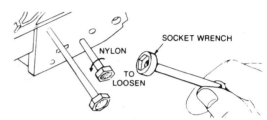

Remove the O-ring and inspect the metering valve

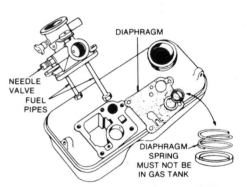

Removing the nylon fuel pipes

tion, tighten the carburetor mounting screws in a staggered sequence. Please note that the insertion of the 3/8 in. bolt opens the choke to an over-center position, which preloads the diaphragm.

Remove the 3/8 in. bolt. The choke valve should now move to a fully closed position. If the choke valve is not fully closed, make sure that the choke spring is properly assembled to the diaphragm, and also properly inserted in its pocket in the tank top.

ADJUSTMENTS

All carburetor adjustments should be made with the air cleaner on the engine. Adjustment is best made with the fuel tank half full. See the "Tune-Up" section.

Carburetors

REBUILDING

Pulsa-Jet and Vacu-Jet
(Model Series 82000 and 92000 Only)

Models 82500 and 92500 have a Vacu-Jet carburetor and Models 82900 and 92900 have a Pulsa-Jet carburetor.

1. Remove the carburetor and fuel tank assembly from the engine by removing the two attaching bolts.

2. Disconnect the governor link at the throttle, leaving the governor link and the governor spring hooked to the governor blade and control lever.

3. Slip the carburetor and tank assembly off of the engine.

4. Remove the carburetor from the tank. Always remove all nylon and rubber parts if the carburetor is soaked in solvent.

5. Remove the O-ring and discard it. Remove and inspect the needle valve, packing and seat.

6. Metering holes in the carburetor body

Removal and inspection of a Pulsa-Jet diaphragm

should be cleaned with solvent and compressed air. Do not clean the holes with a pin or a length of wire because of the danger of alterning their size.

7. Remove the choke parts on models 82500 and 82900 by pulling the nylon choke shaft sideways to separate the choke shaft from the choke valve. On the 92500 and 92900, remove the choke parts by first disconnecting the choke return spring at the pin in the carburetor body. Then pull the nylon choke shaft sideways to separate the choke shaft from the choke valve.

8. If the choke valve is heat-sealed to the choke shaft, loosen it by sliding a sharp pointed tool along the edge of the choke shaft. Do not re-seal parts on assembly.

9. When replacing the choke valve and shaft, install the choke valve so the poppet valve spring is visible when the valve is in full choke position.

On these models, the nylon fuel pipe is threaded into the carburetor body. Use a socket to remove and replace it. Be careful not to overtighten it and do not use any sealer.

The Pulsa-Jet diaphragm also serves as a gasket between the carburetor and the tank. Inspect the diaphragm for punctures, wrinkles, and wear. Replace it if it is damaged in any way.

To assemble the carburetor to the tank, first position the dia phragm on the tank. Then place the spring cap and spring on the diaphragm. Install the carburetor, tightening the mounting screws evenly to avoid distortion.

To install the carburetor and tank assembly onto the engine, make sure that the governor link is hooked to the governor blade. Connect the link to the throttle and slip the carburetor into place. Align the carburetor with the intake tube and breather tube grommet. Hold the choke lever in the open position so it does not catch on the control plate. Be sure the O-ring in the carburetor does not distort when fitting the carburetor to the intake tube. Install the mounting bolts. Adjust the carburetor as described in the Tune-Up section.

PULSA-JET THROTTLE PLATE REMOVAL

Cast throttle plates are removed by backing off the idle speed adjustment screw until the throttle clears the retaining lug on the carburetor housing.

Stamped throttles are removed by using a phillips screwdriver to remove the throttle valve screw. After removal of the valve, the throttle may be lifted out. Installation is the reverse of removal.

Some carburetors may have a spiral in the carburetor bore. To remove it, fasten the carburetor in a vise about ½ in. (13mm) below the top of the jaws. Grasp the spiral firmly with a pair of pliers. Place a screwdriver under the edge of the pliers. Using the edge of the vise, push down on the screwdriver to pry out the spiral. When installing the spiral, keep the top flush, or $\frac{1}{32}$ in. (0.8mm) below the carburetor flange, and parallel with the fuel tank mounting face.

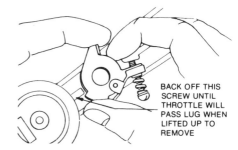

BACK OFF THIS SCREW UNTIL THROTTLE WILL PASS LUG WHEN LIFTED UP TO REMOVE

Removing the cast throttle shafts

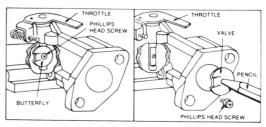

Removing the throttle plate

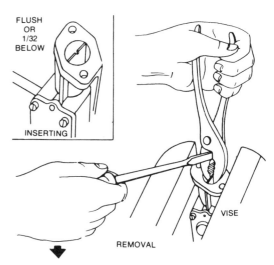

Removing and installing the spiral

FUEL PIPE

Check balls are not used in these fuel pipes. The screen housing or pipe must be replaced if the screen cannot be satisfactorily cleaned. The long pipe supplies fuel from the tank to the pump. The short pipe supplies fuel from the tank cup to the carburetor. Fuel pipes are nylon or brass. Nylon pipes are removed and installed by using a socket, or open-end wrench.

NOTE: *Where brass pipes are used, replace only the screen housing. The housing is driven off the pipe with a screwdriver with the pipe held in a vise. The new housing is installed by lightly tapping it onto the pipe with a soft hammer.*

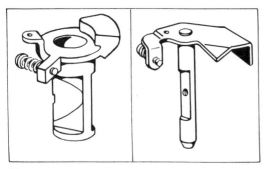

The two types of throttle shafts

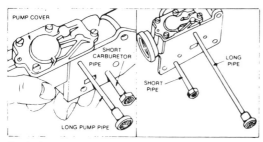

Fuel pipes

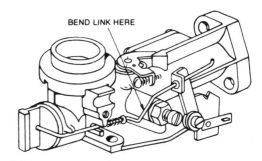

Adjustment of the Choke-a-Matic choke linkage

NEEDLE VALVE AND SEAT

Remove the needle valve to inspect it. If the carburetor is gummy or dirty, remove the seat to allow better cleaning of the metering holes. Do not insert pins or wires in the metering holes. Use solvent or compressed air.

PUMP

Remove the fuel pump cover, diaphragm, spring, and cup. Inspect the diaphragm for punctures, cracks, and fatigue. Replace it if damaged. On early models, the spring cap is solid; on later models, the cap has a hole in it. The new style supersedes the old style. When installing the pump cover, tighten the screws evenly to insure a good seal.

CHOKE-A-MATIC (EXCEPT 100900 MODELS)

To remove the choke link, remove the speed adjustment lever and stop switch insulator plate. Remove the speed adjustment lever from the choke link, then pull out the choke link through the hole in the choke slide.

Replace worn or damaged parts. To assemble, slip the washers and spring over the choke link. Hook the choke link through the hole in the choke slide. Place the other end of the choke link through the hole in the speed adjustment lever and mount the lever and stop switch insulator plate to the carburetor.

Vacu-Jet Carburetors

Vacu-Jet carburetors are removed from the engine together with the fuel tank as one unit. The throttle plates are removed and installed in the same manner as the throttles in the Pulsa-Jet carburetors.

FUEL PIPE

The fuel pipe contains a check ball and a fine mesh screen. To function properly, the screen must be clean and the check ball free. Replace the pipe if the screen and ball cannot be satisfactorily cleaned in carburetor cleaner.

NOTE: *Do not leave the carburetor in the cleaner for more than ½ hour without removing all nylon parts. Nylon fuel pipes are removed and replaced with a $\frac{9}{16}$ in. socket. Brass fuel pipes are removed by clamping the pipe in a vise and prying out the pipe with two screwdrivers.*

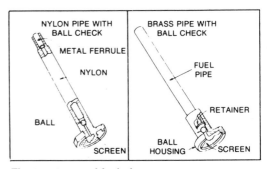

The two types of fuel pipes

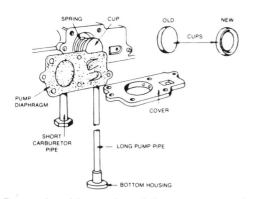

Removal and inspection of the pump cover diaphragm from a Pulsa-Jet carburetor

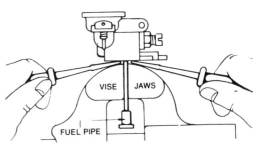

Removal of brass fuel pipes

To install the brass fuel pipes, remove the throttle, if necessary, and place the carburetor and pipe in a vise. Press the pipe into the carburetor until it projects $2\frac{9}{32}-2\frac{21}{16}$ in. (57.9–58.7mm) from the carburetor face.

NEEDLE VALVE AND SEAT

Remove the needle valve assembly to inspect it. If the carburetor is gummy or dirty, remove the seat to allow better cleaning of the metering holes. Do not clean the metering holes with a pin or a length of wire.

CHOKE-A-MATIC LINKAGE

To remove the choke link, remove the speed adjustment lever and the top switch insulator plate. Work the link out through the hole in the choke slide.

Replace all worn or damaged parts. To assemble a carburetor using a choke slide, place the choke return spring and three washers on the choke link. Push the choke link through the hole in the carburetor body, turning the link to line up with the hole in the choke slide. The speed adjustment lever screw and the stop switch insulator plate should be installed as one assembly after placing the choke link through the end of the speed adjustment lever.

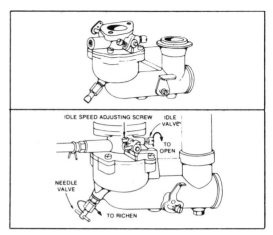

Two piece Flo-Jet carburetor

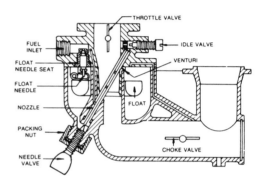

Cutaway view of a two piece Flo-Jet carburetor

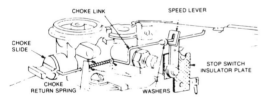

Adjustment of a Choke-a-Matic choke linkage on a Vacu-Jet carburetor

Two Piece Flo-Jet Carburetors (Large and Small Line)

CHECKING THE UPPER BODY FOR WARPAGE

With the carburetor assembled and the body gasket in place, try to insert a 0.002 in. (0.05mm) feeler gauge between the upper and lower bodies at the air vent boss, just below the idle valve. If the gauge can be inserted, the upper body is warped and should be replaced.

CHECKING THE THROTTLE SHAFT AND BUSHINGS

Wear between the throttle shaft and bushings should not exceed 0.010 in. (0.254mm). Check the wear by placing a short iron bar on the upper carburetor body so that it just fits under the throttle shaft. Measure the distance with a feeler gauge while holding the shaft down and then holding it up. If the dif ference is over 0.010 in. (0.254mm), either the upper body should be rebushed, the throttle shaft replaced, or both. Wear on the throttle

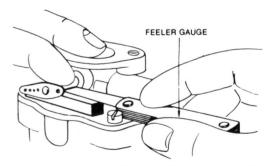

Checking throttle shaft wear with a feeler gauge

shaft can be checked by comparing the worn and unworn portions of the shaft. To replace the bushings, remove the throttle shaft using a thin punch to drive out the pin which holds the throttle stop to the shaft; remove the throttle valve, then pull out the shaft. Place a ¼–20 tap or an E-Z Out in a vise. Turn the carburetor body so as to thread the tap or E-Z Out into the bushings enough to pull the bushings out of the body. Press the new bushings into the carburetor body with a vise. Insert the throttle shaft to be sure it is free in the bushings. If not, run a size $\frac{7}{32}$ in. (5.5mm) drill through both bushings

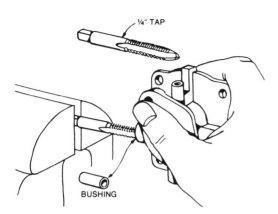

Removing the throttle shaft bushing

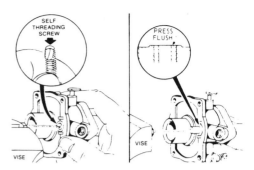

Replacing the float valve seat

to act as a line reamer. Install the throttle shaft, valve, and stop.

DISASSEMBLY OF THE CARBURETOR

1. Remove the idle valve.
2. Loosen the needle valve packing nut.
3. Remove the packing nut and needle valve together. To remove the nozzle, use a narrow, blunt screwdriver so as not to damage the threads in the lower carburetor body. The nozzle projects diagonally into a recess in the upper body and must be removed before the upper body is separated from the lower body, or it may be damaged.
4. Remove the screws which hold the upper and lower bodies together. A pin holds the float in place.
5. Remove the pin to take out the float valve needle. Check the float for leakage. If it contains gasoline or is crushed, it must be replaced. Use a wide, proper fitting screwdriver to remove the float inlet seat.
6. Lift the venturi out of the lower body. Some carburetors have a welch plug. This should be removed only if necessary to remove the choke plate. Some carburetors have nylon choke shaft.

REPAIR

Use new parts where necessary. Always use new gaskets. Carburetor repair kits are available. Tighten the inlet seat with the gasket securely in place, if used. Some float valves have a spring clip to connect the float valve to the float tang. Others are nylon with a stirrup which fits over the float tang. Older float valves and engines with fuel pumps have neither a spring nor a stirrup.

A viton tip float valve is used in later models of the large, two-piece Flo-Jet carburetor. The seat is pressed into the upper body and does not need replacement unless it is damaged.

REPLACING THE PRESSED-IN FLOAT VALVE SEAT

Clamp the head of a #93029 self threading screw in a vise. Turn the carburetor body to thread the screw into the seat. Continue turning the carburetor body, drawing out the seat. Leave the seat fastened to the screw. Insert the new seat #230996 into the carburetor body. The seat has a starting lead.

NOTE: *If the engine is equipped with a fuel pump, install a #231019 seat. Press the new seat flush with the body using the screw and old seat as a driver. Make sure that the seat is not pressed below the body surface or improper float-to-float valve contact will occur. Install the float valve.*

CHECKING THE FLOAT LEVEL

With the body gasket in place on the upper body and the float valve and float installed, the float should be parallel to the body mounting surface. If not, bend the tang on the float until they are parallel. Do not press on the flat to adjust it.

ASSEMBLY OF THE CARBURETOR

Assemble the venturi and the venturi gasket to the lower body. Be sure that the holes in the venturi and the venturi gasket are aligned. Some models do not have a removable venturi.

Float Level Chart

Carburetor Number	Float Setting (in.)
2712-S	$19/64$
2713-S	$19/64$
2714-S	$1/4$
*2398-S	$1/4$
2336-S	$1/4$
2336-SA	$1/4$
2337-S	$1/4$
2337-SA	$1/4$
2230-S	$17/64$
2217-S	$11/64$

*When resilient seat is used, set float level at $9/32 \pm 1/64$.

Install the choke parts and welch plug if previously removed. Use a sealer around the welch plug to prevent entry of dirt.

Fasten the upper and lower bodies together with the mounting screws. Screw in the nozzle with a narrow, blunt screwdriver, making sure that the nozzle tip enters the recess in the upper body. Tighten the nozzle securely. Screw in the needle valve and idle valve until they just seat. Back off the needle valve 1½ turns. Do not tighten the packing nut. Back off the idle valve ¾ of a turn. These settings are about correct. Final adjustment will be made when the engine is running. See the Tune-Up section for mixture and choke adjustments.

One-Piece Flo-Jet Carburetor

The large, one-piece Flo-Jet carburetor has its high speed needle valve below the float bowl. All other repair procedures are similar to the small, one-piece Flo-Jet carburetor.

DISASSEMBLY

1. Remove the idle and needle valves.
2. Remove the carburetor bowl screw. A pin holds the float in place.
3. Remove the pin to take off the float and float valve needle. Check the float for leakage. If it contains gasoline or is crushed, it must be replaced. Use a screwdriver to remove the carburetor nozzle. Use a wide, heavy screwdriver to remove the float valve seat, if used.

If it is necessary to remove the choke valve, venturi throttle shaft, or shaft bushings, proceed as follows:

1. Pry out the welch plug.
2. Remove the choke valve, then the shaft. The venturi will then be free to fall out after the choke valve and shaft have been removed.
3. Check the shaft for wear. (Refer to the "Two-Piece Flo-Jet Carburetor" section for checking wear and replacing bushings.)

REPAIR

Use new parts where necessary. Always use new gaskets. Carburetor repair kits are available. If the venturi has been removed, install the venturi first, then the carburetor nozzle jets. The nozzle jet holds the venturi in place. Replace the choke shaft and valve. Install a new welch plug in the carburetor body. Use a sealer to prevent dirt from entering.

A viton tip float valve is used in the large, one-piece Flo-Jet carburetor. The seat is pressed in the upper carburetor body and does not need replacement unless it is damaged. Replace the seat in the same manner as for the two-piece Flo-Jet carburetor.

CHECKING THE FLOAT LEVEL

With the body gasket in place on the upper body and float valve and the float installed, the float should be parallel to the body mounting surface. If not, bend the tang on the float until they are parallel. Do not press on the float.

Install the float bowl, idle valve, and needle valve. Turn in the needle valve and the idle valve until they just seat. Open the needle valve 2½ turns and the idle valve 1½ turns. On the large carburetors with the needle valve below the float bowl, open the needle valve and the idle valve 1⅛ turns.

These settings will allow the engine to start. Final adjustment should be made when the engine is running and has warmed up to operating temperature. See the "Two-Piece Flo-Jet Carburetor" adjustment procedure.

Governors

The purpose of a governor is to maintain, within certain limits, a desired engine speed even though the load may vary.

AIR VANE GOVERNORS

The governor spring tends to open the throttle. Air pressure against the air vane tends to close the throttle. kThe engine speed at which these two forces balance is called the governed speed. The governed speed can be varied by changing the governor spring tension.

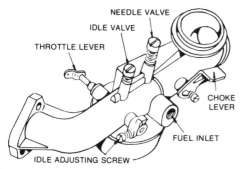

Small one piece Flo-Jet carburetor

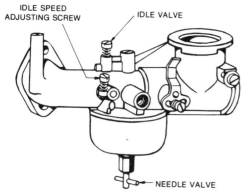

Large one piece Flo-Jet carburetor

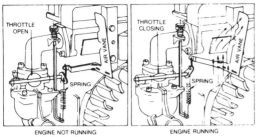

Air vane governor installed on horizontal crank-shaft engine

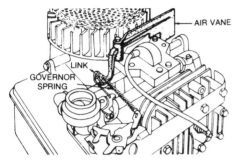

Air vane governor installed on vertical crankshaft engine

Worn linkage or damaged governor springs should be replaced to insure proper governor operation. No adjustment is necessary.

MECHANICAL GOVERNORS

The governor spring tends to pull the throttle open. The force of the counterweights, which are operated by centrifugal force, tends to close the throttle. The engine speed at which these two forces balance is called the governed speed. The governed speed can be varied by changing the governor spring tension.

GOVERNOR REPAIR

The procedures below describe disassembly and assembly of the various kinds of mechanical governors. Look for gears with worn or broken teeth, worn thrust washers, weight pins, cups, followers, etc. Replace parts that are worn and reassemble.

Models N, 6 and 8

DISASSEMBLY

1. Remove the two governor housing mounting screws, and remove the housing.
2. Pull the cup off the governor gear, and then slide the gear off the shaft.
3. Disassemble the governor crank by driving the roll pin out of the end of the governor lever and then remove the crank bushing. Pull the governor crank out of the housing.

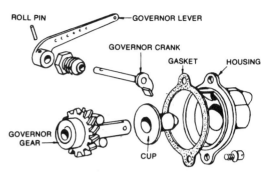

Governor housing and gear assembly

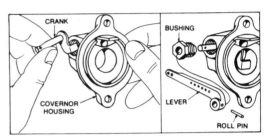

Installing crank and lever

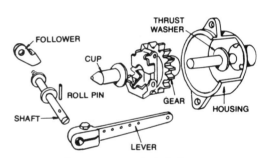

Mechanical governor exploded view

ASSEMBLY

1. Push the governor crank, lever end first, into the housing.
2. Slip the bushing onto the shaft, and then thread it into the housing and tighten securely.
3. Position the lever on the shaft with the lever and shaft pin holes lined up and the lever pointing away from the housing mounting flange. Push in the pin.
4. Push the governor gear onto the shaft in the engine block.
5. Position the gasket on the governor housing, put the hous
ing into position on the block, and install the two housing mounting screws. Connect linkage.

Models 6B, 8B, 60000 and 80000

DISASSEMBLY

1. Loosen the governor lever mounting screw and pull the lever off the shaft.
2. Remove the two housing mounting

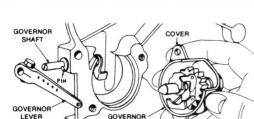

Assembling the mechanical governor

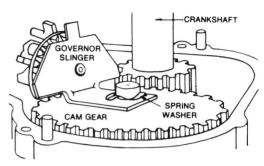

Installing spring on camshaft (Models 100900 and 130900)

screws. Carefully pull the housing off the block being careful to catch the governor gear, which will slip off the shaft. Pull the steel thrust washer off the shaft.

3. Remove the governor lever roll pin and washer. Unscrew the governor lever shaft by turning it clockwise and remove it.

ASSEMBLY

1. Push the governor lever shaft into the crankcase cover, threaded end first. Assemble the small washer onto the inner end of the shaft, and then screw the shaft into the governor crank follower by turning it counterclockwise. Tighten it securely.

2. Turn the shaft until the follower points down slightly, in a position where it would press against the cup when the housing is installed.

3. Place the washer on the outside end of the shaft. Install the rollpin, so the leading end just reaches the outside diameter of the shaft and the back end protrudes.

4. Install the thrust washer and the governor gear on the shaft in the housing (in that order).

5. Hold the crankcase cover in a vertical (the normal) position and install the housing with the gear in position so the point of the steel cup on the gear contacts the follower. Install and tighten the housing mounting screws.

6. Install the lever on the shaft pointing downward at an angle of about 30°. Adjust as described in the Tune-Up section.

Cast Iron Models

DISASSEMBLY

1. Remove the cotter key and washer from the outer end of the governor shaft. Remove the governor crank from inside the crankcase.

2. Slide the governor gear off the shaft.

ASSEMBLY

1. Install the governor gear onto the shaft inside the crankcase. Then, insert the governor shaft assembly through the bushing from inside the crankcase.

2. Install the governor lever to the shaft loosely, and then adjust it as described in the Tune-Up section.

Aluminum Models

DISASSEMBLY

On horizontal shaft models: Remove the governor assembly as a unit from the crankcase cover.

On vertical shaft models: Remove the entire assembly as part of the oil slinger (see the Overhaul Section).

ASSEMBLY

1. Assemble governors on horizontal crankshaft models with crankshaft in a horizontal position. The governor rides on a short stationary shaft which is integral with the crankcase

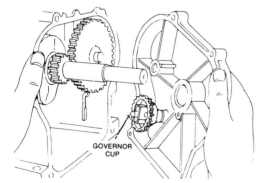

Assembling cover with governor and governor shaft in proper position (horizontal shaft engines)

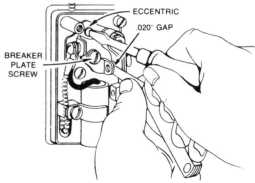

Adjusting the breaker point gap

cover. The governor shaft keeps the governor from sliding off the shaft after the cover is installed. The governor shaft must hang straight down, or it may jam the governor assembly when the crankcase cover is installed, breaking it when the engine is started. The governor shaft adjustment should be made (see the Tune-Up section) as soon as the crankcase cover is in place so that the governor lever will be clamped in the proper position.

2. On both horizontal and vertical crankshaft models, the governor is held together through normal operating forces. For this reason, the governor link and all other external linkages must be in place and properly adjusted whenever the engine is operated.

3. On vertical shaft models 100900 and 130900, be sure the spring washer is in place on the camshaft after the governor is in position.

ENGINE OVERHAUL

Cylinder Head

REMOVAL AND INSTALLATION

Always note the position of the different cylinder head screws so that they can be properly reinstalled. If a screw is used in the wrong position, it may be too short and not engage enough threads. If it is too long, it may bottom on a fin, either breaking the fin, or leaving the cylinder head loose.

1. Remove the cylinder screws and then the cylinder head. Be sure to remove the gasket and all remaining gasket material from the cylinder head and the block.

2. Assemble the cylinder head with a new gasket, cylinder head shield, screws, and washers in their proper places. Graphite grease should be used on aluminum cylinder head screws.

Do not use a sealer of any kind on the head gasket. Tighten the screws down evenly by hand. Use a torque wrench and tighten the head bolts in the correct sequence.

Cylinder Head Bolt Torque Specifications

Basic Model Series	In. lbs. Torque
Aluminum Cylinder	
6B, 60000, 8B, 80000 82000, 92000, 110000, 100000, 130000	140
Cast Iron Cylinder	
5, 6, N, 8, 9	140
14	165

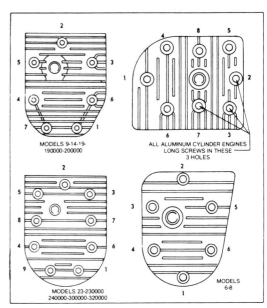

Cylinder head bolt tightening sequences

Valves

REMOVAL AND INSTALLATION

1. Using a valve spring compressor, adjust the jaws so they touch the top and bottom of the valve chamber, and then place one of the jaws over the valve spring and the other underneath, between the spring and the valve chamber. This positioning of the valve spring compressor is for valves that have either pin or collar type retainers.

2. Tighten the jaws to compress the spring. Remove the collars or pin and lift out the valve. Pull out the compressor and the spring.

3. To remove valves with ring type retainers, position the compressor with the upper jaw over the top of the valve chamber and the lower jaw between the spring and the retainer. Compress the spring, remove the retainer, and pull out the valve. Remove the compressor and spring.

To install:

4. Before installing the valves, check the thickness of the valve springs. Some engines use the same spring for the intake and exhaust

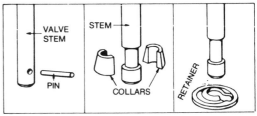

The three types of valve spring retainers

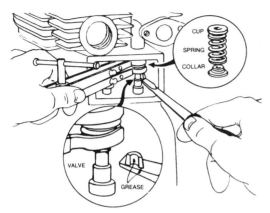

Removing the valve springs with the help of a valve spring compressor

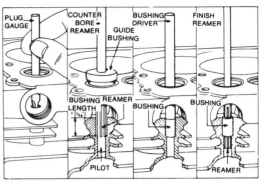

Bushing the valve guide

side, while others use a heavier spring on the exhaust side. Compare the springs before installing them.

5a. If the retainers are held by a pin or collars, place the valve spring and retainer and cup (Models 9–14–19–20–23–24–32) into the valve spring compressor. Compress the spring until it is solid. Insert the compressed spring and retainer into the valve chamber. Then drop the valve into place, pushing the stem through the retainer. Hold the spring up in the chamber, hold the valve down, and insert the retainer pin with needle nose pliers or place the collars in the groove in the valve stem. Loosen the spring until the retainer fits around the pin or collars, then pull out the spring compressor. Be sure the pin or collars are in place.

5b. To install valves with ring type retainers, compress the retainer and spring with the compressor. The large diameter of the retainer should be toward the front of the valve chamber. Insert the compressed spring and retainer into the valve chamber. Drop the valve stem through the larger area of the retainer slot and move the compressor so as to center the small area of the valve retainer slot onto the valve stem shoulder. Release the spring tension and remove the compressor.

Valve Guides

REMOVAL AND INSTALLATION

Aluminum Models

1. First check valve guide for wear with a plug gauge. If the flat end of the valve guide plug gauge can be inserted into the valve guide for a distance of $5/16$ in. (8mm), the valve guide is worn and should be rebushed in the following manner. See the illustation.

2. Procure a reamer and a reamer guide bushing. Lubricate the reamer with kerosene. Use reamer and reamer guide bushing to ream out the worn guide. Ream to only $3/16$ in.

(1.5mm) deeper than valve guide bushing #63709. BE CAREFUL NOT TO REAM THROUGH THE GUIDE!

3. Press in valve guide bushing #63709 until top end of bushing is flush with top end of valve guide. Use a soft metal driver (brass, copper, etc.) or driver #19065 so top end of bushing is not peened over.

4. Finish-ream the bushing. A standard valve can now be used.

NOTE: *It is usually not necessary to bush factory installed brass valve guides. However, if bushing is required, DO NOT REMOVE ORIGINAL BUSHING, but follow standard procedure outlined.*

Cast Iron Models

1. First check valve guide for wear with a plug gauge, Briggs & Stratton part #19151 or equivalent. If the flat end of the valve guide plug gauge can be inserted into the valve guide for a distance of $5/16$ in. (8mm) the guide is worn and should be rebushed in the following manner. See the illustration.

2. Procure a reamer #19183 and reamer guide bushing #19192, and lubricate the reamer with kerosene. Then, use reamer and reamer

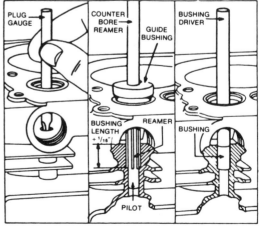

Bushing the valve guide

guide bushing to ream out the worn guide. Ream to only $\frac{3}{16}$ in. (1.5mm) deeper than valve guide bushing #230655. BE CAREFUL NOT TO REAM THROUGH THE GUIDE!

3. Press in valve guide bushing #230655 until top end of bushing is flush with top end of valve guide. Use a soft metal driver (brass, copper, etc .) so top end of bushing is not peened over.

The bushing #230655 is finish reamed to size at the factory, so no further reaming is necessary, and a standard valve can be used.

NOTE: *Valve seating should be checked after bushing the guide, and corrected if necessary by refacing the seat.*

REFACING VALVES AND SEATS

Faces on valves and valve seats should be resurfaced with a valve grinder or cutter to an angle of 45°.

NOTE: *Some engines have a 30° intake valve and seat.*

The valve and seat should then be lapped with a fine lapping compound to remove the grinding marks and ensure a good seat. The valve seat width should be 1.2–1.5mm. If the seat is wider, a narrowing stone or cutter should be used. If either the seat or valve is badly burned, it should be replaced. Replace the valve if the edge thickness (margin) is less than $\frac{1}{64}$ in. (0.4mm) after it has been resurfaced.

CHECK AND ADJUST TAPPET CLEARANCE

Insert the valves in their respective positions in the cylinder. Turn the crankshaft until one of the valves is at its highest position. Turn the crankshaft one revolution. Check the clearance with a feeler gauge. Repeat for the other valve. Grind off the end of the valve stem if necessary to obtain proper clearance.

NOTE: *Check the valve tappet clearance with the en gine cold.*

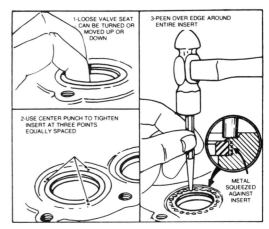

Installing valve seat inserts

Valve Seat Inserts

Cast iron cylinder engines are equipped with an exhaust valve insert which can be removed and replaced with a new insert. The intake side must be counterbored to allow the installation of an intake valve seat insert (see below). Aluminum alloy cylinder models are equipped with inserts on both the exhaust and intake valves.

REMOVAL AND INSTALLATION

NOTE: *Valve seat inserts are removed with a special puller.*

On aluminum alloy cylinder models, it may be necessary to grind the puller nut until the edge is $\frac{3}{32}$ in. (0.8mm) thick in order to get the puller nut under the valve insert.

When installing the valve seat insert, make sure that the side with the chamfered outer edge goes down into the cylinder. Install the seat insert and drive it into place with a driver. The seat should then be ground lightly and the valves and seats lapped lightly with grinding compound.

Valve Tappet Clearance Chart

Model Series	Intake		Exhaust	
	Max	Min	Max	Min
Aluminum Cylinder				
6B, 60000, 8B, 80000	.007	.005	.011	.009
82000, 92000, 100000, 110900	.007	.005	.011	.009
130000	.007	.005	.011	.009
Cast Iron Cylinder				
5, 6, 8, N, 9, 14	.009	.007	.016	.014

Valve Seat Inserts Chart

Basic Model Series	Intake Standard	Exhaust Standard	Exhaust Stellite	Insert # Puller Assembly	Puller Nut
Aluminum Cylinder					
6B, 8B	211291	211291	210452	19138	19140 Ex. 19182 In.
60000, 80000	210879*	211291	210452	19138	19140 Ex. 19182 In.
82000, 92000, 110000	210879	211291	210452	19138	19140 Ex. 19182 In.
100000, 130000	211158	211172	211436	19138	19182 Ex. 19139 In.
Cast Iron Cylinder					
5, 6, N	63838	21865		19138	19140
8	210135	21865		19138	19140
9	63007	63007		19138	19139
14	21880	21880	21612	19138	19141

*21191 used before serial #5810060—210808 used from serial #5810060—6012010
Includes puller and #19182, 19141, 19140 and 19139 nuts

Aluminum alloy cylinder models use the old insert as a spacer between the driver and the new insert. Drive in the new insert until it bottoms. The top of the insert will be slightly below the cylinder head gasket surface. Peen around the insert using a punch and hammer.

NOTE: *The intake valve seat on cast iron cylinder models has to be counterbored before installing the new valve seat insert.*

COUNTERBORING CYLINDER FOR INTAKE VALVE SEAT ON CAST IRON MODELS

1. Select the proper seat insert, cutter shank, counter bore cutter, pilot and driver from the table. These numbers refer to Briggs & Stratton parts — you may get equivalent parts from other sources if available.
2. With cylinder head resting on a flat surface, valve seats up, slide the pilot into the intake valve guide. Then, assemble the correct counterbore cutter to the shank with the cutting blades of the cutter downward.
3. Insert the cutter straight into the valve seat, over the pilot. Cut so as to avoid forcing the cutter to one side, and be sure to stop as soon as the stop on the cutter touches the cylinder head.
4. Blow out all cutting chips thoroughly.

Pistons, Piston Rings, and Connecting Rods
REMOVAL

To remove the piston and connecting rod from the engine, bend down the connecting rod lock. Remove the connecting rod cap. Remove any carbon or ridge at the top of the cylinder bore. This will prevent breaking the rings. Push the piston and rod out of the top of the cylinder.

Pistons used in sleeve bore, aluminum alloy engines are marked with an **L** on top of the piston. These pistons are tin plated and use an ex-

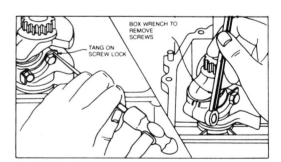

Removing the connecting rod cap

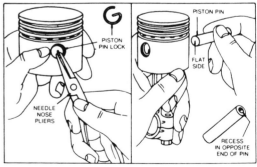

Removing the wrist pin and connecting rod from the piston

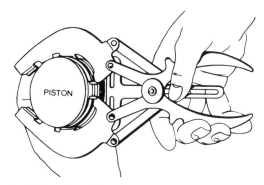

Replacing the piston rings

pander with the oil ring. This piston assembly is not interchangeable with the piston used in the aluminum bore engines (Kool bore).

Pistons used in aluminum bore (Kool bore) engines are not marked on the top.

To remove the connecting rod from the piston, remove the piston pin lock with thin nose pliers. One end of the pin is drilled to facilitate removal of the lock.

Remove the rings one at a time, slipping them over the ring lands. Use a ring expander to remove the rings.

INSPECTION

Check the piston ring fit. Use a feeler gauge to check the side clearance of the top ring. Make sure that you remove all carbon from the top ring groove. Use a new piston ring to check the side clearance. If the cylinder is to be resized, there is no reason to check the piston, since a

Measuring piston ring side gap

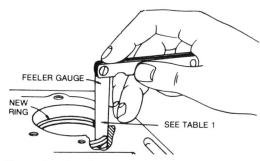

Measuring the piston ring gap

new oversized piston assembly will be installed. If the side clearance is more than 0.007 in. (0.18mm), the piston is excessively worn and should be replaced.

Check the piston ring end gap by cleaning all carbon from the ends of the rings and inserting them one at a time 1 in. (25mm) down into the cylinder. Check the end gap with a feeler gauge. If the gap is larger than recommended, the ring should be replaced.

NOTE: *When checking the ring gap, do not deglaze the cylinder walls by installing piston rings in aluminum cylinder engines.*

Chrome ring sets are available fro all current aluminum and cast iron cylinder models. No honing or deglazing is required. The cylinder bore can be a maximum of 0.005 in. (0.127mm) oversize when using chrome rings.

If the crankpin bearing in the rod is scored, the rod must be replaced. 0.005 in. (0.127mm) oversize piston pins are available in case the connecting rod and piston are worn at the piston pin bearing. If, however, the crankpin bearing in the connecting rod is worn, the rod

Connecting Rod Bearing Specifications

Basic Model Series	Crank Pin Bearing	Piston Pin Bearing
Aluminum Cylinder		
6B, 60000	.876	.492
8B, 80000	1.001	.492
82000, 92000, 110000	1.001	.492
100000	1.001	.555
130000	1.001	.492
Cast Iron Cylinder		
5	.752	.492
6, 8, N	.751	.492
9	.876	.563
14	1.001	.674

Piston Ring Gap Specifications

Basic Model Series	Comp. Ring	Oil Ring
Aluminum Cylinder		
6B, 60000, 8B, 80000		
82000, 92000, 110000, 111000	.035	.045
Cast Iron Cylinder		
5, 6, 8, N, 9	.035	.035

Wrist Pin Specifications

Basic Model Series	Piston Pin	Pin Bore
Aluminum Cylinder		
6B, 60000	.489	.491
8B, 80000	.489	.491
82000, 92000, 110000, 111000	.489	.491
100000	.552	.554
130000	.489	.491
Cast Iron Cylinder		
5, 6, 8, N	.489	.491
9	.561	.563
14	.671	.673

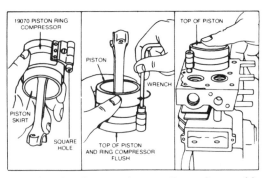

Installing the piston and connecting rod assembly into the cylinder block

should be replaced. Do not attempt to file or fit the rod.

If the piston pin is worn 0.0005 in. (0.0127mm) out of round or below the rejection sizes, it should be replaced.

INSTALLATION

The piston pin is a push fit into both the piston and the connecting rod. On models using a solid piston pin, one end is flat and the other end is recessed. Other models use a hollow piston pin.

1. Place a pin lock in the groove at one side of the piston. From the opposite side of the piston, insert the piston pin, flat end first for solid pins; with hollow pins, insert either end first until it stops against the pin lock. Use thin nose pliers to assemble the pin lock in the recessed end of the piston. Be sure the locks are firmly set in the groove.

2. Install the rings on the pistons, using a piston ring expander. Make sure that they are installed in the proper position. The scraper groove on the center compression ring should always be down toward the piston skirt. Be sure

the oil return holes are clean and all carbon is removed from the grooves.

NOTE: *Install the expander under the oil ring in sleeve bore aluminum alloy engines.*

3. Oil the rings and the piston skirt, then compress the rings with a ring compressor. On cast iron engines, install the compressor with the two projections downward; on aluminum engines, install the compressor with the two projections upward. These instructions refer to the piston in normal position – with skirt downward.

4. Turn the piston and compressor upside down on the bench and push downward so the piston head and the edge of the compressor band are even, all the while tightening the compressor. Draw the compressor up tight to fully compress the rings, then loosen the compressor very slightly.

WARNING: *Do not attempt to install the piston and ring assembly without using a ring compressor.*

5. Place the connecting rod and piston assembly, with the rings compressed, into the cylinder bore.

6. Push the piston and rod down into the cylinder. Oil the crankpin of the crankshaft.

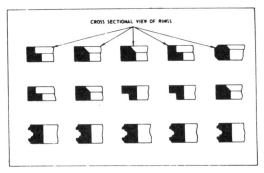

Cross-sectional views and positioning of the various types of piston rings used in Briggs and Stratton engines

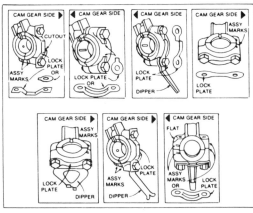

Connecting rod installation

Connecting Rod Capscrew Torque

Basic Model Series	Inch lbs Avg. Torque
Aluminum Cylinder	
6B, 60000	100
8B, 80000	100
82000, 92000, 110000, 111000	100
100000, 130000	100
Cast Iron Cylinder	
5, 6, N, 8	100
9	140
14	190

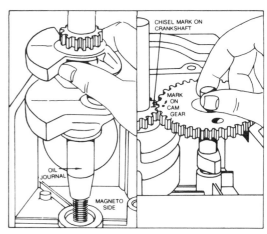

Alignment of the camshaft and crankshaft timing marks

7. Pull the connecting rod against the crankpin and assemble the rod cap so the assembly marks align.

Some rods do not have assembly marks, as the rod and cap will fit together only in one position. Use care to ensure proper installation. On the 251000 engine, the piston has a notch on the top surface. The notch must face the flywheel side of the block when installed. On models 300000 and 320000, the piston has an identification mark **F** located mext to the piston pin bore. The mark must appear on the same side as the assembly mark on the rod. The assembly mark on the rod is also used to identify rod and cap alignment. Note, on these pistons, that the top ring has a beveled upper surface on the outside, while the center ring has a flat outer surface. The **F** mark or notch must face the flywheel when the piston is installed.

Where there are flat washers under the cap screws, remove and discard them prior to installing the rod. Assemble the cap screws and screw locks with the oil dippers (if used), and torque to the figure shown in the chart to avoid breakage or rod scoring later. Turn the crankshaft two revolutions to be sure the rod is correctly installed. If the rod strikes the camshaft, the connecting rod has been installed wrong or the cam gear is out of time. If the crankshaft operates freely, bend the cap screw locks against the screw heads. After tightening the rod screws, the rod should be able to move sideways on the crankpin of the shaft.

Crankshaft and Camshaft Gear
REMOVAL

Aluminum Cylinder Engines

To remove the crankshaft from aluminum alloy engines, remove any rust or burrs from the power take-off end of the crankshaft. Remove the crankcase cover or sump. If the sump or cover sticks, tap it lightly with a soft hammer on alternate sides near the dowel. Turn the crankshaft to align the crankshaft and camshaft timing marks, lift out the cam gear, then remove the crankshaft. On models that have ball bearings on the crankshaft, the crankshaft and the camshaft must be removed together with the timing marks properly aligned — see illustration.

Cast Iron Cylinder Models

To remove the crankshaft from cast iron models, remove the crankcase cover. Revolve the crankshaft until the crankpin is pointing upward toward the breather at the rear of the engine (approximately a 45° angle). Pull the crankshaft out from the drive side, twisting it slightly if necessary. On models with ball bearings on the crankshaft, both the crankcase cover and bearing support should be removed.

On cast iron models with ball bearings on the drive side, first remove the magneto. Drive out the camshaft. Push the camshaft forward into the recess at the front of the engine. Then draw

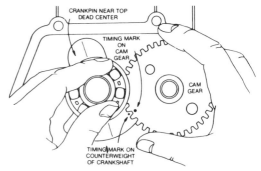

Alignment of the camshaft and crankshaft timing marks on engines equipped with ball bearings

Crankshaft Specifications

Basic Model Series	PTO Journal	Mag. Journal	C Crankpin
Aluminum Cylinder			
6B, 60000	.873	.873	.870
8B, 80000*	.873	.873	.996
82000, 92000*, 110900*	.873	.873	.996
100000, 130000	.998	.873	.996
Cast Iron Cylinder			
5, 6, 8, N	.873	.873	.743
9	.983	.983	.873
14	1.179	1.179	.996

*Auxiliary drive models P.T.O. bearing reject size— 1.003

Camshaft Specifications

Basic Model Series	Cam Gear or Shaft Journals	Cam Lobe
Aluminum Cylinder		
6B, 60000	.498	.883
8B, 80000*	.498	.883
82000, 92000	.498	.883
110900	.436 MAG. .498 PTO.	.870
100000, 130000	.498	.950
Cast Iron Cylinder		
5, 6, 8, N	.372	.875
9	.372	1.124
14	.497	1.115

*Auxiliary drive models P.T.O. .751

the crankshaft from the magneto side of the engine. Double thrust engines have cap screws inside the crankcase which hold the bearing in place. These must be removed before the crankshaft can be removed.

To remove the camshaft from all cast iron models, except the 300400 and 320400, use a long punch to drive the camshaft out toward the magneto side. Save the plug. Do not burr or peen the end of the shaft while driving it out. Hold the camshaft while driving it out. Hold the camshaft while removing the punch, so it will not drop and become damaged.

CHECKING THE CRANKSHAFT

Discard the crankshaft if it is worn beyond the allowable limit. Check the keyways for wear

and make sure they are not spread. Remove all burrs from the keyway to prevent scratching the bearing. Check the three bearing journals, drive end, crankpin, and magneto end, for size and any wear or damage. Check the cam gear teeth for wear. They should not be worn at all. Check the threads at the magneto end for damage. Make sure that the crankshaft is straight.

NOTE: *There are 0.020 in. (0.5mm) undersize connecting rods available for use on reground crakpin bearings.*

BALL BEARINGS REPLACEMENT

The ball bearings are pressed onto the crankshaft. If either the bearing or the crankshaft is to be removed, use an arbor press to remove them.

To install, heat the bearing in hot oil (325°F [163°C] maximum). Don't let the bearing rest on the bottom of the pan in which it is heated. Place the crankshaft in a vise with the bearing side up. When the bearing is quite hot, it will slip fit onto the bearing journal. Grasp the bearing, with the shield down, and thrust it down onto the crankshaft. The bearing will tighten on the shaft while cooling. Do not quench the bearing (throw water on it to cool it).

CHECKING THE CAMSHAFT GEAR

Inspect the teeth for wear and nicks. Check the size of the camshaft and camshaft gear bearing journals. Check the size of the cam lobes. If the cam is worn beyond tolerance, discard it.

Check the automatic spark advance on models equipped with the Magna-Matic ignition system. Place the cam gear in the normal operating position with the movable weight down. Press the weight down and release it. The spring should lift the weight. If not, the spring is stretched or the weight is binding.

INSTALLATION

Aluminum Alloy Engines – Plain Bearing

In aluminum alloy engines, the tappets are inserted first, the crankshaft next, and then the cam gear. When inserting the cam gear, turn the crankshaft and the cam gear so that the timing marks on the gears align.

Aluminum Alloy Engines – Ball Bearing

On crankshafts with ball bearings, the gear teeth are not visible for alignment of the timing marks; therefore, the timing mark is on the counterweight. On ball bearing equipped engines, the tappets are installed first. The crankshaft and the cam gear must be inserted together and their timing marks aligned.

Crankshaft Cover and Crankshaft

INSTALLATION

Models 100900 and 130900

On these models, install the governor slinger onto the cam gear with the spring washer.

To protect the oil seal while assembling the crankcase cover, put oil or grease on the sealing edge of the oil seal. Wrap a piece of thin cardboard around the crankshaft so the seal will slide easily over the shoulder of the crankshaft. If the sharp edge of the oil seal is cut or bent under, the seal may leak.

Cast Iron Engines w/Plain Bearings

1. Assemble the tappets and cylinder, then insert the cam gear.
2. Push the camshaft into the camshaft hole in the cylinder, from the flywheel side, through the cam gear.
3. With a blunt punch, press or hammer the camshaft until the end is flush with the outside of the cylinder on the power takeoff side.
4. Place a small amount of sealer on the camshaft plug, then press or hammer it into the camshaft hole in the cylinder at the flywheel side.
5. Install the crankshaft so the timing marks on the teeth and on the cam gear align.

Cast Iron Engines w/Ball Bearings

1. Assemble the tappets, then insert the cam gear into the cylinder, pushing the cam gear forward into the recess in front of the cylinder.
2. Insert the crankshaft into the cylinder.
3. Turn the camshaft and crankshaft until the timing marks align, then push the cam gear back until it engages the gear on the crankshaft with the timing marks together.
4. Insert the camshaft.
5. Place a small amount of sealer on the camshaft plug and press or hammer it into the camshaft hole in the cylinder at the flywheel side.

Crankshaft End-Play Adjustment

The crankshaft end-play on all models, plain and ball bearing, should be 0.002–0.008 in. (0.05–0.20mm). The method of obtaining the correct end-play varies, however, between cast iron, aluminum, plain, and ball bearing models. New gasket sets include three crankcase cover or bearing support gaskets, 0.005 in. (0.127mm), 0.009 in. (0.228mm), and 0.015 in. (0.381mm) thick.

The end-play of the crankshaft may be checked by assembling a dial indicator on the crankshaft with the pointer against the crankcase. Move the crankshaft in and out. The indicator will show the end-play. Another way to measure the end-play is to assemble a pulley to the crankshaft and measure the end-play with a feeler gauge. Place the feeler gauge between the crankshaft thrust face and the bearing support. The feeler gauge method of measuring crankshaft end-play can only be used on cast iron plain bearing engines with removable bases.

On cast iron engines, the end-play should be 0.002–0.008 in. (0.05–0.20mm) with one 0.015 in. (0.381mm) gasket in place. If the end-play is less than 0.002 in. (0.05mm), which would be the case if a new crankcase or sump cover is used, additional gaskets of 0.005 in. (0.127mm), 0.009 in. (0.228mm), or 0.015 in. (0.381mm) may be added in various combinations to obtain the proper end-play.

ALUMINUM ENGINES ONLY

If the end-play is more than 0.008 in. (0.20mm) with one 0.015 in. (0.381mm) gasket in place, a thrust washer is available to be placed on the crankshaft power take-off end, between the gear and crankcase cover or sump on plain bearing engines. On ball bearing equipped aluminum engines, the thrust washer is added to the magneto end of the crankshaft instead of the power take-off end.

NOTE: *Aluminum engines never use less than the 0.015 in. (0.381mm) gasket.*

Cylinders

INSPECTION

Always inspect the cylinder after the engine has been disassembled. Visual inspection will show if there are any cracks, stripped bolt holes, broken fins, or if the cylinder wall is scored. Use an inside micrometer or telescoping gauge and micrometer to measure the size of the cylinder bore. Measure at right angles.

If the cylinder bore is more than 0.003 in. (0.076mm) oversize, or 0.0015 in. (0.038mm) out of round on lightweight (aluminum) cylinders, the cylinder must be resized (rebored).

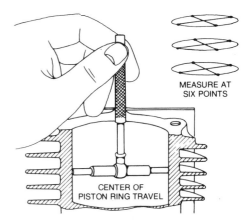

MEASURE AT SIX POINTS

CENTER OF PISTON RING TRAVEL

Checking the cylinder bore

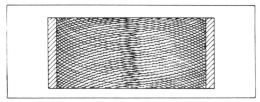

Cross hatch pattern after honing

NOTE: *Do not deglaze the cylinder walls when installing piston rings in aluminum cylinder engines. Also be aware that there are chrome ring sets available for most engines. These are used to control oil pumping in bores worn to 0.005 in. (0.127mm) over standard and do not require honing or glaze breaking to seat.*

RESIZING

Always resize to exactly 0.010 in. (0.254mm), 0.020 in. (0.508mm), or 0.030 in. (0.762mm) over standard size. If this is done accurately, the stock oversize rings and pistons will fit perfectly and proper clearances will be maintained. Cylinders, either cast iron or lightweight, can be quickly resized with a good hone. Use the stones and lubrication recommended by the hone manufacturer to produce the correct cylinder wall finish for the various engine models.

If a boring bar is used, a hone must be used after the boring operation to produce the proper cylinder wall finish. Honing can be done with

Cylinder Bore Specifications

Basic Engine Model or Series	Std. Bore Size Diameter	
	Max	Min
Aluminum Cylinder		
6B		
60000 before Ser. #5810060	2.3125	2.3115
60000 after Ser. #5810030	2.375	2.374
8B, 80000, 82000	2.375	2.374
92000	2.5625	2.5615
100000	2.500	2.449
110000	2.7812	2.7802
130000	2.5625	2.5615
Cast Iron Cylinder		
5, 6, 5S, N	2.000	1.999
8	2.250	2.249
9	2.250	2.249
14	2.625	2.624

a portable electric drill, but it is easaier to use a drill press.

1. Clean the cylinder at top and bottom to remove all burrs and pieces of base and head gaskets.

2. Fasten the cylinder to a heavy iron plate. Some cylinders require shims. Use a level to align the drill press spindle with the bore.

3. Oil the surface of the drill press table liberally. Set the iron plate and the cylinder on the drill press table. Do not anchor the cylinder to the drill press table. If you are using a portable drill, set the plate and the cylinder on the floor.

4. Place the hone driveshaft in the chuck of the drill.

5. Slip the hone into the cylinder. Connect the driveshaft to the hone and set the stop on the drill press so the hone can only extend ¾–1 in. (19–25mm) from the top or bottom of the cylinder. If you are using a portable drill, cut a piece of wood to place in the cylinder as a stop for the hone.

6. Place the hone in the middle of the cylinder bore. Tighten the adjusting knob with your finger or a small screwdriver until the stones fit snugly against the cylinder wall. Do not force the stones against the cylinder wall. The hone should operate at a speed of 300–700 rpm. Lubricate the hone as recommended by the manufacturer.

NOTE: *Be sure that the cylinder and the hone are centered and aligned with the driveshaft and the drill spindle.*

7. Start the drill and, as the hone spins, move it up and down at the lower end of the cylinder. The cylinder is not worn at the bottom but is round so it will act to guide the hone and straighten the cylinder bore. As the bottom of the cylinder increases in diameter, gradually increase your strokes until the hone travels the full length of the bore.

NOTE: *Do not extend the hone more than ¾–1 in. (19–25mm) past either end of the cylinder bore.*

8. As the cutting tension decreases, stop the hone and tighten the adjusting knob. Check the cylinder bore frequently with an accurate micrometer. Hone 0.0005 in. (0.0127mm) oversize to allow for shrinkage when the cylinder cools.

9. When the cylinder is within 0.0015 in. (0.0381mm) of the desired size, change from the rough stone to a finishing stone.

The finished resized cylinder should have a cross-hatched appearance. Proper stones, lubrication, and spindle speed along with rapid movement of the hone within the cylinder during the last few strokes, will produce this finish. Cross-hatching provides proper lubrication and ring break-in.

NOTE: *It is EXTREMELY important that*

the cylinder be thoroughly cleaned after honing to eliminate ALL grit. Wash the cylinder carefully in a solvent such as kerosene. The cylinder bore should be cleaned with a brush, soap, and water.

Bearings

INSPECTION

Plain Type

Bearings should be replaced if they are scored or if a plug gauge will enter. Try the gauge at several points in the bearing.

REPLACING PLAIN BEARINGS

Models 9–14

The crankcase cover bearing support should be replaced if the bearing is worn or scored.

REPLACING THE MAGNETO BEARING

Aluminum Cylinder Engines

There are no removable bearings in these engines. The cylinder must be reamed out so a replacement bushing can be installed.

1. Place a pilot guide bushing in the sump bearing, with the flange of the guide bushing toward the inside of the sump.

2. Assemble the sump on the cylinder. Make sure that the pilot guide bushing does not fall out of place.

3. Place the guide bushing into the oil seal recess in the cylinder. This guide bushing will center the counterbore reamer even though the oil bearing surface might be badly worn.

4. Place the counterbore reamer on the pilot and insert them into the cylinder until the tip of the pilot enters the pilot guide bushing in the sump.

5. Turn the reamer clockwise with a steady, even pressure until it is complltely through the bearing. Lubricate the reamer with kero-

Crankshaft Bearing Specifications

Basic Engine Model or Series	PTO Bearing	Bearing Magneto
Aluminum Cylinder		
6B, 8B	.878	.878
60000, 80000	.878	.878
82000, 92000, 110900	.878	.878
100000, 130000	1.003	.878
Cast Iron Cylinder		
5, 6, N	.878	.878
9	.988	.988
14	1.185	1.185

sene or any other suitable solvent.

NOTE: *Counterbore reaming may be performed without any lubrication. However, clean off shavings because aluminum material builds up on the reamer flutes causing eventual damage to the reamer and an oversize counterbore.*

6. Remove the sump and pull the reamer out without backing it through the bearing. Clean out the remaining chips. Remove the guide bushing from the oil seal recess.

7. Hold the new bushing against the outer end of the reamed out bearing, with the notch in the bushing aligned with the notch in the cylinder. Note the position of the split in the bushing. At a point in the outer edge of the reamed out bearing opposite to the split in the bushing, make a notch in the cylinder hub at a 45° angle to the bearing surface. Use a chisel or a screwdriver and hammer.

8. Press in the new bushing, being careful to align the oil notches with the driver and the support until the outer end of the bushing is flush with the end of the reamed cylinder hub.

9. With a blunt chisel or screwdriver, drive a portion of the bushing into the notch previously made in the cylinder. This is called staking and is done to prevent the bushing from turning.

10. Reassemble the sump to the cylinder with the pilot guide bushing in the sump bearing.

11. Place a finishing reamer on the pilot and insert the pilot into the cylinder bearing until the tip of the pilot enters the pilot guide bushings in the sump bearing.

12. Lubricate the reamer with kerosene, fuel oil, or other suitable solvent, then ream the bushing, turning the reamer clockwise with a steady even pressure until the reamer is completely through the bearing. Improper lubricants will produce a rough bearing surface.

13. Remove the sump, reamer, and the pilot guide bushing. Clean out all reaming chips.

REPLACING THE P.T.O. BEARING

Aluminum Cylinder Engines

The sump or crankcase bearing is repaired the same way as the magneto end bearing. Make sure to complete repair of one bearing before starting to repair the other. Press in new oil seals when bearing repair is completed.

NOTE: *On Models 8B–HA, 80590, 81590, 82590, 80790, 81790, 82990, 92590 and 92990, the magneto bearing can be replaced as described above. However, if the sump bearing is worn, the sump must be replaced.*

REPLACING OIL SEALS

1. Assemble the seal with the sharp edge of leather or rubber toward the inside of the engine.

2. Lubricate the inside diameter of the seal with Lubriplate® or equivalent.

3. Press all seals but those listed below so they are flush with the hub. On models 60000, 80000, 100000 and 13000 with ball bearing which has a mounting flange, the seal must be pressed in until it is $3/16$ in. (4.76mm) below the crannkcase mounting flange.

Extended Oil Filler Tubes and Dipsticks

When installing the extended oil fill and dipstick assembly, the tube must be installed so the O-ring seal is firmly compressed. To do so, push the tube downward toward the sump, then tighten the blower housing screw, which is used to secure the tube and bracket. When the dipstick assembly is fully depressed, it seals the upper end of the tube.

A leak at the seal between the tube and the sump, or at the seal at the upper end of the dipstick can result in a loss of crankcase vacuum, and a discharge of smoke through the exhaust system.

Breathers

The function of the breather is to maintain a vacuum in the crankcase. The breather has a fiber disc valve which limits the direction of air flow caused by the piston moving back and forth in the cylinder. Air can flow out of the crankcase, but the one-way valve blocks the return flow, thus maintaining a vacuum in the crankcase. A partial vacuum must be maintained in the crankcase to prevent oil from being forced out of the engine at the piston rings, oil seals, breaker plunger, and gaskets.

INSPECTION OF THE BREATHER

If the fiber disc valve is stuck or binding, the breather cannot function properly and must be replaced. A 0.045 in. (1.14mm) wire gauge should not enter the space between the fiber disc valve and the body. Use a spark plug wire gauge to check the valve. The fiber disc valve is held in place by an internal bracket which will be distorted if pressure is applied to the fiber disc valve. Therefore, do not apply force when checking the valve with the wire gauge.

If the breather is removed for inspection or valve repair, a new gasket should be used when replacing the breather. Tighten the screws securely to prevent oil leakage.

Most breathers are now vented through the air cleaner, to prevent dirt from entering the crankcase. Check to be sure that the venting el-

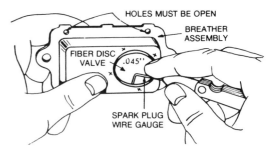

Checking the breather assembly

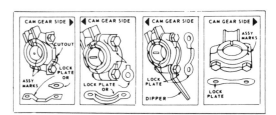

Installing the connecting rod in a horizontal crankshaft engine

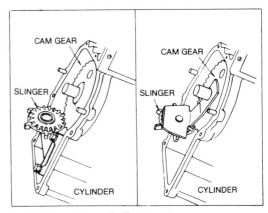

Installation of an oil slinger

bows or the tube are not damaged and that they are properly sealed.

Oil Dippers and Slingers

Oil dippers reach into the oil reservoir in the base of the engine and splash oil onto the internal engine parts. The oil dipper is installed on the connecting rod and has no pump or moving parts.

Oil slingers are driven by the cam gear. Old style slingers using a die cast bracket assembly have a steel bushing between the slinger and the bracket. Replace the bracket on which the oil slinger rides if it is worn to a diameter of 0.490 in. (12.4mm) or less. Replace the steel bushing if it is worn. Newer style oil slingers have a stamped steel bracket.

4

Briggs & Stratton
6 through 12 Hp

ENGINE IDENTIFICATION

The Briggs and Stratton model designation system consists of up to a six digit number. It is possible to determine most of the important mechanical features of the engine by merely knowing the model number. An explanation of what each number means is given below.

1. The first one or two digits indicate the cubic inch displacement (cid).

2. The first digit after the displacement indicates the basic design series, relating to cylinder construction, ignition and general configuration.

3. The second digit after the displacement indicates the position of the crankshaft and the type of carburetor the engine has.

4. The third digit after the displacement indicates the type of bearings and whether or not the engine is equipped with a reduction gear or auxiliary drive.

5. The last digit indicates the type of starter.

Briggs and Stratton Model Numbering System

Cubic Inch Displacement	First Digit After Displacement — Basic Design Series	Second Digit After Displacement — Crankshaft, Carburetor Governor	Third Digit After Displacement — Bearings, Reduction Gears & Auxiliary Drives	Fourth Digit After Displacement — Type of Starter
6	0	0-	0-Plain Bearing	0-Without Starter
8	1	1-Horizontal Vacu-Jet	1-Flange Mounting Plain Bearing	1-Rope Starter
9	2			
10	3	2-Horizontal Pulsa-Jet	2-Ball Bearing	2-Rewind Starter
13	4			
14	5	3-Horizontal Flo-Jet (Pneumatic Governor)	3-Flange Mounting Ball Bearing	3-Electric-110 Volt, Gear Drive
17	6			
19	7	4-Horizontal Flo-Jet (Mechanical Governor)	4-	4-Elec. Starter-Generator-12 Volt, Belt Drive
20	8			
23	9			
24		5-Vertical Vacu-Jet	5-Gear Reduction (6 to 1)	5-Electric Starter Only-12 Volt, Gear Drive
30				
32		6-	6-Gear Reduction (6 to 1) Reverse Rotation	6-Wind-up Starter
		7-Vertical Flo-Jet	7-	7-Electric Starter, 12 Volt Gear Drive, with Alternator
		8-	8-Auxiliary Drive Perpendicular to Crankshaft	8-Vertical-pull Starter
		9-Vertical Pulsa-Jet	9-Auxiliary Drive Parallel to Crankshaft	

General Engine Specifications

Model	Bore Size (in.)	Horsepower
Aluminum Engines		
140000	2.750	6
170000, 171700	3.000	7
190000, 191700	3.000	8
251000	3.4375	10
Cast Iron Engines		
19, 190000, 200000	3.000	8
23, 230000	3.000	9
243000	3.0625	10
300000	3.4375	13
320000	3.5625	16

The model identification plate is usually located on the air baffle surrounding the cylinder.

MAINTENANCE

Air Cleaners

A properly serviced air cleaner protects the engine from dust particles that are in the air. When servicing an air cleaner, check the air cleaner mounting and gaskets for worn or damaged mating surfaces. Replace any worn or damaged parts to prevent dirt and dust from entering the engine through openings caused by improper sealing. Straighten or replace any bent mounting studs.

SERVICING

Oil Foam Air Cleaners

Clean and re-oil the air cleaner element every 25 hours of operation under normal operating conditions. The capacity of the oil-foam air cleaner is adequate for a full season's use without cleaning. Under very dusty conditions, clean the air cleaner every few hours of operation.

The oil-foam air cleaner is serviced in the following manner:

1. Remove the screw that holds the halves of the air cleaner shell together and retains it to the carburetor.
2. Remove the air cleaner carefully to prevent dirt from entering the carburetor.
3. Take the air cleaner apart (split the two halves).
4. Wash the foam in kerosene or liquid detergent and water to remove the dirt.
5. Wrap the foam in a clean cloth and squeeze it dry.
6. Saturate the foam in clean engine oil and squeeze it to remove the excess oil.
7. Assemble the air cleaner and fasten it to the carburetor with the attaching screw.

Oil Bath Air Cleaner

Pour the old oil out of the bowl. Wash the element thoroughly in solvent and squeeze it dry. Clean the bowl and refill it with the same type of oil used in the crankcase.

Dry Element Air Cleaner

Remove the element of the air cleaner and tap (top and bottom) it on a flat surface or wash it in non-sudsing detergent and flush it from the inside until the water coming out is clear. After washing, air dry the element thoroughly before reinstalling it on the engine. NEVER OIL A DRY ELEMENT.

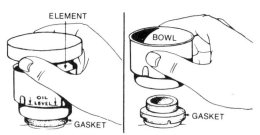

Oil bath air cleaner

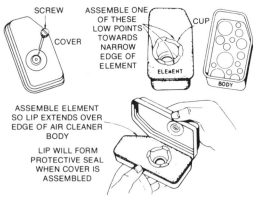

Oil foam air cleaner

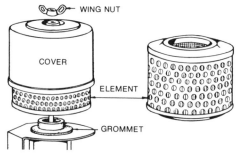

Dry element air cleaner

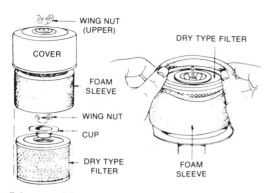

WING NUT (UPPER)

COVER

FOAM SLEEVE

WING NUT

CUP

DRY TYPE FILTER

DRY TYPE FILTER

FOAM SLEEVE

Briggs and Stratton heavy duty air cleaner

Oil Viscosity Recommendations

Winter (under 40°F.)	Summer (above 40°F.)
SAE 5W-20, or SAE 5W-30	SAE 30
If above are not available:	If above is not available:
SAE 10W or SAE 10W-30 (under 0°F.)	SAE 10W-40 or SAE 10W-30
Use SAE 10W or SAE 10W-30 in proportions of 90% motor oil/ 10% kerosene	

Heavy Duty Air Cleaner

Clean and re-oil the foam pre-cleaner at three month intervals or every 25 hours, whichever comes first.

Clean the paper element every year or 100 hours, whichever comes first. Use the dry element procedure for cleaning the paper element of the heavy duty air cleaner.

Use the oil foam cleaning procedure to clean the foam sleeve of the heavy duty air cleaner.

If the engine is operated under very dusty conditions, clean the air cleaner more often.

Oil and Fuel Recommendations

Briggs & Stratton recommends unleaded fuel. Unleaded fuel is preferable because of the reduction in deposits that results from its use, but its use is not required.

Premium fuel is not required, as regular or unleaded will have sufficient knock resistance if the engine is in proper condition. The factory recommends that fuel by purchased in lots small enough to be used up in 30 days or less. When fuel is older than that, it can form gum and varnish, or may be improperly tailored to the prevailing temperature.

You should use a high quality detergent oil designated "For Service SG". Detergent oil is recommended because of its important ability to keep gum and varnish from clogging the lubrication system. Briggs & Stratton specifically recommends that no special oil additives be used.

Oil must be changed every 25 hours of operation. If the atmosphere in which the engine is operating is very dirty, oil changes should be made more frequently, as often as every 12 hours, if necessary. Oil should be changed after 5 hours of operation in the case of brand new engines. Drain engine oil when hot.

In hot weather, when under heavy load, or when brand new, engines may consume oil at a rate which will require you to refill the crank-

case several times between oil changes. Check the oil level every hour or so until you can accurately estimate how long the engine can go between refills. To check oil level, stop the engine and allow it to sit for a couple of minutes, then remove the dipstick or filler cap. Fill the crankcase to the top of the filler pipe when there is no dipstick, or wipe the dipstick clean, reinsert it, and add oil as necessary until the level reaches the upper mark.

On cast iron engines with a gear reduction unit, crankcase and reduction gears are lubricated by a common oil supply. When draining crankcase, also remove drain plug in reduction unit.

On aluminum engines with reduction gear, a

Engine Oil Capacity Chart

Basic Model Series	Capacity Pints
Aluminum	
14, 17 Cu. in. Vert. Crankshaft	2¼
14, 17, 19 Cu. in. Horiz. Crankshaft	2¾
25 Cu. in. Vert. Crankshaft	3
25 Cu. in. Horiz. Crankshaft	3
Cast Iron	
19, 20 Cu. in. Horiz. Crank.	3
23, 24, 30, 32 Cu. in. Horiz. Crank.	4

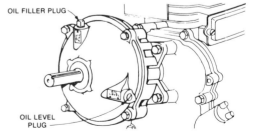

OIL FILLER PLUG

OIL LEVEL PLUG

Location of oil fill and level check plugs, 6-1 gear reduction equipped engines

separate oil supply lubricates the gears, although the same type of oil used in the crankcase is used in the reduction gear cover. On these engines, remove the drain plug every fourth oil change (100 hours), then install the plug and refill. The level in the reduction gear cover must be checked during the refill operation by removing the level plug from the side of the gearcase, removing the filler plug, and then filling the case through the filler plug hole until oil runs out the level plug hole. Then, install both plugs.

On 6–1 gear reduction engines (models 6, 8, 8000, 10000, and 13000), no changes are required for the oil in the reduction gear case, but level must be checked and the case refilled, as described in the paragraph above, every 100 hours. Make sure the oil level plug (with screwdriver slot and no vent) is installed in the hole on the side of the case.

TUNE-UP

Spark Plugs

Remove the spark plug with a ¾ in. (1½ in. plug) or a $^{13}/_{16}$ in. (2 in. plug) deep well socket wrench. Clean carbon deposits off the center and side electrodes with a sharp instrument. If possible, you should also attempt to remove deposits from the recess between the insulator and the threaded portion of the plug. If the electrodes are burned away or the insulator is cracked at any point, replace the plug. Using a wire type feeler gauge, adjust the gap by bending the side electrode where it is curved until the gap is 0.030 in. (0.8mm).

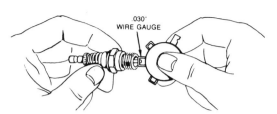

Checking spark plug gap with a wire feeler gauge

When installing the plug, make sure the threads of the plug and the threads in the cylinder head are clean. It is best to oil the plug threads very lightly. Be careful not to overtorque the plug, especially if the engine has an aluminum head. If you use a torque wrench, torque to about 15 ft. lbs.

Breaker Points

All Briggs and Stratton engines have magneto ignition systems. Three types are used: Flywheel Type — Internal Breaker Flywheel Type — External Breaker, and Magna-Matic.

FLYWHEEL TYPE — INTERNAL BREAKER

This ignition system has the magneto located on the flywheel and the breaker points located under the flywheel.

The flywheel is located on the crankshaft with a soft metal key. It is held in place by a nut or starter clutch. The flywheel key must be in good condition to insure proper location of the flywheel for ignition timing. Do not use a steel key under any circumstances. Use only a soft metal key, as originally supplied.

The keyway in both flywheel and crankshaft should not be distorted. Flywheels are made of aluminum, zinc, or cast iron.

Tune-Up Specifications

Model	Plug Type	Plug Gap (in.)	Point Gap (in.)	Armature Gap		Idle Speed
				2 leg	3 leg	
Aluminum Block						
140000, 170000, 190000, 251000	①	.030	.020	.010–.014	.016–.019	1750
Cast Iron Block						
19, 190000, 200000	①	.030	.020	.010–.014	.022–.026	1200
23, 230000	①	.030	.020	.010–.014	.022–.026	1200
243400, 300000, 320000	①	.030	.020	.010–.014	—	1200

① Manufacturer's Code		Manufacturer
1½ in. plug	2 in. plug	
CJ-8	J-8	Champion
RCJ-8	RJ-8	Champion (resistor)
A-7NX	A-71	Autolite
AR-7N	AR-80	Autolite (resistor)
CS-45	GC-46	A.C.
—	R-46	A.C. (resistor)

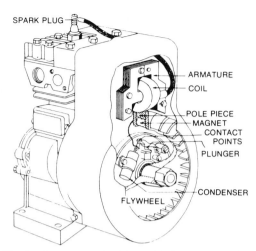

Flywheel magneto ignition with internal breaker points and external armature

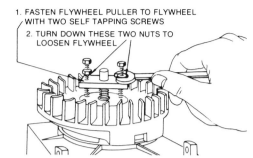

1. FASTEN FLYWHEEL PULLER TO FLYWHEEL WITH TWO SELF TAPPING SCREWS
2. TURN DOWN THESE TWO NUTS TO LOOSEN FLYWHEEL

Removing the flywheel with a puller

Flywheel, Nut, and/or Starter Clutch

REMOVAL AND INSTALLATION

Place a block of wood under the flywheel fins to prevent the flywheel from turning while you are loosening the nut or starter clutch. Be careful not to bend the flywheel. There are special flywheel holders available for this purpose; Briggs & Stratton recommends their use on flywheels of 6¾ in. (171.45mm) diameter or less.

On rope starter engines, the ½ in. flywheel nut has a left-hand thread and the ⅝ in. nut has a right-hand thread. The starter clutch used on rewind or wind-up starters has a right-hand thread.

Some flywheels have two holes provided for the use of a flywheel puller. Use a small gear puller or automotive steering wheel puller to remove the flywheel if a flywheel puller is not available. Be careful not to bend the flywheel if a gear puller is used. On rope starter engines leave the nut on for the puller to bear against. Small cast iron flywheels do not require a puller.

Install the flywheel in the reverse order of removal after inspecting the key and keyway for damage or wear.

Breaker Point Removal and Installation

Remove the breaker cover. Care should be taken when removing the cover, to avoid damaging it. If the cover is bent or damaged, it should be replaced to insure a proper seal.

The breaker point gap on all models is 0.020 in. (0.5mm). Check the points for contact and for signs of burning or pitting. Points that are set too wide will advance the spark timing and may cause kickback when starting. Points that are set too close will retard the spark timing and decrease engine power.

On models that have a separate condenser, the point set is removed by first removing the condenser and armature wires from the break-

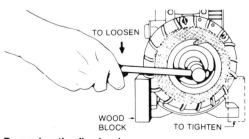

TO LOOSEN

WOOD BLOCK

TO TIGHTEN

Removing the flywheel

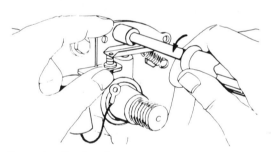

Removing the breaker point assembly

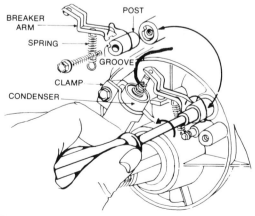

BREAKER ARM
SPRING
POST
GROOVE
CLAMP
CONDENSER

Removing the integral breaker point and condenser assembly

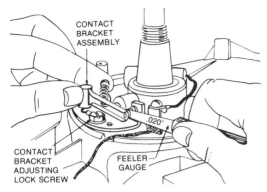

Adjusting the point gap

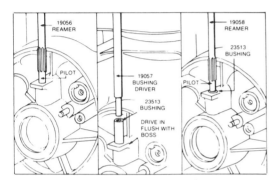

Replacing the breaker plunger bushing

er point clip. Loosen the adjusting lock screw and remove the breaker point assembly.

On models where the condenser is incorporated with the breaker points, loosen the screw which holds the post. The condenser/point assembly is removed by loosening the screw which holds the condenser clamp.

When installing a point set with the separate condenser, be sure that the small boss on the magneto plate enters the hole in the point bracket. Mount the point set to the magneto plate or the cylinder with a lock screw. Fasten the armature lead wire to the breaker points with the clip and screw. If these lead wires do not have terminals, the bare end of the wires can be inserted into the clip and the screw tightened to make a good connection. Do not let the ends of the wire touch either the point bracket or the magneto plate, or the ignition will be grounded.

To install the integral condenser/point set, place the mounting post of the breaker arm into the recess in the cylinder so that the groove in the post fits the notch in the recess. Tighten the mounting screw securely. Use a ¼ in. wrench. Slip the open loop of the breaker arm spring through the two holes in the arm, then hook the closed loop of the spring over the small post protruding from the cylinder. Push the flat end of the breaker arm into the groove in the

mounting post. This places tension on the spring and pulls the arm against the plunger. If the condenser post is threaded, attach the soil primary wire and the ground wire (if furnished) with the lock washer and nut. If the primary wire is fastened to the condenser with a spring fastener, compress the spring and slip the primary wire and ground wire into the hole in the condenser post. Release the spring. Lay the condenser in place and tighten the condenser clamp securely. Install the spring in the breaker arm.

Point Gap Adjustment

Turn the crankshaft until the points are open to the widest gap. When adjusting a breaker point assembly with an integral condenser, move the condenser forward or backward with a screwdriver until the proper gap is obtained − 0.020 in. (0.5mm). Point sets with a separate condenser are adjusted by moving the contact point bracket up and down after the lock screw has been loosened. The point gap is set to 0.020 in. (0.5mm).

Breaker Point Plunger

If the breaker point plunger hole becomes excessively worn, oil will leak past the plunger and may get on the points, causing them to burn. To check the hole, loosen the breaker point mounting screw and move the breaker points out of the way. Remove the plunger. If the flat end of the #19055 plug gauge will enter the plunger hole for a distance of ¼ in. (6mm) or more, the hole should be rebushed.

To install the bushing, it is necessary that the breaker points, armature, and crankshaft be removed. Use a #19056 reamer to ream out the old plunger hole. This should be done by hand. The reamer must be in alignment with the plunger hole. Drive the bushing, #23513, into the hole until the upper end of the bushing is

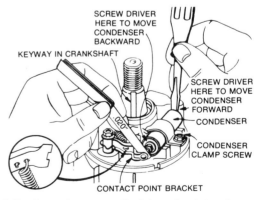

Adjusting point gap on the integral point and condenser assembly

flush with the top of the boss. Remove all metal chips and dirt from the engine.

If the breaker point plunger is worn to a length of 0.870 in. (22mm) or less, it should be replaced. Plungers must be inserted with the groove at the top or oil will enter the breaker box. Insert the plunger into the hole in the cylinder.

Armature Air Gap Adjustment

Set the air gap between the flywheel and the armature as follows: With the armature up as far as possible and just one screw tightened, slip the proper gauge between the armature and flywheel. Turn the flywheel until the magnets are directly below the armature. Loosen the one mounting screw and the magnets should pull the armature down firmly against the thickness gauge. Tighten the mounting screws.

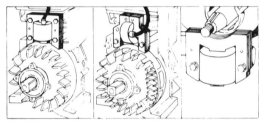

Variations in armature positioning

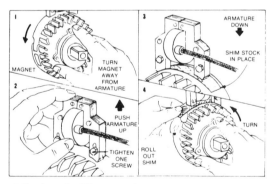

Adjustment of the armature gap

FLYWHEEL TYPE – EXTERNAL BREAKER

Breaker Point Set Removal and Installation

Turn the crankshaft until the points open to their widest gap. This makes it easier to assemble and adjust the points later if the crankshaft is not removed. Remove the condenser and upper and lower mounting screws. Loosen the lock nut and back off the breaker point screw. Install the points in the reverse order of removal.

To avoid the possibility of oil leaking past the breaker point plunger or moisture entering the crankcase between the plunger and the bushing, a plunger seal is installed on the engine

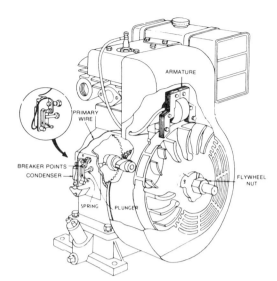

Flywheel magneto ignition with an external breaker assembly

models using this type of ignition system. To install a new seal on the plunger, remove the breaker point assembly and con
denser. Remove the retainer and eyelet, remove the old seal, and install the new one. Use extreme care when installing the seal on the plunger to avoid damaging the seal. Replace the eyelet and retainer and replace the points and condenser.

NOTE: *Apply a small amount of sealer to the threads of both mounting screws and the adjustment screw. The sealer prevents oil from leaking into the breaker point area.*

Point Gap Adjustment

Turn the crankshaft until the points open to their widest gap. Turn the breaker point adjusting screw until the points open to 0.020 in. (0.5mm) and tighten the lock nut. When the cover is installed, seal the point where the primary wire passes under the cover. This area must be resealed to prevent the entry of dust and moisture.

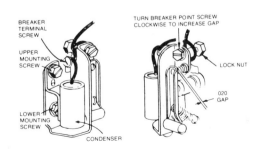

Breaker point gap adjustment

Armature Timing Adjustment

MODELS 193000, 200000, 230000, 243000

Using a puller, remove the flywheel. Set the point gap at 0.020 in. (0.5mm). Position the flywheel on the crankshaft taper. Slip the key in place. Install the flywheel and the crankshaft clockwise until the breaker points are just opening. Use a timing light. When the points just start to open, the arrow on the flywheel should line up with the arrow on the armature bracket.

If the arrows do not match, slip off the flywheel without disturbing the position of the crankshaft. Slightly loosen the mounting screw which holds the armature bracket to the cylinder. Slip the flywheel back onto the crankshaft. Insert the flywheel key. Install the flywheel nut finger tight. Move the armature and bracket assembly to align the arrows. Slip off the flywheel and tighten the armature bracket bolts. Install the key and flywheel. Tighten the flywheel nut to 110–118 ft. lbs. on the 193000 and 200000 series. On all the rest, tighten to 138–150 ft. lbs. Set the armature gap at 0.010–0.014 in. (0.25–0.35mm).

MODELS 19D AND 23D

With the points set at 0.020 in. (0.5mm) and the flywheel key screw finger tight together with the flywheel nut, rotate the flywheel clockwise until the breaker points are just opening. The flywheel key drives the crankshaft while doing this. Using a timing light, rotate the flywheel slightly counterclockwise until the edge of the armature lines up with the edge of the flywheel insert. The crankshaft must not turn while doing this. Tighten the key screw and the flywheel nut. Set the armature air gap at 0.022–0.026 in. (0.56–0.66mm).

Replacing Threaded Breaker Plunger and Bushing

Remove the breaker cover and the condenser and breaker point assembly.

Place a thick ⅜ in. (9.5mm) inside diameter washer over the end of the bushing and screw on the ⅜–24 nut. Tighten the nut to pull the bushing out of the hole. After the bushing has been moved about ⅛ in. (3mm), remove the nut and put on a second thick washer and repeat the procedure. A total stack of ⅜ in. (9.5mm) washers will be required to completely remove the bushing. Be sure the plunger does not fall out of the bushing as it is removed.

Place the new plunger in the bushing with the large end of the plunger opposite the threads on the bushing. Screw the ⅜–24 in. nut onto the threads to protect them and insert the bushing into the cylinder. Place a piece of tub-

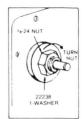

Removing a threaded plunger bushing

ing the same diameter as the nut and, using a hammer, drive the bushing into the cylinder until the square shoulder on the bushing is flush with the face of the cylinder. Check to be sure that the plunger operates freely.

Replacing Unthreaded Breaker Plunger and Bushing

Pull the plunger out as far as possible and use a pair of pliers to break the plunger off as close as possible to the bushing. Use a ¼–20 in. tap or a #93029 self threading screw to thread the hole in the bushing to a depth of about ½–⅝ in. (13–16mm). Use a ¼–20 × ½ in. hex head screw and two spacer washers to pull the bushing out of the cylinder. The bushing will be free when it has been extracted ⁵⁄₁₆ in. (8mm). Carefully remove the bushing and the remainder of the broken plunger. Do not allow the plunger or metal chips to drop into the crankcase.

Correctly insert the new plunger into the new bushing. Insert the plunger and the bushing into the cylinder. Use a hammer and the old bushing to drive the new bushing into the cylinder until the new bushing is flush with the face of the cylinder. Make sure that the plunger operates freely.

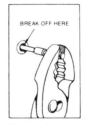

Removing an unthreaded plunger bushing

Plunger Seal

Later models with Flywheel Type — External Breaker Ignition feature a plunger seal. This seal keeps both oil and moisture from entering the breaker box. If the points have become contaminated on an engine manufactured without this feature, the seal may be installed. Parts, part numbers, and their locations are shown in the illustration. Install the seal onto the plunger very carefully to avoid fracturing it.

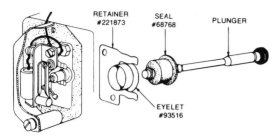

Plunger seal used on later model engines

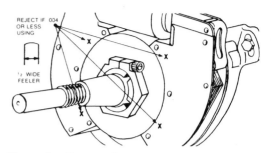

Measuring the armature gap

MAGNA-MATIC IGNITION SYSTEM
Removing the Flywheel

Flywheels on engines with Magna-Matic ignition are removed with pullers similar to factory designs numbered #19068 and 19203. These pullers employ two bolts, which are screwed into holes tapped into the flywheel. The bolts are turned until the flywheel is forced off the crankshaft. Only this type of device should be used to pull these flywheels.

Armature Air Gap

The armature air gap on engines equipped with Magna-Matic ignition system is fixed and can change only if wear occurs on the crankshaft journal and/or main bearing. Check for wear by inserting a ½ in. wide feeler gauge at several points between the rotor and armature. Minimum feeler gauge thickness is 0.004 in. (0.1mm). Keep the feeler gauge away from the magnets on the rotor or you will have a false reading.

Rotor Removal and Installation

The rotor is held in place by a woodruff key and a clamp on later engines, and a woodruff key and set screw on older engines. The rotor clamp must always remain on the rotor, unless the rotor is in place on the crankshaft and within the armature, or a loss of magnetism will occur.

Loosen the socket head screw in the rotor clamp which will allow the clamp to loosen. It may be necessary to use a puller to remove the rotor from the crankshaft. On older models, loosen the small lock screw, then the set screw.

To install the set screw type rotor, place the woodruff key in the keyway on the crankshaft, then slide the rotor onto the crankshaft until

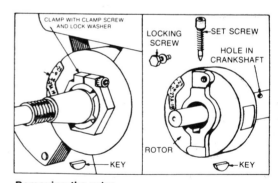

Removing the rotor

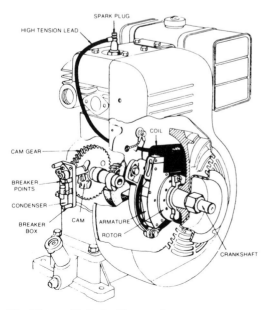

The Magna-Matic ignition system

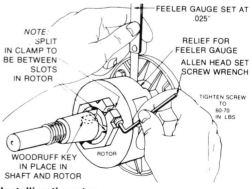

Installing the rotor

the set screw hole in the rotor and the crankshaft are aligned. Be sure the key remains in place. Tighten the set screw securely, then tighten the lock screw to prevent the set screw from loosening. The lock screw is self-threading and the hole does not require tapping.

To install the clamp type rotor, place the woodruff key in place in the crankshaft and align the keyway in the rotor with the woodruff key. If necessary, use a short length of pipe and a hammer to drive the rotor onto the shaft until a 0.025 in. (0.6mm) feeler gauge can be inserted between the rotor and the bearing support. The split in the clamp must be between the slots in the rotor. Tighten the clamp screws to 60–70 inch lbs.

Rotor Timing Adjustment

The rotor and armature are correctly timed at the factory and require timing only if the armature has been removed from the engine, or if the cam gear or crankshaft has been replaced.

If it is necessary to adjust the rotor, proceed as follows: with the point gap set at 0.020 in. (0.5mm), turn the crankshaft in the normal direction of rotation until the breaker points close and just start to open. Use a timing light or insert a piece of tissue paper between the breaker points to determine when the points begin to open. With the three armature mounting screws slightly loose, rotate the armature until the arrow on the armature lines up with the arrow on the rotor. Align with the corresponding number of engine models, for example, on Model 9, align with #9. Retighten the armature mounting screws.

Coil and/or Armature Replacement

Usually the coil and armature are not separated, but left assembled for convenience. However, if one or both need replacement, proceed as follows: the coil primary wire and the coil ground wire must be unfastened. Pry out the clips that hold the coil and coil core to the armature. The coil core is a slip fit in the coil and can be pushed out of the coil.

To reassemble, push the coil core into the coil

with the rounded side toward the ignition cable. Place the coil and core on the armature with the coil retainer between the coil and the armature and with the rounded side toward the coil. Hook the lower end of the clips into the armature, then press the upper end onto the coil core.

Fasten the coil ground wire (bare double wires) to the armature support. Next, place the assembly against the cylinder and around the rotor and bearing support. Insert the three mounting screws together with the washer and lockwasher into the three long oval holes in the armature. Tighten them enough to hold the armature in place but loose enough so the armature can be moved for adjustment of the timing. Attach the primary wires from the coil and the breaker points to the terminal at the upper side of the backing plate. This terminal is insulated from the backing plate. Push the ignition cable through the louvered hole at the left side of the backing plate.

Breaker Point Removal and Installation

Turn the crankshaft until the points open to the widest gap. This makes it easier to assemble and adjust the points later if the crankshaft is not removed. With the terminal screw out, remove the spring screw. Loosen the breaker shaft nut until the nut is flush with the end of the shaft. Tap the nut to free the breaker arm from the tapered end of the breaker shaft. Remove the nut, lockwasher, and breaker arm. Remove the breaker plate screw, breaker plate, pivot, insulating plate, and eccentric. Pry out the breaker shaft seal with a sharp pointed tool.

To install the breaker points, press in the new oil seal with the metal side out. Put the new breaker plate on the top of the insulating plate, making sure that the detent in the breaker plate engages the hole in the insulating plate. Fasten the breaker plate screw enough to put a light tension on the plate. Adjust the eccentric so that the left edge of the insulating plate is

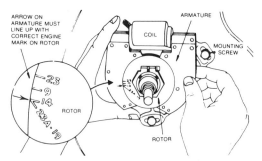

Adjustment of the timing

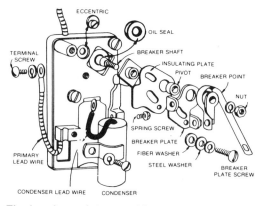

The breaker point assembly

parallel to the edge of the box and tighten the screw. This locates the breaker plate so that the proper gap adjustments may be made. Turn the breaker shaft clockwise as far as possible and hold it in this position. Place the new breaker points on the shaft, then the lockwasher, and tighten the nut down on the lockwasher. Replace the spring screw and terminal screw.

Breaker Box Removal and Installation

Remove the two mounting screws, then remove the breaker box, turning it slightly to clear the arm at the inner end of the breaker shaft. The breaker points need not be removed to remove the breaker box.

To install, pull the primary wire through the hole at the lower left corner of the breaker box. See that the primary wire rests in the groove at the top end of the box, then tighten the two mounting screws to hold the box in place.

Breaker Shaft Removal and Installation

The breaker shaft can be removed, after the breaker points are removed, by turning the shaft one half turn to clear the retaining spur at the inside of the breaker box.

Install by inserting the breaker shaft with the arm upward so the arm will clean the retainer boss. Push the shaft all the way in, then turn the arm downward.

Breaker Point Adjustment

To adjust the breaker points, turn the crankshaft until the breaker points open to the widest gap. Loosen the breaker point plate screw slightly. Rotate the eccentric to obtain a point gap of 0.020 in. (0.5mm). Tighten the breaker plate screw.

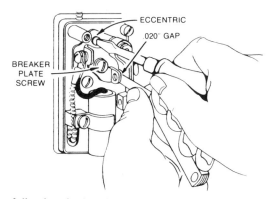

Adjusting the breaker point gap

Mixture Adjustment

Two Piece Flo-Jet

1. Start the engine and run it at 3000 rpm until it warms up.

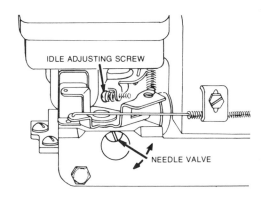

Carburetor adjustment screws

2. Turn the needle valve (flat handle) to both extremes of operation noting the location of the valve at both points. That is, turn the valve inward until the mixture becomes too lean and the engine starts to slow, then note the position of the valve. Turn it outward slowly until the mixture becomes too rich and the engine begins to slow. Turn the valve back inward to the midpoint between the two extremes.

3. Install a tachometer on the engine. Pull the throttle to the idle position and hold it there through the rest of this step. Adjust the idle speed screw until the engine idles at 1750 rpm if it's an aluminum engine, or 1200 rpm, if it's a cast iron engine. Then, turn the idle valve in and out to adjust mixture, as described in Step 2. If idle valve adjustment changes idle speed, adjust speed to specification.

4. Release the throttle and observe the engine's response. The engine should accelerate without hesitation. If response is poor, one of the mixture adjustments is too lean. Readjust either or both as necessary. If idle speed was changed after idle valve was adjusted, readjust the idle valve first.

One Piece Flo-Jet

Follow the instructions for adjusting the Two Piece Flo-Jet carburetor (above). On the large,

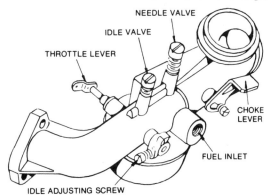

Idle valve and needle valve locations on the One Piece Flo-Jet

One Piece Flo-Jet, the needle valve is located under the float bowl, and the idle valve on top of the venturi passage. On the small One Piece Flo-Jet, both valves are adjusted by screws located on top of the venturi passage. The needle valve is located on the air horn side, is centered above the float bowl, and uses a larger screw head.

Governor Adjustments

SETTING MAXIMUM GOVERNED SPEED WITH ROTARY LAWNMOWER BLADES

NOTE: *Strict limits on engine rpm must be observed when setting top governed speed on rotary lawnmowers. This is done so that blade tip speeds will be kept to less than 19,000 feet per minute. Briggs & Stratton suggests setting the governor 200 rpm low to allow for possible error in the tachometer reading. These figures below, based on blade length, must be strictly adhered to, or a serious accident could result!*

Model 140000

Loosen the screw which holds the governor lever to the governor shaft. Turn the governor lever counterclockwise until the carburetor throttle is wide open. With a screwdriver, turn the governor shaft counterclockwise as far as it will go. Tighten the screw which holds the governor lever to the governor shaft.

Cast Iron Models 19, 190000, 200000, 23, 230000, 240000

Loosen the screw which holds the governor lever to the governor shaft. Push the lever counterclockwise as far as it will go. Hold it in position and turn the governor shaft counterclockwise as far as it will go. This can be done with a screwdriver. Securely tighten the screw that holds the governor lever to the shaft.

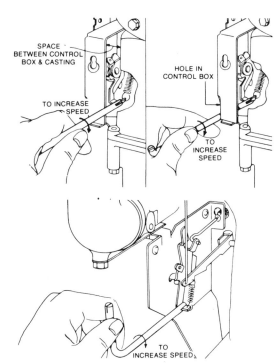

Bending the spring anchor tang to get desired top speed

Aluminum Models 140000, 170000, 190000, 251000

Vertical and horizontal shaft engine governors are adjusted by setting the control lever in the high speed position. Loosen the nut on the governor lever. Turn the governor shaft clockwise with a screwdriver to the end of its travel. Tighten the nut. The throttle must be wide open. Check to see if the throttle can be moved from idle to wide open without binding.

ADJUSTING TOP NO LOAD SPEED

Set the control lever to the maximum speed position with the engine running. Bend the spring anchor tang to get the desired top speed.

ADJUSTMENT FOR CLOSER GOVERNING

Generator Applications Only

1. Snap knob upward to release adjusting nut.

Blade Length (in.)	Max. Governed Speed (R.P.M.)
18	4032
19	3820
20	3629
21	3456
22	3299
23	3155
24	3024
25	2903
26	2791

You can make a tool like the one shown to adjust spring anchor tang

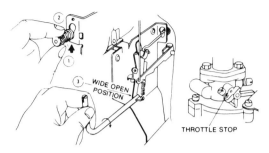

Obtaining closer governing on generator applications

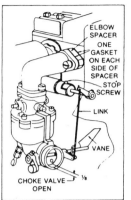
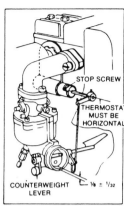

Adjusting automatic choke—Two Piece Flo-Jet

2. Pull knob out against stop.

3. Then, bend the spring anchor tang to get top no-load speed as described below, depending upon the application.

On models 140400, 146400, 170400, 190400 and 251400 with an 1800 rpm generator: temporarily substituting a #260902 governor spring, set the no load speed at 2600 rpm, and then set throttle stop at 1600 rpm.

On models 140400, 146400, 170400, 190400, 251400 and 251400 with an 3600 rpm generator: set no load speed to 4200 rpm with standard governor spring.

4. Snap knob back into its normal position.

5. Adjust the knob for the desired generator speed.

Choke Adjustment

Choke-a-Matic, Pulsa-Jet and Vacu-Jet Carburetors

To check the operation of the choke linkage, move the speed adjustment lever to the choke position. If the choke slide does not fully close, bend the choke link. The speed adjustment lever must make good contact against the top switch.

Install the carburetor and adjust it in the same manner as the Pulsa-Jet carburetor.

Two-Piece Flo-Jet Automatic Choke

Hold the choke shaft so the thermostat lever is free. At room temperature — 68°F (20°C), the screw in the thermostat collar should be in the center of the stops. If not, loosen the stop screw and adjust the screw.

Loosen the set screw on the lever of the thermostat assembly. Slide the lever to the right or left on the shaft to ensure free movement of the choke link in any position. Rotate the thermostat shaft clockwise until the stop screw strikes the tube. Hold it in position and set the lever on the thermostat shaft so that the choke valve will be held open about ⅛ in. (3mm) from a closed position. Then tighten the set screw in the lever.

Rotate the thermostat shaft counterclock-

wise until the stop screw strikes the opposite side of the tube. Then open the choke valve manually until it stops against the top of the choke link opening. The choke valve should now be open approximately ⅛ in. (3mm) as before.

Check the position of the counterweight lever. With the choke valve in a wide open position (horizontal) the counterweight lever should also be in a horizontal position with the free end toward the right.

Operate the choke manually to be sure that all parts are free to move without binding or rubbing in any position.

Compression Checking

You can check the compression in any Briggs & Stratton engine by performing the following simple procedure: spin the flywheel counterclockwise (flywheel side) against the compression stroke. A sharp rebound indicates that there is satisfactory compression. A slight or no rebound indicates poor compression.

It has been determined that this test is an accurate indication of compression and is recommended by Briggs and Stratton. Briggs & Stratton does not supply compression pressures.

Loss of compression will usually be the result of one or a combination of the following:

1. The cylinder head gasket is blown or leaking.

2. The valves are sticking or not seating properly.

3. The piston rings are not sealing, which would also cause the engine to consume an excessive amount of oil.

Carbon deposits in the combustion chamber should be removed every 100 or 200 hours of use (more often when run at a steady load), or whenever the cylinder head is removed.

CARBURETED FUEL SYSTEM

There are three types of carburetors used on Briggs & Stratton engines. They are the Pulsa-Jet, Vacu-Jet and Flo-Jet. The first two types have three models each and the Flo-Jet has two versions.

Before removing any carburetor for repair, look for signs of air leakage or mounting gaskets that are loose, have deteriorated, or are otherwise damaged.

Note the position of the governor springs, governor link, remote control, or other attachments to facilitate reassembly. Be careful not to bend the links or stretch the springs.

AUTOMATIC CHOKE OPERATION

The automatic choke operates in conjunction with engine vacuum, similar to the Pulsa-Jet fuel pump.

A diaphragm under the carburetor is connected to the choke shaft by a link. A calibrated spring under the diaphragm holds the choke closed when the engine is not running. Upon starting, vacuum created during the intake stroke is routed to the bottom of the diaphragm through a calibrated passage, thereby opening the choke.

This system also has the ability to respond in the same manner as an accelerator pump. As speed decreases during heavy loads, the choke valve partially closes, enriching the air/fuel mixture, thereby improving low speed performance and lugging power.

To check the automatic choke, remove the air cleaner and replace the stud. Observe the position of the choke valve; it should be fully closed. Move the speed control to the stop position; the governor spring should be holding the throttle in a closed position. Give the starter rope several quick pulls. The choke valve should alternately open and close.

If the choke valve does not react as stated in the previous paragraph, the carburetor will have to be disassembled to determine the problem. Before doing so, however, check the following items so you know what to look for:

ENGINE IS UNDER-CHOKED

1. Carburetor is adjusted too lean.
2. The fuel pipe check valve is inoperative (Vacu-Jet only).
3. The air cleaner stud is bent.
4. The choke shaft is sticking due to dirt.
5. The choke spring is too short or damaged.
6. The diaphragm is not preloaded.

ENGINE IS OVER-CHOKED

1. Carburetor is adjusted too rich.
2. The air cleaner stud is bent.

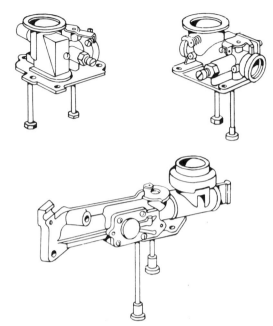

The three types of Pulsa-Jet carburetors

The two types of Flo-Jet carburetors

3. The choke shaft is sticking due to dirt.
4. The diaphragm is ruptured.
5. The vacuum passage is restricted.
6. The choke spring is distorted or stretched.
7. There is gasoline or oil in the vacuum chamber.
8. There is a leak between the link and the diaphragm.
9. The diaphragm was folded during assembly, causing a vacuum leak.

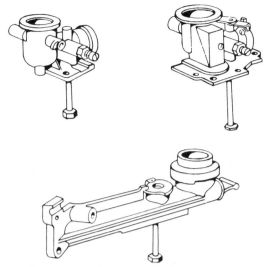

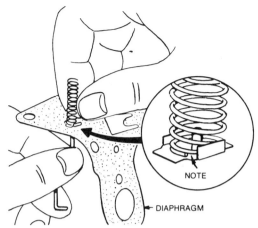

Assembling the diaphragm spring to the new diaphragm

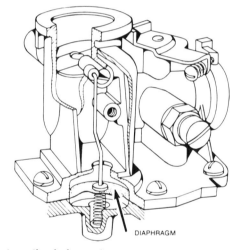

The three types of Vacu-Jet carburetors

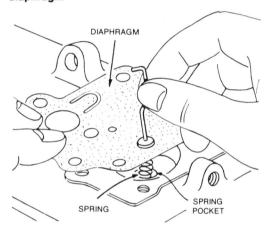

Installing the diaphragm and spring into the spring pocket

Automatic choke system

10. The machined surface on the tank top is not flat.

REPLACING THE AUTOMATIC CHOKE

Inspect the automatic choke for free operation. Any sticking problems should be corrected as proper choke operation depends on freedom of the choke to travel as dictated by engine vacuum.

Remove the carburetor and fuel tank assembly from the engine. The choke link cover may now be removed and the choke link disconnected from the choke shaft. Disassemble the carburetor from the tank top, being careful not to damage the diaphragm.

CHECKING THE DIAPHRAGM AND SPRING

The diaphragm can be reused, provided it has not developed wear spots or punctures. On the

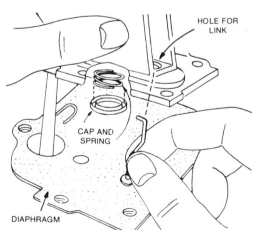

Positioning the diaphragm on top of the fuel tank

Pulsa-Jet models, make sure that the fuel pump valves are not damaged. Also check the choke spring length. The Pulsa-Jet spring minimum length is 1⅛ in. (28.5mm) and the maximum is $1\frac{7}{32}$ in. (31mm) Vacu-Jet spring length minimum is $\frac{15}{16}$ in. (24mm), maximum length 1 in. (25mm). If the spring length is shorter or longer than specified, replace the diaphragm and the spring.

CHECKING THE TANK TOP

The machined surface on the top of the tank must be flat in order for the diaphragm to provide an adequate seal between the carburetor and the tank. If the machined surface on the tank is not flat, it is possible for gasoline to enter the vacuum chamber by passing between the machined surface and the diaphragm. Once fuel has entered the vacuum chamber, it can move through the vacuum passage and into the carburetor. The flatness of the machined surface on the tank top can be checked by using a straight-edge and a feeler gauge. The surface should not vary more than 0.002 in. (0.05mm). Replace the tank if a 0.002 in. (0.05mm) feeler gauge can be passed under the straight-edge.

If a new diaphragm is installed, assemble the spring to the replacement diaphragm, taking care not to bend or distort the spring.
Place the diaphragm on the tank surface, positioning the spring in the spring pocket.

Place the carburetor on the diaphragm ensuring that the choke link and diaphragm are properly aligned between the carburetor and the tank top. On Pulsa-Jet models, place the pump spring and cap on the diaphragm over the recess or pump chamber in the fuel tank. Thread in the carburetor mounting screws to about two threads. Do not tighten them. Close the choke valve and insert the choke link into the choke shaft.

Remove the air cleaner gasket, if it is in place, before continuing. Insert a ⅜ in. bolt or rod into the carburetor air horn. With the bolt in position, tighten the carburetor mounting screws in

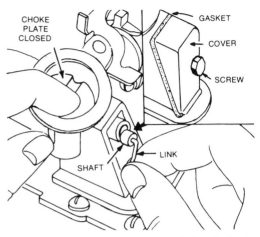

Inserting the choke link into the choke shaft

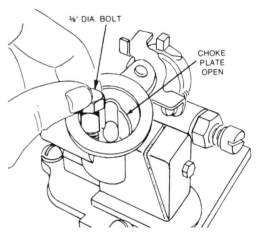

Pre-loading the diaphragm to adjust the choke

a staggered sequence. Please note that the insertion of the ⅜ in. bolt opens the choke to an over-center position, which preloads the diaphragm.

Remove the ⅜ in. bolt. The choke valve should now move to a fully closed position. If the choke valve is not fully closed, make sure that the choke spring is properly assembled to the diaphragm, and also properly inserted in its pocket in the tank top.

All carburetor adjustments should be made with the air cleaner on the engine. Adjustment is best made with the fuel tank half full. See the "Tune-Up" section.

Two Piece Flo-Jet Carburetors Large and Small Line

CHECKING THE UPPER BODY FOR WARPAGE

With the carburetor assembled and the body gasket in place, try to insert a 0.002 in.

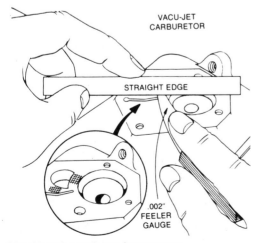

Checking the tank top for warpage

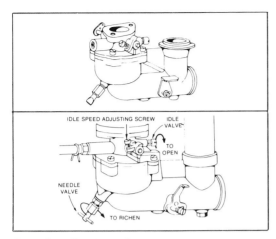

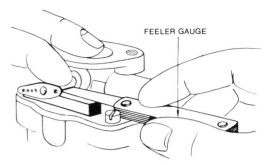

Checking throttle shaft wear with a feeler gauge

Two piece Flo-Jet carburetor

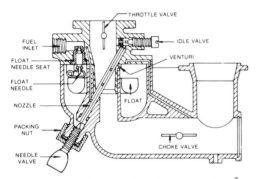

Cutaway view of a two piece Flo-Jet carburetor

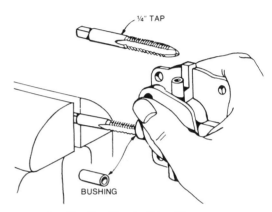

Removing the throttle shaft bushing

(0.05mm) feeler gauge between the upper and lower bodies at the air vent boss, just below the idle valve. If the gauge can be inserted, the upper body is warped and should be replaced.

CHECKING THE THROTTLE SHAFT AND BUSHINGS

Wear between the throttle shaft and bushings should not exceed 0.010 in. (0.25mm). Check the wear by placing a short iron bar on the upper carburetor body so that it just fits under the throttle shaft. Measure the distance with a feeler gauge while holding the shaft down and then holding it up. If the difference is over 0.010 in. (0.25mm), either the upper body should be rebushed, the throttle shaft replaced, or both. Wear on the throttle shaft can be checked by comparing the worn and unworn portions of the shaft. To replace the bushings, remove the throttle shaft using a thin punch to drive out the pin which holds the throttle stop to the shaft; remove the throttle valve, then pull out the shaft. Place a ¼–20 tap or an E-Z Out in a vise. Turn the carburetor body so as to thread the tap or E-Z Out into the bushings enough to pull the bushings out of the body. Press the new bushings into the carburetor

body with a vise. Insert the throttle shaft to be sure it is free in the bushings. If not, run a size ⁷⁄₃₂ in. (5.5mm) drill through both bushings to act as a line reamer. Install the throttle shaft, valve, and stop.

DISASSEMBLY OF THE CARBURETOR

1. Remove the idle valve.
2. Loosen the needle valve packing nut.
3. Remove the packing nut and needle valve together. To remove the nozzle, use a narrow, blunt screwdriver so as not to damage the threads in the lower carburetor body. The nozzle projects diagonally into a recess in the upper body and must be removed before the upper body is separated from the lower body, or it may be damaged.
4. Remove the screws which hold the upper and lower bodies together. A pin holds the float in place.
5. Remove the pin to take out the float valve needle. Check the float for leakage. If it contains gasoline or is crushed, it must be replaced. Use a wide, proper fitting screwdriver to remove the float inlet seat.
6. Lift the venturi out of the lower body. Some carburetors have a welch plug. This should be removed only if necessary to remove the choke plate. Some carburetors have nylon choke shaft.

REPAIR

Use new parts where necessary. Always use new gaskets. Carburetor repair kits are available. Tighten the inlet seat with the gasket securely in place, if used. Some float valves have a spring clip to connect the float valve to the float tang. Others are nylon with a stirrup which fits over the float tang. Older float valves and engines with fuel pumps have neither a spring nor a stirrup.

A viton tip float valve is used in later models of the large, two-piece Flo-Jet carburetor. The seat is pressed into the upper body and does not need replacement unless it is damaged.

Replacing the Pressed-In Float Valve Seat

Clamp the head of a #93029 self threading screw in a vise. Turn the carburetor body to thread the screw into the seat. Continue turning the carburetor body, drawing out the seat. Leave the seat fastened to the screw. Insert the new seat #230996 into the carburetor body. The seat has a starting lead.

NOTE: *If the engine is equipped with a fuel pump, install a #231019 seat. Press the new seat flush with the body using the screw and old seat as a driver. Make sure that the seat is not pressed below the body surface or improper float-to-float valve contact will occur. Install the float valve.*

ously removed. Use a sealer around the welch plug to prevent entry of dirt.

Fasten the upper and lower bodies together with the mounting screws. Screw in the nozzle with a narrow, blunt screwdriver, making sure that the nozzle tip enters the recess in the upper body. Tighten the nozzle securely. Screw in the needle valve and idle valve until they just seat. Back off the needle valve 1½ turns. Do not tighten the packing nut. Back off the idle valve ¾ of a turn. These settings are about correct. Final adjustment will be made when the engine is running. See the Tune-Up section for mixture and choke adjustments.

One-Piece Flo-Jet Carburetor

The large, one-piece Flo-Jet carburetor has its high speed needle valve below the float bowl. All other repair procedures are similar to the small, one-piece Flo-Jet carburetor.

DISASSEMBLY

1. Remove the idle and needle valves.
2. Remove the carburetor bowl screw. A pin holds the float in place.
3. Remove the pin to take off the float and float valve needle. Check the float for leakage. If it contains gasoline or is crushed, it must be replaced. Use a screwdriver to remove the carbu-

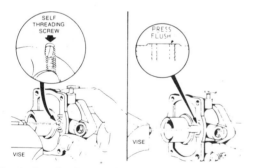

Replacing the float valve seat

Checking the Float Level

With the body gasket in place on the upper body and the float valve and float installed, the float should be parallel to the body mounting surface. If not, bend the tang on the float until they are parallel. Do not press on the flat to adjust it.

ASSEMBLY OF THE CARBURETOR

Assemble the venturi and the venturi gasket to the lower body. Be sure that the holes in the venturi and the venturi gasket are aligned. Some models do not have a removable venturi. Install the choke parts and welch plug if previ-

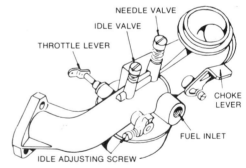

Small one piece Flo-Jet carburetor

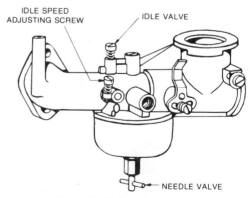

Large one piece Flo-Jet carburetor

retor nozzle. Use a wide, heavy screwdriver to remove the float valve seat, if used.

If it is necessary to remove the choke valve, venturi throttle shaft, or shaft bushings, proceed as follows.

1. Pry out the welch plug.
2. Remove the choke valve, then the shaft. The venturi will then be free to fall out after the choke valve and shaft have been removed.
3. Check the shaft for wear. (Refer to the "Two-Piece Flo-Jet Carburetor" section for checking wear and replacing bushings).

REPAIR OF THE CARBURETOR

Use new parts where necessary. Always use new gaskets. Carburetor repair kits are available. If the venturi has been removed, install the venturi first, then the carburetor nozzle jets. The nozzle jet holds the venturi in place. Replace the choke shaft and valve. Install a new welch plug in the carburetor body. Use a sealer to prevent dirt from entering.

A viton tip float valve is used in the large, one-piece Flo-Jet carburetor. The seat is pressed in the upper carburetor body and does not need replacement unless it is damaged. Replace the seat in the same manner as for the two-piece Flo-Jet carburetor.

Checking the Float Level

With the body gasket in place on the upper body and float valve and the float installed, the float should be parallel to the body mounting surface. If not, bend the tang on the float until they are parallel. Do not press on the float.

Install the float bowl, idle valve, and needle valve. Turn in the needle valve and the idle valve until they just seat. Open the needle valve 2½ turns and the idle valve 1½ turns. On the large carburetors with the needle valve below the float bowl, open the needle valve and the idle valve 1⅛ turns.

Float Level Chart

Carburetor Number	Float Setting (in.)
2712-S	$19/64$
2713-S	$19/64$
2714-S	$1/4$
*2398-S	$1/4$
2336-S	$1/4$
2336-SA	$1/4$
2337-S	$1/4$
2337-SA	$1/4$
2230-S	$17/64$
2217-S	$11/64$

*When resilient seat is used, set float level at $9/32 \pm 1/64$.

These settings will allow the engine to start. Final adjustment should be made when the engine is running and has warmed up to operating temperature. See the "Two-Piece Flo-Jet Carburetor" adjustment procedure.

Governors

The purpose of a governor is to maintain, within certain limits, a desired engine speed even though the load may vary.

AIR VANE GOVERNORS

The governor spring tends to open the throttle. Air pressure against the air vane tends to close the throttle. The engine speed at which these two forces balance is called the governed speed. The governed speed can be varied by changing the governor spring tension.

Worn linkage or damaged governor springs should be replaced to insure proper governor operation. No adjustment is necessary.

MECHANICAL GOVERNORS

The governor spring tends to pull the throttle open. The force of the counterweights, which are operated by centrifugal force, tends to close the throttle. The engine speed at which these two forces balance is called the governed speed. The governed speed can be varied by changing the governor spring tension.

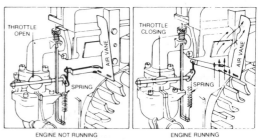

Air vane governor installed on horizontal crankshaft engine

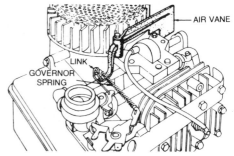

Air vane governor installed on vertical crankshaft engine

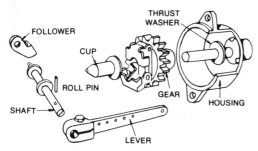

Mechanical governor exploded view

GOVERNOR REPAIR

The procedures below describe disassembly and assembly of the various kinds of mechanical governors. Look for gears with worn or broken teeth, worn thrust washers, weight pins, cups, followers, etc. Replace parts that are worn and reassemble.

Model 140000

DISASSEMBLY

1. Loosen the governor lever mounting screw, and pull the lever off the shaft.
2. Remove the two housing mounting screws. Carefully pull the housing off the block, being careful to catch the governor gear, which will slip off the shaft. Pull the steel thrust washer off the shaft.
3. Remove the governor lever roll pin and washer. Unscrew the governor lever shaft by turning it clockwise and remove it.

ASSEMBLY

1. Push the governor lever shaft into the crankcase cover, threaded end first. Assemble the small washer onto the inner end of the shaft, and then screw the shaft into the governor crank follower by turning it counterclockwise. Tighten it securely.
2. Turn the shaft until the follower points down slightly, in a position where it would press against the cup when the housing is installed.
3. Place the washer on the outside end of the shaft. Install the rollpin, so the leading end just reaches the outside diameter of the shaft and the back end protrudes.

4. Install the thrust washer and the governor gear on the shaft in the housing (in that order).
5. Hold the crankcase cover in a vertical (the normal) position and install the housing with the gear in position so the point of the steel cup on the gear contacts the follower. Install and tighten the housing mounting screws.
6. Install the lever on the shaft pointing downward at an angle of about 30°. Adjust as described in the Tune-Up section.

Cast Iron Models 19, 190000, 20000, 23, 230000, 240000

DISASSEMBLY

1. Remove the cotter key and washer from the outer end of the governor shaft. Remove the governor crank from inside the crankcase.
2. Slide the governor gear off the shaft.

ASSEMBLY

1. Install the governor gear onto the shaft inside the crankcase. Then, insert the governor shaft assembly through the bushing from inside the crankcase.
2. Install the governor lever to the shaft loosely, and then adjust it as described in the Tune-Up section.

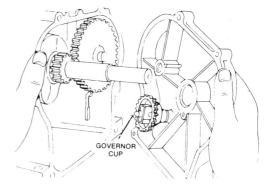

Assembling cover with governor and governor shaft in proper position (horizontal shaft engines)

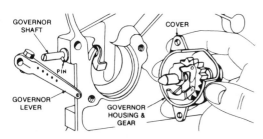

Assembling the mechanical governor

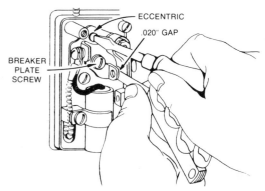

Adjusting the breaker point gap

Aluminum Models 140000, 170000, 190000 and 251000

DISASSEMBLY

On horizontal shaft models: Remove the governor assembly as a unit from the crankcase cover.

On vertical shaft models: Remove the entire assembly as part of the oil slinger (see the Overhaul Section).

ASSEMBLY

1. Assemble governors on horizontal crankshaft models with crankshaft in a horizontal position. The governor rides on a short stationary shaft which is integral with the crankcase cover. The governor shaft keeps the governor from sliding off the shaft after the cover is installed. The governor shaft must hang straight down, or it may jam the governor assembly when the crankcase cover is installed, breaking it when the engine is started . The governor shaft adjustment should be made (see the Tune-Up section) as soon as the crankcase cover is in place so that the governor lever will be clamped in the proper position.

2. On both horizontal and vertical crankshaft models, the governor is held together through normal operating forces. For this reason, the governor link and all other external linkages must be in place and properly adjusted whenever the engine is operated.

ENGINE OVERHAUL

Cylinder Head

REMOVAL AND INSTALLATION

Always note the position of the different cylinder head screws so that they can be properly reinstalled. If a screw is used in the wrong position, it may be to short and not engage enough threads. If it is too long, it may bottom on a fin, either breaking the fin, or leaving the cylinder head loose.

Cylinder Head Bolt Torque Specifications

Basic Model Series	In. lbs. Torque
Aluminum Cylinder	
140000, 170000, 190000, 251000	165
Cast Iron Cylinder	
19, 190000, 200000, 23, 230000, 240000, 300000, 320000	190

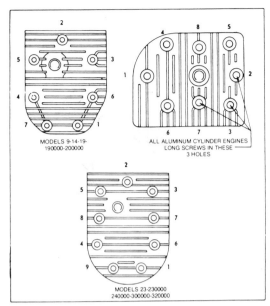

Cylinder head bolt tightening sequences

Remove the cylinder screws and then the cylinder head. Be sure to remove the gasket and all remaining gasket material from the cylinder head and the block. Assemble the cylinder head with a new gasket, cylinder head shield, screws, and washers in their proper places. Graphite grease should be used on aluminum cylinder head screws.

Do not use a sealer of any kind on the head gasket. Tighten the screws down evenly by hand. Use a torque wrench and tighten the head bolts in the correct sequence.

Valves

REMOVAL AND INSTALLATION

1. Using a valve spring compressor, adjust the jaws so they touch the top and bottom of the valve chamber, and then place one of the jaws over the valve spring and the other underneath, between the spring and the valve chamber. This positioning of the valve spring compressor is for valves that have either pin or collar type retainers.

2. Tighten the jaws to compress the spring. Remove the collars or pin and lift out the valve.

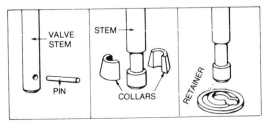

The three types of valve spring retainers

3. Pull out the compressor and the spring.

4a. To remove valves with ring type retainers, position the compressor with the upper jaw over the top of the valve chamber and the lower jaw between the spring and the retainer. Compress the spring, remove the retainer, and pull out the valve. Remove the compressor and spring.

4b. If the retainers are held by a pin or collars, place the valve spring and retainer and cup (Models 14–19–20–23–24–32) into the valve spring compressor. Compress the spring until it is solid. Insert the compressed spring and retainer into the valve chamber. Then drop the valve into place, pushing the stem through the retainer. Hold the spring up in the chamber, hold the valve down, and insert the retainer pin with needle nose pliers or place the collars in the groove in the valve stem. Loosen the spring until the retainer fits around the pin or collars, then pull out the spring compressor. Be sure the pin or collars are in place.

5. Before installing the valves, check the thickness of the valve springs. Some engines use the same spring for the intake and exhaust side, while others use a heavier spring on the exhaust side. Compare the springs before installing them.

6. To install valves with ring type retainers, compress the retainer and spring with the compressor. The large diameter of the retainer should be toward the front of the valve chamber. Insert the compressed spring and retainer into the valve chamber. Drop the valve stem through the larger area of the retainer slot and move the compressor so as to center the small area of the valve retainer slot onto the valve stem shoulder. Release the spring tension and remove the compressor.

Valve Guides

REMOVAL AND INSTALLATION

First check valve guide for wear with a plug gauge, Briggs & Stratton part #19151 or equivalent. If the flat end of the valve guide plug gauge can be inserted into the valve guide for a distance of $5/16$ in. (8mm), the guide is worn and should be rebushed in the following manner.

1. Procure a reamer #19183 and reamer guide bushing #19192, and lubricate the reamer with kerosene. Then, use reamer and reamer guide bushing to ream out the worn guide. Ream to only $1/16$ in. (1.6mm) deeper than valve guide bushing #230655 . BE CAREFUL NOT TO REAM THROUGH THE GUIDE!

2. Press in valve guide bushing #230655 until top end of bushing is flush with top end of valve guide. Use a soft metal driver (brass, cop-

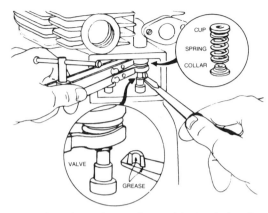

Removing the valve springs with the help of a valve spring compressor

per, etc.) so top end of bushing is not peened over.

NOTE: *The bushing #230655 is finish reamed to size at the factory, so no further reaming is necessary, and a standard valve can be used.*

Valve seating should be checked after bushing the guide, and corrected if necessary by refacing the seat.

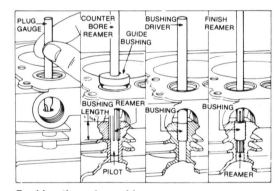

Bushing the valve guide

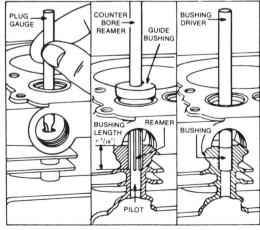

Bushing the valve guide

REFACING VALVES AND SEATS

Faces on valves and valve seats should be resurfaced with a valve grinder or cutter to an angle of 45°.

NOTE: *Some engines have a 30° intake valve and seat.*

The valve and seat should then be lapped with a fine lapping compound to remove the grinding marks and ensure a good seat. The valve seat width should be 1.2–1.6mm. If the seat is wider, a narrowing stone or cutter should be used. If either the seat or valve is badly burned, it should be replaced. Replace the valve if the edge thickness (margin) is less than 0.4mm after it has been resurfaced.

CHECK AND ADJUST TAPPET CLEARANCE

Insert the valves in their respective positions in the cylinder. Turn the crankshaft until one of the valves is at its highest position. Turn the crankshaft one revolution. Check the clearance with a feeler gauge. Repeat for the other valve. Grind off the end of the valve stem if necessary to obtain proper clearance.

NOTE: *Check the valve tappet clearance with the engine cold.*

Valve Seat Inserts

Cast iron cylinder engines are equipped with an exhaust valve insert which can be removed and replaced with a new insert. The intake side must be counter-bored to allow the installation of an intake valve seat insert (see below). Aluminum alloy cylinder models are equipped with inserts on both the exhaust and intake valves.

REMOVAL AND INSTALLATION

Valve seat inserts are removed with a special puller.

NOTE: *On aluminum alloy cylinder models, it may be necessary to grind the puller nut until the edge is 3/32 in. (0.8mm) thick in order to get the puller nut under the valve insert.*

When installing the valve seat insert, make sure that the side with the chamfered outer

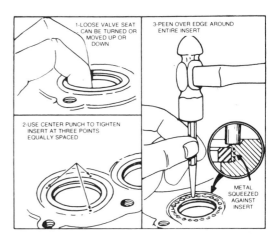

Installing valve seat inserts

edge goes down into the cylinder. Install the seat insert and drive it into place with a driver. The seat should then be ground lightly and the valves and seats lapped lightly with grinding compound.

Aluminum alloy cylinder models use the old insert as a spacer between the driver and the new insert. Drive in the new insert until it bottoms. The top of the insert will be slightly below the cylinder head gasket surface. Peen around the insert using a punch and hammer.

The intake valve seat on cast iron cylinder models has to be counter-bored before installing the new valve seat insert.

COUNTERBORING THE CYLINDER FOR THE INTAKE VALVE SEAT ON CAST IRON MODELS

1. Select the proper seat insert, cutter shank, counter bore cutter, pilot and driver from the table. These numbers refer to Briggs & Stratton parts — you may get equivalent parts from other sources if available.

2. With cylinder head resting on a flat surface, valve seats up, slide the pilot into the intake valve guide. Then, assemble the correct counterbore cutter to the shank with the cutting blades of the cutter downward.

Valve Tappet Clearance Chart

Model Series	Intake		Exhaust	
	Max	Min	Max	Min
Aluminum Cylinder				
140000, 170000, 190000, 251000	.007	.005	.011	.009
Cast Iron Cylinder				
19, 190000, 200000	.009	.007	.016	.014
23, 230000, 240000, 300000, 320000	.009	.007	.019	.017

Valve Seat Inserts Chart

Basic Model Series	Intake Standard	Exhaust Standard	Exhaust Stellite	Insert # Puller Assembly	Puller Nut
Aluminum Cylinder					
140000, 170000, 190000	211661	211661	210940*	19138	19141
250000	211661	211661	210940	19138	19141
Cast Iron Cylinder					
19, 190000	21880	21880	21612	19138	19141
200000, 23, 230000	21880	21880	21612	19138	19141
240000	21880	21612	21612	19138	19141
300000, 320000		21612	21612	19138	19141

* 21191 used before serial #5810060—210808 used from serial #5810060—6012010
# Includes puller and #19182, 19141, 19140 and 19139 nuts

3. Insert the cutter straight into the valve seat, over the pilot. Cut so as to avoid forcing the cutter to one side, and be sure to stop as soon as the stop on the cutter touches the cylinder head.

4. Blow out all cutting chips thoroughly.

Pistons, Piston Rings, and Connecting Rods

REMOVAL

To remove the piston and connecting rod from the engine, bend down the connecting rod lock. Remove the connecting rod cap. Remove any carbon or ridge at the top of the cylinder bore. This will prevent breaking the rings. Push the piston and rod out of the top of the cylinder.

Pistons used in sleeve bore, aluminum alloy engines are marked with an **L** on top of the piston. These pistons are tin plated and use an expander with the oil ring. This piston assembly is not interchangeable with the piston used in the aluminum bore engines (Kool bore).

Pistons used in aluminum bore (Kool bore) engines are not marked on the top.

To remove the connecting rod from the piston, remove the piston pin lock with thin nose

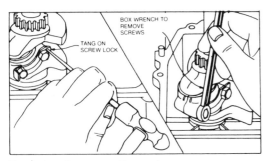

Removing the connecting rod cap

pliers. One end of the pin is drilled to facilitate removal of the lock.

Remove the rings one at a time, slipping them over the ring lands. Use a ring expander to remove the rings.

INSPECTION

Check the piston ring fit. Use a feeler gauge to check the side clearance of the top ring. Make sure that you remove all carbon from the top ring groove. Use a new piston ring to check the side clearance. If the cylinder is to be resized, there is no reason to check the piston, since a new oversized piston assembly will be installed. If the side clearance is more than 0.007 in. (0.178mm), the piston is excessively worn and should be replaced.

Check the piston ring end gap by cleaning all carbon from the ends of the rings and inserting them one at a time 1 in. (25mm) down into the cylinder. Check the end gap with a feeler gauge. If the gap is larger than recommended, the ring should be replaced.

NOTE: *When checking the ring gap, do not deglaze the cylinder walls by installing piston rings in aluminum cylinder engines.*

Chrome ring sets are available for all current aluminum and cast iron cylinder models. No honing or deglazing is required. The cylinder bore can be a maximum of 0.005 in. (0.127mm) oversize when using chrome rings.

If the crankpin bearing in the rod is scored, the rod must be replaced. 0.005 in. (0.127mm) oversize piston pins are available in case the connecting rod and piston are worn at the piston pin bearing. If, however, the crankpin bearing in the connecting rod is worn, the rod should be replaced. Do not attempt to file or fit the rod.

If the piston pin is worn 0.0005 in out of

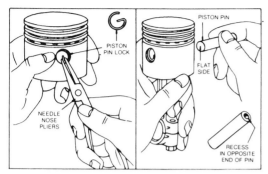

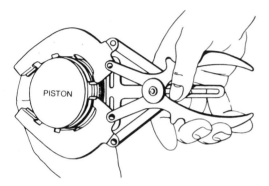

Removing the wrist pin and connecting rod from the piston

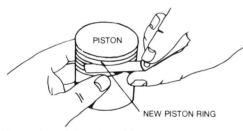

Replacing the piston rings

Measuring piston ring side gap

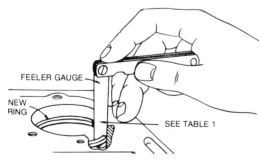

Measuring the piston ring gap

Connecting Rod Bearing Specifications

Basic Model Series	Crank Pin Bearing	Piston Pin Bearing
Aluminum Cylinder		
140000, 170000	1.095	.674
190000	1.127	.674
251000	1.252	.802
Cast Iron Cylinder		
19, 190000	1.001	.674
200000	1.127	.674
23, 230000	1.189	.736
240000	1.314	.674
300000, 320000	1.314	.802

Piston Ring Gap Specifications

Basic Model Series	Comp. Ring	Oil Ring
Aluminum Cylinder		
140000, 170000, 190000, 251000	.035	.045
Cast Iron Cylinder		
19, 190000, 200000, 23, 230000, 240000 300000, 320000	.035	.035

Wrist Pin Specifications

Basic Model Series	Piston Pin	Pin Bore
Aluminum Cylinder		
140000, 170000, 190000	.671	.671
251000	.799	.801
Cast Iron Cylinder		
19, 190000	.671	.673
200000	.671	.673
23, 230000	.734	.736
240000	.671	.673
300000, 320000	.799	.801

round or below the rejection sizes, it should be replaced.

INSTALLATION

The piston pin is a push fit into both the piston and the connecting rod. On models using a solid piston pin, one end is flat and the other end is recessed. Other models use a hollow piston pin. Place a pin lock in the groove at one side of the piston. From the opposite side of the piston, insert the piston pin, flat end first for solid pins; with hollow pins, insert either end first until it stops against the pin lock. Use thin nose pliers to assemble the pin lock in the recessed end of the piston. Be sure the locks are firmly set in the groove.

Install the rings on the pistons, using a piston ring expander. Make sure that they are installed in the proper position. The scraper groove on the center compression ring should always be down toward the piston skirt. Be sure the oil return holes are clean and all carbon is removed from the grooves.

NOTE: *Install the expander under the oil ring in sleeve bore aluminum alloy engines.*

Oil the rings and the piston skirt, then compress the rings with a ring compressor. On cast iron engines, install the compressor with the two projections downward; on aluminum engines, install the compressor with the two projections upward. These instructions refer to the piston in normal position – with skirt downward. Turn the piston and compressor upside down on the bench and push downward so the piston head and the edge of the compressor band are even, all the while tightening the compressor. Draw the compressor up tight to fully

compress the rings, then loosen the compressor very slightly.

WARNING: *Do not attempt to install the piston and ring assembly without using a ring compressor.*

Place the connecting rod and piston assembly, with the rings compressed, into the cylinder bore. Push the piston and rod down into the cylinder. Oil the crankpin of the crankshaft. Pull the connecting rod against the crankpin

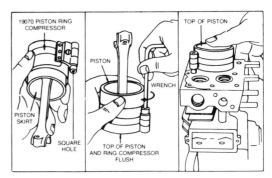

Installing the piston and connecting rod assembly into the cylinder block

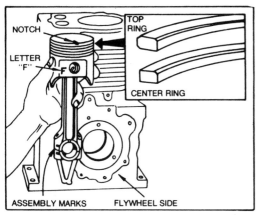

Assembling the piston and connecting rod assembly

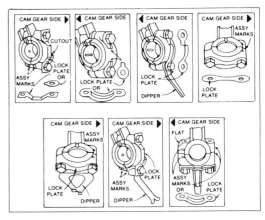

Connecting rod installation

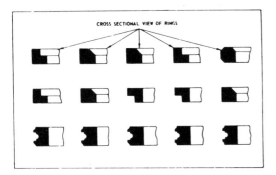

Cross-sectional views and positioning of the various types of piston rings used in Briggs and Stratton engines

Connecting Rod Capscrew Torque

Basic Model Series	Inch lbs Avg. Torque
Aluminum Cylinder	
140000, 170000, 190000	165
251000	185
Cast Iron Cylinder	
19, 190000, 200000	190
23, 230000	190
240000, 300000, 320000	190

and assemble the rod cap so the assembly marks align.

NOTE: *Some rods do not have assembly marks, as the rod and cap will fit together only in one position. Use care to ensure proper installation. On the 251000 engine, the piston has a notch on the top surface. The notch must face the flywheel side of the block when installed.*

Where there are flat washers under the cap screws, remove and discard them prior to installing the rod. Assemble the cap screws and screw locks with the oil dippers (if used), and torque to the figure shown in the chart to avoid breakage or rod scoring later. Turn the crankshaft two revolutions to be sure the rod is correctly installed. If the rod strikes the camshaft, the connecting rod has been installed wrong or the cam gear is out of time. If the crankshaft operates freely, bend the cap screw locks against the screw heads. After tightening the rod screws, the rod should be able to move sideways on the crankpin of the shaft.

Crankshaft and Camshaft Gear

REMOVAL

Aluminum Cylinder Engines

To remove the crankshaft from aluminum alloy engines, remove any rust or burrs from the power take-off end of the crankshaft. Remove the crankcase cover or sump. If the sump or cover sticks, tap it lightly with a soft hammer on alternate sides near the dowel. Turn the crankshaft to align the crankshaft and camshaft timing marks, lift out the cam gear, then remove the crankshaft. On models that have ball bearings on the crankshaft, the crankshaft and the camshaft must be removed together with the timing marks properly aligned – see illustration.

Cast Iron Cylinder Models

To remove the crankshaft from cast iron models, remove the crankcase cover. Revolve the crankshaft until the crankpin is pointing upward toward the breather at the rear of the engine (approximately a 45° angle). Pull the crankshaft out from the drive side, twisting it slightly if necessary. On models with ball bearings on the crankshaft, both the crankcase cover and bearing support should be removed.

On cast iron models with ball bearings on the drive side, first remove the magneto. Drive into the recess at the front of the engine. Then draw the crankshaft from the magneto side of the engine. Double thrust engines have cap screws inside the crankcase which hold the bearing in place. These must be removed before the crankshaft can be removed.

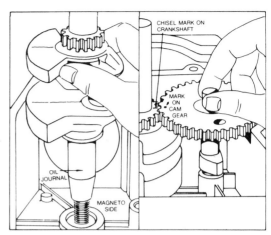

Alignment of the camshaft and crankshaft timing marks

To remove the camshaft from all cast iron models, except the 300400 and 320400, use a long punch to drive the camshaft out toward the magneto side. Save the plug. Do not burr or peen the end of the shaft while driving it out. Hold the camshaft while driving it out. Hold the camshaft while removing the punch, so it will not drop and become damaged.

CHECKING THE CRANKSHAFT

Discard the crankshaft if it is worn beyond the allowable limit. Check the keyways for wear and make sure they are not spread. Remove all burrs from the keyway to prevent scratching the bearing. Check the three bearing journals, drive end, crankpin, and magneto end, for size and any wear or damage. Check the cam gear teeth for wear. They should not be worn at all. Check the threads at the magneto end for damage. Make sure that the crankshaft is straight.

NOTE: *There are 0.020 in. (0.5mm) undersize connecting rods available for use on reground crankpin bearings.*

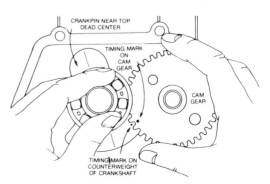

Alignment of the camshaft and crankshaft timing marks on engines equipped with ball bearings

Crankshaft Specifications

Basic Model Series	PTO Journal	Mag. Journal	C Crankpin
Aluminum Cylinder			
140000, 170000	1.179	.997 #	1.090
190000	1.179	.997 #	1.122
251000	1.376	1.376	1.247
Cast Iron Cylinder			
19, 190000	1.179	1.179	.996
200000	1.179	1.179	1.122
23, 230000 †	1.376	1.376	1.184
240000	Ball	Ball	1.309
300000, 320000	Ball	Ball	1.309

\# Synchro balanced magneto bearing reject size— 1.179

†Gear reduction P.T.O.—1.179

Camshaft Specifications

Basic Model Series	Cam Gear or Shaft Journals	Cam Lobe
Aluminum Cylinder		
140000, 170000, 190000	.498	.977
251000	.498	1.184
Cast Iron Cylinder		
19, 190000	.497	1.115
200000	.497	1.115
23, 230000	.497	1.184
240000	.497	1.184
300000	#	1.184
320000	#	1.215

\# Magneto side—.8105, P.T.O. side—.6145

REMOVAL AND INSTALLATION OF THE BALL BEARINGS

The ball bearings are pressed onto the crankshaft. If either the bearing or the crankshaft is to be removed, use an arbor press to remove them.

To install, heat the bearing in hot oil — 325°F (163°C) maximum. Don't let the bearing rest on the bottom of the pan in which it is heated. Place the crankshaft in a vise with the bearing side up. When the bearing is quite hot, it will slip fit onto the bearing journal. Grasp the bearing, with the shield down, and thrust it down onto the crankshaft. The bearing will tighten on the shaft while cooling. Do not quench the bearing (throw water on it to cool it).

CHECKING THE CAMSHAFT GEAR

Inspect the teeth for wear and nicks. Check the size of the camshaft and camshaft gear bearing journals. Check the size of the cam lobes. If the cam is worn beyond tolerance, discard it.

Check the automatic spark advance on models equipped with the Magna-Matic ignition system. Place the cam gear in the normal operating position with the movable weight down. Press the weight down and release it. The spring should lift the weight. If not, the spring is stretched or the weight is binding.

INSTALLATION

Aluminum Alloy Engines — Plain Bearing

In aluminum alloy engines, the tappets are inserted first, the crankshaft next, and then the cam gear. When inserting the cam gear, turn the crankshaft and the cam gear so that the timing marks on the gears align.

Aluminum Alloy Engines — Ball Bearing

On crankshafts with ball bearings, the gear teeth are not visible for alignment of the timing marks; therefore, the timing mark is on the counterweight. On ball bearing equipped engines, the tappets are installed first. The crankshaft and the cam gear must be inserted together and their timing marks aligned.

Crankshaft Cover and Crankshaft

INSTALLATION

Cast Iron Engines w/Plain Bearings

Assemble the tappets to the cylinder, then insert the cam gear. Push the camshaft into the camshaft hole in the cylinder from the flywheel side through the cam gear. With a blunt punch, press or hammer the camshaft until the end is flush with the outside of the cylinder on the power takeoff side. Place a small amount of sealer on the camshaft plug, then press or hammer it into the camshaft hole in the cylinder at the flywheel side. Install the crankshaft so the timing marks on the teeth and on the cam gear align.

Cast Iron w/Ball Bearings

Assemble the tappets, then insert the cam gear into the cylinder, pushing the cam gear forward into the recess in front of the cylinder. Insert the crankshaft into the cylinder. Turn the camshaft and crankshaft until the timing marks align, then push the cam gear back until it engages the gear on the crankshaft with the timing marks together. Insert the camshaft.

Place a small amount of sealer on the camshaft plug and press or hammer it into the camshaft hole in the cylinder at the flywheel side.

CRANKSHAFT END-PLAY ADJUSTMENT

The crankshaft end-play on all models, plain and ball bearing, should be 0.002–0.008 in. (0.2mm). The method of obtaining the correct end-play varies, however, between cast iron, aluminum, plain, and ball bearing models. New gasket sets include three crankcase cover or bearing support gaskets, 0.005 in. (0.127mm), 0.009 in. (0.228mm), and 0.015 in. (0.381mm) thick.

The end-play of the crankshaft may be checked by assembling a dial indicator on the crankshaft with the pointer against the crankcase. Move the crankshaft in and out. The indicator will show the end-play. Another way to measure the end-play is to assemble a pulley to the crankshaft and measure the end-play with a feeler gauge. Place the feeler gauge between the crankshaft thrust face and the bearing support. The feeler gauge method of measuring crankshaft end-play can only be used on cast iron plain bearing engines with removable bases.

On cast iron engines, the end-play should be 0.002–0.008 in. (0.05–0.20mm) with one 0.015 in. (0.381mm) gasket in place. If the end-play is less than 0.002 in. (0.05mm), which would be the case if a new crankcase or sump cover is used, additional gaskets of 0.005 in. (0.127mm), 0.009 in. (0.228mm) or 0.015 in. (0.381mm) may be added in various combinations to obtain the proper end-play.

ALUMINUM ENGINES ONLY

If the end-play is more than 0.008 in. (0.20mm) with one 0.015 in. (0.381mm) gasket in place, a thrust washer is available to be placed on the crankshaft power take-off end, between the gear and crankcase cover or sump on plain bearing engines. On ball bearing equipped aluminum engines, the thrust washer is added to the magneto end of the crankshaft instead of the power take-off end.

NOTE: *Aluminum engines never use less than the 0.015 in. (0.381mm) gasket.*

Cylinders

INSPECTION

Always inspect the cylinder after the engine has been disassembled. Visual inspection will show if there are any cracks, stripped bolt holes, broken fins, or if the cylinder wall is scored. Use an inside micrometer or telescoping gauge and micrometer to measure the size of the cylinder bore. Measure at right angles.

If the cylinder bore is more than 0.003 in.

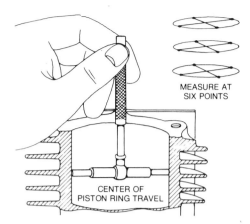

MEASURE AT SIX POINTS

CENTER OF PISTON RING TRAVEL

Checking the cylinder bore

(0.076mm) oversize, or 0.0015 in. (0.381mm) out of round on light-weight (aluminum) cylinders, the cylinder must be resized (rebored).

NOTE: *Do not deglaze the cylinder walls when installing piston rings in aluminum cylinder engines. Also be aware that there are chrome ring sets available for most engines. These are used to control oil pumping in bores worn to 0.005 in. (0.127mm) over standard and do not require honing or glaze breaking to seat.*

RESIZING

Always resize to exactly 0.010 in. (0.254mm), 0.020 in. (0.50mm) or 0.030 in. (0.762mm) over standard size. If this is done accurately, the stock oversize rings and pistons will fit perfectly and proper clearances will be maintained. Cylinders, either cast iron or lightweight, can be quickly resized with a good hone. Use the stones and lubrication recommended by the hone manufacturer to produce the correct cylinder wall finish for the various engine models.

If a boring bar is used, a hone must be used after the boring operation to produce the proper cylinder wall finish. Honing can be done with a portable electric drill, but it is easier to use a drill press.

1. Clean the cylinder at top and bottom to remove all burrs and pieces of base and head gaskets.

2. Fasten the cylinder to a heavy iron plate. Some cylinders require shims. Use a level to align the drill press spindle with the bore.

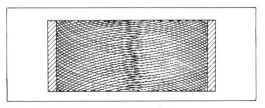

Cross hatch pattern after honing

Cylinder Bore Specifications

Basic Engine Model or Series	Std. Bore Size Diameter	
	Max	Min
Aluminum Cylinder		
140000	2.750	2.749
170000, 190000	3.000	2.999
251000	3.4375	3.4365
Cast Iron Cylinder		
19, 23, 190000, 200000	3.000	2.999
230000	3.000	2.999
243400	3.0625	3.0615
300000	3.4375	3.4365
320000	3.5625	3.5615

3. Oil the surface of the drill press table liberally. Set the iron plate and the cylinder on the drill press table. Do not anchor the cylinder to the drill press table. If you are using a portable drill, set the plate and the cylinder on the floor.

4. Place the hone driveshaft in the chuck of the drill.

5. Slip the hone into the cylinder. Connect the driveshaft to the hone and set the stop on the drill press so the hone can only extend ¾–1 in. (19–25mm) from the top or bottom of the cylinder. If you are using a portable drill, cut a piece of wood to place in the cylinder as a stop for the hone.

6. Place the hone in the middle of the cylinder bore. Tighten the adjusting knob with your finger or a small screwdriver until the stones fit snugly against the cylinder wall. Do not force the stones against the cylinder wall. The hone should operate at a speed of 300–700 rpm. Lubricate the hone as recommended by the manufacturer.

NOTE: *Be sure that the cylinder and the hone are centered and aligned with the driveshaft and the drill spindle.*

7. Start the drill and, as the hone spins, move it up and down at the lower end of the cylinder. The cylinder is not worn at the bottom but is round so it will act to guide the hone and straighten the cylinder bore. As the bottom of the cylinder increases in diameter, gradually increase your strokes until the hone travels the full length of the bore.

NOTE: *Do not extend the hone more than ¾–1 in. (19–25mm) past either end of the cylinder bore.*

8. As the cutting tension decreases, stop the hone and tighten the adjusting knob. Check the cylinder bore frequently with an accurate mi-

crometer. Hone 0.0005 in. (0.0127mm) oversize to allow for shrinkage when the cylinder cools.

9. When the cylinder is within 0.0015 in. (0.038mm) of the desired size, change from the rough stone to a finishing stone.

The finished resized cylinder should have a cross-hatched appearance. Proper stones, lubrication, and spindle speed along with rapid movement of the hone within the cylinder during the last few strokes, will produce this finish. Cross-hatching provides proper lubrication and ring break-in.

NOTE: *It is EXTREMELY important that the cylinder be thoroughly cleaned after honing to eliminate ALL grit. Wash the cylinder carefully in a solvent such as kerosene. The cylinder bore should be cleaned with a brush, soap, and water.*

Bearings

INSPECTION

Plain Type

Bearings should be replaced if they are scored or if a plug gauge will enter. Try the gauge at several points in the bearings.

REPLACING PLAIN BEARINGS

Models 19–20–23

The crankcase cover bearing support should be replaced if the bearing is worn or scored.

REPLACING THE MAGNETO BEARING

Aluminum Cylinder Engines

There are no removable bearings in these engines. The cylinder must be reamed out so a replacement bushing can be installed.

1. Place a pilot guide bushing in the sump bearing, with the flange of the guide bushing toward the inside of the sump.

2. Assemble the sump on the cylinder. Make

Crankshaft Bearing Specifications

Basic Engine Model or Series	PTO Bearing	Bearing Magneto
Aluminum Cylinder		
140000, 170000	1.185	1.004
190000	1.185	1.004
251000	1.383	1.383
Cast Iron Cylinder		
19, 190000, 200000	1.185	1.185
23, 230000	1.382	1.382
240000, 300000	Ball	Ball
320000	Ball	Ball

sure that the pilot guide bushing does not fall out of place.

3. Place the guide bushing into the oil seal recess in the cylinder. This guide bushing will center the counterbore reamer even though the oil bearing surface might be badly worn.

4. Place the counterbore reamer on the pilot and insert them into the cylinder until the tip of the pilot enters the pilot guide bushing in the sump.

5. Turn the reamer clockwise with a steady, even pressure until it is completely through the bearing. Lubricate the reamer with kerosene or any other suitable solvent.

NOTE: *Counterbore reaming may be performed without any lubrication. However, clean off shavings because aluminum material builds up on the reamer flutes causing eventual damage to the reamer and an oversize counterbore.*

6. Remove the sump and pull the reamer out without backing it through the bearing. Clean out the remaining chips. Remove the guide bushing from the oil seal recess.

7. Hold the new bushing against the outer end of the reamed out bearing, with the notch in the bushing aligned with the notch in the cylinder. Note the position of the split in the bushing. At a point in the outer edge of the reamed out bearing opposite to the split in the bushing, make a notch in the cylinder hub at a 45° angle to the bearing surface. Use a chisel or a screwdriver and hammer.

8. Press in the new bushing, being careful to align the oil notches with the driver and the support until the outer end of the bushing is flush with the end of the reamed cylinder hub.

9. With a blunt chisel or screwdriver, drive a portion of the bushing into the notch previously made in the cylinder. This is called staking and is done to prevent the bushing from turning.

10. Reassemble the sump to the cylinder with the pilot guide bushing in the sump bearing.

11. Place a finishing reamer on the pilot and insert the pilot into the cylinder bearing until the tip of the pilot enters the pilot guide bushings in the sump bearing.

12. Lubricate the reamer with kerosene, fuel oil, or other suitable solvent, then ream the bushing, turning the reamer clockwise with a steady even pressure until the reamer is completely through the bearing. Improper lubricants will produce a rough bearing surface.

13. Remove the sump, reamer, and the pilot guide bushing. Clean out all reaming chips.

REPLACING THE P.T.O. BEARING

Aluminum Cylinder Engines

The sump or crankcase bearing is repaired the same way as the magneto end bearing.

Make sure to complete repair of one bearing before starting to repair the other. Press in new oil seals when bearing repair is completed.

REPLACING OIL SEALS

1. Assemble the seal with the sharp edge of leather or rubber toward the inside of the engine.

2. Lubricate the inside diameter of the seal with Lubriplate® or equivalent.

3. Press all seals so they are flush with the hub.

Extended Oil Filler Tubes and Dipsticks

When installing the extended oil fill and dipstick assembly, the tube must be installed so the O-ring seal is firmly compressed. To do so, push the tube downward toward the sump, then tighten the blower housing screw, which is used to secure the tube and bracket. When the dipstick assembly is fully depressed, it seals the upper end of the tube.

A leak at the seal between the tube and the sump, or at the seal at the upper end of the dipstick can result in a loss of crankcase vacuum, and a discharge of smoke through the exhaust system.

Breathers

The function of the breather is to maintain a vacuum in the crankcase. The breather has a fiber disc valve which limits the direction of air flow caused by the piston moving back and forth in the cylinder. Air can flow out of the crankcase, but the one-way valve blocks the return flow, thus maintaining a vacuum in the crankcase. A partial vacuum must be maintained in the crankcase to prevent oil from being forced out of the engine at the piston rings, oil seals, breaker plunger, and gaskets.

INSPECTION OF THE BREATHER

If the fiber disc valve is stuck or binding, the breather cannot function properly and must be

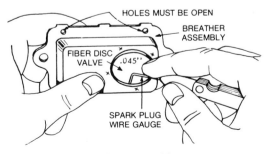

Checking the breather assembly

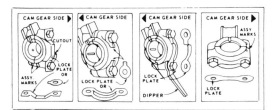

Installing the connecting rod in a horizontal crankshaft engine

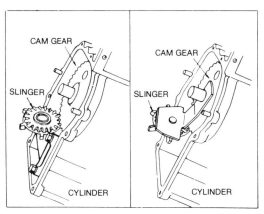

Installation of an oil slinger

replaced. A 0.045 in. (1.14mm) wire gauge should not enter the space between the fiber disc valve and the body. Use a spark plug wire gauge to check the valve. The fiber disc valve is held in place by an internal bracket which will be distorted if pressure is applied to the fiber disc valve. Therefore, do not apply force when checking the valve with the wire gauge.

If the breather is removed for inspection or valve repair, a new gasket should be used when replacing the breather. Tighten the screws securely to prevent oil leakage.

Most breathers are now vented through the air cleaner, to prevent dirt from entering the crankcase. Check to be sure that the venting elbows or the tube are not damaged and that they are properly sealed.

Oil Dippers and Slingers

Oil dippers reach into the oil reservoir in the base of the engine and splash oil onto the internal engine parts. The oil dipper is installed on the connecting rod and has no pump or moving parts.

Oil slingers are driven by the cam gear. Old style slingers using a die cast bracket assembly have a steel bushing between the slinger and the bracket. Replace the bracket on which the oil slinger rides if it is worn to a diameter of 0.490 in. (12.4mm) or less. Replace the steel bushing if it is worn. Newer style oil slingers have a stamped steel brackets.

5

Clinton
2 through 5 Hp

ENGINE IDENTIFICATION

Clinton engines are identified by a name plate that is installed on the engine at the factory. The name plate contains the serial number and the model number, both of which are necessary when obtaining replacement parts.

Two numbering systems are used to identify Clinton engines. The first one applies to engines made prior to 1961, the second pertains to engines made after that year.

The early numbering system has no practical use to the consumer. It is useful only when ordering parts and only to one who has access to a parts manual. No other information can be gained from the model or serial number than what parts fit a particular engine.

The recent numbering system, however, is quite useful in gaining additional information about a certain engine. The serial number, followed by the type letter, is a numerically sequential number and is used to identify the engine in relation to changes that are made in design. The model number consists of a ten digit sequence of numbers that is deciphered in the following manner:

The first digit indicates whether the engine is a 2-stroke or 4-stroke design. The number 4 indicates a 4-stroke engine and the number 5 indicates a 2-stroke engine.

The second and third digits identify the basic engine series and whether the engine has a vertical or horizontal crankshaft. Odd numbers in the third digit position indicate that the engine has a vertical crankshaft and even numbers indicate a horizontal crankshaft.

The fourth digit identifies the type of starter installed on the engine: 0 — a recoil starter, 1 — a rope starter, 2 — an impulse starter, 3 — a crank starter, 4 — a 12 volt electric starter, 5 — a 12 volt starter generator, 6 — a 110 volt electric starter, 7 — a 12 volt generator, 8 — not assigned any specific meaning, 9 — indicates a short block.

The fifth digit indicates what type of bearing is used on the crankshaft; 1 — aluminum or bronze sleeve bearing with a flange mounting surface and pilot diameter on the engine mounting face for mounting equipment concentric to the crankshaft center line; 2 — ball or roller bearing; 3 — ball or roller bearing with a flange mounting surface and pilot diameter on the engine mounting face for mounting equipment concentric to the crankshaft center line; 4–9 — not assigned any meaning.

The sixth digit identifies whether there are any reduction gears or power-take-off units: 0 — not equipped with any such unit; 1 — auxiliary PTO; 2 — 2:1 reduction gears; 3 — not assigned; 4 — 4:1 reduction gears; 5 — not assigned; 6 — 6:1 reduction gears; 7–9 — not assigned.

The eighth through tenth digits are used to identify model variations.

TYPE LETTER

MFD BY CLINTON ENGINES CORP.
MAQUOKETA IOWA U S A

SERIAL NO   10278904   D

MODEL NO   405 0000 070

DIGITS   1·2·3   4·5·6·7   89·10

VARIATION

Numbering system after 1961

The type letter identifies parts that are not interchangeable.

Be sure to give the model number and the type letter when obtaining replacement parts.

MAINTENANCE

Air Cleaner

SERVICE

Metallic Mesh Air Cleaner

1. Loosen the air cleaner screw and remove the air cleaner.
2. Place both element and cover parts in a nonvolatile solvent, and agitate the metal mesh vigorously.
3. Dip the mesh into clean engine oil, and then install air cleaner.

Dry Paper Air Cleaner

1. Remove the air cleaner can from the engine.
2. Brush lightly with a soft bristle brush (not a wire brush).
3. Blow the dirt out, using compressed air. Blow from inside to outside.
4. Make sure the sealing gasket is in place, and install the air cleaner.

Oil Bath Air Cleaner

1. Remove the air cleaner from the engine, disassemble, and soak in a nonvolatile solvent.
2. Inspect the plastic blow carefully for cracks, and replace if necessary.
3. Blow the solvent out of the mesh filter with compressed air.
4. Fill to the correct level with SAE 30 oil, and install.

Polyurethane Air Cleaner

1. Remove the element from the air cleaner container, and wash it in soap and water.
2. Dry it thoroughly. Apply enough engine oil to cover the face of the element (about 1 tablespoon), and install the air cleaner.

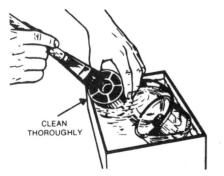

Oil bath air cleaner—washing mesh in solvent

Crankcase Capacity Chart

Model	Capacity
V-100, VS-100, A-300, A-650, VS-2100, VS-3100, VS-4100, and Models 401, 403, 405, 407, 408, 409, 411, 415, 417, 429, 431, 435	1 pint
100, 2100, 3100, H-3100, 4100, 400, 402, 404, 406, 424, 426	1¼ pints
700-A, 700-C, D-700, D-800, A-800, A-900, A-1100, B-1100, C-1100, D-1100, D-1200, A-1200, B-1290, 492, 494, 498	1¼ pints
VS-700, VS-750, VS-800, VS-900, V-1000, V-1100, VS-1100, V-1200, VS-1200, 499	¼ pints
429, 431, 435	1¾ pints

Oil and Fuel Recommendations

FOUR-CYCLE OIL

Follow the recommendations below. Do not use oil of ML (Mostly Light) rating, as it will void the warranty. SG oil is recommended, but best results are obtained with MS rated oil.

- 32°F and above: SAE 30, MM or MS
- –10°F–32°F: SAE 10W, MM or MS
- Below –10°F: SAE 5W, MM or MS rating

TWO-CYCLE OIL

Use a good quality outboard (2-stroke) motor oil, rated MM or MS. Do not use oils rated DM or DS. Use SEA 30 or SAE 40 viscosity.

On sleeve bearing engines, mix the oil in the proportions: ¾ pint to each gallon of gasoline. On needle bearing engines, use ½ pint to each gallon of gasoline.

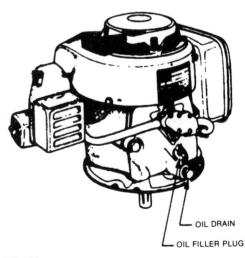

OIL DRAIN

OIL FILLER PLUG

VS-700

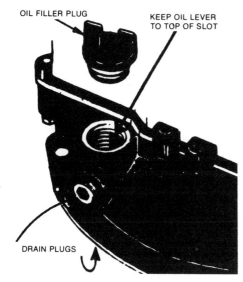

V-100 crankcase fill and drain points

NOTE: *On outboard motors, during the first five hours of operation (break-in), mix ½ pint of oil to each gallon of gasoline. After that, mix ¼ pint to each gallon of fuel. Mix the oil and fuel thoroughly by first supplying one gallon of fuel, pouring the oil in and shaking the can vigorously, and then completely filling the fuel can.*

NOTE: *When the engine uses a screw-in type dipstick, check oil level without screwing dipstick into crankcase.*

Spark Plugs

Remove the spark plug lead and remove the spark plug with a deep well socket. Check for excessive buildup of carbon deposits, burned electrodes, and a cracked insulator. Replace the plug if any of these problems exist. If the plug has only light carbon deposits, wire brush the plug clean and set plug gap with a wire feeler gauge to: 0.028–0.033 in. (0.7–0.8mm) on 2-cycle engines; 0.025–0.028 in. (0.6–0.7mm) on 4-cycle engines.

Breaker Points

CHECKING

1. To check the breaker points, remove the ball, the magneto box cover, and gasket.
2. Look for evidence of excess oil in the box, which would indicate a leaking oil seal or defective breather assembly.
3. Check the point contacts for excessive wear or pitting. Normally the point assembly will last for many years if it is aligned properly, the gap is set correctly, and the rubbing block or shuttle is properly aligned on the actuating cam. If it is necessary to replace the points,

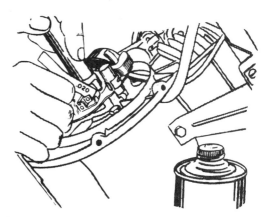

Checking the breaker point gap

make sure that the new set is installed properly.

NOTE: *Do not file the points and bend only the stationary side of the points to align the contact surfaces. Replace the condenser when the points are replaced.*

4. Breaker point gap is critical to engine performance, so make sure it is set to 0.020 in. (0.5mm) unless otherwise specified on the bail cover.

REPLACEMENT

1. Remove the flywheel, as described in the "Engine Disassembly" procedure. Remove the bail and remove the breaker box cover and gasket.
2. Disconnect the primary wire, remove the contact set attaching screws, and remove the contacts.
3. Reverse the removal procedure to install the contact set. Leave the contact set mounting screws slightly loose.
4. Rotate the crankshaft until the points are on the highest point of the cam. Set the gap to the specification shown on the bail cover, or to 0.020 in. (0.5mm) using a flat feeler gauge, as shown. Tighten the mounting screws.
5. Clean the contact surfaces with carbon tetrachloride and then dry with paper. Align the surfaces, if necessary, as described above under "Checking." Reset the gap, if necessary.
6. Grease the cam, rotate the crankshaft, and then remove the excess grease.
7. Replace the cover gasket if it is damaged or oil soaked. Install the cover and snap the bail into position.
8. Install the flywheel, and torque the nut to specification.

Magneto Air Gap

The magneto air gap is the distance between the stationary laminations of the coil and the rotating magnets of the flywheel. In general, the closer the magnets pass to the laminations, the better the magneto will perform. Some extra clearance must be provided for bearing wear, however. The proper clearance for engines under five horsepower is 0.007–0.017 in. (0.18–0.43mm) and 0.012– 0.020 in. (0.3–0.5mm) for engines over five horsepower.

The air gap is measured by placing layers of plastic tape over the laminations, replacing the flywheel and turning the flywheel. Remove the flywheel and check to see if the flywheel touched the tape, and adjust the coil assembly accordingly. Use only one layer of tape at a time. The thickness of common plastic electrician's tape is about 0.008–0.009 in. (0.20–0.23mm).

Breaker Cam

The breaker cam on most Clinton engines is replaceable. Check the fit of the cam over the crankshaft to make sure that it is tight.

Mixture Adjustment

1. If the engine runs very roughly or will not start, first make a preliminary setting as follows:

   a. Very gently turn the main mixture screw in until it seats very lightly.

   b. Turn screw outward (counterclockwise) the specified number of turns:
   - 501 — 1 turn
   - Lift Carburetors — 1¼–1½ turns
   - LMG, LMB, LMV Carburetors — 1¼
   - All others — 1½ turns

2. Following this, start and run the engine until hot. Then, turn the mixture screw inward or outward in ¹⁄₁₆ turn increments, pausing after each adjustment, until best running is obtained. The most accurate adjustment is obtained with a tachometer. Set the mixture so the highest possible rpm is obtained.

Mechanical Governor Adjustment

1. Stop the engine and set any throttle controls so there is tension on the governor spring.

2. Loosen the adjusting screw. Position the throttle to within exactly ¹⁄₃₂ in. (0.8mm) of the stop on the carburetor casting. Tighten the adjusting screw.

Compression Check

1. Remove the spark plug and install a compression gauge in its place.

2. Crank the engine over at normal cranking speed. Gauge readings should be:
   - 2-stroke: above 60 psi
   - 4-stroke up to 4½ hp: 65–70 psi
   - 4-stroke above 4½ hp: 70 psi

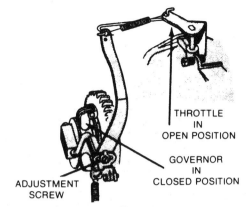

Location of governor adjustment screw

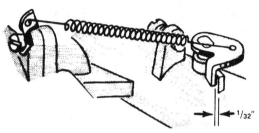

Throttle position and dimension

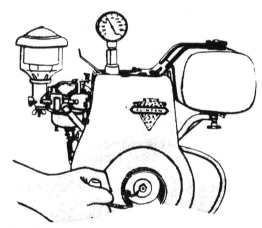

Checking compression

CARBURETED FUEL SYSTEM

Clinton engines use a variety of float type carburetors and one type of suction lift carburetor.

A carburetor can only malfunction as a result of these causes: the presence of foreign matter (dirt, water); out of adjustment (too rich or too lean a mixture), and leakage caused by worn parts or cracks in the casting. Look for any of the above causes before disassembling the carburetor. Of course, it may be required that the carburetor be disassembled to correct the problem, but at least you will have some direction.

NOTE: *Check the throttle shaft/main casting tolerance. This is one place on the carburetor that cannot be repaired.*

501 Engine Carburetor

The 501 engine carburetor is a relatively simple carburetor and can be disassembled after it is removed from the engine.

1. Remove the choke and air filter assembly, remove the mixture adjusting screw and spring, and unscrew the large bolt which holds the float bowl to the rest of the carburetor.

2. Please note that the main fuel nozzle is contained in the top of the large bolt and care should be exercised not to damage the needle seat. Disassemble the float and fuel inlet needle.

NOTE: *The needle seat is not replaceable. The bowl cover, needle pin, spring, and seat assembly must be replaced if any part is worn.*

3. Clean all parts in solvent, blow dry with compressed air, inspect, and replace any worn or damaged parts.

4. Assemble the carburetor in the reverse order of disassembly. Set the float level with the bowl cover inverted and the float and needle installed so that there is $13/64$ in. $\pm$ $1/32$ in. (5mm $\pm$ 0.8mm) clearance between the outer edge of the bowl cover and the free end of the float. Adjust the level by bending the lip of the float with a screwdriver. Use all new gaskets.

5. Set the mixture adjusting needle one turn open from the seat to start the engine. This carburetor does not have an idle mixture orifice and therefore will not operate at speeds below 3000 engine rpm. The operating range is between 3000 and 3800 rpm. Make the final mixture adjustment with a tachometer if possible. If a tachometer is not available, adjust the mixture screw $1/16$ of a turn at a time until you obtain the best engine performance.

Suction Lift Carburetor

THROTTLE PLATE AND SHAFT REPLACEMENT

1. Drill through the plug at the rear of the carburetor body.

2. Force out the plug with a small drift pin.

3. Remove the plastic plug.

4. Remove the screws which retain the throttle plate to the shaft and remove the plate and shaft.

5. Reinstall in the reverse order of removal.

Make sure that the throttle plate and shaft operate without binding. Use a sealer on the new expansion plug.

NOTE: *Horizontal suction lift carburetors do not have a plug.*

The choke plate and shaft is replaced in the same manner as the throttle, except that there is no expansion plug to be removed.

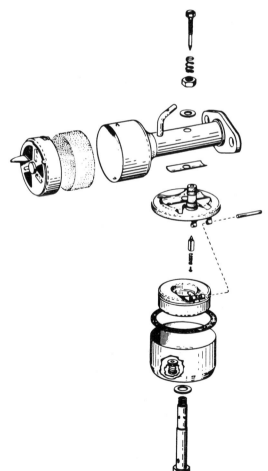

501 Engine carburetor

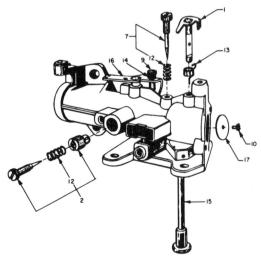

Suction lift carburetor

STAND PIPE REPLACEMENT

The stand pipe is press-fit into the body of the carburetor. Remove the pipe by clamping it in a vise and twisting the carburetor body while at the same time pulling until the pipe is free. To install the pipe, tap it lightly into place until the end of the pipe is 1.94 in. ± 0.45 in. (49mm ± 11mm) from the body of the carburetor. Use a sealer at the point where the pipe is inserted into the carburetor body.

IDLE NEEDLE AND JET REPLACEMENT

The idle needle and jet are replaceable and can be removed as follows:

1. Unscrew the needle and remove it.
2. Remove the expansion plug in the bottom of the carburetor body.
3. To remove the idle jet, push a piece of $\frac{1}{16}$ in. (1.5mm) diameter rod through the fuel well and up the idle passage until the jet is pushed out of the passage.

To install the idle needle and jet:

4. Make a mark exactly 1¼ in. (31.75mm) from the end of the $\frac{1}{16}$ in. (1.5mm) diameter rod and push the new jet into the idle passage until the mark is exactly in the center of the main fuel well.
5. Install the needle and set it at 4–4¼ turns open from being seated.

The high speed needle and seat can be inspected for wear or damage by removing the needle and checking its taper. If the needle taper is damaged, replace it. Inspect the seat for taper and splits. If the seat is split or tapered from the needle being screwed in too tight, the complete carburetor must be replaced, since the seat cannot be replaced separately. When the needle is replaced, the initial adjustment is ¾–1½ turns open from being lightly seated.

LMG, LMB and LMV Type Carburetors

These carburetors are float type carburetors and can be reconditioned in the same manner as the 501 carburetors by taking a note of the following differences in design and specifications.

The main fuel nozzle needle is inserted from the bottom and pushed up through the middle of the float bowl.

The float, fuel inlet needle, and seat are basically the same as that of the 501 carburetor.

NOTE: *Do not remove the main fuel nozzle*

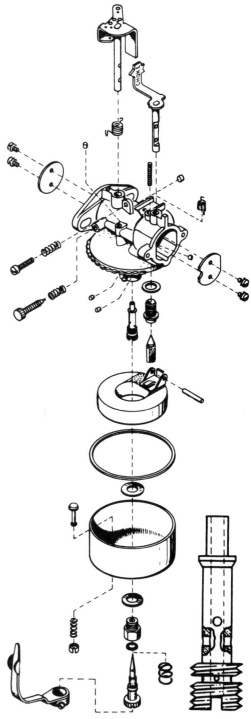

LMG, LMV, LMB type carburetors with an enlarged view of the main jet nozzle

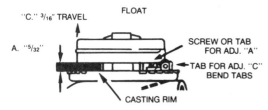

Float adjustment for the LMG, LMV, LMB type carburetors

from the carburetor body unless it is to be replaced. Once it is removed it cannot be reinstalled.

Use all new gaskets.

The throttle valve is installed with the part number or trademark **W** facing toward the mounting flange.

The preliminary setting of the idle adjusting needle is 1¼ turns open after being lightly seated.

Adjust the float in the same manner as the 501 carburetor. There should be $\frac{5}{32}$ in. (4mm) clearance between the float and the casting rim when the carburetor is inverted. When the carburetor is turned over, the float should not drop more than $\frac{3}{16}$ in. (4.8mm).

The preliminary setting for the main fuel adjusting needle is 1¼ turns open after being lightly seated.

H.E.W. Carburetors

H.E.W. carburetors are float type carburetors and can be serviced in the same manner as 501 carburetors. After cleaning and inspecting the parts for wear or damage, assemble the carburetor, noting the following differences:

Install the throttle valve with the part number or **W** toward the mounting flange with the throttle in the closed position. Always use new gaskets during assembly.

The initial setting for the idle adjusting screw is 1½ turns open from being lightly seated.

If any part of the float assembly has to be replaced, replace the whole assembly. Do not replace individual parts.

The float setting is made in the same manner as the 501 carburetor, by turning the main body of the carburetor upside down and measuring the clearance between the float and the body casting rim. The distance in this case is $\frac{3}{16}$ in. (4.8mm) with $\frac{3}{16}$ in. (4.8mm) of travel.

The preliminary setting for the high speed adjusting screw is 1½ turns open from being seated lightly.

U.T. Carburetors

These are also float type carburetors and are serviced in the same manner as 501 carburetors, noting the following differences:

The throttle valve is installed with the trademark **C** on the side toward the idle port when viewed from the mounting flange side. Use new screws.

Set the float level with the float installed and the housing inverted. The measurement is to be taken with the needle seated and the gasket removed. Measure between the float seam and the throttle body. Adjust by bending the lip of the float.

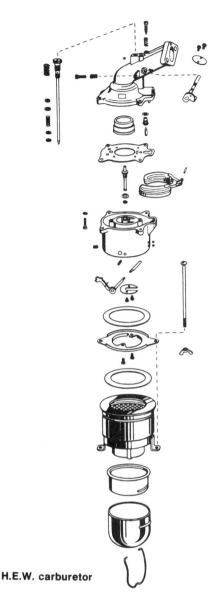

H.E.W. carburetor

The peliminary setting for the high speed adjusting needle is 1¼ turns open from being lightly seated.

The preliminary setting for the idle adjusting needle is 1½ turns open from being lightly seated.

The chart below gives the float level setting dimension as related to the carburetor identification number and part number:

Touch 'N' Start Primer Carburtor

Steps in operation of the primer:
1. Seal the bowl vent with a finger.
2. Depress the bulb to pressurize the bowl.
3. Pressure in carburetor bowl forces the fuel into the carburetor throat.
4. When the engine is cranked, the intake

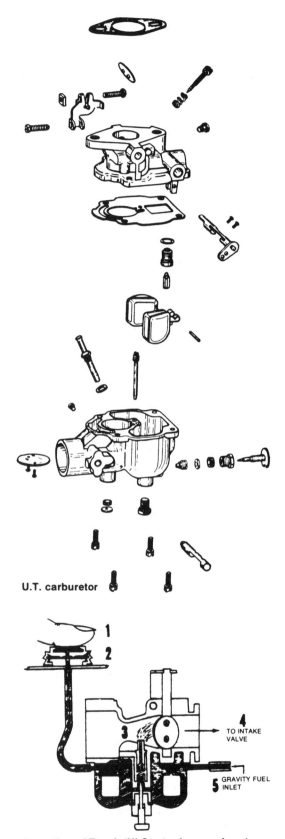

Ident No.	Part No.	Float Setting (in.)
2712–S	39–143–500	$^{19}/_{64}$
2713–S	39–144–500	$^{19}/_{64}$
2714–S	39–140–500	$^1/_4$
*2398-S	39–147–500	$^1/_4$
2336–S	39–146–500	$^1/_4$
2336–SA	39–146–500	$^1/_4$
2337-S	39–145–500	$^1/_4$
2337–SA	39–145–500	$^1/_4$
2230-S	39–343–500	$^{17}/_{64}$
2217-S	39–344–500	$^{11}/_{64}$

*With resilient seat—$^9/_{32}$ + or − $^1/_{64}$

valve opens, letting gasoline into the combustion chamber for quick starting.

5. Gasoline forced from the bowl during priming is replaced by the flow of gasoline from the fuel tank through the gravity fuel inlet.

This primer is applicable to the LMG, LMB, and LMV carburetors. Servicing this carburetor would be the same as listed for the LMG, LMB, and LMV, except a choke lever and choke valve are not used. Note the bowl atmospheric vent is routed back through the primer tube and bulb.

Fixed Speed Carburetor

Steps in operation:

1. Rotate the control knob counterclockwise to open the throttle (4-cycle engines) (2-cycle not equipped with control knob).

2. To stop the engine rotate the control knob clockwise. (4-cycle engines) (2-cycle engines use a shorting device).

NOTE: *The governor spring is located on the throttle shaft between the lever and the carburetor casting. The setting on the high speed*

U.T. carburetor

Operation of Touch 'N' Start primer carburetor

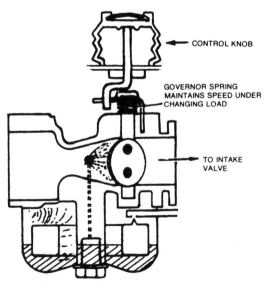

Operation of the Fixed Speed carburetor

screw is 1¼–1½ turns. Servicing this carburetor would be the same as listed for the LMG, LMB, or LMV except there is no main nozzle or idle circuit.

Carter Carburetors

Carter float type carburetors are serviced in the same manner as 501 carburetors, taking note of the following differences:

Do not remove the choke valve and shaft unless they are to be replaced. A spring loaded ball holds the choke in the wide open position. Be sure to use a new ball and spring when replacing the choke shaft and plate assembly.

Install the throttle plate with the trademark C on the side toward the idle port when viewed from the mounting flange side.

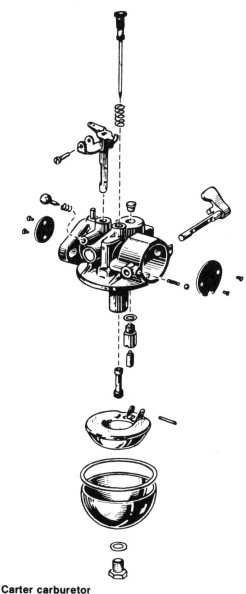

Carter carburetor

The float setting is made in the same manner as the 501 carburetor and the measurement is ³⁄₁₆ in. (4.8mm).

The initial setting for the high speed adjustment screw is 2 turns open from being lightly seated.

The initial adjustment for the idle adjusting screw is 1½ turns open from being lightly seated.

Fuel Pumps

MECHANICAL FUEL PUMPS

These pumps can be rebuilt. See the exploded view below.

The 220-122-500 and 220-145-500 fuel pumps are simple diaphragm units that screw into the inlet side of the carburetor. They are activated by crankcase pressure pulses. They cannot be rebuilt, but must be replaced if they will not lift the fuel six inches.

The diaphragm type fuel pumps used on VS–1200, V–1200, and 499 series engines can be rebuilt. However, construction is so simple no rebuild specifics are supplied by the factory.

Governors

INSPECTION AND ASSEMBLY OF MECHANICAL GOVERNOR

When assembling an engine equipped with the centrifugal weight governor inspect the governor shaft bearing in the block and the governor arm assembly that goes through the bearing, for wear and replace them if necessary. After inspection, insert the arm through the bearing and fasten the arm and weight assembly into the bearing.

Care should be taken on installation of this arm and weight assembly as they may be locked to the outside linkage 180° from the correct position which would tear out the centrifugal weights and damage the arm and weight assembly upon operation of the engine. The weight and arm or yoke should be as close to the cam axle or governor gear as it can be to be properly installed. In this position, it will operate against the governor collar or thimble assembly and will move in conjunction with the governor spring tension and the centrifugal force of the weights which are attached to the camshaft or governor gear.

The collar should be inspected for wear and possible damage, and the weight assembly itself should be inspected for wear and possible damage or bending of the weights or the weight supports.

When servicing a centrifugal governor, check to be certain that the collar or thimble operates freely on the camshaft or governor gear and that the governor shaft moves freely in the bushing. When the bushing in the block is replaced, check carefully freedom of shaft motion as the bushing may be distorted in installation.

Also the governor shaft can be bent easily on disassembly or reassembly and can be bent in usage. Also check range of movement of collar or thimble after assembly of camshaft or governor gear to determine that these parts do not lock against block.

INSPECTION AND ASSEMBLY OF AIR VANE GOVERNOR

The air vane should be inspected visually when reassembling and replaced if bent or damaged. Use care in the hook-up of the air vane link and throttle plate so that they move freely and do not drag at the connections or on the bearing plate or blower housing. Many of the air vane governors have a spring inside of the vane at the pivot. The spring gives a dampening effect on the vane movement. This spring should be replaced if the engine has been out of service for a period of time so that it retains the pressure on the bushing or vane.

When servicing an air vane governor, the condition of the blower housing should be checked carefully. Dents and bends should be removed from it so that the air stream moves as it should to the air vane. The air vane must be in the same condition as when manufactured and replaced when bent because the governor spring tension and the vane are balanced. If the vane does not sit in the air blast properly, the spring will be too strong for the air vane to stretch.

When assembling the air vane governor, apply tension to the governor spring and close the throttle manually to see that it moves open freely, that it does not bind at the governor linkage, air vane, pivot post, bushings, bearing plate, blower housing, etc. It should move freely from closed to open position by governor spring tension.

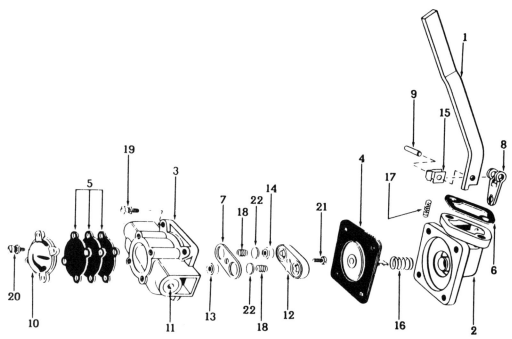

1. Rocker arm
2. Body
3. Top cover
4. Diaphragm assembly
5. Diaphragm pulsator
6. Mounting gasket
7. Valve gasket
8. Linkage
9. Rocker arm pin
10. Cover plate
11. Pipe plug
12. Valve retainer
13. Valve seat (head)
14. Valve seat (retainer)
15. Rocker arm spring clip
16. Diaphragm spring
17. Rocker arm spring
18. Valve spring
19. Screw & lockwasher assembly (cover plate)
20. Screw & lockwasher assembly (top cover)
21. Screw & lockwasher assembly (valve retainer)
22. Valve

Exploded view of mechanical fuel pump-typical

General Engine Specifications

Model Number	Block Construction	Piston Displacement	Type	Model Number	Block Construction	Piston Displacement	Type
E65	Alum.	5.76	2 Cycle	A & B 1100	LLCI	8.3	4 Cycle
				C1100	LLCI	8.3	4 Cycle
100	Alum.	7.2	4 Cycle	D1100	LLCI	8.3	4 Cycle
100–1000	Alum.	7.2	4 Cycle	V1100–1000	LLCI	9.5	4 Cycle
100–2000	Alum.	7.2	4 Cycle	VS1100	LLCI	9.5	4 Cycle
V100–1000	LLCI	7.2	4 Cycle	VS1100–1000	LLCI	9.5	4 Cycle
VS100	Alum.	7.2	4 Cycle				
VS100–1000	Alum.	7.2	4 Cycle	1200	LLCI	10.2	4 Cycle
VS100–2000	Alum.	7.2	4 Cycle	1200–1000	LLCI	10.2	4 Cycle
VS100–3000	Alum.	7.2	4 Cycle	1200–2000	LLCI	10.2	4 Cycle
VS100–4000	Alum.	7.2	4 Cycle	A1200	LLCI	10.2	4 Cycle
				B1290–1000	LLCI	10.2	4 Cycle
200	Alum.	4.5	2 Cycle	V1200–1000	LLCI	10.2	4 Cycle
A200	Alum.	4.5	2 Cycle	VS1200	LLCI	10.2	4 Cycle
AVS200	Alum.	4.5	2 Cycle				
AVS200–1000	Alum.	4.5	2 Cycle	2100	Alum.	7.2	4 Cycle
VS200	Alum.	4.5	2 Cycle	A2100	Alum.	7.2	4 Cycle
VS200–1000	Alum.	4.5	2 Cycle	A2100–1000	Alum.	7.2	4 Cycle
VS200–2000	Alum.	4.5	2 Cycle	A2100–2000	Alum.	7.2	4 Cycle
VS200–3000	Alum.	4.5	2 Cycle				
VS200–4000	Alum.	5.76	2 Cycle	VS2100	Alum.	7.2	4 Cycle
				VS2100–1000	Alum.	7.2	4 Cycle
300	LLCI	4.72	4 Cycle	VS2100–2000	Alum.	7.2	4 Cycle
A300	LLCI	4.72	4 Cycle	VS2100–3000	Alum.	7.2	4 Cycle
VS300	LLCI	4.72	4 Cycle				
350	LLCI	4.72	4 Cycle	VS3000	Alum.	7.2	4 Cycle
A400	Alum.	5.76	2 Cycle	3100	Alum.	8.3	4 Cycle
A400–1000	Alum.	5.76	2 Cycle	3100–1000	Alum.	8.3	4 Cycle
AVS400	Alum.	5.76	2 Cycle	3100–2000	Alum.	8.3	4 Cycle
AVS400–1000	Alum.	5.76	2 Cycle	3100–3000	Alum.	8.3	4 Cycle
BVS400	Alum.	5.76	2 Cycle	H3100–1000	LLCI	8.3	4 Cycle
CVS400–1000	Alum.	5.76	2 Cycle	FV3100–1000	LLCI	8.3	4 Cycle
VS400	Alum.	5.76	2 Cycle	AFV3100–1000	LLCI	8.3	4 Cycle
VS400–1000	Alum.	5.76	2 Cycle	AV3100–1000	LLCI	8.3	4 Cycle
VS400–2000	Alum.	5.76	2 Cycle	AV3100–2000	LLCI	8.3	4 Cycle
VS400–3000	Alum.	5.76	2 Cycle	AVS3100	Alum.	8.3	4 Cycle
VS400–4000	Alum.	5.76	2 Cycle	AVS3100–1000	Alum.	8.3	4 Cycle
				AVS3100–2000	Alum.	8.3	4 Cycle
500	LLCI	5.89	4 Cycle	AVS3100–3000	Alum.	8.3	4 Cycle
GK590	Alum.	5.76	2 Cycle	V3100–1000	LLCI	8.3	4 Cycle
				V3100–2000	LLCI	8.3	4 Cycle
650	LLCI	5.89	4 Cycle	VS3100	Alum.	8.3	4 Cycle
				VS3100–1000	Alum.	8.3	4 Cycle
700–A	LLCI	5.89	4 Cycle	VS3100–2000	Alum.	8.3	4 Cycle
B700	LLCI	5.89	4 Cycle	VS3100–3000	Alum.	8.3	4 Cycle
C700	LLCI	5.89	4 Cycle				
D700	LLCI	6.65	4 Cycle	4100	Alum.	8.3	4 Cycle
D700–1000	LLCI	6.65	4 Cycle	4100–1000	Alum.	8.3	4 Cycle
D700–2000	LLCI	6.65	4 Cycle	4100–2000	Alum.	8.3	4 Cycle
D700–3000	LLCI	6.65	4 Cycle	AVS4100–1000	Alum.	8.3	4 Cycle
VS700	LLCI	5.89	4 Cycle	AVS4100–2000	Alum.	8.3	4 Cycle
VS750	LLCI	5.89	4 Cycle	VS4100–1000	Alum.	8.3	4 Cycle
				VS4100–2000	Alum.	8.3	4 Cycle
800	LLCI	8.3	4 Cycle				
A800	LLCI	8.3	4 Cycle	400–0000–000	Alum.	7.2	4 Cycle
VS800	LLCI	8.3	4 Cycle	401–0000–000	Alum.	7.2	4 Cycle
				402–0000–000	Alum.	7.2	4 Cycle
900	LLCI	8.3	4 Cycle	403–0000–000	Alum.	7.2	4 Cycle
900–1000	LLCI	8.3	4 Cycle	404–0000–000	Alum.	8.3	4 Cycle
900–2000	LLCI	8.3	4 Cycle	405–0000–000	Alum.	8.3	4 Cycle
900–3000	LLCI	8.3	4 Cycle	406–0000–000	LLCI	8.3	4 Cycle
900–4000	LLCI	8.3	4 Cycle	407–0000–000	LLCI	8.3	4 Cycle
VS900	LLCI	8.3	4 Cycle	407–0002–000	LLCI	8.3	4 Cycle
				408–0000–000	Alum.	8.3	4 Cycle
V1000–1000	LLCI	8.3	4 Cycle	409–0000–000	Alum.	8.3	4 Cycle
VS1000	LLCI	8.3	4 Cycle				

General Engine Specifications (cont.)

Model Number	Block Construction	Piston Displacement	Type	Model Number	Block Construction	Piston Displacement	Type
411–0000–000	Alum.	7.2	4 Cycle	492–0300–000	LLCI	8.3	4 Cycle
411–0002–000	Alum.	7.2	4 Cycle	494–0000–000	LLCI	8.3	4 Cycle
415–0000–000	Alum.	8.3	4 Cycle	494–0001–000	LLCI	8.3	4 Cycle
415–0002–000	Alum.	8.3	4 Cycle	497–0000–000	LLCI	10.2	4 Cycle
417–0000–000	LLCI	8.3	4 Cycle	498–0300–000	LLCI	10.2	4 Cycle
424–0000–000	LLCI	8.3	4 Cycle	498–0301–000	LLCI	10.2	4 Cycle
426–0000–000	Alum.	8.3	4 Cycle	499–0000–000	LLCI	10.2	4 Cycle
429–0003–000	LLCI	9.2	4 Cycle	500–0000–000	Alum.	5.76	2 Cycle
431–0003–000	LLCI	9.2	4 Cycle	501–0000–000	Alum.	5.76	2 Cycle
435–0003–000	Alum.	8.3	4 Cycle	501–0001–000	Alum.	5.76	2 Cycle

Alum. = Aluminum
LLCI = Long Life Cast Iron

ENGINE OVERHAUL

The same basic procedure for disassembling a Clinton engine can be used for all engines. The procedure given below pertains to both 2-stroke and 4-stroke Clinton engines; differences are noted. Procedures for servicing individual components are given at a later point in this section.

Engine

DISASSEMBLY

1. Remove the engine from the piece of equipment it powers and then remove any brackets, braces, adapters or pulleys.
2. Clean the exterior of the engine.
3. Drain the lubricating oil from the crankcase.
4. Remove the fuel tank and blower housing.
5. Remove the carburetor and governor assembly, marking the spring and link holes for correct reassembly.
6. Remove the muffler assembly.
7. Remove the flywheel nut, using a flywheel holder to hold the flywheel while the nut is removed.
8. While lifting up on the flywheel, gently tap the crankshaft to loosen the flywheel from the crankshaft taper. Remove the flywheel and flywheel key.
9. Remove the complete magneto assembly which includes the coil, breaker points, condenser, and laminations.
10. Remove the cylinder head and gasket on 4-stroke engines.
11. Remove the valve chamber cover and breather assembly from 4-stroke engines.
12. Remove the valve spring keepers after compressing the valve spring with a valve spring compressor.
13. Remove the valves and springs from the block after removing the valve spring compressor.

NOTE: *Some valves have a burr on the stem that will prevent the valve from being removed up through the valve guide. If present, it will be necessary to remove this burr from the stem in order to remove the valve from the engine. To remove the burr, hold a flat file against the burred area and rotate the valve.*

14. Remove the base plate or end cover assembly on 4-stroke engines.

NOTE: *On some engines the base is an integral part of the block and cannot be removed. If this is the case, remove the side plate on the power take-off side of the engine. Before removing the side plate or crankshaft, make sure all paint, rust, and dirt are cleaned from the area of the crankshaft bearing. This is so the side plate can be easily removed. When removing the side plate from engines that have ball bearings, it will first be necessary to remove the oil seal and the snap-ring from the crankshaft.*

15. Remove the mounting plate and reed plate assembly on 2-stroke engines.
16. Remove the connecting rod cap screws

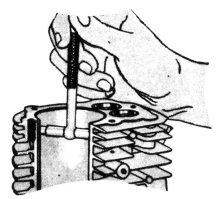

Measuring the cylinder bore—a cutaway view

and cap. Mark the cap and connecting rod so they can be reassembled in the same position.

17. On 4-stroke engines, check for a carbon or metal ridge at the top of the cylinder. If a ridge is present, remove it with a ridge reamer or hone.

18. On 2-stroke engines, push the piston and connecting rod assembly up into the cylinder as far as it will go so it will not hit the crankshaft when it is removed.

19. Remove the piston and connecting rod assembly from a 4-stroke engine's block.

20. Remove the bearing plate on the flywheel side of the block if the engine being disassembled has one.

21. Remove the crankshaft.

NOTE: *On 4-stroke engines with a ball bearing on the PTO side of the engine, it will be necessary to remove the cap screws which hold the bearing in place before the crankshaft can be removed. On some models with ball bearings and tapered roller bearings, it will be necessary to remove the crankshaft oil seal and camshaft axle, and move the camshaft to one side before the crankshaft can be removed. 2-stroke engines having a ball bearing on the PTO side of the crankshaft will have to have the retaining ring, which holds the bearing in place, removed before the crankshaft can be removed.*

22. Remove the camshaft assembly. Drive the camshaft axle out of the PTO side of the block as the flywheel side is smaller.

23. Remove the piston and connecting rod assembly from 2-stroke engines.

24. After the camshaft is removed from a 4-stroke engine, mark the valve tappets as to whether they are the exhaust tappet or the intake tappet, and then remove them. If no valve work is to be done, be sure to replace the valves in the same position from which they were removed.

25. Remove the piston and rod assembly. After disassembling the engine, clean all parts in a safe solvent, removing all deposits of carbon and oil, etc. Check all operating clearances and replace or rebuild parts as necessary.

Cylinder Bore

After disassembling the engine, inspect the cylinder bore to see if it can be reused. Look for score marks on the cylinder walls. If there are marks and they are too deep to be removed, the block will have to be discarded. If there is a hole in the block due to connecting rod failure, the block will have to be replaced. If there are broken cooling fins on the outside of the block, these can cause overheating and replacing the block should be considered.

Check the dimensions of the cylinder bore to determine the extent of wear and whether or not it has to be rebored. The cylinder bore can be rebored to 0.010 in. (0.25mm) or 0.020 in. (0.5mm) oversize since there are oversize pistons available in these sizes. If the cylinder is within serviceable limits and there is no need to rebore it, be sure to deglaze the cylinder before installing the piston assembly with new rings.

Bearings

Clinton engines are equipped with tapered roller bearings, ball bearings, needle bearings, and sleeve bearings. The first thing to determine is whether or not the bearing is worn or damaged and needs replacing. Then clean the bearings in a sofe solvent, inspect them for excessive play due to wear, smoothness of rotation, pitted surfaces, and damage. All of these types of bearings are pressed on the crankshaft and into the bearing plates and are removed by either a bearing splitter and puller or they are driven out of the bearing plates with a punch. In all cases be very careful not to bend, gouge, or otherwise damage the crankshaft or bearing plate when removing and installing the bearings.

With sleeve bearings, first inspect the bearing surface for scoring and damage to determine whether the bearing has to be replaced.

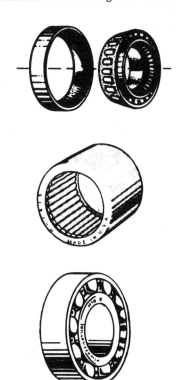

Tapered roller, needle, and ball bearing type bearings, all of which are used in Clinton engines

Check the bearing diameter for wear. In some cases you will find that the bearing surface is the same material as the block. These bearings can be reamed out and sleeve bearings installed. If the original bearing is a sleeve type bearing, it can be removed by driving it out with the proper size driving tool. Install the new bearing so that the oil hole in the bearing is aligned with the oil passage in the block or bearing plate. Drive the bearing into the block or bearing plate until it is recessed about $\frac{1}{32}$ in. (0.8mm) from the crankshaft thrust face of the block or bearing plate. After installing the new piece, it must be finish reamed. After finish reaming, clean all metal filings and debris from the engine, making sure that all oil passages are free from obstruction.

Valve Seats

Standard valve seats, those without inserts, can be reground to remove all of the oxidized surface metal and gain perfect sealing characteristics. After grinding the valve seats, the valves must be lapped in with lapping compound. Not too much lapping is recommended, just enough to obtain a good seal.

If the engine has had a number of valve jobs and the valve seat is too deep, requiring that too much stock be removed from the valve stem to obtain the proper valve-to-tappet clearance, valve seat inserts may be installed. If over half of the metal between the lock groove and the end of the valve stem has been removed to gain the proper stem-to-tappet clearance, you should consider installing valve seat inserts.

On aluminum block engines, iron valve seat inserts are standard equipment. To remove these inserts, it is first necessary to remove the metal that has been rolled over the edge of the insert to hold it in place. This is normally accomplished by using the proper size cutter. If the valve seat insert is loose, a cutter may not be necessary. After the insert has been removed, it is necessary to cut the block to the proper depth of $\frac{3}{16}$-$\frac{7}{32}$ in. (4.8–5.5mm). This is the depth of the insert plus $\frac{1}{32}$ in. (0.8mm) which is used to hold the insert in place. The insert is held to the cylinder block by a definite interference type press fit. The insert should be cooled before attempting to install it in the

block. After the insert is fitted in place, with the bevel facing up, the metal around the edge of the insert must be peened over the edge of the insert in order to hold it in place. Do not strike the block too sharply when peening because of the posibility of distorting the cylinder bore. Finish grind the valve seat insert and lap in the valves.

Valve Guides

First, inspect and measure the valve guide diameter to determine whether the guide is worn enough to necessitate rebuilding. The standard guide size for 4-stroke engines under 5 horsepower is 0.2495–0.2510 in. (6.3373–6.3754mm). On engines over 5 horsepower, the standard guide size is 0.312–0.313 in. (7.925–7.950mm).

When the valve stem-to-valve guide clearance is more than the maximum serviceable clearance and cannot be corrected by installing a new valve, you will have to either replace the valve guide (if it is replaceable), oversize it, or knurl it.

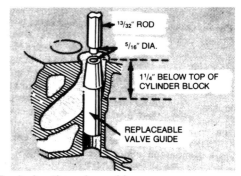

Replacing the valve guides

Valves

Inspect the valves for a burned face, warped stem or head, scored or damaged stem, worn keeper groove in the stem, and a head margin of less than $\frac{1}{64}$ in. (0.4mm). If any one of these conditions exists, the valve should be replaced. Check the valve stem diameter. On engines with less than 5 horsepower, the stem diameter should be 0.2475–0.2465 in. (6.2865–6.2611mm). On engines over 5 horsepower, the stem diameter is to be 0.310–0.309 in. (7.874–7.846mm). Any time the valve stem-to-guide clearance can be reduced more than 0.001 in. (0.025mm) by replacing the valve with a new one, you should do so. Also any time the stem-to-guide clearance is over 0.0045 in. (0.114mm) you should consider doing some rework (new valve guides, seats and valves) to bring the clearance below 0.0045 in. (0.114mm) but not

The valve seat width is to be between $\frac{1}{32}$ and $\frac{3}{64}$ in. (0.030–0.045 in.) and the valve seat angle is to be between $43\frac{1}{2}°$ and $44\frac{1}{2}°$

less than 0.002 in. (0.05mm). If it is determined that the old valve can be reused, then it should be refaced, using an automotive type valve grinder to secure a 45° face angle on the valve with a $\frac{1}{64}$ in. (0.4mm) margin between the head and the face of the valve.

2-Stroke Engine Reed Valves

Inspect the reed valves for the following items: broken reed valves, bent or distorted reed valves, damaged or distorted reed valve seat, or a broken or bent reed valve stop. If any of these conditions exist, the reed valve assembly must be replaced.

Valve Springs

To check the condition of valve springs, simply remove the spring from the engine and stand it on a flat surface next to a new valve spring. If the old spring is shorter and leans to one side, it should be replaced with a new spring. Some of the cast iron engines have a stronger or stiffer valve spring installed on the exhaust valve. Make sure that a stiffer spring is installed on the exhaust valve or, to be sure, install two stiff springs in the engine. When a valve seat is rebuilt, the valve then seats further down into the block and this results in a loss of spring tension. To restore spring tension, install a thin washer on top of the valve spring.

Valve Tappets

The valve tappets should be inspected for wear on the head of the tappet and score marks or burrs anywhere else. The tappet should be replaced if any defects are found. Measure the dimensions of the tappet, checking for stem diameter and length. Oversize tappets are not available; however, the tappet guide can be knurled and rebored to correct size should the tappet-to-guide clearance become too large.

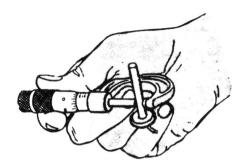

Measuring the tappet stem diameter

Piston Assembly

Inspect the piston assembly for scored walls, damaged ring lands, worn or damaged wrist pin lock ring grooves, and a cracked or broken piston skirt. If any of these defects are present, the piston must be replaced. Check the dimensions of the piston with a micrometer.

NOTE: *The ring land diameter on 4-stroke engines is tapered and the reading at the ring land will be 0.00125 in. (0.03mm) smaller per 1 in. (25mm) of piston length.*

Clean all carbon deposits from the ring grooves. An old broken ring will serve as an excellent tool for cleaning ring grooves.

Check the side clearances of the rings with new rings installed. The minimum and maximum clearances for oil, scraper, and compression rings are as follows: ● 2-stroke engines – 0.0015–0.004 in. (0.038–0.101mm)

● 4-stroke engines under five horsepower – 0.002–0.005 in. (0.05–0.127mm)

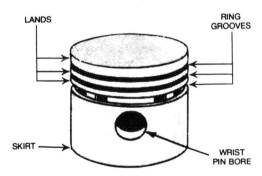

Names of the piston parts

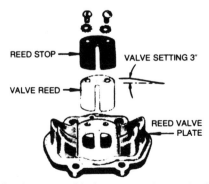

Reed valve assembly for two stroke engines

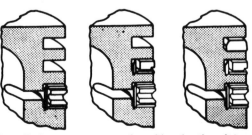

Installation sequence and position for the piston rings

• 4-stroke engines over five horsepower — 0.0025–0.005 in. (0.064–0.127mm)

If an oversized piston is used, the amount of the oversize is stamped on the top of the piston.

The ring gap on all engines except the 1⅞ in. (47.625mm) bore 2-stroke engine is 0.007–0.017 in. (0.18–0.43mm). The ring gap on the 1⅞ in. (47.625mm) bore 2-stroke engine is 0.005–0.013 in. (0.13–0.33mm). Oversize rings are available. Install the rings in the following order: oil ring, scraper ring, and compression ring. The oil ring can be installed with either side up, the scraper ring should have the step on the lower side toward the bottom of the engine's crankcase and the compression ring has to be installed with the bevel on the inside circumference facing upward.

NOTE: *2-stroke engines have wire retainers or pins located in the ring grooves to keep the ring from moving in the groove. Make sure the ring gap is properly located over these retainers.*

Inspect the connecting rod for wear or damage, such as a scored bearing surface, cracks, and damaged threads. Use a micrometer to check all of the connecting rod dimensions. Check the clearance between the wrist pin and the connecting rod at the wrist pin hole. The tolerance for all Clinton engines is 0.0004–0.0011 in. (0.010–0.028mm). When the clearance reaches 0.002 in. (0.05mm), the parts should be replaced with new ones or rebuilt. Clinton, however, does not supply oversize wrist pins.

When installing the piston and connecting rod in a 4-stroke engine, the piston may go either way, but the rod has an oil hole that must face toward the flywheel side of the engine (with the exception of those engines that use a clearance rod in which the marked side faces toward the camshaft of the engine).

On 2-stroke engines, the piston is installed with the downward slope of the piston dome facing the exhaust side of the engine. There is no special way for the connecting rod to be installed.

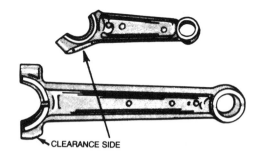

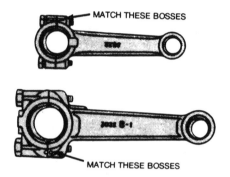

Install clearance rods with the side marked clearance side facing toward the camshaft

Install the connecting rod cap with the match marks opposite each other

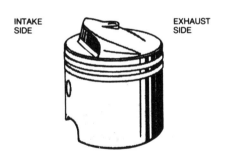

Installation of a two stroke engine piston

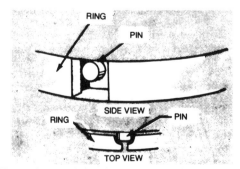

Piston ring retainers in two stroke engines

Wrist Pins

All Clinton wrist pins are a "hand press fit" into the piston. Care should be taken when removing or installing the wrist pin into rod or piston. It is easy to distort or damage the piston or rod. Never lay a piston on a solid object when removing or installing wrist pin. The piston can be supported in the palm of your hand when servicing to keep from damaging it. There is no special way to install the wrist pin into the piston or rod, except on the 2-cycle engines which in some cases have a hollow wrist pin closed on one end. Make sure the closed end is towards exhaust side.

Crankshaft

Before removing the crankshaft, remove the spark plug and rotate the crankshaft with the starter mechanism, while checking for any wobble of the end of the crankshaft. Any wobbling indicates that the crankshaft is bent and must be replaced. Deviance of 0.001 in. (0.025mm) or more is not tolerable. End-play of the crankshaft should be between 0.008–0.018 in. (0.20–0.46mm). If the endplay exceeds 0.025 in. (0.635mm), the condition should be corrected. End-play is adjusted when the engine is assembled by the addition of various size gaskets behind the bearing plate. It is not recommended that the crankshaft be straightened. Check all bearing surfaces for wear with a micrometer. Replace the crankshaft if it is bent or cracked; if the keyway is damaged; if the taper is damaged; if the flywheel end threads are stripped; or if the bearings are scored.

Bearing Plates and Bases

Inspect these visually, to determine whether or not they can be re-used. Reject for the reasons listed:

 a. Broken or cracked, housing mounting flange on the bearing plate or mounting ears or flange base.

 b. Cracked or distorted bearing bases.

 c. Warped or distorted gasket or mounting surface.

 d. Oil seal or bearing pocket oversize.

 e. Stripped threads on the lamination hold-down screw holes in the bearing plates or drain and filler plug holes in the bases.

 f. Worn crankshaft thrust face surfaces on base or bearing plate.

Camshaft

Check the camshaft for extremely worn lobes and broken gear teeth. Oil pump drive camshafts have a pin located below the gear that must have a squared end and must be secure to the crankshaft. Camshafts from engines with vertical crankshafts have a scoop riveted to the bottom of the gear. Make sure that the scoop is secure. Make sure that on those models equipped with centrifugal advance (ignition) that the advance mechanism is free and the springs are not distorted or broken. Check the dimensions of the camshaft axle.

Cylinder

Check the cylinder head for warpage with a straightedge, after removing all dirt and depos-

its. If the head is warped, place a piece of emery cloth, with the rough side facing up, on a flat surface. Move the cylinder head gasket surface over the emery cloth in a figure eight pattern until the surface of the head is flat. If there are any broken cooling fins or if the spark plug hole threads are stripped, the head must be replaced.

Oil Seals

Oil seals serve two purposes, these being to keep the oil from leaking out of the crankcase on 4-cycle engines, and sealing the crankcase on 2-cycle engines, to keep the vacuum and pressure from being affected by the outside atmospheric pressures.

Any time an engine is being disassembled and the oil seals are not going to be replaced with new ones, it is a must that oil seal loaders be installed over the crankshaft or cam gear axle to keep from damaging the seal lips when the base, bearing plate, crankshaft or cam gear is removed. Clinton has oil seal loaders that will fit any diameter shaft used in the Clinton line of engines or you may use an equivalent part designed specifically for this purpose.

Whenever an engine is disassembled or the oil seal removed from it, the oil seal should be given a visual inspection for the following, to determine if it can be reused:

 a. Cut or damaged seal lips.

 b. Distorted or bent seal.

 c. Condition of seal lip to make sure it still is flexible, and has not taken a permanent set.

Any of the above defects, would require replacement of the seal with a new one. To insure that an oil seal will function properly it is recommended that any time an oil seal area of an engine has been worked on new seals be used.

Oil seals should be removed prior to removal and replacement of bearings and reaming of bearings. The oil seals may be removed by prying out or by any means at hand with some care being used not to damage the bearing plate,

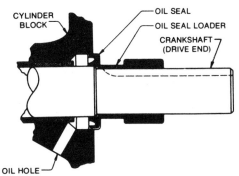

Cross section showing use of an oil seal loader

block, or base to which a new seal must be replaced.

Engine Assembly

4-STROKE ENGINES

This is a general procedure and is intended to be only a guide since deviations may be necessary for some models.

1. Insert the tappets into the block.
2. Assemble the oil pump to the cam gear, if so equipped.
3. Install the mechanical governor shaft, if so equipped.
4. Install the crankshaft and cam gear into the engine, making sure that the crankshaft thrust washer is in place if one is used.
5. Align the crankshaft and camshaft timing marks.
6. Install the piston and rod assembly using a ring compressor and great caution not to break rings or damage the piston.
7. Install the rod cap and oil dipper, if so equipped, and the cap screw and lock. Tighten to the correct torque. Crimp the screw locks securely.
8. Install the bearing plate and base plate or end cover assembly to the cylinder block. Check the crankshaft end-play. Engines using sleeve bearings should have 0.005–0.020 in. (0.13–0.50mm) end-play. Engines using tapered roller bearings should have 0.001–0.006 in. (0.025–0.152mm) end-play. Engines using roller bearings have no end-play specifications; however, care should be taken not to have the crankshaft too tight after assembly. The end-play is adjusted by the installation of various size gaskets between the plate and block.
9. Install the oil seals in the PTO and flywheel side of the crankshaft.
10. Install the valves into the block and check the valve stem-to-tappet clearance. Clearance is checked with the lobe of the tappet facing away from the valve. Clearance for a 4-stroke engine is 0.009–0.012 in. (0.23–0.30mm). Clearance is adjusted by grinding or filing the valve stem.
11. Using a valve spring compressor, assemble the valve springs to the valves.

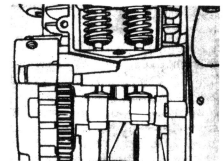
Adjust the valve-to-tappet clearance with the tappets completely off of the cam lobes

12. Install the breather assembly into the valve spring chamber and install the cover.
13. Install the cylinder deflector into the engine.
14. Assemble the magneto assembly to the engine block or bearing plate, whichever is applicable, making sure that the points are clean and adjusted to the correct gap.
15. Install the flywheel, flywheel screen, and starter cup to the crankshaft. Tighten the flywheel nut to the proper specification.
16. Install the carburetor assembly and governor, making sure that the governor assembly links and springs are placed in their original holes.
17. Place the cylinder head on the block. Torque the head bolts in three stages, in the proper sequence, and to the proper torque.
18. Install the blower housing to the engine.
19. Install the spark plug, muffler assembly, and air cleaner.

2-STROKE ENGINES

1. Assemble the piston and rod assembly and install it into the block with the help of a piston ring compressor. Be careful not to damage the rings or the piston.
2. Install the crankshaft into the block, installing the crankshaft thrust washer if the engine is so equipped.
3. Assemble the connecting rod and piston assembly to the crankshaft by installing the

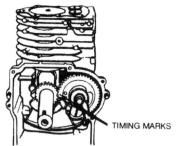
Align the crankshaft and camshaft timing marks

TIMING MARKS

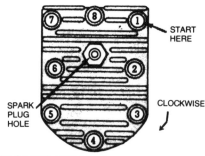
Cylinder head bolt tightening sequence

START HERE

SPARK PLUG HOLE

CLOCKWISE

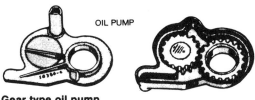

Gear type oil pump

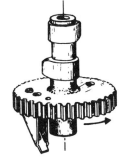

Camshaft mounted oil scoop

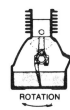 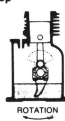

Connecting rod cap mounted oil dipper

connecting rod cap and cap screws. Tighten the cap screws to the correct torque.

4. Install the reed valve plate to the engine.

5. Install the bearing plate. Engines that use sleeve bearings should have a crankshaft end-play measuring 0.005–0.020 in. (0.13–0.50mm). Engines using ball bearings have no specific end-play measurement but make sure that the crankshaft is not tight after assembly. End-play can be adjusted by the addition of various size gaskets behind the bearing plate.

6. Install the bearing oil seals on the PTO side and the flywheel side of the crankshaft.

7. Install the magneto to the bearing plate and adjust the points to the proper gap.

8. Install the flywheel, flywheel screen, and the starter cup to the crankshaft. Tighten the flywheel attaching nut to the correct torque specification.

9. Assemble the carburetor, governor links, springs, and air vane to the engine. Always replace all governor components in the same position from which they were removed.

10. Install the cylinder deflector to the engine.

11. Install the gas tank.

12. Install the air cleaner, spark plug, and muffler.

General Engine Specifications

		1	2	3	4	5	6	7	8	9
Cylinder Bore Dia.	Min.	2.3745	2.3745	2.3745	2.3745	2.000	2.000	2.000	2.125	2.375
	Max.	2.3755	2.3755	2.3755	2.3755	2.001	2.001	2.001	2.126	2.376
Piston Skirt Dia.	Min.	2.3690	2.3690	2.3690	2.3690	1.9935	1.9935	1.9935	2.119	2.3690
	Max.	2.3700	2.3700	2.3700	2.3700	1.9945	1.9945	1.9945	2.120	2.3700
Piston Skirt to Cylinder Clearance	Min.	.0045	.0045	.0045	.0045	.0045	.0045	.0045	.005	.0055
	Max.	.0065	.0065	.0065	.0065	.0065	.0065	.0065	.007	.0075
Piston Ring to Groove Clearance	Min.	.002	.002	.002	.002	.002	.002	.002	.002	.002
	Max.	.005	.005	.005	.005	.005	.005	.005	.005	.005
Ring End Gap in Cylinder	Min.	.007	.007	.007	.007	.007	.007	.007	.007	.007
	Max.	.017	.017	.017	.017	.017	.017	.017	.017	.017
Connecting Rod Bore Crankshaft End	Min.	.8140	.8770	.8140	.8770	.7515	.7515	.8770	.8770	.8770
	Max.	.8145	.8775	.8145	.8775	.7520	.7520	.8775	.8775	.8775
Connecting Rod to Crankshaft Clearance	Min.	.0015	.0015	.0015	.0015	.0018	.0018	.0018	.0018	.0018
	Max.	.0030	.0030	.0030	.0030	.0035	.0035	.0035	.0035	.0035
Connecting Rod to Wrist Pin Clearance	Min.	.0004	.0004	.0004	.0004	.0004	.0004	.0004	.0004	.0004
	Max.	.0011	.0011	.0011	.0011	.0011	.0011	.0011	.0011	.0011
Crankshaft Rod Pin Diameter	Min.	.8119	.8745	.8119	.8745	.7483	.7483	.8745	.8745	.8754
	Max.	.8125	.8752	.8125	.8752	.7490	.7490	.8752	.8752	.8752
Crankpin Out-of-Round	Max.	.001	.001	.001	.001	.001	.001	.001	.001	.001
Crankshaft Main Diameter P.T.O. End	Min.	.8733	.8733	.8733	Note	.7483	.8745	.8745	.8745	.8745
	Max.	.8740	.8740	.8740	#1	.7490	.8752	.8752	.8752	.8752
Crankshaft Main Diameter Flywheel End	Min.	.8120	.8120	.8120	.8120	.7483	.7483	.8745	.8745	.8745
	Max.	.8127	.8127	.8127	.8127	.7490	.7490	.8752	.8752	.8752
Crankshaft to Main Bearing Clearance	Min.	.0018	.0018	.0018	.0018	.0018	.0018	.0018	.0018	.0018
	Max.	.0035	.0035	.0035	.0035	.0035	.0035	.0035	.0035	.0035
Crankshaft End Play	Min.	.008	.008	.008	.008	.004	.004	.008	.008	.008
	Max.	.018	.018	.018	.018	.012	.012	.018	.018	.018
Block or Bearing Plate Main Bearing Bore P.T.O. End	Min.	.8758	.8758	.8758	Note	.7510	.877	.877	.877	.877
	Max.	.8768	.8768	.8768	#5	.7520	.878	.878	.878	.878
Bearing Plate or Block Bearing Bore (Flywheel) End	Min.	.8145	.8145	.8145	.8145	.7510	.7510	.877	.877	.877
	Max.	.8155	.8155	.8155	.8155	.7520	.7520	.878	.878	.878
Valve or Tappet Guide Bore I.D.	Min.	.2495	.2495	.2495	.2495	.2495	.2495	.2495	.2495	.2495
	Max.	.2510	.2510	.2510	.2510	.2510	.2510	.2510	.2510	.2510
Valve Stem to Guide Clearance	Min.	.0015	.0015	.0015	.0015	.0020	.0020	.0020	.0020	.0020
	Max.	.0045	.0045	.0045	.0045	.0045	.0045	.0045	.0045	.0045
Valve Clearance, Intake & Exhaust	Min.	.009	.009	.009	.009	.007	.007	.009	.009	.009
	Max.	.011	.011	.011	.011	.009	.009	.011	.011	.011
Camshaft to Axle Clearance	Min.	.001	.001	.001	.001	.001	.001	.001	.001	.001
	Max.	.003	.003	.003	.003	.003	.003	.003	.003	.003
Camshaft Axle Clearance P.T.O.	Min.	.001	.001	.001	.001					
	Max.	.003	.003	.003	.003					
Camshaft Axle Clearance Flywheel End	Min.	.001	.001	.001	.001					
	Max.	.003	.003	.003	.003					
Point Setting	Min.	.018	.018	.018	.018	.018	.018	.018	.018	.018
	Max.	.021	.021	.021	.021	.021	.021	.021	.021	.021
Spark Plug Gap	Min.	.025	.025	.025	.025	.025	.025	.025	.025	.025
	Max.	.028	.028	.028	.028	.028	.028	.028	.028	.028
Comp. at Cranking Speed, P.S.I.	Min.	65	65	65	65	65	65	65	65	65
Carburetor Float Setting (Clinton)	Min.	$5/32$	$5/32$	$5/32$	$5/32$	$5/32$	$5/32$	$5/32$	$5/32$	$5/32$
	Max.	$11/64$	$11/64$	$11/64$	$11/64$	$11/64$	$11/64$	$11/64$	$11/64$	$11/64$
Carburetor Float Setting (Carter)	Min.	$11/64$	$11/64$	$11/64$	$11/64$	$11/64$	$11/64$	$11/64$	$11/64$	$11/64$
	Max.	$13/64$	$13/64$	$13/64$	$13/64$	$13/64$	$13/64$	$13/64$	$13/64$	$13/64$
Magneto Air Gap	Min.	.007	.007	.007	.007	.007	.007	.007	.007	.007
	Max.	.017	.017	.017	.017	.017	.017	.017	.017	.017
Magneto Edge Gap (Phelon)	Min.	$5/32$	$5/32$	$5/32$	$5/32$	$5/32$	$5/32$	$5/32$	$5/32$	$5/32$
	Max.	$9/32$	$9/32$	$9/32$	$9/32$	$9/32$	$9/32$	$9/32$	$9/32$	$9/32$
Magneto Edge Gap (Clinton)	Min.	$7/64$	$7/64$	$7/64$	$7/64$			$7/64$	$7/64$	$7/64$
	Max.	$1/4$	$1/4$	$1/4$	$1/4$			$1/4$	$1/4$	$1/4$
Oil Recommended A.P.I. Rating	See Bulletin #9 for SAE	MM MS	MM MS	MM MS	MM MS	MM MS	MM MS	MM MS	MM MS	MM MS
Fuel Recommended		Reg. Gas	Reg. Gas	Reg. Gas	Reg. Gas	Reg. Gas	Reg. Gas	Reg. Gas	Reg. Gas	Reg. Gas

Note 1 Crankshaft diameter .8733 to .8740 or .9995 to 1.0002, except 435-0000-000 which is 1.220 to 1.221.
Note 2 Ball, needle or roller bearing used. Check component parts, if worn or defective, replace.
Note 3 Wrist pin clearance, .0004 minimum, .0011 maximum or umits other than listed below. Needle bearing used in D65-1000 Type (C), J9-1000 Type (B), J6-1100 and J6-1101. Check component parts, if worn or defective, replace.
Note 4 412-0000-000, 413-0000-000 with sleeve bearings .002 to .006, 412-0300-000 with roller bearings .001 to .006.
Note 5 Bearing bore diameter .8758 to .8768 or 1.0002 to 1.0003, except 435-0000-000 which is 1.2228 to 1.2235.
Note 6 Valve guides .312 to .313 inside diameter and are replaceable. Tappet guide inside diameter .437 to .438.
Note 7 412-0000-000 .001 minimum, .004 maximum. 413-0000-000 .0005 minimum, .002 maximum.

General Engine Specifications (cont.)

		10	11	12	13	14	15	16	17	18
Cylinder Bore Dia.	Min.	2.375	2.375	2.4685	2.4685	2.4685	2.499	2.8125	2.8125	2.8125
	Max.	2.376	2.376	2.4695	2.4695	2.4695	2.500	2.8135	2.8135	2.8135
Piston Skirt Dia.	Min.	2.3690	2.3690	2.4630	2.4630	2.4630	2.4935	2.8045	2.8045	2.8045
	Max.	2.3700	2.3700	2.4640	2.4640	2.4640	2.4945	2.8055	2.8055	2.8055
Piston Skirt to Cylinder	Min.	.0055	.0055	.0055	.0055	.0055	.0045	.007	.007	.007
Clearance	Max.	.0075	.0075	.0075	.0075	.0075	.0065	.009	.009	.009
Piston Ring to Groove	Min.	.002	.002	.002	.002	.002	.002	.0025	.0025	.0025
Clearance	Max.	.005	.005	.005	.005	.005	.005	.0050	.0050	.0050
Ring End Gap in	Min.	.007	.007	.007	.007	.007	.007	.007	.007	.007
Cylinder	Max.	.017	.017	.017	.017	.017	.017	.017	.017	.017
Connecting Rod Bore	Min.	.8770	.9140	.8770	.9140	.9140	.8770	1.2510	1.1265	1.1265
Crankshaft Ends	Max.	.8775	.9145	.8775	.9145	.9145	.8775	1.2513	1.1268	1.1268
Connecting Rod to Crankshaft	Min.	.0018	.0018	.0018	.0018	.0018	.0015	.001	.0015	.0015
Clearance	Max.	.0035	.0035	.0035	.0035	.0035	.0035	.002	.0025	.0025
Connecting Rod to Wrist	Min.	.0004	.0004	.0004	.0004	.0004	.0004	.0002	.0002	.0002
Pin Clearance	Max.	.0011	.0011	.0011	.0011	.0011	.0011	.0011	.0011	.0011
Crankshaft Rod Pin	Min.	.8745	.9114	.8745	.9114	.9114	.8745	1.2493	1.1243	1.1243
Diameter	Max.	.8752	.9120	.8752	.9120	.9120	.8752	1.2500	1.1250	1.1250
Crankpin Out-of Round	Max.	.001	.001	.001	.001	.001	.001	.001	.001	.001
Crankshaft Main Diameter	Min.	.9995	.9995	Note	Note	.9995	1.220	1.2510	Note	Note
P.T.O. End	Max.	1.0002	1.0002	#2	#2	1.0002	1.221	1.2515	#2	#2
Crankshaft Main Diameter	Min.	.8745	.8745	Note	Note	.8745	.8120	1.2510	Note	Note
Flywheel End	Max.	.8752	.8752	#2	#2	.8752	.8127	1.2515	#2	#2
Crankshaft to Main Bearing	Min.	.0018	.0018	Note	Note	.0018	.0018	.0010	Note	Note
Clearance	Max.	.0035	.0035	#2	#2	.0035	.0035	.0025	#2	#2
Crankshaft End	Min.	.008	.008	.001	.001	.008	.008	Note	.006	.001
Play	Max.	.018	.018	.006	.006	.018	.018	#4	.020	.006
Block or Bearing Plate Main	Min.	1.002	1.002	Note	Note	1.002	1.2228	1.2525	Note	Note
Bearing Bore P.T.O. End	Max.	1.003	1.003	#2	#2	1.003	1.2235	1.2535	#2	#2
Bearing Plate or Block Bearing	Min.	.877	.877	Note	Note	.877	.8145	1.2525	Note	Note
Bore (Flywheel) End	Max.	.878	.878	#2	#2	.878	.8155	1.2535	#2	#2
Valve or Tappet Guide Bore	Min.	.2495	.2495	.2495	.2495	.2495	.2495	.312	Note	Note
I.D.	Max.	.2510	.2510	.2510	.2510	.2510	.2510	.313	#6	#6
Valve Stem to Guide Clearance	Min.	.0020	.0020	.0020	.0020	.0020	.0015	.002	.002	.002
	Max.	.0045	.0045	.0045	.0045	.0045	.0045	.004	.004	.004
Valve Clearance, Intake &	Min.	.009	.009	.009	.009	.009	.009	.011	.010	.010
Exhaust	Max.	.011	.010	.010	.010	.010	.011	.012	.012	.012
Camshaft to Axle	Min.	.001	.001	.001	.001	.001			.0015	.0015
Clearance	Max.	.003	.003	.003	.003	.003			.0035	.0035
Camshaft Axle Clearance	Min.						.001	Note		
P.T.O.	Max.						.003	#7		
Camshaft Axle Clearance	Min.						.001	.001		
Flywheel End	Max.						.003	.003		
Point Setting	Min.	.018	.018	.018	.018	.018	.018	.018	.028	.028
	Max.	.021	.021	.021	.021	.021	.021	.021	.030	.030
Spark Plug Gap	Min.	.025	.025	.025	.025	.025	.025	.025	.025	.025
	Max.	.028	.028	.028	.028	.028	.028	.028	.028	.028
Comp. at Cranking Speed, P.S.I.	Min.	65	65	65	65	65	65	65	70	70
Carburetor Float Setting	Min.	$5/32$	$5/32$	$5/32$	$5/32$	$5/32$	$5/32$	$5/32$		$11/64$
(Clinton)	Max.	$11/64$	$11/64$	$11/64$	$11/64$	$11/64$	$11/64$	$11/64$		$13/64$
Carburetor Float Setting	Min.	$11/64$	$11/64$	$11/64$	$11/64$	$11/64$			$15/64$	$15/64$
(Carter)	Max.	$13/64$	$13/64$	$13/64$	$13/64$	$13/64$			$17/64$	$17/64$
Magneto Air Gap	Min.	.007	.007	.007	.007	.007	.007	.007	.012	.012
	Max.	.017	.017	.017	.017	.017	.017	.017	.020	.020
Magneto Edge Gap (Phelon)	Min.	$5/32$	$5/32$	$5/32$	$5/32$	$5/32$				
	Max.	$9/32$	$9/32$	$9/32$	$9/32$	$9/32$				
Magneto Edge Gap (Clinton)	Min.	$7/64$	$7/64$	$7/64$	$7/64$	$7/64$	$7/64$	$7/64$		
	Max.	$1/4$	$1/4$	$1/4$	$1/4$	$1/4$	$1/4$	$1/4$		
Oil Recommended	See Bulletin	MM	MM	MM	MM	MM	MM	MM	MM	MM
A.P.I. Rating	#9 for SAE	MS	MS	MS	MS	MS	MS	MS	MS	MS
Fuel Recommended		Reg. Gas	Reg. Gas	Reg. Gas	Reg. Gas	Reg. Gas	Reg. Gas	Reg. Gas	Reg. Gas	Reg. Gas

Note 1 Crankshaft diameter .8733 to .8740 or .9995 to 1.0002, except 435-0000-000 which is 1.220 to 1.221.
Note 2 Ball, needle or roller bearing used. Check component parts, if worn or defective, replace.
Note 3 Wrist pin clearance, .0004 minimum, .0011 maximum or umits other than listed below. Needle bearing used in D65-1000 Type (C), J9-1000 Type (B), J6-1100 and J6-1101. Check component parts, if worn or defective, replace.
Note 4 412-0000-000, 413-0000-000 with sleeve bearings .002 to .006, 412-0300-000 with roller bearings .001 to .006.
Note 5 Bearing bore diameter .8758 to .8768 or 1.0002 to 1.0003, except 435-0000-000 which is 1.2228 to 1.2235.
Note 6 Valve guides .312 to .313 inside diameter and are replaceble. Tappet guide inside diameter .437 to .438.
Note 7 412-0000-000 .001 minimum, .004 maximum. 413-0000-000 .0005 minimum, .002 maximum.

General Engine Specification (cont.)

		19	20	21	22	23	24	25	26	27
Cylinder Bore Dia.	Min.	2.9995	3.1245	3.1245	3.1245	3.1245	1.875	1.875	2.125	2.125
	Max.	3.0005	3.1255	3.1255	3.1255	3.1255	1.876	1.876	2.126	2.126
Piston Skirt Dia.	Min.	2.9915	3.117	3.117	3.1185	3.1185	1.8695	1.8695	2.1195	2.1195
	Max.	2.9925	3.118	3.118	3.1195	3.1195	1.8705	1.8705	2.1205	2.1205
Piston Skirt to Cylinder	Min.	.007	.0065	.0065	.005	.005	.0045	.0045	.005	.005
Clearance	Max.	.009	.0085	.0085	.007	.007	.0065	.0065	.007	.007
Piston Ring to Groove	Min.	.0025	.0025	.0025	.0025	.0025	.0015	.0015	.0015	.0015
Clearance	Max.	.0050	.0050	.0050	.0050	.0050	.0040	.0040	.0040	.0040
Ring End Gap in	Min.	.007	.010	.010	.010	.010	.005	.005	.007	.007
Cylinder	Max.	.017	.020	.020	.020	.020	.013	.013	.017	.017
Connecting Rod Bore	Min.	1.1265	1.2510	1.2510	1.2510	1.2510	.7820	.7820	.7820	.7820
Crankshaft End	Max.	1.1268	1.2513	1.2513	1.2513	1.2513	.7827	.7827	.7827	.7827
Connecting Rod to	Min.	.0015	.0010	.0010	.0010	.0010	.0026	.0026	.0026	.0026
Crankshaft Clearance	Max.	.0025	.0018	.0018	.0018	.0018	.0040	.0040	.0040	.0040
Connecting Rod to Wrist	Min.	.0002	.0002	.0002	.0002	.0002	.0004	.0004	.0004	.0004
Pin Clearance	Max.	.0011	.0011	.0011	.0011	.0011	.0011	.0011	.0011	.0011
Crankshaft Rod Pin	Min.	1.1243	1.2495	1.2495	1.2495	1.2495	.7788	.7788	.7788	.7788
Diameter	Max.	1.1250	1.2500	1.2500	1.2500	1.2500	.7795	.7795	.7795	.7795
Crankpin Out-of-Round	Max.	.001	.001	.001	.001	.001	.001	.001	.001	.001
Crankshaft Main Diameter	Min.	Note	Note	Note	Note	Note	.8745	.8745	.8745	.9995
P.T.O. End	Max.	#2	#2	#2	#2	#2	.8752	.8752	.8752	1.0002
Crankshaft Main Diameter	Min.	Note	Note	Note	Note	Note	.7495	.7495	.7495	.7495
Flywheel End	Max.	#2	#2	#2	#2	#2	.7502	.7502	.7502	.7502
Crankshaft to Main Bearing	Min.	Note	Note	Note	Note	Note	.0015	.0015	.0015	.0015
Clearance	Max.	#2	#2	#2	#2	#2	.0035	.0035	.0035	.0035
Crankshaft End	Min.	.001	.006	.001	.006	.001	.005	.005	.005	.005
Play	Max.	.006	.020	.006	.020	.006	.020	.020	.020	.020
Block or Bearing Plate Main	Min.	Note	Note	Note	Note	Note	.8770	.8770	.8770	1.002
Bearing Bore P.T.O. End	Max.	#2	#2	#2	#2	#2	.8780	.8780	.8780	1.003
Bearing Plate or Block Bearing	Min.	Note	Note	Note	Note	Note	.7517	.7517	.7517	.7517
Bore (Flywheel) End	Max.	#2	#2	#2	#2	#2	.7525	.7525	.7525	.7525
Valve or Tappet Guide Bore	Min.	Note	Note	Note	Note	Note				
I.D.	Max.	#6	#6	#6	#6	#6				
Valve Stem to Guide Clearance	Min.	.002	.002	.002	.002	.002				
	Max.	.004	.004	.004	.004	.004				
Valve Clearance, Intake &	Min.	.010	.010	.010	.010	.010				
Exhaust	Max.	.012	.012	.012	.012	.012				
Camshaft to Axle	Min.	.0015	.0015	.0015	.0015	.0015				
Clearance	Max.	.0035	.0035	.0035	.0035	.0035				
Camshaft Axle Clearance	Min.									
P.T.O.	Max.									
Camshaft Axle Clearance	Min.									
Flywheel End	Max.									
Point Setting	Min.	.028	.028	.028	.028	.028	.018	.018	.018	.018
	Max.	.030	.030	.030	.030	.030	.021	.021	.021	.021
Spark Plug Gap	Min.	.025	.025	.025	.025	.025	.025	.025	.025	.025
	Max.	.028	.028	.028	.028	.028	.028	.028	.028	.028
Comp. at Cranking Speed, P.S.I.	Min.	70	70	70	70	70	60	60	60	60
Carburetor Float Setting	Min.	11/64		11/64		11/64	5/32	5/32	5/32	5/32
(Clinton)	Max.	13/64		13/64		13/64	11/64	11/64	11/64	11/64
Carburetor Float Setting	Min.	15/64	15/64	15/64	15/64	15/64	11/64	11/64	11/64	11/64
(Carter)	Max.	17/64	17/64	17/64	17/64	17/64	13/64	13/64	13/64	13/64
Magneto Air Gap	Min.	.012	.012	.012	.012	.012	.007	.007	.007	.007
	Max.	.020	.020	.020	.020	.020	.017	.017	.017	.017
Magneto Edge Gap (Phelon)	Min.						5/32	5/32	5/32	5/32
	Max.						9/32	9/32	9/32	9/32
Magneto Edge Gap (Clinton)	Min.						7/64	7/64	7/64	7/64
	Max.						1/4	1/4	1/4	1/4
Oil Recommended A.P.I. Rating	See Bulletin #9 for SAE	MM MS	MM MS	MM MS	MM MS	MM MS	Outboard Motor Oil or SAE 30 Non Detergent			
Fuel Recommended		Reg. Gas	Reg. Gas	Reg. Gas	Reg. Gas	Reg. Gas	Reg. Gas	Reg. Gas	Reg. Gas	Reg. Gas

Note 1 Crankshaft diameter .8733 to .8740 or .9995 to 1.0002, except 435-0000-000 which is 1.220 to 1.221.
Note 2 Ball, needle or roller bearing used. Check component parts, if worn or defective, replace.
Note 3 Wrist pin clearance, .0004 minimum, .0011 maximum or umits other than listed below. Needle bearing used in D65-1000 Type (C). J9-1000 Type (B), J6-1100 and J6-1101. Check component parts, if worn or defective, replace.
Note 4 412-0000-000, 413-0000-000 with sleeve bearings .002 to .006, 412-0300-000 with roller bearings .001 to .006.
Note 5 Bearing bore diameter .8758 to .8768 or 1.0002 to 1.0003, except 435-0000-000 which is 1.2228 to 1.2235.
Note 6 Valve guides .312 to .313 inside diameter and are replaceble. Tappet guide inside diameter .437 to .438.
Note 7 412-0000-000 .001 minimum, .004 maximum. 413-0000-000 .0005 minimum, .002 maximum.

General Engine Specifications (cont.)

		28	29	30	31	32	33	34	35	36
Cylinder Bore Dia.	Min.	2.125	2.125	1.8750	2.1255	1.8750	1.811	1.8750	2.1255	2.1255
	Max.	2.126	2.126	1.8765	2.1270	1.8765	1.814	1.8765	2.1270	2.1270
Piston Skirt Dia.	Min.	2.1195	2.1195	1.8695	2.120	1.871	1.807	1.871	2.120	2.120
	Max.	2.1205	2.1205	1.8705	2.121	1.872	1.809	1.872	2.121	2.121
Piston Skirt to Cylinder	Min.	.005	.005	.0045	.0045	.0045	.003	.0045	.0045	.0045
Clearance	Max.	.007	.007	.0065	.0070	.0065	.007	.0065	.0070	.0070
Piston Ring to Groove	Min.	.0015	.002	.002	.002	.002	.002	.002	.002	.002
Clearance	Max.	.0040	.004	.004	.004	.004	.005	.004	.004	.004
Ring End Gap in	Min.	.007	.010	.010	.010	.010	.004	.010	.010	.010
Cylinder	Max.	.017	.015	.015	.015	.015	.020	.015	.015	.015
Connecting Rod Bore	Min.	.7820	Note	.7816	Note	Note	Note	Note	Note	Note
Crankshaft End	Max.	.7827	#2	.7825	#2	#2	#2	#2	#2	#2
Connecting Rod to	Min.	.0026	Note	.0021	Note	Note	Note	Note	Note	Note
Crankshaft Clearance	Max.	.0040	#2	.0037	#2	#2	#2	#2	#2	#2
Connecting Rod to Wrist	Min.	.0004	.0004	.0004	Note	.0004	Note	.0004	Note	Note
Pin Clearance	Max.	.0011	.0011	.0011	#3	.0011	#2	.0011	#3	#3
Crankshaft Rod Pin	Min.	.7788	.6594	.7788	.6594	.6594	.4960	.6594	.6594	.6594
Diameter	Max.	.7795	.6599	.7795	.6599	.6599	.4965	.6599	.6599	.6599
Crankpin Out-of-Round	Max.	.001	.001	.001	.001	.001	.001	.001	.001	.001
Crankshaft Main Diameter	Min.	.8745	Note	Note	Note	Note	Note	Note	Note	Note
P.T.O. End	Max.	.8752	#2	#2	#2	#2	#2	#2	#2	#2
Crankshaft Main Diameter	Min.	.7495	.7495	.7495	.7495	.7495	Note	.7495	.7495	.7495
Flywheel End	Max.	.7502	.7502	.7502	.7502	.7502	#2	.7502	.7502	.7502
Crankshaft to Main Bearing	Min.	.0015	Note	.0015	Note	Note	Note	Note	Note	Note
Clearance	Max.	.0035	#2	.0035	#2	#2	#2	#2	#2	#2
Crankshaft End	Min.	.005	Note	Note	Note	Note	.003	.003	.003	Note
Play	Max.	.020	#2	#2	#2	#2	.020	.020	.020	#2
Block or Bearing Plate Main	Min.	.8770	Note	Note	Note	Note	Note	Note	Note	Note
Bearing Bore P.T.O. End	Max.	.8778	#2	#2	#2	#2	#2	#2	#2	#2
Bearing Plate or Block Bearing	Min.	.7517	Note	Note	Note	Note	Note	Note	Note	Note
Bore (Flywheel) End	Max.	.7525	#2	#2	#2	#2	#2	#2	#2	#2
Valve or Tappet Guide Bore	Min.									
I.D.	Max.									
Valve Stem to Guide Clearance	Min.									
	Max.									
Valve Clearance, Intake &	Min.									
Exhaust	Max.									
Camshaft to Axle	Min.									
Clearance	Max.									
Camshaft Axle Clearance	Min.									
P.T.O	Max.									
Camshaft Axle Clearance	Min.									
Flywheel End	Max.									
Point Setting	Min.	.018	.018	.018	.018	.018	.013	.014	.014	.018
	Max.	.021	.021	.021	.021	.021	.017	.016	.016	.021
Spark Plug Gap	Min.	.025	.025	.025	.025	.025	.025	.025	.025	.025
	Max.	.028	.028	.028	.028	.028	.030	.028	.028	.028
Comp. at Cranking Speed, P.S.I.	Min.	60	60	60	60	60	80	60	60	60
Carburetor Float Setting	Min.	$5/32$	$5/32$							$1\ 25/64$
(Clinton)	Max.	$11/64$	$11/64$							$1\ 27/64$
Carburetor Float Setting	Min.	$11/64$	$11/64$							
(Carter)	Max.	$13/64$	$13/64$							
Magneto Air Gap	Min.	.007	.007	.007	.007	.007	.007	.007	.007	.007
	Max.	.017	.017	.017	.017	.017	.017	.017	.017	.017
Magneto Edge Gap (Phelon)	Min.	$5/32$								
	Max.	$9/32$								
Magneto Edge Gap (Clinton)	Min.	$7/64$	$7/64$	$7/64$	$7/64$	$7/64$	$3/32$	$3/32$	$3/32$	$7/64$
	Max.	$1/4$	$1/4$	$1/4$	$1/4$	$1/4$	$5/16$	$5/16$	$5/16$	$1\ 4$
Oil Recommended A.P.I. Rating					Outboard Motor Oil or SAE 30 Non Detergent					
Fuel Recommended		Reg. Gas	Reg. Gas	Reg. Gas	Reg. Gas	Reg. Gas	Reg. Gas	Reg. Gas	Reg Gas	Reg. Gas

Note 1 Crankshaft diameter .8733 to .8740 or .9995 to 1.0002, except 435-0000-000 which is 1.220 to 1.221.
Note 2 Ball, needle or roller bearing used. Check component parts, if worn or defective, replace.
Note 3 Wrist pin clearance, .0004 minimum, .0011 maximum or umits other than listed below. Needle bearing used in D65-1000 Type (C). J9-1000
Type (B), J6-1100 and J6-1101. Check component parts, if worn or defective, replace.
Note 4 412-0000-000, 413-0000-000 with sleeve bearings .002 to .006, 412-0300-000 with roller bearings .001 to .006.
Note 5 Bearing bore diameter .8758 to .8768 or 1.0002 to 1.0003, except 435-0000-000 which is 1.2228 to 1.2235.
Note 6 Valve guides .312 to .313 inside diameter and are replaceble. Tappet guide inside diameter .437 to .438.
Note 7 412-0000-000 .001 minimum, .004 maximum. 413-0000-000 .0005 minimum, .002 maximum.

Torque Specifications

		All 4 Cycle Aluminum Vertical & Horizontal Shaft	V100, V3100, 406, H3100 407, 417	429 & 431	A300	300, VS300, 350, 500, 650, 700A, C700 D700, VS700, VS750, 800, A800, VS800 900, VS900, V1000, A-B-1100, C1100, D1100,V1100, VS1100, 1200, A1200, B1290, V1200, VS1200, 492, 494, 497, 498, 499	412 & 413	1600, 1800, 2500, 2790 414, 416, 418, 420, 422	200, A200, VS200, VS400, A400, 500, 501	E65 & GK590	E10—Chainsaw	D15—Chainsaw D25—Chainsaw	D35, D55, D65—Chainsaws E75, E95,—Chainsaws	J5, J6, J7, J8, J9—Outboards
Connecting Rod Aluminum	Min.	100	100	100	70	70	215	215	35	70	50	55	80	80
	Max.	125	125	125	80	80	235	235	45	80	55	65	90	90
Connecting Rod Forged Steel	Min.									90			90	90
	Max.									100			100	100
Bearing Plate P.T.O. End	Min.	75	75	75			75	160						
	Max.	85	85	85			85	180						
Bearing Plate Flying End	Min.			120		140			75	75		80	80	75
	Max.			150		160			95	95		90	90	95
Back Plate to Block	Min.							70						
	Max.							80						
Head Bolts	Min.	125	225	225	200	200	200	200						
	Max.	150	250	250	220	220	220	220						
Base Bolts	Min.	75	75	75	150	325	75	150	125	125				
	Max.	85	85	85	160	375	85	160	150	150				
End Cover or Gear Box	Min.					120								
	Max.					150								
Speed Reducer Mounting	Min.	110	110		110	110	110	110	110					
	Max.	150	150		150	150	150	150	150					
P.T.O. Housing or Mounting Flange	Min.	75	75	75		120	75	160	125					
	Max.	85	85	85		150	85	180	150					
Carb. Reed Plate or Manifold to Blk.	Min.	60	60	60	60	60	65	60	60	60	45	50	50	50
	Max.	65	65	65	65	65	75	65	65	65	55	60	60	60
Carb. to Reed Plate or Manifold	Min.	35	35	35	60	35	35	60	60	60		50	50	50
	Max.	50	50	50	65	50	50	65	65	65		60	60	60
Blower Housing	Min.	60	60	60	65	65	65	65	65	65	90	80	80	75
	Max.	70	70	70	70	70	75	70	70	70	110	90	90	85
Muffler to Block	Min.	110	110	110	140	140	170	170	40	40	90	60	60	
	Max.	120	120	120	150	150	180	180	60	60	110	70	70	
Flywheel	Min.	375	375	375	375	400	400	*100	375	250	150	375	**250	250
	Max.	400	400	400	400	450	500	*120	400	300	180	425	**300	300
Flywheel Touch & Stop for Brake	Min.	650	650											
	Max.	700	700											
Spark Plug	Min.	275	275	275	275	275	275	275	275	275	250	230	230	230
	Max.	300	300	300	300	300	300	300	300	300	300	270	270	270
Stator Plate	Min.	50	50	50	50	50	50	80	50	50	50	50	50	45
	Max.	60	60	60	60	60	60	100	60	60	60	60	60	65

All torque in inch pounds except those marked with a single*
*Foot Pounds
**D35 Requires Same as D25

Cross Reference Chart

Model No.	Column No.	Model No.	Column No.
E – 65	29		
		D1100	9
100	1	V1100 – 1000	11
100 – 1000	1	VS1100	11
100 – 2000	1	VS1100 – 1000	11
V100 – 1000	3		
VS100	3	1200	12
VS100 – 1000	3	1200 – 1000	12
VS100 – 2000	3		
VS100 – 3000	3	1200 – 2000	13
VS100 – 4000	3	A1200	13
		B1290 – 1000	13
200	24	V1200 – 1000	14
A200	24	VS1200	14
AVS200	24		
AVS200 – 1000	25	1600	17
VS200	24	A1600 – 1000	18
VS200 – 1000	24		
VS200 – 2000	25	1800 – 1000	19
VS200 – 3000	25		
VS200 – 4000	27	2100	1
		A2100	1
300	5	A2100 – 1000	1
A300	5	A2100 – 2000	1
VS300	6	VS2100	3
350	5	VS2100 – 1000	3
		VS2100 – 2000	3
A400	28	VS2100 – 3000	3
A400 – 1000	28		
AVS400	26	2500	20
AVS400 – 1000	27	A2500	22
BVS400	27	B2500 – 1000	21
CVS400 – 1000	27		
VS400	26	2790 – 1000	23
VS400 – 1000	26		
VS400 – 2000	27	VS3000	3
VS400 – 3000	27		
VS400 – 4000	27	3100	2
		3100 – 1000	2
GK590	29	3100 – 2000	2
		3100 – 3000	2
650	7	H3100 – 1000	2
		FV3100 – 1000	4
700 – A	7	AFV3100 – 1000	4
B700	7	AV3100 – 1000	4
C700	7	AV3100 – 2000	4
D700	8	AVS3100	4
D700 – 1000	8	AVS3100 – 1000	4
D700 – 2000	8	AVS3100 – 2000	4
D700 – 3000	8	AVS3100 – 3000	4
VS700	7	V3100 – 1000	4
VS750	7	V3100 – 2000	4
		VS3100	4
800	9	VS3100 – 1000	4
A800	9	VS3100 – 2000	4
VS800	9	VS3100 – 3000	4
900	9	4100	2
900 – 1000	9	4100 – 1000	2
900 – 2000	9	4100 – 2000	2
900 – 3000	9	AVS4100 – 1000	4
900 – 4000	9	AVS4100 – 2000	4
VS900	10	VS4100 – 1000	4
		VS4100 – 2000	4
V1000 – 1000	10		
VS1000	10	J – 5	36
		J – 6	36
A&B1100	9	J – 7	36
C1100	9	J – 8	36

Cross Reference Chart (cont.)

Model No.	Column No.	Model No.	Column No.
J–9	36	415–0000–000	4
E10–1000	33	415–0002–000	4
D15–1000	30	416–1300–000	18
D25–1000	30	417–0000–000	4
D35–1000	31	418–1300–000	19
D55–1000	32	418–1301–000	19
D65–1000	31	420–1300–000	21
E75–1000	34	420–1301–000	21
E95–1000	35	422–1300–000	23
		422–1301–000	23
400–0000–000	1	424–0000–000	2
401–0000–000	3	426–0000–000	2
402–0000–000	1	429–0003–000	15
403–0000–000	3	431–0003–000	15
404–0000–000	2	435–0003–000	4
405–0000–000	4	492–0300–000	9
406–0000–000	2	494–0000–000	9
407–0000–000	4	494–0001–000	9
407–0002–000	4	497–0000–000	14
408–0000–000	2	498–0300–000	13
409–0000–000	4	498–0301–000	13
411–0000–000	3	499–0000–000	14
411–0002–000	3		
412–0000–000	16	500–0000–000	28
413–0000–000	16	501–0000–000	27
414–1300–000	18	501–0001–000	27
414–1301–000	18		

6

Clinton
6 through 12 Hp

ENGINE IDENTIFICATION

Clinton engines are identified by a name plate that is installed on the engine at the factory. The name plate contains the serial number and the model number, both of which are necessary when obtaining replacement parts.

Two numbering systems are used to identify Clinton engines. The first one applies to engines made prior to 1961, the second pertains to engines made after that year.

The early numbering system has no practical use to the consumer. It is useful only when ordering parts and only to one who has access to a parts manual. No other information can be gained from the model or serial number than what parts fit a particular engine.

The recent numbering system, however, is quite useful in gaining additional information about a certain engine. The serial number, followed by the type letter, is a numerically sequential number and is used to identify the engine in relation to changes that are made in design. The model number consists of a ten digit sequence of numbers that is deciphered in the following manner:

The first digit indicates whether the engine is a 2-stroke or 4-stroke design. The number 4 indicates a 4-stroke engine and the number 5 indicates a 2-stroke engine.

The second and third digits identify the basic engine series and whether the engine has a vertical or horizontal crankshaft. Odd numbers in the third digit position indicate that the engine has a vertical crankshaft and even numbers indicate a horizontal crankshaft.

The fourth digit identifies the type of starter installed on the engine: 0 – a recoil starter, 1 – a rope starter, 2 – an impulse starter, 3 – a crank starter, 4 – a 12 volt electric starter, 5 – a 12 volt starter generator, 6 – a 110 volt electric starter, 7 – a 12 volt generator, 8 – not assigned any specific meaning, 9 – indicates a short block.

The fifth digit indicates what type of bearing is used on the crankshaft; 1 – aluminum or bronze sleeve bearing with a flange mounting surface and pilot diameter on the engine mounting face for mounting equipment concentric to the crankshaft center line; 2 – ball or roller bearing; 3 – ball or roller bearing with a flange mounting surface and pilot diameter on the engine mounting face for mounting equipment concentric to the crankshaft center line; 4–9 – not assigned any meaning.

The sixth digit identifies whether there are any reduction gears or power-take off units: 0 – not equipped with any such unit; 1 – auxiliary PTO; 2 – 2:1 reduction gears; 3 – not assigned; 4 – 4:1 reduction gears; 5 – not assigned; 6 – 6:1 reduction gears; 7–9 – not assigned.

The eighth through tenth digits are used to identify model variations.

TYPE LETTER

MFD BY **CLINTON ENGINES CORP.**
MAQUOKETA IOWA U S A

SERIAL NO   10278904   D

MODEL NO   405 0000 070

DIGITS   1·2·3   4·5·6·7   89·10

VARIATION

Numbering system after 1961

The type letter identifies parts that are not interchangeable.

Be sure to give the model number and the type letter when obtaining replacement parts.

MAINTENANCE

Air Cleaner

SERVICE

Metallic Mesh Air Cleaner

1. Loosen the air cleaner screw and remove the air cleaner.

2. Place both element and cover parts in a nonvolatile solvent, and agitate the metal mesh vigorously.

3. Dip the mesh into clean engine oil, and then install air cleaner.

Dry Paper Air Cleaner

1. Remove the air cleaner can from the engine.

2. Brush lightly with a soft bristle brush (not a wire brush).

3. Blow the dirt out, using compressed air. Blow from inside to outside.

4. Make sure the sealing gasket is in place, and install the air cleaner.

Oil Bath Air Cleaner

1. Remove the air cleaner from the engine, disassemble, and soak in a nonvolatile solvent.

2. Inspect the plastic blow carefully for cracks, and replace if necessary.

3. Blow the solvent out of the mesh filter with compressed air.

4. Fill to the correct level with SAE 30 oil, and install.

Polyurethane Air Cleaner

1. Remove the element from the air cleaner container, and wash it in soap and water.

2. Dry it thoroughly. Apply enough engine oil to cover the face of the element (about 1 tablespoon), and install the air cleaner.

Oil and Fuel Recommendations

4-CYCLE OIL

Follow the recommendations below. Do not use oil of ML (Mostly Light) rating, as it will void the warranty. MM oil is recommended, but best results are obtained with MS rated oil. Oil rated DG may be used, but is not particularly recommended, and DM oil is specifically not recommended. Its use will void the warranty.

- 32°F and above: SAE 30, MM or MS
- –10°F–32°F: SAE 10W, MM or MS
- Below –10°F: SAE 5W, MM or MS rating

2-CYCLE OIL

Use a good quality outboard (2-stroke) motor oil, rated MM or MS. Do not use oils rated DM or DS. Use SEA 30 or SAE 40 viscosity.

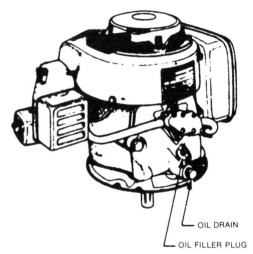

VS-700

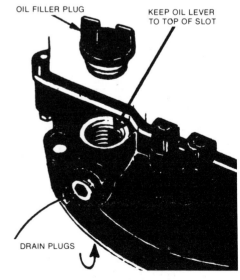

V-100 crankcase fill and drain points

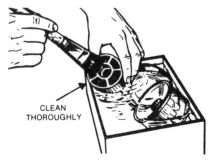

Oil bath air cleaner—washing mesh in solvent

Crankcase Capacity Chart

Model	Capacity
V−100, VS−100, A−300, A−650, VS−2100, VS−3100, VS−4100, and Models 401, 403, 405, 407, 408, 409, 411, 415, 417, 429, 431, 435	1 pint
100, 2100, 3100, H−3100, 4100, 400, 402, 404, 406, 424, 426	1¼ pints
700−A, 700−C, D−700, D−800, A−800, A−900, A−1100, B−1100, C−1100, D−1100, D−1200, A−1200, B−1290, 492, 494, 498	1¼ pints
VS−700, VS−750, VS−800, VS−900, V−1000, V−1100, VS−1100, V−1200, VS−1200, 499	¼ pints
429, 431, 435	1¾ pints
413	2 pints
412	2½ pints
1600, 1800, 414, 418	3 pints
2500, 2790, 420, 422	4½ pints

On sleeve bearing engines, mix the oil in the proportions: ¾ pint to each gallon of gasoline. On needle bearing engines, use ½ pint to each gallon of gasoline.

NOTE: *On outboard motors, during the first five hours of operation (break-in), mix ½ pint of oil to each gallon of gasoline. After that, mix ¼ pint to each gallon of fuel. Mix the oil and fuel thoroughly by first supplying one gallon of fuel, pouring the oil in and shaking the can vigorously, and then completely filling the fuel can.*

NOTE: *When the engine uses a screw-in type dipstick, check oil level without screwing dipstick into crankcase.*

Spark Plugs

Remove the spark plug lead and remove the spark plug with a deep well socket. Check for excessive buildup of carbon deposits, burned electrodes, and a cracked insulator. Replace the plug if any of these problems exist. If the plug has only light carbon deposits, wire brush the plug clean and set plug gap with a wire feeler gauge to : 0.028–0.033 in. (0.7–0.8mm) on 2-cycle engines; 0.025–0.028 in. (0.6–0.7mm) on 4-cycle engines.

Breaker Points

CHECKING

1. To check the breaker points, remove the ball, the magneto box cover, and gasket.
2. Look for evidence of excess oil in the box,

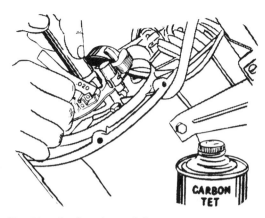

Checking the breaker point gap

which would indicate a leaking oil seal or defective breather assembly.

3. Check the point contacts for excessive wear or pitting. Normally the point assembly will last for many years if it is aligned properly, the gap is set correctly, and the rubbing block or shuttle is properly aligned on the actuating cam. If it is necessary to replace the points, make sure that the new set is installed properly.

NOTE: *Do not file the points and bend only the stationary side of the points to align the contact surfaces. Replace the condenser when the points are replaced.*

4. Breaker point gap is critical to engine performance, so make sure it is set to 0.020 in. (0.5mm) unless otherwise specified on the bail cover.

REPLACEMENT

1. Remove the flywheel, as described in the "Engine Disassembly" procedure. Remove the bail and remove the breaker box cover and gasket.

2. Disconnect the primary wire, remove the contact set attaching screws, and remove the contacts.

3. Reverse the removal procedure to install the contact set. Leave the contact set mounting screws slightly loose.

4. Rotate the crankshaft until the points are on the highest point of the cam. Set the gap to the specification shown on the bail cover, or to 0.020 in. (0.5mm) using a flat feeler gauge, as shown. Tighten the mounting screws.

5. Clean the contact surfaces with carbon tetrachloride and then dry with paper. Align the surfaces, if necessary, as described above under "Checking." Reset the gap, if necessary.

6. Grease the cam, rotate the crankshaft, and then remove the excess grease.

7. Replace the cover gasket if it is damaged

or oil soaked. Install the cover and snap the bail into position.

8. Install the flywheel, and torque the nut to specification.

Magneto Air Gap

The magneto air gap is the distance between the stationary laminations of the coil and the rotating magnets of the flywheel. In general, the closer the magnets pass to the laminations, the better the magneto will perform. Some extra clearance must be provided for bearing wear, however. The proper clearance for engines under five horsepower is 0.007–0.017 in. (0.18–0.43mm) and 0.012–0.020 in. (0.3–0.5mm) for engines over five horsepower.

The air gap is measured by placing layers of plastic tape over the laminations, replacing the flywheel and turning the flywheel. Remove the flywheel and check to see if the flywheel touched the tape, and adjust the coil assembly accordingly. Use only one layer of tape at a time. The thickness of common plastic electrician's tape is about 0.008–0.009 in. (0.20–0.22mm).

Breaker Cam

The breaker cam on most Clinton engines is replaceable. Check the fit of the cam over the crankshaft to make sure that it is tight.

NOTE: *On Model 412 and 413 engines, the breaker cam is machined onto the crankshaft.*

Mixture Adjustment

1. If the engine runs very roughly or will not start, first make a preliminary setting as follows:

   a. Very gently turn the main mixture screw in until it seats very lightly.

   b. Turn screw outward (counterclockwise) the specified number of turns:
   - 501 – 1 turn
   - Lift Carburetors – 1¼–1½ turns
   - LMG, LMB, LMV Carburetors – 1¼
   - All others – 1½ turns

2. Following this, start and run the engine until hot. Then, turn the mixture screw inward or outward in $\frac{1}{16}$ turn increments, pausing after each adjustment, until best running is obtained. The most accurate adjustment is obtained with a tachometer. Set the mixture so the highest possible rpm is obtained.

Mechanical Governor Adjustment

1. Stop the engine and set any throttle controls so there is tension on the governor spring.

2. Loosen the adjusting screw. Position the throttle to within exactly $\frac{1}{32}$ in. (0.8mm) of the stop on the carburetor casting. Tighten the adjusting screw.

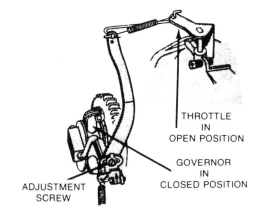

THROTTLE IN OPEN POSITION

GOVERNOR IN CLOSED POSITION

ADJUSTMENT SCREW

Location of governor adjustment screw

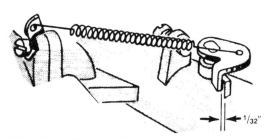

$\frac{1}{32}''$

Throttle position and dimension

Compression Check

1. Remove the spark plug and install a compression gauge in its place.

2. Crank the engine over at normal cranking speed. Gauge readings should be:
- 2-stroke: above 60 psi
- 4-stroke up to 4½ hp: 65–70 psi
- 4-stroke above 4½ hp: 70 psi

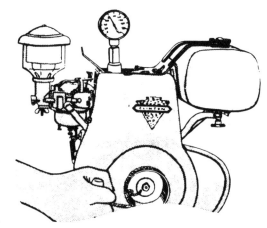

Checking compression

CARBURETED FUEL SYSTEM

Clinton engines use a variety of float type carburetors and one type of suction lift carburetor.

A carburetor can malfunction as a result of these causes: the presence of foreign matter (dirt, water); out of adjustment (too rich or too lean a mixture), and leakage caused by worn parts or cracks in the casting. Look for any of the above causes before disassembling the carburetor. Of course, it may be required that the carburetor be disassembled to correct the problem, but at least you will have some direction.

NOTE: *Check the throttle shaft/main casting tolerance. This is one place on the carburetor that cannot be repaired.*

501 Engine Carburetor
OVERHAUL

The 501 engine carburetor is a relatively simple carburetor and can be disassembled after it is removed from the engine.

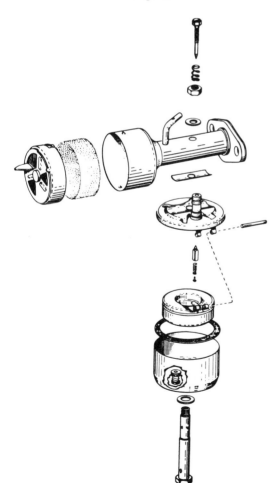

501 Engine carburetor

1. Remove the choke and air filter assembly, remove the mixture adjusting screw and spring, and unscrew the large bolt which holds the float bowl to the rest of the carburetor.

2. Please note that the main fuel nozzle is contained in the top of the large bolt and care should be exercised not to damage the needle seat. Disassemble the float and fuel inlet needle.

NOTE: *The needle seat is not replaceable, The bowl cover, needle pin, spring, and seat assembly must be replaced if any part is worn.*

3. Clean all parts in solvent, blow dry with compressed air, inspect, and replace any worn or damaged parts.

4. Assemble the carburetor in the reverse order of disassembly. Set the float level with the bowl cover inverted and the float and needle installed so that there is $13/64$ in. $\pm$ $1/32$ in. (5.16mm $\pm$ 0.8mm) clearance between the outer edge of the bowl cover and the free end of the float. Adjust the level by bending the lip of the float with a screwdriver. Use all new gaskets.

5. Set the mixture adjusting needle one turn open from the seat to start the engine. This carburetor does not have an idle mixture orifice and therefore will not operate at speeds below 3000 engine rpm. The operating range is between 3000 and 3800 rpm. Make the final mixture adjustment with a tachometer if possible. If a tachometer is not available, adjust the mixture screw $1/16$ of a turn at a time until you obtain the best engine performance.

Suction Lift Carburetor
OVERHAUL

Throttle Plate and Shaft Replacement

1. Drill through the plug at the rear of the carburetor body.

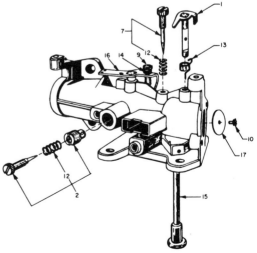

Suction lift carburetor

2. Force out the plug with a small drift pin.

3. Remove the plastic plug.

4. Remove the screws which retain the throttle plate to the shaft and remove the plate and shaft.

5. Reinstall in the reverse order of removal.

Make sure that the throttle plate and shaft operate without binding. Use a sealer on the new expansion plug.

NOTE: *Horizontal suction lift carburetors do not have a plug.*

The choke plate and shaft is replaced in the same manner as the throttle, except that there is no expansion plug to be removed.

Stand Pipe Replacement

The stand pipe is press-fit into the body of the carburetor. Remove the pipe by clamping it in a vise and twisting the carburetor body while at the same time pulling until the pipe is free. To install the pipe, tap it lightly into place until the end of the pipe is 1.94 in. ± 0.45 in. (49.3mm ± 11.4mm) from the body of the carburetor. Use a sealer at the point where the pipe is inserted into the carburetor body.

Idle Needle and Jet Replacement

The idle needle and jet are replaceable and can be removed as follows:

1. Unscrew the needle and remove it.

2. Remove the expansion plug in the bottom of the carburetor body.

3. To remove the idle jet, push a piece of $\frac{1}{16}$ in. (1.5mm) diameter rod through the fuel well and up the idle passage until the jet is pushed out of the passage.

To install the idle needle and jet:

4. Make a mark exactly 1¼ in. (31.75mm) from the end of the $\frac{1}{16}$ in. (1.5mm) diameter rod and push the new jet into the idle passage until the mark is exactly in the center of the main fuel well.

5. Install the needle and set it at 4–4¼ turns open from being seated.

The high speed needle and seat can be inspected for wear or damage by removing the needle and checking its taper. If the needle taper is damaged, replace it. Inspect the seat for taper and splits. If the seat is split or tapered from the needle being screwed in too tight, the complete carburetor must be replaced, since the seat cannot be replaced separately. When the needle is replaced, the initial adjustment is ¾– 1½ turns open from being lightly seated.

LMG, LMB and LMV Type Carburetors

OVERHAUL

These carburetors are float type carburetors and can be reconditioned in the same manner

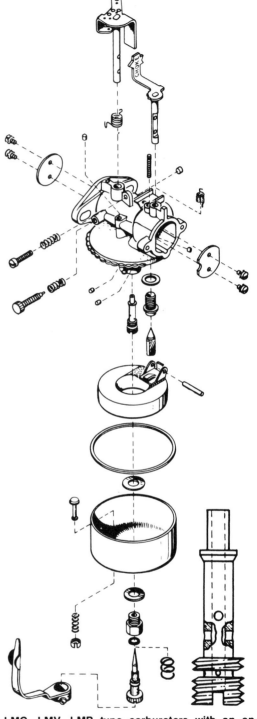

LMG, LMV, LMB type carburetors with an enlarged view of the main jet nozzle

as the 501 carburetors by taking a note of the following differences in design and specifications.

The main fuel nozzle needle is inserted from the bottom and pushed up through the middle of the float bowl.

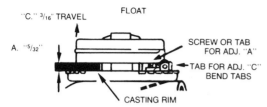

Float adjustment for the LMG, LMV, LMB type carburetors

The float, fuel inlet needle, and seat are basically the same as that of the 501 carburetor.

NOTE: *Do not remove the main fuel nozzle from the carburetor body unless it is to be replaced. Once it is removed it cannot be reinstalled.*

Use all new gaskets.

The throttle valve is installed with the part number or trademark **W** facing toward the mounting flange.

The preliminary setting of the idle adjusting needle is 1¼ turns open after being lightly seated.

Adjust the float in the same manner as the 501 carburetor. There should be $\frac{5}{32}$ in. (3.97mm) clearance between the float and the casting rim when the carburetor is inverted. When the carburetor is turned over, the float should not drop more than $\frac{3}{16}$ in. (4.7mm).

The preliminary setting for the main fuel adjusting needle is 1¼ turns open after being lightly seated.

H.E.W. Carburetors

OVERHAUL

H.E.W. carburetors are float type carburetors and can be serviced in the same manner as 501 carburetors. After cleaning and inspecting the parts for wear or damage, assemble the carburetor, noting the following differences:

Install the throttle valve with the part number or **W** toward the mounting flange with the throttle in the closed position. Always use new gaskets during assembly.

The initial setting for the idle adjusting screw is 1½ turns open from being lightly seated.

If any part of the float assembly has to be replaced, replace the whole assembly. Do not replace individual parts.

The float setting is made in the same manner as the 501 carburetor, by turning the main body of the carburetor upside down and measuring the clearance between the float and the body casting rim. The distance in this case is $\frac{3}{16}$ in. (4.7mm) with $\frac{3}{16}$ in. (4.7mm) of travel.

The preliminary setting for the high speed adjusting screw is 1½ turns open from being seated lightly.

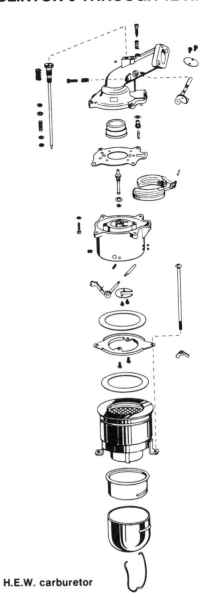

H.E.W. carburetor

U.T. Carburetors

OVERHAUL

These are also float type carburetors and are serviced in the same manner as 501 carburetors, noting the following differences:

The throttle valve is installed with the trademark **C** on the side toward the idle port when viewed from the mounting flange side. Use new screws.

Set the float level with the float installed and the housing inverted. The measurement is to be taken with the needle seated and the gasket removed. Measure between the float seam and the throttle body. Adjust by bending the lip of the float.

The preliminary setting for the high speed

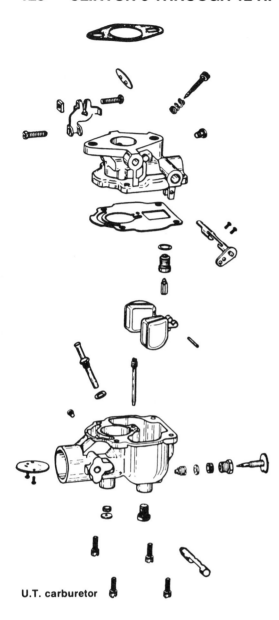

U.T. carburetor

adjusting needle is 1¼ turns open from being lightly seated.

The preliminary setting for the idle adjusting needle is 1½ turns open from being lightly seated.

The chart below gives the float level setting dimension as related to the carburetor identification number and part number:

Touch 'N' Start Priner Carburetor

Steps in operation of the primer:
1. Seal the bowl vent with a finger.
2. Depress the bulb to pressurize the bowl.
3. Pressure in carburetor bowl forces the fuel into the carburetor throat.
4. When the engine is cranked, the intake valve opens, letting gasoline into the combustion chamber for quick starting.
5. Gasoline forced from the bowl during priming is replaced by the flow of gasoline from the fuel tank through the gravity fuel inlet.

This primer is applicable to the LMG, LMB, and LMV carburetors. Servicing this carburetor would be the same as listed for the LMG, LMB, and LMV, except a choke lever and choke valve are not used. Note the bowl atmospheric vent is routed back through the primer tube and bulb.

Fixed Speed Carburetor

Steps in operation:
1. Rotate the control knob counterclockwise to open the throttle (4-cycle engines) (2-cycle not equipped with control knob).
2. To stop the engine rotate the control knob clockwise. (4-cycle engines) (2-cycle engines use a shorting device).

NOTE: *The governor spring is located on the throttle shaft between the lever and the carburetor casting. The setting on the high speed screw is 1¼–1½ turns. Servicing this carburetor would be the same as listed for the LMG,*

Ident No.	Part No.	Float Setting (in.)
2712–S	39–143–500	$^{19}/_{64}$
2713–S	39–144–500	$^{19}/_{64}$
2714–S	39–140–500	¼
*2398–S	39–147–500	¼
2336–S	39–146–500	¼
2336–SA	39–146–500	¼
2337–S	39–145–500	¼
2337–SA	39–145–500	¼
2230–S	39–343–500	$^{17}/_{64}$
2217–S	39–344–500	$^{11}/_{64}$

*With resilient seat—$^9/_{32}$ + or − $^1/_{64}$

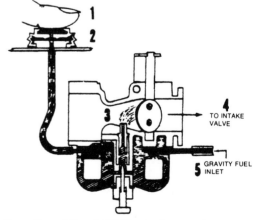

Operation of Touch 'N' Start primer carburetor

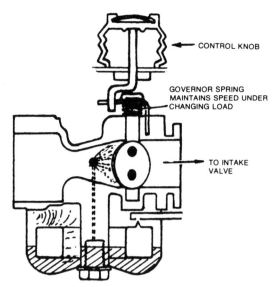

Operation of the Fixed Speed carburetor

LMB, or LMV except there is no main nozzle or idle circuit.

Carter Carburetors

Carter float type carburetors are serviced in the same manner as 501 carburetors, taking note of the following differences:

Do not remove the choke valve and shaft unless they are to be replaced. A spring loaded ball holds the choke in the wide open position. Be sure to use a new ball and spring when replacing the choke shaft and plate assembly.

Install the throttle plate with the trademark **C** on the side toward the idle port when viewed from the mounting flange side.

The float setting is made in the same manner as the 501 carburetor and the measurement is $3/16$ in. (4.7mm).

The initial setting for the high speed adjusting screw is 2 turns open from being lightly seated.

The initial adjustment for the idle adjusting screw is 1½ turns open from being lightly seated.

Fuel Pumps

MECHANICAL FUEL PUMPS

These pumps can be rebuilt. See the exploded view.

The 220–122–500 and 220–145–500 fuel pumps are simple diaphragm units that screw into the inlet side of the carburetor. They are activated by crankcase pressure pulses. They cannot be rebuilt, but must be replaced if they will not lift the fuel six inches.

The diaphragm type fuel pumps used on VS–

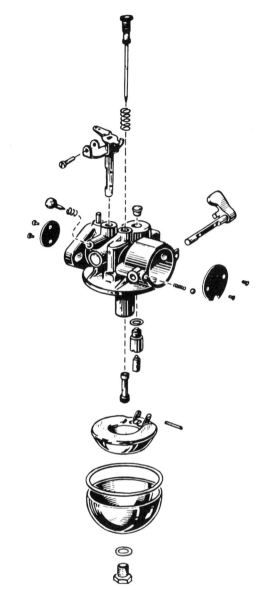

Carter carburetor

1200, V–1200, and 499 series engines can be rebuilt. However, construction is so simple no rebuild specifics are supplied by the factory.

Governors

INSPECTION AND ASSEMBLY OF MECHANICAL GOVERNOR

When assembling an engine equipped with the centrifugal weight governor inspect and governor shaft bearing in the block and the governor arm assembly that goes through the bearing, for wear and replace them if necessary. After inspection, insert the arm through the bearing and fasten the arm and weight assembly into the bearing.

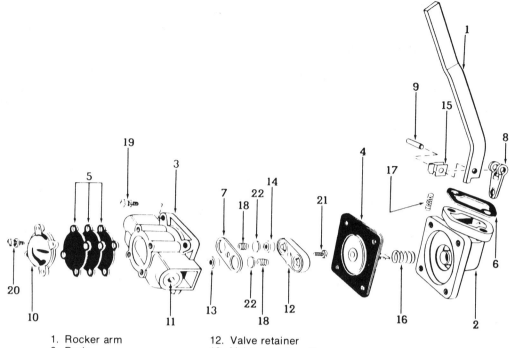

1. Rocker arm
2. Body
3. Top cover
4. Diaphragm assembly
5. Diaphragm pulsator
6. Mounting gasket
7. Valve gasket
8. Linkage
9. Rocker arm pin
10. Cover plate
11. Pipe plug
12. Valve retainer
13. Valve seat (head)
14. Valve seat (retainer)
15. Rocker arm spring clip
16. Diaphragm spring
17. Rocker arm spring
18. Valve spring
19. Screw & lockwasher assembly (cover plate)
20. Screw & lockwasher assembly (top cover)
21. Screw & lockwasher assembly (valve retainer)
22. Valve

Exploded view of mechanical fuel pump-typical

Care should be taken on installation of this arm and weight assembly as they may be locked to the outside linkage 180 degrees from the correct position which would tear out the centrifugal weights and damage the arm and weight assembly upon operation of the engine. The weight and arm or yoke should be as close to the cam axle or governor gear as it can be to be properly installed. In this position, it will operate against the governor collar or thimble assembly and will move in conjunction with the governor spring tension and the centrifugal force of the weights which are attached to the camshaft or governor gear.

The collar should be inspected for wear and possible damage, and the weight assembly itself should be inspected for wear and possible damage or bending of the weights or the weight supports.

When servicing a centrifugal governor, check to be certain that the collar or thimble operates freely on the camshaft or governor gear and that the governor shaft moves freely in the bushing. When the bushing in the block is re-placed, check carefully freedom of shaft motion as the bushing may be distorted in installation.

Also the governor shaft can be bent easily on disassembly or reassembly and can be bent in usage. Also check range of movement of collar or thimble after assembly of camshaft or governor gear to determine that these parts do not lock against block.

INSPECTION AND ASSEMBLY OF AIR VANE GOVERNOR

The air vane should be inspected visually when reassembling and replaced if bent or damaged. Use care in the hook-up of the air vane link and throttle plate so that they move freely and do not drag at the connections or on the bearing plate or blower housing. Many of the air vane governors have a spring inside of the vane at the pivot. The spring gives a dampening effect on the vane movement. This spring should be replaced if the engine has been out of service for a period of time so that it retains the pressure on the bushing or vane.

When servicing an air vane governor, the

General Engine Specifications

Model Number	Block Construction	Piston Displacement	Type	Model Number	Block Construction	Piston Displacement	Type
E65	Alum.	5.76	2 Cycle	A & B 1100	LLCI	8.3	4 Cycle
				C1100	LLCI	8.3	4 Cycle
100	Alum.	7.2	4 Cycle	D1100	LLCI	8.3	4 Cycle
100–1000	Alum.	7.2	4 Cycle	V1100–1000	LLCI	9.5	4 Cycle
100–2000	Alum.	7.2	4 Cycle	VS1100	LLCI	9.5	4 Cycle
V100–1000	LLCI	7.2	4 Cycle	VS1100–1000	LLCI	9.5	4 Cycle
VS100	Alum.	7.2	4 Cycle				
VS100–1000	Alum.	7.2	4 Cycle	1200	LLCI	10.2	4 Cycle
VS100–2000	Alum.	7.2	4 Cycle	1200–1000	LLCI	10.2	4 Cycle
VS100–3000	Alum.	7.2	4 Cycle	1200–2000	LLCI	10.2	4 Cycle
VS100–4000	Alum.	7.2	4 Cycle	A1200	LLCI	10.2	4 Cycle
				B1290–1000	LLCI	10.2	4 Cycle
200	Alum.	4.5	2 Cycle	V1200–1000	LLCI	10.2	4 Cycle
A200	Alum.	4.5	2 Cycle	VS1200	LLCI	10.2	4 Cycle
AVS200	Alum.	4.5	2 Cycle				
AVS200–1000	Alum.	4.5	2 Cycle	1600	LLCI	16.3	4 Cycle
VS200	Alum.	4.5	2 Cycle	A1600–1000	LLCI	16.3	4 Cycle
VS200–1000	Alum.	4.5	2 Cycle				
VS200–2000	Alum.	4.5	2 Cycle	1800–1000	LLCI	18.6	4 Cycle
VS200–3000	Alum.	4.5	2 Cycle				
VS200–4000	Alum.	5.76	2 Cycle	2100	Alum.	7.2	4 Cycle
				A2100	Alum.	7.2	4 Cycle
300	LLCI	4.72	4 Cycle	A2100–1000	Alum.	7.2	4 Cycle
A300	LLCI	4.72	4 Cycle	A2100–2000	Alum.	7.2	4 Cycle
VS300	LLCI	4.72	4 Cycle				
350	LLCI	4.72	4 Cycle	VS2100	Alum.	7.2	4 Cycle
				VS2100–1000	Alum.	7.2	4 Cycle
A400	Alum.	5.76	2 Cycle	VS2100–2000	Alum.	7.2	4 Cycle
A400–1000	Alum.	5.76	2 Cycle	VS2100–3000	Alum.	7.2	4 Cycle
AVS400	Alum.	5.76	2 Cycle				
AVS400–1000	Alum.	5.76	2 Cycle	2500	LLCI	25	4 Cycle
BVS400	Alum.	5.76	2 Cycle	A2500	LLCI	25	4 Cycle
CVS400–1000	Alum.	5.76	2 Cycle	B2500–1000	LLCI	25	4 Cycle
VS400	Alum.	5.76	2 Cycle				
VS400–1000	Alum.	5.76	2 Cycle	2790–1000	LLCI	25	4 Cycle
VS400–2000	Alum.	5.76	2 Cycle				
VS400–3000	Alum.	5.76	2 Cycle	VS3000	Alum.	7.2	4 Cycle
VS400–4000	Alum.	5.76	2 Cycle				
				3100	Alum.	8.3	4 Cycle
500	LLCI	5.89	4 Cycle	3100–1000	Alum.	8.3	4 Cycle
GK590	Alum.	5.76	2 Cycle	3100–2000	Alum.	8.3	4 Cycle
				3100–3000	Alum.	8.3	4 Cycle
650	LLCI	5.89	4 Cycle	H3100–1000	LLCI	8.3	4 Cycle
				FV3100–1000	LLCI	8.3	4 Cycle
700–A	LLCI	5.89	4 Cycle	AFV3100–1000	LLCI	8.3	4 Cycle
B700	LLCI	5.89	4 Cycle	AV3100–1000	LLCI	8.3	4 Cycle
C700	LLCI	5.89	4 Cycle	AV3100–2000	LLCI	8.3	4 Cycle
D700	LLCI	6.65	4 Cycle	AVS3100	Alum.	8.3	4 Cycle
D700–1000	LLCI	6.65	4 Cycle	AVS3100–1000	Alum.	8.3	4 Cycle
D700–2000	LLCI	6.65	4 Cycle	AVS3100–2000	Alum.	8.3	4 Cycle
D700–3000	LLCI	6.65	4 Cycle	AVS3100–3000	Alum.	8.3	4 Cycle
VS700	LLCI	5.89	4 Cycle	V3100–1000	LLCI	8.3	4 Cycle
VS750	LLCI	5.89	4 Cycle	V3100–2000	LLCI	8.3	4 Cycle
				VS3100	Alum.	8.3	4 Cycle
800	LLCI	8.3	4 Cycle	VS3100–1000	Alum.	8.3	4 Cycle
A800	LLCI	8.3	4 Cycle	VS3100–2000	Alum.	8.3	4 Cycle
VS800	LLCI	8.3	4 Cycle	VS3100–3000	Alum.	8.3	4 Cycle
900	LLCI	8.3	4 Cycle	4100	Alum.	8.3	4 Cycle
900–1000	LLCI	8.3	4 Cycle	4100–1000	Alum.	8.3	4 Cycle
900–2000	LLCI	8.3	4 Cycle	4100–2000	Alum.	8.3	4 Cycle
900–3000	LLCI	8.3	4 Cycle	AVS4100–1000	Alum.	8.3	4 Cycle
900–4000	LLCI	8.3	4 Cycle	AVS4100–2000	Alum.	8.3	4 Cycle
VS900	LLCI	8.3	4 Cycle	VS4100–1000	Alum.	8.3	4 Cycle
				VS4100–2000	Alum.	8.3	4 Cycle
V1000–1000	LLCI	8.3	4 Cycle				
VS1000	LLCI	8.3	4 Cycle				

General Engine Specifications (cont.)

Model Number	Block Construction	Piston Displacement	Type	Model Number	Block Construction	Piston Displacement	Type
400–0000–000	Alum.	7.2	4 Cycle	420–1300–000	LLCI	25	4 Cycle
401–0000–000	Alum.	7.2	4 Cycle	420–1301–000	LLCI	25	4 Cycle
402–0000–000	Alum.	7.2	4 Cycle	422–1300–000	LLCI	25	4 Cycle
403–0000–000	Alum.	7.2	4 Cycle	422–1301–000	LLCI	25	4 Cycle
404–0000–000	Alum.	8.3	4 Cycle	424–0000–0000	LLCI	8.3	4 Cycle
405–0000–000	Alum.	8.3	4 Cycle	426–0000–000	Alum.	8.3	4 Cycle
406–0000–000	LLCI	8.3	4 Cycle	429–0003–000	LLCI	9.2	4 Cycle
407–0000–000	LLCI	8.3	4 Cycle	431–0003–000	LLCI	9.2	4 Cycle
407–0002–000	LLCI	8.3	4 Cycle	435–0003–000	Alum.	8.3	4 Cycle
408–0000–000	Alum.	8.3	4 Cycle	492–0300–000	LLCI	8.3	4 Cycle
409–0000–000	Alum.	8.3	4 Cycle	494–0000–000	LLCI	8.3	4 Cycle
411–0000–000	Alum.	7.2	4 Cycle	494–0001–000	LLCI	8.3	4 Cycle
411–0002–000	Alum.	7.2	4 Cycle	497–0000–000	LLCI	10.2	4 Cycle
412–0000–000	LLCI	15.5	4 Cycle	498–0300–000	LLCI	10.2	4 Cycle
413–0000–000	LLCI	15.5	4 Cycle	498–0301–000	LLCI	10.2	4 Cycle
414–1300–000	LLCI	16.3	4 Cycle	499–0000–000	LLCI	10.2	4 Cycle
414–1301–000	LLCI	16.3	4 Cycle	500–0000–000	Alum.	5.76	2 Cycle
415–0000–000	Alum.	8.3	4 Cycle	501–0000–000	Alum.	5.76	2 Cycle
415–0002–000	Alum.	8.3	4 Cycle	501–0001–000	Alum.	5.76	2 Cycle
416–1300–000	LLCI	16.3	4 Cycle				
417–0000–000	LLCI	8.3	4 Cycle				
418–1300–000	LLCI	18.6	4 Cycle	Alum. = Aluminum			
418–1301–000	LLCI	18.6	4 Cycle	LLCI = Long Life Cast Iron			

condition of the blower housing should be checked carefully. Dents and bends should be removed from it is that the air stream moves as it should to the air vane. The air vane must be in the same condition as when manufactured and replaced when bent because the governor spring tension and the vane are balanced. If the vane does not sit in the air blast properly, the spring will be too strong for the air vane to stretch.

When assembling the air vane governor, apply tension to the governor spring and close the throttle manually to see that it moves open freely, that it does not bind at the governor linkage, air vane, pivot post, bushings, bearing plate, blower housing, etc. It should move freely from closed to open position by governor spring tension.

ENGINE OVERHAUL

The same basic procedure for disassembling a Clinton engine can be used for all engines. The procedure given below pertains to both 2-stroke and 4-stroke Clinton engines; differences are noted. Procedures for servicing individual components are given at a later point in this section.

Engine Disassembly

1. Remove the engine from the piece of equipment it powers and then remove any brackets, braces, adapters or pulleys.

2. Clean the exterior of the engine.
3. Drain the lubricating oil from the crankcase.
4. Remove the fuel tank and blower housing.
5. Remove the carburetor and governor assembly, marking the spring and link holes for correct reassembly.
6. Remove the muffler assembly.
7. Remove the flywheel nut, using a flywheel holder to hold the flywheel while the nut is removed.
8. While lifting up on the flywheel, gently tap the crankshaft to loosen the flywheel from the crankshaft taper. Remove the flywheel and flywheel key.
9. Remove the complete magneto assembly which includes the coil, breaker points, condenser, and laminations.
10. Remove the cylinder head and gasket on 4-stroke engines.
11. Remove the valve chamber cover and breather assembly from 4-stroke engines.
12. Remove the valve spring keepers after compressing the valve spring with a valve spring compressor.
13. Remove the valves and springs from the block after removing the valve spring compressor.

NOTE: *Some valves have a burr on the stem that will prevent the valve from being removed up through the valve guide. If present, it will be necessary to remove this burr from the stem in order to remove the valve from the* engine. *To remove the burr, hold a flat file against the burred area and rotate the valve.*

14. Remove the base plate or end cover assembly on 4-stroke engines.

NOTE: *On some engines the base is an integral part of the block and cannot be removed. If this is the case, remove the side plate on the power take-off side of the engine. Before removing the side plate or crankshaft, make sure all paint, rust, and dirt are cleaned from the area of the crankshaft bearing. This is so the side plate can be easily removed. When removing the side plate from engines that have ball bearings, it will first be necessary to remove the oil seal and the snap-ring from the crankshaft.*

15. Remove the mounting plate and reed plate assembly on 2-stroke engines.

16. Remove the connecting rod cap screws and cap. Mark the cap and connecting rod so they can be reassembled in the same position.

17. On 4-stroke engines, check for a carbon or metal ridge at the top of the cylinder. If a ridge is present, remove it with a ridge reamer or hone.

18. On 2-stroke engines, push the piston and connecting rod assembly up into the cylinder as far as it will go so it will not hit the crankshaft when it is removed.

19. Remove the piston and connecting rod assembly from a 4-stroke engine's block.

20. Remove the bearing plate on the flywheel side of the block if the engine being disassembled has one.

21. Remove the crankshaft.

NOTE: *On 4-stroke engines with a ball bearing on the PTO side of the engine, it will be necessary to remove the cap screws which hold the bearing in place before the crankshaft can be removed. On some models with ball bearings and tapered roller bearings, it will be necessary to remove the crankshaft oil seal and camshaft axle, and move the camshaft to one side before the crankshaft can be*

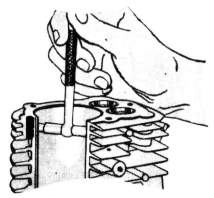
Measuring the cylinder bore—a cutaway view

removed. *2-stroke engines have a ball bearing on the PTO side of the crankshaft will have to have the retaining ring, which holds the bearing in place, removed before the crankshaft can be removed.*

22. Remove the camshaft assembly. Drive the camshaft axle out of the PTO side of the block as the flywheel side is smaller.

23. Remove the piston and connecting rod assembly from 2-stroke engines.

24. After the camshaft is removed from a 4-stroke engine, mark the valve tappets as to whether they are the exhaust tappet or the intake tappet, and then remove them. If no valve work is to be done, be sure to replace the valves in the same position from which they were removed.

25. Remove the piston and rod assembly. After disassembling the engine, clean all parts in a safe solvent, removing all deposits of carbon and oil, etc. Check all operating clearances and replace or rebuild parts as necessary.

Cylinder Bore

After disassembling the engine, inspect the cylinder bore to see if it can be reused. Look for score marks on the cylinder walls. If there are marks and they are too deep to be removed, the block will have to be discarded. If there is a hole in the block due to connecting rod failure, the block will have to be replaced. If there are broken cooling fins on the outside of the block, these can cause overheating and replacing the block should be considered.

Check the dimensions of the cylinder bore to determine the extent of wear and whether or not it has to be rebored. The cylinder bore can be rebored to 0.010 in. (0.25mm) or 0.020 in. (0.5mm) oversize since there are oversize pistons available in these sizes. If the cylinder is within serviceable limits and there is no need to rebore it, be sure to deglaze the cylinder before installing the piston assembly with new rings.

Bearings

Clinton engines are equipped with tapered roller bearings, ball bearings, needle bearings, and sleeve bearings. The first thing to determine is whether or not the bearing is worn or damaged and needs replacing. Then clean the bearings in a safe solvent, inspect them for excessive play due to wear, smoothness of rotation, pitted surfaces, and damage. All of these types of bearings are pressed on the crankshaft and into the bearing plates and are removed by either a bearing splitter and puller or they are driven out of the bearing plates with a punch. In all cases by very careful not to bend, gouge, or otherwise damage the crankshaft or bearing plate when removing and installing the bearings.

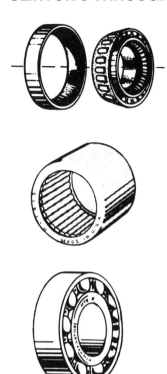

Tapered roller, needle, and ball bearing type bearings, all of which are used in Clinton engines

With sleeve bearings, first inspect the bearing surface for scoring and damage to determine whether the bearing has to be replaced. Check the bearing diameter for wear. In some cases you will find that the bearing surface is the same material as the block. These bearings can be reamed out and sleeve bearings installed. If the original bearing is a sleeve type bearing, it can be removed by driving it out with the proper size driving tool. Install the new bearing so that the oil hole in the bearing is aligned with the oil passage in the block or bearing plate. Drive the bearing into the block or bearing plate until it is recessed about $\frac{1}{32}$ in. (0.8mm) from the crankshaft thrust face of the block or bearing plate. After installing the new piece, it must be finish reamed. After finish reaming, clean all metal filings and debris from the engine, making sure that all oil passages are free from obstruction.

Valve Seats

Standard valve seats, those without inserts, can be reground to remove all of the oxidized surface metal and gain perfect sealing characteristics. After grinding the valve seats, the valves must be lapped in with lapping compound. Not too much lapping is recommended, just enough to obtain a good seal.

If the engine has had a number of valve jobs

The valve seat width is to be between $\frac{1}{32}$ and $\frac{3}{64}$ in. (0.030–0.045 in.) and the valve seat angle is to be between 43½° and 44½°

and the valve seat is too deep, requiring that too much stock be removed from the valve stem to obtain the proper valve-to-tappet clearance, valve seat inserts may be installed. If over half of the metal between the lock groove and the end of the valve stem has been removed to gain the proper stem-to-tappet clearance, you should consider installing valve seat inserts.

On aluminum block engines, iron valve seat inserts are standard equipment. To remove these inserts, it is first necessary to remove the metal that has been rolled over the edge of the insert to hold it in place. This is normally accomplished by using the proper size cutter. If the valve seat insert is loose, a cutter may not be necessary. After the insert has been removed, it is necessary to cut the block to the proper depth of $\frac{3}{16}$–$\frac{7}{32}$ in. (4.7–5.5mm) This is the depth of the insert plus $\frac{1}{32}$ in. (0.8mm) which is used to hold the insert in place. The insert is held to the cylinder block by a definite interference type press fit. The insert should be cooled before attempting to install it in the block. After the insert is fitted in place, with the bevel facing up, the metal around the edge of the insert must be peened over the edge of the insert in order to hold it in place. Do not stroke the block too sharply when peening because of the possibility of distorting the cylinder bore. Finish grind the valve seat insert and lap in the valves.

Valve Guides

First, inspect and measure the valve guide diameter to determine whether the guide is worn enough to necessitate rebuilding. The standard guide size for 4-stroke engines under 5 horsepower is 0.2495–0.2510 in. (6.33–6.37mm). On engines over 5 horsepower, the standard guide size is 0.312–0.313 in. (7.925–7.950mm).

When the valve stem-to-valve guide clearance is more than the maximum serviceable clearance and cannot be corrected by installing a new valve, you will have to either replace the valve guide (if it is replaceable), oversize it, or knurl it.

Valve guides are replaceable in the 1600, 1800, 2500, 2790, 414–0000–000, 418–0000–000, 420–0000–000, and the 422–0000–000 series engines. The valve guides are pressed out of

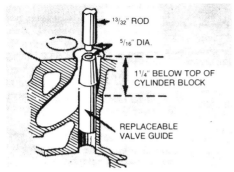

Replacing the valve guides

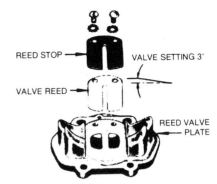

Reed valve assembly for two stroke engines

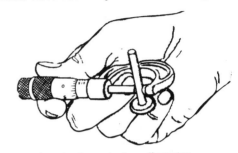

Measuring the tappet stem diameter

the block from the base of the cylinder head side. Note the position of the guide before removing it. Install the new guide by reversing the removal procedure. The new guides should be installed at least 1¼ in. (31.75mm) below the top of the cylinder block. Remove any burrs that might have been created by the installation procedure with a 5/16 in. (7.935mm) reamer.

Valves

Inspect the valves for a burned face, warped stem or head, scored or damaged stem, worn keeper groove in the stem, and a head margin of less than 1/64 in. (0.4mm). If any one of these conditions exists, the valve should be replaced. Check the valve stem diameter. On engines with less than 5 horsepower, the stem diameter should be 0.2475–0.2465 in. (6.2865–6.2611mm). On engines over 5 horsepower, the stem diameter is to be 0.310–0.309 in. (7.87–7.85mm). Any time the valve stem-to-guide clearance can be reduced more than 0.001 in. (0.025mm) by replacing the valve with a new one, you should do so. Also any time the stem-to-guide clearance is over 0.0045 in. (0.1143mm) you should consider doing some rework (new valve guides, seats and valves) to bring the clearance below 0.0045 in. (0.1143mm) but not less than 0.002 in. (0.05mm). If it is determined that the old valve can be reused, then it should be refaced, using an automotive type valve grinder to secure a 45 degree face angle on the valve with a 1/64 in. (0.397mm) margin between the head and the face of the valve.

2-Stroke Engine Reed Valves

Inspect the reed valves for the following items: broken reed valves, bent or distorted reed valves, damaged or distorted reed valve seat, or a broken or bent reed valve stop. If any of these conditions exist, the reed valve assembly must be replaced.

Valve Springs

To check the condition of valve springs, simply remove the spring from the engine and stand it on a flat surface next to a new valve spring. If the old spring is shorter and leans to one side, it should be replaced with a new spring. Some of the cast iron engines have a stronger or stiffer valve spring installed on the exhaust valve. Make sure that a stiffer spring is installed on the exhaust valve or, to be sure, install two stiff springs in the engine. When a valve seat is rebuilt, the valve then seats further down into the block and this results in a loss of spring tension. To restore spring tension, install a thin washer on top of the valve spring.

Valve Tappets

The valve tappets should be inspected for wear on the head of the tappet and score marks or burrs anywhere else. The tappet should be replaced if any defects are found. Measure the dimensions of the tappet, checking for stem diameter and length. Oversize tappets are not available; however, the tappet guide can be knurled and rebored to correct size should the tappet-to-guide clearance become too large.

Piston Assembly

Inspect the piston assembly for scored walls, damaged ring lands, worn or damaged wrist pin lock ring grooves, and a cracked or broken piston skirt. If any of these defects are present, the piston must be replaced. Check the dimensions of the piston with a micrometer.

NOTE: *The ring land diameter on 4-stroke engines is tapered and the reading at the ring land will be 0.00125 in. (0.03mm) smaller per 1 in. (25.4mm) of piston length.*

Clean all carbon deposits from the ring grooves. An old broken ring will serve as an excellent tool for cleaning ring grooves.

Check the side clearances of the rings with new rings installed. The minimum and maximum clearances for oil, scraper, and compression rings are as follows: 2-stroke engines — 0.0015–0.004 in. (0.038–0.101mm); 4-stroke engines under five horsepower — 0.002–0.005 in. (0.05–0.13mm); 4-stroke engines over five horsepower — 0.0025–0.005 in. (0.064–0.13mm).

If an oversized piston is used, the amount of the oversize is stamped on the top of the piston.

The ring gap on all engines except the 1⅞ in.

(47.625mm) bore 2-stroke engine is 0.007–0.017 in. (0.178–0.432mm). The ring gap on the 1⅞ in. (47.625mm) bore 2-stroke engine is 0.005–0.013 in. (0.127–0.330mm). Oversize rings are available. Install the rings in the following order: oil ring, scraper ring, and compression ring. The oil ring can be installed with either side up, the scraper ring should have the step on the lower side toward the bottom of the engine's crankcase and the compression ring has to be installed with the bevel on the inside circumference facing upward.

NOTE: *2-stroke engines have wire retainers or pins located in the ring grooves to keep the ring from moving in the groove. Make sure the ring gap is properly located over these retainers.*

Inspect the connecting rod for wear or damage, such as a scored bearing surface, cracks, and damaged threads. Use a micrometer to check all of the connecting rod dimensions. Check the clearance between the wrist pin and the connecting rod at the wrist pin hole. The tolerance for all Clinton engines is 0.0004–0.0011 in. (0.010–0.028mm). When the clear-

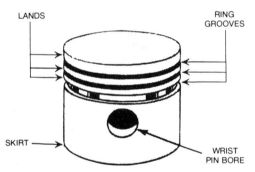

Names of the piston parts

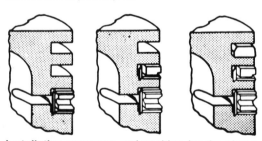

Installation sequence and position for the piston rings

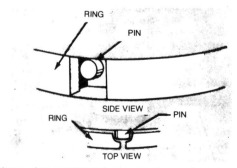

Piston ring retainers in two stroke engines

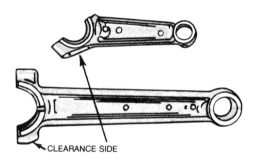

CLEARANCE SIDE

CLEARANCE SIDE

Install clearance rods with the side marked clearance side facing toward the camshaft

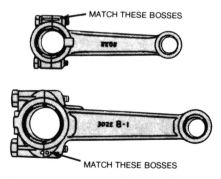

MATCH THESE BOSSES

MATCH THESE BOSSES

Install the connecting rod cap with the match marks opposite each other

INTAKE
SIDE

EXHAUST
SIDE

Installation of a two stroke engine piston

ance reaches 0.002 in. (0.05mm), the parts should be replaced with new ones or rebuilt. Clinton, however, does not supply oversize wrist pins.

When installing the piston and connecting rod in a 4-stroke engine, the piston may go either way, but the rod has an oil hole that must face toward the flywheel side of the engine (with the exception of those engines that use a clearance rod in which the marked side faces toward the camshaft of the engine).

On 2-stroke engines, the piston is installed with the downward slope of the piston dome facing the exhaust side of the engine. There is no special way for the connecting rod to be installed.

Wrist Pins

All Clinton wrist pins are a "hand press fit" into the piston. Care should be taken when removing or installing the wrist pin into rod or piston. It is easy to distort or damage the piston or rod. Never lay a piston on a solid object when removing or installing wrist pin. The piston can be supported in the palm of your hand when servicing to keep from damaging it. There is no special way to install the wrist pin into the piston or rod, except on the 2-cycle engines which in some cases have a hollow wrist pin closed on one end. Make sure the closed end is towards exhaust side.

Crankshaft

Before removing the crankshaft, remove the spark plug and rotate the crankshaft with the starter mechanism, while checking for any wobble of the end of the crankshaft. Any wobbling indicates that the crankshaft is bent and must be replaced. Deviance of 0.001 in. (0.025mm) or more is not tolerable. End-play of the crankshaft should be 0.008–0.018 (0.20–0.45mm). If the endplay exceeds 0.025 in. (0.635mm), the condition should be corrected. End-play is adjusted when the engine is assembled by the addition of various size gaskets behind the bearing plate. It is not recommended that the crankshaft be straightened. Check all

bearing surfaces for wear with a micrometer. Replace the crankshaft if it is bent or cracked; if the keyway is damaged; if the taper is damaged; if the flywheel end threads are stripped; or if the bearings are scored.

Bearing Plates and Bases

Inspect these visually, to determine whether or not they can be re-used. Reject for the reasons listed:

a. Broken or cracked, housing mounting flange on the bearing plate or mounting ears or flange base.

b. Cracked or distorted bearing bases.

c. Warped or distorted gasket or mounting surface.

d. Oil seal or bearing pocket oversize.

e. Stripped threads on the lamination hold-down screw holes in the bearing plates or drain and filler plug holes in the bases.

f. Worn crankshaft thrust face surfaces on base or bearing plate.

Camshaft

Check the camshaft for extremely worn lobes and broken gear teeth. Oil pump drive camshafts have a pin located below the gear that must have a squared end and must be secure to the crankshaft. Camshafts from engines with vertical crankshafts have a scoop riveted to the bottom of the gear. Make sure that the scoop is secure. Make sure that on those models equipped with centrifugal advance (ignition) that the advance mechanism is free and the springs are not distorted or broken. Check the dimensions of the camshaft axle.

Cylinder

Check the cylinder head for warpage with a straight-edge, after removing all dirt and deposits. If the head is warped, place a piece of emery cloth, with the rough side facing up, on a flat surface. Move the cylinder head gasket surface over the emery cloth in a figure eight pattern until the surface of the head is flat. If there are any broken cooling fins or if the spark plug hole threads are stripped, the head must be replaced.

Oil Seals

Oil seals serve two purposes, these being to keep the oil from leaking out of the crankcase on 4-cycle engines, and sealing the crankcase on 2-cycle engines, to keep the vacuum and pressure from being affected by the outside atmospheric pressures.

Any time an engine is being disassembled and the oil seals are not going to be replaced with new ones, it is a must that oil seal loaders be in-

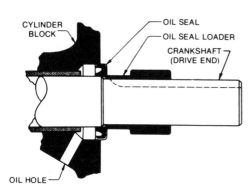

Cross section showing use of an oil seal loader

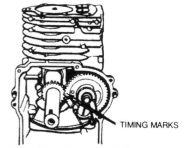

TIMING MARKS

Align the crankshaft and camshaft timing marks

stalled over the crankshaft or cam gear axle to keep from damaging the seal lips when the base, bearing plate, crankshaft or cam gear is removed. Clinton has oil seal loaders that will fit any diameter shaft used in the Clinton line of engines or you may use an equivalent part designed specifically for this purpose.

Whenever an engine is disassembled or the oil seal removed from it, the oil seal should be given a visual inspection for the following, to determine if it can be reused:

    a. Cut or damaged seal lips.
    b. Distorted or bent seal.
    c. Condition of seal lip to make sure it still is flexible, and has not taken a permanent set.

Any of the above defects, would require replacement of the seal with a new one. To insure that an oil seal will function properly it is recommended that any time an oil seal area of an engine has been worked on new seals be used.

Oil seals should be removed prior to removal and replacement of bearings and reaming of bearings. The oil seals may be removed by prying out or by any means at hand with some care being used not to damage the bearing plate, block, or base to which a new seal must be replaced.

Engine Assembly

4-Stroke Engines

This is a general procedure and is intended to be only a guide since deviations may be necessary for some models.

1. Insert the tappets into the block.
2. Assemble the oil pump to the cam gear, if so equipped.
3. Install the mechanical governor shaft, if so equipped.
4. Install the crankshaft and cam gear into the engine, making sure that the crankshaft thrust washer is in place if one is used.
5. Align the crankshaft and camshaft timing marks.

6. Install the piston and rod assembly using a ring compressor and great caution not to break rings or damage the piston.
7. Install the rod cap and oil dipper, if so equipped, and the cap screw and lock. Tighten to the correct torque. Crimp the screen locks securely.
8. Install the bearing plate and base plate or end cover assembly to the cylinder block. Check the crankshaft end-play. Engines using sleeve bearings should have 0.005–0.020 in. (0.13–0.50mm) end-play. Engines using tapered roller bearings should have 0.001–0.006 in. (0.025–0.152mm) end-play. Engines using roller bearings have no end-play specifications; however, care should be taken not to have the crankshaft too tight after assembly. The end-play is adjusted by the installation of various size gaskets between the plate and block.
9. Install the oil seals in the PTO and flywheel side of the crankshaft.
10. Install the valves into the block and check the valve stem-to-tappet clearance. Clearance is checked with the lobe of the tappet facing away from the valve. Clearance for a 4-stroke engine is 0.009–0.012 in. (0.23–0.30mm). Clearance is adjusted by grinding or filing the valve stem.
11. Using a valve spring compressor, assemble the valve springs to the valves.
12. Install the breather assembly into the valve spring chamber and install the cover.
13. Install the cylinder deflector into the engine.

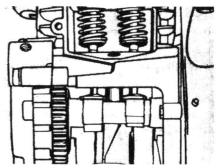

Adjust the valve-to-tappet clearance with the tappets completely off of the cam lobes

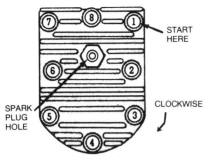

Cylinder head bolt tightening sequence

14. Assemble the magneto assembly to the engine block or bearing plate, whichever is applicable, making sure that the points are clean and adjusted to the correct gap.

15. Install the flywheel, flywheel screen, and starter cup to the crankshaft. Tighten the flywheel nut to the proper specification.

16. Install the carburetor assembly and governor, making sure that the governor assembly links and springs are placed in their original holes.

17. Place the cylinder head on the block. Torque the head bolts in three stages, in the proper sequence, and to the proper torque.

18. Install the blower housing to the engine.

19. Install the spark plug, muffler assembly, and air cleaner.

2-Stroke Engines

1. Assemble the piston and rod assembly and install it into the block with the help of a piston ring compressor. Be careful not to damage the rings or the piston.

2. Install the crankshaft into the block, installing the crankshaft thrust washer if the engine is so equipped.

3. Assemble the connecting rod and piston assembly to the crankshaft by installing the connecting rod cap and cap screws. Tighten the cap screws to the correct torque.

4. Install the reed valve plate to the engine.

5. Install the bearing plate. Engines that use sleeve bearings should have a crankshaft end-play measuring 0.005–0.020 in. (0.13–0.50mm). Engines using ball bearings have no specific end-play measurement but make sure that the crankshaft is not tight after assembly. End-play can be adjusted by the addition of various size gaskets behind the bearing plate.

6. Install the bearing oil seals on the PTO side and the flywheel side of the crankshaft.

7. Install the magneto to the bearing plate and adjust the points to the proper gap.

8. Install the flywheel, flywheel screen, and the starter cup to the crankshaft. Tighten the flywheel attaching nut to the correct torque specification.

9. Assemble the carburetor, governor links, springs, and air vane to the engine. Always replace all governor components in the same position from which they were removed.

10. Install the cylinder deflector to the engine.

11. Install the gas tank.

12. Install the air cleaner, spark plug, and muffler.

Lubrication System

All 4-stroke engines with vertical crankshafts are lubricated by either a camshaft driven gear type oil pump or an oil scoop attached to the camshaft which rotates in the oil lying in the bottom of the crankcase. The gear type pump forces oil up through a steel tube to the upper main bearing. The oil then falls down onto other parts needing to be lubricated.

The oil scoop attached to the camshaft sprays oil to the top of the engine in a circular path. The upper main bearing in oil scoop engines has an oil access slot in the top of the bearing area to catch the oil as it is splashed up.

On 4-stroke engines that have a horizontal crankshaft, there is an oil dipper or distributor located on the bottom of the connecting rod bearing cap. As the crankshaft turns, the dipper

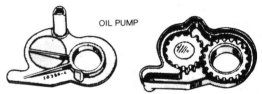

Gear type oil pump

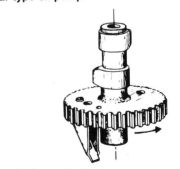

Camshaft mounted oil scoop

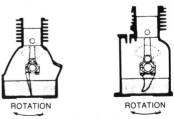

Connecting rod cap mounted oil dipper

churns through the oil in the crankcase and splashes it to all moving parts that need lubrication. There are oil passages, holes, and slots which the oil passes through on its way to the bearing surfaces.

All connecting rods have oil access holes or chambers to insure adequate lubrication. Make sure that all oil access holes are installed facing toward the top main bearing in engines with vertical crankshafts.

7

Kohler K-Series
4-Stroke
2 through 5 Hp
1970–83

ENGINE IDENTIFICATION

An engine identification plate is mounted on the carburetor side of the engine blower housing. The numbers that are important, as far as ordering replacement parts is concerned, are the model, serial, and specification numbers.

The model number indicates the engine model series. It also is a code indicating the cubic inch displacement and the number of cylinders. The model number K181, for instance, indicates the engine is 18 cu. in. in displacement and that it has 1 cylinder. The letters following the model number indicate that a variety of other equipment is installed on the engine. The letters and what they mean are as follows:

- C Clutch model
- G Housed with fuel tank
- H Housed less fuel tank
- P Pump model
- R Reduction gear
- S Electric start
- T Retractable start

NOTE: *A model number without a suffix letter indicates a basic rope start version.*

The specification number indicates a model variation. It indicates a combination of various groups used to build the engine. It may have a letter preceding it which is sometimes important in determining superseding parts. The first two numbers of the specifications number is the code designation the engine model: the remaining numbers are issued in numerical sequence as each new specification is released, for example, 2899, 28100, 28101, etc. The current specification number model code is K91.

The serial number lists the order in which the engine was built. If a change takes place to a model or a specification, the serial number is used to indicate the points at which the change takes place. The first letter or number in the serial number indicates what year the engine was built. The letter prefix to the engine serial number was dropped in 1969 and thereafter the prefix is a number. Engines made in 1969 have either the letter **E** or the number **1**. The code is as follows:

- A – 1965
- B – 1966
- C – 1967
- D – 1968
- E – 1969

First Digit Numbers:

- 1 – 1969
- 2 – 1970
- 3 – 1971
- 4 – 1972
- 5 – 1973
- 6 – 1974

MAINTENANCE

Air Cleaners

A dirty air cleaner can cause rich fuel/air mixture and consequent poor engine operation and sludge deposits. If the filter becomes dirty enough, dirt that otherwise would be trapped can pass through and may wear the engine's moving parts prematurely. It is therefore necessary that all maintenance work be performed precisely as specified.

DRY AIR CLEANERS

Clean dry element air cleaners every 50 hours of operation, or every 6 months (whichever comes first) under good operating conditions. Service more frequently if the operating area is dusty. Remove the element and tap it lightly against a hard surface to remove the bulk of the dirt. If dirt will not drop off easily, replace the element. Do not use compressed air or solvents. Replace the air cleaner every 100–200 hours, under good conditions, and more frequently if the air is dusty.

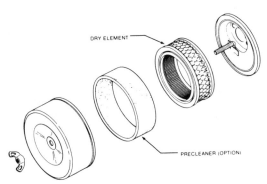

Exploded view of dry type air cleaner with pre-cleaner

Observe the following precautions:

1. Handle the element carefully-do not allow the gasket surfaces to become bent or twisted.

2. Make sure gasket surfaces seal against back plate and cover.

3. Tighten wing nut only finger tight – if it is too tight, cleaner may not seal properly.

If the dry type air cleaner is equipped with a precleaner, service this unit when cleaning the paper element. Servicing consists of cleaning the precleaner in soap and water, squeezing the excess out, and then allowing it to air dry before installation. Do not oil!

OIL BATH AIR CLEANERS

This type of unit may be used to replace the dry type in applications where very frequent replacement of the element is required. The conversion is simple and requires the use of an elbow to fit the oil bath unit onto the engine in a vertical position.

Service the unit every 25 hours of operation under good conditions and, under dusty conditions, as often as every 8 hours of operation.

Service as follows:

1. Remove cover and lift element out of bowl.

2. Drain dirty oil from bowl, and then wash thoroughly in clean solvent.

3. Swish the element in the solvent and then allow it to drip dry. Do not dry with compressed air. Lightly oil the element with engine oil.

4. Inspect air horn, filter bowl, and cover gaskets, and replace as necessary (if grooved or cracked).

5. Install filter bowl gasket on air horn, then put the bowl into position. Fill bowl to indicated level with engine oil.

6. Install element, put the cover in position, and then install copper gasket (if used) and wingnut. Tighten wingnut with fingers only to avoid distorting housing. Make sure all joints in the unit seal tightly.

Lubrication
CRANKCASE

Oil level must be maintained between **F** and **L** marks – do not overfill. Check every day and add as necessary. On new engines, be especially careful to stop engine and check level frequently. When checking, make sure regular type dipstick is inserted fully. On screw type dipstick, check level with dipstick inserted fully but not screwed in. On this type, however, make sure to screw dipstick back in tightly when oil level check is completed.

Use SG type oils meeting viscosity specifications according to the prevailing temperature as shown in the chart below.

Change initial fill of oil on new engines after five hours of operation. Then, change oil every 25 hours of operation. Change oil when engine is hot. Change more frequently in dusty areas. If the engine has just been overhauled, it is best to fill it initially with a non-detergent oil. Then, after 5 hours, refill with SG type oil.

Oil capacities are:

K91 — ½ qt. (473mL)

REDUCTION GEAR UNITS

Every 50 hours, remove the oil plug on the lower part of the reduction unit cover to check level. If oil does not reach the level of the oil plug, remove the vented fill plug from the top of the cover and refill with engine oil until level is correct. This oil need not be changed unless unit has been out of service for several months. In this situation, remove the drain plug, drain oil, then replace plug and fill to proper level as described above.

FUEL RECOMMENDATIONS

Use either leaded or unleaded regular grade fuel of at least 90 octane. Unleaded fuel produces fewer combustion chamber deposits, so its use is preferred.

Purchase fuel from a reputable dealer, and make sure to use only fresh fuel (fuel less than 30 days old). If the engine is stored, drain the fuel system or use a fuel stabilizer that is compatible with the type of fuel tank the engine is equipped with.

Spark Plugs
SERVICE

The spark plug should be removed and serviced every 100 hours of engine operation. The plug should have a light coating of light gray colored deposits. If deposits are black, fuel/air mixture could be too rich due to improper carburetor adjustment or a dirty air cleaner. If deposits are white, the engine may be overheating or a spark plug of too high a heat range could be in use.

Kohler recommends that the plug be replaced rather than sandblasted or scraped if there are excessive deposits. Torque plugs to 18–22 ft. lbs.

TESTING

To test a plug for adequate performance, remove it from the engine, attach the ignition wire, and then rest the side electrode against the cylinder head. Crank the engine vigorously. If there is a sharp spark, the plug and ignition system are all right, although ignition timing should be checked if the engine fires irregularly.

Breaker Points

INSPECTION

Remove the breaker cover and inspect the points for pitting or buildup of metal on either the movable or stationary contact every 100 hours of operation. Replace the points if they are badly burned. If there is a great deal of metal buildup on either contact, the condenser may be faulty and should be replaced.

To replace points, remove the primary wiring connector screw and pull off the primary wire. Then, remove the contact set mounting screws and remove the contact set. Install the new set of points in reverse order, leaving upper mounting screw slightly loose. Then set point gap and timing as described below.

SETTING BREAKER GAP AND TIMING

1. Remove the breaker cover and disconnect the spark plug lead. Rotate the engine in direction of normal rotation until the points reach the maximum opening.

2. Using a clean, flat feeler gauge of 0.020 in. (0.50mm) size, check the gap between the points. Gauge should just slide between the contacts without opening them when flat between them. If the gap is incorrect, loosen the upper mounting screw (if necessary), and shift the breaker base with the blade of the screwdriver until gap is correct.

3. There is a timing sight hole in either the bearing plate or the blower housing. If there is a snap button in the hole, pry it out with a screwdriver.

4. While observing the sight hole, turn the engine slowly in normal direction of rotation. When the T mark appears in the hole, the points should just be beginning to open. If timing is incorrect, breaker gap will have to be reset slightly − 0.018–0.022 in. (0.46–0.56mm). If the points are not yet opening when the timing mark is centered in the hole, make the point gap wider. If points open too early, narrow it. Recheck the setting after tightening the upper breaker mounting screw by turning the engine in normal direction of rotation past the firing point and checking that the points open at just the right time.

NOTE: *This procedure may be performed with the engine running at 1200–1800 rpm if a timing light is available. Connect the timing light according to manufacturer's instructions. You may have to chalk the timing mark to see it adequately.*

TRIGGER AIR GAP

Trigger air gap is set within the range 0.005–0.010 in. (0.13–0.25mm). As long as the gap falls within this range, the ignition system should perform adequately. Optimum ignition performance during cold weather starting is provided if the gap is adjusted to 0.005 in. (0.13mm). If you wish to adjust this or to ensure that the gap falls within the proper range, rotate the flywheel until the flywheel projection is lined up with the trigger assembly. Then,

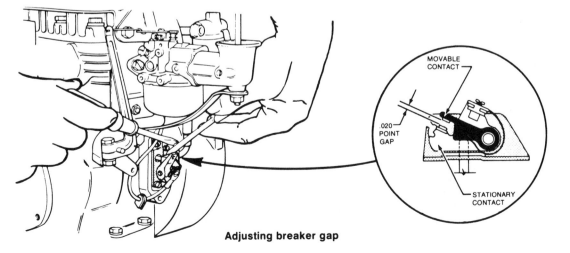

Adjusting breaker gap

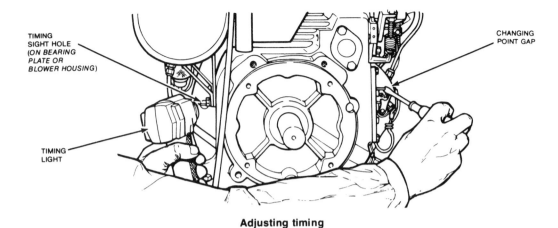

TIMING
SIGHT HOLE
(ON BEARING
PLATE OR
BLOWER HOUSING)

CHANGING
POINT GAP

TIMING
LIGHT

Adjusting timing

loosen the trigger bracket capscrews and slide the trigger back and forth to get the proper gap, as measured with a flat feeler gauge. Then, re-tighten capscrews.

IGNITION COILS

Coils do not require regular service, except to make sure they are kept clean, that the connections are tight, and that rubber insulators are in good condition (replace if cracked). If you suspect poor performance of a breakerless type ignition system and trigger air gap is correct, check resistance with an ohmmeter. To do this, disconnect the high tension lead at the coil and connect the meter between coil terminal and coil mounting bracket. If resistance is not about 11,500 ohms, replace the coil. Also, check the reading with the meter lead going to the coil terminal pulled off and connected to the spark plug connector of the high tension lead. If there is continuity here, replace the coil.

PERMANENT MAGNETS

These may be checked for magnet strength by holding a screwdriver (non-magnetic) blade within one inch of the magnet. If the magnetic field is good, the blade will be attracted to the magnet. Otherwise, replace it.

Mixture Adjustments

NOTE: *Before making any adjustments, be sure that the carburetor air cleaner is not clogged. A clogged air cleaner will cause an over-rich mixture, black exhaust smoke, and may lead you to believe that the carburetor is out of adjustment when, in reality, it is not. The carburetor is set at the factory and rarely needs adjustment unless, of course, it has been disassembled or rebuilt.*

1. With the engine stopped, turn the main and idle fuel adjusting screws all the way in until they bottom lightly. Do not force the screws or you will damage the needles.

2. For a preliminary setting, turn the main fuel screw out 2 full turns and the idle screw out 1¼ turns.

3. Start the engine and allow it to reach operating temperatures; then operate the engine at full throttle and under a load, if possible.

4. For final adjustment, turn the main fuel adjustment screw in until the engine slows down (lean mixture), then out until it slows

Tune-Up Specifications

Model	Plug Gap (in.)	Breaker Point Gap (in.)	Trigger Air Gap (in.)	Normal Timing (deg)	Retard Timing (deg)
K91	.025①	.020	—	20B	—

B—Before
① Shielded plug gap—.020 in.

Spark Plug Specifications

Engine Model	Plug Size	Hex Size	Plug Reach	Standard Plugs		Resistor Plugs	
				Solid Post	Knurled Nut	Non-Shielded	Shielded
K91	14 mm	¹³/₁₆"	³/₈"	J-8 270321-S	J-8 220040-S	XJ-8 232604-S	XEJ-8 220258-S

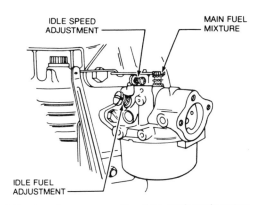

Adjustment screws on the side draft carburetor

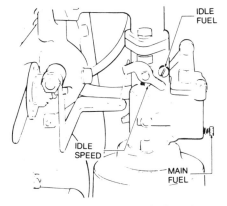

Adjustment screws on the updraft carburetor

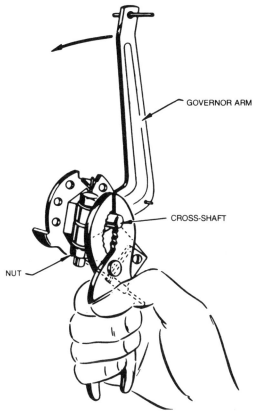

Initial adjustment of the governor installed on the K91, K141, K161, and the K181 engines

down again (rich mixture). Note the positions of the screw at both settings, then set it about halfway between the two positions.

5. Set the idle mixture adjustment screw in the same manner. The idle speed (no-load) on most engines is 1200 rpm; however, on engines with a parasitic load (hydrastatic drives) the engine idle speed may have to be increased to as much as 1700 rpm for best no-load idle.

Governor Adjustment

All Kohler engines use mechanical, camshaft driven governors.

INITIAL ADJUSTMENT

1. Loosen, but do not remove, the nut that holds the governor arm to the governor cross shaft.

2. Grasp the end of the cross shaft with a pair of pliers and turn it in counterclockwise as far as it will go. The tab on the cross shaft will stop against the rod on the governor gear assembly.

3. Pull the governor arm away from the carburetor, then retighten the nut which holds the governor arm to the shaft. With updraft carburetors, lift the arm as far as possible, then retighten the arm nut.

FINAL ADJUSTMENT

After making the initial adjustment and connecting the throttle wire on the variable speed applications, start the engine and check the maximum operating speed with a tachometer.

If adjustment is necessary:

1. Loosen the bushing nut slightly.

2. Move the throttle bracket in a counterclockwise direction to increase speed, or in a clockwise direction to decrease engine speed. Maximum speed is 4000 rpm.

3. With the speed set to the proper range, tighten the bushing nut to lock the throttle bracket in position.

Choke Adjustment

THERMOSTATIC TYPE

If the engine does not start when cranked, continue cranking and move the choke lever first to one side and then to the other to determine whether the setting is too lean or too rich. Once the direction in which lever must be moved has been determined, loosen the adjusting screw on the choke body. Then, move the bracket downward to increase choking or upward to decrease it. Then, tighten the

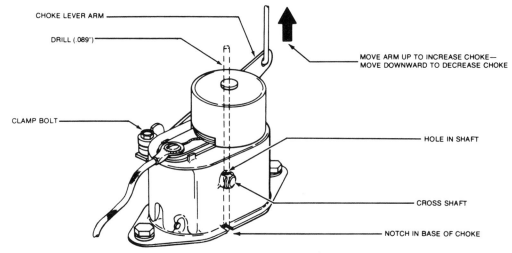

CHOKE LEVER ARM

DRILL (.089")

MOVE ARM UP TO INCREASE CHOKE—
MOVE DOWNWARD TO DECREASE CHOKE

CLAMP BOLT

HOLE IN SHAFT

CROSS SHAFT

NOTCH IN BASE OF CHOKE

Adjusting electric-thermostatic choke

lockscrew. Try starting it again and readjust as necessary.

ELECTRIC-THERMOSTATIC TYPE

Remove the air cleaner from the carburetor and check the position of the choke plate. The choke should be fully closed when engine is at outside temperature and the temperature is very low. In milder temperatures, slightly less closure is required.

If adjustment is required, move the choke arm until the hole in the brass shaft lines up with the slot in the bearings. Insert a #43 (0.089 in.) drill through the shaft and push it downward so it engages the notch in the base of the choke unit. Then, loosen the clamp bolt on the choke lever and push the arm upward to move the choke plate toward the closed position. When the desired position is obtained, tighten the clamp bolt. Then, remove the drill.

Remount the air cleaner, and then check for any binding in the choke linkage. Correct as necessary. Finally, run the engine until hot, and make sure the choke opens fully. If not, readjust it toward the open position as necessary.

Compression Check

Compression is checked by removing the spark plug lead and spinning the flywheel forward against compression. If the piston does not bounce backward with considerable force, checking with a gauge may be necessary. On Automatic Compression Release engines, rotate the flywheel backward against power stroke-if little resistance is felt, check compression with a gauge.

The compression gauge check requires rapid motoring (spinning) of the crankshaft, at about 1000 rpm. Install the gauge in the spark plug

hole and motor the engine. Gauge should read 110–120 psi. If reading is less than 100 psi, the engine requires major repair to piston rings or valves.

FUEL SYSTEM

Carburetor

If a carburetor will not respond to mixture screw adjustments, then you can assume that there are dirt, gum, or varnish deposits in the carburetor or worn/damaged parts. To remedy these problems, the carburetor will have to be completely disassembled, cleaned, and worn parts replaced and reassembled.

Parts should be cleaned with solvent to remove all deposits. Replace worn parts and use all new gaskets. Carburetor rebuilding kits are available.

REBUILDING

Side Draft Carburetors

1. Remove the carburetor from the engine.
2. Remove the bowl nut, gasket, and bowl. If the carburetor has a bowl drain, remove the drain spring, spacer and plug, and gasket from inside the bowl.
3. Remove the float pin, float, needle, and needle seat. Check the float for dents, leaks, and wear on the float lip or in the float pin holes.
4. Remove the bowl ring gasket.
5. Remove the idle fuel adjusting needle, main fuel adjusting needle, and springs.
6. Do not remove the choke and throttle plates or shafts. If these parts are worn, replace the entire carburetor assembly.

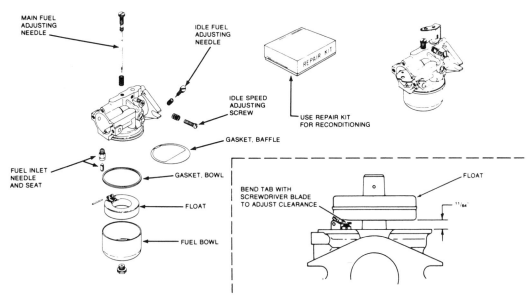

Exploded view of the sidedraft carburetor. Inset shows float adjustment procedure

To assemble:

1. Install the needle seat, needle, float, and float pin.

2. Set the float level. With the carburetor casting inverted and the float resting against the needle in its seat, there should be $^{11}/_{64}$ in. ± $^{1}/_{32}$ in. (4.4mm ± 0.8mm) clearance between the machined surface of the casting and the free end of the float.

3. Adjust the float level by bending the lip of the float with a small screwdriver.

4. Install the new bowl ring gasket, new bowl nut gasket, and bowl nut. Tighten the nut securely.

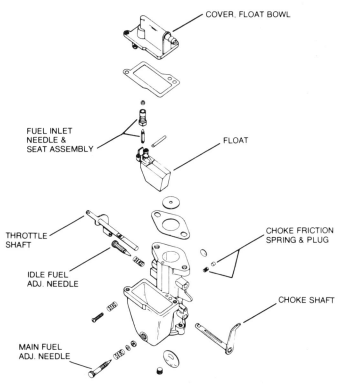

Exploded view of the updraft carburetor

5. Install the main fuel adjustment needle. Turn it in until the needle seats in the nozzle and then back out two turns.

6. Install the idle fuel adjustment needle. Back it out about 1¼ turns after seating it lightly against the jet.

7. Install the carburetor on the engine.

Updraft Carburetors

1. Remove the carburetor from the engine.

2. Remove the bowl cover and the gasket.

3. Remove the float pin, float, needle and needle seat. Check the float pin for wear.

4. Remove the idle fuel adjustment needle, main fuel adjustment needle, and the springs. Do not remove the choke plate or the shaft unless the replacement of these parts is necessary.

To assemble:

1. Install the throttle shaft and plate. The elongated side of the valve must be toward the top.

2. Install the needle seat. A ⁵⁄₁₆ in. socket should be used. Do not overtighten.

3. Install the needle, float, and float pins.

4. Set the float level. With the bowl cover casting inverted and the float resting lightly against the needle in its seat, there should be ⁷⁄₁₆ in. ± ¹⁄₃₂ in. (11mm ± 0.8mm) clearance between the machined surface casting and the free end of the float.

5. Adjust the float level by bending the lip of the float with a small screwdriver.

6. Install the new carburetor bowl gasket, bowl cover, and bowl cover screws. Tighten the screws securely.

7. Install the main fuel adjustment needle. Turn it in until the screw seats in the nozzle and then back it out 2 turns.

8. Install the idle fuel adjustment needle. Back it out about 1½ turns after seating the screw lightly against the jet. Install the idle speed screw and spring. Adjust the idle to the desired speed with the engine running.

9. Install the carburetor on the engine.

Fuel Pump

Fuel pumps used on single cylinder Kohler engines are either the mechanical or vacuum actuated type. The mechanical type is operated by an eccentric on the camshaft and the vacuum type is operated by the pulsating negative pressures in the crankcase. The K91 vacuum type pump is not serviceable and must be replaced when faulty. The mechanical pump is serviceable and rebuilding kits are available.

1. Disconnect fuel lines, remove mounting screws, and pull the pump off the engine.

2. File a mark across some point at the union of pump body and cover. Remove the screws and remove the cover.

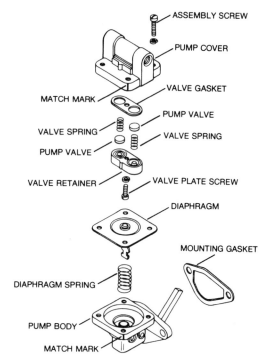

Exploded view of the fuel pump

3. Turn the cover upside down and remove the valve plate screw and washer. Remove the valve retainer, valves, valve springs, and valve gasket, after noting the position of each part. Discard the valve springs, valves and valve retainer gasket.

4. Clean the fuel head with solvent and a soft wire brush. Hold the pump cover with the diaphragm surface upward; position a new gasket into the cavity. Put the valve spring and valves into position in the cavity and reassemble the valve retainer. Lock the retainer into position by installing the fuel pump valve retainer screw.

5. Rebuild the lower diaphragm section.

6. Hold the mounting bracket and press down on the diaphragm to compress the spring underneath. Turn the bracket 90 degrees to unhook the diaphragm and remove it.

7. Clean the mounting bracket with solvent and a wire brush.

8. Stand a new diaphragm spring in the casting, put the diaphragm into position, and push downward to compress the spring. Turn the diaphragm 90 degrees to reconnect it.

9. Position the pump cover on top of the mounting bracket with the indicating marks lined up. Install the screws loosely on mechanical pumps; on vacuum pumps, tighten the screws.

10. Holding only the mounting bracket, push the pump lever to the limit of its travel, hold it there, and then tighten the four screws.

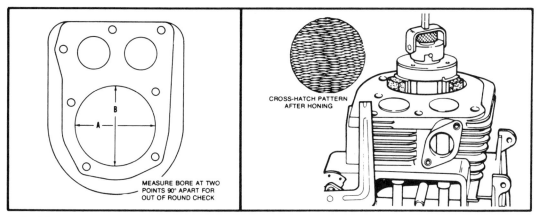

Left side—measuring the cylinder bore. Right side—honing must produce a cross-hatch pattern as shown

11. Remount the fuel pump on the engine with a new gasket, tighten the mounting bolts, and reconnect the fuel lines.

ENGINE OVERHAUL

Disassembly

The following procedure is designed to be a general guide rather than a specific and all-inclusive disassembly procedure. The sequence may have to be varied slightly to allow for the removal of special equipment or accessory items such as motor/generators, starters, instrument panels, etc.

1. Disconnect the high tension spark plug lead and remove the spark plug.

2. Close the valve on the fuel sediment bowl and remove the fuel line at the carburetor.

3. Remove the air cleaner from the carburetor intake.

4. Remove the carburetor.

5. Remove the fuel tank. The sediment bowl and brackets remain attached to the fuel tank.

6. Remove the blower housing, cylinder baffle, and head baffle.

7. Remove the rotating screen and the starter pulley.

8. The flywheel is mounted on the tapered portion of the crankcase and is removed with the help of a puller. Do not strike the flywheel with any type of hammer.

9. Remove the breaker point cover, breaker point lead, breaker assembly, and the push-rod that operates the points.

10. Remove the magneto assembly.

11. Remove the valve cover and breather assembly.

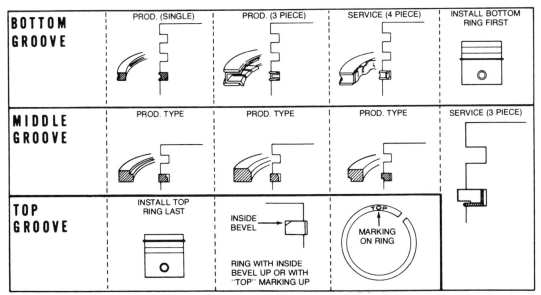

Positioning of production and service type piston rings on the piston

12. Remove the cylinder head.

13. Raise the valve springs with a valve spring compressor and remove the valve spring keepers from the valve stems. Remove the valve spring retainers, springs, and valves.

14. Remove the oil pan base and unscrew the connecting rod can screws. Remove the connecting rod cap and piston assembly from the cylinder block.

NOTE: *It will probably be necessary to use a ridge reamer on the cylinder walls before removing the piston assembly, to avoid breaking the piston rings.*

15. Remove the crankshaft, oil seals and, if necessary, the anti-friction bearings.

NOTE: *It may be necessary to press the crankshaft out of the cylinder block. The bearing plate should be removed first, if this is the case.*

16. Turn the cylinder block upside down and drive the camshaft pin out from the power take-off side of the engine with a small punch. The pin will slide out easily once it is driven free of the cylinder block.

17. Remove the camshaft and the valve tappets.

18. Loosen and remove the governor arm from the governor shaft.

19. Unscrew the governor bushing nut and remove the governor shaft from the inside of the cylinder block.

20. Loosen, but do not remove, the screw located at the lower right of the governor bushing nut until the governor gear is free to slide off of the stub shaft.

CYLINDER BLOCK SERVICE

Make sure that all surfaces are free of gasket fragments and sealer materials. The crankshaft bearings are not to be removed unless replacement is necessary. One bearing is pressed into the cylinder block and the other is located in the bearing plate. If there is no evidence of scoring or grooving and the bearings turn easily and quietly it is not necessary to replace them.

The cylinder bore must not be worn, tapered, or out-of-round more than 0.005 in. (0.13mm). Check at two locations 90 degrees apart and compare with specifications. If it is, the cylinder must be rebored. If the cylinder is very badly scored or damaged it may have to be replaced, since the cylinder can only be rebored to either 0.010 in. (0.25mm) or 0.020 in. (0.50mm) and 0.030 in. (0.76mm) maximum. Select the nearest suitable oversize and bore it to that dimension. On the other hand, if the cylinder bore is only slightly damaged, only a light deglazing may be necessary.

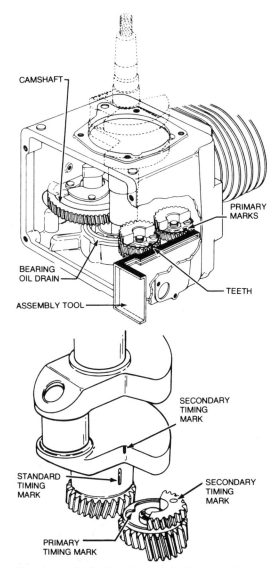

Timing marks for the dynamic balance system

HONING THE CYLINDER BORE

1. The hone must be centered in relation to the crankshaft crossbore. It is best to use a low speed drill press. Lubricate the hone with kerosene and lower it into the bore. Adjust the stones so they contact the cylinder walls.

2. Position the lower edge of the stones even with the lower edge of the bore, hone at about 600 rpm. Move the hone up and down continuously. Check bore size frequently.

3. When the bore reaches a dimension 0.0025 in. (0.0635mm) smaller than desired size, replace the coarse stones with burnishing stones. Use burnishing stones until the dimension is within 0.0005 in. (0.013mm) of desired size.

4. Use finishing stones and polish the bore to

final size, moving the stones up and down to get a 60 degree cross-hatch pattern. Wash the cylinder wall thoroughly with soap and water, dry, and apply a light coating of oil.

CRANKSHAFT SERVICE

Inspect the keyway and the gears that drive the camshaft. If the keyways are badly worn or chipped, the crankshaft should be replaced. If the cam gear teeth are excessively worn or if any are broken, the crankshaft must be replaced.

Check the crankpin for score marks or metal pickup. Slight score marks can be removed with a crocus cloth soaked in oil. If the crankpin is worn more than 0.002 in. (0.05mm), the crankshaft is to be either replaced or the crankpin reground to 0.010 in. (0.254mm) undersize. If the crankpin is reground to 0.010 in. (0.254mm) undersize, a 0.010 in. (0.254mm) undersize connecting rod must be used to achieve proper running clearance.

CONNECTING ROD SERVICE

Check the bearing area for wear, score marks, and excessive running and side clearance. Replace the rod and cap if they are worn beyond the limits allowed.

PISTON AND RINGS SERVICE

Rings are available in the standard size as well as 0.010 in. (0.25mm), 0.020 in. (0.50mm), and 0.030 in. (0.76mm) oversize sets.

NOTE: *Never reuse old rings.*

The standard size rings are to be used when the cylinder is not worn or out-of-round. Oversize rings are only to be used when the cylinder has been rebored to the corresponding oversize. Service type rings are used only when the cylinder is worn but within the wear and out-of-round limitations; wear limit is 0.005 in. (0.127mm) oversize and out-of-round limit is 0.004 in. (0.10mm).

The old piston may be reused if the block does not need reboring and the piston is within wear limits. Never reuse old rings. After removing old rings, thoroughly remove deposits from ring grooves. New rings must each be positioned in its running area of the cylinder bore for an end clearance check, and each must meet specifications.

The cylinder must be deglazed before replacing the rings. If chrome plated rings are used, the chrome plated ring must be installed in the top groove. Make sure that the ring grooves are free from all carbon deposits. Use a ring expander to install the rings. Then check side clearance.

PISTON AND ROD SERVICE

Normally very little wear will take place at the piston boss and piston pin. If the original piston and connecting rod can be used after rebuilding, the piston pin may also be used. However if a new piston or connecting rod or both have to be used, a new piston pin must also be installed. Lubricate the pin before installing it with a loose to light interference fit. Use new piston pin retainers whether or not the pin is new. Make sure they're properly engaged.

VALVES AND VALVE MECHANISM SERVICE

Inspect the valve mechanism, valves, and valve seats or inserts for evidence of wear, deep pitting, cracks or distortion. Check the clearance between the valve stems and the valve guides.

Valve guides must be replaced if they are worn beyond the limit allowed. K91 model engines do not use valve guides. To remove valve guides, press the guide down into the valve chamber and carefully break off the protruding end until the guide is completely removed. Be careful not to damage the block when removing the old guides. Use an arbor press to install the new guides. Press the new guides to the depth specified, then use a valve guide reamer to gain the proper inside diameter.

Make sure that replacement valves are the correct type (special hard faced valves are needed in some cases). Exhaust valves are always hard faced.

Intake valve seats are usually machined into the block, although inserts are used in some engines. Exhaust valve seats are made of special hardened material. The seating surfaces should be held as close to $\frac{1}{32}$ in. (0.8mm) in width as possible. Seats more than $\frac{1}{16}$ in. (1.6mm) wide must be reground with 45 degree and 15 degree cutters to obtain the proper width. Reground or new valves and seats must be lapped in for a proper fit.

After resurfacing valves and seats and lapping them in, check the valve clearance. Hold the valve down on its seat and rotate the cam-

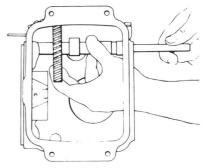

Installing the camshaft

shaft until it has no effect on the tappet, then check the clearance between the end of the valve stem and the tappet. If the clearance is not sufficient (it will always be less after grinding), it will be necessary to grind off the end of the valve stem until the correct clearance is obtained.

CYLINDER HEAD SERVICE

Remove all carbon deposits and check for pitting from hot spots. Replace the head if metal has been burned away because of head gasket leakage. Check the cylinder head for flatness. If the head is slightly warped, it can be resurfaced by rubbing it on a piece of sandpaper placed on a flat surface. Be careful not to nick or scratch the head when removing carbon deposits.

Engine Assembly

REAR MAIN BEARING

Install the rear main bearing by pressing it into the cylinder block with the shielded side toward the inside of the block. If it does not have a shielded side, then either side may face inside.

GOVERNOR SHAFT

1. Place the cylinder block on its side and slide the governor shaft into place from the inside of the block. Place the speed control disc on the governor bushing nut and thread the nut into the block, clamping the throttle bracket into place.
2. There should be a slight end-play in the governor shaft and that can be adjusted by moving the needle bearing in the block.
3. Place a space washer on the stub shaft and slide the governor gear assembly into place.
4. Tighten the holding screw from outside the cylinder block.
5. Rotate the governor gear assembly to be sure that the holding screw does not contact the weight section of the gear.

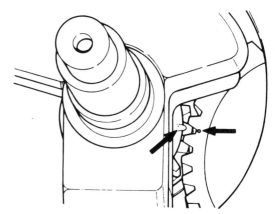

Alignment of the timing marks for the crankshaft and the camshaft

CAMSHAFT

1. Turn the cylinder block upside down.
2. The tappets must be installed before the camshaft is installed. Lubricate and install the tappets into the valve guides.
3. Position the camshaft inside the block.
NOTE: *Align the marks on the camshaft and the automatic spark advance, if so equipped.*
4. Lubricate the rod and insert it into the bearing plate side of the block. Install one 0.005 in. (0.127mm) washer between the end of the camshaft and the block. Push the rod through the camshaft and tap it lightly until the rod just starts to enter the bore at the PTO end of the block. Check the endplay and adjust it with additional washers if necessary. Press the rod into its final position.
5. The fit at the bearing plate for the camshaft rod is a light to loose fit to allow oil that might leak past to drain back into the block.

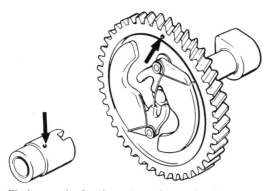

Timing marks for the automatic spark advance

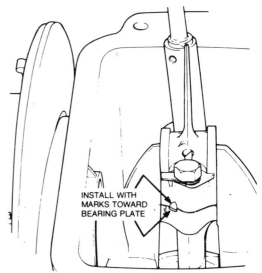

INSTALL WITH MARKS TOWARD BEARING PLATE

Connecting rod and cap alignment marks

CRANKSHAFT

1. Place the block on the base of an arbor press and carefully insert the tapered end of the crankshaft through the inner race of the anti-friction bearing.

2. Turn the crankshaft and camshaft until the timing mark in the shoulder of the crankshaft lines up with the mark on the cam gear.

3. When the marks are aligned, press the crankshaft into the bearing, making sure that the gears mesh as it is being pressed in. Recheck the alignment of the timing marks on the crankshaft and the camshaft.

4. The end-play of the crankshaft is controlled by the application of various thickness gaskets between the bearing plate and the block. Normal end-play is achieved by installing 0.020 in. (0.50mm) and 0.010 in. (0.25mm) gaskets, with the thicker gaskets on the inside.

BEARING PLATE

1. Press the front main bearing into the bearing plate. Make sure that the bearing is straight.

2. Press the bearing plate onto the crankshaft and into position on the block. Install the cap screws and secure the plate to the block. Draw up evenly on the screws.

3. Measure the crankshaft end-play, which is very critical on gear reduction engines.

PISTON AND ROD ASSEMBLY

1. Lubricate the pin and assemble it to the connecting rod and piston. Install the wrist pin retaining ring. Use new retaining rings.

2. Lubricate the entire assembly, stagger the ring gaps and, using a ring compressor, slide the piston and rod assembly into the cylinder bore with the connecting rod marks on the flywheel side of the engine.

3. Place the block on its end and oil the connecting rod end and the crankpin.

4. Attach the rod cap, lock or lock washers, and the cap screws. Tighten the screws to the correct torque.

NOTE: *Align the marks on the cap and the connecting rod.*

5. Bend the lock tabs to lock the screws.

CRANKSHAFT OIL SEALS

Apply a coat of grease to the lip and guide the oil seals onto the crankshaft. Make sure no foreign material gets onto the knife edges of seal, and make sure the seal does not bend. Place the block on its side and drive the seals squarely into the bearing plate and block.

OIL PAN BASE

Using a new gasket on the base, install pilot studs to align the cylinder block, gasket, and base. Tighten the four attaching screws to the correct torque.

VALVES

1. See the engine rebuilding section of the "Clinton" chapter for details concerning installation of the seats and guides. Clean the valves, seats, and parts thoroughly. Grind and lap-in the valves and seats for proper seating. Valve seat width must be $\frac{1}{32}$–$\frac{1}{16}$ in. (0.8–1.6mm). After grinding and lapping, slide the valves into position and check the clearance between stem and tappet. If the clearance is too small, grind the stem ends square and remove all burrs. On engines with adjustable valves, make the adjustment at this time.

2. Place the valve springs, retainers, and rotators under the valve guides. Lubricate the valve stems, and then install the valves down through the guides, compress the springs, and place the locking keys or pins in the grooves of the valve stems.

CYLINDER HEAD

1. Use a new cylinder head gasket.

2. Lubricate and tighten the head bolts evenly, and in sequence, to the proper torque.

3. Install the spark plug.

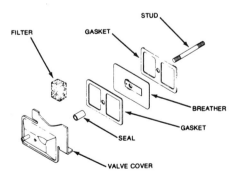
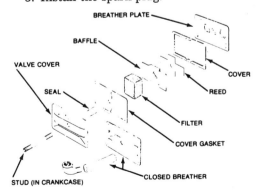

Exploded views of two common types of breathers showing assembly sequence

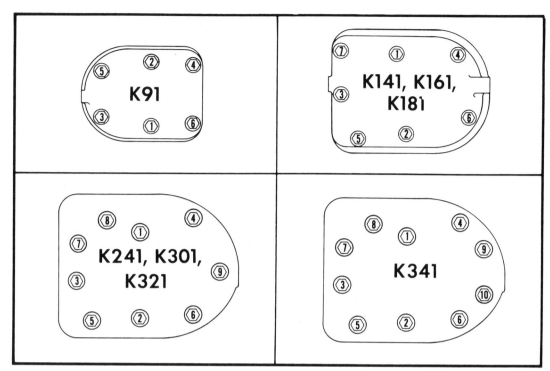

Cylinder head torquing sequences

BREATHER ASSEMBLY

Assemble the breather assembly, making sure that all parts are clean and the cover is securely tightened to prevent oil leakage.

MAGNETO

On flywheel magneto systems, the coil-core assembly is secured onto the bearing plate. On magneto-alternator systems, the coil is part of the stator assembly, which is secured to the bearing plate. On rotor type magneto systems, the rotor has a keyway and is press fitted onto the crankshaft. The magnet rotor is marked "engine-side" for proper assembly. Run all leads through the hole provided at the 11 o'clock position on the bearing plate.

Engine Rebuilding Specifications

Specification	K91
Displacement	
Cubic Inches	8.86
Cubic Centimeters	145.19
Horsepower (Max RPM)	4.0
Cylinder Bore	
New Diameter	2.375
Maximum Wear Diameter	2.378
Maximum Taper	.0025
Maximum out of Round	.005
Crankshaft	
End Play (Free)	.0228/.0038

Engine Rebuilding Specifications (cont.)

Specification	K91
Crankpin	
New Diameter	.936
Maximum Out of Round	.0005
Maximum Taper	.001
Camshaft	
Run Clearance on Pin	.001/.0025
End Play	.005/.020
Connecting Rod	
Big End Maximum Diameter	.9385
Rod-Crankpin Max Clear	.0035
Small (Pin) End-New Dia	.56315
Rod to Pin Clearance	.0007/.0008
Piston	
Thrust Face-Max Wear Dia*	2.359
Thrust Face*-Bore Clear	.0035/.006
Ring-Max Slide Clearance	.006
Ring-End Gap in New Bore	.007/.017
Ring-End Gap in Used Bore	.027
Valve-Intake	
Valve-Tappet Cold Clear	.005/.009
Valve Lift (Zero Lash)	.2095
Stem to Guide Max Wear	
Clear	.004
Valve-Exhaust	
Valve-Tappet Cold Clear	.011/.015
Valve Lift (Zero Lash)	.1828
Stem to Guide Max Wear	
Clear	.006

Engine Rebuilding Specifications (cont.)

Specification	K91
Tappet	
Clearance in Guide	.0005/.002
Ignition	
Spark Plug Gap-Gasoline	.025
Spark Plug Gap-Gas	.018
Spark Plug Gap (Shielded)	.020
Breaker Point Gap	.020
Trigger Air Gap (Breakerless)	NOT USED
SparkRun ° BTDC	20°
Spark Retard	NO RETARD
Torque Valves	
(Also See Pages 15.3)	
Spark Plug (foot lbs)	18–22
Cylinder Head	200 in. lbs
Connecting Rod	140 in. lbs
Flywheel Nut	40–50 ft lbs

*Measured just below oil ring and at right angles to piston pin

FLYWHEEL

1. Place the washer in place on the crankshaft and place the flywheel in position. Install the key.
2. Install the starter pulley, lock washer, and retaining nut. Tighten the retaining nut to the specified torque.

BREAKER POINTS

1. Install the pushrod.
2. Position the breaker points and fasten them with the two screws.

3. Place the cover gasket into position and attach the magneto lead.
4. Set the gap and install the cover.

CARBURETOR

Insert a new gasket and assemble the carburetor to the intake port with the two attaching screws.

GOVERNOR ARM AND LINKAGE

1. Insert the carburetor linkage in the throttle arm.
2. Connect the governor arm to the carburetor linkage and slide the governor arm into the governor shaft.
3. Position the governor spring in the speed control disc.
4. Before tightening the clamp bolt, turn the shaft counterclockwise with pliers as far as it will go; pull the arm as far as it will go to the left (away from the carburetor), tighten the nut,

Valve Specifications

	Dimension	Model K91	
		Intake	Exhaust
A	Seat Angle	89°	89°
B	Seat Width	.037/.045	.037/.045
C	Insert OD	—	.972/.973
D	Guide Depth	None	None
E	Guide ID	None	None
F	Valve Head Diameter	.979/.989	.807/.817
G	Valve Face Angle	45°	45°
H	Valve Stem Diameter	.2480/.2485	.2460/.2465

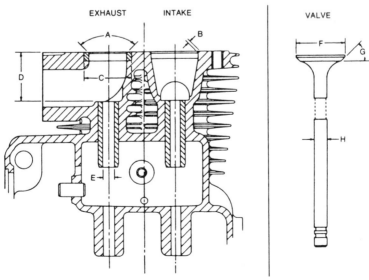

Key to valve specifications chart

and check for freedom of movement. Adjust the governor.

BLOWER HOUSING AND FUEL TANK

Install the head baffle, cylinder baffle, and the blower housing, in that order. The smaller cap screws are used on the bottom of the crankcase. Install the fuel tank and connect the fuel line.

RUN-IN PROCEDURE

1. Fill the crankcase with a non-detergent oil and run it under load for 5 hours to break it in.

2. Drain oil and refill crankcase with the recommended detergent type oil. Non-detergent oil must not be used except for break-in.

8

Kohler K-Series
4-Stroke
6 through 12 Hp
1970–83

ENGINE IDENTIFICATION

An engine identification plate is mounted on the carburetor side of the engine blower housing. The numbers that are important, as far as ordering replacement parts is concerned, are the model, serial, and specification numbers.

The model number indicates the engine model series. It also is a code indicating the cubic inch displacement and the number of cylinders. The model number K181, for instance, indicates the engine is 18 cu in. in displacement and that it has 1 cylinder. The letters following the model number indicate that a variety of other equipment is installed on the engine. The letters and what they mean are as follows:
- C Clutch model
- G Housed with fuel tank

General Engine Specifications

Model	Bore & Stroke (in.)	Displacement	Horsepower
K141 (—29355)	$2^7/_8$ x $2^1/_2$	16.22	6.25
K141 (29356—)	$2^{15}/_{16}$ x $2^1/_2$	16.9	6.25
K161 (—281161)	$2^7/_8$ x $2^1/_2$	16.22	6.25
K161 (281162—)	$2^{15}/_{16}$ x $2^1/_2$	16.9	6.25
K181	$2^{15}/_{16}$ x $2^3/_4$	18.6	8.0
K241	$3^1/_4$ x $2^7/_8$	23.9	10.0
K241A	$3^1/_4$ x $2^7/_8$	23.9	8.0
K301	$3^3/_8$ x $3^1/_4$	29.07	12.0
K301A	$3^3/_8$ x $3^1/_4$	29.07	12.0
K321	$3^1/_2$ x $3^1/_4$	31.27	14.0
K321A	$3^1/_2$ x $3^1/_4$	31.27	14.0
K341	$3^3/_4$ x $3^1/_4$	35.89	16.0
K341A	$3^3/_4$ x $3^1/_4$	35.89	16.0

- H Housed less fuel tank
- P Pump model
- R Reduction gear
- S Electric Start
- T Retractable start

NOTE: *A model number without a suffix letter indicates a basic rope start version.*

The specification number indicates a model variation. It indicates a combination of various groups used to build the engine. It may have a letter preceding it which is sometimes important in determining superseding parts. The first two numbers of the specifications number is the code designating the engine model; the remaining numbers are issued in numerical sequence as each new specification is released, for example, 2899, 28100, 28101, etc. The current specification number model code is as follows:

K141–29
K161–28
K181–30
K241–46
K301–47

The serial number lists the order in which the engine was built. If a change takes place to a model or a specification, the serial number is used to indicate the points at which the change takes place. The first letter or number in the serial number indicates what year the engine was built. The letter prefix to the engine serial number was dropped in 1969 and thereafter the prefix is a number. Engines made in 1969 have either the letter **E** or the number **1**. The code is as follows:
- A — 1965
- B — 1966–
- C — 1967
- D — 1968
- E — 1969

First Digit Numbers:
- 1 — 1969
- 2 — 1970
- 3 — 1971

- 4 – 1972
- 5 – 1973
- 6 – 1974

MAINTENANCE

Air Cleaners

A dirty air cleaner can cause rich fuel/air mixture and consequent poor engine operation and sludge deposits. If the filter becomes dirty enough, dirt that otherwise would be trapped can pass through and may wear the engine's moving parts prematurely. It is therefore necessary that all maintenance work be performed precisely as specified.

DRY AIR CLEANERS

Clean dry element air cleaners every 50 hours of operation, or every 6 months (whichever comes first) under good operating conditions. Service more frequently if the operating area is dusty. Remove the element and tap it lightly against a hard surface to remove the bulk of the dirt. If dirt will not drop off easily, replace the element. Do not use compressed air or solvents. Replace the air cleaner every 100–200 hours, under good conditions, and more frequently if the air is dusty.

Observe the following precautions:

1. Handle the element carefully – do not allow the gasket surfaces to become bent or twisted.

2. Make sure gasket surfaces seal against back plate and cover.

3. Tighten wing nut only finger tight – if it is too tight, cleaner may not seal properly.

If the dry type air cleaner is equipped with a precleaner, service this unit when cleaning the paper element. Servicing consists of cleaning the precleaner in soap and water, squeezing the excess out, and then allowing it to air dry before installation. Do not oil!

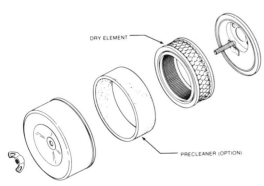

DRY ELEMENT

PRECLEANER (OPTION)

Exploded view of dry type air cleaner with precleaner

OIL BATH AIR CLEANERS

This type of unit may be used to replace the dry type in applications where very frequent replacement of the element is required. The conversion is simple and requires the use of an elbow to fit the oil bath unit onto the engine in a vertical position.

Service the unit every 25 hours of operation under good conditions and, under dusty conditions, as often as every 8 hours of operation. Service as follows:

1. Remove cover and lift element out of bowl.

2. Drain dirty oil from bowl, and then wash thoroughly in clean solvent.

3. Swish the element in the solvent and then allow it to drip dry. Do not dry with compressed air. Lightly oil the element with engine oil.

4. Inspect air horn, filter bowl, and cover gaskets, and replace as necessary (if grooved or cracked).

5. Install filter bowl gasket on air horn, then put the bowl into position. Fill bowl to indicated level with engine oil.

6. Install element, put the cover in position, and then install copper gasket (if used) and wingnut. Tighten wingnut with fingers only to avoid distorting housing. Make sure all joints in the unit seal tightly.

Lubrication

CRANKCASE

Oil level must be maintained between **F** and **L** marks – do not overfill. Check every day and add as necessary. On new engines, be especially careful to stop engine and check level frequently. When checking, make sure regular type dipstick is inserted fully. On screw type dipstick, check level with dipstick inserted fully but not screwed in. On this type, however, make sure to screw dipstick back in tightly when oil level check is completed.

Use SG type oils meeting viscosity specifications according to the prevailing temperature as shown in the chart below.

Change initial fill of oil on new engines after five hours of operation. Then, change oil every 25 hours of operation. Change oil when engine is hot. Change more frequently in dusty areas.

Oil Viscosity Chart

Air Temperature	Oil Viscosity	Oil Type
Above 30° F	SAE 30	API Service SC*
30° to 0° F	SAE 10W-30	API Service SC*
Below 0° F	SAE 5W-20	API Service SC*

* SC standard recommendation—CC (MIL-2104B) and SD class oils may also be used.

If the engine has just been overhauled, it is best to fill it initially with a non-detergent oil. Then, after 5 hours, refill with SG type oil.

Oil capacities are:
- K141, K161, K181 — 1qt. (0.9L)
- K241, K301 — 2 qts. (1.9L)
- On K241A, K301A, install 1 qt. (0.9L), then fill to **F** mark on dipstick.

REDUCTION GEAR UNITS

Every 50 hours, remove the oil plug on the lower part of the reduction unit cover to check level. If oil does not reach the level of the oil plug, remove the vented fill plug from the top of the cover and refill with engine oil until level is correct. This oil need not be changed unless unit has been out of service for several months. In this situation, remove the drain plug, drain oil, then replace plug and fill to proper level as described above.

FUEL RECOMMENDATIONS

Use either leaded or unleaded regular grade fuel of at least 90 octane. Unleaded fuel produces fewer combustion chamber deposits, so its use is preferred.

Purchase fuel from a reputable dealer, and make sure to use only fresh fuel (fuel less than 30 days old). If the engine is stored, drain the fuel system or use a fuel stabilizer that is compatible with the type of fuel tank the engine is equipped with.

Spark Plugs
SERVICE

The spark plug should be removed and serviced every 100 hours of engine operation. The plug should have a light coating of light gray colored deposits. If deposits are black, fuel/air mixture could be too rich due to improper car-

buretor adjustment or a dirty air cleaner. If deposits are white, the engine may be overheating or a spark plug of too high a heat range could be in use.

Kohler recommends that the plug be replaced rather than sandblasted or scraped if there are excessive deposits. Torque plugs to 18–22 ft. lbs.

TESTING

To test a plug for adequate performance, remove it from the engine, attach the ignition wire, and then rest the side electrode against the cylinder head. Crank the engine vigorously. If there is a sharp spark, the plug and ignition system are all right, although ignition timing should be checked if the engine fires irregularly.

Breaker Points
INSPECTION

Remove the breaker cover and inspect the points for pitting or buildup of metal on either the movable or stationary contact every 100 hours of operation. Replace the points if they are badly burned. If there is a great deal of metal buildup on either contact, the condenser may be faulty and should be replaced.

To replace points, remove the primary wiring connector screw and pull off the primary wire. Then, remove the contact set mounting screws and remove the contact set. Install the new set of points in reverse order, leaving upper mounting screw slightly loose. Then set point gap and timing as described below.

SETTING BREAKER GAP AND TIMING

1. Remove the breaker cover and disconnect the spark plug lead. Rotate the engine in direc-

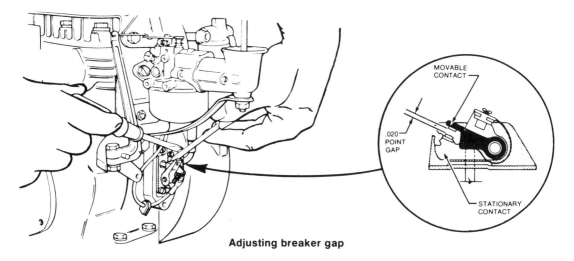

Adjusting breaker gap

Adjusting timing

tion of normal rotation until the points reach the maximum opening.

2. Using a clean, flat feeler gauge of 0.020 in. (0.50mm) size, check the gap between the points. Gauge should just slide between the contacts without opening them when flat between them. If the gap is incorrect, loosen the upper mounting screw (if necessary), and shift the breaker base with the blade of the screwdriver until gap is correct.

3. There is a timing sight hole in either the bearing plate or the blower housing. If there is a snap button in the hole, pry it out with a screwdriver.

4. While observing the sight hole, turn the engine slowly in normal direction of rotation. When the **S** or **SP** mark (engines with Automatic Compression Release) or the **T** mark on engines without ACR, appears in the hole, the points should just be beginning to open. If timing is incorrect, breaker gap will have to be reset slightly – 0.018–0.022 in. (0.46–0.56mm).

If the points are not yet opening when the timing mark is centered in the hole, make the point gap wider. If points open too early, narrow it. Recheck the setting after tightening the upper breaker mounting screw by turning the engine in normal direction of rotation past the firing point and checking that the points open at just the right time.

NOTE: *This procedure may be performed with the engine running at 1200–1800 rpm if a timing light is available. Connect the timing light according to manufacturer's instructions. You may have to chalk the timing mark to see it adequately.*

TRIGGER AIR GAP

Trigger air gap is set within the range 0.005–0.010 in. (0.127–0.254mm). As long as the gap falls within this range, the ignition system should perform adequately. Optimum ignition performance during cold weather starting is provided if the gap is adjusted to 0.005 in.

Tune-Up Specifications

Model	Plug Gap (in.)	Breaker Point Gap (in.)	Trigger Air Gap (in.)	Normal Timing (deg)	Retard Timing (deg)
K141 (small bore)	.025 ①	.020	.005 – .010	20	3B
K141 (large bore)	.025 ①	.020	.005 – .010	20	—
K161 (small bore)	.025 ①	.020	.005 – .010	20	3B
K161 (large bore)	.025 ①	.020	.005 – .010	20	—
K181	.025 ①	.020	.005 – .010	20	3B
K241	.025 ①	.020	.005 – .010	20	3A
K301	.025 ①	.020	.005 – .010	20	3A
K321	.025 ①	.020	.005 – .010	20	—
K341	.025 ①	.020	.005 – .010	20	—

B—Before
A—After
① Shielded plug gap—.020 in.

Spark Plug Specifications

Engine Model	Plug Size	Hex Size	Plug Reach	Standard Plugs		Resistor Plugs	
				Solid Post	Knurled Nut	Non-Shielded	Shielded
K141	14 mm	$13/16''$	$3/8''$	J-8 270321-S	J-8 220040-S	XJ-8 232604-S	XEJ-8 220258-S
K161	14 mm	$13/16''$	$3/8''$	J-8 270321-S	J-8 220040-S	XJ-8 232604-S	XEJ-8 220258-S
K181	14 mm	$13/16''$	$3/8''$	J-8 270321-S	J-8 220040-S	XJ-8 232604-S	XEJ-8 220258-S
K241	14 mm	$13/16''$	$7/16''$	H-10 235040-S	Not Available	XH-10 235041-S	XEH-10 235259-S
K301	14 mm	$13/16''$	$7/16''$	H-10 235040-S	Not Available	XH-10 235041-S	XEH-10 235259-S
K321	14 mm	$13/16''$	$7/16''$	H-10 235040-S	Not Available	XH-10 235041-S	XEH-10 235259-S
K341	14 mm	$13/16''$	$7/16''$	H-10 235040-S	Not Available	XH-10 235041-S	XEH-10 235259-S

Gap Setting—Gasoline .025″ (Shielded .020″) Tightening Torque—All plugs 18 to 22 foot lbs.
(Champion plugs listed—use Champion or equivalent plugs.)

(0.127mm). If you wish to adjust this or to ensure that the gap falls within the proper range, rotate the flywheel until the flywheel projection is lined up with the trigger assembly. Then, loosen the trigger bracket capscrews and slide the trigger back and forth to get the proper gap, as measured with a flat feeler gauge. Then, retighten capscrews.

IGNITION COILS

Coils do not require regular service, except to make sure they are kept clean, that the connections are tight, and that rubber insulators are in good condition (replace if cracked). If you suspect poor performance of a breakerless type ignition system and trigger air gap is correct, check resistance with an ohmmeter. To do this, disconnect the high tension lead at the coil and connect the meter between coil terminal and coil mounting bracket. If resistance is not about 11,500 ohms, replace the coil. Also, check the reading with the meter lead going to the coil terminal pulled off and connected to the spark plug connector of the high tension lead. If there is continuity here, replace the coil.

PERMANENT MAGNETS

These may be checked for magnet strength by holding a screwdriver (non-magnetic) blade within one inch of the magnet. If the magnetic field is good, the blade will be attracted to the magnet. Otherwise, replace it.

Mixture Adjustments

NOTE: *Before making any adjustments, be sure that the carburetor air cleaner is not clogged. A clogged air cleaner will cause an over-rich mixture, black exhaust smoke, and may lead you to believe that the carburetor is out of adjustment when, in reality, it is not. The carburetor is set at the factory and rarely needs adjustment unless, of course, it has been disassembled or rebuilt.*

1. With the engine stopped, turn the main and idle fuel adjusting screws all the way in until they bottom lightly. Do not force the screws or you will damage the needles.

2. For a preliminary setting, turn the main fuel screw out 2 full turns and the idle screw out $1\frac{1}{4}$ turns.

3. Start the engine and allow it to reach operating temperatures; then operate the engine at full throttle and under a load, if possible.

4. For final adjustment, turn the main fuel

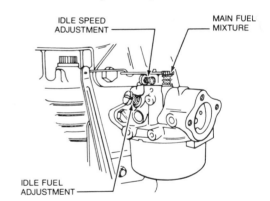

Adjustment screws on the side draft carburetor

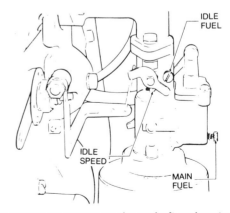

Adjustment screws on the updraft carburetor

adjustment screw in until the engine slows down (lean mixture), then out until it slows down again (rich mixture). Note the positions of the screw at both settings, then set it about halfway between the two positions.

5. Set the idle mixture adjustment screw in the same manner. The idle speed (no-load) on most engines is 1200 rpm; however, on engines with a parasitic load (hydrastatic drives) the engine idle speed may have to be increased to as much as 1700 rpm for best no-load idle.

Governor Adjustment

All Kohler engines use mechanical, camshaft driven governors.

INITIAL ADJUSTMENT

1. Loosen, but do not remove, the nut that holds the governor arm to the governor cross shaft.
2. Grasp the end of the cross shaft with a pair of pliers and turn it in counterclockwise as far as it will go. The tab on the cross shaft will stop against the rod on the governor gear assembly.
3. Pull the governor arm away from the carburetor, then retighten the nut which holds the

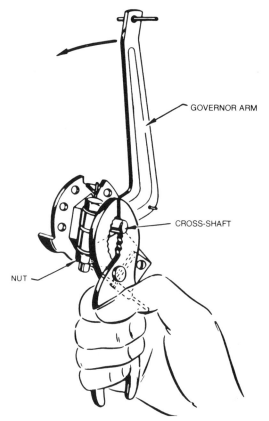

GOVERNOR ARM

CROSS-SHAFT

NUT

Initial adjustment of the governor installed on the K91, K141, K161, and the K181 engines

governor arm to the shaft. With updraft carburetors, lift the arm as far as possible, then retighten the arm nut.

FINAL ADJUSTMENT

K141–K181

After making the initial adjustment and connecting the throttle wire on the variable speed applications, start the engine and check the maximum operating speed with a tachometer.

If adjustment is necessary:

1. Loosen the bushing nut slightly.
2. Move the throttle bracket in a counterclockwise direction to increase speed, or in a clockwise direction to decrease engine speed. Maximum speed for the K141 and K181 is 3600 rpm.
3. With the speed set to the proper range, tighten the bushing nut to lock the throttle bracket in position.

K241

Engine must be adjusted to 3600 rpm.

1. Start the engine and measure the speed with a tachometer.
2. If the speed is incorrect, adjust as follows:

   a. Constant Speed Governor – Tighten the governor adjusting screw to increase speed, or loosen to decrease speed until the correct speed is attained.

   b. Variable Speed Governor – Loosen the capscrew, move the high speed stop bracket until the correct speed is attained, and then retighten the capscrew.

If the governor is too sensitive (causing hunting or surging), or not sensitive enough (causing too great a drop in speed when load is applied), the governor sensitivity should be adjusted. Make the governor more sensitive by moving the spring to holes further apart. Make it less sensitive by moving it to holes that are closer together. Standard setting is the third hole from the bottom on the governor arm and second hole from the top on the speed control bracket.

Choke Adjustment

THERMOSTATIC TYPE

If the engine does not start when cranked, continue cranking and move the choke lever first to one side and then to the other to determine whether the setting is too lean or too rich. Once the direction in which lever must be moved has been determined, loosen the adjusting screw on the choke body. Then, move the bracket downward to increase choking or upward to decrease it. Then, tighten the lockscrew. Try starting it again and readjust as necessary.

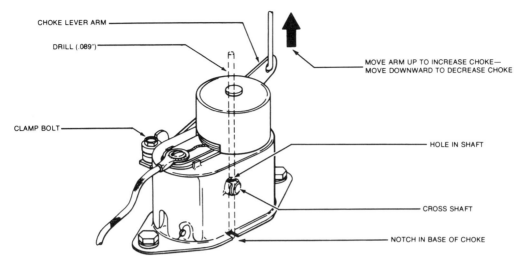

Adjusting electric-thermostatic choke

ELECTRIC-THERMOSTATIC TYPE

Remove the air cleaner from the carburetor and check the position of the choke plate. The choke should be fully closed when engine is at outside temperature and the temperature is very low. In milder temperatures, slightly less closure is required.

If adjustment is required, move the choke arm until the hole in the brass shaft lines up with the slot in the bearings. Insert a #43 (0.089 in.) drill through the shaft and push it downward so it engages the notch in the base of the choke unit. Then, loosen the clamp bolt on the choke lever and push the arm upward to move the choke plate toward the closed position. When the desired position is obtained, tighten the clamp bolt. Then, remove the drill.

Remount the air cleaner, and then check for any binding in the choke linkage. Correct as necessary. Finally, run the engine until hot, and make sure the choke opens fully. If not, readjust it toward the open position as necessary.

Valve Adjustment

On K241 and K301 engines, adjustable valve tappets are provided. With the engine cold, turn crankshaft until it reaches Top Dead Center timing mark. If valves are slightly open, turn the crankshaft another turn until valves are closed and engine is again at Top Center. Check valve clearances with a flat feeler gauge. Note that exhaust and intake clearances are different, and make sure you're using the right gauge for each valve. If the valve clearance is correct, a gauge can just be inserted between tappet and valve stem. A slight pull is required to bring it back out. If clearance is incorrect, loosen the locking nut and turn the adjusting nut in or out to get the proper clearance. Hold the adjusting nut while tightening the locknut and recheck clearance.

Compression Check

Compression is checked by removing the spark plug lead and spinning the flywheel forward against compression. If the piston does not bounce backward with considerable force, checking with a gauge may be necessary. On Automatic Compression Release engines, rotate the flywheel backward against power stroke-if little resistance is felt, check compression with a gauge.

The compression gauge check requires rapid motoring (spinning) of the crankshaft, at about 1000 rpm. Install the gauge in the spark plug hole and motor the engine. Gauge should read 110–120 psi. If reading is less than 100 psi, the engine requires major repair to piston rings or valves.

FUEL SYSTEM

Carburetor

If a carburetor will not respond to mixture screw adjustments, then you can assume that there are dirt, gum, or varnish deposits in the carburetor or worn/damaged parts. To remedy these problems, the carburetor will have to be completely disassembled, cleaned, and worn parts replaced and reassembled.

Parts should be cleaned with solvent to remove all deposits. Replace worn parts and use all new gaskets. Carburetor rebuilding kits are available.

REBUILDING

Side Draft Carburetors

1. Remove the carburetor from the engine.
2. Remove the bowl nut, gasket, and bowl. If the carburetor has a bowl drain, remove the drain spring, spacer and plug, and gasket from inside the bowl.
3. Remove the float pin, float, needle, and needle seat. Check the float for dents, leaks, and wear on the float lip or in the float pin holes.
4. Remove the bowl ring gasket.
5. Remove the idle fuel adjusting needle, main fuel adjusting needle, and springs.
6. Do not remove the choke and throttle plates or shafts. If these parts are worn, replace the entire carburetor assembly.

To assemble:

1. Install the needle seat, needle, float, and float pin.
2. Set the float level. With the carburetor casting inverted and the float resting against the needle in its seat, there should be $^{11}/_{64} \pm ^{1}/_{32}$ in. (4.4mm $\pm$ 0.8mm) clearance between the machined surface of the casting and the free end of the float.
3. Adjust the float level by bending the lip of the float with a small screwdriver.
4. Install the new bowl ring gasket, new bowl nut gasket, and bowl nut. Tighten the nut securely.
5. Install the main fuel adjustment needle. Turn it in until the needle seats in the nozzle and then back out two turns.
6. Install the idle fuel adjustment needle.

Back it out about $1^{1}/_{4}$ turns after seating it lightly against the jet.
7. Install the carburetor on the engine.

Updraft Carburetors

1. Remove the carburetor from the engine.
2. Remove the bowl cover and the gasket.
3. Remove the float pin, float, needle and needle seat. Check the float pin for wear.
4. Remove the idle fuel adjustment needle, main fuel adjustment needle, and the springs. Do not remove the choke plate or the shaft unless the replacement of these parts is necessary.

To assemble:

1. Install the throttle shaft and plate. The elongated side of the valve must be toward the top.
2. Install the needle seat. A $^{5}/_{16}$ in. socket should be used. Do not over-tighten.
3. Install the needle, float, and float pins.
4. Set the float level. With the bowl cover casting inverted and the float resting lightly against the needle in its seat, there should be $^{7}/_{16}$ in. $\pm$ $^{1}/_{32}$ in. (11mm $\pm$ 0.8mm). clearance between the machined surface casting and the free end of the float.
5. Adjust the float level by bending the lip of the float with a small screwdriver.
6. Install the new carburetor bowl gasket, bowl cover, and bowl cover screws. Tighten the screws securely.
7. Install the main fuel adjustment needle. Turn it in until the screw seats in the nozzle and then back it out 2 turns.
8. Install the idle fuel adjustment needle.

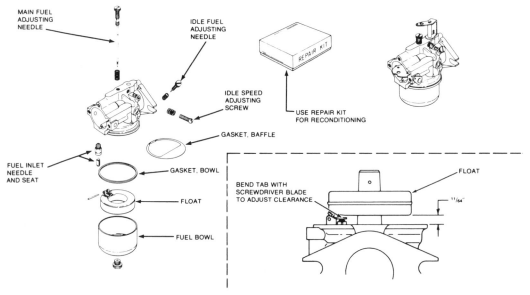

Exploded view of the sidedraft carburetor. Inset shows float adjustment procedure

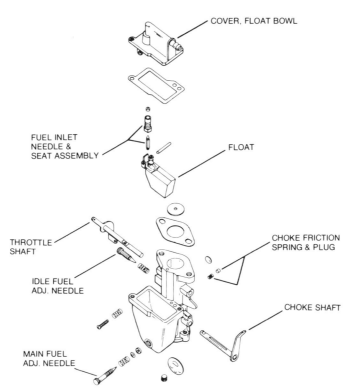

Exploded view of the updraft carburetor

Back it out about $1\frac{1}{2}$ turns after seating the screw lightly against the jet. Install the idle speed screw and spring. Adjust the idle to the desired speed with the engine running.

9. Install the carburetor on the engine.

Fuel Pump

Fuel pumps used on single cylinder Kohler engines are either the mechanical or vacuum actuated type. The mechanical type is operated by an eccentric on the camshaft and the vacuum type is operated by the pulsating negative pressures in the crankcase. The K91 vacuum type pump is not serviceable and must be replaced when faulty. The mechanical pump is serviceable and rebuilding kits are available.

1. Disconnect fuel lines, remove mounting screws, and pull the pump off the engine.

2. File a mark across some point at the union of pump body and cover. Remove the screws and remove the cover.

3. Turn the cover upside down and remove the valve plate screw and washer. Remove the valve retainer, valves, valve springs, and valve gasket, after noting the position of each part.

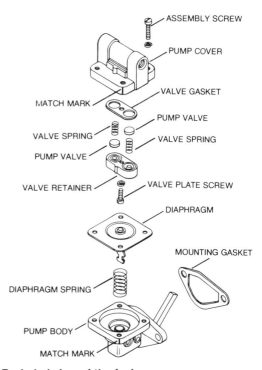

Exploded view of the fuel pump

Discard the valve springs, valves and valve retainer gasket.

4. Clean the fuel head with solvent and a soft wire brush. Hold the pump cover with the diaphragm surface upward; position a new gasket into the cavity. Put the valve spring and valves into position in the cavity and reassemble the valve retainer. Lock the retainer into position by installing the fuel pump valve retainer screw.

5. Rebuild the lower diaphragm section.

6. Hold the mounting bracket and press down on the diaphragm to compress the spring underneath. Turn the bracket 90 degrees to unhook the diaphragm and remove it.

7. Clean the mounting bracket with solvent and a wire brush.

8. Stand a new diaphragm spring in the casting, put the diaphragm into position, and push downward to compress the spring. Turn the diaphragm 90 degrees to reconnect it.

9. Position the pump cover on top of the mounting bracket with the indicating marks lined up. Install the screws loosely on mechanical pumps; on vacuum pumps, tighten the screws.

10. Holding only the mounting bracket, push the pump lever to the limit of its travel, hold it there, and then tighten the four screws.

11. Remount the fuel pump on the engine with a new gasket, tighten the mounting bolts, and reconnect the fuel lines.

ENGINE OVERHAUL

Disassembly

The following procedure is designed to be a general guide rather than a specific and all inclusive disassembly procedure. The sequence may have to be varied slightly to allow for the removal of special equipment or accessory items such as motor/generators, starters, instrument panels, etc.

1. Disconnect the high tension spark plug lead and remove the spark plug.

2. Close the valve on the fuel sediment bowl and remove the fuel line at the carburetor.

3. Remove the air cleaner from the carburetor intake.

4. Remove the carburetor.

5. Remove the fuel tank. The sediment bowl and brackets remain attached to the fuel tank.

6. Remove the blower housing, cylinder baffle, and head baffle.

7. Remove the rotating screen and the starter pulley.

8. The flywheel is mounted on the tapered portion of the crankcase and is removed with the help of a puller. Do not strike the flywheel with any type of hammer.

9. Remove the breaker point cover, breaker point lead, breaker assembly, and the pushrod that operates the points.

10. Remove the magneto assembly.

11. Remove the valve cover and breather assembly.

12. Remove the cylinder head.

13. Raise the valve springs with a valve spring compressor and remove the valve spring keepers from the valve stems. Remove the valve spring retainers, springs, and valves.

14. Remove the oil pan base and unscrew the connecting rod can screws. Remove the connecting rod cap and piston assembly from the cylinder block.

NOTE: *It will probably be necessary to use a ridge reamer on the cylinder walls before removing the piston assembly, to avoid breaking the piston rings.*

15. Remove the crankshaft, oil seals and, if necessary, the anti-friction bearings.

NOTE: *It may be necessary to press the crankshaft out of the cylinder block. The bearing plate should be removed first, if this is the case.*

16. Turn the cylinder block upside down and drive the camshaft pin out from the power take-off side of the engine with a small punch. The pin will slide out easily once it is driven free of the cylinder block.

17. Remove the camshaft and the valve tappets.

18. Loosen and remove the governor arm from the governor shaft.

19. Unscrew the governor bushing nut and remove the governor shaft from the inside of the cylinder block.

20. Loosen, but do not remove, the screw located at the lower right of the governor bushing nut until the governor gear is free to slide off of the stub shaft.

CYLINDER BLOCK SERVICE

Make sure that all surfaces are free of gasket fragments and sealer materials. The crankshaft bearings are not to be removed unless replacement is necessary. One bearing is pressed into the cylinder block and the other is located in the bearing plate. If there is no evidence of scoring or grooving and the bearings turn easily and quietly it is not necessary to replace them.

The cylinder bore must not be worn, tapered, or out-of-round more than 0.005 in. (0.127mm). Check at two locations 90 degrees apart and compare with specifications. If it is, the cylinder must be rebored. If the cylinder is very badly scored or damaged it may have to be replaced, since the cylinder can only be rebored to either 0.010 in. (0.254mm) or 0.020 in. (0.500mm) and 0.030 in. (0.762mm) maximum. Select the nearest suitable oversize and bore it to that dimension. On the other hand, if the cylinder bore is only slightly damaged, only a light deglazing may be necessary.

HONING THE CYLINDER BORE

1. The hone must be centered in relation to the crankshaft crossbore. It is best to use a low speed drill press. Lubricate the hone with kerosene and lower it into the bore. Adjust the stones so they contact the cylinder walls.

2. Position the lower edge of the stones even with the lower edge of the bore, hone at about 600 rpm. Move the hone up and down continuously. Check bore size frequently.

3. When the bore reaches a dimension 0.0025 in. (0.0635mm) smaller than desired size, replace the coarse stones with burnishing stones. Use burnishing stones until the dimension is within 0.0005 in. (0.0127mm) of desired size.

4. Use finishing stones and polish the bore to final size, moving the stones up and down to get a 60 degree cross-hatch pattern. Wash the cylinder wall thoroughly with soap and water, dry, and apply a light coating of oil.

CRANKSHAFT SERVICE

Inspect the keyway and the gears that drive the camshaft. If the keyways are badly worn or chipped, the crankshaft should be replaced. If the cam gear teeth are excessively worn or if any are broken, the crankshaft must be replaced.

Check the crankpin for score marks or metal pickup. Slight score marks can be removed with a crocus cloth soaked in oil. If the crankpin is worn more than 0.002 in. (0.05mm), the crankshaft is to be either replaced or the crankpin reground to 0.010 in. (0.254mm) undersize. If the crankpin is reground to 0.010 in. (0.254mm) undersize, a 0.010 in. (0.254mm) undersize connecting rod must be used to achieve proper running clearance.

CONNECTING ROD SERVICE

Check the bearing area for wear, score marks, and excessive running and side clearance. Replace the rod and cap if they are worn beyond the limits allowed.

PISTON AND RINGS SERVICE

Production and Service Type

Rings are available in the standard size as well as 0.010 in. (0.254mm), 0.020 in. (0.500mm), and 0.030 in. (0.762mm) oversize sets.

NOTE: *Never reuse old rings.*

The standard size rings are to be used when the cylinder is not worn or out-of-round. Oversize rings are only to be used when the cylinder has been rebored to the corresponding oversize. Service type rings are used only when the cylinder is worn but within the wear and out-of-round limitations; wear limit is 0.005 in. (0.127mm) oversize and out-of-round limit is 0.004 in. (0.10mm).

NOTE: *Never reuse old rings.*

The standard size rings are to be used when the cylinder is not worn or out-of-round. Oversize rings are only to be used when the cylinder has been rebored to the corresponding oversize. Service type rings are used only when the cylinder is worn but within the wear and out-of-round limitations; wear limit is 0.005 in. (0.127mm) oversize and out-of-round limit is 0.004 in. (0.10mm).

The old piston may be reused if the block does not need reboring and the piston is within wear limits. Never reuse old rings. After removing old rings, thoroughly remove deposits from ring

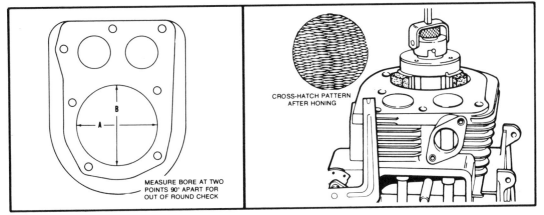

Left side—measuring the cylinder bore. Right side—honing must produce a cross-hatch pattern as shown

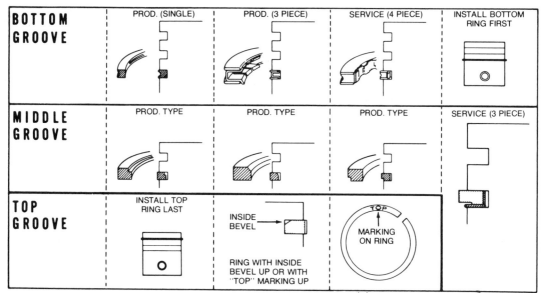

Positioning of production and service type piston rings on the piston

grooves. New rings must each be positioned in its running area of the cylinder bore for an end clearance check, and each must meet specifications.

The cylinder must be deglazed before replacing the rings. If chrome plated rings are used, the chrome plated ring must be installed in the top groove. Make sure that the ring grooves are free from all carbon deposits. Use a ring expander to install the rings. Then check side clearance.

PISTON AND ROD SERVICE

Normally very little wear will take place at the piston boss and piston pin. If the original piston and connecting rod can be used after rebuilding, the piston pin may also be used. However if a new piston or connecting rod or both have to be used, a new piston pin must also be installed. Lubricate the pin before installing it with a loose to light interference fit. Use new piston pin retainers whether or not the pin is new. Make sure they're properly engaged.

VALVES AND VALVE MECHANISM SERVICE

Inspect the valve mechanism, valves, and valve seats or inserts for evidence of wear, deep pitting, cracks or distortion. Check the clearance between the valve stems and the valve guides.

Valve guides must be replaced if they are worn beyond the limit allowed. K91 model engines do not use valve guides. To remove valve guides, press the guide down into the valve chamber and carefully break off the protruding end until the guide is completely removed. Be careful not to damage the block when removing

the old guides. Use an arbor press to install the new guides. Press the new guides to the depth specified, then use a valve guide reamer to gain the proper inside diameter.

Make sure that replacement valves are the correct type (special hard faced valves are needed in some cases). Exhaust valves are always hard faced.

Intake valve seats are usually machined into the block, although inserts are used in some engines. Exhaust valve seats are made of special hardened material. The seating surfaces should be held as close to $\frac{1}{32}$ in. (0.8mm) in width as possible. Seats more than $\frac{1}{16}$ in. (1.6mm) wide must be reground with 45 degree and 15 degree cutters to obtain the proper width. Reground or new valves and seats must be lapped in for a proper fit.

After resurfacing valves and seats and lapping them in, check the valve clearance. Hold the valve down on its seat and rotate the camshaft until it has no effect on the tappet, then check the clearance between the end of the valve stem and the tappet. If the clearance is not sufficient (it will always be less after grinding), it will be necessary to grind off the end of the valve stem until the correct clearance is obtained. This is necessary on all engines except the K141 and K301 engines which all have adjustable tappets.

CYLINDER HEAD SERVICE

Remove all carbon deposits and check for pitting from hot spots. Replace the head if metal has been burned away because of head gasket leakage. Check the cylinder head for flatness. If the head is slightly warped, it can be resurfaced by rubbing it on a piece of sandpaper placed on a flat surface. Be careful not to nick or scratch the head when removing carbon deposits.

DYNAMIC BALANCE SYSTEM SERVICE

The dynamic balance system consists of two balance gears which run on needle bearings. The gears are assembled on two stub shafts that are pressed into special bosses in the crankcase. Snap-rings hold the gears and spacer washers are used to control end-play. The gears are driven off of the crankgear. The dynamic balance system is found on special versions of K241 and K301 models.

If the stub shaft is worn or damaged, press the old shaft out. The new shafts must be pressed in a specified distance which depends upon the distance between the stub shaft boss and main bearing boss. Measure the distance the stub shaft boss protrudes above the main bearing boss and then press the shaft in for a protrusion of the shaft end beyond stub shaft boss as specified. If stub shaft boss protrudes about $7/16$ in. (11mm) beyond main bearing boss, press the shaft in until it is 0.735 in. (18.7mm) above stub shaft boss. If protrusion is about $1/16$ in. (1.6mm), press the stub shaft in until it is 1.110 in. (28mm) above the stub shaft boss, and then use a $3/8$ in. (9.5mm) spacer.

When installing the balance gears, slip one 0.010 in. (0.254mm) spacer onto the stub shaft, then install the gear/bearing assembly onto the stub shaft with the timing marks facing out. Proper end-play of 0.002–0.010 in. (0.05–0.25mm) is attained with one 0.005 in. (0.127mm) spacer, one 0.010 in. (0.254mm) spacer, and one 0.020 in. (0.50mm) spacer which are all installed on the snap-ring retainer end of the shaft. Install the thickest spacer next to the retainer. Check the end-play and adjust it by adding or subtracting 0.005 in. (0.127mm) spacers.

To time the balance gears, first press the crankshaft into the block and align the primary timing mark on the top of the balance gear with the standard timing mark next to the crankgear. Press the shaft in until the crankgear is engaged $1/16$ in. (1.6mm) into the top gear (narrow side). Rotate the crankshaft to align the timing marks on the crankgear and cam gear. Press the crankshaft the remainder of the way into the block.

Rotate the crankshaft until it is about 15 degrees past BDC and slip one 0.010 in. (0.25mm) spacer over the stub shaft before installing the bottom gear/bearing assembly.

Align the secondary timing mark on this gear with the secondary timing mark on the counterweight of the crankshaft and then install the gear on the shaft. The secondary timing mark will also be aligned with the standard timing mark on the crankshaft after installation. Use one 0.005 in. (0.127mm) spacer and one 0.020 in. (0.50mm) spacer (with larger spacer next to retainer) to get proper end play of 0.002–0.010 in. (0.05–0.25mm). Install the snap-ring retainer, then check and adjust the endplay.

Engine Assembly

REAR MAIN BEARING

Install the rear main bearing by pressing it into the cylinder block with the shielded side toward the inside of the block. If it does not have a shielded side, then either side may face inside.

GOVERNOR SHAFT

1. Place the cylinder block on its side and slide the governor shaft into place from the in-

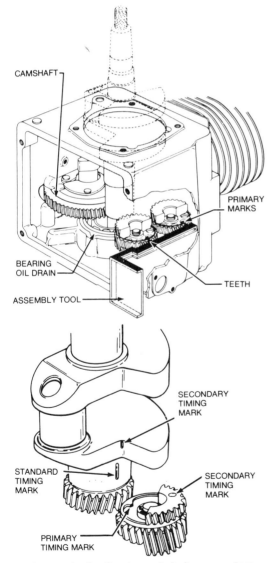

CAMSHAFT

PRIMARY MARKS

BEARING OIL DRAIN

TEETH

ASSEMBLY TOOL

SECONDARY TIMING MARK

STANDARD TIMING MARK

SECONDARY TIMING MARK

PRIMARY TIMING MARK

Timing marks for the dynamic balance system

side of the block. Place the speed control disc on the governor bushing nut and thread the nut into the block, clamping the throttle bracket into place.

2. There should be a slight end-play in the governor shaft and that can be adjusted by moving the needle bearing in the block.

3. Place a space washer on the stub shaft and slide the governor gear assembly into place.

4. Tighten the holding screw from outside the cylinder block.

5. Rotate the governor gear assembly to be sure that the holding screw does not contact the weight section of the gear.

CAMSHAFT

1. Turn the cylinder block upside down.

2. The tappets must be installed before the camshaft is installed. Lubricate and install the tappets into the valve guides.

3. Position the camshaft inside the block. NOTE: *Align the marks on the camshaft and the automatic spark advance, if so equipped.*

4. Lubricate the rod and insert it into the bearing plate side of the block. Install one 0.005 in. (0.127mm) washer between the end of the camshaft and the block. Push the rod through the camshaft and tap it lightly until the rod just starts to enter the bore at the PTO end of the block. Check the endplay and adjust it with additional washers if necessary. Press the rod into its final position.

5. The fit at the bearing plate for the camshaft rod is a light to loose fit to allow oil that might leak past to drain back into the block.

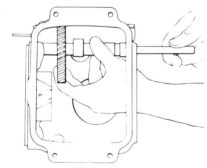

Installing the camshaft

CRANKSHAFT

1. Place the block on the base of an arbor press and carefully insert the tapered end of the crankshaft through the inner race of the antifriction bearing, or sleeve bearing on the K141.

2. Turn the crankshaft and camshaft until the timing mark in the shoulder of the crankshaft lines up with the mark on the cam gear.

3. When the marks are aligned, press the

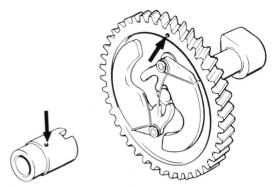

Timing marks for the automatic spark advance

crankshaft into the bearing, making sure that the gears mesh as it is being pressed in. Recheck the alignment of the timing marks on the crankshaft and the camshaft.

4. The end-play of the crankshaft is controlled by the application of various thickness gaskets between the bearing plate and the block. Normal end-play is achieved by installing 0.020 in. (0.50mm) and 0.010 in. (0.25mm) gaskets, with the thicker gaskets on the inside.

BEARING PLATE

1. Press the front main bearing into the bearing plate. Make sure that the bearing is straight.

2. Press the bearing plate onto the crankshaft and into position on the block. Install the cap screws and secure the plate to the block. Draw up evenly on the screws.

3. Measure the crankshaft end-play, which is very critical on gear reduction engines.

PISTON AND ROD ASSEMBLY

1. Lubricate the pin and assemble it to the connecting rod and piston. Install the wrist pin retaining ring. Use new retaining rings.

2. Lubricate the entire assembly, stagger the

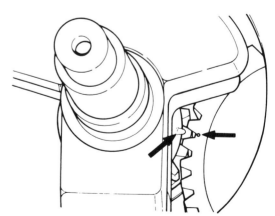

Alignment of the timing marks for the crankshaft and the camshaft

ring gaps and, using a ring compressor, slide the piston and rod assembly into the cylinder bore with the connecting rod marks on the flywheel side of the engine.

3. Place the block on its end and oil the connecting rod end and the crankpin.

4. Attach the rod cap, lock or lock washers, and the cap screws. Tighten the screws to the correct torque.

NOTE: *Align the marks on the cap and the connecting rod.*

5. Bend the lock tabs to lock the screws.

CRANKSHAFT OIL SEALS

Apply a coat of grease to the lip and guide the oil seals onto the crankshaft. Make sure no foreign material gets onto the knife edges of seal, and make sure the seal does not bend. Place the block on its side and drive the seals squarely into the bearing plate and block.

OIL PAN BASE

Using a new gasket on the base, install pilot studs to align the cylinder block, gasket, and base. Tighten the four attaching screws to the correct torque.

VALVES

1. See the engine rebuilding section of the "Clinton" chapter for details concerning installation of the seats and guides. Clean the valves, seats, and parts thoroughly. Grind and lap-in the valves and seats for proper seating. Valve seat width must be $\frac{1}{32}$–$\frac{1}{16}$ in. (0.8–1.6mm). After grinding and lapping, slide the valves into position and check the clearance between stem and tappet. If the clearance is too small, grind the stem ends square and remove all burrs. On engines with adjustable valves, make the adjustment at this time.

2. Place the valve springs, retainers, and rotators under the valve guides. Lubricate the valve stems, and then install the valves down through the guides, compress the springs, and place the locking keys or pins in the grooves of the valve stems.

CYLINDER HEAD

1. Use a new cylinder head gasket.

2. Lubricate and tighten the head bolts evenly, and in sequence, to the proper torque.

3. Install the spark plug.

BREATHER ASSEMBLY

Assemble the breather assembly, making sure that all parts are clean and the cover is securely tightened to prevent oil leakage.

MAGNETO

On flywheel magneto systems, the coil-core assembly is secured onto the bearing plate. On magneto-alternator systems, the coil is part of the stator assembly, which is secured to the bearing plate. On rotor type magneto systems, the rotor has a keyway and is press fitted onto the crankshaft. The magnet rotor is marked "engine-side" for proper assembly. Run all leads through the hole provided at the 11 o'clock position on the bearing plate.

FLYWHEEL

1. Place the washer in place on the crankshaft and place the flywheel in position. Install the key.

2. Install the starter pulley, lock washer, and retaining nut. Tighten the retaining nut to the specified torque.

BREAKER POINTS

1. Install the pushrod.

2. Position the breaker points and fasten them with the two screws.

3. Place the cover gasket into position and attach the magneto lead.

4. Set the gap and install the cover.

CARBURETOR

Insert a new gasket and assemble the carburetor to the intake port with the two attaching screws.

GOVERNOR ARM AND LINKAGE

1. Insert the carburetor linkage in the throttle arm.

2. Connect the governor arm to the carburetor linkage and slide the governor arm into the governor shaft.

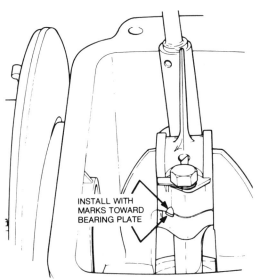

INSTALL WITH MARKS TOWARD BEARING PLATE

Connecting rod and cap alignment marks

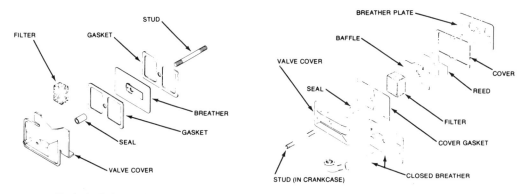

Exploded views of two common types of breathers showing assembly sequence

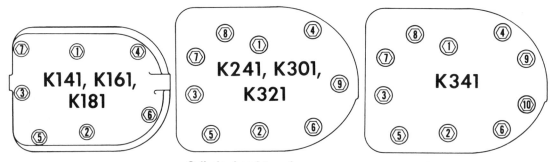

Cylinder head torquing sequences

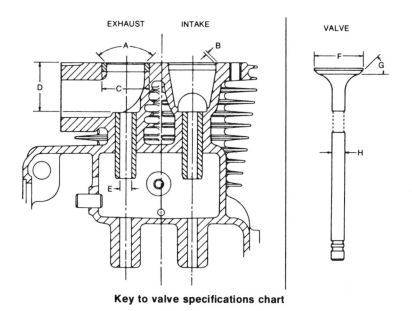

Key to valve specifications chart

3. Position the governor spring in the speed control disc on the K141, K161, and K181.

4. Before tightening the clamp bolt, turn the shaft counterclockwise with pliers as far as it will go; pull the arm as far as it will go to the left (away from the carburetor), tighten the nut, and check for freedom of movement. Adjust the governor.

BLOWER HOUSING AND FUEL TANK

Install the head baffle, cylinder baffle, and the blower housing, in that order. The smaller cap screws are used on the bottom of the crankcase. Install the fuel tank and connect the fuel line.

RUN-IN PROCEDURE

1. Fill the crankcase with a non-detergent oil and run it under load for 5 hours to break it in.

2. Drain oil and refill crankcase with the recommended detergent type oil. Non-detergent oil must not be used except for break-in.

Valve Specifications

Dimension	Model K141, K161, K181		K241, K301, K321, K341	
	Intake	Exhaust	Intake	Exhaust
A Seat Angle	89°	89°	89°	89°
B Seat Width	.037/.045	.037/.045	.037/.045	.037/.045
C Insert OD	—	1.2535/1.2545	—	1.2535/1.2545
D Guide Depth	1.312	1.312	1.586	1.497
E Guide ID	.312/.313	.312/.313	.312/.313	.312/.313
F Valve Head Diameter	$1^3/_8$	$1^1/_8$	1.370/1.380	1.120/1.130*
G Valve Face Angle	45°	45°	45°	45°
H Valve Stem Diameter	.3105/.3110	.3090/.3095	.3105/.3110	.3084/.3091

*2.125″ on all K341 and K321 engines with spec suffix "D" and later.

Engine Rebuilding Specifications

Specifications	K141		K161			K181	K241	K301	K321	K341
	2⅞" Bore	2¹⁵/₁₆" Bore	2¹⁵/₁₆" Bore	2⅞" Bore	2¹⁵/₁₆" Bore					
Displacement										
Cubic Inches	16.22	16.9	16.9	16.22	16.9	18.6	23.9	29.07	31.27	35.89
Cubic Centimeter	265.8	276.99	276.99	265.8	276.99	304.8	391.65	476.37	528.46	588.24
Horsepower (Max RPM)	6.25	6.25	6.25	7.0	7.0	8.0	10.0	12.0	14.0	16.0
Cylinder Bore										
New Diameter	2.875	2.9375	2.9375	2.875	2.9375	2.9375	3.251	3.375	3.500	3.750
Maximum Wear Diameter	2.878	2.9405	2.9405	2.878	2.9405	2.9405	3.2545	3.3785	3.503	3.753
Maximum Taper	.0025	.0025	.0025	.0025	.0025	.0025	.0015	.0015	.0015	.0015
Maximum out of Round	.005	.005	.005	.005	.005	.005	.005	.005	.005	.005
Crankshaft										
End Play (Free)	.002/.023	.002/.023	.002/.023	.002/.023	.002/.023	.002/.023	.003/.020	.003/.020	.003/.020	.003/.020
Crankpin										
New Diameter	1.186	1.186	1.186	1.186	1.186	1.186	1.500	1.500	1.500	1.500
Maximum Out of Round	.0005	.0005	.0005	.0005	.0005	.0005	.0005	.0005	.0005	.0005
Maximum Taper	.001	.001	.001	.001	.001	.001	.001	.001	.001	.001
Camshaft										
Run Clearance on Pin	.0005/.003	.0005/.003	.0005/.003	.0005/.003	.0005/.003	.0005/.003	.001/.0035	.001/.0035	.001/.0035	.001/.0035
End Play	.005/.010	.005/.010	.005/.010	.005/.010	.005/.010	.005/.010	.005/.010	.005/.010	.005/.010	.005/.010
Connecting Rod										
Big End Maximum Diameter	1.1885	1.1885	1.1885	1.1885	1.1885	1.1885	1.5025	1.5025	1.5025	1.5025
Rod-Crankpin Max Clear	.0035	.0035	.0035	.0035	.0035	.0035	.0035	.0035	.0035	.0035
Small (Pin) End-New Dia	.62565	.62565	.62565	.62565	.62565	.62565	.85975	.87585	.87585	.87585
Rod to Pin Clearance	.0006/.0011	.0006/.0011	.0006/.0011	.0006/.0011	.0006/.0011	.0006/.0011	.0003/.0008	.0003/.0008	.0003/.0008	.0003/.0008
Piston										
Thrust Face-Max Wear Dia*	2.866	2.9305	2.9305	2.866	2.9305	2.9305	3.2445	3.3625	3.4945	3.7425
Thrust Face*-Bore Clear	.006/.0075	.006/.008	.006/.008	.006/.0075	.006/.008	.006/.008	.0075/.0085	.0065/.0095	.007/.010	.007/.010
Ring-Max Side Clearance	.006	.006	.006	.006	.006	.006	.006	.006	.006	.006
Ring-End Gap in New Bore	.007/.017	.007/.017	.007/.017	.007/.017	.007/.017	.007/.017	.010/.020	.010/.020	.010/.020	.010/.020
Ring-End Gap in Used Bore	.027	.027	.027	.027	.027	.027	.027	.030	.030	.030

Valve-Intake									
Valve-Tappet Cold Clear	.006/.008	.006/.008	.006/.008	.006/.008	.006/.008	.008/.010	.008/.010	.008/.010	.008/.010
Valve Lift (Zero Lash)	.2778	.2778	.2778	.2778	.2778	.324	.324	.324	.324
Stem to Guide Max Wear Clear	.0045	.0045	.0045	.0045	.0045	.0045	.0045	.0045	.0045
Valve-Exhaust									
Valve-Tappet Cold Clear	.015/.017	.015/.017	.015/.017	.015/.017	.015/.017	.017/.020	.017/.020	.017/.020	.017/.020
Valve Lift (Zero Lash)	.2542	.2542	.2542	.2542	.2542	.324	.324	.324	.324
Stem to Guide Max Wear Clear	.006	.006	.006	.006	.006	.0065**	.0065**	.0065**	.0065**
Tappet									
Clearance in Guide	.0005/.002	.0005/.002	.0005/.002	.0005/.002	.0005/.002	.0008/.0023	.0008/.0023	.0008/.0023	.0008/.0023
Ignition									
Spark Plug Gap-Gasoline	.025	.025	.025	.025	.025	.025	.025	.025	.025
Spark Plug Gap-Gas	.018	.018	.018	.018	.018	.018	.018	.018	.018
Spark Plug Gap (Shielded)	.020	.020	.020	.020	.020	.020	.020	.020	.020
Breaker Point Gap	.020	.020	.020	.020	.020	.020	.020	.020	.020
Trigger Air Gap (Breakerless)									
Spark Run °BTDC	.005/.010 20°	.005/.010 20°	.005/.010 20°	.005/.010 20°	.005/.010 20°	.005/.010 20°	.005/.010 20°	.005/.010 20°	.005/.010 20°
Spark Retard	3° BTDC*** (ACR-NONE)	ACR ONLY (No Retard)	3° BTDC*** (ACR-NONE)	ACR ONLY (No Retard)	3° BTDC*** (ACR-NONE)	3° ATDC*** (ACR-NONE)	3° ATDC*** (ACR-NONE)	ACR ONLY (No Retard)	ACR ONLY (No Retard)
Torque Values (Also See Page 15.3)									
Spark Plug (ft. lbs.)	18–22	18–22	18–22	18–22	18–22	18–22	18–22	18–22	18–22
Cylinder Head	15–20 ft. lbs.	15–20 ft. lbs.	15–20 ft. lbs.	15–20 ft. lbs.	15–20 ft. lbs.	25–30 ft. lbs.	25–30 ft. lbs.	25–30 ft. lbs.	25–30 ft. lbs.
Connecting Rod	200 in. lbs.	200 in. lbs.	200 in. lbs.	200 in. lbs.	200 in. lbs.	300 in. lbs.	300 in. lbs.	300 in. lbs.	300 in. lbs.
Flywheel Nut	50–60 ft. lbs.	50–60 ft. lbs.	50–60 ft. lbs.	50–60 ft. lbs.	50–60 ft. lbs.	60–70 ft. lbs.	60–70 ft. lbs.	60–70 ft. lbs.	60–70 ft. lbs.

* Measured just below oil ring and at right angles to piston pin

** Measured at top of guide with valve closed

*** Engines built before automatic compression release (ACR)

9

Kohler K-Series Engines 1984–92 2 through 12 Hp

AIR CLEANER AND AIR INTAKE SYSTEM

K series engines are equipped with a high-density paper air cleaner element. Engines of some specifications are also equipped with an oiled foam precleaner that surrounds the paper element.

AIR CLEANER DISASSEMBLY

1. Remove the wing nut and air cleaner cover.
2. Remove the precleaner (if so equipped), paper element and seal.
3. Remove the base screws, air cleaner base, gasket and hose.

AIR CLEANER SERVICE

Precleaner

If so equipped, wash and re-oil the precleaner every 25 operating hours (more often under extremely dusty or dirty conditions).

1. Wash the precleaner in warm eater and detergent.
2. Rinse the precleaner thoroughly until all traces of detergent are eliminated. Squeeze out excess water (do not wring). Allow precleaner to dry.
3. Saturate the precleaner with clean, fresh engine oil. Squeeze out excess oil.
4. Reinstall the precleaner over the paper element.

Paper Element

Every 100 operating hours (more often under extremely dusty or dirty conditions) check the paper element. Replace the element as follows:
1. Remove the precleaner (if so equipped), element cover nut, element cover and paper element.
2. Replace a dirty, bent or damaged element with a new genuine Kohler element. Handle

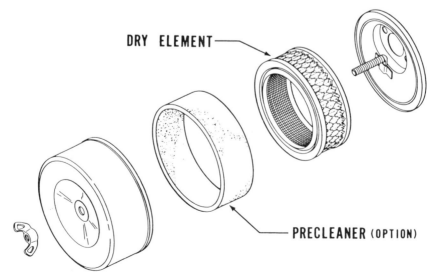

DRY ELEMENT

PRECLEANER (OPTION)

Air cleaner assembly—exploded view

HORSEPOWER (Maximum RPM) Engine Model		4 / K91	7 / K161 *	8 / K181	10 / K241	12 / K301	14 / K321	16 / K341
GENERAL	Bore x Stroke	2.375x2.000	2.938x2.500	2.938x2.750	3.251x2.875	3.375x3.250	3.500x3.250	3.750x3.250
	Displacement Cu. In.	8.86	16.94	18.64	23.85	29.07	31.27	35.90
	Max. Operating RPM	4000	3600	3600	3600	3600	3600	3600
BALANCE GEAR	Shaft O.D. New	—	—	—	.4998/.5001	.4998/.5001	.4998/.5001	.4998/.5001
	Shaft O.D. Maximum Wear Limit	—	—	—	.4996	.4996	.4996	.4996
	End Play	—	—	—	.002/.010	.002/.010	.002/.010	.002/.010
CAMSHAFT	Sleeve I.D. Installed	—	—	—	—	—	—	—
	End Play	.005/.020	.005/.010	.005/.010	.005/.010	.005/.010	.005/.010	.005/.010
CONNECTING ROD	Running Clearance Rod To Crank-Pin (New)	.001/.0025	.001/.002	.001/.002	.001/.002	.001/.002	.001/.002	.001/.002
	Rod To Crank-Pin Wear Limit	.003	.0025	.0025	.0025	.0025	.0025	.0025
	Rod To Piston Pin (New)	.0007/.0008	.0006/.0011	.0006/.0011	.0003/.0008	.0003/.0008	.0003/.0008	.0003/.0008
	Small End I.D. (New)	.5630/.5633	.6255/.6258	.6255/.6258	.8596/.8599	.8757/.8760	.8757/.8760	.8757/.8760
CRANKSHAFT — MAINS	PTO & Flywheel End O.D. New	.9841/.9844	1.1811/1.1814	1.1811/1.1814	1.5745/1.5749	1.5745/1.5749	1.5745/1.5749	1.5745/1.5749
	Maximum Wear Limit	.9841	1.1811	1.1811	1.5745	1.5745	1.5745	1.5745
	Max. Out of Round (Sleeve)	—	—	—	—	—	—	—
	Max. Taper (Sleeve)	—	—	—	—	—	—	—
	Running Clearance (Sleeve) Maximum New	—	—	—	—	—	—	—
	Wear Limit ①	—	—	—	—	—	—	—
	New Sleeve Bearing I.D. Installed	—	—	—	—	—	—	—
CRANKPIN	New	.9360/.9355	1.1860/1.1855	1.1860/1.1855	1.5000/1.4995	1.5000/1.4995	1.5000/1.4995	1.5000/1.4995
	Max. Wear Limit	.9350	1.1850	1.1850	1.4990	1.4990	1.4990	1.4990
	Max. Out of Round	.0005	.0005	.0005	.0005	.0005	.0005	.0005
	Max. Taper	.001	.001	.001	.001	.001	.001	.001
	End Play	.004/.023	.002/.023	.002/.023	.003/.020	.003/.020	.003/.020	.003/.020
CYLINDER BORE	Inside Diameter New	2.3755/2.3745	2.9380/2.9370	2.9380/2.9370	3.2515/3.2505	3.3755/3.3745	3.5005/3.4995	3.7505/3.7495
	Maximum Wear Limit	2.378	2.941	2.941	3.254	3.378	3.503	3.753
	Max. Out of Round	.003	.003	.003	.003	.003	.003	.003
	Max. Taper	.003	.003	.003	.002	.002	.002	.002
CYLINDER HD.	Max. Out of Flatness	.003	.003	.003	.003	.003	.003	.003
IGNITION	Spark Plug Type⑥	RCJ-8	RCJ-8	RCJ-8	RH-10	RH-10	RH-10	RH-10
	Plug Type & Gap — Battery	.025	.025	.025	.035	.035	.035	.035
	Magneto	.025	.025	.025	.025	.025	.025	.025
	Gaseous Fuels	.018	.018	.018	.018	.018	.018	.018
	Nominal Point Gap	.020	.020	.020	.020	.020	.020	.020
PISTON ⑦	Service Replacement Sizes				.003 — .010 — .020 — .030			
	Thrust Face O.D.⑦ New	2.371/2.369	2.9297/2.9281	2.9297/2.9281	3.2432/3.2413	3.368/3.365	3.4941/3.4925	3.7425/3.7410⑨
	Maximum Wear Limit	2.366	2.925	2.925	3.238	3.363	3.491	3.738⑨
	Thrust Face To Bore Clearance (New)①②	.0035/.006	.007/.010	.007/.010	.007/.010	.007/.010	.007/.010	.007/.010⑨
	Ring End Gap New Bore	.007/.017	.007/.017	.007/.017	.010/.020	.010/.020	.010/.020	.010/.020
	Ring End Gap Used Bore (Max.)	.027	.027	.027	.030	.030	.030	.030
	Max. Ring Side Clearance	.006	.006	.006	.006	.006	.006	.006
PISTON ⑨	Service Replacement Sizes				.003 — .010 — .020 — .030			
	Thrust Face O.D.⑨ New	—	—	2.9329/2.9336	—	3.3700/3.3693	3.4945/3.4938	3.7465/3.7455
	Maximum Wear Limit	—	—	2.931	—	3.367	3.492	3.744
	Thrust Face To Bore Clearance (New)①③	—	—	.0034/.0051	—	.0045/.0062	.0050/.0067	.0030/.0050
	Ring End Gap New Bore⑤	—	—	.010/.023	—	.010/.020	.010/.020	.010/.020
	Ring End Gap Used Bore (Max.)	—	—	.032	—	.030	.030	.030
	Max. Ring Side Clearance	—	—	.006	—	.006	.006	.006
PISTON PIN	Outside Diameter	.5623/.5625	.6247/.6249	.6247/.6249	.8591/.8593	.8752/.8754	.8752/.8754	.8752/.8754
VALVES	Guide Reamer Size	.250	.3125	.3125	.3125	.3125	.3125	.3125
	Tappet Clearance (Cold) Intake	.005/.009	.006/.008	.006/.008	.008/.010	.008/.010	.008/.010	.008/.010⑨
	Exhaust	.011/.015	.017/.019	.017/.019	.017/.019	.017/.019	.017/.019	.017/.019
	Minimum Lift (Zero Lash) Intake	.2035	.2718	.2718	.318	.318	.318	.318
	Exhaust	.1768	.2482	.2482	.318	.318	.318	.318
	Minimum Valve Stem O.D. Intake	.2478	.3103	.3103	.3103	.3103	.3103	.3103
	Exhaust	.2458	.3088	.3088	.3074	.3074	.3074	.3074
	Nominal Angle Valve Seat	45°	45°	45°	45°	45°	45°	45°
	Guide I.D. Maximum Wear Limit① Intake	.005	.005	.005	.006	.006	.006	.006
	Exhaust	.007	.007	.007	.008	.008	.008	.008

① Maximum limits combination of I.D. and O.D. measurements
② Ball bearing 1.3779/1.3784, Maximum Wear 1.3779
③ Ball bearing 1.7716/1.7721, Maximum Wear 1.7716
④ Pre Series II 1.3733/1.3738, Maximum Wear 1.3728
⑤ Ball bearing .002/.023
⑥ Champion spark plugs or equivalent
⑦ Measure just below oil ring groove and at right angles to piston pin
⑧ 1800 RPM generator sets .005/.007
⑨ Measure ½" above the bottom of the piston skirt.
⑩ Top and center compression rings.

* Includes K141

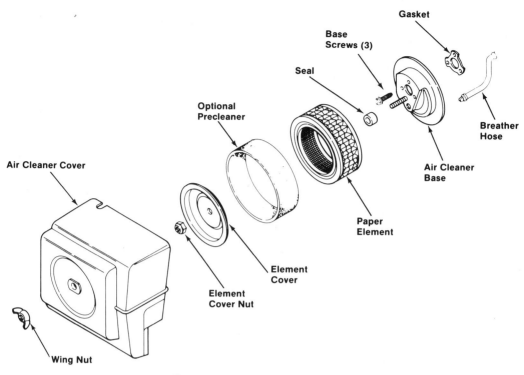

K181 new look, air cleaner assembly

new elements carefully; do not use if surfaces are bent or damaged.

NOTE: *Do not wash the paper element or use compressed air as this will damage the element.*

3. Reinstall the paper element.

4. Install the precleaner (cleaned and oiled) over the paper element.

5. Install the air cleaner cover and wing nut. Tighten wing nut. Make sure element is sealed tightly against air cleaner base.

Inspect Air Cleaner Components

Whenever the air cleaner cover is removed, or when servicing the paper element or precleaner, check the following components:

1. Air cleaner Base - Make sure it is secured tightly to carburetor and is not bent or damaged.

2. Element Cover and Element Cover Nut - On K181 New Look engines only, make sure element cover is not bent or damaged. Check that

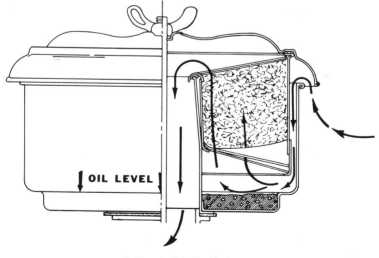

Optional oil bath air cleaner

element cover nut is secured tightly to seal element between air cleaner base and element cover. Tighten nut to 50 inch lbs. torque.

3. Breather Tube - Make sure it is sealed tightly in the air cleaner base and breather cover.

NOTE: *On Model K181 New Look engines of certain specifications, the element cover may contact the breather tube, making it impossible to maintain crankcase vacuum. To prevent this problem, cut the end of the breather tube that protrudes through the air cleaner base at approximately a 45 degree angle.*

WARNING: *Damaged, worn or loose air cleaner components could allow unfiltered air into the engine causing premature wear and failure. Replace any damaged or worn components.*

OPTIONAL OIL BATH AIR CLEANER

If the engine has an oil bath type air cleaner, clean and service it after every 25 hours of operation or more frequently if conditions warrant.

1. Remove the cover, lift the element out of the bowl and drain the oil from the bowl.

2. Thoroughly wash bowl and cover in clean solvent. Swish the element in the solvent and allow it to dry.

NOTE: *Do not use compressed air to dry the element. The filtering material could be damaged.*

3. Lightly re-oil the element with engine oil.

4. Inspect base and cover gaskets. Replace if damaged.

5. Install base gasket and place filter on air horn.

6. Add engine oil to filter and fill to the OIL LEVEL mark.

7. Install filter element, cover gasket and cover. Secure with wing nut finger tight only.

COOLING AIR INTAKE SYSTEM

Effective cooling of an air cooled engine depends on an unobstructed flow of air over the cooling fins. Air is drawn into the cooling shroud by fins located on the flywheel. The blower housing, cooling shroud, air screen covering the flywheel and cooling fins on the cylinder and cylinder head must be kept clean and unobstructed at all times.

Never operate the engine with the blower housing or cooling shroud - removed. These devices direct air flow over the cooling fins.

NOTE: *Some engines use a plastic grass screen and some use metal. The two are not interchangeable unless other modifications are made to the engine.*

FUEL SYSTEM AND GOVERNOR

Fuel System

The typical gasoline fuel system and related components include the fuel tank with vented cap, shutoff valve screen, in-line fuel filter, fuel pump (some models), carburetor and interconnecting fuel line.

Operation

The fuel from the tank is moved through the screen and shutoff valve, in-line filter and fuel lines by the fuel pump (if so equipped) or gravity. Fuel enters the carburetor float bowl and is moved into the carburetor body where it is mixed with air. The fuel-air mixture is drawn into the combustion chamber where it is compressed, then ignited by the spark plug.

CAUTION: *Gasoline may be present in the carburetor and fuel system. Gasoline is extremely flammable and it can explode if ignited. Keep sparks, open flames, and other sources of ignition away from the engine. Disconnect and ground the spark plug lead to prevent the possibility of sparks from the ignition system.*

Fuel Tank

Engine-mounted fuel tanks on K series engines are constructed of steel. They are fitted with a vented cap. The venting properties of the cap should be checked regularly. A clogged vent can cause pressure buildup in the tank, which could result in fuel spraying from the filler when the cap is loosened. It can also cause a partial vacuum in the tank, stopping the engine.

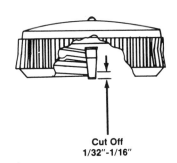

Cut Off
1/32"-1/16"

Fuel tank cap. ("new look" only)

Fuel Shutoff Valve

Some engines are equipped with a fuel shutoff valve with a wire mesh screen. On engines without a shutoff valve, a straight outlet fitting is used. The wire mesh prevents relatively large particles in the tank from reaching the carburetor. The shutoff valve permits work on the fuel system without the need for draining the tank.

Fuel Filter

Some engines covered by this manual may be equipped with a see-through inline fuel filter. When the interior of the filter appears to be dirty, it should be replaced.

Fuel Pump

All K series except the K91 have provisions for mounting a mechanically operated fuel pump. If no fuel pump is mounted on these engines, a cover is placed over the pump mounting pad on the crankcase.

Older fuel pumps have a metal body. Later models have a body made of plastic. The plastic body better insulates the fuel from the hot engine, minimizing the chance of vapor lock.

OPERATION

The mechanical fuel pump is operated by a lever that rides on the engine camshaft. The lever transmits a pumping action to the flexible diaphragm inside the pump body. The pumping action draws fuel in through the inlet check valve on the downward stroke of the diaphragm. On the upward stroke, the fuel is forced out through the outlet check valve.

REMOVAL

1. Disconnect the fuel lines from the inlet and outlet fittings of the pump.
2. Remove the fillister head screws, flat washers, fuel pump and gasket.
3. If required, remove the fittings from the pump body.

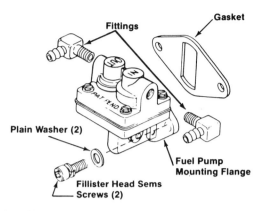

Installing fuel pump

REPAIR

Plastic bodied fuel pumps are not serviceable and must be replaced when faulty. Replacement pumps are available in kits which include the pump, mounting gasket and plain washers.

INSTALLATION

1. Fittings - Apply a small amount of Permatex Aviation Perm A Gasket® (or equivalent gasoline resistant thread sealant) to fittings. Turn fittings into pump six full turns; continue turning fittings in the same direction until desired direction is reached.

2. Install new gasket, fuel pump, flat washers, lock washers and fillister head screws.

NOTE: *Make sure that the fuel pump lever is positioned above the camshaft. Damage to the fuel pump ad severe damage to the engine could result if the lever is positioned below the camshaft.*

Make sure that the flat washers are installed next to the mounting flange to prevent damage from the lock washers.

If a metal bodied pump was replaced by a plastic bodied pump, make sure that the old thick gasket is discarded and the new thin gasket is used.

3. Torque screws 37 - 45 inch lbs.

4. Connect fuel lines to inlet and outlet fittings.

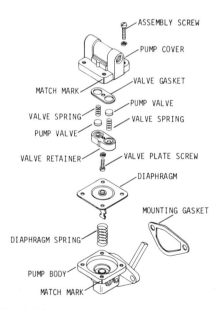

Mechanical fuel pump

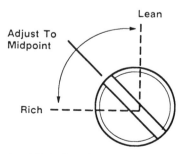

Optimum low idle fuel setting

PRELIMINARY SETTINGS – K-SERIES MODELS

	KOHLER ADJUSTABLE JET		WALBRO FIXED JET	
	Low Idle	High Idle	Low Idle	NOTE: Refer to publication TP2377B Carburetor Reference Manual for additional information.
K91	1–1/2 turns	2 turns	NOT APPL.	
K141	1–1/2 turns	3 turns	NOT APPL.	
K161*	1–1/2 turns	3 turns	NOT APPL.	
K181*	1–1/4 turns	2 turns	2–1/2 turns	
K241	2–1/2 turns	2 turns	1–1/4 turns	
K301	2–1/2 turns	2 turns	1–1/4 turns	
K321	2–1/2 turns	3–1/4 turns	1–1/2 turns	
K341	2–1/2 turns	3–1/2 turns	1 turn	

* Includes "New Look" Models

Preliminary low idle and high idle fuel needle settings

Carburetor

CAUTION: *Gasoline may be present in the carburetor and fuel system. Gasoline is extremely flammable and it can explode if ignited. Keep sparks, open flames, and other sources of ignition away from the engine. Disconnect and ground the spark plug lead to prevent the possibility of sparks from the ignition system.*

ADJUSTMENT

The carburetor is designed to deliver the correct fuel/air mixture to the engine under all operating conditions. Carburetors are set at the factory and normally do not need adjustment. If the engine exhibits conditions like those found in the table that follows, it may be necessary to adjust the carburetor.

In general, turning the adjusting needles in (clockwise) decreases the supply of fuel to the carburetor. This gives a leaner fuel-to-air mixture. Turning the adjusting needles out (counterclockwise) increases the supply of fuel to the carburetor. This gives a richer fuel-to-air mixture. Setting the needles midway between the lean and rich positions will usually give the best results. Adjust the carburetor as follows:

1. With the engine stopped, turn the low idle

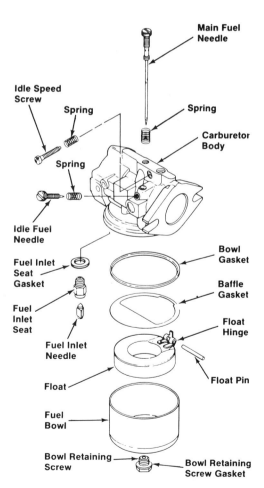

Kohler-built adjustable jet carburetor—exploded view

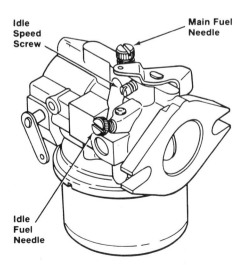

Kohler-built adjustable jet carburetor

fuel adjusting needle in (clockwise) until it bottoms lightly.

NOTE: *The tip of the low idle fuel and high idle fuel adjusting needles are tapered to critical dimensions. Damage to the needles and the seats in carburetor body will result if the needles are forced.*

2. Preliminary Settings: Turn the adjusting needles out (counterclockwise) from lightly bottomed according to the table shown.

3. Start the engine and run at half throttle for five to ten minutes to warm up. The engine must be warm before making final settings (Steps 4, 5, 6, and 7).

4. High Idle Fuel Needle Setting: This adjustment is required only for adjustable high idle (main) jet carburetors. If the carburetor is a fixed main jet type, go to step 5.

a. Place the throttle into the "fast" position. If possible, place the engine under load.

b. Turn the high idle fuel adjusting needle out — counterclockwise — from the preliminary setting until the engine speed decreases (rich). Note the position of the needle.

c. Now turn the adjusting needle in (clockwise). The engine sped may increase, then it will decrease as the needle id turned in (lean). Note the position of the needle.

d. Set the adjusting needle midway between the rich and lean settings.

5. Low Idle Speed Setting: Place the throttle control into the "idle" or "slow" position. Set the low idle speed to 1200 rpm ± 75rpm by turning the low idle speed adjusting screw in or out. Check the speed using a tachometer.

NOTE: *The actual low idle speed depends on the application. Refer to the equipment manufacturer's instructions for specific low idle speed settings. The recommended low idle speed for Basic Engines is 1200 rpm. To ensure best results when setting the low idle fuel needle, the low idle speed must not exceed 1500 rpm.*

6. Low Idle Fuel Setting: Place the throttle into the "idle" or "slow" position.

a. Turn the low idle fuel adjusting needle out (counterclockwise) from the preliminary setting until the engine speed decreases (rich). Note the position of the needle.

b. Now turn the adjusting needle in (clockwise). The engine speed may increase, then it will decrease as the needle is turned in (lean). Note the position of the needle.

c. Set the adjusting needle midway between the rich and lean settings.

7. Recheck the low idle speed using a tachometer. Readjust the speed as necessary.

DISASSEMBLY

1. Remove the bowl retaining screw, retaining screw gasket and fuel bowl.

2. Remove the float pin, float, fuel inlet needle, baffle gasket and bowl gasket.

3. Remove the fuel inlet seat and inlet seat gasket. Remove the idle fuel and main fuel adjusting needles and springs. Remove the idle speed adjusting screw and spring.

4. Further disassembly to remove the throttle and choke shafts is recommended only if these parts are to be replaced. Refer to "Throttle and Choke Shaft Replacement" later in this section.

Cleaning

CAUTION: *Carburetor cleaners and solvents are extremely flammable. Keep sparks, flames and other sources of ignition away from the area. Follow the cleaner manufacturer's warnings and instructions on its proper and safe use. Never use gasoline as a cleaning agent.*

All parts should be carefully cleaned using a carburetor cleaner (such as acetone). Be sure all gum deposits are removed from the following areas:

• Carburetor body and bore; especially the areas where throttle plate, choke plate and shafts are seated.

• Float and hinge.

• Fuel bowl.

• Idle fuel and "off-idle" ports in carburetor bore, ports in main fuel adjusting needle and main fuel seat.

NOTE: *These areas can be cleaned using a piece of fine wire in addition to cleaners. Be careful not to enlarge the ports or break the cleaning wire within the ports.*

Blow out all passages with compressed air.

NOTE: *Do not submerge carburetor in cleaner or solvent when fiber or rubber seals are installed. The cleaner may damage these seals.*

INSPECTION

1. Carefully inspect all components and replace those that are worn or damaged.

2. Inspect the carburetor body for cracks, holes and other wear or damage.

3. Inspect the float for dents or holes. Check the float hinge for wear and missing or damaged float tabs.

4. Inspect the inlet needle and seat for wear or grooves.

5. Inspect the tips of the main and idle adjusting needles for wear or grooves.

6. Inspect the throttle and choke shafts and plate assemblies for wear or excessive play.

CHOKE PLATE MODIFICATION

The choke action has been changed on production carburetors to reduce the chances of over choking. On production carburetors now used on the K241 and K301, one relief hole is

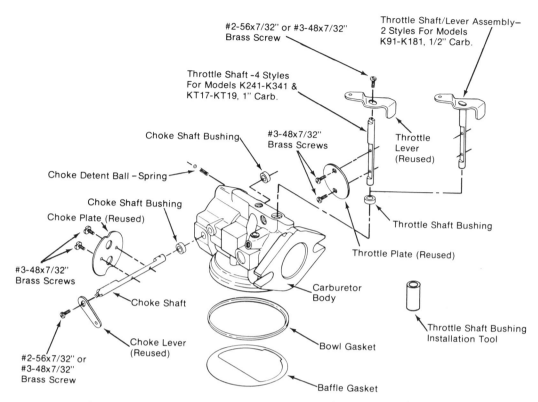

Throttle and choke shaft replacement kits

now $\frac{11}{32}$ in. and the other is $\frac{3}{16}$ in. If you find that the relief holes are smaller than this, enlarge them to these dimensions.

NOTE: *When redrilling the holes, take the necessary precautions to prevent chips from entering the engine.*

REPAIR

Always use new gaskets when servicing and reinstalling carburetors. Several repair kits,

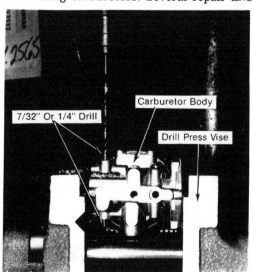

Aligning/drilling carburetor body

which include the gaskets and other components, are available. Always refer to the Parts Manual for the engine being serviced to ensure that the correct carburetor repair kits and replacement parts are ordered.

CAUTION: *Suitable eye protection (safety glasses, goggles, or face hood) should be worn for any procedure involving the use of compressed air, punches, hammers, chisels, drills, or grinding tools.*

Throttle And Choke Shaft Replacement

Two kits are available that allow replacement of the carburetor throttle and choke shafts.

1. To ensure correct reassembly, mark choke plate and carburetor body with a marking pen. Also take note of choke plate position in bore and choke lever position.

2. Carefully and slowly remove the screws securing choke plate to choke shaft. remove and save the choke plate as it will be reused.

3. File off any burrs which may have been left on the choke shaft when the screws were removed. Place carburetor on workbench with choke side down. Remove choke shaft; the detent ball and spring will fall out.

4. Note the position of the choke lever with respect to the cut out portion of the choke shaft.

5. Carefully grind or file away the riveted portion of the shaft. remove and save the choke lever; discard the old choke shaft.

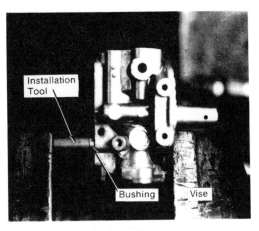

Installing throttle shaft bushing

6. Attach the choke lever to the new choke shaft from the kit. Make sure the lever is installed correctly as noted in step 4. Secure lever to choke shaft as follows:

- Models K91 - K181; Apply Loctite® to threads of 1 #2-56 x $\frac{7}{32}$ in. brass screw. Secure lever to shaft.
- Models K241 - K341; Apply Loctite® to threads of 1 #3-48 x $\frac{7}{32}$ in. brass screw. Secure lever to shaft.

Throttle Plate and Throttle Shaft; Transfer Throttle Lever

1. To ensure correct reassembly, mark throttle plate and carburetor body with a marking pen. Also take note of the throttle plate position in the bore and the throttle lever position.

2. Carefully and slowly remove the screws securing the throttle plate to throttle shaft. Remove and save the throttle plate for reuse.

3. File off any burrs that may have been left on the throttle shaft when screws were removed.

NOTE: *Failure to remove burrs from the throttle shaft may cause permanent damage to carburetor body when shaft is removed.*

4. Remove throttle shaft from carburetor body. Remove and discard the foam rubber dust seal from the throttle shaft.

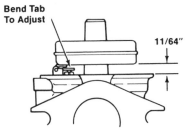

Inverted Carburetor

Setting float level

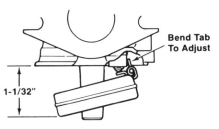

Setting float drop

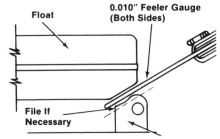

Inverted Carburetor

Checking float clearance

5. Remove and transfer the throttle lever as follows:

- Models K91 - K181 (½ in. Carb.): Carefully grind or file away the riveted portion of the throttle shaft. Save the throttle shaft as it will be used to install the new throttle shaft bushing. Discard the throttle lever.
- Models K241 - K341 (1 in. Carb.):

a. Note the position of the throttle lever with respect to the cutout portion of the throttle shaft.

b. Carefully grind or file away the riveted portion of the shaft. Remove the throttle lever.

c. Compare the old shaft with the new shafts in the kit. Select the appropriate new shaft and discard the old shaft.

d. Attach throttle lever to throttle shaft.

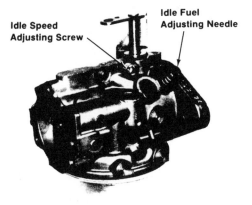

Fixed main jet carburetor

Make sure lever is installed correctly as noted in step a.

e. Apply Loctite® to threads of 1 #2-56 x $^7/_{32}$ in. brass screw (use #3-48 x $^7/_{32}$ in. screw if shaft is $2^{49}/_{64}$ in. long. Secure lever to shaft.

Drilling Choke Shaft Bores Using A Drill Press

1. Mount the carburetor body in a drill press vise. Keep the vise jaws slightly loose.
2. Install a drill bit of the following size in

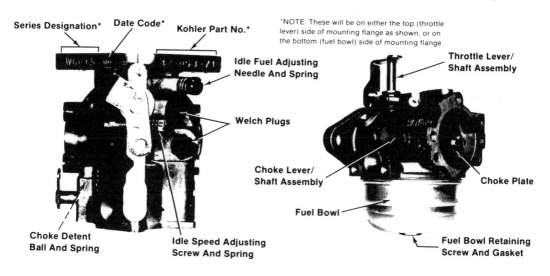

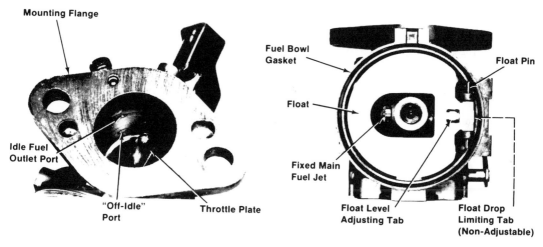

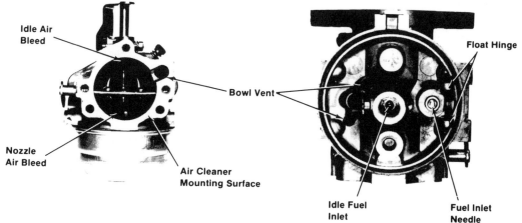

Major components and service locations—typical fixed jet carburetor

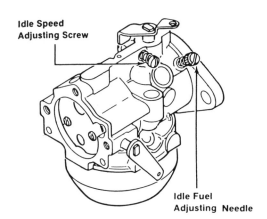

Fixed main jet carburetor

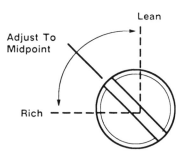

Optimum low idle fuel setting

the drill press chuck. Lower the bit (not rotating) through both choke shaft bores; then tighten vise. This ensures accurate alignment of the carburetor body with the drill press chuck.
- Models K91 - K181 (½ in. Carb.); Use a $\frac{7}{32}$ in. diameter drill bit.
- Models K241 - K341 (1 in. Carb.) Use a ¼ in. diameter drill bit.

3. install a $\frac{19}{64}$ in. drill bit in the chuck. Set drill press to a low speed suitable for aluminum. Drill slowly to ensure a good finish.

4. Ream the choke shaft bores to a final size of $\frac{5}{16}$ in.. For best results use a piloted $\frac{5}{16}$ in. reamer.

5. Blow out all metal chips using compressed air. Thoroughly clean the carburetor body in carburetor cleaner.

Installing Choke Shaft Bushings

1. Install screws in the tapered holes that enter the choke shaft bores until the screws bottom lightly.

2. Coat the outside surface of the kit-supplied choke shaft bushings with Loctite® from the kit. Carefully press the bushings into the carburetor body using a smooth-jawed vise. Stop pressing when bushings bottom against screws. On Models K91 - K181 (½ in. Carb.); Make sure the bushing is pressed below the surface of the large choke shaft boss until the bushing bottoms against the screw.

3. Allow Loctite® to "set" for 5 to 10 minutes, then remove screws.

4. Install new choke shaft in bushings. Rotate shaft and check that it does not bind.

NOTE: *If binding occurs, locate and correct the cause before proceeding. Use choke shaft to align bushings if necessary.*

5. Remove choke shaft and allow Loctite® to "set" for an additional 30 minutes before proceeding.

6. Wipe away any excess Loctite® from bushings and choke shaft.

Installing throttle Shaft Bushing

1. Make sure the dust seal counterbore in the carburetor body is thoroughly clean and free of chips and burrs.

PRELIMINARY SETTINGS

K–SERIES MODELS	KOHLER ADJUSTABLE JET		WALBRO FIXED JET	WALBRO ADJUSTABLE JET	
	Low Idle	High Idle	Low Idle	Low Idle	High Idle
				2 B DETERMD	2 B DETERMD
K91	1–1/2 turns	2 turns	NOT APPL.	NOT APPL.	NOT APPL.
K141	1–1/2 turns	3 turns	NOT APPL.	2 B DETERMD	2 B DETERMD
K161*	1–1/2 turns	3 turns	NOT APPL.	2–1/2 turns	3/4 turn
K181*	1–1/4 turns	2 turns	2–1/2 turns	1–3/4 turns	1–1/8 turns
K241	2–1/2 turns	2 turns	1–1/4 turns	1–3/4 turns	1–1/8 turns
K301	2–1/2 turns	2 turns	1–1/4 turns	2 B DETERMD	2 B DETERMD
K321	2–1/2 turns	3–1/4 turns	1–1/2 turns	2 B DETERMD	2 B DETERMD
K341	2–1/2 turns	3–1/2 turns	1 turn	1–1/4 turns	1–1/4 turns
KT17	1 turn	2–1/2 turns	1–1/4 turns	1–1/4 turns	1 turn
KT19	1 turn	2–1/2 turns	1–1/4 turns	2 B DETERMD	2 B DETERMD
K582	1–1/4 turns	3 turns	NOT APPL.		

*Includes "New Look" Models

Preliminary low idle and high idle fuel needle settings

2. Install a throttle shaft (without throttle lever) in carburetor body to use as a pilot:
- Models K91 - K181 (½ in. Carb.); Use the old throttle shaft removed previously.
- Models K141 - K341 (1 in. Carb.); Use one of the remaining new throttle shafts from the kit.

3. Coat the outside surface of the throttle shaft bushing with Loctite® from the kit. Slip the bushing over the shaft. Using a vise and the installation tool from the kit, press the bushing into the counterbore until it bottoms in the carburetor body.

4. Allow the Loctite® to "set" for 5 to 10 minutes, then remove the throttle shaft.

5. Install the new throttle shaft and lever in carburetor body. Rotate the shaft and check that it does not bind.

NOTE: *If binding occurs, locate the cause and correct before proceeding. use throttle shaft to align bushing if necessary.*

6. Remove the shaft and allow the Loctite® to "set" for an additional 30 minutes before proceeding.

7. Wipe away all excess Loctite® from bushing and throttle shaft.

Installing Detent Spring and Ball, Choke Shaft and Choke Plate

1. Install new detent spring and ball in carburetor body in the side opposite the choke lever.

2. Compress detent ball and spring and insert choke shaft through bushings. Make sure the choke lever is on the correct side of the carburetor body.

3. Compress choke plate to choke shaft. Make sure marks are aligned and plate is positioned properly in the bore. Apply Loctite® to threads of 2 #3-48 x $\frac{7}{32}$ in. brass screws. Install screws so that they are slightly loose.

4. Operate the choke lever. Check that there is no binding between choke plate and carburetor bore. Loosen screws and adjust plate as necessary; then tighten screws.

Installing Throttle Shaft and Throttle Plate

1. Install throttle shaft in carburetor with cutout portion of the shaft facing out.

2. Attach throttle plate to throttle shaft. Make sure marks are aligned and plate is positioned properly in the bore. Apply Loctite® to threads of 2 #3-48 x $\frac{7}{32}$ in. brass screws. Install screws so that they are slightly loose.

3. Apply finger pressure to throttle shaft to keep it firmly seated against pivot in carburetor body. Rotate the throttle shaft until the throttle plate fully closes the bore around its perimeter; then tighten screws.

4. Operate the throttle lever and check that the throttle plate does not bind in the bore. Loosen screws and adjust plate if necessary; then tighten screws securely.

CARBURETOR ASSEMBLY

1. Install the fuel inlet seat gasket and fuel inlet seat into the carburetor body. Torque seat to 35-45 inch lbs.

2. Install the fuel inlet needle into inlet seat. Install float and slide float pin through float hinge and float hinge towers on carburetor body.

3. Set float level: Invert carburetor so the float tab rests on the fuel inlet needle. There should be $\frac{11}{64}$ in. ± $\frac{1}{32}$ in.) clearance between the machined surface of the body and the free end of the float. Bend the float tab with a small screwdriver to adjust.

4. Set float drop: Turn the carburetor over to its normal operating position and allow float to drop to its lowest level. The float drop should be limited to $1\frac{1}{32}$ in. between the machined surface of body and the bottom of the free end of float. Bend the float tab with a small screwdriver to adjust.

5. Check float-to-float hinge tower clearance: Invert the carburetor so the float tab rests on the fuel inlet needle. Insert a 0.010 in. feeler gauge between the float and float hinge towers. If the feeler gauge cannot be inserted, or there is interference between the float and towers, file the towers to obtain the proper clearance.

6. Install the bowl and baffle gasket. Position baffle gasket so the inner edge is against the float hinge towers.

7. Install the fuel bowl so it is centered on the baffle gasket. Make sure the baffle gasket and bowl are positioned properly to ensure a good seal.

8. Install the bowl retaining screw gasket and bowl retaining screw Torque screw to 50-60 inch lbs.

9. Install the idle speed adjusting screw and spring. Install the idle fuel and main fuel adjusting needles and springs. Turn the adjusting needles clockwise until they are bottomed lightly.

NOTE: *The ends of adjusting needles are tapered to critical dimensions. Damage to needles and seats will result if needles are forced.*

10. Reinstall the carburetor to the engine using a new gasket.

11. Adjust the carburetor as outlined under the "Adjustment" portion of this section.

WALBRO FIXED/ADJUSTABLE CARBURETOR

This section covers the idle adjustment, disassembly, cleaning, inspection, repair, and reassembly of the Walbro-built, side draft, fixed/adjustable main jet carburetors.

CAUTION: *Before servicing the carburetor, engine, or equipment, always remove the spark plug leads to prevent the engine from starting accidentally. Ground the leads to prevent sparks that could cause fires.*

Gasoline may be present in the carburetor and fuel system. Gasoline is extremely flammable and its vapors can explode if ignited. Keep sparks, open flame, and other sources of ignition away from the area to prevent the possibility of fires or explosions.

Suitable eye protection (safety glasses, goggles, or face shield) should be worn for any procedure involving the use of compressed air, punches, hammmers, chisels, drills, or grinding tools.

TROUBLESHOOTING

If engine troubles are experienced that appear to be fuel system related, check the following areas before adjusting or disassembling the carburetor.

- Make sure the fuel tank is filled with clean, fresh gasoline.
- Make sure the fuel tank cap vent is not blocked and that it is operating properly.

- Make sure fuel is reaching the carburetor. This includes checking the fuel shut-off valve, fuel tank filler screen, in-line fuel filter, fuel lines, and fuel pump for restrictions or faulty components as necessary.
- Make sure the carburetor is securely fastened to the engine using gaskets in good condition.
- Make sure the air cleaner element is clean and all air cleaner components are fastened securely.
- Make sure the ignition system, governor system, exhaust system, and throttle and choke controls are operating properly.
- If, after checking the items listed above, starting problems or other conditions similar to those listed in the following table exist, it may be necessary to adjust or service the carburetor.

CARBURETOR ADJUSTMENT

NOTE: *The tip of the low idle fuel and high idle fuel adjusting needles are tapered to critical dimensions. Damage to the needles and the seats in carburetor body will result if the needles are forced.*

In general, turning the adjusting needles in (clockwise) decreases the supply of fuel to the carburetor. This gives a leaner fuel-to-air mix-

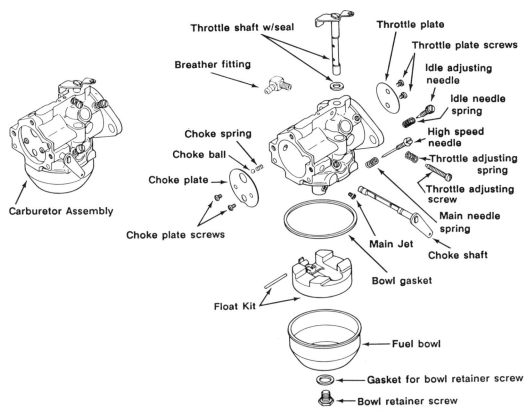

Throttle shaft w/seal Throttle plate Throttle plate screws Breather fitting Idle adjusting needle Idle needle spring High speed needle Choke spring Throttle adjusting spring Choke ball Throttle adjusting screw Choke plate Main needle spring Carburetor Assembly Choke shaft Choke plate screws Main Jet Bowl gasket Float Kit Fuel bowl Gasket for bowl retainer screw Bowl retainer screw

Walbro fixed/adjustable jet carburetor—exploded view

ture. Turning the adjusting needles out (counterclockwise) increases the supply of fuel to the carburetor. This gives richer fuel-to-air mixture. Setting the needles midway between the lean and rich positions will usually give the best results.

Adjust the carburetor as follows:

1. With the engine stopped, turn the low idle fuel adjusting needles in (clockwise) until it bottoms lightly.

2. Preliminary Settings: Turn the adjusting needles out (counterclockwise) from lightly bottomed according to the table shown.

3. Start the engine and run at half throttle for five to ten minutes to warm up. The engine must be war, before making final settings (Steps 4, 5, 6, and 7).

4. High Idle Fuel Needle Setting: This adjustment is required only for adjustable high idle (main) jet carburetors. If the carburetor is fixed main jet type, go to step 5.

    a. Place the throttle into the "fast" position. If possible, place the engine under load.

    b. Turn the high idle fuel adjusting needle out (counterclockwise) from the preliminary setting until the engine speed decreases (rich). Note the position of the needle.

    c. Now turn the adjusting needle in (clockwise). The engine speed may increase, then it will decrease as the needle is turned in (lean). Note the position of the needle.

    d. Set the adjusting needle midway between the rich and lean settings.

5. Low Idle Speed Setting: Place the throttle control control into the "idle" or "slow" position. Set the low idle speed to 1200 rpm ± 75 rpm by turning the low idle speed adjusting screw in or out. Check the speed using a tachometer.

NOTE: *The actual low idle speed depends on the application. Refer to the equipment manufacturer's instructions for specific low idle speed settings. The recommended low idle speed for Basic Engines is 1200 rpm. To ensure best results when setting the low idle fuel needle, the low idle speed must not exceed 1500 rpm.*

6. Low Idle Fuel Needle setting: Place the throttle into the "idle" or "slow" position.

    a. Turn the low idle fuel adjusting needle out (counterclockwise) from the preliminary setting until the engine speed decreases (rich). Note the position of the needle.

    b. Now turn the adjusting needle in (clockwise). The engine speed may increase, then it will decrease as the needle is turned in (lean). Note the position of the needle.

    c. Set the adjusting needle midway between the rich and lean settings.

7. Recheck the low idle speed using a tachometer. Readjust the speed as necessary.

DISASSEMBLY

1. Remove the bowl retaining screw, retaining screw gasket, and fuel bowl.

2. Remove the bowl gasket, float pin, float, and fuel inlet needle.

CAUTION: *To prevent damage to the carburetor, do not attempt to remove the fuel inlet seat as it is not serviceable. Replace the carburetor if the fuel inlet seat is damaged.*

3. Remove the idle fuel adjusting needle and spring. Remove the idle speed adjusting screw and spring.

4. Remove the main fuel jet.

5. In order to clean the "off-idle" ports and the bowl vent channel thoroughly, the welch plugs covering these areas must be removed. Use tool No. K01018 and the following procedure to remove the welch plugs.

    a. Pierce the welch plug with the tip of the tool.

CAUTION: *To prevent damage to the carburetor, do not allow the tool to strike the carburetor body.*

    b. Pry out the welch plug using the tool.

Throttle And Choke Shaft Removal

Further disassembly to remove the throttle shaft and choke shaft is recommended only if these parts are to be cleaned or replaced.

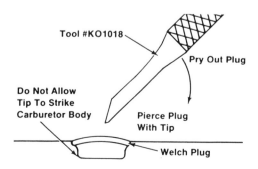

Tool #KO1018

Pry Out Plug

Do Not Allow Tip To Strike Carburetor Body

Pierce Plug With Tip

Welch Plug

Removing welch plugs

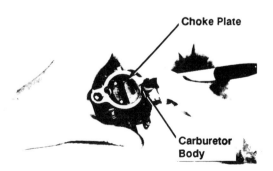

Choke Plate

Carburetor Body

Marking throttle plate and carburetor body

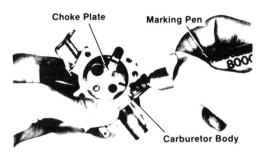

Marking choke plate and carburetor body

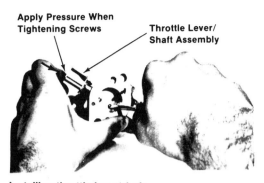

Installing throttle lever/shaft

THROTTLE SHAFT REMOVAL

1. Because the edges of the throttle plate are beveled, mark the throttle plate and carburetor body with a marking pen to ensure correct reassembly. Also take note of the throttle plate position in bore, and the position of the throttle lever.

2. Carefully and slowly remove the screws securing the throttle plate to throttle shaft. Remove the throttle plate.

3. File off any burrs which may have been left on the throttle shaft when the screws were removed. Do this before removing the throttle shaft from carburetor body.

4. Remove the throttle lever/shaft assembly with foam dust seal from carburetor body.

CHOKE SHAFT REMOVAL

1. Because the edges of choke plate are beveled, mark the choke pate and carburetor body with a marking pen to ensure correct reassembly. Also take note of the choke plate position in bore, and the position of the choke lever.

2. Carefully and slowly remove the screws securing the choke plate to choke shaft. Remove the choke plate.

3. file off any burrs which may have been left on the choke shaft when the screws were removed. Do this before removing the choke shaft from carburetor body.

4. Rotate the choke shaft until the cutout portion of shaft is facing the air cleaner mounting surface. Place the carburetor body on the work bench with choke side down. Remove the

choke lever/shaft assembly from carburetor body; the detent ball and spring will drop out.

CLEANING

CAUTION: *Carburetor cleaners and solvents are extremely flammable. Keep sparks, flames, and other sources of ignition away from the area. Follow the cleaner manufacturer's warnings and instructions on its proper and safe use. Never use gasoline as a cleaning agent.*

All parts should be carefully cleaned using a carburetor cleaner (such as acetone). Be sure all gum deposits are removed form the following areas:

• Carburetor body and bore; especially the areas where the throttle plate, choke plate, and shafts are seated.

• Idle fuel and "off-idle" ports in carburetor bore, main jet, bowl vent, and fuel inlet seat.

NOTE: *These areas can be cleaned using a piece of fine wire in addition to cleaners. Be careful not to enlarge the ports, or break the cleaning wire within ports. Blow out all passages with compressed air.*

• Float and Float hinge.

• Fuel Bowl.

• Throttle plate, choke plate, throttle shaft, and choke shaft.

CAUTION: *Do not submerge the carburetor*

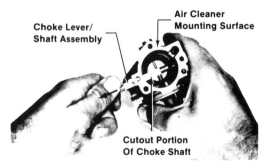

Removing choke lever/shaft

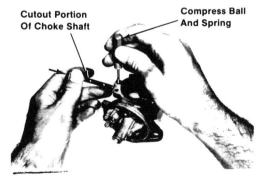

Installing choke lever/shaft

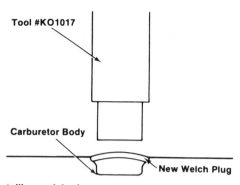

Installing welch plugs

in cleaner or solvents when fiber, rubber, or foam seals or gaskets, or the fuel inlet needle are installed. The cleaner may damage these parts.

INSPECTION

- Carefully inspect all components and replace those that are worn or damaged.
- Inspect the carburetor body for cracks, holes, and other wear or damage.
- Inspect the float for cracks or holes. Check the float hinge for wear, and missing or damaged float tabs.
- Inspect the fuel inlet needle for wear or grooves.
- Inspect the tip of the idle fuel adjusting needle for wear or grooves.
- Inspect the throttle and choke shaft and plate assemblies for wear or excessive play.

REPAIR

Always use new gaskets when servicing and reinstalling carburetors. Repair kits are available which include new gaskets and other components. These kits are described below.

Components such as the throttle and choke shaft assemblies, throttle plate, choke plate, idle fuel needle, main jet, and others, are available separately.

REASSEMBLY

Throttle Shaft Installation

1. Install the foam dust seal on throttle shaft. Insert the throttle lever/shaft assembly into carburetor body with the cutout portion of shaft facing the carburetor mounting flange.
2. Install the throttle plate to throttle shaft. Make sure the plate is positioned properly in bore as marked and noted during disassembly (the numbers stamped on plate should face the carburetor mounting flange). Apply Loctite®

#609 to threads of 2 plate retaining screws. Install screws so they are slightly loose.
3. Apply finger pressure to the throttle lever/shaft to keep it firmly seated against pivot in carburetor body. Rotate the throttle shaft until the throttle plate fully closes the bore around its entire perimeter; then tighten screws.
4. Operate the throttle lever; check for binding between the throttle plate and carburetor bore. Loosen screws and adjust throttle plate as necessary; then torque screws to 8-12 inch lbs.

Choke Shaft Installation

1. Install the detent spring and ball into the carburetor body.
CAUTION: *If the detent ball does not drop through the tapped air cleaner base screw hole by its own weight, do not force it. Forcing the ball could permanently lodge it in the hole. Install the ball through the choke shaft bore instead.*
2. Compress the detent ball and spring. Insert the choke lever/shaft assembly into carburetor body with the cutout portion of shaft facing the air cleaner mounting surface. Make sure the choke lever is on the correct side of carburetor body.
3. Install the choke plate to choke shaft. Make sure the plate is positioned properly in bore as marked and noted during disassembly. (The numbers stamped on plate should face the air cleaner mounting surface and be upright.) Apply Loctite® #609 to threads of 2 plate retaining screws. Install the screws so they are slightly loose.
4. Operate the choke lever; check for binding between the choke plate and carburetor bore. Adjust plate as necessary; then torque screws to 8-12 inch lbs.

Carburetor Reassembly

1. If the welch plugs have been removed for cleaning, new welch plugs must be installed. Use tool No. K01017 and the following procedure to install the welch plugs.

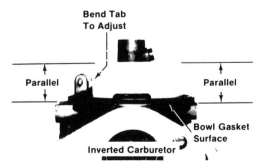

Setting float level

a. Position the carburetor body securely with the welch plug cavities to the top.

b. Place a new welch plug into the cavity with the raised portion up. Use the end of the tool that is about the same size as plug and flatten the plug. Do not force the plug below the top surface.

c. After welch plugs are installed, seal the exposed surface with sealant. Allow the sealant to dry.

NOTE: *If a commercial sealant is not available, fingernail polish can be used.*

2. Install the main fuel jet.

3. Install fuel inlet needle into inlet seat. Install float and slide float pin through float hinge and float hinge towers on carburetor body.

4. Set Float Level: Invert the carburetor so the float tab rests on the fuel inlet needle. The exposed surface of float should be parallel with the bowl gasket surface of the carburetor body (exposed, free end of float 0.690-0.720 in. from bowl gasket surface). Bend the float tab with a small screwdriver to adjust.

5. Install a new bowl gasket and the fuel bowl. Make sure the bowl gasket and bowl are centered and positioned properly to ensure a good seal.

6. Install a new bowl retaining screw gasket and the bowl retaining screw. Torque screw to 45-55 inch lbs.

7. Install the idle speed adjusting screw and spring.

8. Install the idle fuel adjusting needle and spring. turn the adjusting needle in (clockwise) until it bottoms lightly.

CAUTION: *The tip of the idle fuel adjusting needle is tapered to critical dimensions. Damage to the needle and the seat in carburetor body will result if the needle is forced.*

9. Turn the idle fuel needle out (counterclockwise) from lightly bottomed according to the instructions in the "Adjustment" section of this Bulletin.

HIGH ALTITUDE OPERATION (FIXED JET)

When operating the engine at high altitudes, the main fuel mixture tends to get overrich. An overrich mixture can cause conditions such as black, sooty exhaust smoke, misfiring, loss of speed and power, poor fuel economy, and poor or slow governor response.

To compensate for this, a special high altitude main fuel jet is available for each carburetor. The high altitude main fuel jet is sold in a kit which includes the jet and necessary gaskets.

High Altitude Jet Installation (Fixed Jet)

1. Remove the fuel bowl retaining screw, retaining screw gasket, fuel bowl, and bowl gasket.

NOTE: *I necessary, remove the air cleaner and carburetor from engine to make fuel bowl removal easier.*

2. Remove the float pin, float, and fuel inlet needle.

3. Remove the existing main fuel jet.

4. Install the new high altitude main fuel jet and torque to 12-16 inch lbs.

5. Reinstall the fuel inlet needle, float, and float pin.

6. Install the new bowl gasket from kit and the fuel bowl. Make sure the bowl gasket and bowl are centered and positioned properly to ensure a good seal.

7. Install the new bowl retaining screw gasket from kit and the bowl retaining screw. Torque screw to 45-55 inch lbs.

8. Reinstall the carburetor and air cleaner to engine as necessary using the new gaskets from kit.

IDLE ADJUSTMENT PROCEDURE FOR K341AQS ENGINES WITH ANTI-DIESELING SOLENOID

The idle speed of some vibro-mounted K341AQS engines has been increased to allow smoother operation at low idle and an anti-dieseling solenoid has been added to prevent dieseling during shut-down at the higher idle speed. If called upon to adjust the idle on any K341AQS engine with this solenoid, use the following procedure.

STEP 1 - IDLE FUEL MIXTURE ADJUSTMENT: With engine stopped, turn the idle fuel adjusting screw all the way in (clockwise) until it bottoms lightly then back out ½ turn.

STEP 2 - IDLE SPEED ADJUSTMENT: Start engine and check idle speed with a hand tachometer. Idle, no load, speed should be 2100 RPM. To set the idle speed, loosen the jam nut on the anti-dieseling solenoid and turn the solenoid in or out until 2100 RPM idle speed is attained - retighten jam nut to lock solenoid in position.

Thermostatic Type Automatic Chokes

The automatic choke is a heat sensitive thermostatic unit. At room temperature, choke lever will be set in a vertical position. If engine should fail to start when cranked, adjust choke lever by hand to determine if choke setting is too lean or too rich. Once this has been established, adjustment can be made to remedy the situation.

ADJUSTMENT

1. Loosen adjustment lock screw on choke body. This allows the position of adjustment to be changed.

2. Moving adjustment bracket downward will increase the amount of choking. Upward movement will result in less choking.

3. After adjustment is made, tighten adjustment lock screw.

Electric-Thermostatic Type Automatic Chokes

Remove air cleaner from carburetor to observe position of choke plate. Choke adjustment must be made on cold engine. If starting in extreme cold, choke should be in full closed position before engine is started. A lesser degree of choking is needed in milder temperatures.

ADJUSTMENT

1. Move choke arm until hole in brass shaft lines up with slot in bearings.

2. Insert #43 drill (0.089 in.) and push all the way down to engine manifold to engage in notch in base of choke unit.

3. Loosen clamp bolt choke lever, push arm upward to move choke plate toward closed position. After desired position is attained, tighten clamp bolt then remove drill.

4. After replacing air cleaner, check for evidence of binding in linkage, adjust as needed. Be sure chokes are fully open when engine is at normal operating temperature.

TROUBLESHOOTING

Check resistance of heater terminal using an ohmmeter. Resistance should be 3 ohms or more. If resistance is less than 3 ohms, replace the choke.

CHOKE REPLACEMENT AND ADJUSTMENT

1. Position the choke unit on the two mounting screws so that it is slightly loose.

2. Hold the choke plate in the wide open position.

3. Rotate the choke unit clockwise on the carburetor (viewed from the choke side) with a slight pressure until it can no longer be rotated.

4. While holding the choke unit in the above position, tighten the two mounting screws.

NOTE: *With engine not running and before any cranking, the choke plate will be closed 5-10° at a temperature of about 75°F. As the temperature decreases the choke plate will close even more.*

5. Check choke function by removing the spark plug lead and cranking the engine. The choke plate should close a minimum of 45 degrees at temperatures above 75 degrees F. The plate will close more at lower temperatures.

NOTE: *During cranking, the choke will remain closed only 5 to 10 seconds, as choke closing time is controlled by the Decision Maker.*

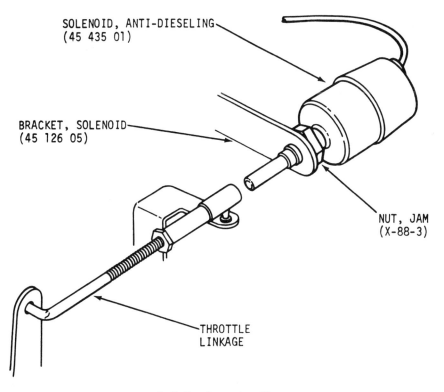

SOLENOID, ANTI-DIESELING
(45 435 01)

BRACKET, SOLENOID
(45 126 05)

NUT, JAM
(X-88-3)

THROTTLE
LINKAGE

Anti-dieseling solenoid

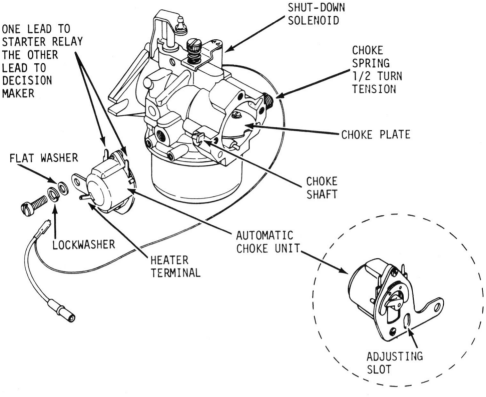

Thermo-electric automatic choke

CHOKE SHAFT SPRING ADJUSTMENT

To adjust the choke spring, hold the plate in the wide open position. Windup the spring ½ turn and then place the straight end of the spring through the hole in the shaft.

FUEL SYSTEM

The main components of the fuel system as used on K series engines are:
- Fuel tank
- Primary regulator
- Secondary regulator
- Carburetor

In some applications, the primary and secondary regulators are combined in one two-stage unit. The gas carburetor and secondary regulator (or two stage regulator) are normally furnished with the engine. Other components are furnished by the fuel supplier.

There are some isolated instances in which the equipment manufacturer supplies the entire fuel system for operation with gas. Information on servicing these systems must be obtained from the equipment manufacturer.

Depending on the air temperature and the mixture of gasses in the tank, pressure at the outlet of the tank can be as high as 180 to 200 psi.

Secondary Regulator

The secondary regulators used on Kohler engines are compact single diaphragm types. This

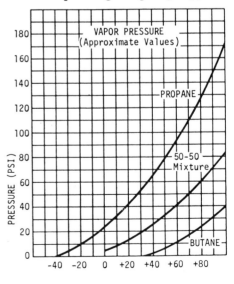

LP gas vapor pressure curve

type regulator accurately regulates the flow of gas to the carburetor and shuts the gas off automatically when the demand for gas ceases. If the regulator fails, it must be replaced or reconditioned by an authorized gas equipment repair shop. Do not attempt to repair a faulty regulator.

Secondary regulators used on Kohler engines require only one adjustment. This adjustment should be performed while the engine is running.

Garretson Model S, SD and KN regulators have a lockoff or fuel control adjustment. Use the following procedure to make this adjustment.

NOTE: *The regulator should be mounted as close to vertical as possible, and adjusted in the position in which it will be mounted on the engine.*

1. Connect regulator inlet to a source of clean compressed air, not over 10 psi. Do not connect to a gas supply.

2. Turn air supply on.

3. If the regulator being adjusted is a Model KN, open the lock off adjusting screw until air just starts flowing through the regulator.

4. Turn the lock off adjusting screw in slowly until air flow stops.

NOTE: *A soap bubble test is a good way to check for complete shutoff. If bubbles indicate that air is still flowing, turn the screw in one more full turn.*

The lock off adjusting screw may be used to adjust fuel flow while the engine is idling. Never adjust at any speed above idle.

5. If the regulator being adjusted is a Model S or SD, depress the primer button for an instant. This will allow air to flow through the regulator.

6. Check the air flow stops when the primer is released.

7. If air flow does not stop completely, loosen the adjustment screw lock nut and turn the adjustment screw in until air flow stops, then one more full turn.

8. Repeat steps 5 through 7 until air flow sops every time.

9. Tighten adjustment screw lock nut.

Primary Regulator

The primary regulator provides initial control of the fuel under pressure as it comes from the fuel supply tank. The inlet pressure for primary regulators should never exceed 250 psi. The primary regulator is adjusted for outlet pressure of approximatelly 6 ounces per square inch (11 in. W.C.). If the regulator does not function properly, replace it or have it serviced by an authorized gas equipment shop. Never attempt to service a faulty primary regulator.

Upon demand for fuel, pressure drops on the outside of the regulator diaphragm. The gas inlet valve then begins to open, allowing fuel to pass through the regulator to the secondary regulator. As the need for more fuel increases, the fuel inlet valve opens further, allowing more fuel to pass.

Pressure may be adjusted by removing the bonnet cap and turning the spring tension adjustment with a large screwdriver. Turning clockwise increases the pressure; turning counterclockwise decreases it.

Two Stage Regulator

The two stage regulator used on Kohler engines is a double diaphragm type regulator designed for use with air-cooled engines. It combines primary and secondary regulation in one unit. The regulator fuel inlet is connected to the fuel tank. Its outlet is connected to the carburetor. If the regulator fails to operate properly, replace it or have it serviced by an authorized gas equipment shop. Never attempt to service a faulty regulator.

Vaporized fuel is admitted to the regulator at fuel tank pressure (up to 250 psi). Because the secondary valve is closed (engine not running), the pressure on the internal side of the primary diaphragm builds until the pressure overcomes the spring action on the opposite side of the diaphragm. This primary diaphragm spring has sufficient tension to require approximately 10 psi pressure on the internal side of the diaphragm to counteract the opening force due to the spring. When the pressure reaches this lev-

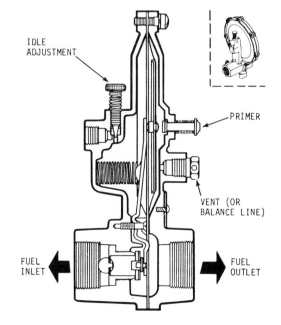

Model F and F1 secondary regulators

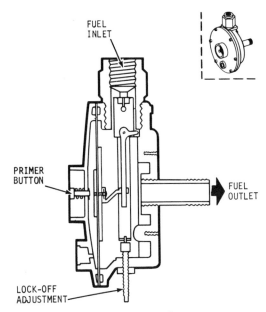

Models S and SD secondary regulators

el, the valve is closed, preventing further pressure rise.

The secondary diaphragm acts against the secondary valve spring. Its action results from vacuum caused by the carburetor. As the vacuum begins acting on the diaphragm, the diaphragm is moved nearer to the center of the regulator, opening the secondary valve until equilibrium is reached. As more fuel is needed, vacuum from the carburetor increases, causing the secondary valve to open further. When fuel is flowing, pressure on the primary diaphragm is lowered slightly, permitting the spring to open the primary valve in an attempt to bring the pressure back to 10 psi.

ADJUSTMENT

1. Turn the secondary adjustment counterclockwise as far as it will go. Then turn it clockwise 3 turns.

2. Connect a source of clean compressed air of at least 25 psi to the regulator inlet an depress primer button 3 times.

3. Connect a 0 to 15 psi pressure gauge to the fuel outlet and press and hold the primer button. The pressure gauge should read approximately 2 psi and hold steady at this reading. If pressure rises slowly, the primary valve is leaking and the regulator must be replaced. If pressure remains constant, proceed.

4. Remove pressure gauge and cover outlet with a film of soap solution. If a bubble forms, the secondary valve is leaking.

5. Slowly turn the secondary adjustment to the left until the bubble expands, then to the right one complete turn to stop the leak. If leaking persists, replace the regulator.

GOVERNOR

Engine speed governors in the K series of engines (with the exception of the K91) are of the centrifugal flyweight mechanical type. The K91 utilizes a flyball. The governor gear and flyweight mechanism are contained within the crankcase. The governor gear is driven by a gear on the camshaft.

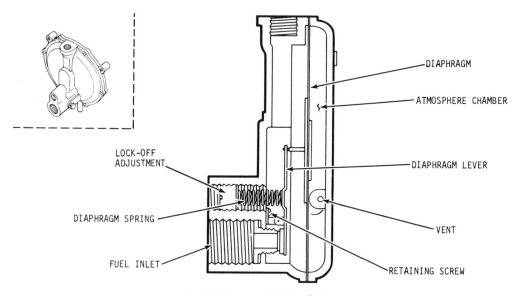

Model KN secondary regulator

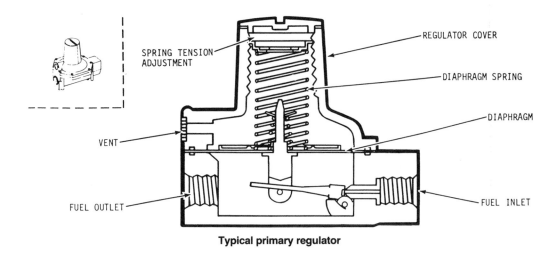

Typical primary regulator

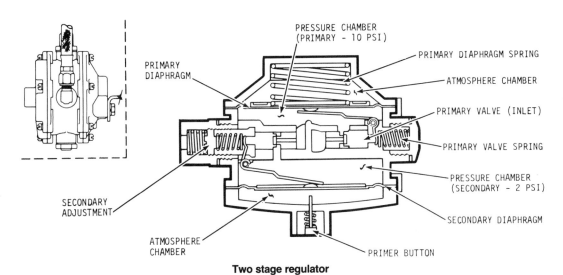

Two stage regulator

Operation

In operation, centrifugal force causes the flyweights (or flyball) to move outward with an increase in speed and inward with a decrease. As the flyweights move outward, they force the regulating pin of the assembly to move outward. The regulating pin contacts the tab on the cross shaft, causing the shaft to rotate with changing speed. One end of the cross shaft protrudes through the side of the crankcase. Through external linkage attached to the cross-shaft, the rotating action is transmitted to the throttle on the carburetor.

When the engine is not running, the governor spring holds the throttle in the open position. When a normal load is applied to an operating engine, the speed tends to decrease. The resulting rotation of the cross shaft acts against the governor spring, opening the throttle wider. This action admits more fuel, restoring engine speed. As speed again reaches the governed setting, the shaft rotates to close the throttle valve enough to maintain governed speed.

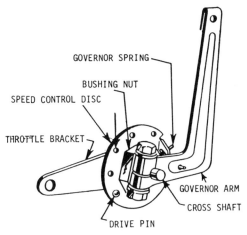

Governor components

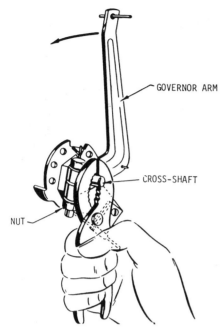

Initial adjustment

Governed speed may be at a fixed point as constant speed applications or variable as determined by a throttle control setting.

INITIAL ADJUSTMENT

K91, K141, K161, K181

Governors are adjusted at the factory. Further adjustment should not be necessary unless the governor arm or linkage work loose or become disconnected. The need for governor adjustment may be indicated by engine speed surges or hunting with changes in load or by a considerable drop in engine speed when a normal speed is applied. The internal governor mechanism is different on the K241 through K341 models. Be sure to follow the adjustment procedure for the model engine being serviced.

1. Loosen, but do not remove, the nut that holds the governor arm to the governor cross shaft.

2. Grasp the end of the cross shaft with pliers and turn counterclockwise as far as possible. The tab on the cross shaft will touch the rod on the governor gear assembly.

3. Pull the governor arm away from the carburetor as far as it will go, then tighten nut holding governor arm to cross shaft.

THROTTLE WIRE INSTALLATION

In those applications where a throttle is to be connected to the engine, connect it as follows.

1. Bend the end of the throttle wire.

2. Place throttle control in open position. Insert throttle wire in speed control disc hole nearest the throttle bracket.

3. Install throttle cable clamp and bolt it to the throttle bracket.

4. Remove drive pin from speed control disc and operate the throttle control, rotating the disc from idle to full speed.

SPEED ADJUSTMENT

CAUTION: *The maximum allowable speed for Model K91 is 4000 RPM. Models K161 and K181 are restricted to 3600 RPM maximum. Never tamper with the governor setting to increase engine speed above these limits. Severe personal injury and damage to the engine or equipment can result if the engine is operated at speeds above these maximums.*

After making an initial adjustment or connecting a throttle wire, set speed adjustment as follows.

1. Start the engine and allow a few minutes for warmup.

2. Open the throttle to full speed and check engine speed with a tachometer. Speed should be approximately 4000 RPM for Model K91 and 3600 RPM for Model K161 or K181.

3. If speed is not as required, slightly loosen the bushing nut at the speed control disc.

4. Move the throttle bracket counterclockwise to increase engine speed or clockwise to decrease speed.

5. When proper speed is set, tighten the bushing nut.

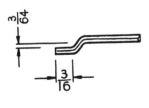

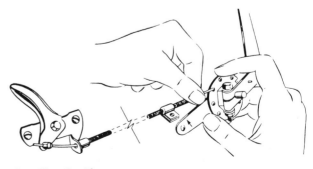

Installing throttle

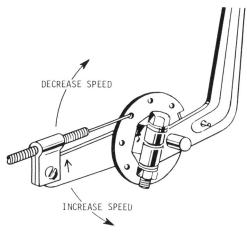

Speed adjustment

NOTE: *Do not use excessive force in tightening the bushing nut. Excessive force could cause binding or stripping of threads.*

OPERATION

Centrifugal force acting on the rotating governor gear assembly causes the flyweights to move outward as speed increases and inward as speed decreases. As the flyweights move outward they force the regulating pin of the assembly to move outward. The regulating pin contacts the tab on the cross shaft, causing the shaft to rotate with changing speed. One end of the cross shaft protrudes through the side of the crankcase. Through external attached to the cross shaft, the rotating action is transmitted to the throttle plate of carburetor.

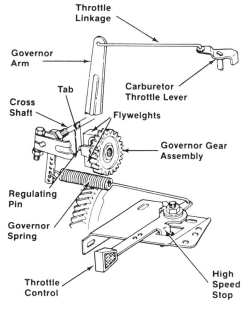

Centrifugal flyweight mechanical governor

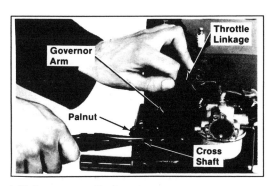

Initial governor adjustment

When the engine is at rest and the throttle is in the "fast" position, the tension of the governor spring holds the throttle valve open. When the engine is operating (governor gear assembly is rotating), the force applied by the regulating pin against the cross shaft tends to close the throttle valve. The governor spring tension and the force applied by the regulating pin are in "equilibrium" during operation, holding the engine speed constant.

When a load is applied and the engine speed (and governor speed) decreases, the governor spring tension moves the governor arm to open the throttle plate wider. This admits more fuel and restores engine speed. (This action takes place very rapidly, so a reduction in speed is hardly noticed.) As the speed reaches the governed setting, the governor spring tension and the force applied by the regulating pin will again be in equilibrium. This maintains engine speed at a relatively constant level.

Governed speed may be at a fixed point as on constant speed applications, or variable as determined by a throttle control lever.

ADJUSTMENT

CAUTION: *The maximum allowable speed for these engines is 3600 RPM, no load. Never tamper with the governor setting to increase the maximum speed. Severe personal injury and damage to the engine or equipment can result if operated at speeds above maximum.*

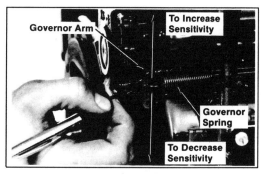

Governor sensitivity adjustment

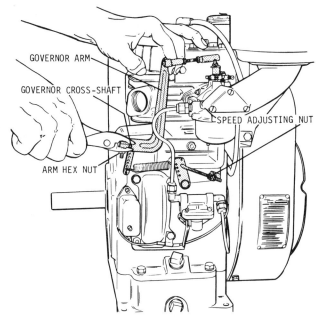

Initial adjustment

Initial Adjustment

Make this initial adjustment whenever the governor arm is loosened or removed from cross shaft. Make sure the throttle linkage is connected to governor arm and throttle lever on carburetor to ensure proper setting.

1. Pull the governor arm away from the carburetor as far as it will go.

2. Grasp the end of cross shaft with pliers and turn counterclockwise as far as it will go.

3. Tighten the pall nut on governor arm to 15 inch lbs. torque.

NOTE: *Make sure there is at least $\frac{1}{16}$ in. clearance between governor arm and cross shaft bushing nut to prevent interference.*

High Speed Adjustment

The maximum allowable speed is 3600 RPM, no load. The actual high speed setting depends

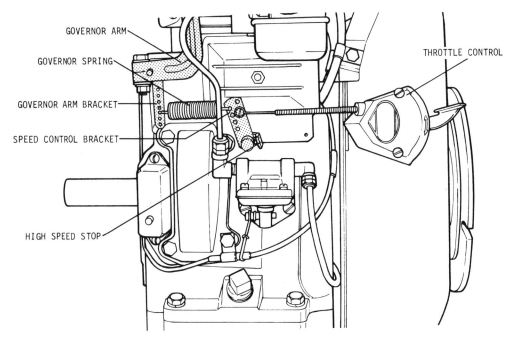

Variable speed governor

on the application. Refer to the equipment manufacturer's instructions for specific high speed settings. Check the operating speed with a tachometer; do not exceed the maximum. To adjust high speed stop:

1. Loosen the lock nut on high speed adjusting screw.

2. Turn the adjusting screw in or out until desired speed is reached. Tighten the lock nut.

3. Recheck the speed with the tachometer; readjust if necessary.

Sensitivity Adjustment

Governor sensitivity is adjusted by repositioning the governor spring in the holes in governor arm. If set too sensitive, speed surging will occur with a change in load. If a big drop in speed occurs when normal load is applied, the governor should be set for greater sensitivity.

The standard spring position is in the third hole from the cross shaft. the position can vary, depending on the engine application. Therefore, make a note of (or mark) the spring position before removing it from the governor arm.

RETRACTABLE STARTERS

Retractable starters are lubricated during manufacturer and should require no further lubrication until disassembly for cord or rewind spring replacement or for other repair.

Frequently check mounting screws to make sure starter is securely tightened on blower housing of engine. If screws are loose, starter realignment may be necessary. Also make sure that the air intake screen is maintained in clean condition at all times.

Model K91 w/Fairbanks-Morse Starters

Starters have die cast aluminum housings. A friction shoe assembly under spring tension is used and engages in the drive cup when the starter handle is pulled. The drive cup is held in place on the engine with flywheel nut. A pin on the cup is engaged in crankshaft keyway to prevent slippage of the drive cup.

OPERATION

1. Be sure starter screen is kept clean when operating engine or serious engine damage can result from lack of cooling air.

2. After engine has started, do not allow starter rope to snap back into starter housing. Continue to hold handle and allow starter rope to rewind slowly.

NOTE: *Releasing handle when starter rope is extended will shorten life of starter.*

3. Do not use starter in a rough manner, such as jerking or pulling starter rope all the way out. A smooth, steady pull will start engine under normal conditions.

4. Always pull starter handle straight out so that rope will not receive excessive wear from friction against guide. Proper procedure will prevent unnecessary wear.

5. If coil starter should ever fail, starter assembly can be removed and engine cranked with a rope. The starter drive cup will serve as a pulley for emergency purposes.

DISASSEMBLY

If starting rope breaks or if staring spring fails, the following procedure should be followed.

NOTE: *Handle rewind springs with caution.*

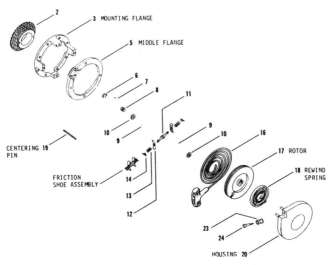

Fairbanks-Morse starter—exploded view

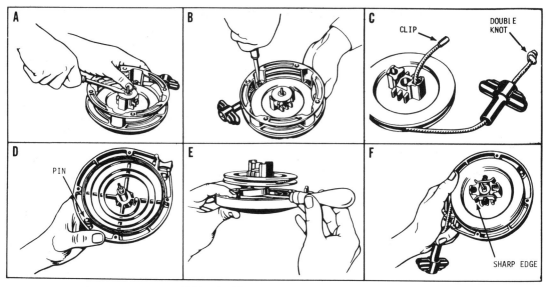

Fairbanks-Morse starter disassembly

1. To remove starter from engine, remove four mounting bolts.

2. Hold washer (Key 7) in position with thumb while removing retainer ring (Key 6) with a screwdriver.

3. Remove washer (Key 7), spring (Key 8), washers (Keys 9 and 10) then remove friction shoe assembly (Keys 11, 12, 13, and 14).

4. Prevent rewind spring from escaping from cover by carefully lifting rotor about ½ in. and detach inside spring loop from rotor.

NOTE: *If spring should escape, it can easily be replaced in cover by coiling in turns.*

STARTING ROPE REPLACEMENT

When installing a new rope (Key 16) in rotor, thread through rotor hole, then wind rope onto rotor, as explained in "Reassembly." Replace handle and washer, if used, and tie a double knot in the end of the rope.

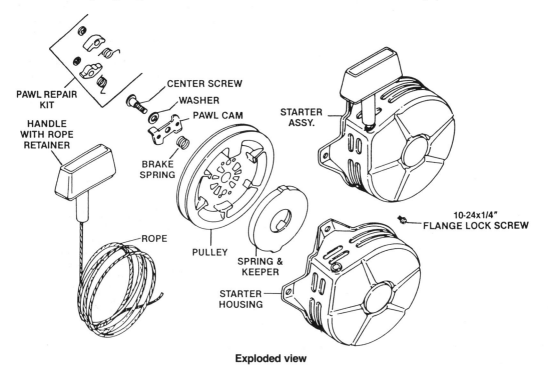

Exploded view

REWIND SPRING REPLACEMENT

1. Start with the inside loop, remove spring carefully from cover by pulling out one loop at a time, holding back the rest of the turns. When replacing with new spring, note the position of spring loop.

2. Spring holders furnished with replacement springs simplify the assembly procedure. Place spring in proper position as shown, with the outside loop engaged around the pin. Then press the spring into cover cavity thus releasing the spring holder. A few drops of SAE 20 or 30 oil should then be applied to spring and light grease on cover shaft.

REASSEMBLY

1. Replace washers (Keys 9 and 10), friction shoe assembly, washers (Keys 9 and 10), spring (Key 8), washer (Key 7), and retaining ring (Key 6).

2. Starter rope is now completely wound on rotor in the direction shown.

3. The starter will be damaged if not centered properly. To ensure the proper centering of the starter, pull out the centering pin (Key 19) about ⅛ in.. Place the starter on the four screws, make sure the centering pin engages the center hole in the crankshaft and press into position. Hold the starter with one hand and place the lock washers and nuts on the screws and tighten securely.

INSTALLING STARTER

1. To align the starter, place it on the blower housing in the desired position, with the centering pin engaged in the center hole of the crankshaft. (If the centering pin is too short to reach the crankshaft, use a pair of pliers and pull the pin out to the correct length.).

2. Press the starter into position and install the four screws with lock washers and flat washers.

3. Hold the starter assembly in this centered position and securely tighten the four screws.

Stamped Housing Models

CAUTION: *Retractable starters contain a powerful wire recoil spring that is under tension. Do not remove the center screw from the starter until the tension is released. Removing the center screw before releasing spring tension, or improper starter disassembly, can cause the sudden and potentially dangerous release of the spring.*

Always wear safety goggles when servicing retractable starters - full face protection is recommended.

To ensure personal safety and proper starter disassembly, the following procedures must be followed carefully.

REMOVAL

Remove the five screws securing the starter assembly to blower housing.

INSTALLATION

1. Install starter to blower housing using the five mounting screws. Leave screws slightly loose.

2. Pull the handle out approximately 8 in. to 10 in. until the pawls engage in the drive cup. Hold the handle in this position and tighten the screws securely.

STARTER PAWLS REPLACEMENT

A pawl repair kit, No. 41 757 02 is available. This kit includes two starter pawls, two pawl springs, two retaining rings, and installation instructions.

1. Remove starter from engine.

CAUTION: *Do not remove the center screw of the starter when replacing pawls. Removal of the center screw can cause the sudden and potentially dangerous release of the recoil spring. It is not necessary to remove the center screw when making this repair.*

2. Carefully not position of the pawls, pawl springs, and retaining ring before disassembly. (Components must be assembled correctly for proper operation.).

3. Remove the retaining rings, pawls, and pawl spring springs from pawl pins on pulley.

4. Clean pins and lubricate with any commercially available bearing bearing grease.

5. Install new pawl springs, pawls, and retaining rings. When properly installed, the pawl springs will hold the pawls against the pawl cam.

NOTE: *Make sure the snap rings are securely seated in grooves of pawl pins. Failure to seat the snap ring can cause pawls to dislodge during operation.*

6. Pull rope to make sure pawls operate properly.

Starter pawls

Removing handle

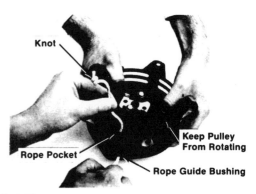

Installing rope

7. Install starter to engine as instructed under "To Install Starter."

ROPE REPLACEMENT

The rope can be replaced without complete starter disassembly.

1. Remove the starter from engine.

2. Pull the rope out approximately 12 in. and tie a temporary (slip) knot in it to keep it from retracting into starter.

3. Remove the rope retainer from inside handle. Untie the knot and remove the retainer and handle.

4. Hold the pulley firmly with thumb and untie the slip knot. Allow the pulley to rotate slowly as the spring tension is released.

5. When all spring tension on the starter pulley is released, remove old rope from pulley.

6. Tie a single knot in one end of new rope.

7. Rotate the pulley counterclockwise (when viewed from pawl side of pulley) until the spring is tight. (Approx. 6 full turns of pulley).

8. Rotate the pulley clockwise until the rope pocket is aligned with the rope guide bushing of housing.

NOTE: *Do not allow pulley/spring to unwind. Enlist the aid of a helper if necessary,*

or use a c-clamp to hold the pulley in position.

9. Insert the new rope into the rope pocket of pulley and through rope guide bushing in housing.

10. Tie a slip knot approximately 12 in. from the free end of rope. Hold pulley firmly with thumb and allow pulley to rotate slowly until the temporary knot reaches the rope guide bushing in housing.

11. Slip the handle and rope retainer onto rope. Tie a single knot at the end of rope and install rope retainer into handle.

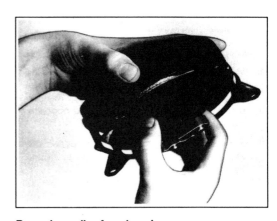

Removing pulley from housing

Releasing spring tension

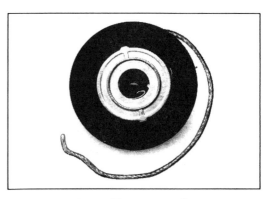

Position of spring and keeper on pulley

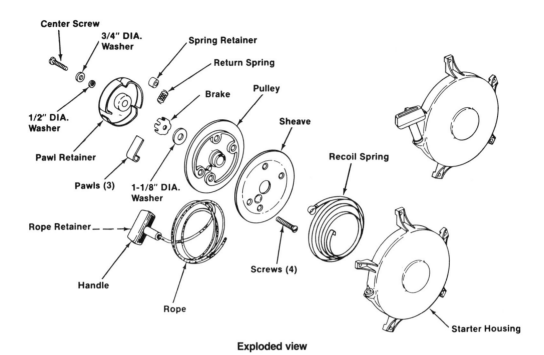

Exploded view

12. Untie the slip knot in rope and pull the handle out until the rope is fully extended. Slowly retract the rope into the starter. If the spring has been properly tensioned, the rope will fully retract until the handle hits the housing.

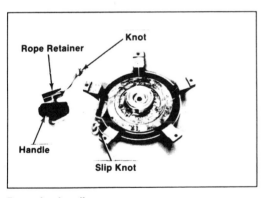

Removing handle

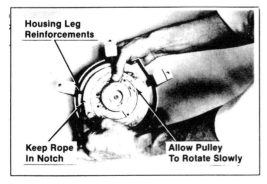

Releasing spring tension

DISASSEMBLY

1. Remove starter from engine.

CAUTION: *Do not remove the center screw of the starter until the tension of recoil spring has been released. Removing the center screw before releasing spring tension, or improper starter disassembly can cause the sudden and potentially dangerous release of the recoil spring. Follow these instructions carefully to ensure personal safety and proper starter disassembly. Make sure adequate face protection is worn by all persons in the area.*

2. Pull the rope out approximately 12 in. and tie a temporary (slip) knot in it to keep it from retracting into starter.

3. Remove the rope retainer from inside han-

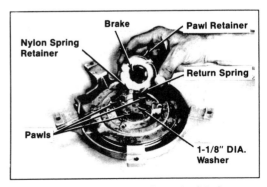

Removing pawl retainer, pawls, and related components

Removing pulley from housing

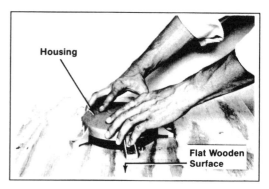

Removing spring from housing

dle and untie the knot to remove retainer and handle.

4. Hold the pulley firmly with thumb and untie the slip knot. Allow pulley to rotate slowly as the spring tension is released.

5. When all spring tension on the starter pulley has been released, remove the rope from the pulley.

6. Remove the center screw, washer, pawl cam, and brake spring.

7. Rotate the pulley clockwise 2 full turns. This will ensure the pulley is disengaged from the spring.

8. Hold the pulley into starter housing and invert starter so the pulley is away from your face, and away from others in the area.

9. Rotate the pulley slightly from side to side and carefully separate the pulley from the starter housing.

NOTE: *If the pulley and housing do not separate easily, the spring could be engaged with the pulley, or there is still tension on the spring. Return the pulley to the housing and repeat step 7 before separating the pulley and housing.*

10. Note the position of the spring and keeper assembly on the pulley. (The spring and keeper assembly must be correctly positioned on pulley for proper operation.) Remove the spring and keeper assembly from the pulley as a package.

CAUTION: *Do not remove the spring from the keeper. Severe personal injury could result from sudden uncoiling of the spring.*

11. Remove the rope from pulley. If necessary, remove the starter pawl components from pulley as instructed under "To Replace Starter Pawls."

INSPECTION AND SERVICE

1. Carefully inspect rope, starter paws, housing, center screw, and other components for wear or damage.

2. Replace all worn or damaged components.

3. Do not attempt to rewind a spring that has come out of the keeper. Order and install a new spring and keeper assembly.

4. Clean away all old grease and dirt from starter components. Generously lubricate the spring and center shaft of starter housing with any commercially available bearing grease.

REASSEMBLY

1. Make sure spring is well lubricated with grease. Position the spring and keeper assembly to pulley (side opposite pawls). The outside spring tail must be positioned opposite rope pocket.

2. Install the pulley with spring and keeper assembly into starter housing.

NOTE: *The pulley is in position when the*

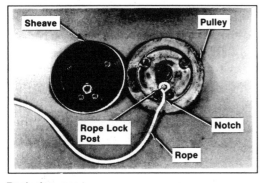

Replacing rope

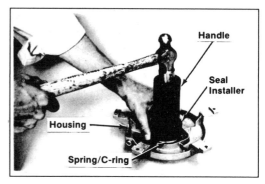

Installing spring using seal installer and handle

center shaft is extending slightly above the face of the pulley. Do not wind the pulley and recoil spring at this time.

3. Lubricate the brake spring sparingly with grease. Install the brake spring into the recess in center shaft of starter housing. (Make sure the threads in center shaft remain clean, dry, and free of grease or oil.).

4. Apply a small amount of Loctite® #271 to the threads to center screw. Install the center screw with washer and cam to the center shaft. Torque screw to 65-75 inch lbs.

5. If necessary, install the pawl springs, pawls, and retaining rings to pins on starter pulley. Refer to "To Replace Starter Pawls."

6. Tension the spring and install the rope and handle as instructed in steps 5 through 12 under "To Replace Rope."

7. Install the starter to engine.

Cast Housing Models

DISASSEMBLY

1. Remove the starter from engine.

CAUTION: *Do not remove the center screw of the starter until the tension of recoil spring has been released. Removing the center screw before releasing spring tension, or improper starter disassembly can cause the sudden and potentially dangerous release of the recoil spring. Follow these instructions carefully to ensure personal safety and proper starter disassembly. Make sure adequate face protection is worn by all persons in the area.*

2. Pull the rope out approximately 12 in. and tie a temporary (slip) knot in it to keep it from retracting into starter.

3. Remove the rope retainer from inside handle. Untie the knot and remove the retainer and handle.

4. Rotate the pulley counterclockwise until the notch in pulley is next to the rope guide bushing.

5. Hold the pulley firmly to keep it from turning. Untie the slip knot and pull the rope through the bushing.

6. Place the rope into the notch in pulley. This will keep the rope from interfering with the starter housing leg reinforcements as the pulley is rotated (step 7).

7. Hold the housing and pulley with both hands. Release pressure on the pulley and allow it to rotate slowly as the spring tension is released. Be sure to keep the rope in the notch.

8. Make sure the spring tension is fully released. (the pulley should rotate easily in either direction.).

9. When all spring tension on the pulley is released, remove the center screw, ¾ in. DIA. washer, and ½ in. DIA. washer.

10. Carefully lift the pawl retainer from pulley.

NOTE: *A small return spring and nylon spring retainer (spacer) are located under the pawl retainer. These parts are fragile and can be easily lost or damaged. If necessary, use a small screwdriver to loosen the spring retainer from the post on pulley. Replace the spring if it is broken, stretched, or shows other signs of damage.*

11. Remove the 1⅛ in. DIA. thrust washer, brake, return spring, nylon spring retainer, and pawls.

12. Rotate the pulley clockwise 2 full turns. There should be no resistance to this rotation. This will ensure the pulley is disengaged from the recoil spring.

13. Hold the pulley into starter housing and invert starter so the pulley is away from your face and others in the area.

14. Rotate the pulley slightly from side to side and carefully separate the pulley from the starter housing.

NOTE: *Pulley and housing do not separate easily, the spring could be engaged with pulley, or there is still tension on the spring. Return the pulley to the housing and repeat step 12 before separating the pulley and housing.*

15. Only if it is necessary for the repair of starter, remove the spring from the starter housing as instructed under "To Replace Recoil Spring." Do not remove the spring unless it is absolutely necessary.

INSPECTION AND SERVICE

1. Carefully inspect the rope, starter pawls, housing, center screw, center shaft, spring and other components for wear or damage.

2. Replace all worn or damaged components.

3. Carefully clean all old grease and dirt from starter components. Lubricate the spring, center shaft, and certain other components as specified in these instructions with any commercially available bearing grease.

ROPE REPLACEMENT

The starter must be completely disassembled to replace the rope.

1. Remove the starter from engine.

2. Disassemble starter as instructed in steps 2 through 14 under "Disassembly."

3. Remove the 4 Phillips head screw securing the pulley and sheave. Separate the pulley and sheave and remove the old rope.

4. Position the new rope in the notch in the pulley and around the rope lock post.

NOTE: *Use only a genuine Kohler replacement rope which is designed for this starter. Using rope of the incorrect diameter and/or type will not lock properly in the pulley.*

5. Install the sheave to the pulley and install the 4 Phillips head screws. Use care not to strip or cross-thread the threads in pulley.

6. Inspect the pulley to make sure the sheave is securely joined to the pulley. Pull firmly on the rope to make sure it is securely retained in the pulley.

RECOIL SPRING REPLACEMENT

CAUTION: *Do not attempt to pull or pry the recoil spring from the housing. Doing so can cause the sudden and potentially dangerous release of the spring from the housing. Follow these instructions carefully to ensure personal safety and proper spring replacement. Make sure adequate face protection is worn throughout the following procedure.*

1. Carefully not the position of the spring in the housing. The new spring must be installed in the proper position - it is possible to install it backwards in the housing.

2. Place the housing on a flat wooden surface with the recoil spring and center shaft down and away from you.

3. Grasp the housing by the top so that your fingers are protected. Do not wrap your fingers around the edge of the housing.

4. Lift the housing and rap it firmly against the wooden surface. repeat this procedure until the spring is released from the spring pocket in housing.

5. Discard the old spring.

CAUTION: *Do not attempt to rewind or reinstall a spring once it has been removed from the starter housing. Severe personal injury could result from the sudden uncoiling of the spring. Always order and install a new spring which is held in a specially designed "C-ring" spring retainer.*

6. Thoroughly clean the starter housing removing all old grease and dirt.

7. Carefully remove the masking tape surrounding the new spring/C-ring.

8. Position the spring/C-ring to the housing

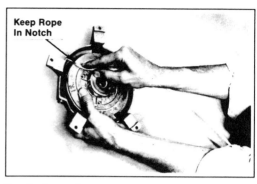
Tensioning spring

so the spring hook is over the post in the housing. Make sure the spring is coiled on the correct direction.

9. Obtain Deal Installer #11791 and Handle #11795. (Refer to "Special Tools" Section.) Hook the spring hook over the post in housing. Make sure the spring/C-ring is centered over the spring pocket in housing. Drive the spring out of the c-ring and into the spring pocket using the seal installer and handle.

10. Make sure all of the spring coils are bottomed against ribs in spring pocket. Use the seal installer and handle to bottom the coils, as necessary.

11. Lubricate the spring moderately with wheel bearing grease before reassembling the starter.

ASSEMBLY

1. Install the recoil spring into the starter housing as instructed under Replace Recoil Spring.

2. Sparingly lubricate the center shaft of starter with wheel bearing grease.

3. Make sure the rope is in good condition. If necessary, replace the old rope as instructed under "To Replace Rope."

NOTE: *Ready the pulley and rope for assembly by unwinding all of the rope from the pulley. Place the rope in the notch in the pulley. This will keep the rope from interfering with the starter leg reinforcements as the pulley is rotated later during reassembly.*

4. Install the pulley onto the center shaft.

NOTE: *If the pulley does not fully seat, it is resting on the inner center spring coil. Rotate the pulley slightly from side to side while exerting slight downward pressure. This should move the inner spring coil out of the way and allow the pulley to drop into position.*

The pulley is in position when the center shaft is flush with the face of the pulley. Do not wind the pulley and recoil spring at this time.

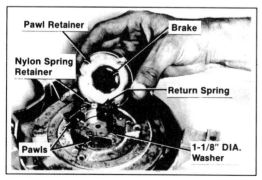
Installing pawls, pawl retainer, and related components

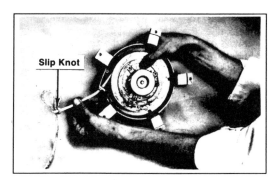

Winding rope onto pulley

5. Install the starter pawls into the appropriate pockets in the pulley.

6. Sparingly lubricate the underside of the 1⅛ in. DIA. washer with grease and install it over the center shaft. Make sure the threads in center shaft remain clean, dry, and free of grease or oil.

7. Sparingly lubricate the insides of the "legs" of the brake spider with grease. Instal the brake to the retainer.

8. Install the small return ring to the pawl retainer. Make sure it is positioned properly.

9. Position the pawl retainer and return spring next to the small post on pulley. Install the free loop of the return spring over the post. Install the nylon spring retainer over the post.

10. Invert the pawl retainer over the pawls and center hub of pulley. Take great care not to damage or unhook the return spring. Make sure the pawls are positioned in the slots of pawl retainer.

11. As a test, rotate the pawl retainer slightly clockwise. Pressure from the return spring should be felt. In addition, the pawl retainer should return to its original position when released. If no spring pressure is felt or the retainer does not return, the spring is damaged, unhooked, or improperly assembled. Repeat steps 8, 9, and 10 to correct the problem.

12. Sparingly lubricate the ½ in. DIA. washer and ¾ in. DIA. washer in the center of pawl retainer. Make sure the threads in center shaft remain clan, dry, and free of grease or oil.

13. Apply a small amount of Loctite® #271 to the threads of center screw. Install the center screw to center shaft. Torque screw to 55-70 inch lbs.

14. Rotate the pulley counterclockwise (when viewed from the pawl side of pulley) until the spring is tight. (Approximately 4 full turns of pulley.) Make sure the fully extended rope is held in the notch in pulley to prevent interference with the housing leg reinforcements.

15. Rotate the pulley clockwise until the notch is aligned with the rope guide bushing of housing.

NOTE: *Do not allow the pulley/spring to unwind. Enlist the aid of a helper, or use a c-clamp to hold pulley in position.*

16. Insert the free end of rope through rope guide bushing. Tie a temporary (slip) knot approximately 12 in. from the free end of the rope.

17. Hold the pulley firmly with thumbs and allow the pulley to rotate slowly until the slip knot reaches the rope guide bushing of housing.

18. Slip the handle and rope retainer onto rope. Tie a single knot at the end of rope and install retainer into handle.

19. Untie the slip knot and pull the handle out until the rope is fully extended. Slowly retract the rope into the starter. If the spring has been properly tensioned, the rope will fully retract until the handle hits the housing.

IGNITION SYSTEMS

Kohler K series are fitted with one of three types of ignition systems, each available in different versions. Most parts in one system are not interchangeable with parts from another system. Care should be taken in selection of replacement parts to ensure the right parts are used. The three types of systems and their available versions are:

Magneto Ignition System
1. Magneto rotor type; ignition only
2. Magneto flywheel type (magnet ring; ignition only)
3. Magneto flywheel type with 3 Amp lighting coils
4. Magneto flywheel type with 10 Amp alternator

Battery Ignition Systems
1. Battery ignition with motor generator
2. Battery ignition with 10 Amp alternator
3. Battery ignition with 15 Amp alternator
4. Battery ignition with 30 Amp alternator

Breakerless Ignition System
1. Breakerless ignition with 10 Amp alternator
2. Breakerless ignition with 15 Amp alternator

Magneto Ignition System
OPERATION

In all magneto ignition systems, high-strength permanent magnets provide the energy for ignition. In rotor type systems, the magnet is pressed onto the crankshaft and is rotated inside a coil-core assembly (stator) mounted

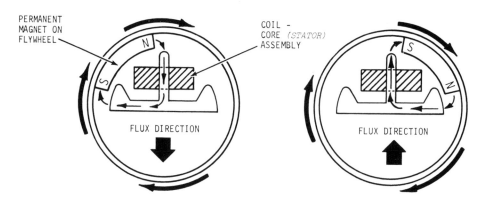

Magneto cycle showing flux reversal

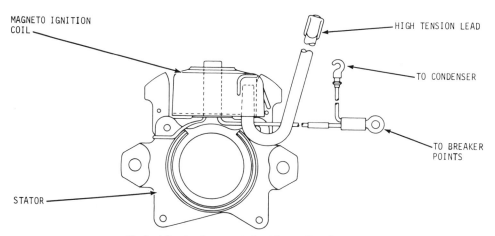

Typical flywheel magneto ignition coil and starter

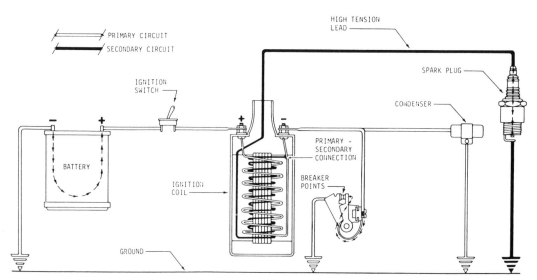

Wiring diagram—battery ignition system

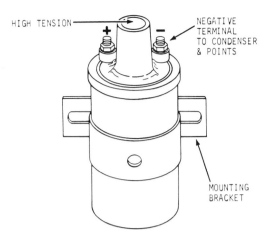

Typical battery ignition coil

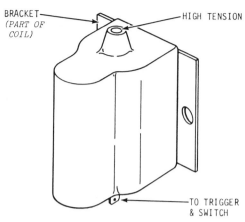

Typical breakerless ignition coil

on the breaking plate. In the other systems, a permanent magnet ring on the inside of the flywheel revolves around the stator. Movement of the magnets past the stator induces electric current flow in the stator coil (and in alternator and lighting coils if provided). The magnets are mounted with alternate North and South poles so that the direction of magnetic flux constantly changes, producing an alternating current (AC) in the stator coil windings.

The stator windings are connected to the magneto ignition coil. Current flow in the ignition coil reaches its highest peak at the instant the magnetic flux reverses direction. This is the point at which the system is timed to provide a spark at the spark plug.

The ignition coil has a low tension primary winding and a high tension secondary winding. The secondary winding has approximately 100 turns of wire for evert 1 turn in the primary. This relationship causes the voltage induced in the secondary winding to be about 100 times higher than in the primary. If the magneto produces 250 volts in the primary winding, the secondary winding voltage will be 25,000 volts.

When ignition is required, the breaker points open to break the primary circuit. The resultant sudden collapse of the field around the primary winding causes sufficient energy to be produced in the secondary winding to bridge the spark plug gap. The collapsing field also induces energy in the primary winding, but the condenser shunts this energy to ground, preventing it from bridging the breaker point gap.

TIMING

Engines are equipped with a timing sight hole either in the bearing plate or in the blower housing. If a snap button covers the hole, pry it out with a screwdriver or similar tool so that the timing marks may be seen. Two marks will be present on the flywheel; T for top dead center, and S or SP for the firing point (20 deg. before top dead center).

There are two ways to time a magneto ignition system, static and timing light. The timing light method is the more accurate of the two. A

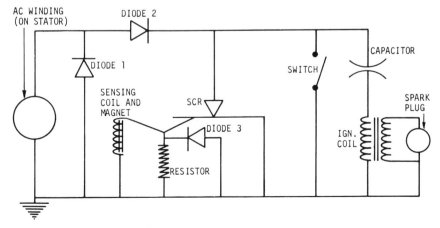

Schematic oil typical breakerless ignition system

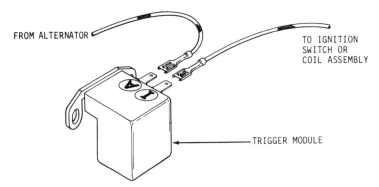

FROM ALTERNATOR

TO IGNITION
SWITCH OR
COIL ASSEMBLY

TRIGGER MODULE

Trigger module lead connections

storage battery is needed for use with most timing lights.

Static Timing Method

1. Remove the breaker point cover.
2. Remove the spark plug lead to prevent unintentional starting of the engine.
3. Rotate the engine slowly by hand in the direction of normal operation. Rotation should be clockwise when viewed from the flywheel end.
4. The breaker points should just begin to open when the S or SP mark (Y mark on Model K91) appears in the center of the timing sight hole. Continue rotating the engine until the breaker points are fully opened.
5. Measure the breaker point gap with a feeler gauge. The gap should be 0.020 in..
6. If the gap is not 0.020 in., loosen the gap adjustment screw and adjust the gap.
7. Tighten the gap adjustment screw.
8. Replace the breaker point cover.

Timing Light Timing Method

Several different types of timing lights are available. Follow the manufacturer's directions for use. Perform timing with a timing light as follows.

1. Remove the lead from the spark plug.

2. Wrap one end of a short piece of fine bare wire around the spark plug terminal and replace the lead. The free end of the wire must protrude from beneath the rubber boot on the lead.

NOTE: *The preceding is for timing lights using an alligator clip to connect the spark plug. If the light in use has a sharp prong on the spark plug lead, simply penetrate the rubber boot with the prong and make contact with spark plug lead metal connector.*

3. Connect one timing light lead to the wire wrapped around the spark plug terminal.
4. Connect one timing light lead to the hot (ungrounded) terminal of the battery.
5. Connect the third timing light lead to engine ground.
6. Start the engine and run it at 1200 to 1800 RPM.
7. Aim the timing light at the timing sight hole. The light should flash just as the S or SP mark is centered in the sight hole or is in line with the center mark on the bearing plate or blower housing.
8. If timing is not as specified, carefully remove the breaker point and slightly loosen the gap adjusting screw, shift the breaker point plate until the timing mark is properly positioned, and tighten the screw.

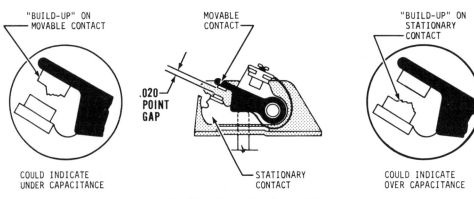

"BUILD-UP" ON
MOVABLE CONTACT

MOVABLE
CONTACT

"BUILD-UP" ON
STATIONARY
CONTACT

.020
POINT
GAP

STATIONARY
CONTACT

COULD INDICATE
UNDER CAPACITANCE

COULD INDICATE
OVER CAPACITANCE

Metal transfer on breaker points

9. Shut off the engine and replace the breaker point cover.

Battery Ignition System

OPERATION

The battery ignition system operates in a manner similar to the magneto system. the major difference is that, in the battery system, energy is provided by a battery. The battery is maintained at full charge by an engine mounted motor-generator or alternator.

The coil in a battery ignition system is connected as follows:

a. The positive (+) terminal is connected to the positive terminal of the battery.

b. The negative (-) terminal is connected to the breaker points.

c. The high tension (center) terminal is connected to the spark plug.

TIMING

The timing procedure for the battery ignition system is the same as for the magneto system. When using a timing light, refer to the manufacturer's instructions.

NOTE: *The model K341QS Specification 71276A engine is unique in that it is timed slightly differently then other K series engines. These engines operate at lower speed, so the timing is set at 16 degrees before top dead center to improve running smoothness. Instead of having an S or SP at the timing mark on the flywheel, these engines have a 1 above and a 6 below the mark. When timing these engines, the timing mark is centered as with other engines.*

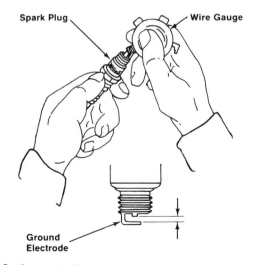

Setting spark plug gap

IGNITION SERVICE

Single Cylinder Models

Ignition problems and poor performance on these models are often the result of using an incorrect ignition coil, spark plug, or plug gap setting. When replacing an ignition coil always use the genuine Kohler replacement. Use of the correct spark plug and gap setting is also important. The specified plug is a Champion H10/RH10, or equivalent, gapped at 0.035 in. (.9mm). Failure to follow these recommendations will result in erratic high speed ignition misfire or cutting-out under load.

Breakerless Ignition System

OPERATION

The breakerless ignition system operates on the same general principle as the magneto system but does not use breaker points and conventional ignition condenser to time the spark. A trigger module containing solid state electronics performs the same function as the breaker points.

The breakerless system consists of four major components:

- Ignition winding on alternator stator
- Trigger module
- Ignition coil assembly
- Flywheel-mounted trigger

The ignition winding is separate from other windings on the alternator stator. It functions like the magneto winding. The trigger module contains three diodes, a resistor, a sensing coil and magnet and an SCR, a sort of electronic switch. The ignition coil assembly includes a capacitor and a pulse transformer that serves the same purpose as the ignition coil in other systems. The flywheel has a projection that triggers ignition.

In some applications a 22 ohm, ½ watt resistor has been placed between the key switch and the ignition coil. This has been added to prevent current feedback through a dirty or wet switch. This feedback, if not held in check by a resistor, can damage the trigger unit.

TIMING

Because there are no breaker points in this system, there is no requirement for timing. However, there is a requirement for positioning the trigger module for proper relationship with the flywheel projection. The gap between the projection and trigger module is normally set between 0.005 in. and 0.010 in.. This setting is not critical, but selecting a 0.005 in. gap promotes better cold weather starting. Set the gap as follows.

1. Remove the spark plug lead to prevent starting.

2. Rotate the flywheel so that the projection is aligned with the trigger module.

3. Loosen the cap screws on the trigger module bracket and insert a 0.005 in. feeler gauge in the gap.

4. Move the trigger module until it touches the feeler gauge, making sure that the flat surfaces of module and projection are parallel.

5. Tighten the cap screws and replace the spark plug lead.

Trigger Module

The trigger module used on breakerless ignition systems is a solid state device which includes diodes, resistor, sensing coil and magnet plus an electronic switch called an SCR. The terminal marked A must be connected to the alternator while terminal I must be connected to the ignition switch or ignition coil. Operating with these leads reversed will cause damage to the solid state devices. If a faulty trigger module is suspected, disconnect and remove the trigger from the engine and perform the following tests with a flashlight tester. Reset air gap when reinstalling trigger.

Didoe Test

Turn tester switch ON and connect one lead to the I terminal and the other to the A terminal then reverse these leads--light should come on with leads one way but not the other way. If light stays on or off both ways, this indicates diodes are faulty--replace trigger module.

SCR Test

Turn tester on then connect one lead to the I terminal and the other to the trigger mounting bracket.

NOTE: *If light comes on, reverse the leads as the light must be off initially for this test.*

Lightly tap magnet with a metal object--when this is done, tester light should come on and stay on until leads are disconnected. If light does not come on, this indicates SCR is not switching properly in which case trigger module should be replaced.

Ignition Coils

Breakerless Type Ignition Coil

Use an ohmmeter to test breakerless type coil assembly. (A) -- Remove high tension lead from terminal on coil. Insert one ohmmeter lead in coil terminal and the other to the coil mounting bracket. A resistance of about 11,500 ohms should be indicated here. (B) -- Connect one tester lead to the coil mounting bracket and the other to the ignition switch wire. Continuity

should not be indicated here. Replace ignition coil assembly if wrong results are obtained from either of these tests.

Magneto and Battery System Breaker Points

Engine operation is greatly affected by breaker point condition and adjustment of the gap. If points are burned or badly oxidized, little or no current will pass. The engine may not operate at all or may miss at high speed. Size of the breaker point gap affects the amount of time the points are open and closed. If the gap is set too wide, they will open too early and close too late. A definite period of time is required for the field to build in the ignition coil. If the points are closed for too long or too short a period, a weak spark will be produced by the coil.

Severe metal buildup on either contact indicates that the condenser is not properly matched to the rest of the system and should be replaced.

Spark Plugs

Engine misfire and starting difficulty are often caused by the spark plug's being in poor condition or being improperly gapped. The spark plug should be removed after every 100 hours of operation for a check of its condition. At this time the gap should be reset or the spark plug replaced as necessary.

SERVICE

1. Clean the area around the base of the spark plug to keep dirt out of the engine upon removal.

2. Remove the spark plug and check its condition. Replace it if it is badly worn or if re-use is questionable. Clean it if it re-useable.

NOTE: *Do not clean the spark plug in a machine that uses abrasive grit. Some grit could remain in recesses and enter the engine, causing extensive wear and damage.*

3. Check the gap with a wire type feeler gauge. set the gap a s shown in the following table by carefully bending the side electrode.

4. Install the spark plug and torque it to 18 to 20 ft. lbs.

Alternator

OPERATION

There are five different models of alternators used in the K series of engines. They are rated at 1.25, 3, 10, 15 and 30 amperes. the 1.25 amp system is intended for battery charging only. The 3 amp device is intended for battery charging and lighting.

There are no adjustments provided for in these systems. Replace if faulty.

NOTE: *To prevent damage to the electrical system and components:*

a. Make sure the battery polarity is correct. A negative (-) ground system is used with K series engines.

b. Disconnect the rectifier-regulator leads and/or wiring harness plug if electric (arc) welding is to be done on the equipment powered by the engine. Disconnect any other electrical accessories that share a common ground with the engine.

c. Make sure the stator (AC) leads do not touch. Shorting them together could permanently damage the stator.

d. Do not operate the engine with the battery disconnected.

NOTE: *If a battery has discharged to less than 4 volts, there may not be sufficient power to activate the rectifier-regulator. If the battery fails to accept a charge from the alternator, charge it on a battery charger and reinstall.*

ELECTRIC STARTING SYSTEMS

There are three types of electric starters used in the K series of engines. The three types are: **Motor-Generator** - This starter also functions as a DC generator. In the starting mode, it turns the crankshaft through a V belt arrangement. The V belt transmits turning force from a small pulley on the motor-generator to a large pulley on the crankshaft.

Wound-Field Bendix Drive Starter - In the field-wound starters, electrical current flows through coils to build up a strong magnetic field to turn the armature. When the armature starts to rotate, a drive pinion moves forward on the armature shaft and meshes with a ring gear on the flywheel. The armature and ring

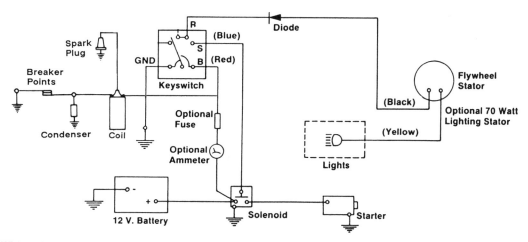

Wiring diagram—electric start engines 1.25 amp or 3 amp unregulated battery charging system/70 watt lighting

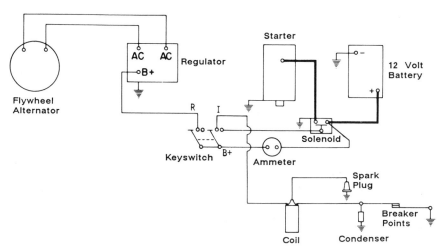

Wiring diagram—electric start engines/16 amp engines/15 amp regulated battery charging sytem

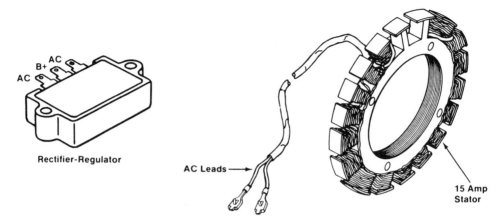

15 amp stator and rectifier-regulator

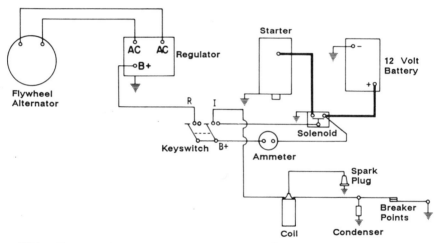

Wiring diagram—electric start engines/25 amp regulated battery charging system

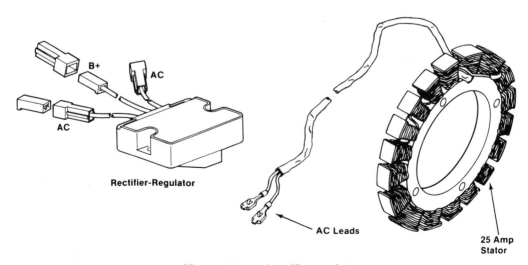

25 amp stator and rectifier-regulator

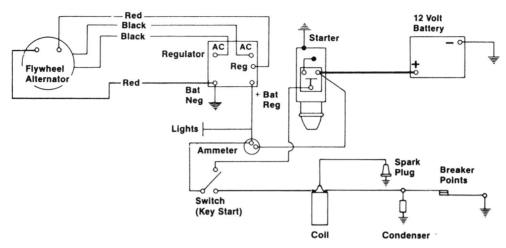

Wiring diagram—electric start engines/30 amp regulated battery charging system

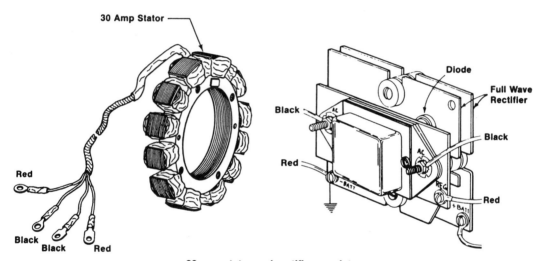

30 amp stator and rectifier-regulator

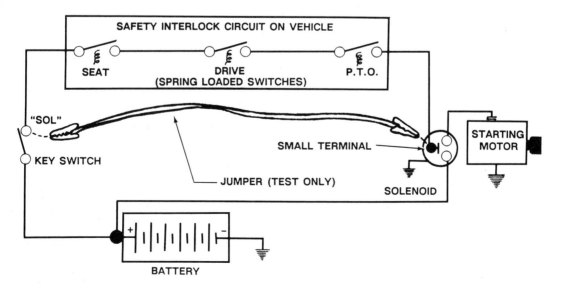

Battery ignition interlock bypass

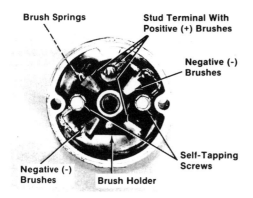

Brush Springs

Stud Terminal With
Positive (+) Brushes

Negative (-)
Brushes

Self-Tapping
Screws

Negative (-)
Brushes

Brush Holder

Commutator end cap with brushes

gear remain engaged until the engine starts to run. When the flywheel begins to turn faster than the starter, the pinion is thrown from the ring gear and returns to the disengaged position. A small anti-drift spring on the armature shaft holds the pinion in this position as the starter slows to a stop.

Permanent Magnet Bendix Drive Starter - Operation of this type starter is the same as that of the wound-filed starter. the major difference between the two is in the method of generating the magnetic field to turn the armature. This starter uses strong permanent magnets in place of field coils.

Safety Interlocks

In an effort to enhance safe operation of their equipment, many manufacturers install safety interlocks to prevent engine start before certain safety requirements are met. These interlocks are usually incorporated in the starter circuit.

Unless all interlock switches are closed, the starter will not function.

Before servicing a starter that has failed, always check the safety interlock system first. This is done by bypassing the interlock switches with a temporary jumper wire.

CAUTION: *Other than interlock testing, never operate an engine with the safety interlock system removed or bypassed. Great bodily harm or equipment damage could result!*

Interlocks connected to an engine with a battery ignition system are bypassed simply by placing a jumper wire as shown.

CAUTION: *Make sure all safety conditions have been observed before starting as engine with the interlocks bypassed.*

The safety interlock system on manual start magneto ignition engines is placed in the ignition system. The series connected interlock switches are connected to a solid state module that is connected to the ignition system. The module serves two functions. It grounds the ignition system until all interlocks have closed and, after the engine has started, it prevents the ignition from grounding as the individual interlocks are opened in normal operation (transmission placed in Drive, PTO engaged, etc.).

Motor-Generator Type Starter
BRUSH REPLACEMENT

1. Remove the brush springs from the pockets in brush holder.
2. Remove the self-tapping screws and negative (-) brushes.
3. Remove the stud terminal with positive

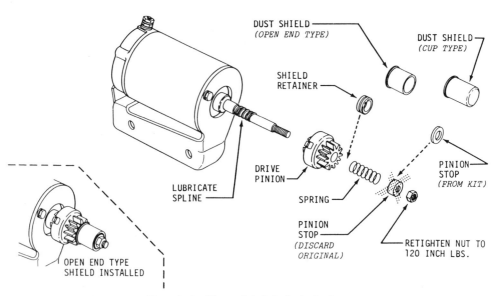

DUST SHIELD
(OPEN END TYPE)

DUST SHIELD
(CUP TYPE)

SHIELD
RETAINER

DRIVE
PINION

LUBRICATE
SPLINE

SPRING

PINION
STOP
(FROM KIT)

PINION
STOP
*(DISCARD
ORIGINAL)*

RETIGHTEN NUT TO
120 INCH LBS.

OPEN END TYPE
SHIELD INSTALLED

Magneto ignition safety interlock stystem

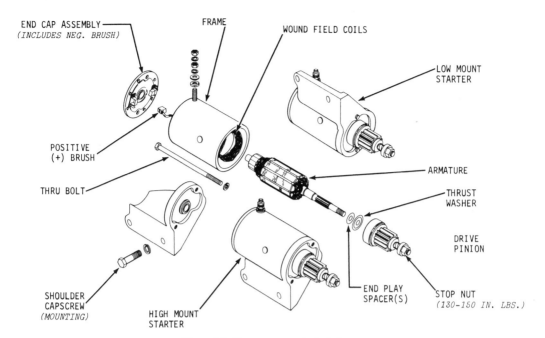

Wound-field starter—exploded view

(+) brushes, and plastic brush holder from end cap.

4. Reinstall the brush holder and new holder and new stud terminal with positive (+) brushes into end cap. Secure with the fiber washer, plain washer, split lock washer, and hex nut.

CAUTION: *To prevent electric arcing, make sure the stud terminal and braided brush leads do not touch the end cap.*

5. Install the new negative (-) brushes and secure with the self-tapping screws.

6. Install the brush springs and brushes into the pockets in brush holder. Make sure the chamfered sides of brushes are away from the springs.

NOTE: *Use a brush holder tool to keep the brushes in the pockets. A brush holder tool can easily be made from thin sheet metal.*

COMMUTATOR SERVICE

Clean the commutator with a coarse, lint free cloth. Do not use emery cloth. if the commutator is badly worn or grooved, turn down on a lathe, or replace the armature.

REASSEMBLY

1. Insert the armature into the starter frame. Make sure the magnets are closer to the drive shaft end of armature. the magnets will hold the armature inside the frame.

2. Install the thrust washer and drive end cap. Make sure the match marks on end cap and frame are aligned.

3. Install the brush holder tool to keep the brushes in the pockets of commutator end cap.

4. Install the commutator end cap to armature and starter frame. Firmly hold the drive end cap and commutator end cap to the starter frame. Remove the brush holder tool.

5. Make sure the match marks on end cap and frame are aligned. Install the through-bolts.

6. Install the drive pinion, dust cover spacer, anti-drifting spring, stop gear spacer, stop nut, and dust cover. Refer to "Starter Drive Service."

NOTE: *If the engine being serviced is equipped with special shouldered cap screws and lock washers for mounting, make sure these same parts are used for reinstalling the starter. these special parts ensure alignment of the pinion and ring gear.*

Wound-Field Bendix Drive Starter

WARNING: *In the event of a false start (engine starts but fails to keep running) the engine must be allowed to come to a complete stop before the starter is re-engaged. If the flywheel is still rotating when the starter is engaged, the pinion and ring gear may be damaged.*

Do not crank the engine for longer than 10 seconds. A 60-second cool-down period must be allowed between starting attempts. Failure to follow this procedure could result in starter burnout.

NOTE: *If the engine being serviced is a Model K161 or K181 and has special shouldered cap screws and lock washers for mounting. Make sure these same parts are used for reinstalling the starter. These special parts ensure alignment of the pinion and ring gear.*

SERVICE

1. Remove the end cap assembly by taking out the two through bolts and carefully slipping the end cap off the armature.
2. Lift the spring holding the positive brush and remove the brush.
3. Carefully remove the armature.
4. Inspect both brushes (positive on frame; negative on end cap). If brushes are worn unevenly or are shorter than $5/16$ in., replace them.
5. Remove the negative brush by drilling out the rivet holding it to the end cap. Install the replacement brush and rivet.
6. Remove the positive brush by peeling back insulating material on the field winding and unclipping or unsoldering. Install the replacement brush and clip or solder in place.
7. Use a coarse cloth to clean the commutator. If the commutator is grooved or extremely dirty, use a commutator stone or fine sandpaper.
NOTE: *Never use emery cloth to clean a commutator.*
8. Carefully insert the armature.
9. Lightly coat the end cap bushing and armature shaft with light engine oil.
10. hold the positive brush spring back and carefully place end in position on armature

shaft. Release spring after brushes are contacting commutator.
11. insert two through bolts and torque to 40 to 55 inch lbs.
12. inspect pinion and splined shaft. If any damage is noted, replace the Bendix drive.
13. If the Bendix drive is in good condition, wipe everything clean and apply a very thin coat of special silicone grease (Kohler Part No. 52 357 01) to the splined portion of the armature shaft.

Permanent Magnet Bendix Drive Starter

SERVICE

WARNING: *In the event of a false start (engine starts but fails to keep running) the engine must be allowed to come to a complete stop before the starter is re-engaged. If the flywheel is still rotating when the starter is engaged, the pinion and ring gear may be damaged.*

Do not crank the engine for longer than 10 seconds. A 60-second cool-down period must be allowed before starting attempts. Failure to follow this procedure could result in starter burnout.

1. Remove the stop nut and the remainder of the Bendix drive.
2. Remove both through bolts.
3. Remove the end bracket capscrew from the end cap.
4. Remove mounting bracket and frame by

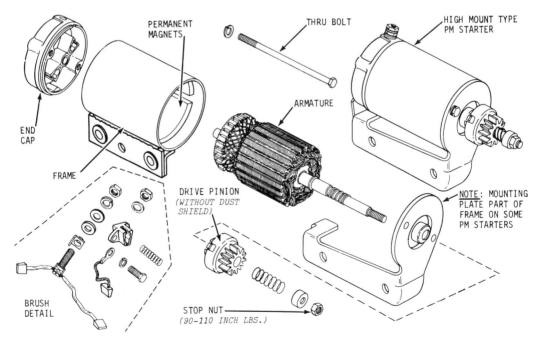

Permanent magnet starter—exploded view

rotating the end bracket and slipping the mounting bracket and frame off of the drive end of the armature.

5. Separate the end cap from the armature, being careful to restrain the brushes in the end cap.

6. Inspect the commutator. If dirty, clean it with a coarse, lint-free cloth. If grooved, dress it with a commutator stone or turn it down on a lathe and undercut the mica.

TROUBLESHOOTING

Starter failures from overcranking or cranking with an abnormal parasitic load on the engine, will display one or a number of the following signs:

1. The armature wire insulation or coating will appear discolored and may be swollen. In many cases, you may be able to detect an odor from the burnt wire coating or see it oozing from the starter housing.

2. One or a number of the armature windings may have wires or wire connections that have burnt in tow. Wires may have insulation missing or be partially fused together.

3. The starter brushes will show heavy surface galling and brush material transfer. Additionally, in many instances the starter brushes will be welded or stuck in the brush holders.

Some of the frequent causes of abnormal parasitic load at cranking are:

• Improper viscosity engine crankcase oil.

• Incorrect fluid in a direct coupled hydrostatic unit - remember, even in the idle or neutral position, a direct coupled hydrostatic pump will place a parasitic load on the engine at cranking.

• Malfunctioning or inoperative direct coupled clutch assembly.

• Engaged accessory or drive clutch assembly.

• Overcranking - cranking the starter continuously for more than the recommended period and/or not allowing a sufficient cool down period between starting attempts.

• Parasitic Load at cranking - a load or force on the engine at cranking that opposes normal engine rotation.

BATTERY

BATTERY TEST

If the battery does not have enough charge to crank the engine, recharge it.

NOTE: *Do not attempt to jump-start the engine with another battery. Starting with a battery larger than recommended can burn out the starter motor.*

The battery is tested by connecting a DC volt-meter across the battery terminals and cranking the engine. If the battery voltage drops below 9 while cranking, the batter is in need of a charge or replacement.

BATTERY CHARGING

CAUTION: *Batteries contain sulfuric acid. To prevent acid burns, avoid contact with skin, eyes and clothing.*

Batteries produce explosive hydrogen gas while being charged. Charge the battery only in a well ventilated area. Keep cigarettes, sparks, open flame and other sources of ignition away from the battery at all times.

To prevent accidental shorting and the resultant sparks, remove all jewelry before servicing the battery.

When disconnecting battery cables, always disconnect the negative (-) cable first. When connecting battery cables, always connect the negative cable last.

Before disconnecting the negative (-) cable, make sure all switches are OFF. If any switch is ON, a spark will occur at the ground terminal. This could result in an explosion if hydrogen gas or gasoline vapors are present.

Keep batteries and acid out of the reach of children.

BATTERY MAINTENANCE

Regular maintenance will ensure that the battery will ensure that the battery will accept and hold a charge.

CAUTION: *Always turn the ignition switch OFF or disconnect the battery cables before charging the battery. failure to do this could result in overheating and explosion of the ignition coil.*

1. Check the level of the electrolyte regularly. Add distilled water to maintain it at its recommended level.

NOTE: *Do not overfill the battery. Poor performance or early failure will result.*

2. Keep the cables, terminals and external battery surfaces clean. A buildup of corrosive acid or dirt on the surfaces can cause the battery to self-discharge. Wash the cables, terminals and external surfaces with a baking soda and water solution. Rinse thoroughly with clean water.

NOTE: *Do not allow the baking soda solution to enter the battery cells. The solution will chemically destroy the electrolyte.*

AUTOMATIC COMPRESSION RELEASE

All K-series cylinder engines, except the K91, are equipped with Automatic Compression Release (ACR). The ACR mechanism lowers compression at cranking speeds to make starting easier.

OPERATION

The ACR mechanism consists of two flyweights and a spring attached to the gear on camshaft. When the engine is rotating at low cranking speeds (600 RPM or lower) the flyweights are held by the spring in the position shown. In this position, the tab on the larger flyweight protrudes above the exhaust cam lobe. This lifts the exhaust valve off its seat during the first part of the compression stroke. The reduced compression results in an effective compression ratio of about 2:1 during cranking.

After the engine speed increases to about 600 RPM, centrifugal force moves the flyweights to the position shown. In this position the tab on the larger flyweight drops into the recess in the exhaust cam lobe. When in the recess, the tab has no effect on the exhaust valve and the engine operates at full compression and full power.

When the engine is stopped, the spring returns the flyweights to the position shown, ready for the next start.

INSPECTION AND SERVICE

The ACR mechanism is extremely rugged and virtually trouble-free. If hard starting is ex-

perienced, check the exhaust valve for lift as follows:

1. Check exhaust valve to tappet clearance and adjust as necessary to specification.
2. Remove cylinder head and turn the crankshaft clockwise by hand and observe the exhaust valve carefully. When the piston is approximately ⅔ of the way up the cylinder during the compression stroke, the exhaust valve should lift off the seat slightly.

NOTE: *If the exhaust valve does not lift, the ACR spring may be unhooked or broken. To service the spring, remove the oil pan and rehook spring or replace it. The camshaft does not have to be removed.*

The flyweights are not serviceable. If they are stuck or worn excessively, the camshaft must be replaced.

NOTE: *The tab on the flyweights is hardened and is not adjustable. Do not attempt to bend the tab - it will break and a new camshaft will be required.*

COMPRESSION TESTING

Because of the ACR mechanism, it is difficult to obtain an accurate compression reading.

To check the condition of the combustion chamber, and related mechanisms, physical inspection and a crankcase vacuum test are recommended.

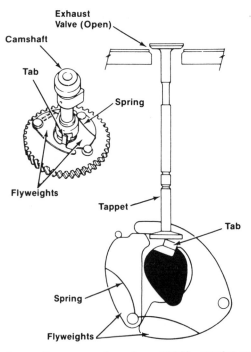

Automatic compression release (ACR)—starting position

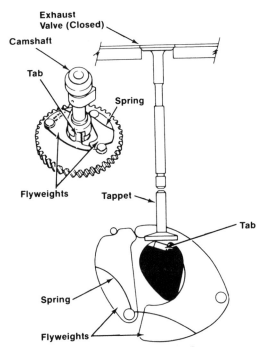

Automatic compression release (ACR)—running position

AUTOMATIC COMPRESSION RELEASE (ACR) CHANGES

New ACR Tests

Engines with serial no. 9006118 and after have hardened and ground steel ACR tabs on the camshaft assemblies. These new assemblies are manufactured with improved techniques, which permanently set the ACR mechanism, making adjustments to the mechanism unnecessary and impossible.

NOTE: *Do not attempt to bend these hardened steel ACR tabs. These tabs will break if bent.*

Procedure For Checking And Adjusting ACR On Engines Prior To Serial No. 9006118

On engines manufactured before serial no. 9006118 the ACR can still be checked and reset using the procedure described below.

ACR is set according to the amount of valve lift on the exhaust valve. The correct amount of lift is established by the height of the lifting tab in relation to the camshaft. if improper lift is suspected, the setting can be checked and adjusted as follows:

1. Check valve tappet clearances and adjust as necessary to specification.

2. Remove cylinder head and turn the engine over by hand until you reach BDC of the intake stroke (intake valve will be closing).

3. Mount a dial indicator on the top of the exhaust valve and set a 0.

4. Slowly turn the flywheel clockwise and watch the dial indicator. When the piston is about ⅔ of the way up the cylinder, the exhaust valve should open for ACR. Exhaust valve opening as indicated on the dial indicator should be 0.031-0.042 in.

If the exhaust valve does not open to the specified amount, adjust the ACR according to STEP 5.

NOTE: *Caution must be exercised in the bending of the tab as it is hardened and may crack or break if bent back and forth more than 3 or 4 times.*

5. If the valve lift was above 0.042 in., hold a wooden dowel or peg on the top of the valve and tap it down carefully to within the 0.031-0.042 in. range. If the valve lift was below 0.031, remove the camshaft cover on the side of the engine exposing the cam gear and bend the ACR tab carefully upward until the valve lift is within the specified range.

ENGINE MECHANICAL

DISASSEMBLY

CAUTION: *Before servicing the engine or equipment, always remove the spark plug*

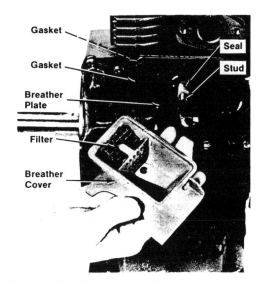

Removing breather components

lead to prevent the engine from starting accidentally. Ground the lead to prevent sparks that could cause fires.

Clean all parts thoroughly as the engine is disassembled. Only clean parts can be accurately inspected and gauged for wear or damage. There are many commercially available cleaners that quickly remove grease, oil, and grime rpm engine parts. When such a cleaner is used, follow the manufacturer's instructions carefully. Make sure all traces of the cleaner are removed before the engine is reassembled and placed in operation - even small amounts of these cleaners quickly break down the lubricating properties of engine oil. Check all parts for evidence of:

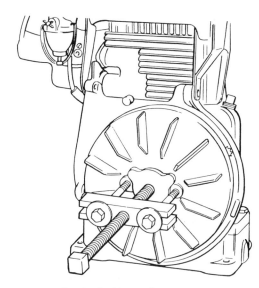

Removing flywheel with a puller

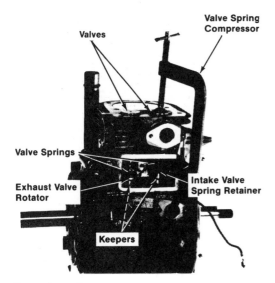

Removing valves

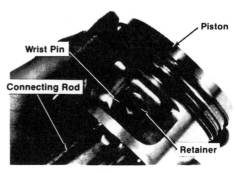

Removing piston from connecting rod

- Excessive sludge and varnish
- Scoring of the cylinder wall
- Piston damage
- Evidence of external oil leaks
- Evidence of overheating

Any of the listed problems could be the result of improper engine servicing or maintenance. The owner should be made aware of the benefits of proper servicing and maintenance.

1. Disconnect the spark plug lead and position it away from the spark plug terminal.

2. Unscrew the oil drain plug(s) and drain the crankcase oil into a suitable container for disposal.

3. Remove the wing nut, air cleaner cover, precleaner (if so equipped), paper element, three base screws, base, and base gasket.

4. If the engine is equipped with a flat muffler, remove muffler and gasket by unscrewing cap screws. If equipped with a round muffler remove by turning the threaded exhaust pipe between the muffler and engine with a pipe wench.

CAUTION: *Gasoline may be present in the carburetor and fuel system. Gasoline is extremely flammable and it can explode if ignited. Keep sparks, open flames, and other sources of ignition away from the engine. Disconnect and ground the spark plug lead to prevent the possibility of sparks from the ignition system.*

5. Close the fuel shut-off valve at fuel tank (if so equipped) or drain fuel from tank.

6. Loosen the hose clamp and remove fuel line from the carburetor inlet.

7. Remove two slotted hex cap screws, the carburetor, and gasket.

8. Remove the throttle linkage from the carburetor throttle lever.

9. Note the position of the governor spring in governor arm.

10. Loosen pawl nut. Remove governor arm and space from cross shaft.

NOTE: *Loosening pawl nut or removing governor arm will disrupt governor arm to cross shaft adjustment. Readjustment will be required upon reassembly.*

11. Remove the governor spring from the governor arm.

12. Remove the hex cap screw, plain washer, spacer, bracket and throttle lever.

CAUTION: *Gasoline may be present in the carburetor and fuel system. Gasoline is extremely flammable and can explode if ignited. Keep sparks, open flames, and other sources of ignition away from the engine. Dis-*

Removing connecting rod and piston

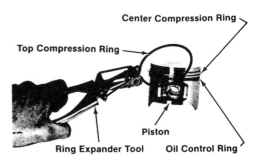

Removing piston rings

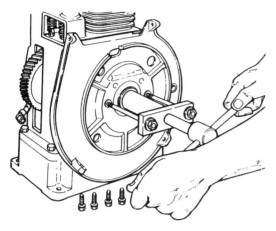

Removal of bearing plate with puller

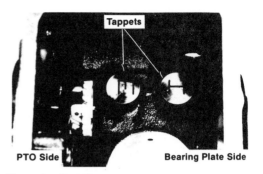

Removing tappets

connect and ground the spark plug lead to prevent the possibility of sparks from the ignition system.

13. Disconnect the fuel line from the fuel pump inlet fitting.

14. Disconnect the fuel line from the fuel pump outlet fitting.

15. Remove the fillister head screws, plain washers, fuel pump, and gasket.

16. With retractable starter: Remove screws, washers and the retractable starter assembly.

17. With electric starter:

a. Disconnect electrical connector(s) from back of key switch.

b. Disconnect lead from electrical starter.

c. Remove key switch panel.

d. Remove hex cap screws which mount electric starter to engine.

e. Remove electric starter.

CAUTION: *Gasoline may be present in the carburetor and fuel system. Gasoline is extremely flammable and it can explode if ignited. Keep sparks, open flames, and other sources of ignition away from the engine. Disconnect and ground the spark plug lead to prevent the possibility of sparks from the ignition system.*

18. Remove fuel line from fuel tank outlet fitting.

19. Remove tank with bracket(s).

20. Remove the dipstick.

21. Remove the cylinder head baffle.

22. Remove the carburetor side air baffle.

23. Remove the starter side air baffle.

24. Remove pawl nut, breather cover, and gasket.

25. Remove the filter, seal, reed stop, reed, breather plate, gasket, and stud.

26. Remove the spark plug, cylinder head, and gasket.

27. Remove breaker point cover, gasket, breaker point lead, breaker assembly and push rod.

NOTE: *Always use a flywheel strap wrench to hold the flywheel when loosening or tightening flywheel and fan retaining fasteners. Do not use any type of bar or wedge between fins of cooling fan as the fins could become cracked or damaged. Always use a puller to remove flywheel from crankshaft. Do not strike the crankshaft or flywheel, as these parts could become cracked or damaged.*

28. On rope start models:

a. Remove the grass screen retainer and wire mesh grass screen from rope pulley.

b. Hold the flywheel with a strap wrench and loosen the hex cap screw. Remove the hex cap screw, Remove the hex cap screw, plain washer, rope pulley, and spacer. Remove the nylon grass screen from the fan.

29. On retractable start models:

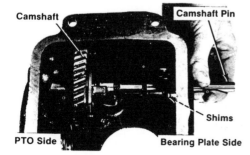

Removing camshaft

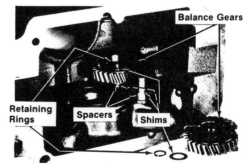

Removing balance gears

a. Hold the flywheel with a strap wrench and loosen hex cap screw securing flywheel to crankshaft. Remove the hex cap screw, plain washer, and drive cup.

b. Remove the grass screen from the drive cup.

30. On electric start models:

a. remove the grass screen from the fan.

b. Hold the flywheel with a strap wrench and loosen hex cap screw or hex nut securing flywheel to crankshaft. Remove the hex cap screw or hex nut. remove plain washer.

31. On all models

Flywheel is mounted on tapered portion of crankshaft. Use of a puller is recommended for removing flywheel. Bumping end of crankshaft with a hammer to loosen flywheel should be avoided as this can damage crankshaft.

NOTE: *Ignition magnet is not removable or serviceable!*

Do not attempt to remove ignition magnet from flywheel. Loosening or removing magnet mounting screws could cause the magnet to come off during engine operation and be thrown from the engine causing severe injury. Replace the flywheel if magnet is damaged.

32. remove the screws and stator.

33. Rotate the crankshaft until the piston is at top dead center of compression stroke (both valves closed and piston flush with top of bore).

34. Compress the valve springs with a valve spring compressor and remove the keepers.

35. Remove the valve spring compressor, then remove the valves, intake valve spring lower retainer, exhaust valve rotator, valve springs, and valve spring upper retainers.

NOTE: *Some models use a valve rotator on both valves.*

Make sure the piston is at top dead center in bore to prevent damage to oil dipper on connecting rod.

36. Remove the hex cap screws, oil pan, and gasket.

37. Remove the connecting rod cap.

NOTE: *If a carbon ridge is present at top of bore, use a ridge reamer tool to remove it before attempting to remove piston.*

38. Carefully push the connecting rod and piston out top of bore.

39. Remove the retainer and wrist pin. Separate the piston from the connecting rod.

40. remove the top and center compression rings and the oil control ring spacer using a ring expander tool.

41. Remove the rails and expander spring(s).

42. Remove the hex cap screws securing the bearing plate to crankcase.

43. Remove the bearing plate from the crankshaft using a puller.

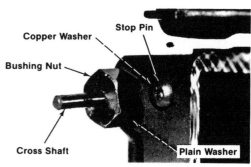
Removing cross shaft and stop pin

NOTE: *The front bearing may remain either in the bearing plate or on the crankshaft when the bearing plate is removed.*

44. Press the crankshaft out of the crankcase from the PTO side. It may be necessary to press crankshaft out of cylinder block. Bearing plate should be removed first if this is done.

NOTE: *If the repair does not require separating the bearing plate from crankshaft, the crankshaft and bearing plate can be pressed out as necessary.*

45. Drive the camshaft pin (and cup plug on bearing side plate) out of the crankcase from the PTO side.

46. Remove the camshaft pin, camshaft, and shim(s) on bearing plate side of camshaft.

47. Mark the tappets as being either intake or exhaust. Remove the tappets from the crankcase.

NOTE: *The intake valve tappet is closest to the bearing plate side of crankcase. The exhaust valve tappet is closest to the PTO side of crankcase.*

48. Remove the retaining rings, shims, balance gears with needle bearings, shims and spacers.

NOTE: *Extreme care must be taken when handling the new needle bearings or when removing balance gears containing the new bearings. The needles are no longer caged and will drop out. If this should occur, the*

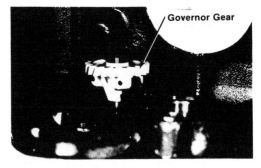
Removing governor gear

bearing case should be greased and the needles reset. There are 27 individual needles in each bearing.

49. Remove the stop pin, copper washer, governor gear, and thrust washer.

50. Remove bushing nut and sleeve. Remove cross shaft from inside crankcase.

51. Remove the oil seals from the crankcase and bearing plate.

52. Press the bearings out of the bearing plate and crankcase.

NOTE: *If the bearings have remained on the crankshaft, remove bearing by using a puller.*

INSPECTION AND REPAIR

All parts should be thoroughly cleaned. Dirty parts cannot be accurately gauged or inspected properly for wear or damage. There are many commercially available cleaners that quickly remove grease, oil and grime accumulation from engine parts. If such a cleaner is used, follow the manufacturer's instructions carefully, and make sure that all of the cleaner is removed before the engine is reassembled and placed in operation. Even small amounts of these cleaners quickly break down the lubricating properties of engine oils.

Flywheel Inspection

Inspect the flywheel for cracks, and the flywheel keyway for damage. Replace flywheel if cracked. Replace the flywheel, the crankshaft, and the key if flywheel key is sheared or the keyway is damaged.

Inspect ring gear for cracks or damage. Kohler no longer provides ring gears as a serviceable part. Replace flywheel if the ring gear is damaged.

Flywheel Key Inspection

Shearing is possible on engines with flywheel drives and battery ignition systems. Check conditions such as overload, ignition timing and spark plug gap when flywheel key shearing occurs.

Spark plug gap on battery ignition engines must be set as specified. If improperly gaped, a maverick spark can occur, which can cause improper ignition of unburned gases and can create a force causing the flywheel key to shear.

When repairing this type of failure, replace the flywheel, crankshaft, key, flywheel washer and nut or bolt.

Cylinder Head Inspection

Blocked cooling fins often cause localized "hot spots" which can result in a "blown" cylinder head gasket. If the gasket fails, high temperature gases can burn away portions of the aluminum alloy head. A cylinder head in this condition must be replaced.

If the cylinder head appears in good condition, use a block of wood or plastic scraper to scrape away carbon deposits. Be careful not to nick or scratch the aluminum, especially in gasket seating area.

The cylinder head should be checked for flatness. Use a feeler gauge and a surface plate or a piece of plate glass to make this check. Cylinder head flatness should not vary more than 0.003 in.; if it does, replace the cylinder head.

NOTE: *Measure cylinder head flatness between each cap screw hole.*

In cases where the head is warped or burned, it will also be necessary to replace the head screws. The high temperatures that warped or burned the head could have made the screws ductile which will cause them to stretch when tightened.

Cylinder Block Inspection and Reconditioning

Check all gasket surfaces to make sure they are free of gasket fragments. Gasket surfaces must also be free of deep scratches or nicks.

Scoring of the Cylinder Wall: Unburned fuel, in severe case, can cause scuffing and scoring of the cylinder wall. As raw fuel seeps down the cylinder wall, it washes the necessary lubricating oils off the piston and cylinder wall so that the piston rings make metal to metal contact with the wall. Scoring of the cylinder wall can also be caused by localized hot spots resulting from blocked fins or from inadequate or contaminated lubrication.

Measuring cylinder bore

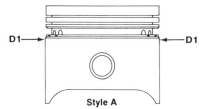

Style A—Measure piston diameter (D1) perpendicular to piston pin just below the oil ring groove.

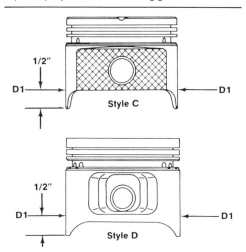

Styles C and D—Measure piston diameter (D1) perpendicular to piston pin at 1/2″ above the bottom of the skirt.

Measuring piston diameter

If the cylinder bore is badly scored, excessively worn, tapered, or out of round, resizing is necessary. Use an inside micrometer to determine the amount of wear (see "general Information", Section 1), then select the nearest suitable oversize of either 0.003 in., 0.010 in., 0.020 in., or 0.030 in.. Resizing to one of these oversizes will allow usage of the available oversize piston and ring assemblies. Initially, resize

using a boring bar, then use the following procedures for honing the cylinder:

HONING

While most commercially available cylinder hones can be used with either portable drills or drill presses, the use of a low speed drill press is preferred as it facilitates more accurate alignment of the bore in relation to the crankshaft crossbore. Honing is best accomplished at a drill speed of about 250 RPM and 60 strokes per minute. After installing coarse stones in hone, proceed as follows:

1. Lower hone into bore and after centering, adjust so that stones are in contact with the cylinder wall. Use of a commercial cutting-cooling agent is recommended.

2. With the lower edge of each stone positioned even with the lowest edge of the bore, start drill and honing process. Move hone up and down while resizing to prevent formation of cutting ridges. Check size frequently.

NOTE: *Keep in mind the temperatures caused by honing may cause inaccurate measurements. make sure the block is cool when measuring.*

3. When bore is within 0.0025 in. of desired size, remove coarse stones and replace with burnishing stones. Continue with burnishing stones until within 0.0025 in. of desired size and then use finish stones (220-280 grit) and polish to final size. A crosshatch should be observed if honing is done correctly. The crosshatch should intersect at approximately 23 degrees to 33 degrees off the horizontal. Too flat an angle could cause the rings to skip and wear excessively, too high an angle will result in high oil consumption.

4. After resizing, check the bore for roundness, taper, and size. Use an inside micrometer, telescoping gauge, or bore gauge to take measurements. The measurements should be taken

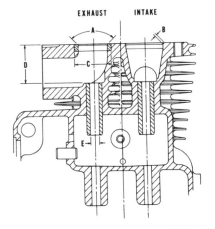

Valve details

at three locations in the cylinder - at the top, middle, and bottom. Two measurements should be taken (perpendicular to each other) at each of the three locations.

5. Thoroughly clean cylinder wall with soap and hot water. Use a scrub brush to remove all traces or boring/honing process. Dry thoroughly and apply a light coat of SAE 10 oil to prevent rust.

MEASURING PISTON-TO-BORE CLEARANCE

Before installing the piston into the cylinder bore, it is necessary that the clearance be accurately checked. This step is often overlooked, and if the clearances are not within specifications, generally engine failure will result.

NOTE: *Do not use a feeler gauge to measure piston-to-bore clearance, it will yield inaccurate measurements. use a micrometer.*

The following procedures should be used to measure the piston-to-bore clearance:

1. Use a micrometer and measure the diameter of the piston as shown.

2. Use an inside micrometer and measure the diameter of the piston as shown.

3. Use an inside micrometer, telescoping gauge, or bore gauge and measure the cylinder bore. take the measurement approximately 2½ in. below the top of the bore and perpendicular to the piston pin.

4. Piston-to-bore clearance is the difference between the bore and the piston diameter (step 2 minus step 1). For style A pistons only, clearance should be: 0.0035-0.006 in. for K91, 0.007-0.010 in. for K161-K341. For piston styles C and D, clearance should be: 0.0034-0.0051 in. for K181, 0.0045-0.0062 in. for K301.

VALVE INSPECTION AND SERVICE

Carefully inspect valve mechanism parts. Inspect valve springs and related hardware for excessive wear or distortion. Valve spring free height should be approximately the dimension given in the chart below. Check valves and valve seat area or inserts for evidence of deep pitting, cracks or distortion. Check clearance of valve stems in guides.

Hard starting, or loss of power accompanied by high fuel consumption may be symptoms of faulty valve. Although these symptoms could also be attributed to worn rings, remove and check valves first. After removal, clean valve head, face and stem with power wire brush and then carefully inspect for defects such as warped valve head, excessive corrosion or worn stem end. Replace valves found to be in bad condition. A normal valve and valves in bad condition are shown in the accompanying illustrations.

Valve Guides

If a valve guide is worn beyond specifications, it will not guide the valve in a straight line. This may result in a burnt valve face or seat, loss of comp ession, and excessive oil consumption.

To check valve guide to valve stem clearance, thoroughly clean the valve guide and, using a split-ball gauge, measure the inside diameter. Then, using an outside micrometer, measure the diameter of the valve stem at several points on the stem where it moves in the valve guide. Use the largest stem diameter to calculate the clearance. On models K91, K161, and K181, the clearance should not exceed 0.005 in. for intake and 0.007 in. for exhaust valves. On models K241, K301, the clearance should not exceed 0.006 in. for intake and 0.008 in. for exhaust valves. If the clearance exceeds these specifications, determine whether the valve stem or the guide is responsible for the excessive clearance.

NOTE: *The exhaust valves on these engines have a slightly tapered valve stem to help prevent sticking. Because of the taper, the valve stem must be measured in two places to determine if the valve stem is worn. If the valve stem diameter is within specifications, replace the valve guide.*

VALVE GUIDE REMOVAL

The valve guides are a tight press fit in the cylinder block. A valve guide removal tool is recommended to remove valve guides (refer to "Special Tools" section). To remove valve guide, proceed as follows:

1. Install ⁵⁄₁₆-18 NC nut on coarse threaded end of 2½ in. long stud (K161 and K181) or 3½ in. long stud (K241, K301).

2. Insert other end of stud through valve guide bore and install ⁵⁄₁₆-24 NF nut. Tighten both ruts securely.

NOTE: *Valve guide must be held firmly by the stud assembly so that all slide hammer force will act on the guide.*

3. Assemble the valve guide removal adapter to the stud and then slide hammer to the adapter.

4. Use the slide hammer to pull the guide out.

VALVE GUIDE INSTALLATION

1. Make sure valve guide bore is clean and free of nicks or burrs.

2. Using valve guide driver (refer to "Special Tools" section), align and then press guide in until valve guide driver bottoms on valve guide counterbore.

3. Valve guides are often slightly compressed during insertion. Use a piloted reamer and then a finishing reamer to resize the guide bore to 0.3125 in. for K161, K181, K241, K301.

Valve Seat Inserts

The intake valve seat is usually machined into the cylinder block, however, certain applications may specify a hard alloy insert. If the seat becomes badly pitted, cracked, or distorted, the insert must be replaced.

The insert is a tight press fit in the cylinder block. A valve seat removal tool is recommended for this job (refer to "Special Tools" section). Since insert removal causes loss of metal in the insert bore area, use only Kohler service replacement inserts, which are slightly larger to provide proper retention in the cylinder block. Make sure new insert is properly started and pressed into bore to prevent cocking of the insert.

VALVE SEAL INSERT REMOVAL

1. Install valve seat puller on forcing screw and lightly secure with washer and nut.

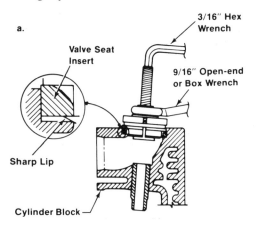

a.

Valve Seat Insert

3/16" Hex Wrench

9/16" Open-end or Box Wrench

Sharp Lip

Cylinder Block

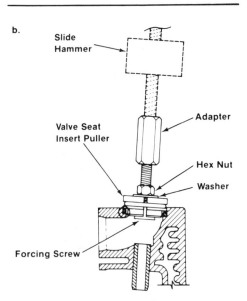

b.

Slide Hammer

Adapter

Valve Seat Insert Puller

Hex Nut

Washer

Forcing Screw

Pulling valve seat insert (typical)

2. Center the puller assembly on valve seat insert.

3. Hold forcing screw with a hexing wrench to prevent turning and slowly tighten nut.

NOTE: *Make sure sharp lip on puller (see insert) engages in joint between bottom of valve seat insert and cylinder block counterbore, all the way around.*

4. Continue to tighten nut until puller is tight against valve seat insert.

5. Assemble adapter to valve seat puller forcing screw and slide hammer to adapter.

6. Use slide hammer to remove valve seat insert.

VALVE SEAT INSERT INSTALLATION

1. Make sure valve seat insert bore is clean and free of nicks and burrs.

2. Align valve seat insert in counterbore and using valve seat installer and driver (refer to "Special Tools" section), press seat in until bottomed.

3. Use a standard valve seat cutter and cut seat to dimensions shown.

Reground or new valves must be lapped in to provide proper fit. Use a hand valve grinder with suction for final lapping. Lightly coat valve face with "fine" grade of grinding compound, then rotate valve on seat with grinder. Continue grinding until smooth surface is obtained on seat and on valve face. Thoroughly clean cylinder block in soap and hot water to remove all traces of grinding compound. After drying cylinder block apply a light coating of SAE 10 oil to prevent rusting.

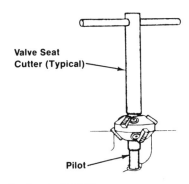

Valve Seat Cutter (Typical)

Pilot

Standard valve seat cutter

PISTON AND RINGS

Identification

Three different styles of pistons are currently being used in Kohler K-series engines.

Style "A" pistons can be used in all K-series engines. The style A piston can be identified by its full skirt and its lack of an installation direction identifier on its crown (a new piston can be installed facing either direction).

The Style "C" piston is used on the K341 engines only. It can be identified by its partial skirt and raised criss-cross design in the recessed area around the piston pin bore. In addition, it has an installation direction identifier (a notch) at its top. the style C piston is to be installed with the notch facing the flywheel.

The Style "D" piston has been used on the K181 and K301 engines. It can be identified by its partial skirt and rectangular recessed area around the piston pin bore. In addition, it has an installation direction identifier, Fly, which is stamped into the top of the piston. the style D piston is to be installed with the arrow of the Fly mark pointing towards the flywheel.

Piston Sizes - All Styles

In order to ensure a correct fit between piston and cylinder we utilize two cylinder bore sizes at the factory. Cylinder blocks are honed to the Standard (STD) size or 0.003: (.075mm) oversize with corresponding pistons. Blocks using the oversize are stamped on the cylinder head gasket surface with 0.003 in.. It is essential that 0.003 in. oversize pistons are used in these blocks to prevent possible failure such as noisy engine or eventual piston skirt cracking. These pistons are available from Kohler. Standard Service Rings should be used with both Standard and 0.003 in. oversize pistons. ring end gap will increase slightly when installed on 0.003 in. oversize pistons; however, sealing is maintained due to the ring design.

Inspection

Scuffing and scoring of piston and cylinder wall occur when internal temperatures approach the melting point of the piston. Temperatures high enough to do this are created by friction, which is usually attributed to improper lubrication, and/or overheating of the engine.

Normally, very little wear takes place in the piston boss-piston pin area. If the original piston and connecting rod can be reused after new rings are installed, the original pin can also be reused but new piston pin retainers are required. The piston pin is included as part of the piston assembly - if the pin boss in piston, or the pin are worn or damaged, a new piston assembly is required.

Ring failure is usually indicated by excessive oil consumption and blue exhaust smoke. When

Stuck, Broken Rings

Abrasive Worn Rings

Abrasive Scratched Rings

Scored Piston and Rings

Common types of piston and ring damage

rings fail, oil is allowed to enter the combustion chamber where it is burned along with the fuel. High oil consumption can also occur when the piston ring end gap is incorrect because the ring cannot properly conform to the cylinder wall under this condition. Oil control is also lost when ring gaps are not staggered during installation.

When cylinder temperatures get too high, lacquer and varnish collect on piston causing rings to stick which results in rapid wear. A worn ring usually takes on a shiny or bright appearance. Scratches on rings and piston are caused by abrasive material such as carbon, dirt, or pieces of hard metal.

Detonation damage occurs when a portion of the fuel charge ignites spontaneously from heat and pressure shortly after ignition. This creates two frame fronts which meet and explode to create extreme hammering pressures on a specific area of the piston. detonation generally occurs from using fuels with too low of an octane rating.

Pre-ignition of the fuel charge before the timed spark can cause damage similar to detonation. Pre-ignition damage is often more sever than detonation damage - often, a hole is quickly burned right through the piston dome. Pre-ignition is caused by a hot spot in the combustion chamber from sources such as: glowing carbon deposits, blocked fins, improperly seated valves or wrong spark park plug.

Service

K-series replacement pistons are available in STD bore size, and in 0.003 in., 0.010 in., 0.020 in. and 0.030 in. oversizes. Replacement pistons include new piston ring sets and new piston pins.

Service replacement piston ring sets are also available separately for STD-0.003 in. (same ring set for both sizes), 0.010 in., 0.020 in. and 0.030 in. oversized pistons. Always use new piston rings when installing pistons. Never reuse old rings.

The cylinder bore must be deglazed before service ring sets are used.

Some important points to remember when servicing piston rings:

1. If the cylinder block does not need reboring and if the old piston is within wear limits (refer to section 1, "General Information") and free of score or scuff marks, the old piston may be reused.

2. Remove old rings and clean up grooves. Never reuse old rings.

3. Before installing new rings on piston, place top two rings, each in turn, into its running area in cylinder bore and check end gap.

Measuring piston ring clearance

4. After installing the new compression (top and middle) rings on piston, check piston-to-ring side clearance. Maximum recommended side clearance is 0.006 in.. If side clearance is greater than 0.006 in., a new piston must be used.

Oil Ring End Gaps

Although 4 sizes of service ring sets are available (Std., ± 0.010 in., ± 0.020 in., ± 0.030 in.), only two sizes of oil rings are supplied (Std. and 0.020 in. oversize). When using 0.010 in. and 0.030 in. oversize ring sets, the oil rings appear to have excessive end gap. This is not detrimental and proper sealing will be achieved due to the additional scraper rings and expander.

NOTE: *Scraper and main ring end gaps should be staggered around the groove to prevent combustion blow-by.*

Piston Ring Installation

NOTE: *Rings must be installed correctly. Ring installation instructions are usually included with new ring sets. Follow instructions carefully. Use a piston ring expander to install rings. Install the bottom (oil control) ring first and the top compression last.*

POSI-LOCK CONNECTING RODS

Posi-Lock connecting rods are used in some K-series engines. On model K181 engines with

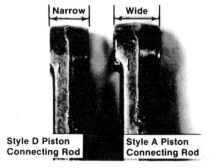

Style D Piston
Connecting Rod

Style A Piston
Connecting Rod

Posi-lock connecting rods

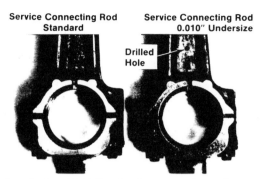

Service Connecting Rod Standard

Service Connecting Rod 0.010″ Undersize

Drilled Hole

Standard and 0.010″ undersize connecting rods

the style D pistons (refer to "Piston and Rings, Identification" earlier in this section), the connecting rods have a narrower piston pin end than on the earlier (style A) Posi-Lock connecting rods. Therefore, the Posi-Lock connecting rods used with the style D pistons are not interchangeable with the Posi-Lock connecting rods used with style A pistons.

Inspection and Service

Check bearing area (big end) for excessive wear, score marks, running and side clearances (refer to Section 1, "General Information"). Replace rod and cap if scored or excessively worn.

Service replacement connecting rods are available in STD crank pin size and 0.010 in. undersize. The 0.010 in. undersize can be identified by the drilled hole located in the lower end of the rod shank. Always refer to the appropriate parts information to ensure the correct replacements are used..

BALANCE GEARS AND STUB SHAFTS

Some K241 and K301 engines are equipped with a balance gear system.

The system consists of two gears and spacer (used to control end play) mounted on stub shafts which are pressed into the crankcase. The gears and spacer s are held on the shafts with snap-ring retainers. The gears are timed with and driven by the engine crankshaft.

Inspection and Repair

Use a micrometer and measure the stub shaft diameter. If the diameter is less then 0.4996 in., replace the stub shaft. Use an arbor press to push old shaft out and new shaft in. The stub shaft must protrude a specific distance above the stub shaft boss. If the stub shaft boss is about $7/16$ in. above the main bearing boss, press the shaft in until it is 0.735 in. above the stub shaft boss. On blocks where the stub shaft boss is only about $1/16$ in. above the main bearing boss, press shaft in until is 1.110 in. above the stub shaft boss. A $3/8$ in. spacer must be used with the shaft which protrudes 1.110 in..

Inspect the gears for worn or chipped teeth and for worn needle bearings, if required.

BALANCE GEAR BEARING AND BALANCE GEAR ASSEMBLY

A new needle bearing for the Dynamic Balance System is now being used on 10-16 HP Kohler engines. the new bearing (part number 47030 01) has been in use beginning with serial number 9641311. It is not interchangeable with the old needle bearing, part number 236506.

Complete balance gear assemblies are interchangeable - and old style gear assemblies have been superceded with a new gear assembly, part number 47 042 01.

Critical consideration is required when only the needle bearing is to be replaced. The engine serial number alone can correctly determine which needle bearing is involved on original equipment engines. However should a bearing replacement be required after a complete bal-

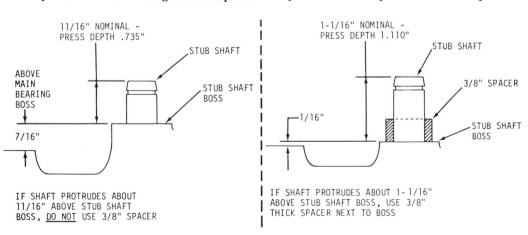

Stub shaft press depth

ance gear has been replaced on an engine with a serial number prior to 9641311, the following methods will assist in identifying the correct bearing:

Method #1 - I.D. of Balance Gear Bore
0.6825 - 236506
0.6821
0.6865 - 47 030 01
0.6869

Method #2 - O.D. of Old Bearing
0.6825 - 236506
0.6828
0.6870 - 47 030 01
0.6875

GOVERNOR GEAR

Inspection

Inspect the governor gear teeth. Look for any evidence of worn, chipped or cracked teeth. If one or more of these problems is noted, replace the governor gear.

CAMSHAFT AND CRANKSHAFT

Inspection and Service

Inspect the gear teeth on both the crankshaft and camshaft. If the teeth are badly worn, chipped or some are missing, replacement of the damaged components will be necessary.

Also, inspect the crankshaft bearings for scoring, grooving, etc. Do not replace bearings unless they show signs of damage or are out of running clearance specifications. If crankshaft turns easily and noiselessly, and there is not evidence of scoring, grooving, etc., on the races of bearing surfaces, the bearings can be reused.

Check crankshaft keyways. If worn or chipped, replacement of the crankshaft will be necessary. Also inspect the crank pin for score marks or metallic pickup. Slight score marks can be cleaned with crocus cloth soaked in oil. If wear limits, as stated in Section 1, "General Information", are exceeded, it will be necessary to either replace the crankshaft or regrind the crank pin to 0.010 in. undersize. If reground, a 0.010 in. undersize connecting rod (big end) must then be used to achieve proper running clearance. measure the crank pin for size, taper and out-of-round.

NOTE: *If the crank pin is reground, visually check to ensure that the fillet blends smoothly with the crank pin surface.*

When replacing a crankshaft with external threads on the flywheel end with one that has internal threads, different mounting hardware is required. The internally threaded crankshafts are solid in kits which include the hard-

ware. The mounting hardware can also be purchased separately.

1. Use a $^{13}/_{32}$ I.D. x 1¼ O.D. x ⅛ TH. plain washer (Part No. 52114 01) when installing drive cups with a 1¼ in. Dia. spot face (machined, recessed area around mounting hole). These drive cups are primarily used on International Harvester applications, but may be found on other applications. Therefore, use the drive cup to identify which washer should be used.

2. Required for drive cups with ⅝ in. mounting hole.

OPTIONAL GEAR REDUCTION UNIT

The reduction unit consists of a driven gear which is pressed on the power take off (PTO) shaft. The drive gear is an integral part of the engine crankshaft. The gear reduction on the K91 and K181 units is 6:1. The gear reduction on the K301 engines is 4:1. The PTO shaft is supported by two bearings, one in the cover and the other in the housing. Oil seals are provided at both ends of the shaft.

Removal

1. Drain lubricating oil from unit.
2. Remove four cap screws from gear housing and slide cover off along drive gear.
3. Remove four cap screws holding gear housing to engine.
4. Wash all parts and inspect shaft, bushing and gear for wear. Replace worn parts.
5. Remove old oil seals and install new seals (flat side out) in the gear housing and cover.

Installation

1. Wrap piece of tape or roll paper around crankshaft gear to protect the oil seal, slide housing over the shaft and attach to the block. Two lock washers are used on the outside of housing and copper washers inside.

2. Tape or paper should be wrapped around the shaft to prevent the keyway from damaging the cover oil seal. Install the gasket(s) and reduction gear cover and tighten cap screws.

3. Adjust shaft end clearance to 0.001-0.006

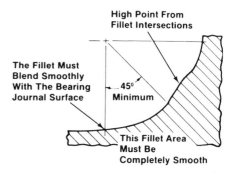

Crankpin fillets

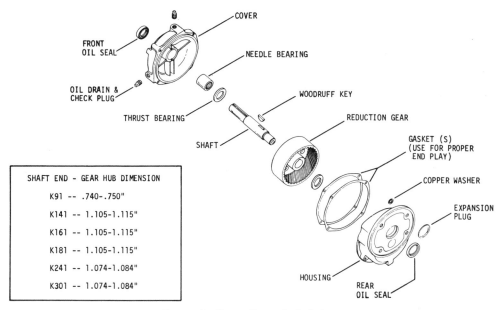

SHAFT END - GEAR HUB DIMENSION

K91 -- .740-.750"

K141 -- 1.105-1.115"

K161 -- 1.105-1.115"

K181 -- 1.105-1.115"

K241 -- 1.074-1.084"

K301 -- 1.074-1.084"

Gear reduction unit—exploded view

in. by varying the total gasket thickness, adding or removing gaskets as required.

4. Remove oil fill plug and level plug, fill unit to the oil level hole. Use the same grade of oil as used in the engine.

ENGINE REASSEMBLY

The following sequence is suggested for complete engine reassembly. This procedure assumes that all components are new or have been reconditioned, and all component subassembly work has been completed. This procedure may have to varied slightly to accommodate options or special equipment.

NOTE: *Make sure the engine is assembled using all specified torque values, tightening sequences, and clearances. failure to observe specifications could cause severe engine wear or damage. Always use new gaskets.*

1. Install the rear bearing into crankcase using the #4747 handle and appropriate bearing installer. (Refer to the "Special Tools" section).

Make sure the bearing is bottomed fully, and is straight and true in bore. Install the rear main bearing by pressing it into cylinder block. If using a shielded type bearing, install with shielded side facing toward inside of block.

2. Slide cross shaft into place from inside of block.

3. Place speed control disc on governor bushing nut and thread bushing nut into block. On earlier models, the cross shaft has an extension riveted in place to line up with governor gear. Torque bushing nut as follows:

- K91 70-90 inch lbs.
- K161, K181 – 130-150 inch lbs.
- K241, K301 – 100-120 inch lbs.

4. Install the thrust washer, governor gear, copper washer, and stop pin.

5. Rotate governor gear assembly to be sure stop pin does not contact weight section governor gear.

6. Install the intake valve tappet and exhaust valve tappet into crankcase. (Intake valve

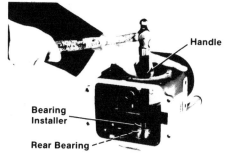

Installing rear bearing

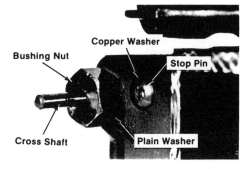

Installing cross shaft and stop pin

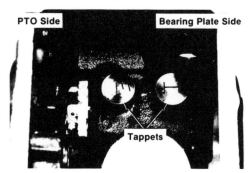

Installing tappets

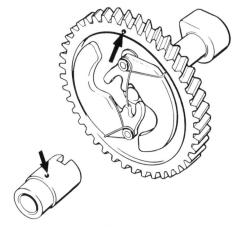

Timing marks—pre-ACR camshaft

tappet towards bearing plate side; exhaust valve tappet towards PTO side of crankcase.).

NOTE: *On K161 and K181 ACR engines, install the shorter tappet in the exhaust bore guide. Intake and exhaust tappets are interchangeable on other models.*

7. Install the camshaft, one 0.005 in. shim spacer, and the camshaft pin (from bearing plate side). Do not driver the camshaft pin into its final position at this time.

NOTE: *On pre-ACR models with the automatic spark advance camshaft, spread actuators and insert cam. Align the timing marks on cam and gear as shown.*

8. Measure the camshaft end play between the spacer and crankcase boss using a flat feeler gauge. Recommended camshaft end play is 0.005-0.020 in. for model K91 and 0.005-0.010 in. - for all other K-series models. Add or subtract 0.005 in. and/or 0.010 in. shim spacers as necessary to obtain the proper end play.

9. the K-Series engines now use a new camshaft pin, the new camshaft pins are shorter than the old pins originally used in K-Series engines.

10. To install the new (shorter) camshaft pin, drive the camshaft pin from the bearing plate side of crankshaft into the PTO side of crankcase:

a. For Models K161 and K181 - drive the camshaft pin to a depth of 0.275-0.285 in.

from the machined baring plate gasket surface.

b. For Models K241, K301 - drive the camshaft pin to a depth of 0.300-0.330 in. from the machined bearing plate gasket surface.

To install the old (longer) camshaft pin, drive the camshaft pin into the crankcase until the PTO end of camshaft pin is flush with the mounting surface on PTO side of crankcase.

11. On Engines So Equipped: The balance gears must be timed to the crankshaft whenever the crankshaft is installed. Use a balance gear timing tool to simplify this procedure (refer to the "Special Tools" section in this manual). if the balance gears must be timed without using the tool, do not install the lower balance gear (closest to the oil pan) until after the crankshaft has been installed.

12. Install the ⅜ in. spacer, one 0.010 in. shim spacer, balance gear, one 0.020 in. shim spacer, and retaining ring (rounded edge towards balance gear). A new style needle bearing is now being used on the K-Series balance gear assembly.

NOTE: *Extreme care must be taken when handling the new needle bearings. The needles are no longer caged and will drop out. If*

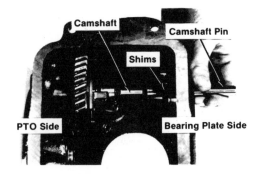

Installing camshaft

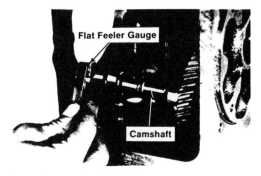

Measuring camshaft end play

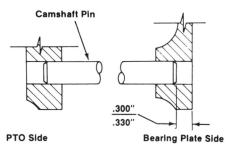

PTO Side   **Bearing Plate Side**

.300"
.330"

Installing camshaft pin

this should occur, the bearing case should be greased and the needles reset. There are 27 individual needles in each bearing.

13. Check end play with a flat feeler gauge. Recommended end play is 0.002-0.010 in.. If end play is not within range, install or remove 0.005 in. and 0.010 in. spacers, as necessary.

14. On Engines Without Balance Gears

a. Lubricate the crankshaft rear bearing surface. Insert the crankshaft through the rear bearing.

NOTE: *If the crankshaft and bearing plate have not been separated, position the fuel line and wiring harness between the bearing plate and crankcase before pressing the crankshaft all the way in.*

b. Align the primary timing mark on crankshaft with the timing mark on camshaft. Press the crankshaft into rear bearing. Make sure the camshaft and crankshaft gears mesh and that the timing marks remain aligned while pressing.

15. On Engines With Balance Gears:

K-Series have two styles of balance gear assemblies. To provide improved vibration reducing characteristics, redesigned balance gear assemblies are being used in the K241 and K301 single cylinder engines. These new balance gear assemblies (Part No. 45 043 03) are being used in engines with a Serial No. of 1613600013 and later, and for service replacement.

Because of the physical differences of the gear, new procedures for installing the crankshaft, and timing the balance gears, crankshaft, and camshaft are required.

The following crankshaft installation procedures are broken down into four sections:

1A) OLD STYLE BALANCE GEAR ASSEMBLY - WITH A BALANCE GEAR TIMING TOOL

1B) OLD STYLE BALANCE GEAR ASSEMBLY - WITHOUT A BALANCE GEAR TIMING TOOL

2A) NEW STYLE BALANCE GEAR ASSEMBLY - WITH A BALANCE GEAR TIMING TOOL

2B) NEW STYLE BALANCE GEAR ASSEM-

BLY - WITHOUT A BALANCE GEAR TIMING TOOL METHOD

1A) OLD STYLE BALANCE GEAR ASSEMBLY - WITH A BALANCE GEAR TIMING TOOL

1. Align the primary timing marks of balance gears with the teeth on timing tool. Insert tool so it meshes with gears. Hold or clamp tool against oil pan gasket surface.

2. lubricate the crankshaft rear bearing surface. Insert the PTO end of crankshaft through rear bearing. "Straddle" the primary and secondary timing marks on crankshaft over the rear bearing oil drain. Press the crankshaft into rear bearing until the crankgear is just above the camshaft gear but not in mesh with it.

NOTE: *If the crankshaft and bearing plate have not been separated, position the fuel line and wiring harness between the bearing plate and crankcase before pressing the crankshaft all the way in.*

3. Remove the balance gear timing tool and align the primary timing mark on the crankshaft with the timing mark on the camshaft gear. Press the crankshaft all the way in to the rear bearing. Make sure the camshaft and crankshaft gears mesh and that the timing marks align while pressing.

4. Check the timing of the crankshaft, camshaft, and balance gears:

a. The primary timing mark on crankshaft should align with the secondary timing mark on lower balance gear.

b. The primary timing mark should mark on crankshaft should align with the timing mark on camshaft.

c. If the mark do not align, the timing is incorrect and must be corrected.

1B) OLD STYLE BALANCE GEAR ASSEMBLY - WITHOUT A BALANCE GEAR TIMING TOOL

NOTE: *The balance gear should be installed after the crankshaft has been installed.*

1. Lubricate the crankshaft rear bearing surface. Insert the PTO end of crankshaft through rear bearing. Align the primary timing mark on

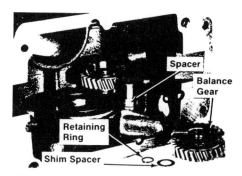

Installing balance gears

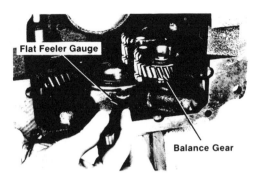

Measuring balance gear end play

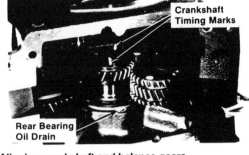

Aligning crankshaft and balance gears

NEW   OLD

Old and new style balance gear assemblies

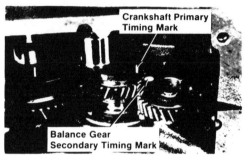

Checking crankshaft and balance gear alignment

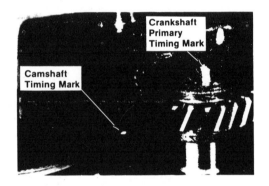

Aligning crankshaft and camshaft timing marks

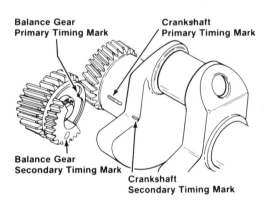

Timing marks on balance gear and crankshaft

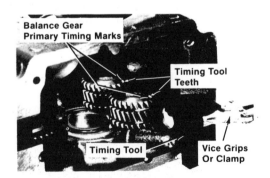

Installing balance gear timing tool

crankshaft with the primary timing mark on upper balance gear. Press the crankshaft into rear bearing until the crankgear just starts to mesh (about $\frac{1}{16}$ in.) with the center ring of balance gear teeth.

NOTE: *If the crankshaft and bearing plate have not been separated, position the fuel line and wiring harness between the bearing plate and crankcase before pressing the crankshaft all the way in.*

2. Align the primary timing mark on the crankshaft with the timing mark on the camshaft gear. Press the crankshaft all the way into the rear bearing. Make sure the camshaft and crankshaft gears mesh and that the timing marks align while pressing.

3. Position the crankshaft so it is about 15 degrees past BDC. Install ⅜ in. spacer, and one 0.010 in. shim spacer. Align the secondary timing mark on the lower balance gear with the secondary timing mark on the crankshaft. In-

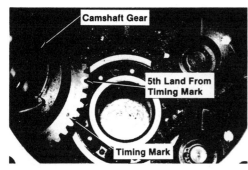

Marking load on camshaft gear

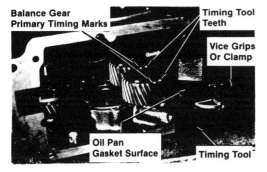

Installing balance gear timing tool

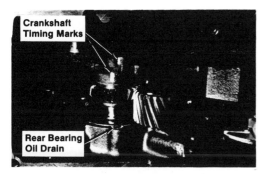

Aligning crankshaft and rear bearing oil drain

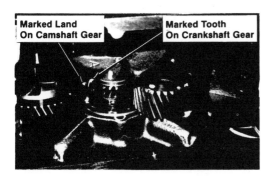

Aligning camshaft gear and crankshaft gear

stall the lower balance gear on the stub shaft. If properly timed, the primary timing mark on the crankshaft will now be aligned with the secondary timing mark on the lower balance gear.

4. Install one (1) 0.020: shim spacer and retaining ring (rounded edge towards gear). Check end play of lower balance gear as instructed under ''INSTALL BALANCE GEARS.''

5. Check the timing mark on crankshaft, camshaft, and balance gears. The primary mark on crankshaft should align with the primary timing mark on upper balance gear. The primary mark on crankshaft should align with the secondary timing mark on lower balance gear. The primary mark on crankshaft should align with timing mark on camshaft. If the marks do not align, the timing is incorrect and must be corrected.

2A) NEW STYLE BALANCE GEAR ASSEMBLY - WITH A BALANCE GEAR TIMING TOOL

1. Count and mark the teeth on the crankshaft gear, and the lands (notches between teeth) on the camshaft gear as follows:

a. Crankshaft - Locate the primary timing mark on crankshaft. While looking at the PTO end of crankshaft, start with the tooth directly below timing mark and count five (5) teeth in a counterclockwise direction. mark the fifth tooth.

b. Camshaft - Locate the timing mark on camshaft. starting with the land next to the timing mark, count five (5) lands in a counterclockwise direction. Mark the fifth land.

2. Align the primary timing marks on balance gears with the teeth on timing tool. Insert the tool so it meshes with the gears. Hold or clamp the tool against oil pan gasket surface of crankcase.

3. Lubricate the rear bearing surface of crankshaft. Insert the PTO end of crankshaft through the rear bearing. ''Straddle'' the primary and secondary timing marks on crankshaft over the rear bearing oil drain. Press the crankshaft into the rear bearing until the crankshaft gear is just above the camshaft gear, but not in mesh with it. Do not remove the balance gear timing tool at this time.

4. Align the fifth (5th) land marked on cam-

Crankshaft gear/lower balance gear alignment

shaft gear with the fifth (5th) tooth marked on camshaft gear. Press the crankshaft all the way into the rear bearing. Make sure the camshaft and crankshaft gears mesh and the marks align while pressing.

5. Remove the balance gear timing tool. Check the timing of the crankshaft, camshaft, and balance gears. The primary timing mark on crankshaft should align with the secondary timing mark on lower balance gear. The primary timing mark on crankshaft should align with the timing mark on camshaft.

2B) NEW STYLE BALANCE GEAR ASSEMBLY - WITHOUT A BALANCE GEAR TIMING TOOL

NOTE: *The lower balance gear should be installed after the crankshaft has been installed.*

1. Count and mark the teeth on the crankshaft gear, and the land (notches between teeth) on the upper balance gear as follows:

a. Crankshaft - Locate the primary timing mark on crankshaft. While looking at the PTO end of crankshaft, start with the tooth directly below timing mark and count twelve (12) teeth in a counterclockwise direction. Mark the twelfth tooth.

b. Upper Balance Gear - Locate the secondary timing mark on balance gear. Starting with the land next to the timing mark, count seven (7) lands in a clockwise direction. Mark the seventh land.

2. Lubricate the rear bearing surface of crankshaft. Insert the PTO end of crankshaft through the rear bearing. Align the twelfth (12th) tooth marked on crankshaft gear with the seventh (7th) land marked on upper balance gear. Press the crankshaft into the rear bearing until the crankshaft gear is just above the camshaft gear, but not in mesh with it.

3. Align the timing mark on camshaft with the primary timing mark on crankshaft.

NOTE: *Align the timing mark on camshaft with the primary timing mark on crankshaft. To align the marks, rotate the camshaft only - do not rotate the crankshaft. Rotating the*

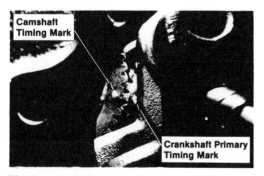

Aligning camshaft gear and crankshaft gear

Aligning lower balance gear and crankshaft

Crankshaft gear/lower balance gear alignment

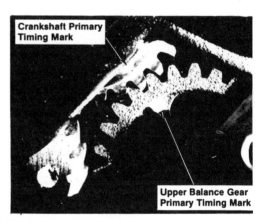

Crankshaft gear/upper balance gear alignment

crankshaft could cause the crankshaft gear to come out of mesh and the marks align while pressing.

4. Install the ³⁄₈ in. spacer and one (1) 0.010 in. shim spacer to the stub shaft for the lower balance gear.

5. Position the crankshaft so it is about 15 degrees past bottom dead center (BDC). Align the secondary timing mark on crankshaft. Install the lower balance gear to the stub shaft. If properly timed, the secondary timing mark on lower balance gear will now be aligned with the primary timing mark on crankshaft.

6. Secure the lower balance gear to stub

shaft using one (1) 0.020 in. shim spacer and re-taining ring (rounded edge towards gear). Check end play of lower balance gear as in-structed in "INSTALL BALANCE GEARS".

7. Check the timing of the crankshaft, cam-shaft, and balance gears. The primary timing mark on crankshaft should align with the sec-ondary timing mark on lower balance gear. The primary timing mark on crankshaft should align with the timing mark on camshaft. The primary timing mark on crankshaft should align with the primary timing mark on upper balance gear. If the marks do not align, the tim-ing is incorrect and must be corrected.

Front Bearing Installation

Install the front bearing into the bearing plate using the #4747 handle and appropriate bearing installer. (Refer to the "Special Tools" section). Make sure the bearing is bottomed fully, and straight and true in the bore.

CONTINUE ENGINE ASSEMBLY

16. Position the fuel line and wiring harness (if so equipped) to crankcase.

17. Adjust the fuel line and wiring harness to their final positions just before securing the bearing plate to the crankcase.

18. The installation of bearing plate and gas-kets can be made considerably easier with the use of two simple, easy to make alignment guides. Using 2½ in. long bolts with the hexa-gon heads removed and screwdriver slots cut in the stem, screw the two headless bolts into the cylinder block diagonally from each other. Bolt thread sizes are ¼-20 U.N.C. for K91-K181; ⅜-16 U.N.C. for K241-K361.

19. Lubricate the bearing surface of crank-shaft and bearing. Install the gasket, two or three 0.005 in. shims (as required), and bearing plate over studs.

NOTE: *Crankshaft end play is determined*

Installing oil seals using sleeves

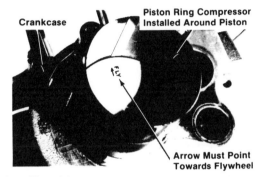

Installing pistons

by the thickness of the gasket and shims be-tween crankcase and bearing plate. Check the end play after the bearing plate is installed.

20. Install two hex cap screws and hand tight-en. Remove the locating studs, and install the remaining two hex cap screws and hand tighten.

21. Tighten the screws evenly, drawing bear-ing plate to crankcase. Torque K91-K181 to 115 inch lbs. Torque K241-K341 to 35 ft. lbs.

22. Check crankshaft end play between the inner bearing race and shoulder of crankshaft

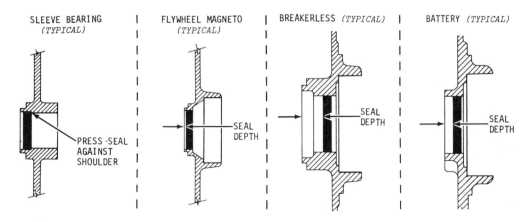

Front oil seal location

Installing connecting rod cap

Adjusting valve-to-tappet clearance

using a flat feeler gauge. Recommended total end play is:

- K91 − 0.004-0.023 in.
- K161, K181 − 0.002-0.023 in.
- K241, K301 − 0.003-0.020 in.

If measured end play is not within limits, remove the bearing plate and, remove or install shims as necessary.

NOTE: *Crankshaft end play is especially critical on gear reduction engines.*

23. Slide the appropriate seal sleeves over the crankshaft (refer to the "Special Tools" section). Generously lubricate the lips of the oils seals with light grease. Slide the oil seals over the sleeves.

24. Use the #11795 handle and appropriate seal drivers to install the front oil seals to the following depths. Note that the front oil seal depth varies with engine model and type of bearing plate used-bearing plate configuration differs with type of ignition system used.

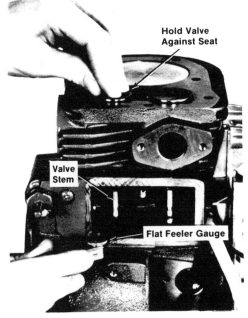

Measuring valve-to-tappet clearance

NOTE: *For detailed piston inspection and piston ring installation procedures, refer to the "Inspection And Repair/Reconditioning" section.*

25. Style A pistons: Install wrist pin and retainers.

26. Style "C" And "D" Pistons:

NOTE: *Proper orientation of the piston to the connecting rod is extremely important. Improper orientation may cause extensive wear or damage.*

27. Orient piston and connecting rod so that the notch (Style "C" piston) or Fly symbol (Style "D" piston) on piston and the match mark on connecting rod are facing the same direction.

28. Install wrist pin and retainers.

NOTE: *Proper orientation of the piston to the connecting rod is extremely important. Improper orientation may cause extensive wear or damage.*

29. Stagger the piston rings in their grooves until end gaps are 120 degrees apart.

30. Lubricate the piston and rings with engine oil. Install the piston ring compressor around piston.

31. Orient the notch (on style "C" piston) or Fly symbol (Style "D" piston) and match marks on connecting rod towards the flywheel end of crankshaft. Gently push the piston/connecting rod into bore - do not pound on piston.

32. Lubricate the crankshaft and connecting rod journal surfaces with engine oil. Install the connecting rod cap - make sure the match marks are aligned and the oil hole is towards the camshaft. It is important that marks on the connecting rod and cap line up and face flywheel end of engine.

33. Torque the capscrew to 20% over the nominal torque value listed below. Loosen cap screws to below the nominal value--do not leave overtorqued. Retorque bolts to the nominal value.

NOTE: *To prevent damage to connecting rod and engine, do not overtorque-loosen--and retorque the hex nuts on Posi-Lock connecting* rods. *Torque nuts, in increments, directly to the specified value.*

34. Rotate the crankshaft until the piston is at top dead center in bore to protect the dipper on the connecting rod. If locking tabs are used, bend tabs to lock cap screws.

35. Install screws and oil drain plug as specified in "General Information".

36. Rotate the crankshaft until piston is at top dead center of compression stroke.

37. Install the valves and measure the valve-to-tappet clearance using a flat feeler gauge.

NOTE: *Valve faces and seats must be lapped-in before checking /adjusting valve clearance. Refer to the "Inspection And Repair/Reconditioning" section.*

38. Adjust valve-to-tappet clearance, as necessary.

   a. On models K91, K141, K161, and K181: If clearance is too small, grind end of valve stems until correct clearance is obtained. Make sure stems are ground perfectly flat and smooth. If clearance is too large, replace the valves and recheck clearance.

NOTE: *Large clearances can also be reduced by grinding the valves and/or valve seats. Refer to the "Inspection And Repair/Reconditioning" section for valve specifications.*

   b. On Models K241 and K301, adjust valve-to-tappet clearance by turning the adjusting screw on tappets.

39. On Models K91, K161, and K181, install the valve springs (close coils to top), intake valve spring retainer, exhaust valve rotator or retainer, and valves.

40. On Models K241 and K301, install the valve spring upper retainers, valve springs (close coils to top), intake valve spring lower retainer, exhaust valve rotator or retainer, and valves.

NOTE: *Some models use a valve rotator on both valves.*

41. Compress springs using a valve spring compressor and install keepers.

42. On flywheel-magneto ignition systems, the magneto coil-core assembly ignition systems, the magneto coil-core assembly is secured in stationary position on the bearing plate. On the magneto-alternator systems, the coil is part of the stator assembly which is also secured to the bearing plate. Permanent magnets are affixed to the inside rim of the flywheel except in rotor type magneto systems. On these the magnet or rotor has a keyway and is press fitted on crankshaft. The magnet rotor is marked "engine-side" for proper assembly.

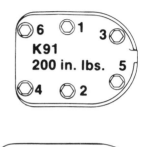

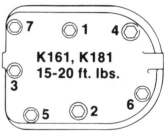

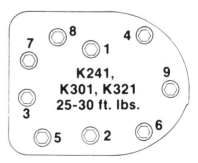

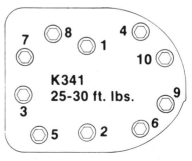

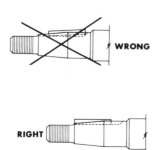

Installing a square flywheel key

Cylinder head fastener torque sequence

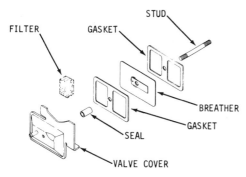

K181 breather assembly

43. After installing magneto components, run all leads out through holes provided (in 11 o'clock position) on bearing plate.

CAUTION: *Damaging Crankshaft and Flywheel Could Cause Personal Injury!*

Using improper procedures to install the flywheel can crack or damage the crankshaft and/or flywheel. This not only causes extensive engine damage, but also is a serious threat to the safety of persons nearby, since broken fragments could be thrown from the engine. Always observe and use the following precautions and procedures when installing the flywheel.

NOTE: *Before installing the flywheel, make sure the crankshaft taper and flywheel hub are clean dry and completely free of lubricants. The presence of lubricants can cause the flywheel to be overstressed and damaged when the cap screw is torqued to specification.*

Make sure square flywheel key is installed only in the flat area of keyway, not in the rounded area. The flywheel can become cracked or damaged if the key is installed in the rounded area of keyway.

Always use a flywheel strap wrench to hold flywheel when tightening flywheel fastener. Do not use any type of bar or wedge between the cooling fins or flywheel ring gear, as these parts could become cracked or damaged.

Do not use impact wrenches to install the flywheel retaining nut as this may overstress the nut and crack the flywheel hub.

Do not reuse a flywheel if it has been dropped or damaged in any way.

Do make a through visual inspection of the flywheel and crankshaft before installation to make sure they are in good condition and fee of cracks.

The old crankshaft design has a externally threaded end and uses a square key, plain washer, and marsden nut to align and secure the flywheel.

The new crankshaft design has an internally threaded end and uses a woodruff key,

washer, and/or brushing, hex cap screw or hexnut.

44. Position key properly in keyway as shown, and carefully guide key slot in flywheel hub over the key while installing to avoid pushing the key inward.

45. On models K91, K161, and K181 w/Rope Start: Install rope pulley, plain washer, and hex nut (lubricate threads with oil). Hold flywheel with strap wrench and torque hex nut to 40-50 ft. lbs. for K91 and 85-90 ft. lbs. for K161 and K181. If a hex head screw is used, torque screw to 250 inch lbs.

46. On models K91, K161, and K181 w/Retractable Start:

a. Install the grass screen.

b. Install the drive cup , plain washer, and hex nut (lubricate threads with oil). Hold the flywheel with strap wrench and torque hex nut to 40-50 ft. lbs. for K91 and 85-90 ft. lbs. for K161 and K181. If a hex head screw is used, torque screw to 250 inch lbs.

47. On models K91, K161, and K181 w/Electric Start:

a. Install the plain washer and hex nut (lubricate threads with oil). Hold the flywheel with strap wrench and torque hex nut to 40-50 ft. lbs. for K91 and 85-90 ft. lbs. for K161 and K181. If a hex head screw is used, torque screw to 250 inch lbs.

b. Install the grass screen.

48. On models K241, K301 w/Rope Start:

a. Install the nylon grass screen.

b. Install the spacer, rope pulley, plain washer, and hex cap screw (lubricate threads with oil). Hold the flywheel with a strap wrench and torque hex cap screw to 35-40 ft. lbs. If a hex nut is used, torque to 50-60 ft. lbs.

c. Install the wire mesh grass screen and grass screen retainer to rope pulley.

49. On models K241, K301 w/Retractable Start:

a. Install the grass screen.

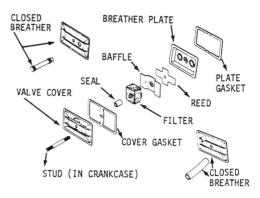

K241 breather assembly

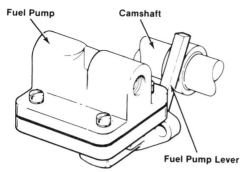

Fuel Pump   Camshaft

Fuel Pump Lever

Mechanical fuel pump

b. Install the drive cup, plain washer, and hex cap screw (lubricate threads with oil). Hold the flywheel with a strap wrench and torque hex cap screw to 35-40 ft. lbs. If a hex nut is used, torque to 50-60 ft. lbs.

50. On models K241, K301 w/Electric Start:

a. Install the plain washer and hex cap screw (lubricate threads with oil). Hold the flywheel with a strap wrench and torque hex cap screw to 35-40 ft. lbs. If a hex nut is used, torque to 50-60 ft. lbs.

b. Install the grass screen.

51. For all models, torque the grass screen fasteners to 70-140 ft. lbs. for a metal grass screen and 20-30 inch lbs. for a plastic grass screen.

52. Install the spark plug lead and kill lead into the slots in the baffle.

53. Install the remaining self-tapping screws and the blower housing.

NOTE: *On some models, the grass screen must be installed before installing the blower housing.*

54. Install push rod, breaker assembly, and breaker point lead.

55. Set breaker point gap at 0.020 in. full open.

56. Install gasket and breaker point cover.

57. Install the gasket and cylinder head. Always use a new gasket when head has been removed for service work.

58. Torque the hex cap screws and hex nuts (in increments) in the sequence and torques shown.

NOTE: *The importance of torquing cylinder head bolts to specified values and following the recommended sequences cannot be overemphasized. Blown head gaskets and cylinder head distortion may result from improper torquing. Following is the recommended torquing procedure:*

1. Lubricate the cylinder head bolts with oil before installation.

2. Initially torque each bolt to 10 ft. lbs. following the recommended torque sequence.

3. Sequentially tighten each bolt in 10 ft. lbs.

increments until the specified torque values are reached.

After reaching the final torque value, run the engine for 15 minutes, stop, and allow to cool. Then, sequentially retorque the head bolts to the specified torque value.

4. Make sure the spark plug is properly gapped.

5. Install the spark plug and torque it to 18-22 ft. lbs.

59. Install the stud, gasket, breather plate, reed, reed stop, seal, and filter. The accompanying illustrations show the correct order of assembly for two types of breather assemblies. Make sure reed valve is installed properly and that oil drain hole on breather plate is down.

NOTE: *All K181 Specifications have been changed to call for 2 pieces of breather filter 231419 instead of 1. Testing has revealed the use of two filters prevents oil droplets from being expelled through the breather system. All K181 engines are now being built with two filters and when serviced, two should always be used.*

60. Install the gasket, breather cover, and pawlnut.

70. Install the starter side air baffle, plain washer, and hex cap screws. Leave the screws loose.

71. Install the carburetor side air baffle, plain washer, and hex cap screws. Leave the screws loose.

72. Install the cylinder head baffle, plain washer, and hex cap screws. Leave the screws loose.

73. Tighten the screws securely when all pieces are in position.

NOTE: *Shorter screws go into lower portion of blower housing.*

74. Install dipstick.

CAUTION: *Gasoline may be present in the carburetor and fuel system. Gasoline is extremely flammable and it can explode if ignited. Keep sparks, open flames, and other sources of ignition away from the engine. Disconnect and ground the spark plug lead to*

Cap Screws

Muffler

Heat Shield

Gasket

Installing muffler

prevent the possibility of sparks from the ignition system.

75. Install fuel tank with brackets.
76. Install fuel line on fuel tank outlet fitting.
77. Install electric starter.
78. Install hex cap screws which mount electric starter to engine.
79. Install key switch panel.
80. Connect lead to electrical starter.
81. Connect electrical connector(s).
82. Install the retractable starter and hex cap screws. Leave the screws slightly loose.
83. Pull the starter handle out 8-10 in. until the pawls engage in the drive cup. Hold the handle in this position and tighten screws securely.
84. Install the gasket, fuel pump, plain washers, and fillister head screws. Torque the screws to 37-45 inch lbs.

NOTE: *Make sure the fuel pump lever is positioned above the camshaft. Damage to the fuel pump, and subsequent severe engine damage could result if the lever is positioned below the camshaft.*

85. Connect the fuel lines to fuel pump inlet and outlet fittings.
86. Install the throttle lever, bracket, spacer, plain washer and hex cap screw.
87. Install the governor spring to the governor arm. Install the governor arm to the cross shaft. Leave the pawlnut slightly loose as the governor arm and cross shaft will be adjusted after the carburetor and throttle linkage are installed.
88. Install the fuel line and hose clamps.
89. Install the gasket, carburetor, and slotted hex cap screws.
90. Install the throttle linkage into the nylon inserts in the governor arm and carburetor throttle lever.
91. Adjust the governor as instructed below.
92. Refer to "Fuel System And Governor" section for carburetor adjustment procedure.

GOVERNOR ADJUSTMENT

The governor cross shaft/governor arm must be adjusted every time the governor arm is loosened or removed from cross shaft.

a. Pull the governor arm away from the carburetor as far as it will go.
b. Grasp end of cross shaft with pliers and turn counterclockwise as far as it will go. The governor shaft can be adjusted for end clearance by moving needle bearing in block. Set bearing to allow a slight back-and-forth movement of shaft.

c. Torque the pawlnut on governor arm to 15 inch lbs.

NOTE: *Make sure there is at least $\frac{1}{16}$ in. clearance between the governor arm and the upper-left cam gear cover fastener to prevent interference.*

93. If the engine is equipped with a flat muffler, install muffler and gasket using cap screws. If equipped with a round muffler, install muffler and threaded exhaust pipe between the muffler and engine using a pipe wrench.
94. Install the base gasket, base, and air cleaner.

PREPARE THE ENGINE FOR OPERATION

Before operating the engine, be sure to do the following:
- Make sure all hardware is tightened securely and oil drain plugs are installed.
- Fill the crankcase with the right amount, weight, and type of oil. Refer to the oil recommendations and procedures in the "General Information" and "Periodic Maintenance" sections.
- Fill the fuel tank with the proper type of gasoline and open fuel shut-off valve (if equipped).
- Adjust the carburetor main fuel needle, idle fuel needle, or idle speed adjusting screw as necessary. Refer to the "Fuel System And Governor" section.
- Make sure the maximum engine speed does not exceed 3600 RPM (4000 RPM for model K91 only). Adjust the high speed stop as necessary. Refer to the "Fuel System And Governor" section.

RUN-IN PROCEDURES (RECONDITIONED ENGINES)

For overhauled engines or those rebuilt with a new short block or miniblock, use straight SAE 30, SG-quality oil for the first 5 hours of operation. Change the oil after this initial run-in period. Refill with SG-quality oil as specified under "Oil Types".

10
Kohler Command 5 Hp

AIR CLEANER

This engine is equipped with a replaceable, high density paper air cleaner element and an oil-foam precleaner (which covers the paper element).

AIR CLEANER SERVICE

Check the air cleaner daily or before starting the engine. Check for and correct heavy buildup of dirt and debris, and loose or damaged components.

NOTE: *Operating the engine with loose or damaged air cleaner components could allow unfiltered air into the engine, causing premature wear and failure.*

PRECLEANER SERVICE

Wash and reoil the precleaner every 25 hours of operation (more often under dusty or dirty conditions).

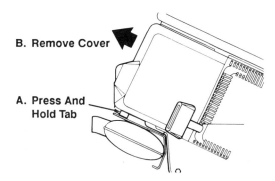

B. Remove Cover

A. Press And Hold Tab

Removing air cleaner cover

1. Press and hold the tab at the bottom of the air cleaner cover.

NOTE: *Choke control must be in the* **OFF** position.

2. Slide the air cleaner cover off of the air cleaner base (away from the retractable starter).

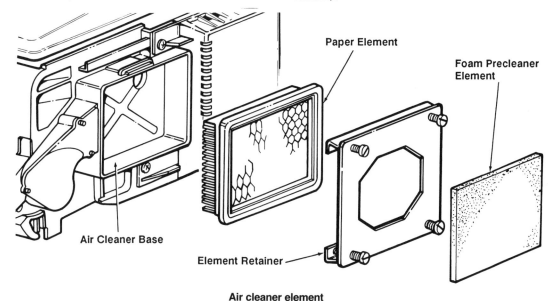

Paper Element

Foam Precleaner Element

Air Cleaner Base

Element Retainer

Air cleaner element

SPECIFICATIONS, TOLERANCES, AND SPECIAL TORQUE VALUES[1]

DESCRIPTION	C5 (5 Hp)
General Specifications	
Power (@ 3600 rpm, corrected to SAE J1349)	3.73 kW (5 hp)
Peak Torque (@ 2200 rpm)	11.4 N•m (8.4 lbf-ft)
Bore	67 mm (2.64 in)
Stroke	51 mm (2.01 in)
Displacement	180 cu cm (10.98 cu in)
Compression Ratio	8.5 : 1
Approx. Weight	16.33 kg (36 lb)
Approx. Oil Capacity	0.66 liter (0.7 U.S. qt)
Air Cleaner	
Base Nut Torque	6.8 N•m (58 lbf-in)
Angle Of Operation — Maximum (At Full Oil Level)	
Intermittent — All Directions	35°
Continuous — All Directions	20°
Camshaft	
End Play	0.15−0.55 mm (0.0059−0.0217 in)
Bore I.D. — Max. Wear Limit Crankcase	16.030 mm (0.6311 in)
Closure Plate	25.430 mm (1.0012 in)
Camshaft Bearing Surface O.D. — Max. Wear Limit Crankcase End	15.954 mm (0.6281 in)
Closure Plate End	25.350 mm (0.9980 in)
Carburetor	
Preliminary Low Idle Fuel Needle Setting	1 Turn
Fuel Bowl Retaining Screw Torque	9.8 N•m (87 lbf-in)

Throttle Plate Retaining Screw Torque . . . . 0.9 – 1.4 N•m (8 – 12 lbf-in)

Charging

Stator Air Gap . . . . 0.203 – 0.305 mm (0.008 – 0.012 in)

Stator Mounting Screw Torque . . . . 4.0 N•m (35 lbf-in)

Closure Plate

Closure Plate Fastener Torque . . . . 22.6 N•m (200 lbf-in)

Connecting Rod

Connecting Rod Cap Fastener Torque . . . . 9.0 N•m (80 lbf-in)

Connecting Rod-To-Crankpin Running Clearance
  New . . . . 0.030 – 0.056 mm (0.0012 – 0.0022 in)

  Max. Wear Limit . . . . 0.0635 mm (0.0025 in)

Connecting Rod-To-Crankpin Side Clearance . . . . 0.431 – 0.661 mm (0.0170 – 0.0260 in)

Connecting Rod-To-Piston Pin Running Clearance . . . . 0.015 – 0.003 mm (0.0006 – 0.0011 in)

Piston Pin End I.D.
  New . . . . 19.015 – 19.023 mm (0.7486 – 0.7489 in)

  Max. Wear Limit . . . . 19.036 mm (0.7495 in)

Crankshaft

End Play (Free) . . . . 0.000 – 0.056 mm (0.0000 – 0.0022 in)

Connecting Rod Journal
  O.D. – New . . . . 30.947 – 30.960 mm (1.2184 – 1.2189 in)

  O.D. – Max. Wear Limit . . . . 30.934 mm (1.2179 in)

  Max. Taper . . . . 0.025 mm (0.0010 in)

  Max. Out-Of-Round . . . . 0.013 mm (0.0005 in)

Crankshaft T.I.R. – PTO End . . . . 0.10 mm (0.004 in)

Cylinder Bore

Cylinder Bore I.D. – New . . . . 67.000 – 67.030 mm (2.6378 – 2.6390 in)

Cylinder Bore I.D. – Max. Wear Limit . . . . 67.049 mm (2.6397 in)

Cylinder Bore I.D. — Max. Out-Of-Round .... 0.150 mm (0.0059 in)

Cylinder Bore I.D. — Max. Taper .... 0.100 mm (0.0039 in)

Cylinder Head

Cylinder Head Fastener Torque .... 22.6 N•m (200 lbf-in)

Max. Out-Of-Flatness .... 0.076 mm (0.003 in)

Electric Starter

Drive Pinion Fastener Torque .... 17.0 – 19.0 N•m (150 – 170 lbf-in)

Drive Pinion-To-Flywheel Ring Gear Backlash .... 0.127 – 0.635 mm (0.0050 – 0.0250 in)

Flywheel

Flywheel Retaining Screw Torque .... 67.8 N•m (50 lbf-ft)

Fuel Tank

Fuel Tank Fastener Screw Torque .... 17.0 N•m (150 lbf-in)

Governor

Governor Cross Shaft Bore I.D. — Max. Wear Limit .... 6.425 mm (0.2530 in)

Governor Cross Shaft-To-Closure Plate Bore Running Clearance .... 0.020 – 0.122 mm (0.0008 – 0.0048 in)

Governor Cross Shaft O.D. — Max. Wear Limit .... 6.296 mm (0.2479 in)

Governor Gear Shaft-To-Governor Gear Running Clearance .... 0.025 – 0.111 mm (0.0010 – 0.0044 in)

Governor Gear Shaft O.D. — Max. Wear Limit .... 9.960 mm (0.3921 in)

Ignition

Spark Plug Type (Champion Or Equivalent) RC12YC

Spark Plug Gap .... 0.76 mm (0.030 in)

Spark Plug Torque .... 24.4 – 29.8 N•m (18 – 22 lbf-ft)

Ignition Module Air Gap .... 0.203 – 0.305 mm (0.0080 – 0.0120 in)

Ignition Module Fastener Torque[2] .... 4.0 or 6.2* N•m (35 or 55* lbf-in)

Muffler

Muffler Retaining Nut Torque . . . . 22.6 N•m (200 lbf-in)

Oil Sentry

Oil Sentry Float Switch Torque . . . . 13.6 N•m (120 lbf-in)

Piston, Piston Rings, And Piston Pin

Piston-To-Piston Pin Clearance . . . . 0.005−0.018 mm (0.0002−0.0007 in)

Piston Pin Bore I.D. − New . . . . 14.006−14.014 mm (0.5514−0.5517 in)

Piston Pin O.D. − New . . . . 13.996−14.000 mm (0.5510−0.5512 in)

Top Compression Ring-To-Groove Side Clearance . . . . 0.040−0.085 mm (0.0016−0.0033 in)

Middle Compression Ring-To-Groove Side Clearance . . . . 0.040−0.072 mm (0.0016−0.0028 in)

Oil Control Ring-To-Groove Side Clearance . . . . 0.140−0.275 mm (0.0055−0.0108 in)

Top And Center Compression Ring End Gap − New . . . . 0.25−0.45 mm (0.010−0.018 in)

Piston Thrust Face (@D_1)-To-Cylinder Bore Running
    Clearance − New[3] . . . . 0.016−0.059 mm (0.0006−0.0023 in)

Retractable Starter

Center Screw Torque . . . . 7.4−8.5 N•m (65−75 lbf-in)

Throttle Control

Throttle Control lever Fastener Torque . . . . 4.3 N•m (38 lbf-in)

Valve Cover

Valve Cover Fastener Torque . . . . 3.4 N•m (30 lbf-in)

Valves And Valve Lifters

Intake Valve Stem-To-Valve Guide Running Clearance . . . . 0.0392−0.0749 mm (0.00154−0.00295 in)

Exhaust Valve Stem-To-Valve Guide Running Clearance . . . . 0.0610−0.0991 mm (0.00240−0.00390 in)

Intake Valve Guide I.D. − New . . . . 4.990−5.010 mm (0.1965−0.1972 in)

Intake Valve Guide I.D. − Max. Wear Limit . . . . 5.085 mm (0.2002 in)

Exhaust Valve Guide I.D. − New . . . . 4.990−5.010 mm (0.1965−0.1972 in)

Exhaust Valve Guide I.D. — Max. Wear Limit	5.080 mm (0.2000 in)
Valve Guide Reamer Size — STD	5.000 mm (0.1968 in)
Valve Guide Reamer Size — Oversize	5.250 mm (0.2066 in)
Intake Valve Minimum Lift	5.40 mm (0.213 in)
Exhaust Valve Minimum Lift	5.40 mm (0.213 in)
Nominal Valve Seat Angle	45°
Valve-To-Tappet Clearance (Cold)	0.000−0.051 mm (0.0000−0.0020 in)

NOTES:

1. Values are in Metric units. Values in parenthesis are English equivalents. Lubricate threads with engine oil prior to assembly.

2. For self-tapping (thread forming) fasteners: the higher torque value* is for initial installation into a new cored hole; the lower torque value is for subsequent installation and installation into tapped holes and weld nuts.

3. Measure 6 mm (0.236 in) above the bottom of the piston skirt at right angles to the piston pin.

3. Remove the precleaner from the air cleaner element retainer.

4. Wash the precleaner in warm water with detergent. Rinse the precleaner thoroughly until all traces of detergent are eliminated. Squeeze out excess water (do not wring). Allow the precleaner to air-dry.

5. Saturate the precleaner with new engine oil. Squeeze out all excess oil.

6. Reinstall the precleaner in the element retainer.

7. Reinstall the air cleaner cover. Make sure the air cleaner cover latch snaps securely.

PAPER ELEMENT SERVICE

Every 100 hours of operation (more often under extremely dusty or dirty conditions), check the paper element. Replace the element as necessary.

1. Remove the air cleaner cover.

2. Remove the precleaner form the air cleaner element retainer.

3. Remove the element retainer and paper element from the air cleaner base as follows:

a. Loosen the four slot head screws in the element retainer.

NOTE: *Do not remove screws.*

b. When screws are loosened sufficiently, unhook element retainer from bottom tabs on air cleaner base. Remove element retainer.

c. Remove paper element.

4. Replace a dirty, bent, or damaged element

with a genuine Kohler element. Do not wash the paper element or use pressurized air, as this will damage the element. Handle new elements carefully; do not use if the sealing surfaces are bent or damaged.

5. When servicing the air cleaner, check the air cleaner base. make sure it is secured and not bent or damaged. Also check the air cleaner element retainer for damage or improper fit. Replace all bent or damaged air cleaner components.

6. Reinstall the paper element , element retainer, and precleaner as follows:

a. Place the paper element into the air cleaner base.

NOTE: *The pleats must run parallel to the cylinder.*

b. Unhook the element retainer into the top of the air cleaner base. Then hook the retainer into the bottom of the base to hold the paper element in place.

NOTE: *Be sure retainer is hooked in tabs.*

c. Tighten the four slot head screws evenly.

NOTE: *These screws must be snug to eliminate any air leaks around paper element.*

d. Reinstall the precleaner in the element retainer.

INSPECTION

Whenever the air cleaner cover is removed, or the paper element or precleaner are serviced, check the following areas/components:

Air Cleaner Base — Make sure the base is secured and not cracked or damaged. Since the air cleaner base and carburetor are secured to the intake port with common hardware, it is extremely important that the nuts securing these components are tight at all times.

Breather Tube — Make sure the tube is installed to both the air cleaner base and valve cover.

NOTE: *Damaged, worn, or loose air cleaner components can allow unfiltered air into the engine causing premature wear and failure. Tighten or replace all loose or damaged components.*

DISASSEMBLY

The following procedure is for complete disassembly of all air cleaner components.

1. Remove the air cleaner cover.

2. Remove the precleaner from the air cleaner element retainer.

3. Remove the element retainer and paper element from the air cleaner base.

4. Remove the two air cleaner base mounting screws and the two air cleaner base mounting nuts.

5. Disconnect the breather tube from the air cleaner base, and remove the air cleaner base and gasket.

ASSEMBLY

Before reinstalling an air cleaner base that has been removed, make sure the four metal bushings, which reinforce the base mounting holes and maintain the proper torque of the mounting hardware, are in place.

1. Install the gasket and air cleaner vase, and connect the breather tube to the air cleaner base.

2. Install the air cleaner base mounting nuts and screws. Torque each fastener to 6.8 N-m (58 inch lbs.).

3. Install the paper element, element retainer and precleaner.

AIR INTAKE/COOLING SYSTEM

CLEANING AIR INTAKE/COOLING AREAS

To ensure proper cooling, make sure the grass screen, cooling fins, and other external surfaces of the engine are kept clean at all times.

Every 100 hours of operation (more often under extremely dusty or dirty conditions), remove the blower housing and other cooling shrouds. Clean the cooling fins and external surfaces as necessary. Make sure the cooling shrouds are reinstalled.

NOTE: *Operating the engine with a blocked grass screen, dirty or plugged cooling fins,* *and/or cooling shrouds removed, will cause engine damage due to overheating.*

FUEL SYSTEM

CAUTION: *Gasoline is extremely flammable and its vapors can explode if ignited. Before servicing the fuel system, make sure there are no sparks, open flames, or other sources of ignition nearby as these can ignite gasoline vapors. Disconnect and ground the spark plug lead to prevent the possibility of sparks from the ignition system.*

FUEL RECOMMENDATIONS

For best results use only clean, fresh, regular grade, unleaded gasoline with a pump sticker octane rating of 87 or higher. In countries using the Research method, it should be 90 octane minimum.

Unleaded gasoline is recommended since it leaves less combustion chamber deposits. Regular grade, leaded gasoline can also be used; however be aware that the combustion chamber and cylinder head may require more frequent cleaning.

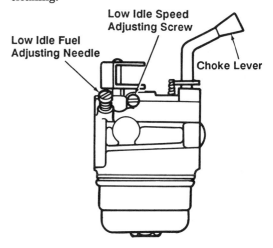

Fixed main jet carburetor

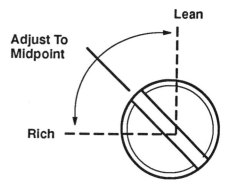

Optimum low idle fuel setting

Use fresh gasoline to ensure it is blended for the season and to reduce the possibility of gum deposits forming which could clog the fuel system. Do not use gasoline left over from the previous season.

Do not add oil to the gasoline!

Gasoline/Alcohol Blends

Up to 10% ethyl alcohol/90% unleaded gasoline can be used as fuel for Kohler engines. Do not use other gasoline/alcohol blends.

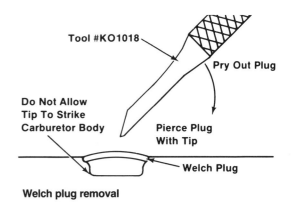

Welch plug removal

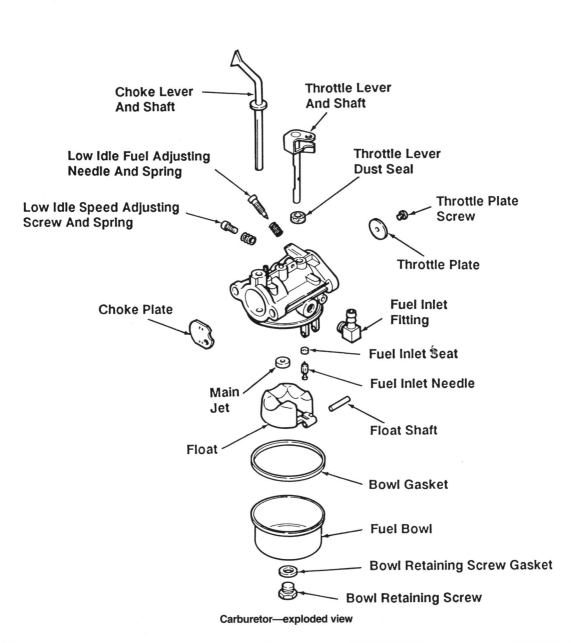

Carburetor—exploded view

Operation

The typical fuel system and related components include the fuel tank, in-line fuel filter, fuel pump, carburetor, and interconnecting fuel lines.

The fuel from the tank is moved through the carburetor inlet, fuel moves by gravity feed from the fuel tank, through the fuel line(s) and in-line filter (if equipped), to the carburetor.

Fuel then enters the carburetor float bowl and is moved into the carburetor body. There, the fuel is mixed with air. This air-fuel mixture is then burned in the engine combustion chamber.

Fuel Filter

Some engines are equipped with an in-line fuel filter. Visually inspect the filter periodically, and replace with a genuine Kohler filter wen dirty.

Carburetor

CAUTION: *Gasoline may be present in the carburetor and fuel system. Gasoline is extremely flammable and its vapors can explode if ignited. Keep sparks, open flames, and other sources of ignition away from the engine. Disconnect and ground the spark plug lead to prevent the possibility of sparks from the ignition system.*

TROUBLESHOOTING

This engine is equipped with a fixed main jet carburetor. If engine troubles are experienced that appear to be fuel system related, check the following areas before adjusting or disassembling the carburetor.

Make sure the fuel tank is filled with clean, fresh gasoline.

Make sure the fuel tank vent cap is not blocked and that it is operating properly.

- Make sure fuel line(s) is unrestricted.
- Make sure the fuel tank filter screen is clean and unobstructed.
- If the fuel tank is equipped with a shutoff valve, make sure it is open and unobstructed.
- If the engine is equipped with an in-line fuel filter, make sure it is clean and unobstructed. Replace the filter if necessary.
- Make sure the air cleaner base and carburetor are securely fastened to the engine using gaskets in good condition.
- Make sure the air cleaner element is clean and all air cleaner components are fastened securely.
- Make sure the ignition system, governor system, exhaust system, and throttle and choke controls are operating properly.
- If, after checking the items listed above, engine starting/running problems still exist, it may be necessary to adjust or service the carburetor.

ADJUSTMENT

NOTE: *Carburetor adjustments should be made only after the engine has warmed up.*

This engine is equipped with a fixed main jet carburetor. The carburetor is designed to deliver the correct fuel-to-air mixture to the engine under all operating conditions. The main fuel jet is calibrated at the factory and is not adjustable. The idle fuel adjusting needle is also set at the factory and normally does not need adjustment.

If, however, the engine is hard-starting or does not operate properly, it may be necessary to adjust or service the carburetor.

1. With the engine stopped, turn the low idle fuel adjusting needle in (clockwise) until it bottoms lightly.

NOTE: *The tip of the idle fuel adjusting needle is tapered to critical dimensions. Damage to the needle and the seat in the carburetor body will result if the needle is forced.*

2. Preliminary Low Idle Fuel Needle Setting: Turn the low idle fuel adjusting needle out (counterclockwise) 1 full turn from lightly bottomed.

3. Start the engine and run at half throttle for five to ten minutes to warm up. the engine must be warm before making final settings (Steps 4,5, and 6).

4. Low Idle Speed setting: Place the throttle control into the idle or slow position. Set the low idle speed to 1200 rpm (± 75 rpm) by turning the low idle speed adjusting screw in or out. Check the speed using a tachometer.

NOTE: *The actual low idle speed depends on the application; refer to equipment manufacturer's recommendations. The recommended low idle speed for basic engines is 1200 rpm. To ensure best results when setting the low idle fuel needle, the low idle speed must not exceed 1500 rpm.*

5. Low Idle Fuel Needle Setting: Place the throttle into the idle or slow position. Turn the low idle fuel adjusting needle out (counterclockwise) from the preliminary setting until the engine speed decreases (rich). Note the position of the needle.

Now turn the adjusting needle in (clockwise). The engine speed may increase, then it will decrease as the needle is turned in further (lean). Note the position of the needle.

Set the adjusting needle midway between the rich and lean settings.

6. Recheck the idle speed using a tachometer. Readjust the speed as necessary.

DISASSEMBLY

1. Remove the bowl retaining screw, retaining screw gasket, and fuel bowl.

2. Remove the bowl gasket, float shaft, float, and fuel inlet needle.

3. Remove the low idle fuel adjusting needle and spring. Remove the low idle speed adjusting screw and spring.

NOTE: *Further disassembly of the carburetor (removal of the welch plugs, fuel inlet seat, throttle plate and shaft, and choke plate and shaft) is recommended only if these parts are to be cleaned or replaced.*

Welch Plug Removal

In order to clean the off-idle ports and bowl vent thoroughly, remove the welch plugs covering these areas.

Use tool no. KO-1018, or equivalent, and the following procedure to remove the welch plugs.

1. Pierce the welch plug with the tip of the tool.

NOTE: *To prevent damage to the carburetor, do not allow the tool to strike the carburetor body.*

2. Pry out the welch plug with the tip of the tool.

Fuel Inlet Set Removal

To remove the fuel inlet seat, pull it out of the carburetor body using a screw, drill bit, or similar tool.

NOTE: *Always install a new fuel inlet seat. Do not reinstall a seat that has been removed.*

Choke Shaft Removal

1. Because the edges of the choke plate are beveled, mark the choke plate and carburetor body to ensure correct reassembly. Also take note of the choke plate position in the bore, and the position of the choke lever.

2. Grasp the choke plate with a pliers. Pull it out of the slot in the choke shaft.

3. Remove the choke shaft.

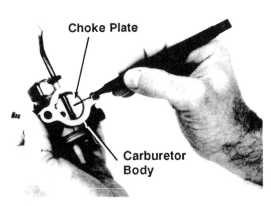

Marking choke plate and carburetor body

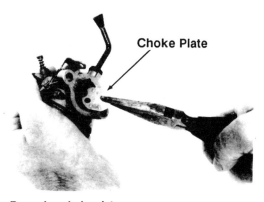

Removing choke plate

Throttle Shaft Removal

1. Because the edges of the throttle plate are beveled, mark the throttle plate and carburetor body to ensure correct reassembly. Also take not of the throttle plate position in the bore, and the position of the throttle lever.

2. Carefully and slowly remove the screw which secures the throttle plate to the throttle shaft. Remove the throttle plate.

3. File off any burrs which may have been left on the throttle shaft when the screw was removed. Do this before removing the throttle shaft from the carburetor body.

4. Remove the throttle lever/shaft assembly with the foam dust seal.

CLEANING

CAUTION: *Carburetor cleaners and solvents are extremely flammable. Keep sparks, flames, and other sources of ignition away from the area. Follow the cleaner manufacturer's warnings and instructions on its proper and safe use. Never use gasoline as a cleaning agent.*

All parts should be cleaned thoroughly using a carburetor cleaner (such as acetone). Make sure all gum deposits are removed from the following areas:

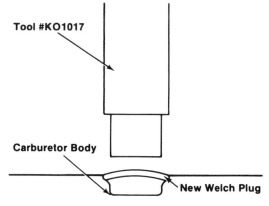

Installing welch plugs

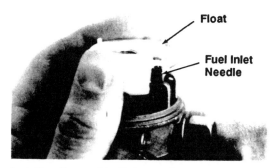

Installing float and fuel inlet needle

Carburetor body and bore – especially the areas where the throttle plate, choke plate and shafts are seated.

Idle fuel and off-idle ports in carburetor bore, main jet, bowl vent, and fuel inlet needle and seat.

NOTE: *These areas can be cleaned with a piece of fine wire in addition to cleaners. Be careful not to enlarge the ports, or break the wire inside the ports. Wearing proper eye protection, blow out all passages with compressed air.*

Float and float hinge.

Fuel bowl.

Throttle plate, choke plate, throttle shaft, and choke shaft.

CAUTION: *NOTE:*

Do not submerge the carburetor in cleaner or solvent when fiber, rubber, or foam seals or gaskets are installed. The cleaner may damage these components.

INSPECTION

Carefully inspect all components and replace those that are worn or damaged.

Inspect the carburetor body for cracks, holes, and other wear or damage.

Inspect the float for cracks, holes, and missing or damaged float tabs. Check the float hinge and shaft for wear or damage.

Inspect the fuel inlet needle and seat for wear or damage.

Inspect the tip of the low idle fuel adjusting needle for wear or grooves.

Inspect the throttle and choke shaft and plate assemblies for wear or excessive play.

REPAIR

Always use new gaskets when servicing or re-installing carburetors. Repair kits are available which include new gaskets and other components.

Components such as the throttle and choke shaft assemblies, throttle plate, choke plate, low idle fuel needle, and others are available separately.

ASSEMBLY

Throttle Shaft Installation

1. Install the foam dust seal on the throttle shaft.

2. Insert the throttle lever/shaft assembly into the carburetor body. Position the cutout portion of the shaft so it faces the carburetor mounting flange.

3. Install the throttle plate to the throttle shaft. Make sure the plate is positioned properly in the bore as noted and marked during disassembly. Apply Loctite® no. 609 to the threads of the throttle plate retaining screw so that it is slightly loose.

4. Apply finger pressure to the throttle lever/shaft to keep it firmly seated against the pivot in the carburetor body. Rotate the throttle shaft until the throttle plate closes the bore around its entire perimeter; then tighten the screw.

5. Operate the throttle lever. Check for binding between the throttle plate and carburetor bore. Loosen the screw and adjust the throttle plate as necessary. Torque the screw to 0.9-1.4 N-m (8-12 inch lbs.).

Choke Shaft Installation

1. Insert the choke shaft into the carburetor body until the choke shaft detent collar touches the top of the detent spring on the carburetor.

2. Lift the detent spring away from the choke shaft detent collar using a small screwdriver, and insert the choke shaft further into the carburetor body until it bottoms. Spring should now engage with detents of collar.

3. Position the choke as noted and marked during disassembly. Insert the choke plate into the slot in the choke shaft. Make sure that the choke plate is inserted far enough that its locking tabs are positioned on each side of the choke shaft.

Fuel Inlet Seat Installation

Press the fuel inlet seat into the bore in the carburetor body until it bottoms.

Welch Plug Installation

Use tool no. KO-1017, or equivalent.

1. Position the carburetor body with the welch plug cavities to the top.

2. Place a new welch plug into the cavity with the raised surface up.

3. Use the end of the tool that is about the same size as the plug and flatten the plug. Do not force the plug below the surface of the cavity.

4. After the plugs are installed, seal them with fingernail polish or lacquer (or an equivalent sealant). Allow the sealant to dry completely.

CARBURETOR BODY REASSEMBLY

1. Install the low idle speed adjusting screw and spring.

2. Install the low idle fuel adjusting needle and spring. Turn the adjusting needle in (clockwise) until it bottoms lightly.

NOTE: *The tip of the fuel adjusting needle is tapered to critical dimensions. Damage to the needle and the seat in the carburetor body will result if the needle is forced.*

3. Turn the low idle fuel adjusting needle out (counterclockwise) 1 full turn from lightly bottomed.

NOTE: *Upon installation of the reassembled carburetor, follow the final adjustment procedures in this Section.*

4. Insert the fuel inlet needle into the float. Lower the float/needle into the carburetor body. Install the float shaft.

5. Install the bowl gasket, fuel bowl, bowl retaining screw gasket, and bowl retaining screw. Torque the bowl retaining screw to 9.8 N-m (87 inch lbs.).

GOVERNOR

This engine is equipped with a centrifugal flyweight mechanical governor. It is designed to hold the engine speed constant under changing load conditions. The governor gear/flyweight mechanism is mounted inside the crankcase and is driven off the gear on the camshaft.

Operation

Centrifugal force acting on the rotating governor gear assembly causes the flyweights to move outward as speed increases, and inward as speed decreases. As the flyweights move outward, they cause the regulating pin to extend from the governor gear assembly.

The regulating pin contacts the tab on the cross shaft, causing the shaft to rotate when the engine speed changes. One end of the cross shaft protrudes through the side of the crank-

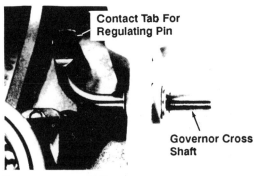

Governor cross shaft

case. Through external linkage attached to the cross shaft, the rotating action is transmitted to the throttle lever of the carburetor.

When the engine is at rest, and the throttle control is in the **fast** position, the tension of the governor spring holds the throttle plate open. When the engine is operating (the governor gear assembly is rotating), the force applied by the regulating pin against the cross shaft tends to close the throttle plate. The governor spring tension and the force applied by the regulating pin are in equilibrium during operation, holding the engine speed constant.

When load is applied and the engine speed (and governor gear speed) decreases, the governor spring tension moves the governor lever to open the throttle plate wider. This allows more fuel into the engine, increasing engine speed. (This action occurs very rapidly, so a reduction in speed is hardly noticed.) As the speed reaches the governed setting, the governor spring tension and the force applied by the regulating pin will again be in equilibrium. This maintains the engine speed at a relatively constant level.

The governed speed setting is determined by the position of the throttle control. It can be variable or constant, depending on the application.

INITIAL ADJUSTMENT

Make this initial adjustment whenever the governor lever is loosened or removed from the

Governor gear assembly

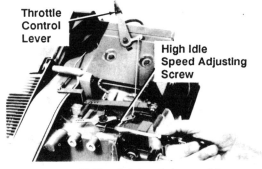

High idle speed/kill switch bracket assembly

cross shaft. To ensure proper setting, make sure the throttle linkage is connected to the governor lever and to the carburetor throttle lever.

1. Loosen the governor lever hex nut.
2. Pull and hold the governor lever away from the carburetor so that the carburetor throttle plate is in the wide open throttle position.
3. Grasp the governor cross shaft with a pliers and turn the shaft counterclockwise as far as it will go.
4. Tighten the hex nut securely.

HIGH IDLE SPEED ADJUSTMENT

The recommended maximum no-load high idle speed for this engine speed is 3600 rpm. The actual high idle speed depends on the application. Refer to the equipment manufacturer's instructions for specific information.

CAUTION: *Do not tamper with the governor setting. Overspeed is hazardous and could cause personal injury.*

The high idle speed is set by turning the high speed adjusting screw on the high idle speed/kill switch bracket assembly in or out.

NOTE: *Although certain engine components have been removed for clarity of the photograph, never run the engine with the air cleaner assembly removed. Damage to the engine might otherwise result.*

1. Start the engine and allow it to warm up. Place the throttle control lever into the fast or high idle position.
2. Check the engine speed with a tachometer.
3. To increase the high idle speed, turn the high idle speed adjusting screw out (counterclockwise), while applying light pressure to (and thereby gradually moving) the throttle control lever in the high idle speed direction (toward the carburetor), until the desired speed is attained.

LOW IDLE SPEED ADJUSTMENT

The low idle speed is set by turning the low idle speed adjusting screw on the carburetor in or out. This setting must be made in conjunction with the idle fuel mixture setting.

SENSITIVITY ADJUSTMENT

Governor sensitivity is adjusted by repositioning the governor spring in the holes in the governor lever. If speed surging occurs with a change in load, the governor is set too sensitive. If a big drop in speed occurs when normal load is applied, the governor should be set for greater sensitivity.

The governor lever has five holes for use in adjusting governor sensitivity. For the least

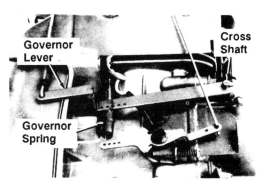

Governnor sensitivity adjustment

governor sensitivity, the governor spring should be inserted in the lever hole closest to the governor cross shaft. The lever holes become increasingly sensitive the farther they are from the cross shaft. For the greatest governor sensitivity, the governor spring should be inserted in the lever hole farthest from the governor cross shaft.

LUBRICATION SYSTEM

OIL RECOMMENDATIONS

Using the proper type and weight of oil in the crankcase is extremely important. So is checking oil daily and changing oil regularly. Failure to use the correct oil, or using dirty oil, causes premature engine wear and failure.

Use high-quality detergent oil of API (American Petroleum Institute) service class SF or SG. Select the viscosity based on the air temperature at the time of operation as shown in the following table.

NOTE: *Using other than service SF or SG oil or extending oil change intervals longer than recommended can cause engine damage.*

A logo or symbol on oil containers identifies the API service class and SAE viscosity grade.

OIL LEVEL CHECK

The importance of checking and maintaining the proper oil level in the crankcase cannot be overemphasized. Check oil BEFORE EACH USE as follows:

Engines With Extended Oil Fill Tube/Dipstick

1. Make sure the engine is stopped, level, and is cool so the oil has had time to drain into the sump.
2. To keep dirt, grass clippings, etc., out of the engine, clean the area around the oil fill cap/dipstick before removing it.
3. Unthread and remove the oil fill cap/dipstick; wipe oil off. Reinsert the dipstick into the tube and rest the oil fill cap on the tube. Do not thread the cap onto the tube.

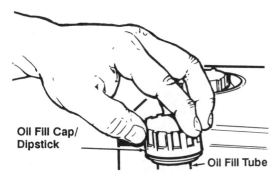

Oil Fill Cap/ Dipstick — **Oil Fill Tube**

Checking oil level—engines with extended oil fill tube/ dipstick

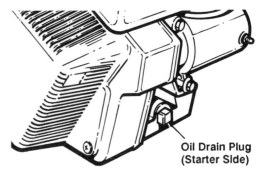

Oil Drain Plug (Starter Side)

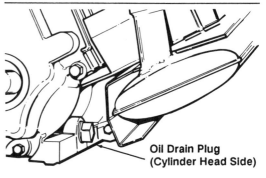

Oil Drain Plug (Cylinder Head Side)

Oil drain plugs

4. Remove the dipstick and check the oil level. The oil level should be up to, but not over, the **F** mark on the dipstick.

5. If the level is low, add oil of the proper type, up to the **F** mark on the dipstick. Always check the level with the dipstick before adding more oil.

NOTE: *To prevent extensive engine wear or damage, always maintain the proper oil level in the crankcase. Never operate the engine with the oil level below the L mark or over the F mark on the dipstick.*

Oil Sentry

Some engines are equipped with an optional Oil Sentry oil level monitor. If the oil level gets low, Oil Sentry will either shut off the engine or activate a warning signal, depending on the application.

NOTE: *Make sure the oil level is checked BEFORE EACH USE and is maintained up to the F mark on the dipstick. This includes engines equipped with Oil Sentry.*

OIL CHANGE

For a new engine, change oil after the first 5 hours of operation. Thereafter, change oil after every 100 hours of operation.

For an overhauled engine or those rebuilt

with a new short block, use 10W-30-weight service class SF oil for the first 5 hours of operation. Change the oil after this initial run-in period. Refill with service class SF.

Change the oil while the engine is still warm. The oil will flow more freely and carry away more impurities. Make sure the engine is level when filling, checking, and changing the oil.

1. Remove the oil drain plug and oil fill cap/dipstick. Be sure to allow ample time for complete drainage.

2. Reinstall the drain plug. Make sure it is tightened to 17.6 N-m (13 foot lbs.) torque.

3. Fill the crankcase, with new oil of the proper type, to the **F** mark on the dipstick. Always check the level with the dipstick before adding more oil.

4. Reinstall the oil fill cap/dipstick and tighten securely.

NOTE: *To prevent extensive engine wear or damage, always maintain the proper oil level in the crankcase. Never operate the engine with the oil level below the L mark or over the F mark on the dipstick.*

RETRACTABLE STARTER

CAUTION: *Retractable starters contain a powerful, flat wire recoil spring that is under tension. Do not remove the center screw from the starter until the spring tension is released. Removing the center screw before re-*

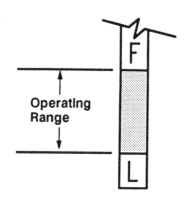

Operating Range

Oil level dipstick

leasing spring tension, or improper starter disassembly, can cause the sudden and potentially dangerous release of the spring.

Always wear safety goggles when servicing retractable starters; full face protection is recommended.

To ensure personal safety, and proper starter disassembly and reassembly, follow the procedures in this section carefully.

REMOVAL

1. Remove air cleaner cover.
2. Remove the four hex. flange screws securing the starter to blower housing.
3. Remove the starter.

INSTALLATION

1. Install the retractable starter and four hex. flange screws to blower housing. Leave the screws slightly loose.
2. Pull the starter handle out until the pawls engage in the drive cup. Hold the handle in this position and tighten the screws securely.
3. Install the air cleaner cover.

ROPE REPLACEMENT

The rope can be replaced without complete starter disassembly.

1. Remove the starter from the engine blower housing.
2. Pull the rope out approx. 12 in. and tie a

Brake spring and washer, pawls, and pawl springs

temporary (slip) knot in it to keep it from retracting into the starter.

3. Remove the rope retainer from inside the starter handle. Untie the single knot and remove the rope retainer and handle.
4. Hold the pulley firmly and untie the slip knot. Allow the pulley to rotate slowly as the spring tension is released.
5. When all spring tension on the starter pulley is released, remove the rope from pulley.
6. Tie a single knot in one end of the new rope.
7. Rotate the pulley counterclockwise (when viewed from pawl side of pulley) until the spring is tight. (Approx. 5 full turns of pulley.).
8. Rotate the pulley clockwise until the rope

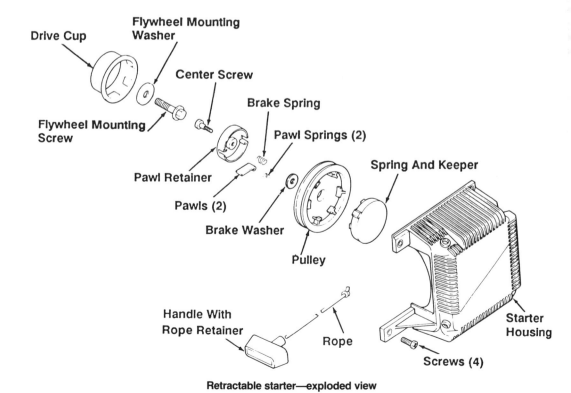

Retractable starter—exploded view

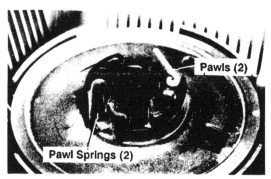

Spring & Keeper

Inner Spring Hook

Rope Hole In Pulley

Position of spring and keeper in pulley

Installing pawls and pawl springs

Pawls (2)

Pawl Springs (2)

Installing pawls and pawl springs

hole in pulley is aligned with rope guide bushing of starter housing.

NOTE: *Do not allow the pulley/spring to unwind. Enlist the aid of a helper if necessary, or use a C-clamp to hold the pulley in position.*

9. Insert the new rope through the rope hole in starter pulley and rope guide bushing of housing.

10. Tie a slip knot approx. 12 in. from the free end of rope. Hold the pulley firmly and allow it to rotate slowly until the slip knot reaches the guide bushing of housing.

11. Slip the handle and rope retainer onto the rope. Tie a single knot at the end of the rope. Install the rope retainer into the starter handle.

12. Untie the slip knot and pull on the handle until the rope is fully extended. Slowly retract the rope into thew starter.

NOTE: *When the spring is properly tensioned, the rope will retract fully and the handle will stop against the starter housing.*

PAWLS (DOGS) REPLACEMENT

The starter must be completely disassembled to replace the starter pawls. A pawl repair kit is available which includes the following components:

DISASSEMBLY

CAUTION: *Do not remove the center screw from starter until the spring tension is re-*

Pulley & Spring

Housing

Installing pulley and spring into housing

leased. *Removing the center screw before releasing spring tension, or improper starter disassembly, can cause the sudden and potentially dangerous release of the spring. Follow these instructions carefully to ensure personal safety and proper starter disassembly. Make sure adequate face protection is worn by all persons in the area.*

1. Release spring tension and remove the handle and starter rope.

2. Remove the center screw and pawl retainer.

3. Remove the brake spring and brake washer.

4. Carefully note the positions of the pawls and pawl springs before removing them. Remove the pawls and pawl springs from the starter pulley.

5. Rotate the pulley clockwise 2 full turns. This will ensure the spring is disengaged from the starter housing.

6. Hold the pulley into the starter housing. Invert the pulley/housing so the pulley is away from your face, and away from the others in the area.

7. Rotate the pulley slightly from side to side and carefully separate the pulley from the housing.

NOTE: *If the pulley and the housing do not separate easily, the spring could be engaged in the starter housing, or there is still tension on the spring. Return the pulley to the housing and repeat step 5 before separating the pulley and housing.*

8. Note the position of the spring and keeper assembly in the pulley. Remove the spring and keeper assembly from the pulley as a package.

CAUTION: *Do not remove the spring from the keeper. Severe personal injury could result from the sudden uncoiling of the spring.*

INSPECTION AND SERVICE

1. Carefully inspect the rope, pawls, housing, center screw, and other components for wear or damage.

2. Replace all worn or damaged components.

3. Do not attempt to rewind a spring that has come out of the keeper. Order and install a new spring and keeper assembly.

4. Clean all old grease and dirt from the starter components. Generously lubricate the spring and center shaft with any commercially-available bearing grease.

REASSEMBLY

1. Make sure the spring is well-lubricated with grease. Place the spring and keeper assembly inside the pulley (with spring towards pulley).

2. Install the pulley with spring and keeper assembly into the starter housing.

NOTE: *Make sure the pulley is fully seated against the starter housing. Do not wind the pulley and recoil spring at this time.*

3. Install the pawl springs and pawls into the starter pulley.

4. Place the brake washer in the recess in the starter housing hub.

5. Lubricate the brake spring sparingly with grease. Place the spring on the plain washer. (Make sure the threads in center shaft remain clean, dry, and free of grease and oil.).

6. Apply a small amount of Loctite® #271 to the threads of the center screw. Install the center screw, with retainer, to the center shaft. Torque the screw to 7.4-8.5 N-m (65-75 inch lbs.).

7. Tension the spring and install the rope and handle as instructed in steps 6 though 12 under Rope Replacement above.

8. Install the starter to the engine blower housing.

ELECTRICAL SYSTEM

Major electrical systems and components covered in this Section include the sprak plug, ignition system and ignition module; in addition to the following optional electrical systems and components; battery, battery charging system, electric starter, and Oil Sentry oil level monitor.

Spark Plug

Engine misfire or starting problems are often caused by a spark plug that is in poor condition or with an improper gap setting.

This engine is factory-equipped with the following spark plug:

Type – Champion RC12YC (or equivalent)
Gap – 0.030 in.
Thread Size – 14 mm
Reach – ¾ in.
Hex Size – ⅝ in.

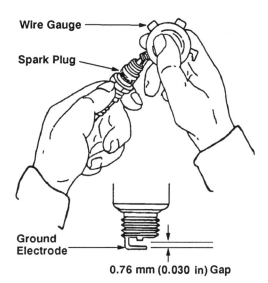

Servicing spark plug

SPARK PLUG SERVICE

Every 100 hours of operation, remove the spark plug, check its condition, and reset the gap or replace with a new plug as necessary.

1. Before removing the spark plug, clean the area around the base of the plug to keep dirt and debris out of the engine.

2. remove the plug and check its condition. Replace the plug if worn or if reuse is questionable.

NOTE: *Do not clean the spark plug in a machine which uses abrasive grit. Some grit could remain on the spark plug and enter the engine, causing extensive wear and damage.*

3. Check the gap using a feeler gauge. Adjust the gap to 0.76 mm (0.030 in) by carefully bending the ground electrode.

4. reinstall the spark plug into the cylinder head. Torque the spark plug into the cylinder head. Torque the spark plug to 24.4-29.8 Nm (18-22 foot lbs.).

INSPECTION

Inspect the spark plug as soon as it is removed from the cylinder head. the deposits on the tip are an indication of the internal condition of the piston rings, valves, and carburetor.

ELECTRONIC MAGNETO IGNITION SYSTEM

This engine is equipped with a dependable electronic magneto ignition system. The system consists of the following components:

A magneto assembly – which is permanently affixed to the flywheel.

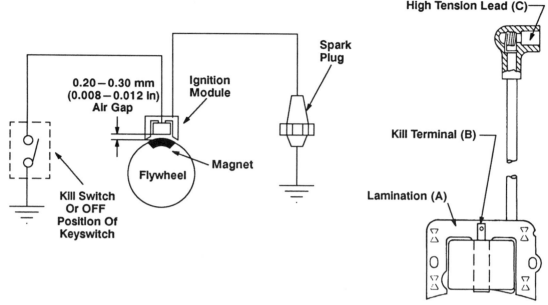

Electronic magneto ignition system

An electronic magneto ignition module — which mounts on the engine crankcase.
A kill switch — (or key switch) which grounds the module to stop the engine.
A spark plug.

OPERATION

As the flywheel rotates and the magnet assembly moves past the ignition module, a low voltage is induced in the primary windings of the module. When the primary voltage is precisely at its peak, the module induces a high voltage in it s secondary windings. This high voltage creates a spark plug at the tip of the spark plug. this spark ignites the air-fuel mixture in the combustion chamber.

The timing of the spark is automatically controlled by the module. Therefore, other than periodically checking/replacing the spark plug, no maintenance, timing, or adjustments are necessary or possible with this system.

Ignition Module
REMOVAL AND INSTALLATION

Refer to the Engine Disassembly and Reassembly Sections for complete ignition module removal and installation procedures.

Battery

A 12-volt battery with a rating of approximately 32-amp hours-250 cold cranking amps, is normally used.

If the battery charge is not sufficient to crank the engine, recharge the battery.

NOTE: *Do not attempt to jump start the engine with another battery. Starting the engine with batteries larger than those recommended can burn out the starter motor.*

BATTERY CHARGING

CAUTION: *Batteries contain sulfuric acid. To prevent acid burns, avoid contact with skin, eyes, and clothing. Batteries produce explosive hydrogen gas while being charged. To prevent a fire or explosion, charge batteries only in well ventilated areas. Keep sparks, open flames, and other sources of ignition away from the battery at all times. Keep batteries out of the reach of children. Remove all jewelry when servicing batteries.*

Before disconnecting the negative (-) ground cable, make sure all switches are OFF. If ON, a spark will occur at the ground cable terminal which could cause an explosion if hydrogen gas or gasoline vapors are present.

BATTERY MAINTENANCE

1. Regularly check the level of electrolyte. Add distilled water as necessary to maintain the recommended level.
NOTE: *Do not overfill the battery. Poor performance or early failure due to loss of electrolyte will result.*
2. Keep the cables, terminals, and external surfaces of battery clean. A build-up of corrosive acid or grime on the external surface can self-discharge the battery. Self-discharging happens rapidly when moisture is present.

3. Wash the cables, terminals, and external surfaces with a baking soda and water solution. Rinse thoroughly with clear water.

NOTE: *Do not allow the baking soda solution to enter the cells as this will destroy the electrolyte.*

BATTERY TEST

Test the battery voltage by connecting D.C. voltmeter across the battery terminals – crank the engine. If the battery drops below 9 volts while cranking, the battery is discharged or faulty.

TROUBLESHOOTING

This engine is equipped with a 0.5 Amp unregulated battery charging system.

NOTE: *Observe the following guidelines to prevent damage to the electrical system and components.*

Electric Start Engines
0.5 Amp Unregulated Battery Charging System
PRECAUTIONS

1. Make sure the battery polarity is correct. A negative (-) ground system is used.
2. Disconnect the stator lead, wiring harness, and any other electrical accessories in common ground with the engine before performing electric welding on the equipment powered by the engine.
3. Prevent the stator (AC) lead from touching or shorting while the engine is running. This could damage the stator.

TROUBLESHOOTING GUIDE

Minimum Output
Engine Speed (rpm) – Output (Volts)
    1600 – 2.49-3.39
    2000 – 4.19-5.57
    2400 – 7.18-9.10
    2800 – 9.68-11.90
    3200 – 1.90-14.00
    3600 – 13.29-14.97
If voltage is significantly lower than listed values replace stator.

NOTE: *Voltmeter must have an integrating time (RMS) function to yield a true DC reading, and a high input impedence (>10 M ohms) such that the output voltage is not artificially lowered due to meter loading.*

ELECTRIC STARTER

Precautions

• Do not crank the engine for more than 10 seconds at a time. If the engine does not start, allow a 60-second cool-down period between starting attempts. Failure to follow these guidelines can burn out the starter motor.

• If the engine develops sufficient speed to disengage the starter but does not keep running (a false start), the engine rotation must be allowed to come to a complete stop before attempting to restart the engine. If the starter is engaged while the flywheel is rotating, the starter pinion and flywheel ring gear may clash, resulting in damage to the starter.

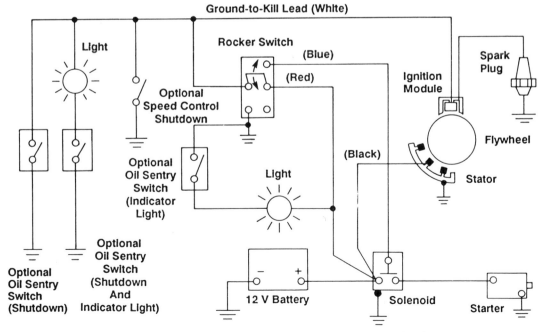

Wiring diagram—electric start engines 0.5 amp unregulated battery charging system

• If the starter does not crank the engine, shut off the starter immediately. Do not make further attempts to start the engine until the condition is corrected. Do not attempt to jump start the engine with another battery. Starting with batteries larger than those recommended can burn out the stator motor.

• Do not drop the starter or strike the starter frame. Doing so can damage the ceramic permanent magnets inside the starter frame.

Bendix Drive Electric Starter

OPERATION

When power is applied to the starter, the armature rotates. As the armature rotates, the drive pinion moves out on the splined drive shaft and into mesh with flywheel ring gear. When the pinion reaches the end of the drive shaft, it rotates the flywheel and cranks the engine.

When the engine starts, the flywheel rotates faster than the starter armature and drive pinion. This moves the drive pinion out of mesh while the ring gear and into the retracted position. When power is removed from the starter, the armature stops rotating and the drive pinion is held in the retraced position by the anti-drift spring.

REMOVAL AND INSTALLATION

Refer to the Engine Disassembly and Assembly sections for starter removal and installation procedures.

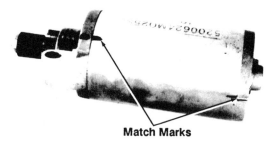

Match Marks

Starter assembly match marks

STARTER DRIVE SERVICE

Every 100 hours of operation (or annually, whichever occurs first), clean and lubricate the splines on the starter drive shaft. If the drive pinion is worn, or has chipped or broken teeth, it must be replaced.

It is not necessary to completely disassemble the starter to service the drive components. Service the drive as follows:

1. Remove the starter from the engine.
2. Remove the dust cover.
3. Hold the drive pinion in a vice with soft jaws when removing and installing the stop nut. The armature will rotate with the nut until the drive pinion stops against internal spacers.

NOTE: *Do not overtighten the vice as this can distort the drive pinion.*

4. Remove the stop nut, stop gear spacer, anti-drift spring, dust cover spacer, and drive pinion.

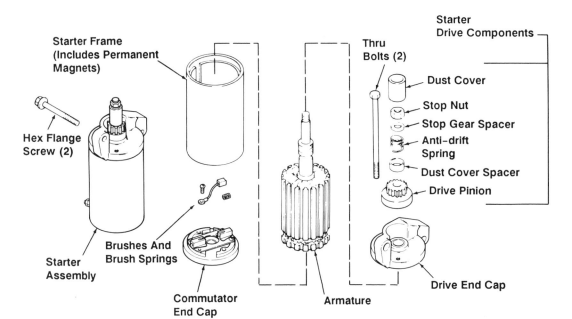

Bendix drive electric starter

5. Clean the splines on drive shaft thoroughly with solvent. Dry the splines thoroughly.

6. Apply a small amount of Kohler electric starter drive lubricant, part no. 52 357 01, or equivalent, to the splines.

NOTE: *Kohler electric starter drive lubricant, part no. 52 357 01, or equivalent, must be used on all Kohler electric starter drives. The use of other lubricants can cause the drive pinion to stick or bind.*

7. Apply a small amount of Loctite® no. 271 to the stop nut threads.

8. Install the drive pinion, dust cover spacer, anti-drift spring, stop gear spacer, and stop nut. Torque the stop nut to 17.0-19.2 N-m (150-170 inch lbs.).

9. Install the dust cover.

DISASSEMBLY

1. Remove the dust cover, stop nut, gear spacer, anti-drift spring, dust cover spacer, and drive pinion. Refer to Starter Drive Service above.

2. Scribe a small line on the drive end cap, opposite the line on the starter frame. These lines will serve as match marks when reassembling the starter.

3. Remove the through bolts.

4. Remove the commutator end cap with brushes and brush springs.

NOTE: *The wiring lead of the positive (+) brush is attached to the insulated terminal on the starter frame. When the commutator end cap is removed, the positive (+) brush should be removed from the brush guide of the brush holder, and will remain attached to the starter frame insulated terminal.*

5. Remove the drive end cap.

6. Remove the armature and thrust washer from inside the starter frame.

Brush Replacement

1. Remove the brush springs from the brush guides of the brush holder.

2. Brush the brush holder screws, negative (−) brush, and plastic brush holder.

3. Remove the hex nuts from the stud terminal. Remove the stud terminal with positive (+) brush and rubber insulating grommet from the starter frame.

4. Reinstall the insulating grommet to the new stud terminal with positive (+) brush. Install the stud terminal with grommet onto the starter frame. Secure the stud with the hex nut.

5. Install the brush holder, new negative (-) brush, and brush holder screws.

6. Install the brush springs and brushes into the brush guides of the brush holder. Make sure the chamfered sides of the brushes are facing away from brush springs.

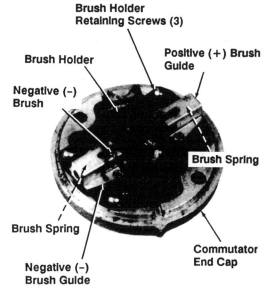

Commutator end cap with brushes

Commutator Service

Clean the commutator with a coarse, lint free cloth. Do not use emery cloth.

If the commutator is badly worn or grooved, turn it down on a lathe or replace the armature.

ASSEMBLY

1. Place the thrust washer over the drive shaft of armature.

2. Insert the armature into the starter frame. Make sure the magnets are closer to the drive shaft end of armature. The magnets will hold the armature inside the frame.

3. Install the drive end cap over the drive shaft. Make sure the match marks on the end cap and starter frame are aligned.

4. Install the brush holder tool to keep the brushes in the pockets of the commutator end cap.

5. Align the match marks on the commutator end cap and starter frame. Hold the drive end cap commutator end caps firmly to the starter frame. Remove the brush holder tool.

6. Install the through bolts and tighten securely.

7. Lubricate the drive shaft with Kohler electric starter drive lubricant. Install the pinion, dust cover spacer, anti-drift spring, stop gear spacer, stop nut, and dust cover. Refer to Starter Drive Service above.

OIL SENTRY OIL LEVEL MONITOR

Operation

Some engines are equipped with optional Oil Sentry system. Oil sentry uses a float switch in the oil pan to detect a low engine oil level. On stationary or unattended applications (pumps, generators, etc.) the float switch can be used to ground the ignition module to stop the engine. On vehicular applications (garden tractors, mowers, etc.) and those equipped with a battery or electric start, the float switch can be used to activate a **low oil** warning light.

Float Switch

REMOVAL

1. Make sure the engine/equipment is resting on a level surface.
2. Remove the oil drain plug and drain oil from crankcase.
3. Disconnect float switch leads.

4. Using a $\frac{9}{16}$ in. open end wrench, turn switch counterclockwise ¼ TURN to loosen. STOP turning switch when flat surface on float switch is in a horizontal position. (Flat surface parallel with base of oil pan and N.C./N.O. markings down.).
5. Turn the switch counterclockwise in ½ TURN INCREMENTS using a smooth, continuous action. Pause briefly between increments and keep the flat surface of float switch in a horizontal position (parallel with base of oil pan).

WARNING: *To prevent damage to the float switch, and to enable you to feel if the float strikes the oil pan, REMOVE THE SWITCH*

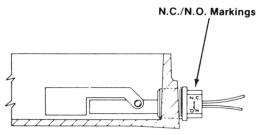

Float switch removal

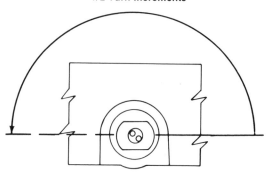

Remove Switch In 1/2 Turn Increments

Float switch removal

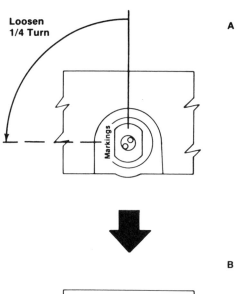

Float switch removal

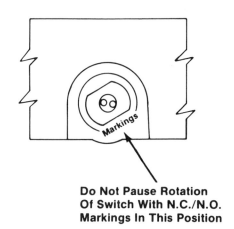

Do Not Pause Rotation Of Switch With N.C./N.O. Markings In This Position

Float switch removal

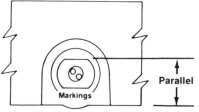

Float switch removal

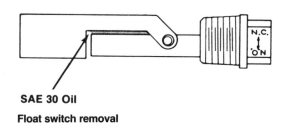

SAE 30 Oil

Float switch removal

BY HAND as soon as it is loose enough for you to do so.

NOTE: *When turning the float switch, use a smooth, continuous action for the ENTIRE ½ turn increment.*

6. If the float does not strike the oil pan, STOP turning the switch, then use the following procedure:

    a. Turn the switch clockwise until the flat surface is in a vertical position. (N.C./N.O. markings on left.) This will allow the float to return against the switch body.

    b. Turn the switch counterclockwise ¼ TURN. STOP turning switch when flat surface is in a horizontal position. (Flat surface parallel with base of oil pan and N.C./N.O. markings down.

    c. Turn the switch counterclockwise in ½ TURN INCREMENTS as instructed in step 5 above.

INSTALLATION

1. Make sure the engine/equipment is resting on a level surface.

2. Remove the oil drain plug and drain oil from crankcase.

3. When adding this switch as an accessory, remove and discard the ½ in. NPSF pipe plug from the location in oil pan where switch will be installed.

WARNING: *To prevent damage to the float switch, and to enable you to feel if the float strikes the oil pan, INSTALL THE SWITCH BY HAND as long as it is loose enough for you to do so.*

4. Apply Loctite® No. 592 Teflon® sealant (or equivalent) to the entire thread area of switch.

5. Apply a thick film of clean SAE 30 oil to the float and switch body.

6. Hold the switch with the flat surface in a vertical position . (N.C./N.O. marking stop the left.) Insert the switch into the oil pan and turn

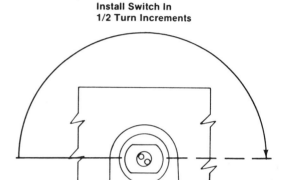

**Install Switch In
1/2 Turn Increments**

Float switch installation

A

1/4 Turn

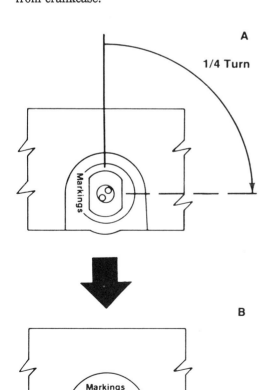

B

Float switch installation

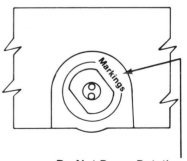

**Do Not Pause Rotation
Of Switch With N.C./N.O.
Markings In This Position**

Float switch installation

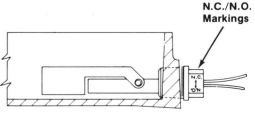

**N.C./N.O.
Markings**

Float switch installation

the switch ¼ turn. STOP turning the switch when the flat surface on switch is in a horizontal position. Flat surface parallel with base of oil pan and N.C./N.O. markings up.).

NOTE: *Several ½ turn increments may be required until the threads on switch engage in oil pan.*

When turning the float switch, use a smooth continuous action for the entire ½ turn increment. Pausing the rotation of the switch may cause the float to strike the oil pan.

7. If the float does not strike the oil pan, STOP turning the switch, then use the following procedure.

a. Turn the switch counterclockwise until the flat is in a vertical position, (N.C./N.O. markings on left.) This will allow the float to return against the switch body.

b. Turn the switch clockwise ¼ TURN. STOP turning switch when flat surface is in a horizontal position. (Flat surface parallel with base of oil pan and N.C./N.O. markings up.).

c. Turn the switch clockwise in ½ TURN INCREMENTS as instructed in step 6 above.

8. Turn in the switch approximately five (5) to six (6) full turns to obtain the proper position. Use a $9/16$ in. open end wrench to tighten the switch. The N.C. markings on switch will be at the top when the switch is positioned properly.

Float Switch Test

Test switch for continuity by placing an ohmmeter or continually test light across leads.
Switch Position A – No Continuity (Switch open)
Switch Position B – Continuity (Switch closed)
Perform the following tests to ensure that the float switch is positioned and working properly before connecting the leads.

NOTE: *These tests apply to engines equipped with a standard oil pan and dipstick. Special oil pan and/or dipstick arrangements can give inaccurate test results.*

1. Connect a continuity test light across float switch leads. The light should be off after oil is above the **L** mark on the dipstick.

2. If the float switch fails this test:

a. Make sure the switch is in the proper position with the N.C. markings at the top.

b. If switch is positioned properly, drain oil and remove switch (see Float Switch Removal). If the float is not attached to the switch body, the oil pan must be removed.

c. Replace a faulty or broken switch with a new one. (See Float Switch Installation.)

Operational Test

Reconnect the leads and perform the following test.

1. Make sure the oil level is up to, but not over the **F** mark on dipstick.

2. Start the engine. If the switch is wired as a low oil level shutdown, the engine should start. If the switch is wired to activate a low oil warning light, the light should be off.

3. Stop the engine. Drain the oil until the oil level is below the **L** mark on the dipstick. If properly wired, the engine will not start, or the light will be **on**.

4. If the test results of steps 2 and 3 are not as indicated, check for improper wiring and/or improper float installation.

ENGINE MECHANICAL SERVICE

DISASSEMBLY

CAUTION: *Before servicing the engine or equipment, always disconnect the spark plug lad to prevent the engine from starting accidentally. Ground the lead to prevent sparks which could cause fires.*

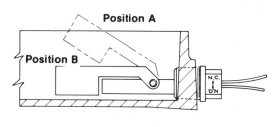

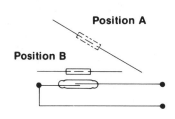

Float switch test

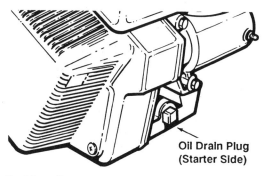

Draining oil

The following sequence is suggested for complete engine disassembly. This procedure can be varied to accommodate options or special equipment.

Clean all parts thoroughly as the engine is disassembled. Only clean parts can be accurately inspected and gauged for wear or damage. There are many commercially available cleaners that will quickly remove grease, oil, and grime from engine parts. When such a cleaner is used, follow the manufacturer's instructions and safety precautions carefully.

Make sure all traces of the cleaner are removed before the engine is reassembled and put into operation. Even small amounts of these cleaners can quickly break down the lubricating properties of engine oil.

1. Disconnect the spark plug.
2. Drain the oil.
3. Remove the oil drain plug and oil fill cap/dipstick.
4. Allow ample time for the oil to drain from the crankcase. Tip engine speed draining.
5. Remove the air cleaner cover as follows:
   a. Press and hold the tab at the bottom of the air cleaner cover.
NOTE: *Choke control must be in the OFF position.*
   b. Slide the air cleaner cover off of the air cleaner base (away from retractable starter).
6. Loosen the slot-head screws and remove the air cleaner element retainer.

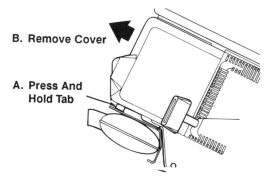

B. Remove Cover

A. Press And Hold Tab

Removing air cleaner cover

Oil Fill Tube   Hex Flange Screw

Removing oil fill tube

7. Remove the Phillips head screws from the air cleaner base.
8. Remove the hex flange nuts, air cleaner, and gasket from the intake studs.
9. On models so equipped, remove Phillips head screws and the retractable starter.
10. Remove the hex flange screw and nut securing the oil fill tube to the fuel tank.
   CAUTION: *Gasoline may be present in the carburetor and fuel system. Gasoline is extremely flammable, and its vapors can explode if ignited. Keep sparks, open flames, and other sources of ignition away from the engine.*
11. Turn the fuel shut-off valve to the OFF position.
12. Disconnect the fuel line from the inlet fitting of the carburetor.
13. Remove the hex flange screws securing the fuel tank to the engine.
14. Remove the fuel tank and fuel line.
15. Remove the throttle linkage from the throttle lever clip.
16. Remove the carburetor and gasket from intake manifold studs.
17. Remove hex flange nuts from exhaust studs and hex flange screws from muffler bracket.
18. Remove muffler and gasket from exhaust from exhaust outlet flange.
19. Loosen four hex flange screws and remove

Retractable Starter   Phillips Head Screws

Removing retractable starter

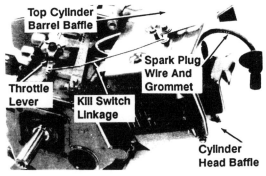

Top Cylinder Barrel Baffle

Spark Plug Wire And Grommet

Throttle Lever

Kill Switch Linkage

Cylinder Head Baffle

Removing baffles

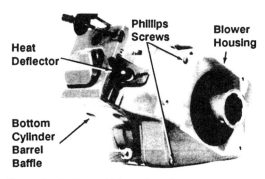

Removing baffle and blower housing

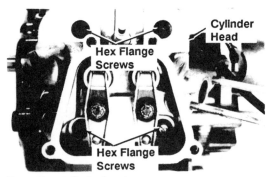

Removing cylinder head

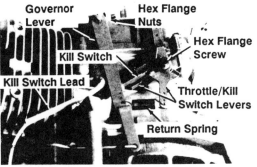

Removing governor, throttle, and kill-switch linkages

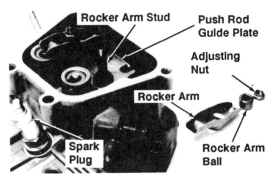

Removing spark plug and rocker arm

Removing valve cover

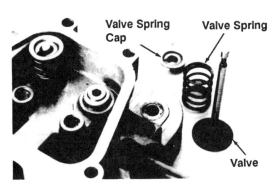

Removing valves

the cylinder head baffle. Remove the spark plug wire grommet from the cylinder head baffle.

20. Remove hex flange screws from the top cylinder barrel baffle. Remove the baffle and disconnect the kill-switch linkage from the throttle lever.

21. Remove the hex flange screws from the bottom cylinder baffle. Remove the baffle.

22. Remove the Phillips head screws from the blower housing. Remove the blower housing.

23. Remove the heat deflector and gaskets from the intake studs.

24. Loosen hex flange nut on governor lever and remove lever from governor shaft. Disconnect return spring from the governor lever.

25. Disconnect the kill-switch lead from the kill-switch.

26. Remove the hex flange screw from the throttle/kill-switch levers.

27. Remove throttle lever, bushing, and kill-switch lever from engine.

28. Remove the hex flange screws from the valve cover. Remove the valve cover from the cylinder head.

29. Remove the breather assembly and valve cover gasket from the cylinder head.

30. Remove the hex flange screws, cylinder head, push rods, and cylinder head gasket.

31. Remove the spark plug.

32. Remove the rocker arm adjusting nuts,

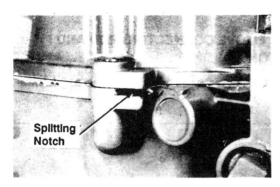

Splitting the closure plate/crankcase

rocker arms and balls, rocker arm studs, and pushrod guide plate.

33. Compress the valve springs by pushing down on the valve spring cap.

34. Remove the valve spring caps, valve springs, and valves.

35. Position the flywheel so the magnet is away from the ignition module.

36. Remove the hex flange screws securing the ignition module to the crankcase.

NOTE: *Always use a flywheel strap wrench to hold the flywheel when loosening or tightening the flywheel retaining fastener. Do not use any type of bar or wedge between the cooling fins as the fins could be cracked or damaged.*

Always use a puller to remove the flywheel from the crankshaft. Do not strike the fly-

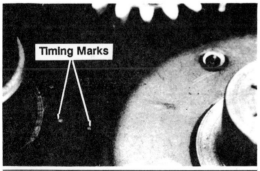

Removing camshaft

wheel or crankshaft, as these parts could be cracked or damaged.

37. Remove the hex flange screw, plain washer, and drive cup.

38. Remove the flywheel from the crankshaft using a puller.

39. Remove the six hex flange screws securing the closure plate to the crankcase.

40. Locate the splitting tabs in the seam of the closure plate and crankcase. Pry the closure plate from the crankcase using a large, flat-blade screwdriver.

NOTE: *Insert the screwdriver only in the splitting tabs. Do not pry on the gasket surfaces of the crankcase or closure plate as this can cause leaks.*

41. Align the timing marks on the camshaft and crankshaft.

42. Mark the tappets as wither intake or exhaust.

NOTE: *The intake tappet is the one farthest from the crankcase gasket surface. The exhaust tappet is nearest to the crankcase gasket surface.*

43. Remove the snap ring and plain washer from the governor cross shaft.

44. Remove the governor cross shaft and small plain washer from the closure.

45. Remove the governor gear and plain washer from the governor shaft.

46. Remove hex flange screw and oil sentry float switch baffle.

47. Use a rubber band to hold float switch.

48. Remove oil sentry float switch from crankcase.

49. Remove the two hex flange screws and connecting rod cap.

NOTE: *If a carbon ridge is present at the top of the bore, use a ridge reamer tool to remove it before attempting to remove the piston.*

50. Carefully push the connecting rod and piston away from the crankshaft and out of the cylinder bore.

51. Remove the wrist pin retainer and the wrist pin. Separate the piston from the connecting rod.

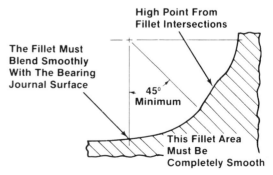

Crankpin fillets

52. Remove the top and center compression rings using a ring expander tool.
53. Remove the oil control ring rails, then remove the rails spacer.
54. Remove the woodruff key from the flywheel taper end of the crankshaft.
55. Press the crankshaft from the crankcase.
56. Remove the oil seals from the crankcase and closure plate.
57. Remove the bearings from the crankcase and closure plate.

CLEANING AND INSPECTION

Clean all parts thoroughly. Only clean parts can be accurately inspected and gauged for war or damage. There are many commercially available cleaners that will quickly remove grease, oil, and grime from engine parts. When such a cleaner is used, follow the manufacturer's instructions and safety precautions carefully.

Make sure all traces of the cleaner are removed before the engine is reassembled and placed into operation. Even small amounts of the these cleaners can quickly break down the lubricating properties of engine oil.

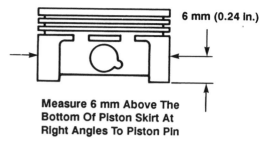

6 mm (0.24 In.)

Measure 6 mm Above The Bottom Of Piston Skirt At Right Angles To Piston Pin

Measuring piston diameter

Camshaft Inspection and Service

Inspect the gear teeth of the camshaft. If the teeth are badly worn, chipped, or some are missing, replacement of the camshaft will be necessary.

Crankshaft Inspection and Service

Inspect the gear teeth of the crankshaft. If the teeth are badly worn, chipped, or some are missing, replacement of the crankshaft will be necessary.

Inspect the crankshaft bearings for scoring, grooving, etc. Do not replace bearings unless

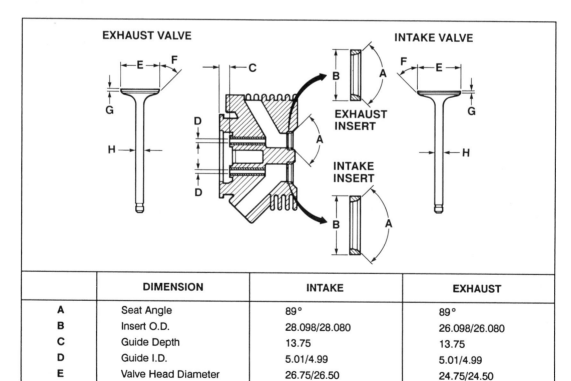

	DIMENSION	INTAKE	EXHAUST
A	Seat Angle	89°	89°
B	Insert O.D.	28.098/28.080	26.098/26.080
C	Guide Depth	13.75	13.75
D	Guide I.D.	5.01/4.99	5.01/4.99
E	Valve Head Diameter	26.75/26.50	24.75/24.50
F	Valve Face Angle	45°	45°
G	Valve Margin (Min.)	1.0	1.0
H	Valve Stem Diameter	4.934/4.952	4.911/4.929

Valve details

they show signs of damage or are out of running clearance specifications. If the crankshaft turns easily and noiselessly, and there is no evidence of scoring, grooving, etc., on the races or bearing surfaces, the bearings can be reused.

Inspect the crankshaft keyways. If worn or chipped, replacement of the crankshaft will be necessary.

Inspect the crankpin for score marks or metallic pickup. Slight score marks can be cleaned with crocus cloth soaked in oil. If wear limits are exceeded, it will either be necessary to replace the crankshaft or regrind the crankpin to 0.25 mm (0.010 in) undersize. If reground, a 0.25 mm (0.010 in) undersize connecting rod (big end) must then be used to achieve proper running clearance. Measure the crankpin for size, taper, and out-of-round.

NOTE: *If the crankpin is reground, visually check to insure that the fillet blends smoothly with the crankpin surface.*

Crankcase Inspection and Service

Check all gasket surfaces to make sure they are free of gasket fragments. Gasket surfaces must also be free of deep scratches or nicks.

Check the cylinder bore wall for scoring. In severe cases, unburned fuel can cause scuffing and scoring of the cylinder wall. It washes the necessary lubricating oils off the piston and cylinder wall. As raw fuel seeps down the cylinder wall, the piston rings make metal to metal contact with the wall. Scoring of the cylinder wall can also be caused by localized hot spots resulting from blocked cooling fins or from inadequate or contaminated lubrication.

If the cylinder bore is badly scored, excessively worn, tapered, or out of round, resizing i necessary. Use a measuring device (inside micrometer, etc.) to determine amount of wear, then select the nearest suitable oversize of either 0.25 mm (0.010 in) or 0.50 mm (0.020 in). Resizing to one of these oversizes will allow usage of the available oversize piston and ring assemblies. Initially, resize using a boring bar, then use the following procedures for honing the cylinder.

Honing

While most commercially available cylinder hones can be used with either portable drills or drill presses, the use of a low speed drill press is preferred as it facilitates more accurate alignment of the bore in relation to the crankshaft crossbore. Honing is best accomplished at a drill speed of about 250 RPM and 60 strokes per minute. After installing coarse stones in hone, proceed as follows:

1. Lower hone into bore and after centering, adjust so that the stones are in contact with the cylinder wall. Use of a commercial cutting-cooling agent is recommended.

2. With the lower edge of each stone positioned even with the lowest edge of the bore, start drill and honing process. Move the hone up and down while resizing to prevent the formation of cutting ridges. Check the size frequently.

NOTE: *Measure the piston diameter and resize the bore to the piston to obtain the specified running clearances. Keep in mind the temperatures caused by honing may cause inaccurate measurements. Make sure the bore is cool when measuring.*

3. When the bore is within 0.064 mm (0.0025 in) of desired size, remove the coarse stones and replace with burnishing stones. Continue with the burnishing stones until within 0.013 mm (0.0005 in) of desired size and then use finish stones (220-280 grit) and polish to final size. A crosshatch should be observed if honing is done correctly. The crosshatch should intersect at approximately 23-33 degrees off the horizontal. Too flat of an angle could cause the rings to skip and wear excessively, too steep of an angle will result in high oil consumption.

4. After resizing, check the bore for roundness, taper, and size. Use am inside micrometer, telescoping gauge, or bore gauge to take measurements. The measurements should be taken at three locations in the cylinder — at the top, middle, and bottom. Two measurements should be taken (perpendicular to each other) at each of the three locations.

Measuring Piston-To-Bore Clearance

Before installing into the cylinder bore, it is necessary that the clearance be accurately checked. This step is often overlooked, and if the clearances are not within specifications, engine failure will usually result.

NOTE: *Do not use a feeler gauge to measure piston-to-bore clearance — it will yield inaccurate measurements. Always use a micrometer.*

Use the following procedure to accurately measure the piston-to-bore clearance:

1. Use a micrometer and measure the diameter of the piston 6 mm (0.24 in) above the bottom of the piston skirt and perpendicular to the piston pin.

2. Use an inside micrometer, telescoping gauge, or bore gauge and measure the cylinder bore. Take the measurement approximately 40 mm (1.6 in) below the top of the bore and perpendicular to the piston pin.

3. Piston-to-bore clearance in the difference between the bore diameter and the piston diameter (step 2 minus step 1).

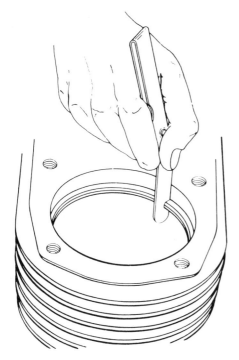

Measuring piston ring end gap

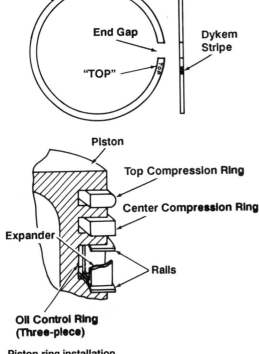

Piston ring installation

Flywheel Inspection

Inspect the flywheel for cracks, and the flywheel keyway for damage. Replace flywheel if cracked. Replace the flywheel, the crankshaft, and the key if flywheel key is sheared or the keyway damaged.

Inspect the ring gear for cracks or damage. Kohler does not provide ring gears as a serviceable part. Replace the flywheel if the ring gear is damaged.

Cylinder Head and Valves Inspection And Service

Carefully inspect the valve mechanism parts. Inspect the valve springs and related hardware for excessive war or distortion. Check the valves and valve seat area or inserts for evidence of deep pitting, cracks, or distortion. Check clearance of the valve stems in guides.

Hard stating, or loss of power accompanied by high fuel consumption may be symptoms of faulty valves. Although these symptoms could also be attributed to worn rings, remove and check the valves first. After removal, clean the valve heads, faces, and stems with a power brush. Then, carefully inspect each valve for defects such as warped head, excessive corrosion, or worn stem end. Replace valves found to be in bad condition. A normal valve and valves in bad condition are shown in the accompanying illustrations.

VALVE GUIDES

If a valve guide is worn beyond specifications, it will not guide the valve in a straight line. This may result in burnt valve aces or seats, loss of compression, and excessive oil consumption.

To check valve guide-to-valve stem clearance, thoroughly clean the valve guide and, using a split-ball gauge, measure the inside diameter. Then, using an outside micrometer, measure the diameter of the valve stem at several points

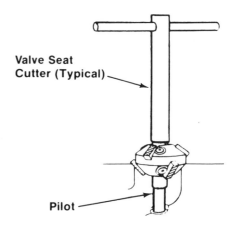

Standard valve cutter

on the stem where it moves in the valve guide. Use the largest stem diameter to calculate the clearance. If the clearance exceeds 7.134 mm (0.2809 in) on intake valve or 7.159 mm (0.2819 in) on exhaust valve, determine whether the valve stem or the guide is responsible for the excessive clearance.

Maximum allowable inside diameter is 5.085 mm (0.2002 in) on the intake valve guide and 5.080 mm (0.2000 in) on the exhaust valve guide.

If the valve stem diameter is within specifications, then recondition the valve guide.

RECONDITIONING VALVE GUIDE

The valve guides in the cylinder head are not removable. Use a 0.25 mm (0.010 in) O/S reamer. Tool no. KO-1033, or equivalent.

VALVE SEAT INSERTS

The valve seats are not replaceable. If the seats become badly pitted, cracked, or distorted, the inserts can be reconditioned.

Use a standard valve seat cutter and cut seat to the required dimensions.

LAPPING VALVES

Reground or new valves must be lapped in, to provide fit. Use a hand valve grinder with suction cup for final lapping. Lightly coat valve face with fine grade of grinding compound, then rotate valve on seat with grinder. Continue grinding until smooth surface is obtained on seat and on valve face. Thoroughly clean cylinder head in soap and hot water to remove all traces of grinding compound. After drying cylinder head apply a light coating of SAE 10 oil to prevent rusting.

Piston and Rings
Inspection and Service

Scuffing and scoring of pistons and cylinder walls occurs when internal temperatures approach the welding point of the piston. Temperatures high enough to do this are created by friction, which is usually attributed to to improper lubrication, and/or overheating of the engine.

Normally, very little wear takes place in the piston boss-piston area. If the original piston and connecting rod can be reused after new rings are installed, the original pin can also be reused but new piston pin retainers are required. The piston pin is included as part of the piston assembly – if the piston pin or the pin boss of the piston is worn or damaged, a new piston assembly is required.

Ring failure is usually indicated by excessive oil consumption and blue exhaust smoke. When rings fail, oil is allowed to enter the combustion

chamber where it burned along with the fuel. High oil consumption can also occur when the piston ring end gap is incorrect because the ring cannot properly conform to the cylinder wall under this condition. Oil control is also lost when ring gaps are not staggered during installation.

When cylinder temperatures get too high, lacquer and varnish collect on pistons causing rings to stick, which results in rapid wear. A worn ring usually takes on a shiny or bright appearance. Scratches on rings and pistons are caused by abrasive material such as carbon, dirt, or pieces of hard metal.

Detonation damage occurs when a portion of the fuel charge ignites spontaneously from heat and pressure shortly after ignition. This creates two flame fronts which meet and explode to create extreme hammering pressures on a specific area of the piston. Detonation generally occurs from using fuels with too low an octane rating.

Preignition, or ignition of the fuel charge before the timed spark, can cause damage similar to detonation. Preignition damage is often more sever than detonation damage – often a hole is quickly burned right through the piston dome. Preignition is caused by a hot spot in the combustion chamber from sources such as: glowing carbon deposits, blocked fins, improperly seated valve, or wrong spark plug.

Replacement pistons are available in STD bore size, and in 0.25 mm (0.010 in) and 0.50 mm (0.20 in) oversizes. Replacement pistons include new piston ring sets and new piston pins.

Service replacement piston rings sets are also available separately for STD pistons, and for 0.25 mm (0.010 in) and 0.50 mm (0.020 in) oversized pistons.

Always use new piston rings when installing pistons. Never reuse old rings.

The cylinder bore must be deglazed before service ring sets are used.

Some important points to remember when servicing piston rings:

1. If the cylinder bore does not need reboring and if the old piston is within wear limits and

NU-4747 Handle And NU-12018 Bearing Installer

Installing crankshaft bearings

Arrow Must Point Towards Flywheel

Piston installation identifier

free of score or scuff marks, the old piston may be reused.

2. Remove old rings and clean up grooves. Never reuse old rings.

3. Before installing the rings on piston, place the top two rings, each in turn, in its running area in cylinder bore and check end gap. This gap should be 0.75 mm (0.030 in) max. in a used cylinder bore and 0.25-0.45mm (0.010-0.018 in) in a new cylinder bore.

4. After installing the new rings on piston, check piston-to-ring side clearance.

Maximum recommended side clearance is:

Top ring − 0.040-0.085 mm (0.0016-0.0033 in)

Middle ring − 0.040-0.072 mm (0.0016-0.0028 in)

Oil control ring − 0.140-0.275 mm (0.0055-0.0108 in)

If side clearance is greater than specified, a new piston must be used.

To install piston rings, proceed as follows:

NOTE: *Rings must be installed correctly. Ring installation instructions are usually included with new rings sets. Follow instructions carefully. Use a piston ring expander to install rings. Install the bottom (oil control) ring first and the top compression ring last.*

1. Oil Control Ring (Bottom Groove): Install expander and then the rails. Make sure the ends of expander are not overlapped.

2. Compression Ring (Center Groove): Install the center ring using a piston ring installation tool. Make sure the **top** mark is up and the PINK stripe is to the left of end gap.

3. Compression Ring (Top Groove): Install the top ring using a piston ring installation tool. Make sure the **top** mark is up and the BLUE stripe is to the left of end gap.

Connecting Rods
Inspection And Service

Check bearing area (big end) for excessive wear, score marks, running and side clearances.

Replace rod and cap if scored or excessively worn.

Service replacement connecting rods are available in STD crankpin size and 0.25 mm (0.010 in) undersize. The 0.25 mm (0.010 in) undersize rod can be identified by the drilled hole located in the lower end of the rod shank.

Governor Gear Inspection

Inspect the governor gear teeth. Look for any evidence of worn, chipped, or cracked teeth. If one or more of these problems is noted, replace the governor gear.

ASSEMBLY

The following sequence is suggested for complete engine reassembly. This procedure assumes that all components are new or have been reconditioned, and all components subassembly work has been completed. This procedure may be varied to accommodate options or special equipment.

NOTE: *Make sure the engine is assembled using all specified torque values, tightening sequences, and clearances. Failure to observe*

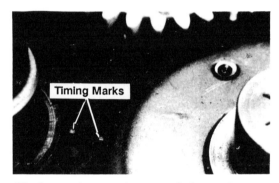

Timing Marks

Aligning crankgear and camgear timing marks

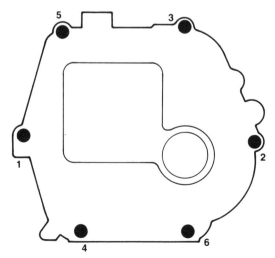

Closure plate fastener torque pattern

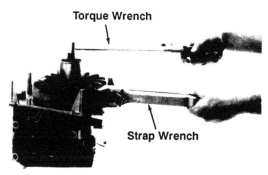

Tightening flywheel fastener

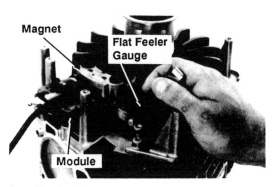

Installing ignition module

specification could cause severe engine wear or damage. Always use new gaskets.

1. Assemble the NU-12018 bearing installer to the NU-4747 handle, or equivalent.

2. Position the installer/bearing to the bearing bore of the crankcase or closure plate.

3. Drive the bearing into the bearing bore. Make sire the bearing is installed straight and true, and bottoms in the bore.

4. Lubricate the flywheel and bearing surface of the crankshaft.

5. Insert the crankshaft through the flywheel and bearing.

6. Assemble the piston, connecting rod, wrist pin and wrist pin retainers.

NOTE: *The connecting rod must be assembled so the side with the cast numbers is opposite the FLY mark on the piston.*

Proper orientation of the piston/connecting rod inside the engine is extremely important. Improper orientation can cause extensive wear or damage.

7. Stagger the piston rings in the grooves until the end gaps are 120 degrees apart.

8. Lubricate thew cylinder bore, piston and rings with engine oil. Compress the piston rings using a piston ring compressor.

9. Orient the FLY mark on piston towards the flywheel side of crankcase. Gently push the piston/connecting rod into bore. Do not pound on the piston.

10. Lubricate the crankshaft journal and connecting rod bearing surfaces with engine oil. Install the connecting rod cap to the connecting rod.

NOTE: *The connecting rod cap must be installed with its match mark aligned with the connecting rod match mark. Improper installation can cause serious engine damage.*

11. Install the hex flange screws and torque in several increments to 9 N-m (80 inch lbs.).

12. Rotate the crankshaft until the piston is at top dead center in the cylinder bore.

13. Install oil sentry float switch in crankcase. Torque the float switch to 13.6 N-m (120 inch lbs.).

NOTE: *The oil sentry float switch must be installed so the float arm is free to pivot toward the center of the crankcase.*

14. Install the oil sentry float switch baffle and hex flange screw.

15. Install plain washer and governor on crankcase stud.

16. Install small plain washer on cross shaft and install cross shaft (from inside closure plate) through bore in closure plate.

17. Install plain washer and hitch pin.

18. Lubricate the tappets and tappet bores in crankcase with engine oil.

19. Install the tappets into the appropriate intake or exhaust tappet bore in the crankcase.

NOTE: *The intake tappet is the one farthest from the crankcase gasket surface. The exhaust tappet is nearest to the crankcase gasket surface.*

20. Lubricate the camshaft bearing surfaced with engine oil.

21. Align the timing marks on the camshaft gear and crankshaft gear. Lower the camshaft into the bearing surface in crankcase. Make sure the camshaft, crankshaft, and governor gears mesh and the timing marks are aligned.

22. Prepare the sealing surfaces of the closure plate and crankcase as directed by the sealant manufacturer.

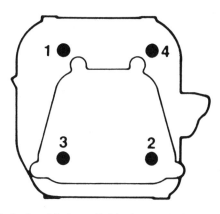

Cylinder head fastener tightening sequence

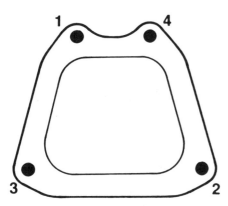

Valve cover fastener tightening sequence

NOTE: *Do not scrape the surfaces when cleaning as this will damage the surfaces and could cause leaks. The use of a gasket-removing solvent is recommended.*

23. RTV silicone sealant is used as a gasket between the closure plate and crankcase. GE Silmate® type RTV-1473 or RTV-108 silicone sealant (or equivalent) is recommended.

24. Apply a $\frac{1}{16}$ in. bead of sealant to the closure plate.

25. Install the closure plate to the crankcase and install the six hex flange screws. Tighten the screws hand tight.

NOTE: *Turn governor cross shaft clockwise before installing the closure plate. Cross shaft must rest on governor for proper operation.*

26. Torque the fasteners, in several increments in the sequence shown, to 22.6 N-m (200 inch lbs.).

27. Slide the seat protector sleeve NU-12021, or equivalent, over the crankshaft. Generously lubricate the lips of the oil seal with light grease. Slide the oil seal over he sleeve.

28. Assemble handle and seal driver. Install the crankcase seal until the driver bottoms against the crankcase. Assemble handle and seal driver. Install the closure plate seal until the driver bottoms against the closure plate.

NOTE: *Oil Seal on PTO side of crankshaft*

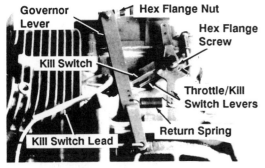

Installing kill-switch, throttle and governor linkage

should be installed to a depth of 5-7 mm (0.020-0.28 in) below lip of crankshaft bore.

CAUTION: *Damaging Crankshaft And Flywheel Can Cause Personal Injury! Using improper procedures to install the flywheel can crack or damage the crankshaft and/or flywheel. This not only causes extensive engine damage, but can also cause personal injury, since broken fragments could be thrown from the engine. Always observe and use the following precautions and procedures when installing the flywheel.*

NOTE: *Before installing the flywheel, make sure the crankshaft taper and flywheel hub are clean, dry and completely free of lubricants. The presence of lubricants can case the flywheel to be over-stressed and damaged when the flange screw is torqued to specification.*

Make sure the flywheel key is installed properly in the keyway. The flywheel can become cracked or damaged if the key is not installed properly in the keyway.

Always use a flywheel strap wrench to hold the flywheel when tightening the flywheel fastener. Do not use any type of bar wedge between the cooling fins or flywheel ring gear, as these parts could become cracked or damaged.

29. Install the woodruff key into the keyway in the crankshaft.

30. Place the flywheel over the keyway/crankshaft. Install the drive cup, plain washer (flat side of washer towards the drive cup), and the hex flange screw.

31. Hold the flywheel with a strap wrench and torque the hex flange screw to 67.8 N-m (50 foot lbs.).

32. Install the ignition module and hex flange screws to the bosses on crankcase. Move the module as far away from the flywheel/magnet as possible. Tighten the hex flange screws slightly.

33. Insert a 0.203-0.305 mm (0.008-0.012 in) flat feeler gauge or shim stock between the magnet and ignition module.

34. Tighten the hex flange screws as follows:
First Time Installation On A New Short Block: 6.2 N-m (55 inch lbs.).
All Reinstallations: 4.0 N-m (35 inch lbs.).

35. Rotate the flywheel back and forth; check to make sure the magnet does not strike the module. Check the gap with a feeler gauge and readjust if necessary.

36. Lubricate with engine oil, and install the valves, valve springs, and valve spring caps.

37. Compress the valve spring by pushing down on the valve spring cap. Lock the valve spring cap in place on the valve stem.

NOTE: *Support valves from beneath the cylinder head to make installing the valve spring caps easier.*

38. Install the pushrod guide plate, rocker arm studs, rocker arms and balls, and rocker arm adjusting nuts. Lubricate with engine oil.

39. Install a new cylinder head gasket.

40. Install the cylinder head and tighten the hex flange screws in several increments in the sequence shown, to 22.6 N-m (200 inch lbs.).

41. Set spark plug gap at 0.76 mm (0.030 in). Install spark plug in cylinder head and torque to 24.4-29.8 N-m (18-22 foot lbs.).

42. Install the push rods. Check that the push rods are seated on the tappets and rocker arms.

43. Adjust valve to tappet clearance as follows:

   a. Position the crankshaft so the piston is at the top of the compression stroke (the camshaft is not pushing the tappets and push rods).

   b. Insert a flat feeler gauge between the rocker arm and valve stem. The recommended valve to rocker arm clearance for both intake and exhaust is 0.038-0.051 mm (0.0015-0.0020 in).

   c. Adjust clearance by turning the adjusting nut clockwise to decrease valve to rocker arm clearance, counterclockwise to increase valve to rocker arm clearance.

44. Install a new valve cover gasket. Install the breather assembly on the cylinder head.

45. Install a valve cover. Torque the hex flange screws to 3.4 N-m (30 inch lbs.) using the sequence shown.

46. Install kill-switch lever, bushing, and throttle lever on the crankcase using hex flange screw.

47. Connect the kill-switch lead to the kill-switch.

48. Install the return spring in the first hole of the throttle lever (the hole nearest the end of the throttle lever).

49. Install the governor lever on the governor cross shaft. install the return spring in the third (middle) hole of the governor lever.

NOTE: *Leave all hardware slightly loose until all sheet metal parts are in position.*

50. Install the blower housing using Phillips head screws in the locations shown.

51. Install the heat detector and gaskets on the intake studs.

52. Install the bottom cylinder baffle using hex flange screws.

53. Connect the kill-switch linkage in the first hole of the throttle lever. Install the top cylinder barrel baffle using hex flange screws.

54. Install the spark plug wire and grommet into the cylinder head baffle. Install the cylinder head baffle onto the top and bottom cylinder baffles.

55. Tighten all hardware.

56. Install new gasket and muffler on exhaust outlet flange.

57. install hex flange nuts onto exhaust studs and hex flange screws in muffler bracket. Torque hex flange nuts to 22.6 N-m (200 inch lbs.).

58. Install new gasket and carburetor onto intake manifold studs.

59. Install the throttle linkage to the carburetor throttle lever using the linkage clip.

CAUTION: *Gasoline may be present in the carburetor and fuel system. Gasoline is extremely flammable, and its vapors can explode if ignited. Keep sparks, flames, and other sources of ignition away from the engine.*

60. Install the fuel tank and fuel line.

61. Secure the fuel tank to the engine using hex flange screws. Torque the hex flange screws to 17 N-m (150 inch lbs.).

62. Install the fuel line on the carburetor inlet fitting. Secure the fuel line with a hose clamp.

63. Make sure the two O-rings on the oil fill tube and the O-ring in the oil fill cap are in place.

64. Install oil fill tube into the hole in the crankcase.

65. Secure the oil fill tube to the fuel tank with the hex flange screw and lock nut.

66. Install the retractable starter and Phillips head screws to the blower housing.

67. Install gasket, air cleaner, and hex flange nuts on intake studs.

68. Install Phillips head screws to air cleaner.

69. Instal the precleaner and air cleaner element retainer. Be sure the retainer is hooked on tabs. Tighten the four slot head screws evenly.

70. Install the air cleaner cover as follows:

   a. Slide the air cleaner cover onto the air cleaner base.

   b. Be sure the tab at the bottom of the air cleaner cover snaps in place to lock the cover on the air cleaner base.

PREPARE THE ENGINE FOR OPERATION

The engine is now completely reassembled. Before starting or operating the engine, be sure to do the following:

1. Make sure all hardware is tightened securely.

2. Make sure the oil drain plug and oil sentry pressure switch are tightened securely.

3. Fill the crankcase with the correct amount, weight, and type of oil.

4. Adjust the governor. Refer to the Fuel System and Governor section.

5. Adjust the carburetor idle fuel needle or idle sped adjusting screw as necessary. Refer to the Fuel System and Governor section.

6. Make sure the maximum engine speed does not exceed 3600 rpm. Adjust the throttle and choke controls and the high speed stop as

necessary. Refer to the Fuel System and Governor section.

AUTOMATIC COMPRESSION RELEASE (ACR)

This engine is equipped with an Automatic Compression Release (ACR) mechanism. ACR lowers compression at cranking speeds to make starting easier.

Operation

The ACR mechanism consists of a lever and control pin assembly attached to the gear on the camshaft. At cranking speeds (700 RPM or lower), the control pin protrudes above the exhaust cam lobe. This pushes the exhaust valve off its seat during the first part of the compression stroke. The reduced compression results in an effective compression ratio of about 2:1 during cranking.

After starting, engine speed increases to over 700 RPM. Centrifugal force moves the lever, and the control pin drops into the recess in the exhaust valve and the engine operates at full power.

When the engine is stopped, the spring returns the lever and control pin assembly to the compression release position ready for the next start.

11

Kohler Command
11 and 12.5 Hp

AIR CLEANER & AIR INTAKE SYSTEM

Air Cleaner

These engines are equipped with a replaceable, high-density paper air cleaner element. Some engines are also equipped with an oiled-foam precleaner which surrounds the paper element.

SERVICE

Check the air cleaner daily or before starting the engine. Check for and correct heavy buildup of dirt and debris, and loose components.

NOTE: *Operating the engine with loose or damaged air cleaner components could allow unfiltered air into the engine causing premature wear and failure.*

Precleaner Service

If so equipped, wash and reoil the precleaner every 25 hours of operation (more often under extremely dusty or dirty conditions).

1. Remove the precleaner from the paper element.

2. Wash the precleaner in warm water with detergent. Rinse the precleaner thoroughly un-

til all traces of detergent are eliminated. Squeeze out excess water (do not wring). Allow the precleaner to air-dry.

3. Saturate the precleaner with new engine oil. Squeeze out all excess oil.

4. Reinstall the precleaner over the paper element.

5. Reinstall air cleaner cover, and air cleaner cover retaining knob. Make sure the knob is tightened securely.

Servicing the Paper Element

Every 100 hours of operation (more often under extremely dusty or dirty conditions), check the paper element. Replace the element as necessary.

1. Remove the precleaner (if so equipped) from the paper element.

2. Remove the wing nut, washer, element cover, and air cleaner element.

3. Do not wash the paper element or use pressurized air, as this will damage the element. Replace a dirty, bent, or damaged element with a new element. Handle new elements carefully; do not use if the sealing surfaces are bent or damaged.

4. Reinstall the paper element, element cov-

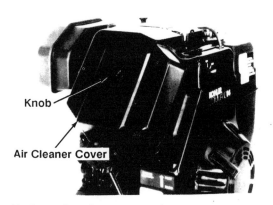

Air cleaner housing components

Knob

Air Cleaner Cover

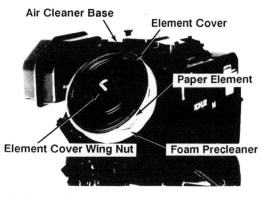

Air cleaner elements

Air Cleaner Base

Element Cover

Paper Element

Element Cover Wing Nut

Foam Precleaner

SPECIFICATIONS, TOLERANCES, AND SPECIAL TORQUE VALUES[1]

DESCRIPTION   **Command 11, 12.5, 14 Hp**
General Specifications

Power (@ 3600 rpm, corrected to SAE J1349)
    Command 11 . . . . 8.20 kW (11 hp)
    Command 12.5 . . . . 9.33 kW (12.5 hp)
    Command 14 . . . . 10.50 kW (14 hp)
Peak Torque
    Command 11 . . . . 27.4 N•m (20.2 lbf•ft)
    Command 12.5 . . . . 27.8 N•m (20.5 lbf•ft)
    Command 14 . . . . 28.9 N•m (21.3 lbf•ft)
Bore . . . . 87 mm (3.43 in)
Stroke . . . . 67 mm (2.64 in)
Displacement . . . . 398 cm³ (24.3 in³)
Compression Ratio 8.5:1
Approx. Weight . . . . 36.3 kg (80 lb)
Approx. Oil Capacity . . . . 1.9 L (2.0 U.S. qt)

Air Cleaner

Base Nut Torque . . . . 9.9 N•m (88 lbf•in)

Angle Of Operation — Maximum (At Full Oil Level)

Intermittent — All Directions . . . . 35°
Continuous — All Directions . . . . 25°

Balance Shaft

End Play (Free) . . . . 0.0575/0.3625 mm (0.0023/0.0143 in)
Running Clearance . . . . 0.025/0.063 mm (0.0009/0.0025 in)
Bore I.D. — New . . . . 20.000/20.025 mm (0.7874/0.7884 in)
Bore I.D. — Max. Wear Limit . . . . 20.038 mm (0.7889 in)
Balance Shaft Bearing Surface O.D. — New . . . . 19.962/19.975 mm (0.7859/0.7864 in)
Balance Shaft Bearing Surface O.D. — Max. Wear Limit . . . . 19.959 mm (0.7858 in)

Camshaft

End Play (With Shims) . . . . 0.076/0.127 mm (0.003/0.005 in)
Running Clearance . . . . 0.025/0.063 mm (0.0010/0.0025 in)
Bore I.D. — New . . . . 20.000/20.025 mm (0.7874/0.7884 in)
Bore I.D. — Max. Wear Limit . . . . 20.038 mm (0.7889 in)
Camshaft Bearing Surface O.D. — New . . . . 19.962/19.975 mm (0.7859/0.7864 in)
Camshaft Bearing Surface O.D. — Max. Wear Limit . . . . 19.959 mm (0.7858 in)

Carburetor

Preliminary Low Idle Fuel Needle Setting
    Command 11 . . . . 1-1/4 Turn
    Command 12.5 . . . . 1-1/4 Turn
    Command 14 . . . . 1-3/4 Turn
Fuel Bowl Nut Torque . . . . 5.1/6.2 N•m (45/55 lbf•in)

Charging

Stator Mounting Screw Torque . . . . 4.0 N•m (35 lbf•in)

Closure Plate

Oil Filter Torque . . . . 5.7/9.0 N•m (50/80 lbf•in)
Oil Filter Drain Plug (1/8" NPT) Torque . . . . 7.3/9.0 N•m (65/80 lbf•in)
Closure Plate Fastener Torque . . . . 24.4 N•m (216 lbf•in)
Oil Sentry Pressure Switch Torque . . . . 7.9 N•m (70 lbf•in)
Oil Pump Cover Fastener Torque[2] . . . . 4.0*6.2 N•m (35*55 lbf•in)
Oil Filter Adapter Fastener Torque . . . . 11.3 N•m (100 lbf•in)

Connecting Rod

Connecting Rod Cap Fastener Torque . . . . 22.6 N•m (200 lbf•in)
Connecting Rod To Crankpin Running Clearance — New . . . . 0.030/0.055 mm (0.0012/0.0022 in)
Connecting Rod To Crankpin Running Clearance —
    Max. Wear Limit . . . . 0.07 mm (0.0025 in)
Connecting Rod To Crankpin Side Clearance . . . . 0.18/0.41 mm (0.007/0.016 in)
Connecting Rod To Piston Pin Running Clearance . . . . 0.015/0.028 mm (0.0006/0.0011 in)
Piston Pin End I.D. — New . . . . 19.015/19.023 mm (0.7486/0.7489 in)
Piston Pin End I.D. — Max. Wear Limit . . . . 19.036 mm (0.7495 in)

Crankcase

Governor Cross Shaft Bore I.D. — New . . . . 6.025/6.050 mm (0.2372/0.2382 in)
Governor Cross Shaft Bore I.D. — Max. Wear Limit . . . . 6.063 mm (0.2387 in)

Crankshaft

End Play (Free) . . . . 0.0575/0.4925 mm (0.0023/0.0194 in)
Crankshaft Sleeve Bearing I.D. — (Installed) New . . . . 44.965/45.003 mm (1.7703/1.7718 in)
Crankshaft Sleeve Bearing I.D. — Max. Wear Limit . . . . 45.016 mm (1.7723 in)
Crankshaft To Sleeve Bearing Running Clearance — New . . . . 0.03/0.09 mm (0.0012/0.0035 in)
Crankshaft Bore (In Oil Pan) To Crankshaft Running
    Clearance — New . . . . 0.03/0.09 mm (0.0012/0.0035 in)
Flywheel End Main Bearing
    (O.D. — New) . . . . 44.913/44.935 mm (1.7682/1.7691 in)
    (O.D. — Max. Wear Limit) . . . . 44.84 mm (1.765 in)
    (Max. Taper) . . . . 0.022 mm (0.0009 in)
    (Max. Out Of Round) . . . . 0.025 mm (0.0010 in)

Closure Plate End Main Bearing Journal
    (O.D. − New) . . . . 41.915/41.935 mm (1.6502/1.6510 in)
    (O.D. − Max. Wear Limit) . . . . 41.86 mm (1.648 in)
    (Max. Taper) . . . . 0.020 mm (0.0008 in)
    (Max. Out Of Round) . . . . 0.025 mm (0.0010 in)

Connecting Rod Journal
    (O.D. − New) . . . . 38.958/38.970 mm (1.5338/1.5343 in)
    (O.D. − Max. Wear Limit) . . . . 38.94 mm (1.5328 in)
    (Max. Taper) . . . . 0.012 mm (0.0005 in)
    (Max. Out Of Round) . . . . 0.025 mm (0.0010 in)

Crankshaft T.I.R.
    (PTO End, Crank In Engine) . . . . 0.15 mm (0.0059 in)
    (Entire Crank, In V-Blocks) . . . . 0.10 mm (0.0039 in)

Cylinder Bore

Cylinder Bore I.D. − New . . . . 87.000/87.025 mm (3.4252/3.4262 in)
Cylinder Bore I.D. − Max. Wear Limit . . . . 87.063 mm (3.4277 in)
Cylinder Bore I.D. − Max. Out Of Round . . . . 0.12 mm (0.0047 in)
Cylinder Bore I.D. − Max. Taper . . . . 0.05 mm (0.0020 in)

Cylinder Head

Cylinder Head Fastener Torque . . . . 40.7 N•m (30 lbf•ft)
Max. Out Of Flatness . . . . 0.076 mm (0.003 in)
Rocker Pedestal Fastener Torque . . . . 9.9 N•m (88 lbf•in)

Electric Starter

Drive Pinion Fastener Torque . . . . 15.3 N•m (135 lbf•in)
Drive Pinion To Flywheel Ring Gear Backlash . . . . 0.025/1.56 mm (0.001/0.061 in)

Fan/Flywheel

Fan Fastener Torque . . . . 9.9 N•m (88 lbf•in)
Flywheel Retaining Screw Torque . . . . 66.4 N•m (49 lbf•ft)

Fuel Pump

Fuel Pump/Cover Fastener Screw Torque[2] . . . . 7.3*9.0 N•m (65*80 lbf•in)

Fuel Tank

Fuel Tank Fastener Torque . . . . 7.3 N•m (65 lbf•in)

Governor

Governor Cross Shaft To Crankcase Running Clearance . . . . 0.025/0.075 mm (0.0010/0.0030 in)
Governor Cross Shaft O.D. − New . . . . 5.975/6.000 mm (0.2352/0.2362 in)
Governor Cross Shaft O.D. − Max. Wear Limit . . . . 5.962 mm (0.2347 in)
Governor Gear Shaft To Governor Gear Running Clearance . . . . 0.015/0.140 mm (0.0006/0.0055 in)
Governor Gear Shaft O.D. − New . . . . 5.990/6.000 mm (0.2358/0.2362 in)
Governor Gear Shaft O.D. − Max. Wear Limit . . . . 5.977 mm (0.2353 in)

Ignition

Spark Plug Type (Champion Or Equiv.) RC12YC
Spark Plug Gap . . . . 1.02 mm (0.040 in)
Spark Plug Torque . . . . 38.0/43.4 N•m (28/32 lbf•ft)
Ignition Module Air Gap . . . . 0.203/0.305 mm (0.008/0.012 in)
Ignition Module Fastener Torque[2] . . . . 4.0*6.2 N•m (35*55 lbf•in)

Muffler

Muffler Retaining Nuts . . . . 24.4 N•m (216 lbf•in)

Piston, Piston Rings, And Piston Pin

Piston To Piston Pin (Selective Fit) . . . . 0.006/0.017 mm (0.0002/0.0007 in)
Piston Pin Bore I.D. − New . . . . 19.006/19.012 mm (0.7483/0.7485 in)
Piston Pin Bore I.D. − Max. Wear Limit . . . . 19.025 mm (0.7490 in)
Piston Pin O.D. − New . . . . 18.995/19.000 mm (0.7478/0.7480 in)
Piston Pin O.D. − Max. Wear Limit . . . . 18.994 mm (0.74779 in)
Top Compression Ring To Groove Side Clearance . . . . 0.040/0.105 mm (0.0016/0.0041 in)
Middle Compression Ring To Groove Side Clearance . . . . 0.040/0.072 mm (0.0016/0.0028 in)
Oil Control Ring To Groove Side Clearance . . . . 0.551/0.675 mm (0.0217/0.0266 in)
Top And Center Compression Ring End Gap − New Bore . . . . 0.3/0.5 mm (0.012/0.020 in)
Top And Center Compression Ring End Gap − Used
   Bore (Max.) . . . . 0.77 mm (0.030 in)
Piston Thrust Face (@D_1) To Cylinder Bore Running
   Clearance − New[3] . . . . 0.041/0.044 mm (0.0016/0.0017 in)

Retractable Starter

Center Screw Torque . . . . 7.4/8.5 N•m (65/75 lbf•in)

Throttle/Choke Controls

Governor Control Lever Fastener Torque . . . . 9.9 N•m (88 lbf•in)
Speed Control Bracket Assembly Fastener Torque[2] . . . . 7.3*10.7 N•m (65*95 lbf•in)

Valve Cover/Rocker Arms

Valve Cover Fastener Torque[2] . . . . 7.3*10.7 N•m (65*95 lbf•in)
Rocker Arm I.D. — New . . . . 15.837/16.127 mm (0.63/0.64 in)
Rocker Arm I.D. — Max. Wear Limit . . . . 16.13 mm (0.640 in)
Rocker Shaft O.D. — New . . . . 15.90/15.85 mm (0.63 in)
Rocker Shaft O.D. — Max. Wear Limit . . . . 15.727 mm (0.619 in)

Valves And Valve Lifters

Hydraulic Valve Lifter To Crankcase Running Clearance . . . . 0.0124/0.0501 mm (0.0005/0.0020 in)
Intake Valve Stem To Valve Guide Running Clearance . . . . 0.038/0.076 mm (0.0015/0.0030 in)
Exhaust Valve Stem To Valve Guide Running Clearance . . . . 0.050/0.088 mm (0.0020/0.0035 in)
Intake Valve Guide I.D. — New . . . . 7.038/7.058 mm (0.2771/0.2779 in)
Intake Valve Guide I.D. — Max. Wear Limit . . . . 7.134 mm (0.2809 in)
Exhaust Valve Guide I.D. — New . . . . 7.038/7.058 mm (0.2771/0.2779 in)
Exhaust Valve Guide I.D. — Max. Wear Limit . . . . 7.159 mm (0.2819 in)
Valve Guide Reamer Size — STD . . . . 7.048 mm (0.2775 in)
Valve Guide Reamer Size — 0.25 mm O.S. . . . . 7.298 mm (0.2873 in)
Intake Valve Minimum Lift . . . . 8.96 mm (0.353 in)
Exhaust Valve Minimum Lift . . . . 9.14 mm (0.360 in)
Nominal Valve Seat Angle . . . . 45°

NOTES:

[1] Values are in Metric units. Values in parenthesis are English equivalents. Lubricate threads with engine oil prior to assembly.

[2] For self-tapping (thread forming) fasteners: the higher torque value is for initial installation into a new cored hole*the lower torque value is for subsequent installation and installation into tapped holes and weld nuts.

[3] Measure 6 mm (0.236 in) above the bottom of the piston skirt at right angles to the piston pin.

English Fastener Torque Recommendations For Standard Applications

Tightening Torque: N•m (lbf•in) + or – 20%			
Bolts, Screws, Nuts And Fasteners Assembled Into Cast Iron Or Steel			**Grade 2 Or 5 Fasteners Into Aluminum**
Grade 2	Grade 5	Grade 8	
Size			
8–32	2.3 (20)	2.8 (25)	———	2.3 (20)
10–24	3.6 (32)	4.5 (40)	———	3.6 (32)
10–32	3.6 (32)	4.5 (40)	———	
1/4–20	7.9 (70)	13.0 (115)	18.7 (165)	7.9 (70)
1/4–28	9.6 (85)	15.8 (140)	22.6 (200)	
5/16–18	17.0 (150)	28.3 (250)	39.6 (350)	17.0 (150)
5/16–24	18.7 (165)	30.5 (270)	———	———
3/8–16	29.4 (260)	———	———	———
3/8–24	33.9 (300)	———	———	———

Tightening Torque N•m (lbf•ft) + or – 20%			
Size			
5/16–24	———	———	40.7 (30)	———
3/8–16	———	47.5 (35)	67.8 (50)	———
3/8–24	———	54.2 (40)	81.4 (60)	———
7/16–14	47.5 (35)	74.6 (55)	108.5 (80)	———
7/16–20	61.0 (45)	101.7 (75)	142.4 (105)	———
1/2–13	67.8 (50)	108.5 (80)	155.9 (115)	———
1/2–20	94.9 (70)	142.4 (105)	223.7 (165)	———
9/16–12	101.7 (75)	169.5 (125)	237.3 (175)	———
9/16–18	135.6 (100)	223.7 (165)	311.9 (230)	———
5/8–11	149.2 (110)	244.1 (180)	352.6 (260)	———
5/8–18	189.8 (140)	311.9 (230)	447.5 (330)	———
3/4–10	199.3 (150)	332.2 (245)	474.6 (350)	———
3/4–16	271.2 (200)	440.7 (325)	637.3 (470)	———

Metric Fastener Torque Recommendations For Standard Applications

Tightening Torque: N•m (lbf•in) + or – 10%

Size	Property Class 4.8	5.8	8.8	10.9	12.9	Noncritical Fasteners Into Aluminum
M4	1.2 (11)	1.7 (15)	2.9 (26)	4.1 (36)	5.0 (44)	2.0 (18)
M5	2.5 (22)	3.2 (28)	5.8 (51)	8.1 (72)	9.7 (86)	4.0 (35)
M6	4.3 (38)	5.7 (50)	9.9 (88)	14.0 (124)	16.5 (146)	6.8 (60)
M8	10.5 (93)	13.6 (120)	24.4 (216)	33.9 (300)	40.7 (360)	17.0 (150)

Tightening Torque: N•m (lbf•ft) + or – 10%

	Property Class 4.8	5.8	8.8	10.9	12.9	Noncritical Fasteners Into Aluminum
M10	21.7 (16)	27.1 (20)	47.5 (35)	66.4 (49)	81.4 (60)	33.9 (25)
M12	36.6 (27)	47.5 (35)	82.7 (61)	116.6 (86)	139.7 (103)	61.0 (45)
M14	58.3 (43)	76.4 (55)	131.5 (97)	184.4 (136)	219.7 (162)	94.9 (70)

Oil Drain Plugs Tightening Torque: N•m (English Equiv.)

Size	Into Cast Iron	Into Aluminum
1/8" NPT	-------------	4.5 (40 lbf•in)
1/4"	17.0 (150 lbf•in)	11.3 (100 lbf•in)
3/8"	20.3 (180 lbf•in)	13.6 (120 lbf•in)
1/2"	27.1 (20 lbf•ft)	17.6 (13 lbf•ft)
3/4"	33.9 (25 lbf•ft)	21.7 (16 lbf•ft)
X–708–1	27.1/33.9 (20/25 lbf•ft)	27.1/33.9 (20/25 lbf•ft)

Torque Conversions

N•m = lbf•in x 0.113
N•m = lbf•ft x 1.356
lbf•in = N•m x 8.85
lbf•ft = N•m x 0.737

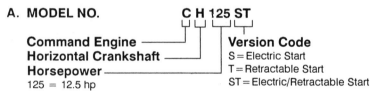

A. MODEL NO.   C H 125 ST

Command Engine
Horizontal Crankshaft
Horsepower
125 = 12.5 hp

Version Code
S = Electric Start
T = Retractable Start
ST = Electric/Retractable Start

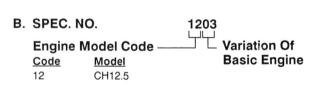

B. SPEC. NO.   1203

Engine Model Code —————— **Variation Of Basic Engine**

Code	Model
12	CH12.5

KOHLERengine

MODEL NO. CH125ST   — A
SPEC. NO.   1203   — B
SERIAL NO. 2005810334   — C

REFER TO OWNER'S MANUAL
FOR OPERATION/MAINTENANCE
INSTRUCTIONS AND SAFETY
PRECAUTIONS.

K KOHLER COMPANY
KOHLER WISCONSIN USA

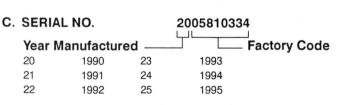

C. SERIAL NO.   2005810334

Year Manufactured ————   ——— Factory Code

20	1990	23	1993
21	1991	24	1994
22	1992	25	1995

er, washer, wing nut, precleaner, air cleaner cover, and air cleaner cover retaining knob. Make sure the knob is tightened securely.

Inspect Air Cleaner Components

Whenever the air cleaner cover is removed, or the paper element or precleaner are serviced, check the following areas/components:

• Covered Air Cleaner Element – Inspect the rubber grommet in the hole of the air cleaner element cover. Replace the grommet if it is worn or damaged.

• Air Cleaner Base – Make sure the base is secured and not cracked or damaged. Since the air cleaner base and carburetor are secured to the intake port with common hardware, it is extremely important that the nuts securing these components are tight at all times.

• Breather Tube – Make sure the tube is installed to both the air cleaner base and valve cover.

NOTE: *Damaged, worn, or loose air cleaner components can allow unfiltered air into the engine causing premature wear and failure. Tighten or replace all loose or damaged components.*

DISASSEMBLY

1. Remove the air cleaner cover retaining knob and air cleaner cover.
2. If so equipped, remove the precleaner from paper element.
3. Remove the wing nut, washer, element cover, and air cleaner element.
4. Disconnect the breather hose from the valve cover.
5. Remove the air cleaner base mounting nuts, air cleaner base, and gasket.
6. If necessary, remove the self-tapping screws and elbow from air cleaner base.

ASSEMBLY

1. Install the elbow and self-tapping screws to air cleaner base.
2. Install the gasket, air cleaner base, and base mounting nuts. Torque the nuts to 9.9 N-m (88 inch lbs.).
3. Connect the breather hose to the air cleaner base (and valve cover). Secure with hose clamps.
4. If necessary, install the grommet into the cover of air cleaner element. Install the air cleaner element, element cover, washer, and wing nut.
5. If equipped, install the precleaner (washed and oiled) over the paper element.
6. Install the air cleaner cover and air cleaner cover retaining knob. Tighten the knob securely.

AIR INTAKE/COOLING SYSTEM

CLEANING

To ensure proper cooling, make sure the grass screen, cooling fins, and other external surfaces of the engine are kept clean at all times.

Every 100 hours of operation (more often under extremely dusty, dirty conditions), remove the blower housing and other cooling shrouds. Clean the cooling fins and external surfaces as necessary. Make sure the cooling shrouds are reinstalled.

NOTE: *Operating the engine with a blocked grass screen, dirty or plugged cooling fins, and/or cooling shrouds removed, will cause engine damage due to overheating.*

FUEL SYSTEM AND GOVERNOR

CAUTION: *Gasoline is extremely flammable and its vapors can explode if ignited. Before servicing the fuel system, make sure there are no sparks, open flames, or other sources of ignition nearby as these can ignite gasoline vapors. Disconnect and ground the spark plug lead to prevent the possibility of sparks from the ignition system.*

FUEL RECOMMENDATIONS

General Recommendations

• Purchase gasoline in small quantities and store in clean, approved containers. A container with a capacity of 2 gallons or less with a pouring spout is recommended. Such a container is easier to handle and helps to eliminate spoilage during refueling.

• Do not use gasoline left over from the pre-

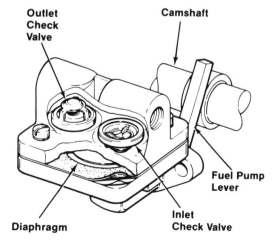

Cutaway—typical fuel pump

vious season, to minimize gum deposits in your fuel system and to ensure easy starting.

- Do not add oil to the gasoline.
- Do not overfill the fuel tank. Leave room for the fuel to expand.

Fuel Type

For best results, use only clean, fresh, unleaded gasoline with a pump sticker octane rating of 87 or higher. I countries using the Research method, it should be 90 octane minimum.

Unleaded gasoline is recommended, as it leaves less combustion chamber deposits. Leaded gasoline may be used is areas where unleaded is not available and exhaust emissions are not regulated. Be aware however, that the cylinder head will require more frequent service.

Gasoline/Alcohol blends

Gasohol (up to 10% ethyl alcohol, 90% unleaded gasoline by volume) is approved as a fuel for Kohler engines. Other gasoline/alcohol blends are not approved.

Gasoline/Ether blends

Methyl Tertiary Butyl Ether (MTBE) and unleaded gasoline blends (up to a maximum of 15% MTBE by volume) are approved as a fuel for Kohler engines. Other gasoline/ether blends are not approved.

Fuel System Operation

The typical fuel system and related components include the fuel tank, in-line fuel filter, fuel pump, carburetor, and interconnecting fuel lines.

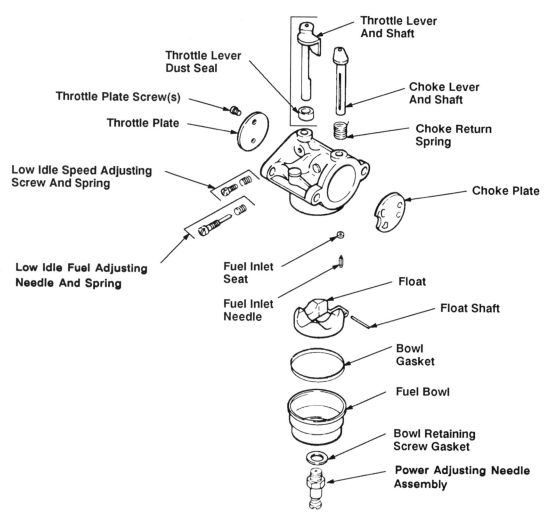

Carburetor—exploded view

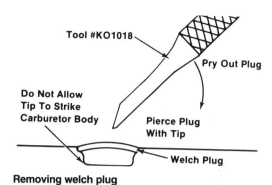

Tool #KO1018

Pry Out Plug

Do Not Allow
Tip To Strike
Carburetor Body

Pierce Plug
With Tip

Welch Plug

Removing welch plug

The fuel from the tank is moved through the in-line filter and fuel lines by the pump. On engines not equipped with a fuel pump, the fuel tank outlet is located above the carburetor inlet; gravity moves the fuel.

Fuel then enters the carburetor float bowl and is moved into the carburetor body. There, the fuel is then burned in the engine combustion chamber.

Fuel Filter

Some engines are equipped with an in-line fuel filter. Visually inspect the filter periodically, and replace when dirty with a genuine Kohler filter.

Fuel Pump

Some engines are equipped with an optical mechanically operated fuel pump. On applications using a gravity feed fuel system, the fuel pump mounting pad is covered with a metal plate.

The fuel pump body is constructed of nylon. The nylon body insulates the fuel from the engine crankcase. This prevents the fuel from vaporizing inside the pump.

The mechanical pump is operated by a lever which rides on the engine camshaft. This lever transmits a pumping action to the diaphragm inside the pump body. On the downward stroke of the diaphragm, fuel is drawn in through the inlet check valve. On the upward stroke of the diaphragm, fuel is forced out through the outlet check valve.

REMOVAL

1. Disconnect the fuel lines from the inlet and outlet fittings of pump.
2. Remove the hex, flange screws, fuel pump, and gasket.
3. If necessary, remove the fittings from the pump body.

REPAIR

Nylon-bodied fuel pumps are not serviceable and must be replaced when faulty. Replace-

ment pumps are available in kits that include the pump and mounting gasket.

INSTALLATION

1. Fittings - Apply a small amount of Permatex Aviation Perm-A-Gasket® (or equivalent) gasoline resistant thread sealant to the threads of fittings. Turn the fittings into the pump 6 full turns; continue turning the fittings in the same direction until the desired position is reached.
2. Install new gasket, fuel pump, and hex, flange screws.
NOTE: *Make sure the fuel pump lever is positioned to the RIGHT of the camshaft (when looking at fuel pump mounting pad). Damage to the fuel pump, and subsequent severe damage could result if the lever is positioned to the left of the camshaft.*
Torque the hex, flange screws as follows:
- First Time Installation On A New Short Block — 9.0 N-m (80 inch lbs.)
- All Reinstallations — 7.3 N-m (65 inch lbs.)
3. Connect the fuel lines to the inlet and outlet fittings.

Carburetor

These engines are equipped with an adjustable main jet carburetor. This subsection covers the troubleshooting, idle adjustment, and service procedures for the carburetor.
CAUTION: *Gasoline may be present in the carburetor and fuel system. Gasoline is extremely flammable and its vapors can explode if ignited. Keep sparks, open flames, and other sources of ignition away from the engine. Disconnect and ground the spark plug lead to prevent the possibility of sparks from the ignition system.*

TROUBLESHOOTING

If engine troubles are experienced that appear to be fuel related, check the following area before adjusting or disassembling the carburetor.
- Make sure the fuel tank is filled with clean, fresh gasoline.
- Make sure the fuel tank cap vent is not blocked and that it is operating properly.
- Make sure fuel is reaching the carburetor. This includes checking the fuel shut-off valve, fuel tank filter screen, in-line fuel filter, fuel lines, and fuel pump for restrictions or faulty components as necessary.
- Make sure the air cleaner base and carburetor is securely fastened to the engine using gaskets in good condition.
- Make sure the air cleaner element is clean

and all air cleaner components are fastened securely.

● Make sure the ignition system, governor system, exhaust system, and throttle and choke controls are operating properly.

● If the engine is hard-starting or runs roughly or stalls at low idle speed, it may be necessary to adjust or service the carburetor.

ADJUSTMENT

NOTE: *Carburetor adjustments should only be made after the engine has warmed up.*

The carburetor is designed to deliver the correct fuel-to-air mixture to the engine under all operating conditions. The main fuel jet (power screw) is calibrated at the factory and is adjustable. The idle fuel adjusting needle is also set at the factory and is adjustable. The idle fuel adjusting needle is also set at the factory and normally does not need adjustment.

If the engine is hard-starting or runs roughly or stalls at low idle speed, it may be necessary to adjust or service the carburetor.

1. With the engine stopped turn the low idle and high idle fuel adjusting needles in (clockwise) until they bottom lightly.

NOTE: *The tip of the idle fuel and high idle fuel adjusting needles are tapered to critical dimensions. Damage to the needles and the seats in carburetor body will result if the needles are forced.*

2. Preliminary settings: Turn the adjusting needles out (counterclockwise) from lightly bottomed to the positions in the chart.

3. Start the engine and run at half-throttle for 5 to 10 minutes to warm up. The engine must be warm before making final settings. Check that the throttle and choke plates can fully open.

4. High idle fuel needle setting: Place the throttle into the "fast" position. If possible place the engine under load. Turn the high idle adjusting needle in (slowly) until engine speed decreases and then back out approximately ¼ turn for best high-speed performance.

5. Low idle speed setting: Place the throttle control into the "idle" or "slow" position. Set the low idle sped to 1500 rpm and ± 75 rpm by turning the low idle speed adjusting screw in or out. Check the speed using a tachometer.

NOTE: *The actual low idle speed depends on the application - refer to equipment manufacturer's recommendations. The recommended low idle speed for basic engines is 1500 rpm. To ensure best results when setting the low idle speed should not exceed 1500 rpm ± 75 rpm.*

6. Low idle fuel needle setting: Place the throttle into the "idle" or "slow" position. Turn the low idle fuel adjusting needle in (slow-

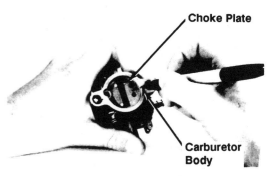

Marking choke plate and carburetor body

ly) until the engine speed decreases and then back out approximately ⅛-¼ turn to obtain best low speed performance.

7. Recheck the idle speed using a tachometer. Readjust the speed as necessary.

DISASSEMBLY

1. Remove the power screw, needle and spring, main jet, power screw gasket and fuel bowl.

2. Remove the bowl gasket, float shaft, shaft, float, and fuel inlet needle.

3. Remove the low idle fuel adjusting needle and spring. Remove the low idle speed adjusting screw and spring.

NOTE: *Further disassembly to remove the welch plug, fuel inlet seat, throttle plate and shaft is recommended only if these parts are to be cleaned or replaced.*

Welch Plug Removal

In order to clean the "off-idle" ports and bowl vent thoroughly, remove the welch plug covering these areas. Use tool no. KO-1018 and the following procedure to remove the welch plug.

1. Pierce the welch plug with the tip of the tool,

NOTE: *To prevent damage to the carburetor, do not allow the tool to strike the carburetor body.*

2. Pry out the welch plug with the tip of the tool.

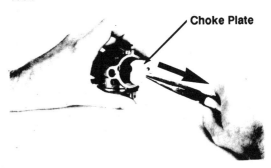

Removing choke plate

Fuel Inlet Seat Removal

To remove the fuel inlet seat, pull it out of the carburetor body using a screw, drill bit, or similar tool.

NOTE: *Always install a new fuel inlet seat. Do not reinstall a seat that has been removed.*

Choke Shaft Removal

1. Because the edges of the choke plate are beveled, mark the choke plate and carburetor body to ensure correct reassembly. Also take note of the choke plate position in bore, and the position of the choke lever and return spring.
2. Grasp the choke plate with pliers. Pull it out the slot in the choke shaft.
3. Remove the choke shaft and choke return spring.

Throttle Shaft Removal

1. Because the edges of the throttle plate are beveled, mark the throttle plate and carburetor body to ensure correct reassembly. Also take note of the throttle plate position in bore, and the position of the throttle lever.
2. Carefully and slowly remove the screws securing the throttle plate to the throttle shaft. Remove the throttle plate.
3. File off any burrs which may have been left on the throttle shaft when the screws were removed. Do this before removing the throttle shaft from the carburetor body.
4. Remove the throttle lever/shaft assembly with foam dust seal.

Cleaning

CAUTION: *Carburetor cleaners and solvents are extremely flammable. Keep sparks, flames, and other sources of ignition away from the area. Follow the cleaner manufacturer's warnings and instructions on its proper and safe use. Never use gasoline as a cleaning agent.*

All parts should be cleaned thoroughly using a carburetor cleaner (such as acetone). Make sure all gum deposits are removed from the following areas:

- Carburetor body and bore — especially the areas where the throttle plate, choke plate and shafts are seated.
- Idle fuel and "off-idle" ports in carburetor bore, power screw, bowl vent, and fuel inlet needle and seat.

NOTE: *These areas can be cleaned with a fine piece of wire in addition to cleaners. Be careful not to enlarge the ports, or break the wire inside the ports. Blow out all passages with compressed air.*

- Float and float hinge.
- Fuel bowl.

- Throttle plate, choke plate, throttle shaft, and choke shaft.

NOTE: *Do not submerge the carburetor in cleaner or solvent when fiber, rubber, or foam seals or gaskets are installed. The cleaner may damage these components.*

Inspection

- Carefully inspect all components and replace those that are worn or damaged.
- Inspect the carburetor body for cracks, holes, and other wear or damage.
- Inspect the float for cracks, holes, and other wear or damage.
- Inspect the fuel inlet needle and seat for wear or damage.
- Inspect the tip of the low idle fuel adjusting needle and power screw needle for wear or grooves.
- Inspect the throttle and choke shaft and plate assemblies for wear or excessive play.

Repair

Always use new gaskets when servicing or reinstalling carburetors. Repair kits are available which include new gaskets and other components. These kits are described below.

Components such as the throttle and choke shaft assemblies, throttle plate, choke plate, low idle fuel needle, power screw, and others, are available separately.

Always refer to the Parts Manual for the engine being serviced to ensure the correct repair kits and replacement parts are ordered.

REASSEMBLY

Throttle Shaft Installation

1. Install the foam dust seal on the throttle shaft.
2. Insert the throttle/shaft assembly into the carburetor body. Position the cutout portion of the shaft so it faces the carburetor mounting flange.
3. Install the throttle plate to the throttle shaft. Make sure the plate is positioned properly in the bore as noted and marked during disassembly. Apply Loctite® no. 609 to the threads of the throttle plate retaining screws. Install the screws so they are slightly loose.
4. Apply finger pressure to the throttle lever/shaft to keep it firmly seated against the pivot in the carburetor body. Rotate the throttle shaft until the throttle shaft until the throttle plate closes the bore around its perimeter; then tighten the screws.
5. Operate the throttle lever. Check for binding between the throttle plate and carburetor bore. Loosen the screws and adjust the throttle plate as necessary. Torque the screws to 0.9/1.4 N-m (8/12 inch lbs.).

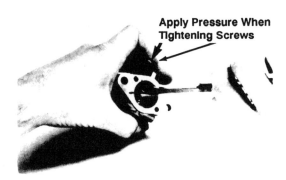

Installing the throttle lever/shaft

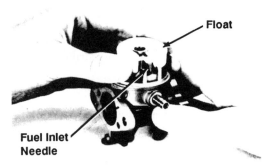

Installing float and fuel inlet needle

Choke Shaft Installation

1. Install the choke return spring to the choke shaft.
2. Insert the choke lever with return spring into the carburetor body.
3. Rotate the choke lever approximately 1/2 turn counterclockwise. Make sure the choke return spring hooks on the carburetor body.
4. Position the choke plate as noted and marked during disassembly. Insert the choke plate into the slot in the choke shaft. Make sure the choke shaft is locked between the tabs on the choke plate.

Fuel Inlet Seat Installation

Press the fuel inlet seat into the bore in carburetor body until it bottoms.

Welch Plug Installation

Use tool no. KO-1017 and install new plugs as follows:
1. Position the carburetor body with the welch plug cavity to the top.
2. Place a new welch plug into the cavity with the raised surface up.
3. Use the end of the tool that is about the same size as the plug and flatten the plug. Do not force the plug below the surface of the cavity.

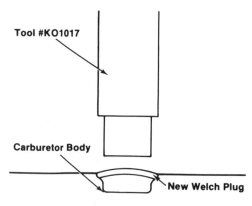

Installing welch plug

4. After the plug is installed, seal it with sealant. Allow the sealant to dry.

NOTE: *If a commercial sealant is not available, fingernail polish can be used.*

Carburetor Reassembly

1. Install the low idle speed adjusting screw and spring.
2. Install the low idle fuel adjusting needle and spring. Turn the adjusting needle in (clockwise) until it bottoms lightly.

NOTE: *The tip of the idle fuel adjusting needle is tapered to critical dimensions. Damage to the needle and the seat in carburetor body will result if the needle is forced.*

3. Turn the low idle fuel adjusting out (counterclockwise) as specified in the "Adjustment" portion of this section.
4. Insert the fuel inlet needle into the float. Lower the float/needle into the carburetor body.
5. Install the float shaft.
6. Install the bowl gasket, fuel bowl, bowl retainer gasket, and power screw.
7. Torque the power screw to: 5.1/6.2 N-m (45/55 inch lbs.).

High Altitude Operation

When operating the engine at altitudes of 1830 m (6000 ft.) and above, the main fuel mixture tends to get overrich. An overrich mixture can cause conditions such as black, sooty exhaust smoke, misfiring, loss of speed and power, poor fuel economy, and poor or slow governor response.

To compensate for the effects of high altitude, a special high altitude main fuel jet can be installed. High altitude jets are sold in kits which include the jet and necessary gaskets. Refer to the Parts Manual for the engine being serviced for the correct kit number.

Governor

these engines are equipped with a centrifugal flyweight mechanical governor. It is designed to hold the engine speed constant under changing

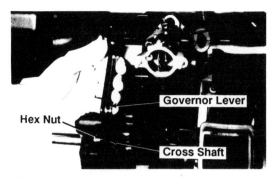

Initial governor adjustment

load conditions. The governor gear/flyweight mechanism is mounted inside the crankcase and is driven off the gear on the camshaft.

Centrifugal force acting on the rotating governor gear assembly causes the flyweights to move outward as speed increases and inward as speed decreases. As the flyweights move outward, they cause the regulating pin to move outward.

The regulating pin contacts the tab on the cross shaft, causing the shaft to rotate when the engine speed changes. One end of the cross shaft protrudes through the side of the crankcase. Through external linkage attached to the cross shaft, the rotating action is transmitted to the throttle lever of the carburetor.

When the engine is at rest, and the throttle is in the "fast" position, the tension of the governor spring holds the throttle plate open. When the engine is operating (the governor gear assembly is rotating), the force applied by the regulating pin against the cross shaft tends to close the throttle plate. The governor spring tension and the force applied by the regulating pin are in "equilibrium" during operation, holding the engine speed constant.

When load is applied and the engine speed (and governor gear speed) decreases, the governor spring tension moves the governor arm to open the throttle plate wider. This allows more fuel into the engine; increasing engine speed. (This action takes place very rapidly, so a reduction in speed is hardly noticed.) As the speed reaches the governed setting, the governor spring tension and the force applied by the regulating pin will again be in equilibrium. This maintains the engine speed at a relatively constant level.

The governed speed setting is determined by the position of the throttle control. It can be variable or constant, depending on the application.

INITIAL ADJUSTMENT

Make this initial adjustment whenever the governor arm is loosened or removed from the cross shaft. To ensure proper setting, make sure the throttle linkage is connected to the governor arm and the throttle lever on the carburetor.

1. Pull the governor lever away from the carburetor (wide open throttle).
2. Insert a nail in the cross shaft hole or grasp the cross shaft with pliers and turn the shaft counterclockwise as far as it will go.
3. Tighten the hex nut securely.

SENSITIVITY ADJUSTMENT

Governor sensitivity is adjusted by repositioning the governor spring in the holes in the governor lever. If speed surging occurs with a change in load, the governor is set too sensitive. If a big drop in speed occurs when normal load is applied, the governor should be set for greater sensitivity.

REMOTE THROTTLE AND CHOKE ADJUSTMENT

1. Adjust the throttle lever. see this section.
2. Install remote throttle cable in hole in the throttle lever.
3. Install remote choke cable in hole in the choke lever.
4. Secure remote cables loosely with the cable clamps.
5. Position the throttle cable so that the throttle lever is against stop.
6. Tighten the throttle cable clamp.
7. Position the choke cable so that the carburetor choke plate is fully closed.
8. Tighten the choke cable clamp.
9. Check carburetor idle speed. See Adjust Carburetor in this section.

LUBRICATION SYSTEM

Using the proper type and weight of oil in the crankcase is extremely important. So, is checking oil daily and changing oil regularly. Failure to use the correct oil, or using dirty oil, causes premature engine wear and failure.

Oil Type

Use a high-quality oil of API (American Petroleum Institute) service class SF or SG. Select the viscosity based on the air temperature at the time of operation as shown in the following table.

CHECK OIL LEVEL

The importance of checking and maintaining the proper oil level in the crankcase cannot be overemphasized. Check oil BEFORE EACH USE as follows:

1. Make sure the engine is stopped, level, and

is cool so the oil has had time to drain into the sump.

NOTE: *Using other than service class SF or SG oil or extending oil change intervals longer than recommended can cause engine damage.*

2. To keep dirt, grass clippings, etc., out of the engine, clean the area around the oil fill cap/dipstick before removing it.

3. Remove the oil fill cap/dipstick; wipe oil off. Reinsert the dipstick into the tube and seat the oil fill cap on the tube.

4. Remove the dipstick and check the oil level. The oil level should up to, but not over, the "F" mark on the dipstick.

5. If the oil level is low, add oil of the proper type, up to the "F" mark on the dipstick. Always check the level with the dipstick before adding more oil.

NOTE: *To prevent extensive engine wear or damage, always maintain the proper oil level in the crankcase. Never operate the engine with the oil level below the "L" mark or over the "F" mark on the dipstick.*

Oil Sentry

Some engines are equipped with an optional Oil Sentry oil pressure monitor. If the oil pressure gets low, Oil Sentry will either shut off the engine or activate a warning signal, depending on the application.

NOTE: *Make sure the oil level is checked BE-FORE EACH USE and is maintained up to the "F" mark on the dipstick. This includes engines equipped with Oil Sentry.*

CHANGING OIL AND OIL FILTER

Changing Oil

For a new engine, change oil after the first 5 hours of operation. Thereafter, change oil after every 100 hours of operation.

For an overhauled engine or those rebuilt with a new short block, use 10W-30-weight service class SF oil for the first 5 hours of operation. Change the oil after this initial run-in period. Refill with service class SF oil as specified in the "Viscosity Grades" table.

Change the oil while the engine is still warm. The oil will flow freely and carry away more impurities. Make sure the engine is level when filling, checking, and changing the oil.

Change the oil as follows:

1. Remove the oil drain plug and oil fill cap/dipstick. Be sure to allow ample time for complete drainage.

2. Reinstall the drain plug. Make sure it is tightened to 13.6 N-m (10 inch lbs.) torque.

3. Fill the crankcase, with new oil of the proper type, to the "F" mark on the dipstick. Always check the level with the dipstick before adding more oil.

4. Reinstall the oil fill cap/dipstick.

NOTE: *To prevent extensive engine wear or damage, always maintain the proper oil level in the crankcase. Never operate the engine with the oil level below the "L" mark over the "F" mark on the dipstick.*

Changing Oil Filter

Replace the oil filter after every oil change (every 200 hours of operation).

1. Drain the oil from the engine crankcase.

2. Allow the oil filter to drain.

3. Remove the old filter and wipe off the filter adapter.

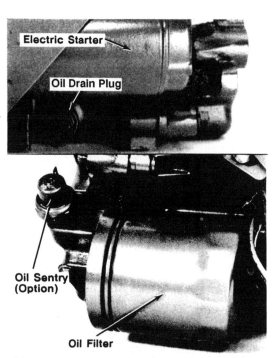

Oil drain plug (starter side shown, also located behind oil filter), oil filter, and optional oil sentry switch

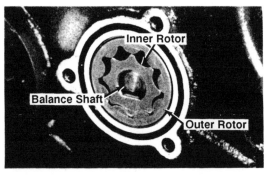

Gerotor oil pump

Oil pickup

4. Apply a thin coat of new oil to the rubber gasket on the replacement oil filter.

5. Install the replacement oil filter to the filter adapter. Turn the filter clockwise until the rubber gasket contacts the filter adapter, then tighten the filter an additional 1/2 turn.

6. Reinstall the drain plug. Torque the drain plug to 7.3/9.0 N-m (65/80 inch lbs.).

7. Fill the crankcase with new oil as instructed under "Change Oil." Add an additional 0.24 L (1/2 pint) of oil for the filter capacity.

8. Start the engine and check for oil leaks. Correct any leaks before placing the engine into service.

Oil Pump

SERVICE

The oil pump rotors can be serviced without removing the closure plate. Remove the oil pump cover on the PTO side of closure plate to service the rotors.

The closure plate must be removed to service the oil pickup and oil pressure relief valve.

Oil Sentry Oil Pressure Monitor

Some engines are equipped with an optional Oil Sentry oil pressure monitor. Oil Sentry will either stop the engine or activate a "low oil" warning light, if the pressure gets low. Actual Oil Sentry use will depend on the engine application.

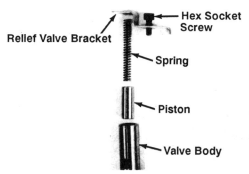

Oil pressure relief valve components

The pressure switch is designed to break contact as the oil pressure increases and make contact as the oil pressure decreases. At oil pressure above approx. 3.0 to 5.0 psi., the switch contacts open. At oil pressures below approx. 3.0 to 5.0 psi., the switch contact close.

On stationary or unattended applications (pumps, generators, etc.), the pressure switch can be used the activate a "low oil" warning light.

NOTE: *Oil sentry is not a substitute for checking the oil level BEFORE EACH USE. Make sure the oil level is maintained up to the "F" mark on the dipstick.*

INSTALLATION

The pressure switch is installed in the oil filter adapter in one of the main oil galleries of the closure plate. On engines not equipped with Oil Sentry, the installation hole is sealed with a 1/8-27 N.P.T.F. pipe plug.

To install the Oil Sentry switch to the oil filter adapter of closure plate:

1. Apply Loctite® #592 pipe sealant with Teflon® (or equivalent) to the threads of the switch.

2. Install the switch into the tapped hole in oil filter adapter. Torque the switch to 7/9 N-m (70 inch lbs.).

TESTING

The Oil Sentry pressure monitor is a normally closed type switch. It is calibrated to open (break contact) with increasing pressure and close (make contact) with decreasing pressure within the range of 3.0/5.0 psi.

Compressed air, a pressure regulator, pressure gauge and a continuity tester are required to test the switch.

1. Connect the continuity tester across the blade terminal and the metal case of switch. With 0 psi pressure applied to the switch, the tester should indicate continuity (switch closed).

2. Gradually increase the pressure to thew switch. The tester should indicate a change to no continuity (switch open) as the pressure increases through the range of 3.0/5.0 psi. The switch should remain open as the pressure is increased to 90 psi maximum.

3. Gradually decrease the pressure to the switch. The tester should indicate a change to continuity (switch closed) as the pressure decreases through the range of 3.0/5.0 psi; approaching 0 psi. If the switch does not operate as specified, replace the switch.

RETRACTABLE STARTER

CAUTION: *The spring is under tension! Retractable starters contain a powerful, flat wire recoil spring that is under tension. Do not remove the center screw from the starter until the spring is released. Removing the center screw before releasing spring tension, or improper starter disassembly, can cause the sudden and potentially dangerous release of the spring.*

Always wear safety goggles when servicing retractable starters - full face protection is recommended.

To ensure personal safety and proper starter disassembly and reassembly, follow the procedures in this section carefully.

REMOVAL

1. remove the five hex flange screws securing the starter blower housing.
2. Remove the starter.

INSTALLATION

1. Install the retractable starter and five hex flange screws to blower housing. Leave the screws slightly loose.
2. Pull the starter handle out until the pawls engage in this position and tighten the screws securely.

ROPE REPLACEMENT

The rope can be replaced without complete starter disassembly.

1. Remove the starter from the engine blower housing.

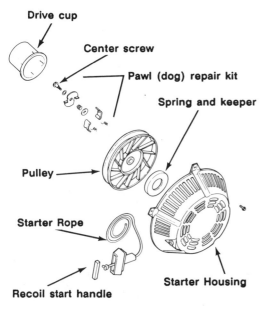

Retractable starter—exploded view

Drive cup
Center screw
Pawl (dog) repair kit
Spring and keeper
Pulley
Starter Rope
Recoil start handle
Starter Housing

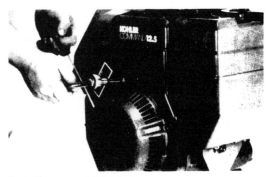

Installing retractable starter

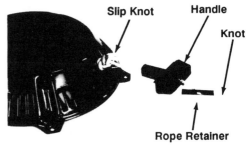

Slip Knot   Handle   Knot
Rope Retainer

Removing starter handle

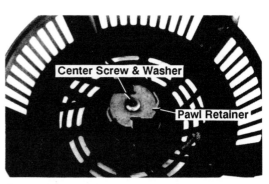

Center Screw & Washer
Pawl Retainer

Center screw, washer and pawl retainer

2. Pull the rope out approx. 12″ and tie a temporary (slip) knot in it to keep it from retracting into the starter.
3. Remove the rope retainer from inside the starter handle. Untie the single knot and remove the rope retainer and handle.
4. Hold the pulley firmly and untie the slip knot. Allow the pulley to rotate slowly as the spring tension is released.
5. When all spring tension on the starter pulley is released, remove the rope from the pulley.
6. Tie a single knot in one end of the new rope.
7. Rotate the pulley counterclockwise (when viewed from pawl side of pulley) until the spring is tight. (Approx. 6 full turns of pulley.)
8. Rotate the pulley counterclockwise until

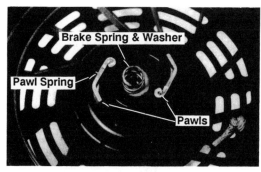

Brake spring and washer, pawls, and pawl springs

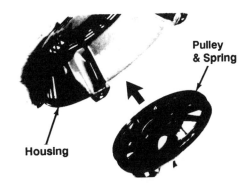

Installing pulley and spring into housing

the rope hole in pulley is aligned with rope guide bushing of starter housing.

NOTE: *Do not allow the pulley/spring to unwind. Enlist the aid of a helper if necessary, or use a C-clamp to hold the pulley in position.*

9. Insert the new rope through the rope hole in starter pulley and rope guide bushing of housing.

10. Tie a slip knot approx. 12″ from the free end of rope. Hold the pulley firmly and allow it to rotate slowly until the slip knot reaches the guide bushing of housing.

11. Slip the handle and rope retainer onto the rope. Tie a single knot at the end of the rope. Install the rope retainer into the starter handle.

12. Untie the slip knot and pull on the handle until the rope is fully extended. Slowly retract the rope into the starter.

When the spring is properly tensioned, the rope will retract fully and the handle will stop against the starter housing.

PAWLS (DOGS) REPLACEMENT

The starter must be completely disassembled to replace the starter pawls. a pawl repair kit is available which includes the following components:

DISASSEMBLY

CAUTION: *Spring Under Tension! Do not remove the center screw from starter until the spring tension is released. Removing the cen-* *ter screw before releasing spring tension, or improper starter disassembly, can cause the sudden and potentially dangerous release of the spring. Follow these instructions carefully to ensure personal safety and proper starter disassembly. Make sure adequate face protection is worn by all persons in the area.*

1. Release spring tension and remove the handle and starter rope. (Refer to ″Rope Replacement″, steps 2 through 5 above.)

2. Remove the center screw, washer, and pawl retainer.

3. Remove the brake spring and brake washer.

4. Carefully note the positions of the pawls and pawl springs before removing them. Remove the pawls and pawl springs from the starter pulley.

5. Rotate the pulley clockwise 2 full turns. This will ensure the spring is disengaged from the starter housing.

6. Hold the pulley into the starter housing. Invert the pulley/housing so the pulley is away from your face, and away from others in the area.

7. Rotate the pulley slightly from side to side and carefully separate the pulley from the housing.

NOTE: *If the pulley and the housing do not separate easily, the spring could be engaged*

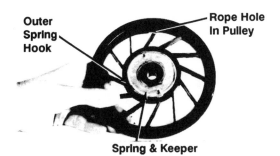

Position of spring and keeper in pulley

Installing pawls and pawl springs

in the starter housing, or there is still tension on the spring. Return the pulley to the housing and repeat step 5 before separating the pulley and housing.

8. Note the position of the spring and keeper assembly in the pulley. Remove the spring and keeper assembly from the pulley as a package. CAUTION: *Do not remove the spring from the keeper. Severe personal injury could result from the sudden uncoiling of the spring.*

INSPECTION AND SERVICE

1. Carefully inspect the rope, pawls, housing, center screw, and other components for wear or damage.

2. Replace all worn or damaged components.

3. Do not attempt to rewind a spring that has come out of the keeper. Order and install a new spring and keeper assembly.

4. Clean all old grease and dirt from the starter components. Generously lubricate the spring and center shaft with any commercially available bearing grease.

REASSEMBLY

1. Make sure the spring is well lubricated with grease. Place the spring and keeper assembly inside the pulley (with spring towards pulley).

2. Install the pulley with spring and keeper assembly into the starter housing. Make sure the pulley is fully seated against the starter housing. Do not wind the pulley and recoil spring at this time.

3. Install the pawls springs and pawls into the starter pulley.

4. Place the brake washer in the recess in starter pulley; over the center shaft.

5. Lubricate the brake spring sparingly with grease. Place the spring on the plain washer. (Make sure the threads in center shaft remain clean, dry, and free of grease and oil.)

6. Apply a small amount of Loctite® #271 to the threads of the center screw. Install the center screw, with washer and retainer, to the center shaft. Torque the screw 7.4/8.5 N-m (65/75 inch lbs.).

7. Tension the spring and install the rope and handle as instructed in steps 6 through 12 under "Rope Replacement" above.

8. Install the starter to the engine blower housing.

ELECTRICAL SYSTEM AND COMPONENTS

Spark Plug

Engine misfire or starting problems are often caused by a spark plug that is in poor condition or with an improper gap setting.

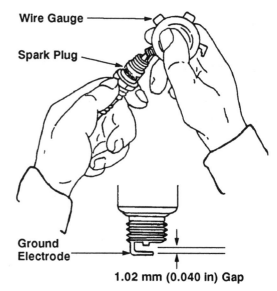

Servicing spark plug

This engine is equipped with the following spark plug:
Type: Champion RC12YC (or equivalent)
Gap: 1.02mm (0.040 in.)
Thread Size: 14mm
Reach: 19.1mm (3/4 in.)
Hex Size: 15.9mm (5/8 in)

REMOVAL AND INSTALLATION

Every 100 hours of operation, remove the spark plug, check its condition, and reset the gap or replace with a new plug as necessary.

1. Before removing the spark plug, clean the area around the base of the plug to keep dirt and debris out of the engine.

2. Remove the plug and check its condition. Replace the plug if worn or reuse is questionable.
NOTE: *Do not clean the spark plug in a machine using abrasive grit. Some grit could remain in the spark plug and enter the engine causing extensive wear and damage.*

3. Check the gap using a wire feeler gauge. Adjust the gap to 1.02 mm (0.040 in) by carefully bending the ground electrode.

4. Reinstall the spark plug into the cylinder head. Torque the spark plug to 38.0/43.4 N-m (28/32 ft. lbs.).

INSPECTION

Inspect the spark plug as soon as it is removed from the cylinder head. The deposits on the tip are an indication of the general condition of the piston rings, valves, and carburetors.

Battery

A 12-volt with a rating of approximately 32-amp hours/250 cold cranking amps, is normally

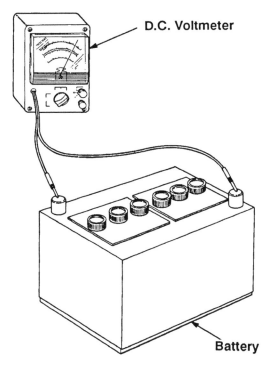

Checking battery voltage

used. Refer to the operating instructions of the equipment this engine powers for specific information.

If the battery charge is not sufficient to crank the engine, recharge the battery.

NOTE: *Do not attempt to "jump start" the engine with another battery. Starting the engine with batteries larger than those recommended can burn out of the starter motor.*

BATTERY CHARGING

CAUTION: *Batteries contain sulfuric acid. To prevent acid burns, avoid contact with skin, eyes, and clothing. Batteries produce explosive hydrogen gas while being charged.*

To prevent a fire or explosion, charge batteries only in well ventilated areas. Keep sparks, open flames, and other sources of ignition away from the battery at all times.

Keep batteries out of the reach of children. Remove all jewelry when servicing batteries.

Before disconnecting the negative (-) ground cable, make sure all switches are OFF. If ON, a spark will occur at the ground cable terminal which could cause an explosion if hydrogen gas or gasoline vapors are present.

BATTERY MAINTENANCE

1. Regularly check the level of electrolyte. Add distilled water as necessary to maintain the recommended level.

NOTE: *Do not overfill the battery. Poor performance or early failure due to loss of electrolyte will result.*

2. Keep the cables, terminals, and external surfaces of battery clean. A build-up of corrosive acid or grime on the external surfaces can self-discharge the battery. Self-discharging happens rapidly when moisture is present.

3. Wash the cables, terminals, and external surfaces with a baking soda and water solution. Rinse thoroughly with clear water.

NOTE: *Do not allow the baking soda solution to enter the cells as this will destroy the electrolyte.*

Battery Test

Test the battery voltage by connecting D.C. voltmeter across the battery terminals - crank the engine. If the battery drops below 9 volts while cranking, the battery is discharged or faulty.

Electronic Magneto Ignition System

These engines are equipped with a dependable electronic magneto ignition system. The system consists of the following components:
- A magnet assembly which is permanently affixed to the flywheel.
- An electronic magneto ignition module which mounts on the engine crankcase.
- A kill switch (or key switch) which grounds the module to stop the engine.
- A spark plug.

OPERATION

As the flywheel rotates and the magnet assembly moves past the ignition module, a low voltage is induced in the primary windings of the module. When the primary voltage id precisely at its peak, the module induces a high voltage in its secondary windings. This high voltage creates a spark at the tip of the spark plug. This spark ignites the fuel-air mixture in the combustion chamber.

The timing of the spark is automatically controlled by the module. Therefore, other than periodically checking/replacing the spark plug, no maintenance, timing, or adjustments are necessary or possible with this system.

NOTE: *Use a low-voltage (2 volts or less) ohmmeter when ohmmeter is required. Always zero ohmmeter on each scale before testing to ensure accurate readings.*

BatterY Charging Systems

This engine is equipped with a 15 Amp regulated battery charging system.

NOTE: *Observe the following guidelines to prevent damage to the electrical system and components.*

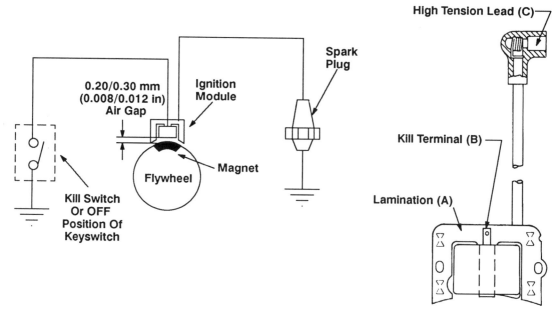

Electronic magneto ignition system

1. Make sure the battery polarity is correct. A negative (-) ground system is used.

2. Disconnect the rectifier-regulator leads and/or wiring harness plug before doing electric welding on the equipment powered by engine. Also disconnect other electrical accessories in common ground with the engine.

3. Prevent the stator (AC) leads from touching or shorting while the engine is running. This could damage the stator.

ELECTRIC STARTER

• Do not crank the engine continuously for more than 10 seconds at a time. If the engine does not start, allow a 60-second cool-down period between starting attempts. Failure to follow these guidelines can burn out the starter motor.

• If the engine develops sufficient speed to disengage the starter but does not keep running (a false start), the engine rotation must be allowed to come to a complete stop before attempting to restart the engine. If the starter is engaged while the flywheel is rotating, the starter pinion and flywheel ring gear may clash, resulting in damage to the starter.

• If the starter does not crank the engine, shut off the starter immediately. Do not make further attempts to start the engine until the condition is corrected. Do not attempt to jump start the engine with another battery. Starting with batteries larger than those recommended can burn out the starter motor.

• Do not drop the starter or strike the starter frame. Doing so can damage the ceramic permanent magnets inside the starter frame.

Bendix Drive Electric Starter

When power is applied to the starter, the armature rotates. As the armature rotates, the drive pinion moves out on the splined drive shaft and into mesh with the flywheel ring gear. When the pinion reaches the end of the drive shaft, it rotates the flywheel and "cranks" the engine.

When the engine starts, the flywheel rotates faster than the starter armature and drive pinion. This moves the drive pinion out of mesh with the ring gear and into the retracted position. When power is removed from the starter, the armature stops and the drive pinion is held in the retracted position by the anti-drift spring.

REMOVAL AND INSTALLATION

Refer to the Engine Disassembly and Reassembly sections for starter removal and installation procedures.

STARTER DRIVE SERVICE

Every 500 hours of operation (or annually, whichever occurs first), clean and lubricate the splines on the starter drive shaft. If the drive pinion is worn, or has chipped or broken teeth, it must be replaced.

It is not necessary to completely disassemble the starter to service the drive components. Service the drive as follows:

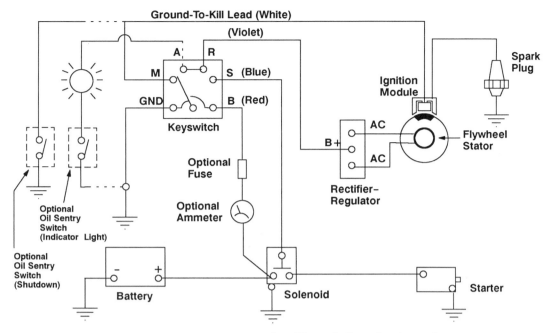

Wiring diagram—electric start engines/15 amp battery charging system

1. Remove the starter from the engine.
2. remove the dust cover.
3. Hold the drive pinion in a vice with soft jaws when removing and installing the stop nut. The armature will rotate with the nut until the drive pinion stops against internal spacers.

NOTE: *Do not overtighten the vice as this can distort the drive pinion.*

4. Remove the stop nut, stop gear spacer, anti-drift spring, dust cover spacer, and drive pinion.
5. Clean the splines on drive shaft thoroughly with solvent. Dry the splines thoroughly.
6. Apply a small amount of Kohler electric starter drive lubricant to the splines.

NOTE: *Kohler electric starter drive lubricant must be used on all Kohler electric start-*

er drives. The use of other lubricants can cause the drive pinion to stick or bind.

7. Apply a small amount of Loctite® no. 271 to the stop nut threads.
8. Install the drive pinion, dust cover spacer, anti-drift spring, stop gear spacer, and stop nut. Torque the stop nut to 17.0/19.2 N-m (135 inch lbs.).
9. Install the dust cover.

STARTER DISASSEMBLY

1. Remove the dust cover, stop nut, stop gear spacer, anti-drift spring, dust cover spacer, and drive pinion. Refer to "Starter Drive Service" above.
2. Scribe a small line on the drive end cap, opposite the line on the starter frame. These

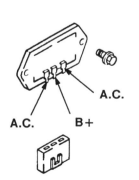

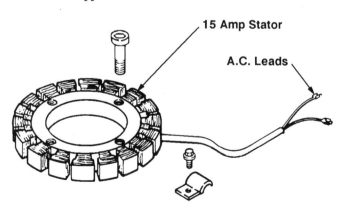

15 amp stator and rectifier-regulator

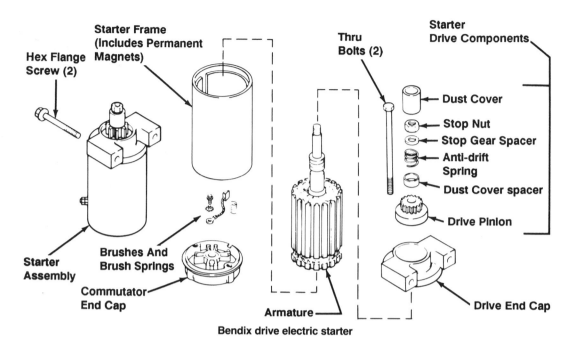

Bendix drive electric starter

lines will service as match marks when reassembling the starter.

3. Remove the through bolts.

4. Remove the commutator end cap with brushes and brush springs.

5. remove the drive end cap.

6. remove the armature and thrust washer from inside the starter frame.

Brush Replacement

1. Remove the brush springs from the pockets in brush holder.

2. Remove the self-tapping screws, negative (-) brushes, and plastic brush holder.

3. Remove the hex flange nut and fiber washer from the stud terminal.

Remove the stud terminal with positive (+) brushes and plastic insulating bushing from the end cap.

4. Reinstall the insulating bushing to the new stud terminal with positive (+) brushes. Install the stud terminal with bushing into the commutator end cap. Secure the stud with the fiber washer and hex flange screw.

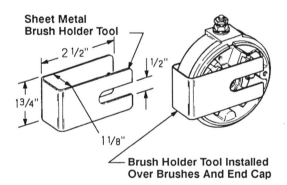

Brush holder tool

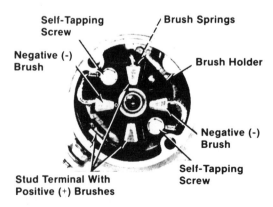

Commutator end cap with brushes

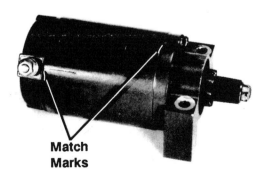

Starter assembly match marks

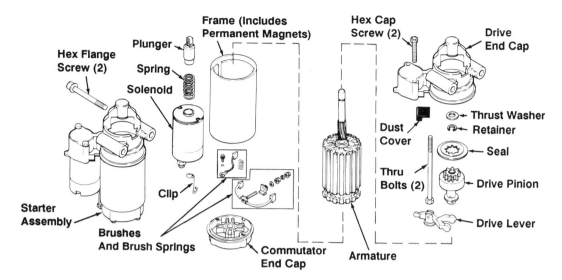

Solenoid shift electric starter

5. Install the brush holder, new negative (-) brushes, and self-tapping screws.

6. Install the brush springs and brushes into the pockets in brush holder. Make sure the chamfered sides of brushes are away from the brush springs.

NOTE: *Use a brush holder tool to keep the brushes in the pockets. A brush holder tool can easily be made from thin sheet metal.*

Commutator Service

Clean the commutator with a coarse, lint free cloth. Do not use emery cloth.

If the commutator is badly worn or grooved, turn it down on a lathe or replace the armature.

STARTER REASSEMBLY

1. Place the thrust washer over the drive shaft of armature.

2. Insert the armature into the starter frame. Make sure the magnets are closer to the drive shaft end of armature. The magnets will hold the armature inside the frame.

3. Install the drive end cap over the drive shaft. Make sure the match marks on the end cap and starter frame are aligned.

4. Install the brush holder tool to keep the brushes in the pockets of the commutator end cap.

5. Align the match marks on the commutator end cap and starter frame. Hold the drive end and commutator end caps firmly to the starter frame. Remove the brush holder tool.

6. Install the through bolts and tighten securely.

7. Lubricate the drive shaft with Kohler electric starter drive lubricant. Install the drive pinion, dust cover spacer, anti-drift spring, stop gear spacer, stop nut, and dust cover. Refer to "Starter Drive Service" above.

Solenoid Shift Electric Starter

When power is applied to the starter the electric solenoid moves the drive pinion out onto the drive shaft and into mesh with the flywheel ring gear. When the pinion reaches the end of the drive shaft it rotates the flywheel and cranks the engine.

When the engine starts and the start switch is released the starter solenoid is deactivated, the drive lever moves back, and the drive pinion moves out of mesh with the ring gear into the retracted position.

STARTER REMOVAL AND INSTALLATION

Refer to the Engine Disassembly and Assembly sections for starter removal and installation procedures.

STARTER DISASSEMBLY

1. Remove clip.

2. Remove cap screws and solenoid. Scribe alignment marks on caps and frame to aid assembly.

3. Remove through bolts, drive end cap, commutator end cap, and frame.

4. Remove drive lever.

5. Remove thrust washer and retainer to remove drive pinion from shaft.

Brush Replacement

See the procedure as explained in the Bendix Drive section, above.

Commutator Service

See the procedure as explained in the Bendix Drive section, above.

STARTER REASSEMBLY

1. Slide frame over armature and place commutator end cap in position. Hold in position temporarily with tape.

NOTE: *Be sure alignment marks on caps and frame are in proper position.*

2. Place drive pinion (with seal), thrust washer and retainer on drive shaft.

3. Place lever in position on drive shaft.

4. Place solenoid plunger on drive lever and position drive end cap over drive shaft. (Be sure the rubber dust cover is in place at the drive lever.)

5. Fasten the end caps with the through bolts.

6. Place the spring in the solenoid and fasten solenoid to drive end cap using hex cap screws.

7. Replace the clip.

ENGINE MECHANICAL

ENGINE DISASSEMBLY

CAUTION: *Before servicing the engine or equipment, always disconnect the spark plug lead to prevent the engine from starting accidentally. Ground the lead to prevent sparks which could cause fires.*

The following sequence is suggested for complete engine disassembly. This procedure can be varied to accommodate options or special equipment.

Clean all parts thoroughly as the engine is disassembled. Only clean parts can be accurately inspected and gauged for wear or damage. There are many commercially available cleaners that will quickly remove grease, oil, and grime from engine parts. When such a cleaner is used, follow the manufacturer's instructions and safety precautions carefully.

Make sure all traces of the cleaner are removed before the engine is reassembled and placed into operation. Even small amounts of these cleaners can quickly break down the lubricating properties of engine oil.

1. Remove spark plug.
2. Drain oil.
3. Remove muffler and bracket.
4. Remove air cleaner cover.
5. Remove air cleaner element, base, and breather hose.
6. Remove choke control.
7. Remove fuel tank and bracket.
8. Remove retractable starter.
9. Remove fuel pump.
10. Remove starter cover - electrical starter.
11. Remove rectifier-regulator.
12. Remove Oil Sentry.
13. Remove throttle control bracket.
14. Remove carburetor,
15. Remove valve cover.
16. Remove cylinder head baffle.

Removing muffler

Removing air cleaner cover

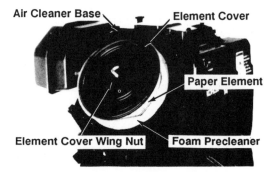

Removing air cleaner elements

Removing muffler

17. Remove blower housing and baffles.
18. Remove ignition module.
19. Remove fuel line.
20. Remove cylinder head push rods/gasket.
21. Remove drive cup, grass screen, flywheel and fan.
22. Remove stator and wiring harness.
23. Remove oil fill tube - if necessary.
24. Remove closure plate.
25. Remove camshaft and hydraulic lifters.
26. Remove balance shaft.
27. Remove connecting rod.
28. Remove piston.
29. Remove crankshaft.
30. Remove main bearing.
31. Remove governor gear.
32. Remove governor cross shaft seal.

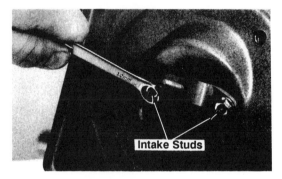

Removing air cleaner base

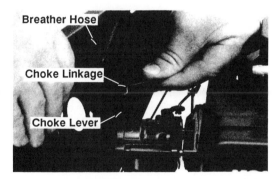

Removing air cleaner base

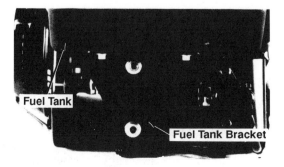

Removing fuel tank

Removing fuel tank

33. Disconnect spark plug lead.
   NOTE: *Pull on boot only, to prevent damage to spark plug lead.*
34. Drain the oil and remove the filter.
35. Remove the muffler
36. Remove the knob and air cleaner cover.
37. Remove the wing nut, washer, element cover, element and precleaner.
38. Remove the hex flange nuts from the intake studs, and the air cleaner base and gasket from the studs.
39. Loosen the hose clamp and disconnect the breather hose from the rocker arm cover. Remove the air cleaner base from the studs and disconnect choke linkage from the carburetor choke lever.
   CAUTION: *Gasoline may be present in the carburetor and fuel system. Gasoline is extremely flammable, and its vapors can explode if ignited. Keep sparks, open flames, and other sources of ignition away from the engine.*
40. Turn fuel shut-off valve to OFF (horizontal) position.
41. Remove hex flange nuts from lower bracket and hex flange screws from upper bracket of fuel tank.
42. Remove the fuel tank and disconnect fuel hose from shut-off valve.

Retractable Starter Removal

Remove the five hex flange screws and retractable starter.

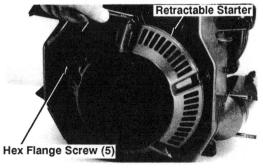

Removing retractable starter

Fuel Pump Removal

CAUTION: *Gasoline may be present in the carburetor and fuel system. Gasoline is extremely flammable, and it's vapors can explode if ignited. Keep sparks, open flames, and other sources of ignition away from the engine.*

1. Disconnect the fuel line from the outlet and inlet fittings of the fuel pump.
2. Remove the two hex flange screws, fuel pump, and gasket.

Electric Starter Removal

1. Disconnect the lead from the stud terminal. Disconnect both leads on Solenoid Shift Starter.
2. Remove the two hex flange screws and starter cover.
3. Remove the starter assembly and spacers from the studs.

Rectifier-Regulator Removal

1. Remove the wire connector from the rectifier-regulator.
2. Remove the two hex flange screws and rectifier-regulator.

Oil Sentry Removal

1. Disconnect the lead from the Oil Sentry switch.
2. Remove Oil Sentry switch from the oil filter adapter.

Throttle Control Bracket Removal

1. Remove two hex flange screws from throttle control bracket.
2. Remove governor lever spring from throttle control bracket.

Carburetor Removal

CAUTION: *Gasoline may be present in the carburetor and fuel system. Gasoline is extremely flammable, and it's vapors can explode if ignited. Keep sparks, open flames, and other sources of ignition away from the engine.*

1. Remove fuel line from carburetor inlet fitting.
2. Disconnect the throttle linkage from the bushing in carburetor governor lever.
3. Remove carburetor and gasket from intake studs.

Valve Cover Removal

Remove the five hex flange cover screws and valve cover from the cylinder head assembly.
NOTE: *The valve cover is sealed to the cylinder head using RTV silicone sealant. When removing valve cover, use care not to damage the gasket surfaces of cover and cylinder head.*

Cylinder Head Baffle Removal

Remove the hex flange screws securing the cylinder head baffle to the cylinder head. Remove the baffle.

Blower Housing and Baffles Removal

Remove the hex flange screws from blower housing and baffles. Disconnect the wire harness from the key switch, if equipped. Remove the blower housing and baffles.

Ignition Module Removal

1. Disconnect the kill lead from the ignition module terminal.
2. Rotate flywheel magnet away from ignition module.

Removing oil sentry

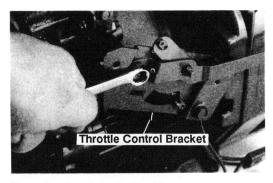

Removing throttle control bracket

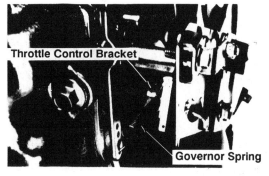

Removing governor spring

3. Remove the two hex flange screws and ignition module.

Fuel Line Removal

Remove the hex flange screw, clip, and fuel line.

Cylinder Head Removal

Remove the hex flange screws, spacer (from the screw by the exhaust port), cylinder head, push rods, and cylinder head gasket.

Cylinder Head Disassembly

1. Remove the spark plug.
2. Remove the hex flange screw, breather reed retainer, and breather reed.
3. Remove the rocker shaft (from the breather side of head), and rocker arms.

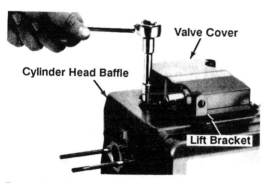

Removing carburetor

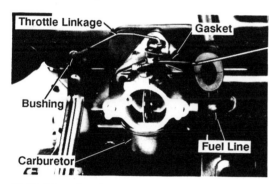

Removing valve cover

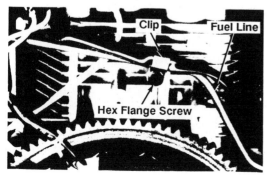

Removing fuel line

4. Remove the valves:
   a. Compress the valve springs using a valve spring compressor.
   b. Remove the keepers, valve spring caps, valve springs, exhaust valve rotator, intake valve spring seat, and intake valve stem seal.
5. Remove the two hex cap screws and rocker bridge.

Drive Cup, Grass Screen, Flywheel, and Fand Removal

NOTE: *Always use the flywheel strap wrench to hold the flywheel when loosening or tightening the flywheel and fan retaining fasteners. Do not use any type of bar or wedge between the fins of cooling fan as the fins could become cracked or damaged.*

Always use a puller to remove the flywheel from the crankshaft. Do not strike the crankshaft or flywheel, as these parts could become cracked or damaged.
1. Remove the hex flange screw, plain washer, and driver cup.
2. Unsnap and remove the grass screen from fan.
3. Remove the flywheel from the crankshaft using a puller.
4. Remove the four hex flange screws and fan from flywheel.

Stator and Wiring Harness Removal

1. Remove the stator leads from connector body.

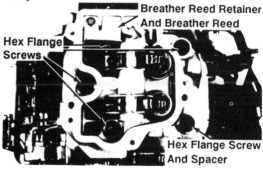

Removing cylinder head

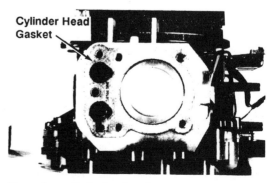

Removing cylinder head gasket

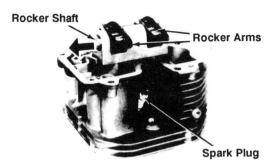

Removing spark plug and rocker arms

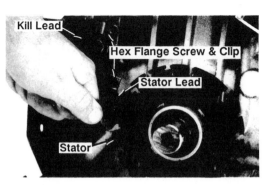

Removing stator

2. Remove the hex flange screw and clip securing the stator leads to the crankcase.

3. Remove the hex flange screw and clip securing the kill lead to the crankcase. Remove the four hex socket head screws and stator.

Closure Plate Removal

1. Remove the twelve hex flange screws securing the closure plate to the crankcase.

2. Locate the splitting notches in the seam of the closure plate and crankcase. Pry the closure plate from the crankcase using a large flatblade screwdriver.

NOTE: *Insert the screwdriver only in the splitting notches. Do not pry on the gasket surfaces of the closure plate or crankcase as this can cause leaks.*

Oil Pickup, Oil Pressure Relief Valve, Oil Pump, and Oil Seal

1. Remove the oil seal from the closure plate.

2. Remove the hex flange screw, clip, oil pickup, and O-ring seal.

3. Remove the hex socket screw, oil pressure relief bracket, relief valve body, piston, and spring.

4. Remove the three hex flange screws, oil pump cover, O-ring, and oil pump rotors.

Camshaft and Hydraulic Lifters Removal

1. Remove the camshaft and shim.

2. Mark or identify the hydraulic lifters as either intake or exhaust. Remove the lifters from the crankcase.

NOTE: *The intake hydraulic lifter is farthest from the crankcase gasket surface. The exhaust hydraulic lifter is nearest to the crankcase gasket surface.*

Balance Shaft Removal

Remove the balance shaft from the crankcase.

Connecting Rod and Piston Removal

1. Remove the two hex flange screws and connecting rod cap.

NOTE: *If a carbon ridge is present at the top of the bore, use a ridge reamer tool to remove it before attempting to remove the piston.*

2. Carefully push the connecting rod and the piston away from the crankshaft and out of the cylinder bore.

3. Remove the wrist pin retainer and wrist pin. Separate the piston from the connecting rod.

4. Remove the top and center compression rings using a ring expander tool.

5. Remove the oil control ring rails, then remove the rails spacer.

Crankshaft Removal

1. Remove the woodruff key from the flywheel taper end of crankshaft.

Removing closure plate

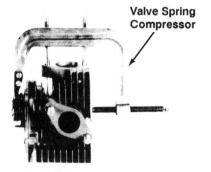

Removing valves with valve spring compressor

Splitting notch of closure plate/crankcase

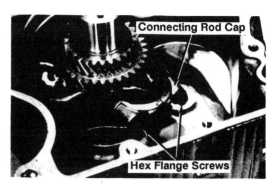

Removing connecting rod

2. Remove the crankshaft from the crankcase.

Flywheel End Oil Seal and Bearing Removal

1. Remove the oil seal from crankcase.
2. Remove the bearing from the crankcase using handle #NU-4747 and bearing remover #KO-1029.

Governor Cross Shaft and Governor Gear Removal

1. Remove the hitch in and plain washer from governor cross shaft.
2. Remove the cross shaft and plain washer from the crankcase.
3. Remove the governor cross shaft oil seal from the crankcase.
4. If necessary, remove the governor gear and regulating pin.

NOTE: *The governor gear is held onto the governor gear shaft by small molded tabs in the gear. When the gear is removed from the shaft these tabs are destroyed. This will require replacement of the gear; therefore, remove the gear only if absolutely necessary (such as when reboring, doing major engine rebuilding, etc.).*

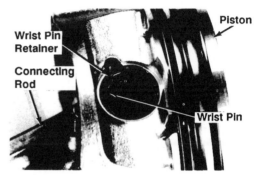

Removing piston from connecting rod

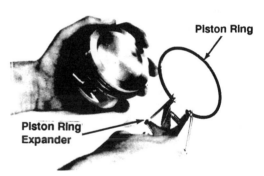

Removing piston rings

ENGINE COMPONENT OVERHAUL

Clean all parts thoroughly. Only clean parts can be accurately inspected and gauged for

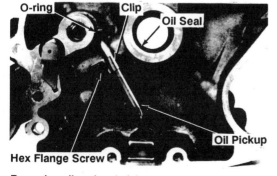

Removing oil seal and pickup

wear or damage. There are many commercially available cleaners that will quickly remove grease, oil, and grime from engine parts. When such a cleaner is used, follow the manufacturer's instructions and safety precautions carefully.

Make sure all traces of the cleaner are removed before the engine is reassembled and placed into operation. Even small amounts of these cleaners can quickly break down the lubricating properties of engine oil.

Camshaft

Inspect the gear teeth of the camshaft. If the teeth are badly worn, chipped, or some are

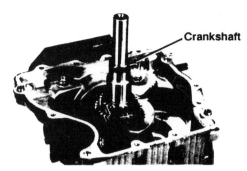

Removing crankshaft

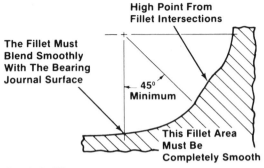

High Point From Fillet Intersections

The Fillet Must Blend Smoothly With The Bearing Journal Surface

45° Minimum

This Fillet Area Must Be Completely Smooth

Crankpin fillets

missing, replacement of the camshaft will be necessary.

Crankshaft

Inspect the gear teeth of the crankshaft. If the teeth are badly worn, chipped or some are missing, replacement of the crankshaft will be necessary.

Inspect the crankshaft bearings for scoring, grooving, etc. Do not replace bearings unless they show signs of damage or are out of running clearance specifications. If the crankshaft turns easily and noiselessly, and there is no evidence of scoring, grooving, etc., on the races of bearing surfaces, the bearings can be reused.

Inspect the crankshaft keyways. If worn or chipped, replacement of the crankshaft will be necessary.

Inspect the crankpin for score marks or metallic pickup. Slight score marks can be cleaned with crocus cloth soaked in oil. If wear limits, as stated in "Specifications and Tolerances" are exceeded, it will be necessary to either replace the crankshaft or regrind the crankpin to 0.25 mm (0.010 in) undersize. If reground, a 0.25 mm (0.010 in) undersize connecting rod (big end) must then be used to achieve proper running clearance. Measure the crankpin for size, taper, and out-of-round.

NOTE: *If the crankpin is reground, visually check to ensure that the fillet blends smoothly with the crankpin surface.*

When regrinding a crankshaft, grinding stone deposits can get caught in oil passages which could cause severe engine damage. Remove the sealing plug each time the crankshaft is ground to provide easy access for cleaning any grinding deposits that may collect in the oil passages.

Crankcase

Check all gasket surfaces to make sure they are free of gasket fragments. Gasket surfaces must also be free of deep scratches or nicks.

Check a the cylinder bore wall for scoring. In severe cases, unburned fuel can cause scuffing and scoring of the cylinder wall. It washes the necessary lubricating oils off the piston and cylinder wall. As raw fuel seeps down the cylinder wall, the piston rings make metal to metal contact with the wall. Scoring of the cylinder wall can also be caused by localized hot spots resulting from blocked cooling fins or from inadequate or contaminated lubrication.

If the cylinder bore is badly scored, excessively worn, tapered, or out of round, resizing is necessary. Use an inside micrometer to determine amount of wear (refer to the "Specification, Tolerances, And Special Torque Values", in Section 1), then select the nearest suitable oversize of either 0.25 mm (0.010 in) or 0.50 mm (0.020 in). Resizing to one of these oversizes will allow usage of the available oversize piston and ring assemblies. Initially, resize using a boring bar, then use the following procedures for honing the cylinder.

HONING

While most commercially available cylinder hones can be used with either portable drills or drill presses, the use of a low speed drill press id preferred as it facilitates more accurate alignment of the bore in relation to the crankshaft crossbore. Honing is best accomplished at a drill speed of about 2500 RPM and 60 strokes per minute. After installing coarse stones in hone, proceed as follows:

1. Lower hone into bore and after centering, adjust so that the stones are in contact with the cylinder wall. Use of a commercial cutting-cooling agent is recommended.

2. With the lower edge of each stone positioned even with the lowest edge of the bore, start drill and honing process. Move the hone up and down while resizing to prevent the formation of cutting ridges. Check the size frequently.

NOTE: *Measure the piston diameter and resize the bore to the piston to obtain the specified running clearances. Keep in mind the temperatures caused by honing may cause in-*

accurate measurements. make sure the bore is cool when measuring.

3. When the bore is within 0.064 mm (0.025 in) of desired size, remove the coarse stones and replace with burnished stones. Continue with the burnishing stones until within 0.013 mm (0.0005 in) of desired size, and then use finish stones (220-280 grit) and polish to final size. A crosshatch should be observed if honing is done correctly. The crosshatch should intersect at approximately 23-33 degrees off the horizontal. Too flat of an angle could cause the rings to skip and wear excessively, to steep of an angle will result in high oil consumption.

4. After resizing, check the bore for roundness, taper, and size. Use an inside micrometer, telescoping gauge, or bore gauge to take measurements. The measurements should be taken at three locations in the cylinder - at the top, middle, and bottom. Two measurements should be taken (perpendicular to each other) at each of the three locations.

MEASURING PISTON-TO-BORE CLEARANCE

Before installing the piston into the cylinder bore, it is necessary that the clearance be accurately checked. This step is often overlooked, and if the clearances are not within specifications, engine failure will usually result.

NOTE: *Do not use a feeler gauge to measure piston-to-bore clearance - it will yield inaccurate measurements. Always use a micrometer.*

Use the following procedure to accurately measure the piston-to-bore clearance:

1. Use a micrometer and measure the diameter of the piston 6 mm (.024 in) above the bottom of the piston skirt and perpendicular to the piston pin.

2. Use an inside micrometer, telescoping gauge, or bore gauge and measure the cylinder bore. Take the measurement approximately 63.5 mm (2.5 in) below the top of the bore and perpendicular to the piston pin.

3. Piston-to-bore clearance is the difference between the bore diameter (step 2 minus step 1).

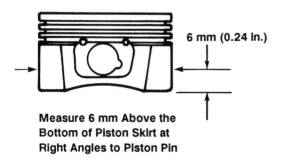

6 mm (0.24 in.)

Measure 6 mm Above the Bottom of Piston Skirt at Right Angles to Piston Pin

Measuring piston diameter

Flywheel

Inspect the flywheel for cracks, and the flywheel keyway for damage. Replace flywheel if cracked. Replace the flywheel, the crankshaft, and the key if flywheel key is sheared or the keyway damaged.

Inspect the ring gear for cracks or damage. Kohler does not provide ring gears as a serviceable part. Replace the flywheel if the ring gear is damaged.

Cylinder Head and Baffles

Carefully inspect the valve mechanism parts. Inspect the valve springs and related hardware for excessive wear or distortion. Check the valves and valve seat area or inserts for evidence of deep pitting, cracks, or distortion. Check clearance of the valve stems in guides.

Hard starting, or loss of power accompanied by high fuel consumption may be symptoms of faulty valves. Although these symptoms could also be attributed to worn rings, remove and check the valves first. After removal, clean the valve heads, faces, ad stems with a power wire brush. Then, carefully inspect each valve for defects such as warped head, excessive corrosion, or worn stem end. Replace valves found to be in bad condition. A normal valve and valves in bad condition are shown in the accompanying illustrations.

VALVE GUIDES

If a valve guide is worn beyond specifications, it will not guide the valve in a straight line. This may result id burnt valve faces or seats, loss of compression, and excessive oil consumption.

To check valve guide to valve stem clearance, thoroughly clean the valve guide and, using a split-ball gauge, measure the inside diameter. Then, using an outside micrometer, measure the diameter of the valve stem at several points in the stem where it moves in the valve guide. Use the largest stem diameter to calculate the clearance. If the clearance exceeds 7.134 mm (0.2809 in) on intake or 7.159 mm (0.2819 in) on exhaust valve, determine whether the valve stem or the guide is responsible for the excessive clearance.

If the valve stem diameter is within specifications, then recondition the valve guide.

The valve guides in the cylinder head are not removable. Use a 0.25 mm (0.010 in) O/S reamer. Tool no. KO-1026.

VALVE SEAT INSERTS

Intake valve seats are usually machined into the cylinder head, however, certain applications may specify hard alloy inserts. The valve seats are not replaceable. If the seats become badly

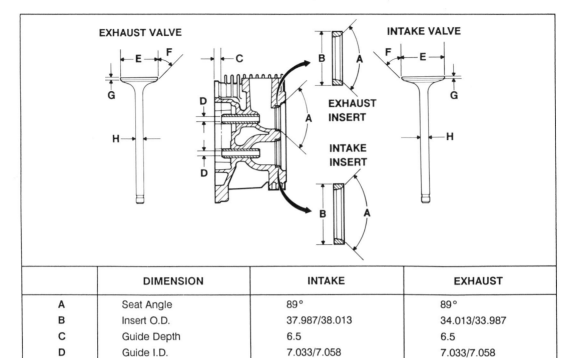

	DIMENSION	INTAKE	EXHAUST
A	Seat Angle	89°	89°
B	Insert O.D.	37.987/38.013	34.013/33.987
C	Guide Depth	6.5	6.5
D	Guide I.D.	7.033/7.058	7.033/7.058
E	Valve Head Diameter	35.63/35.37	31.63/31.37
F	Valve Face Angle	45°	45°
G	Valve Margin (Min.)	1.5	1.5
H	Valve Stem Diameter	6.982/7.000	6.970/6.988

Valve details

pitted, cracked, or distorted, the inserts can be reconditioned.

Use a standard valve seat cutter and cut seat to dimensions shown.

LAPPING VALVES

Reground or new valves must be lapped in, to provide fit. Use a hand valve grinder with suction cup for final lapping. Lightly coat valve face with "fine" grade of grinding compound, then rotate valve on seat with grinder. Continue grinding until smooth surface is obtained on seat and on valve face. Thoroughly clean cylinder head in soap and hot water to remove all traces of grinding compound. After drying cylinder head, apply a light coating of SAE 10 oil to prevent rusting.

INTAKE VALVE STEM SEAL

These engines use valve stem seals on the intake valves. Always use a new seal when valves are removed from cylinder head. The seals should also be replaced if deteriorated or damaged in any way. Never reuse an old seal.

Pistons and Rings

Scuffing and scoring of pistons and cylinder walls occurs when internal temperature ap-

proach the welding point of the piston. Temperatures high enough to do this are created by friction, which is usually attributed to improper lubrication, and/or overheating of the engine.

Normally, very little wear takes place in the piston boss-piston pin area. If the original piston and connecting rod can be reused after new rings are installed, the original pin can also be reused but new piston pin retainers are required. The piston pin is included as part of the

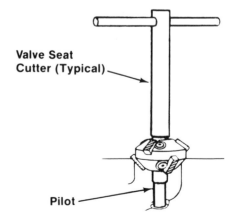

Valve Seat Cutter (Typical)

Pilot

Standard valve seat cutter

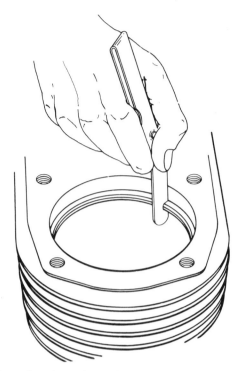

Measuring piston ring end gap

piston assembly - if the pin boss in piston or the pin, are worn or damaged, a new piston assembly is required.

Ring failure is usually indicated by excessive oil consumption and blue exhaust smoke. When rings fail, oil is allowed to enter the combustion chamber where it is burned along with the fuel. High oil consumption can also occur when the piston ring end gap is incorrect because the ring cannot properly conform to the cylinder wall under this condition. Oil control is also lost when ring gaps are not staggered during installation.

When cylinder temperatures get too high, lacquer and varnish collect on pistons causing rings to stick which results in rapid wear. A worn ring usually takes on a shiny or bright appearance.

Scratches on rings and pistons are caused by abrasive materials such as carbon dirt, or pieces of hard metal.

Detonation damage occurs when a portion of the fuel charge ignites spontaneously from heat and pressure shortly after ignition. This creates two flame fronts which meet and explode to create extreme hammering pressures on a specific area of the piston. Detonation generally occurs from using fuels with too low of an octane rating.

Preignition or ignition of the fuel charge before the timed spark can cause damage similar to detonation. Preignition damage is often more sever than detonation damage - often a hole is quickly burned right through the piston dome. Preigntion is caused by a hot spot in the combustion chamber from sources such as: glowing carbon deposits, blocked fins, improperly seated valve, or wrong plug.

Replacement pistons are available in STD bore size and in .025 mm (0.010 in), and 0.50 mm (0.20 in), oversizes. Replacement pistons include new piston ring sets and new piston pins.

Service replacement piston ring sets are also available separately for STD, 0.25 mm (0.010 in), and 0.50 mm (0.020 in), oversized pistons. Always use new piston rings when installing pistons. Never reuse old rings.

The cylinder bore must be deglazed before service ring sets ar used.

Some important points to remember when servicing piston rings:

1. If the cylinder bore does not need reboring and if the old piston is within wear limits and fee of score or scuff marks, the old piston may be reused.

2. Remove old rings and clean up grooves. Never reuse old rings.

3. Before installing the rings on piston, place the top two rings, each in turn, in its running area in cylinder bore and check end gap. This gap should be 0.75 mm (0.030 in) max. in a used

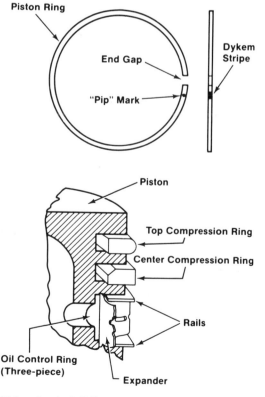

Piston ring installation

cylinder bore and 0.3/0.5 mm (0.012 in) in a new cylinder bore.

4. After installing the new compression (top and middle) rings on piston, check piston-to-ring side clearance. Maximum recommended side clearance is 0.040/0.105 mm (0.0016/0.0041 in). If side clearance is grater than specified, a new piston must be used.

INSTALL PISTON RINGS

NOTE: *Rings must be installed correctly. Ring installation instructions are usually included with new ring sets. Follow instructions carefully. Use a piston ring expander to install rings. Install the bottom (oil control) ring first and the top compression ring last.*

1. Oil Control Ring (Bottom Groove): Install the expander and then the rail. Make sure the ends of the expander are not overlapped.

2. Compression Ring (Center Groove): Install the center ring using a piston ring installation tool. Make sure the "pip" mark is up and the PINK stripe is to the left of end gap.

3. Compression Ring (Top Groove): Instal the top ring using a piston ring installation tool. Make sure to "pip" mark is up and the BLUE stripe is to the left of the end gap.

Connecting Rods

Offset Stepped-cap Connecting Rods are used in all of these engines.

Check bearing area (big end) for excessive wear, score marks, running and side clearances (Refer to Section 1, "Specifications, Tolerances, And Special Torque Values"). Replace rod and cap if scored or excessively worn.

Service replacement connecting rods are available in STD crankpin size and 0.25 mm (0.010 in.) undersize. The 0.25 mm (0.010 in) undersized rod can be identified by the drilled hole located in the lower end of the rod shank. Always refer to the correct replacements are used.

Oil Pump

Pump can be checked/replaced without removing closure plate.

Check oil pressure relief valve body, piston, and spring. Piston and body should be free of nicks or burrs. Check spring for ear or distortion. Spring free length should be approximately 0.992 in. Replace spring if distorted or worn.

Governor Gear

Inspect the governor gear teeth. Look for any evidence of worn, chipped, or cracked teeth. If one or more of these problems is noted, replace the governor gear.

The governor gear must be replaced once it is removed from the engine.

ENGINE REASSEMBLY

The following sequence is suggested for complete engine reassembly. This procedure assumes that all components are new or have been reconditioned, and all component subassembly work has been completed. This procedure may be varied to accommodate options or special equipment.

NOTE: *Make sure the engine is assembled using all specified torque values, tightening sequences, and clearances. Failure to observe specifications could cause severe engine wear or damage. Always use new gaskets.*

1. Install flywheel end bearing.
2. Install governor gear and crosshaft.
3. Install crankshaft.
4. Install piston rings.
5. Install piston to connecting rod.
6. Install piston and rod to crankshaft.
7. Install balance shaft.
8. Install hydraulic lifters and camshaft.
9. Check camshaft end play.
10. Install and torque closure plate.
11. Install oil pump.
12. Install pro end oil seal.
13. Install flywheel end oil seal.
14. Install stator and leads.
15. Install flywheel, grass screen and drive cup.
16. Install fuel line.
17. Install and adjust ignition module.

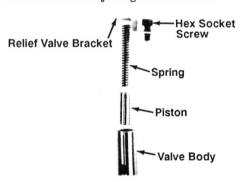

Oil pressure relief valve

Marking position of oil gallery

18. Assemble cylinder head.
19. Install cylinder head.
20. Install baffles and blower housing.
21. Install cylinder head baffle.
22. Install valve cover.
23. Install fuel pump.
24. Install electric starter and cover.
25. Install fuel tank.
26. Install rectifier-regulator.
27. Install carburetor.
28. Install and adjust governor arm.
29. Install throttle bracket.
30. Install choke and air cleaner base plate.
31. Install air cleaner element/precleaner and cover.
32. Install oil filter and Oil Sentry.
33. Install dipstick.
34. Install retractable starter.
35. Install muffler and bracket.

Flywheel End Bearing

1. Mark the position of one of the crankcase bearing oil galleries on the crankcase.
2. Assemble the KO-1028 bearing installer to the NU-4747 handle. Install the sleeve bearing to the bearing installer. Align the oil hole in the bearing with the alignment notch on the installer.
3. Position the installer/bearing to the bearing bore of crankcase. Make sure the alignment notch of installer and mark on crankcase are aligned.
4. Drive the bearing into the crankcase. Make sure the bearing is installed straight and true in bore and that the tool bottoms against the crankcase.
NOTE: *Make sure the hole in the sleeve bearing is aligned with the oil gallery in crankcase. Improper positioning of the bearings can cause engine failure due to lack of lubrication.*

Governor Gear and Cross Shaft

NOTE: *Reuse of an old (removed) governor gear is not recommended.*
1. Install the thrust washer to governor gear shaft.
2. Position the regulating pin to governor gear/flyweights as shown. Slide the governor gear/regulating pin over the governor gear shaft.
3. Using the KO-1030 oil seal installer, install a new governor cross shaft oil seal into the crankcase.
4. Install one plain washer to the cross shaft and insert the cross shaft (from inside crankcase) thorough the crankcase and oil seal.
5. Install one plain washer and hitch pin.

Crankshaft

1. Lubricate the flywheel end bearing surfaces of the crankshaft and crankcase with engine oil.
2. Insert the crankshaft through the flywheel end bearing.

Piston and Connecting Rod

1. Install the piston, connecting rod, piston pin, and piston pin retainers.
NOTE: *Proper orientation of the piston/connecting rod inside the engine is extremely important. Improper orientation can cause extensive wear or damage.*
2. Stagger the piston rings in the grooves until the end gaps are 120 degrees apart.

Cross shaft oil seal

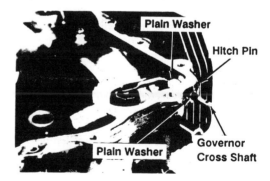

Installing cross shaft

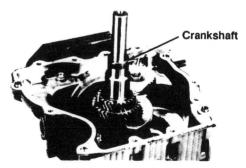

Installing crankshaft

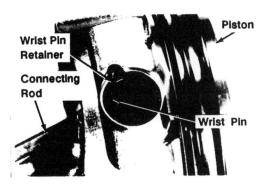

Installing piston to connecting rod

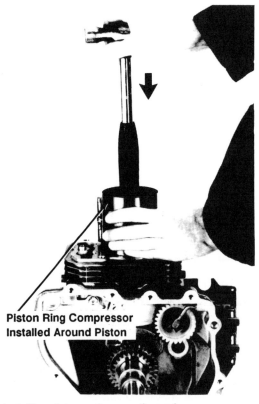

Piston Ring Compressor Installed Around Piston

Installing piston and connecting rod

3. Lubricate the cylinder bore, piston, and rings with engine oil. Compress the piston rings using a piston ring compressor.

4. Orient the "Fly" mark on piston towards the flywheel side of crankcase. Gently push the piston/connecting rod into bore. Do not pound on the piston.

5. Lubricate the crankshaft journal and connecting rod bearing surfaces with engine oil. Install the rod cap to connecting rod.

6. Install the hex flange screws and torque in increments to 22.6 N-m (200 inch lbs.).

7. Rotate the crankshaft until the piston is at the top dead center in the cylinder bore.

Balance Shaft

1. Lubricate the balance shaft bearing surfaces of crankshaft and balance shaft with engine oil.

2. Align the timing mark on the balance shaft gear and the larger gear on crankshaft. Lower the balance shaft into the bearing surface in the crankcase.

Make sure the balance shaft gear, large crankshaft gear and the governor gear teeth mesh and the timing marks are aligned.

Hydraulic Lifters and Camshaft

1. Lubricate the hydraulic lifters and lifter bores in crankcase with engine oil.

2. Install the hydraulic lifters into the appropriate intake or exhaust lifter bore in the crankcase.

NOTE: *Install the lifters from inside the crankcase. The chamfered edge of the lifter must be inserted towards the cylinder head gasket surface. The intake hydraulic lifter is farthest from the crankcase gasket surface. The exhaust hydraulic lifter is nearest to the crankcase gasket surface.*

3. Lubricate the camshaft bearing surfaces of crankcase and camshaft with engine oil.

4. Align the timing marks on the camshaft gear and the smaller gear on crankshaft. Lower the camshaft into the bearing surface in crankcase.

Installing hydraulic lifters

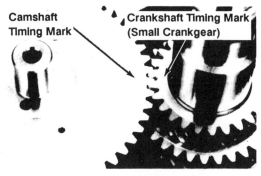

Aligning timing marks on crankgear and camgear

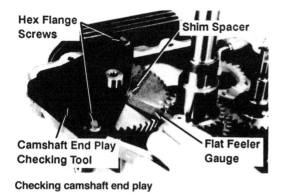

Checking camshaft end play

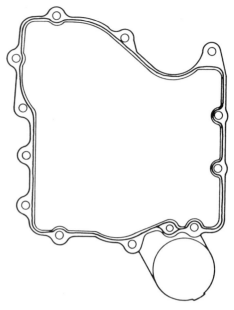

Closure plate sealant pattern

Make sure the camshaft gear and smaller gear on crankshaft mesh and the timing marks are aligned.

DETERMINE CAMSHAFT END PLAY

1. Install the shim spacer, removed during disassembly, to the camshaft.

2. Install the camshaft end play checking tool no. KO-1031 to the crankcase and camshaft. secure the tool to the crankcase with the hex flange screws provided.

3. Using a flat feeler gauge, measure the camshaft end play between the shim spacer and the end play checking tool. Camshaft end play should be 0.076/0.127 mm (0.003/0.005 in).

4. If the camshaft end play is not within the specified range, remove the end play checking tool and add, remove, or replace shims as necessary.

Several color shims are available:

White: 0.69215/0.73025 mm (0.02725/0.02875 in)
Blue: 0.74295/0.78105 mm (0.02929/0.03075 in)
Red: 0.79375/0.83185 mm (0.03125/0.03275 in)
Yellow: 0.84455/0.88265 mm (0.03325/0.03475 in)
Green: 0.89535/0.99345 mm (0.03525/0.03675 in)
Gray: 0.94615/0.98425 mm (0.03725/0.03875 in)
Black: 0.99695/1.03505 mm (0.03925/0.04075 in)

5. Reinstall the end play checking tool and recheck end play.

6. Repeat steps 4 and 5 until the end play is within the specified range.

Oil Pressure Relief Valve

1. Place the relief valve body in the cavity of the closure plate.

2. Insert the piston and spring into the body.

3. Install the bracket and hex flange screw.

Oil Pickup

Install the oil pickup, O-ring, and hex flange screw.

NOTE: *Lightly grease O-ring and install before oil pickup.*

Closure Plate to Crankshaft

RTV sealant is used as a gasket between the closure plate and crankcase. GE Silmate® type RTV-1473 or RTV-108 silicone sealant (or equivalent) is recommended.

1. Prepare the sealing surfaces of the crankcase and closure plate as directed by the sealant manufacture.

NOTE: *Do not scrape the surfaces when cleaning as this will damage the surfaces. This could result in leaks. The use of a gasket removing solvent is recommended.*

2. Apply a 1/16″ bead of sealant to the closure plate as shown.

3. Install the closure plate to the crankcase and install the twelve hex flange screws. Tighten the screws hand tight.

4. Torque the fasteners, in the sequence shown to 24.4 N-m (216 inch lbs.).

Oil Pump

1. Lubricate the oil pump cavity and oil pump rotors with engine oil. Install the outer and inner oil pump rotors.

2. Install the O-ring in the groove in the closure plate.

3. Install the oil pump cover (machined side towards O-ring). Secure with three hex flange screws.

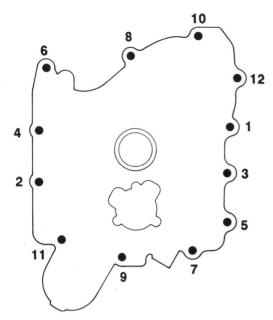

Closure plate fastener torque pattern

NOTE: *Apply sealant to the oil pump cover hex flange screws to prevent leakage.*
4. Torque the screws as follows:
- First Time Installation On A New Closure Plate:
  6.2 N-m (55 inch lbs.).
- Reinstallation On A Used Closure Plate: 4.0 N-m (35 inch lbs.)

Oil Seals

1. Slide the seal protector sleeve, no. KO-1037, over the crankshaft. Generously lubricate the lips of oil seal with light grease. Slide the oil seal over the sleeve.
2. Use handle no. KO-1036 and seal driver no. KO-1027. Install the seals until the driver bottoms against the crankcase of closure plate.

Stator and Wiring Harness

1. Position the stator leads towards the hole i the crankcase. Insert the stator leads through the hole to the outside of the crankcase.

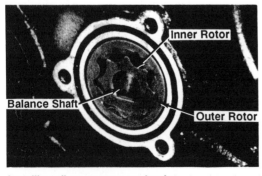

Installing oil pump gears and o-ring

2. Install the stator using four hex socket head screws. Torque the screws to 4.0 N-m (35 inch lbs.).
3. Secure the stator leads to the crankcase with the clip and hex flange screw.
4. Install the connector body to the stator leads.
5. Secure the kill lead to the crankcase with the clip and hex flange screw.

Fan and Flywheel

CAUTION: *Using improper procedures to install the flywheel can crack or damage the crankshaft and/or flywheel. This not only causes extensive engine damage, but can also cause personal injury, since broken fragments could be thrown from the engine.*

Installing stator

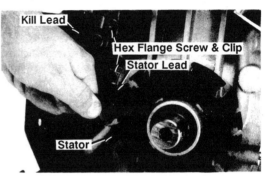

Installing fan to flywheel

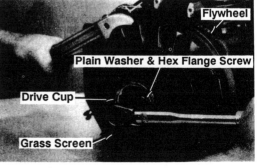

Installing flywheel

Always observe and use the following precautions and procedures when installing the flywheel.

NOTE: *Before installing the flywheel make sure the crankshaft taper and flywheel hub are clean, dry and completely free of lubricants. The presence of lubricants can cause the flywheel to be over-stressed and damaged when the flange screw is torqued to specification.*

Make sure the flywheel key is installed properly in the keyway. The flywheel can become cracked or damaged if the key is not installed properly in the keyway.

Always use a flywheel strap wrench to hold the flywheel when tightening the flywheel fastener. Do not use any type of bar wedge between the cooling fins or flywheel ring gear, as these parts could become cracked or damaged.

1. Install the fan, spacers and hex flange screws to the flywheel. Torque the hex flange screws to 9.9 N-m (88 inch lbs.).

2. Install the woodruff key into the keyway in the crankshaft.

3. Place the flywheel over the keyway/crankshaft. Install grass screen, drive cup, plain washer (flat side of plain washer towards the drive cup), and the hex flange screw.

4. Hold the flywheel with a strap wrench and torque the hex flange screw to 66.4 N-m (491 inch lbs.).

Fuel Line

Install the fuel line, clamp and hex flange screw.

Ignition Module

1. Install the ignition module and hex flange screws to the bosses on crankcase. Move the module as far from the flywheel/magnet as possible. Tighten the hex flange screws slightly.

2. Insert a 10 mm (0.394 in) flat feeler gauge or shim stock between the magnet and ignition module. Loosen the hex flange screws so the magnet pulls the module against the feeler gauge.

3. Tighten the hex flange screws as follows:
• First Time Installation On A New Short Block: 6.2 N-m (55 inch lbs.)
• All Reinstallations: 4.0 N-m (35 inch lbs.).

4. Rotate the flywheel back and forth; check to make sure the magnet does not strike the module.

5. Check the gap with feeler gauge and readjust if necessary. Final Air Gap: 0.203/0.305 mm (0.008/0.012 in)

6. Connect the kill lead to the tab terminal on ignition module.

Cylinder Head Components

1. Install the rocker bridge to the cylinder head. Make sure the small (counterbored) hole is towards the exhaust port side of the cylinder head. Secure the rocker bridge with two hex cap screws.

2. Install the intake valve stem seal, intake valve, intake valve spring seat, intake valve spring, and valve spring cap. Compress the valve spring using a valve spring compressor and install the keeper.

3. Position the rocker arms over the valve stems and rocker arm bridge. Insert the pin (from breather reed side) through the rocker bridge and rocker arms.

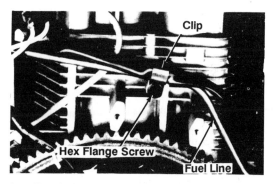

Installing fuel line

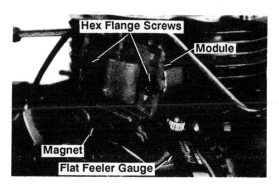

Installing ignition module

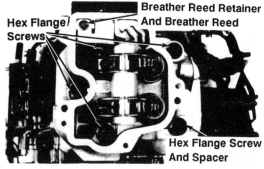

Installing cylinder head

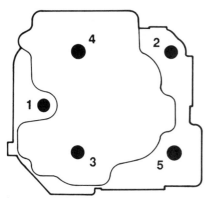

Cylinder head fastener tightening sequence

Cylinder Head

1. Install a new cylinder head gasket.
2. Install the cylinder head spacer (closest to the exhaust port) and hex flange screws. Torque the screws in increments of 10 ft. lbs. in the sequence shown to 40.7 N-m (30 inch lbs.).
3. Install the push rods and compress the valve springs. Snap the push rods underneath the rocker arms.
4. Install the spark plug into the cylinder head. Torque the spark plug to 38.0/43.4 N-m (28/32 inch lbs.).
5. Install the breather reed, breather reed retainer, and hex flange screw.

Baffles and Blower Housing

NOTE: *Leave all hardware slightly loose until all sheet metal pieces are in position.*

1. Install the heat deflector, intake manifold, and gaskets to the cylinder head intake port using two hex socket screws. Torque the hex socket screws to 9.9 N-m (88 inch lbs.).
2. Install the grommet around the high tension lead. Insert the grommet into the slot in the blower housing. Install the blower housing and baffles using hex flange screws.

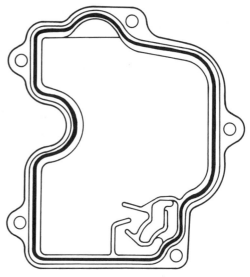

Valve cover sealant pattern

3. Install cylinder head baffle to the cylinder head using hex flange screws.
4. Tighten all hardware.

Valve Cover and Muffler Bracket

RTV silicone sealant is used as a gasket between the valve cover and crankcase. GE Silmate® type RTV-1473 or RTV-108 silicone sealant (or equivalent) is recommended.

1. Prepare the sealing surfaces of the cylinder head and valve cover as directed by the sealant manufacturer.

NOTE: *Do not scrape surfaces when cleaning as this will damage the surface and could cause leaks. The use of a gasket removing solvent is recommended.*

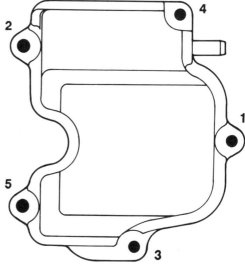

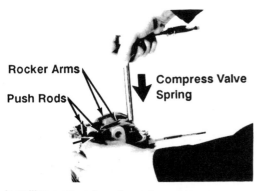

Installing push rods under rocker arms

Valve cover torque sequence

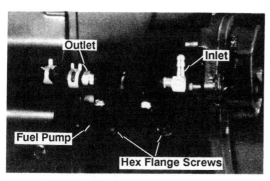

Installing fuel pump

2. Apply a 1/16″ bead of sealant to the cylinder head as shown.

3. Install the valve cover, lift bracket (lifting hole towards flywheel), and two hex flange screws.

4. Torque the screws in the sequence shown, as follows:
- First Time Installation On A New Cylinder Head: 10.7 N-m (95 inch lbs.).
- All Reinstallation: 7.3 N-m (65 inch lbs.).

Fuel Pump

1. Install the rubber line and two hose clamps to the fuel pump end of the metal fuel line. Secure the rubber fuel line to the steel fuel line with on of the clamps.

2. Install the gasket, fuel pump, and two hex flange screws. Torque the screws as follows:
- First Time Installation On A New Short Block: 9.0 N-m (80 inch lbs.).
- All Reinstallations: 7.3 N-m (65 inch lbs.).

Electric Starter

ELECTRIC STARTER (BENDIX DRIVE OR SOLENOID SHIFT)

1. Install the starter and spacers on the mounting studs.

2. Install the starter cover and the two hex flange screws.

3. Connect the lead to the starter terminal(s).

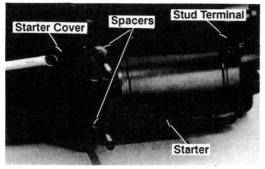

Installing electric starter

Fuel Tank

1. Connect the fuel hose to the shut-off valve.

2. Install the hex flange screws to upper bracket of fuel tank. Install hex flange nuts to studs in lower bracket of fuel tank.

Rectifier-Regulator

1. Install the rectifier-regulator and hex flange screws.

2. Install the connector to the rectifier-regulator,

Carburetor and External Governor Components

1. Install the rubber fuel line and tow hose clamps to the metal fuel line. Secure the metal fuel line with one of the hose clamps.

2. Install the bushing and the throttle linkage to the carburetor throttle lever.

3. Install the gasket and carburetor over the intake studs. Install the free end of the rubber fuel line to the carburetor fuel inlet fitting as the carburetor is inserted over the studs. Secure the fuel line with the other hose clamp.

4. Install the throttle linkage and bushing to governor lever.

5. Install the governor lever to governor cross shaft. Do not tighten the hex nut on the governor lever until the lever is adjusted (step 6).

6. Adjust the governor lever/governor gear.
   a. Pull the governor lever away from the carburetor (wide open throttle).
   b. Insert a nail in the cross shaft hole or grasp the cross shaft with a pliers and turn the shaft counterclockwise as far as it will go,
   c. Tighten the hex nut securely.

Throttle Bracket

1. Install the throttle bracket assembly with two hex flange screws.

2. Install the governor spring in the appropriate hole in the governor arm and throttle control lever, as indicated in the chart. Note that hole positions are counted from the top of the lever. RPM should be checked with a tachometer.

Air Cleaner

1. Connect choke linkage to the carburetor choke lever. Install the base plate to the studs and connect the breather hose to the rocker arm cover.

2. Install the air cleaner base and gasket to the studs and torque the hex flange nuts to 9.9 N-m (88 inch lbs.).

3. Install the element and precleaner, element cover, washer, and wing nut.

4. Install the air cleaner cover and knob.

Retractable Starter

1. Install the retractable starter and five hex flange screws to blower housing. Leave the screws slightly loose.

2. Pull the starter handle out until the pawls engage in the drive cup. Hold the handle in this position and tighten the screws securely.

Muffler

1. Install the gasket, muffler, and hex flange nuts to the exhaust port studs. Leave the nuts slightly loose.

2. Secure the muffler bracket using the two hex flange screws.

3. Torque the hex flange nuts to 24.4 N-m (215 inch lbs.), screws to 9.9 N-m (88 inch lbs.).

12
Kohler Magnum

AIR CLEANER

These engines are equipped with a high-density paper air cleaner element. Some models may also be equipped with an oiled foam precleaner which surrounds the paper element.

ELEMENT REPLACEMENT

1. Remove the wing nut and air cleaner cover.

2. Remove the precleaner (if so equipped), element cover nut, element cover, paper element, and seal.

3. Remove the base screws, air cleaner base, gasket, and breather hose.

4. Install the breather hose, gasket, air cleaner base, and screws.

NOTE: *Make sure breather hose seals tightly in air cleaner base and breather cover to prevent unfiltered air from entering engine.*

5. Install the seal, paper element, element cover, and element cover nut. Tighten nut to 50 in. lbs. torque.

6. if so equipped, install the precleaner (cleaned and oiled) over the paper element.

7. Install the air cleaner cover and wing nut.

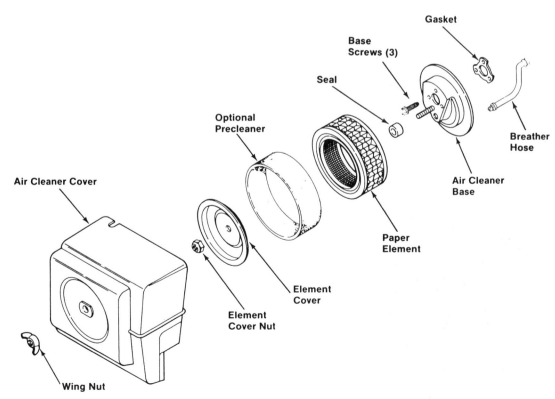

Air cleaner assembly—exploded view

Tighten wing nut until it is snug against cover — do not overtighten.

SERVICE

Precleaner

1. If so equipped, wash and reoil the precleaner every 25 operating hours (more often under extremely dusty or dirty conditions).

2. Rinse the precleaner thoroughly until all traces of detergent are eliminated. Squeeze out excess water (do not wring). Allow precleaner to air dry.

3. Saturate the precleaner in clean, fresh engine oil. Squeeze out excess oil.

4. Reinstall the precleaner over paper element.

Paper Element

Every 100 operating hours (more often under extremely dusty or dirty conditions) check the paper element. Replace the element as follows:

1. Remove the precleaner (if so equipped), element cover nut, element cover, and paper element.

2. Replace a dirty, bent or damaged element with a new element. Handle new elements carefully; do not use if surfaces are bent or damaged.

NOTE: *Do not wash the paper element or use compressed air as this will damage the element.*

3. Reinstall the paper element, element cover, and element cover nut. Make sure nut is tightened securely and element is sealed tightly against the element cover and air cleaner base.

4. Install the precleaner (cleaned and oiled) over the paper element.

5. Install the air cleaner cover and wing nut. Tighten wing nut until it is snug against cover — do not overtighten.

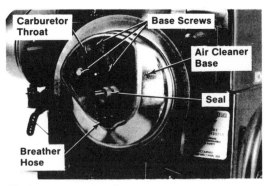

Air cleaner components

Inspect Air Cleaner Components

Whenever the air cleaner cover is removed, or servicing the element or precleaner, check the following components:

Air Cleaner Base — Make sure it is secured tightly to carburetor and is not bent or damaged.

Element Cover and Element Cover Nut — Make sure element cover is not bent or damaged. Make sure element cover nut is secured tightly to seal element between air cleaner base and element cover. Tighten nut to 50 in. lbs. torque.

Breather Tube — Make sure it is sealed tightly in air cleaner base and breather cover.

NOTE: *Damaged, worn, or loose air cleaner components could allow unfiltered air into the engine causing premature wear and failure. Replace all damaged or worn components.*

FUEL SYSTEM

The typical fuel system and related components include the fuel tank with vented cap, shutoff valve with screen, in-line fuel filter, fuel pump, carburetor, and interconnecting fuel line.

Operation

The fuel from the tank is moved through the screen and shutoff valve, in-line filter, and fuel lines by the fuel pump. Fuel then enters the carburetor float bowl and is moved into the carburetor body where it is mixed with air. This fuel-air mixture is then burned in the engine combustion chamber.

CAUTION: *Gasoline is extremely flammable and its vapors can explode if ignited. Before troubleshooting the fuel system, make sure there are no sources of heat, flames, or sparks nearby as these can ignite gasoline vapors. Disconnect and ground the spark plug lead to*

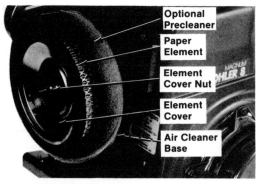

Air cleaner components

	Model M8	Model M10	Model M12	Model M14	Model M16
Air Cleaner					
Element Cover Nut					
Torque (in. lb.)	50	50	50	50	50
Angle of Operation - Maximum					
(At Full Oil Level; Intermittent Operation)					
With Oil Sentry™					
Carb. Side Up	15°	15°	15°	15°	15°
Carb. Side Down	35°	23°	23°	23°	23°
Flywheel End Up	35°	30°	30°	30°	30°
Flywheel End Down	45°	45°	45°	45°	45°
Without Oil Sentry™					
Carb. Side Up	45°	45°	45°	45°	45°
Carb. Side Down	35°	23°	23°	23°	23°
Flywheel End Up	35°	30°	30°	30°	30°
Flywheel End Down	45°	45°	45°	45°	45°
Balance Gear					
End Play	—	.002/.010	.002/.010	.002/.010	.002/.010
New Stub Shaft O.D.	—	.4998/.5001	.4998/.5001	.4998/.5001	.4998/.5001
Stub Shaft O.D. Max Wear					
Limit	—	.4996	.4996	.4996	.4996
Camshaft					
End Play	.005/.010	.005/.010	.005/.010	.005/.010	.005/.010
Camshaft to Camshaft Pin					
Running Clearance	.0010/.0035	.0010/.0035	.0010/.0035	.0010/.0035	.0010/.0035
Camgear Cover Fastener					
Torque (in. lbs.)	—	115	115	115	115
Camshaft Pin Depth					
From Crankcase Surface	.275/.285	.300/.330	.300/.330	.300/.330	.300/.330
Cup Plug Depth from					
Crankcase Surface	.055/.065	.000/.030	.000/.030	.000/.030	.000/.030
Carburetor					
Preliminary Main Fuel					
Screw Setting (Turns)	2	1-1/2	1-1/2	2-1/2	2-1/2
Preliminary Idle Fuel					
Screw Setting (Turns)	1-1/4	2-1/2	2-1/2	2-1/2	2-1/2
Float Level	11/64 (± 1/32)	11/64 (± 1/32)	11/64 (± 1/32)	11/64 (± 1/32)	11/64 (± 1/32)
Float Drop	1-1/32	1-1/32	1-1/32	1-1/32	1-1/32
Fuel Inlet Seat					
Torque (in. lb.)	35	35	35	35	35
Bowl Retaining Screw					
Torque (in. lb.)	50	50	50	50	50
Float to Float Pin					
Tower Clearance	.010	.010	.010	.010	.010
Connecting Rod (Posi-Lock)					
New Service Rod Nut					
Torque (in. lb.)[4, 6]	140	260	260	260	260
Used Rod Nut					
Torque (in. lb.)[4, 6]	100	200	200	200	200
Rod to Crankpin Running					
Clearance - New	.001/.002	.001/.002	.001/.002	.001/.002	.001/.002
Rod to Crankpin Max. Wear					
Limit	.0025	.0025	.0025	.0025	.0025
Rod to Piston Pin Running					
Clearance - New	.0006/.0011	.0003/.0008	.0003/.0008	.0003/.0008	.0003/.0008
Piston Pin End I.D.					
- New	.6255/.6258	.8596/.8599	.8757/.8760	.8757/.8760	.8757/.8760
Rod Side Play on					
Crankpin	.005/.016	.007/.016	.007/.016	.007/.016	.007/.016

	Model M8	Model M10	Model M12	Model M14	Model M16
Crankshaft					
Crankshaft End Play	.002/.023	.003/.020	.003/.020	.003/.020	.003/.020
Main Bearing Surface					
O.D. - New	1.1811/1.1814	1.5745/1.5749	1.5745/1.5749	1.5745/1.5749	1.5745/1.5749
Main Bearing Surface Max.					
Wear Limit	1.1811	1.5745	1.5745	1.5745	1.5745
Crankpin O.D. - New	1.1860/1.1855	1.5000/1.4995	1.5000/1.4995	1.5000/1.4995	1.5000/1.4995
Crankpin O.D. Max.					
Out of Round	.0005	.0005	.0005	.0005	.0005
Crankpin O.D. Max. Taper	.001	.001	.001	.001	.001
Cylinder Bore					
I.D. - New	2.9380/2.9370	3.2515/3.2505	3.3755/3.3745	3.5005/3.4995	3.7505/3.7495
I.D. Max. Wear Limit	2.941	3.254	3.378	3.503	3.753
I.D. Max. Out of Round	.005	.005	.005	.005	.005
I.D. Max. Taper	.003	.002	.002	.002	.002
Cylinder Head					
Cap Screw Torque					
(ft. lb.)[4]	15/20	25/30	25/30	25/30	25/30
Max. Out of Flatness	.003	.003	.003	.003	.003
Fan/Flywheel					
Fan Fastener					
Torque (in. lbs.)	115	115	115	115	115
Flywheel Fastener					
Torque (ft. lb.)[4]	85/90	40/45	40/45	40/45	40/45
Fuel Pump					
Mounting Screw					
Torque (in. lb.)	40/45	40/45	40/45	40/45	40/45
Fuel Tank					
Isolation Mount Torque	Hand Tight[7]	Hand Tight	Hand Tight	Hand Tight	Hand Tight
Upper Bracket to Tank					
Fastener Torque (in. lb.)	90	—	—	—	—
Lower Bracket to Tank					
Fastener Torque (in. lb.)	90	—	—	—	—
Lower Bracket to Crankcase					
Bracket Fastener Torque					
(in. lb.).....................	70	—	—	—	—
Top Tank Bracket to Cyl.					
Head Fastener Torque					
(in. lb.).....................	150	—	—	—	—
Gear Reduction Unit					
Gear Reduction Shaft					
End Play	.001/.030	.008/.030	.005/.030	.005/.030	.005/.030
Governor					
Governor Bushing					
Torque (in. lb.)	100/120	100/120	100/120	100/120	100/120
Governor Bushing to Cross					
Shaft Running Clearance	.0005/.0020	.0010/.0025	.0010/.0025	.0010/.0025	.0010/.0025
Governor Gear to Stub					
Shaft Running Clearance	.0005/.0020	.0005/.0020	.0005/.0020	.0005/.0020	.0005/.0020
Governor Cross Shaft					
End Play	.001/.056	.001/.069	.001/.069	.001/.069	.001/.069

	Model M8	Model M10	Model M12	Model M14	Model M16
Ignition					
Ignition Module to Magnet Air Gap	.012/.016	.012/.016	.012/.016	.012/.016	.012/.016
Spark Plug Type (Champion® or Equiv.).......	RCJ-8	RH-10	RH-10	RH-10	RH-10
Spark Plug Gap	.025	.025	.025	.025	.025
Spark Plug Torque (ft. lb.)	18/22	18/22	18/22	18/22	18/22
Ignition Module Mounting Screw Torque (in. lbs.)	32	32	32	32	32
Keyswitch Nut Torque (in. lbs.)	—	90/100	90/100	90/100	90/100
Oil Pan/Oil Sentry™					
Oil Sentry Switch Max. Torque (in. lb.)[10]	90	90	90	90	90
Piston and Piston Rings (Style "A" Pistons)					
Thrust Face O.D. @ D1 - New[11]	2.9297/2.9281	3.2432/3.2413	3.368/3.365	3.4941/3.4925	—
Thrust Face O.D. @ D1 - Max.[11] Wear Limit	2.925	3.238	3.363	3.491	—
Thrust Face to Bore Clearance @ D1 - New[11]	.007/.010	.007/.010	.007/.010	.007/.010	—
Piston Ring End Gap - New	.007/.017	.010/.020	.010/.020	.010/.020	—
Piston Ring End Gap - Used (Max.)	.027	.030	.030	.030	—
Piston Ring Side Clearance - Max.	.006	.006	.006	.006	—
Piston Pin O.D. - New	.6247/.6249	.8591/.8593	.8752/.8754	.8752/.8754	—
Piston and Piston Rings (Styles "C" And "D" Pistons)					
Thrust Face O.D. @ D1 - New[12]	2.9336/2.9329	—	—	—	3.7455/3.7465
Thrust Face O.D. @ D1 - Max. Wear Limit[12]..........	2.9312	—	—	—	3.7435
Thrust Face to Bore Clearance @ D1 - New[12]	.0034/.0051	—	—	—	.0030/.0050
Piston Ring End Gap - New[9]	.010/.023	—	—	—	.010/.020
Piston Ring End Gap - Used (Max.)[9]	.032	—	—	—	.030
Piston Ring Side Clearance - Max.	.006	—	—	—	.006
Piston Pin O.D. - New	.6247/.6249	—	—	—	.8752/.8754
Valves and Tappets					
Intake Valve to Tappet Clearance - Cold	.006/.008	.008/.010	.008/.010	.008/.010	.008/.010
Exhaust Valve to Tappet Clearance - Cold	.017/.019	.017/.019	.017/.019	.017/.019	.017/.019
Intake Valve Minimum Lift - Zero Lash	.2718	.318	.318	.318	.318
Exhaust Valve Minimum Lift - Zero Lash	.2482	.318	.318	.318	.318
Intake Valve Minimum Stem O.D...................	.3103	.3103	.3103	.3103	.3103
Exhaust Valve Minimum Stem O.D...................	.3074	.3074	.3074	.3074	.3074

	Model M8	Model M10	Model M12	Model M14	Model M16
Valves and Tappets (Cont.)					
Nominal Valve Seat Angle	45°	45°	45°	45°	45°
Valve Guide Reamer Size	.3125	.3125	.3125	.3125	.3125
Intake Valve Guide I.D.					
Max. Wear Limit	.006	.006	.006	.006	.006
Exhaust Valve Guide I.D.					
Max. Wear Limit	.008	.008	.008	.008	.008
Throttle Control Lever					
Remote Throttle Control					
Nut Torque (in. lb.)[8]	10/15	10/15	10/15	10/15	10/15
Engine Mtd. Throttle Control					
Nut Torque (in. lb.)	15/25	15/25	15/25	15/25	15/25
Fixed Speed Applications					
(Shortened Throttle Control)					
Nut Torque (in. lb.)	70	70	70	70	70

eliminate the possibility of sparks from the ignition system.

Fuel Tank

The fuel tank is made of a tough, impact resistant material. If the tank does become cracked or damaged, it is not repairable and must be replaced.

Refer to the "Engine Disassembly and Reassembly" sections for complete fuel tank removal and installation procedures.

Fuel Shutoff Valve

Some engines are equipped with a fuel shutoff valve with a wire mesh screen. On engines without the shutoff valve, a straight outlet fitting is installed. The shutoff valve or outlet fitting are installed into the bottom of the fuel tank with a rubber grommet.

REMOVAL

1. Grasp the shutoff valve or outlet fitting and pull from tank using a side-to-side twisting motion.

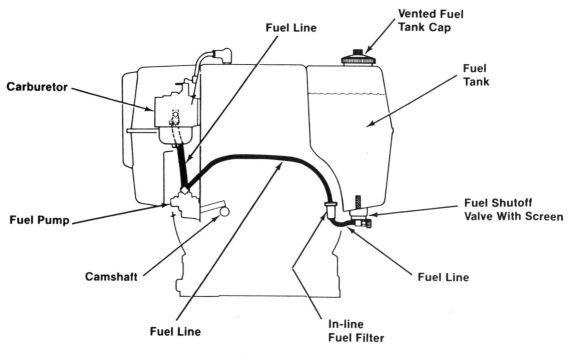

Typical fuel system

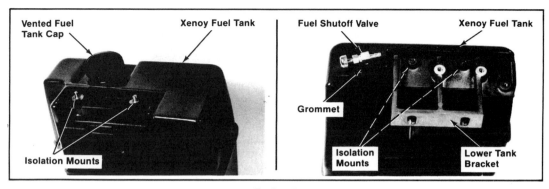

Fuel tank

2. Remove the grommet from tank, or from shutoff valve or outlet fitting.

INSTALLATION

1. Install the grommet into the bottom of the fuel tank.
2. Press the shutoff valve or outlet fitting securely into the grommet.

Isolation Mounts

Isolation mounts are used on model M8 engines with top mounted tank, and on Models M10, and M12 engines with side mounted tanks. Install isolation mounts into fuel tank hand tight.

Fuel Filter

Some engines are equipped with an in-line fuel filter. Visually inspect the filter periodically. Replace when dirty with a new filter.

Fuel Pump

Most Magnum engines are equipped with a mechanically operated fuel pump. On applica-

tions using a gravity feed fuel system, the fuel pump is not used and the pump mounting pad on the crankcase is covered.

The fuel pump body is constructed of a nylon material. The nylon body insulates the fuel from the hot engine crankcase and prevents fuel from vaporizing inside the pump.

The mechanical fuel pump is operated by a lever which rides on the engine camshaft. The lever transmits a pumping action to the diaphragm inside the pump body. This pumping action draws fuel in through the inlet check valve on the downward stroke of the diaphragm. On the upward stroke of the diaphragm, the fuel is forced out through the outlet check valve.

REMOVAL

1. Disconnect the fuel lines from the inlet and outlet fittings of the pump.
2. Remove the fillister head screws, plain washers, fuel pump, and gasket.
3. If necessary, remove the fittings from pump body.

REPAIR

Nylon-bodied fuel pumps are not serviceable and must be replaced when faulty. Replacement pumps are available in kits which include the pump, mounting gasket, and plain washers.

1. Apply a small amount of Permatex Aviation Perm-A-Gasket® (or equivalent) gasoline resistant thread sealant to fittings. Turn fittings into pump 6 full turns; continue turning fittings in same direction until desired position is reached.

2. Install new gasket, fuel pump, plain washers, and fillister head screws.

WARNING: *Make sure the fuel pump lever is positioned above the camshaft. Damage to the fuel pump, and subsequent severe engine damage could result if the lever is positioned below the camshaft.*

Make sure the plain washers are installed

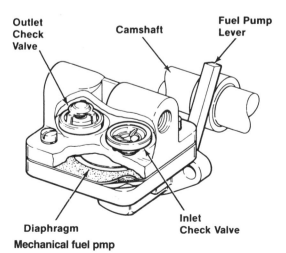

Mechanical fuel pmp

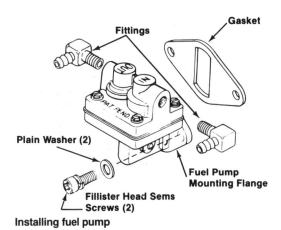

Installing fuel pump

next to the mounting flange to prevent damage from the lockwasher.

3. Torque screws 40-45 inch lbs.

4. Connect fuel lines to inlet and outlet fittings.

Carburetor

CAUTION: *Gasoline may be present in the carburetor and fuel system. Gasoline is extremely flammable and its vapors can explode if ignited. Keep sparks, open flame, and other sources of ignition away from the engine. Wipe up spilled fuel immediately.*

ADJUSTMENT

Turning the adjusting needles in (clockwise) decreases the supply of fuel to the carburetor. This gives a leaner fuel/air mixture. Turning the adjusting needles out (counterclockwise) in-

creases the supply of fuel to the carburetor. This gives a richer fuel/air mixture.

WARNING: *Incorrect settings can cause a fouled spark plug, overheating, excessive valve wear, and other problems. To ensure correct settings, make sure the following adjustment procedures are used.*

Make carburetor adjsutments after the engine has warmed.

1. Stop the engine. Turn the main fuel and idle fuel adjusting needles in (clockwise) until they bottom lightly.

WARNING: *The ends of the main fuel and idle fuel adjusting needles are tapered to critical dimensions. Damage to needles and seats will result if needles are forced.*

2. Preliminary Settings: Turn the main fuel and idle fuel adjusting needles out (counterclockwise) from lightly bottomed as follows: Start the engine and run at half-throttle for 5-10 minutes to warm up. Engine must be warm before making final settings (steps 4-6).

3. Final Setting — Main Fuel: Place throttle in wide open position; and if possible, place engine under load. Turn main fuel adjusting needle out (counterclockwise) from preliminary setting until the engine speed decreases (rich). Note the position of the needle. Now turn the adjusting needle in (clockwise). The engine speed may increase, then it will decrease as the needle is turned in (lean). Note the position of the needle.

4. Final Setting — Idle Fuel: Place throttle into idle or slow position. Set idle fuel adjusting needle using the same procedure as in step 4.

NOTE: *To ensure best results when setting idle fuel mixture, the idle speed must not exceed 1500 RPM. Typical idle speed is 1200 RPM. See step 6.*

5. Idle Speed Setting: Place throttle into idle or slow position. Set idle speed to 1200 rpm ± 75 RPM by turning the idle speed adjusting screw in or out.

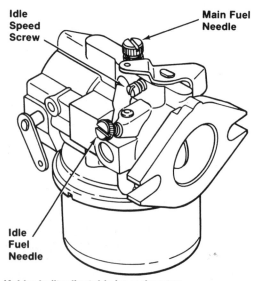

Kohler-built adjustable jet carburetor

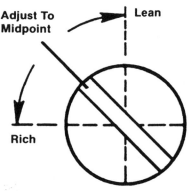

Carburetor adjustment

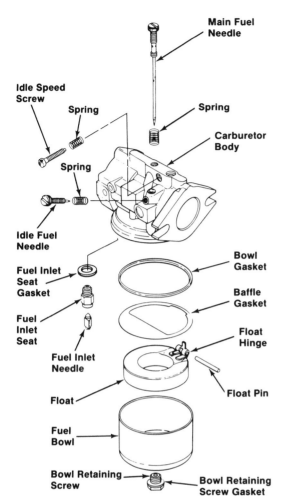

Main Fuel Needle

Idle Speed Screw

Spring

Spring

Carburetor Body

Spring

Idle Fuel Needle

Bowl Gasket

Fuel Inlet Seat Gasket

Baffle Gasket

Fuel Inlet Seat

Float Hinge

Fuel Inlet Needle

Float

Float Pin

Fuel Bowl

Bowl Retaining Screw

Bowl Retaining Screw Gasket

Kohler-built adjustable jet carburetor—exploded view

NOTE: *The actual idle speed depends on the application. Refer to the equipment manufacturer's instructions for specific idle speed settings.*

DISASSEMBLY

1. Remove the bowl retaining screw, retaining screw gasket, and fuel bowl.
2. Remove the float pin, float fuel inlet needle, baffle gasket, and bowl gasket.
3. Remove the fuel inlet seat and inlet seat gasket. Remove the idle fuel and main fuel adjusting needles and springs. Remove the idle speed adjusting screw and spring.
4. Further disassembly to remove the throttle and choke shafts is recommended only if these parts are to be replaced. Refer to "Throttle And Choke Shaft Replacement."

CLEANING

CAUTION: *Carburetor cleaners and solvents are extremely flammable. Keep sparks,*

flames, and other sources of ignition away from area. Follow the cleaner manufacturer's warnings and instructions on its proper and safe use. Never use gasoline as a cleaning agent.

All parts should be carefully cleaned using a carburetor cleaner (such as acetone). Be sure all gum deposits are removed from the following areas:

Carburetor body and bore: especially the areas where throttle plate, choke plate, and shafts are seated.

Float and float hinge.

Fuel bowl.

Idle fuel and "off-idle" ports in carburetor bore, ports in main fuel adjusting needle, and main fuel seat. These areas can be cleaned a piece of fine wire in addition to cleaners. Be careful not to enlarge the ports, or break the cleaning wire within ports.

Blow out all passages with compressed.

WARNING: *Do not submerge carburetor in cleaner or solvent when fiber and rubber seals are installed. The cleaner may damage these seals.*

INSPECTION

1. Carefully inspect all components and replace those that are worn or damaged.
2. Inspect the carburetor body for cracks, holes, and other wear or damage.
3. Inspect the float for dents or holes. Check the float hinge for wear, and missing or damaged float tabs.
4. Inspect the inlet needle and seat for wear or grooves.
5. Inspect the tips of the main fuel and idle fuel adjusting needles for wear or grooves.
6. Inspect the throttle and choke shaft and plate assemblies for wear or excessive play.

REPAIR

Always use new gaskets when servicing and reinstalling carburetors. Several repair kits are available which include the gaskets and other components.

Two kits are available for replacement of the throttle and choke shafts in Kohler-built carburetors.

Kit no. 25 757 04 services the Model M8 carburetor with ½ in. venturi.

Kit no. 25 757 05 services Models M10 and M12 carburetors with 1 in. venturi.

CAUTION: *Suitable eye protection (safety glasses, goggles, or face hood) should be worn for any procedure involving the use of compressed air, punches, hammers, chisels, drills, or grinding tools.*

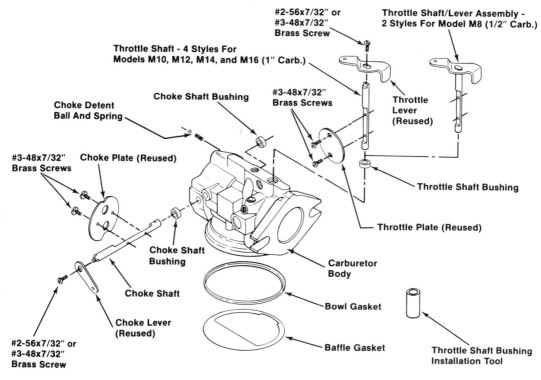

Throttle and choke shaft replacement kits

Carburetor Disassembly

1. To ensure correct reassembly, mark choke plate and carburetor body with a marking pen. Also take note of choke plate position in bore, and choke lever position.

2. Carefully and slowly remove the screws securing choke plate to choke shaft. Remove and save the choke plate as it will be reused.

3. File off any burrs which may have been left on choke shaft when screws were removed. Place carburetor on work bench with choke side down. Remove choke shaft; the detent ball and spring will drop out.

4. Note the position of the choke lever with respect to the cutout portion of choke shaft.

5. Carefully grind or file away the riveted portion of shaft. Remove and save choke lever; discard old choke shaft.

6. Install choke lever to new choke shaft from kit. Make sure lever is installed correctly as noted in step 4. Secure lever to choke shaft as follows:

   a. For Model M8 (½ in. Carb.) — Apply Loctite® to threads of (1) #2-56x⁷⁄₃₂ in. brass screw; secure lever to shaft.

   b. For Models M10, M12 (1 in. Carb) — Apply Loctite® to threads of (1) #3-48x⁷⁄₃₂ in. brass screw; secure lever to shaft.

7. To ensure correct reassembly, mark throttle plate and carburetor body with a marking pen. Also take note of throttle plate position in bore, and throttle lever position.

8. Carefully and slowly remove the screws securing the throttle plate to throttle shaft. Remove and save the throttle plate as it will be reused.

9. File off any burrs which may have been left on throttle shaft when screws were removed.

WARNING: *Failure to remove burrs from the throttle shaft may cause permanent damage to carburetor body when shaft is removed.*

10. Remove the throttle shaft from carburetor body. Remove and discard the foam rubber dust seal from throttle shaft.

11a. For Model M8 (½ in. Carb.) — Carefully grind or file away the riveted portion of throttle shaft. Save the throttle shaft as it will be used to install the new throttle shaft bushing. Discard the throttle lever.

11b. For Models M10, M12 (1 in. Carb.)

   a. Note the position of the throttle lever with respect to the cutout portion of throttle shaft.

   b. Carefully grind or file away the riveted portion of shaft; remove throttle lever.

   c. Carefully compare the old shaft to the new shafts from kit. Select the appropriate new shaft and discard the old shaft.

   d. Install throttle lever to throttle shaft.

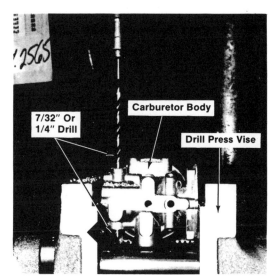

Aligning/drilling carburetor body

Make sure lever is installed correctly as noted in step a.

e. Apply Loctite® to threads of (1) #2-56x⁷⁄₃₂ in. brass screw (use #3-48x⁷⁄₃₂ in. screw with 2⁴⁹⁄₆₄ in. shaft); secure lever to shaft.

12. Mount the carburetor body in a drill press vise. Keep vice slightly loose.

13. Install a drill of the following specified size in drill press chuck. Lower drill (not rotating) through both choke shaft bores; then tighten vice. This ensures the carburetor body and drill are perpendicular and in correct alignment.

- For Model M8 (½ in. Carb.) — Use a ⁷⁄₃₂ in. dia. drill
- For Models M10, M12 (1 in. Carb.) — Use a ¼ in. dia drill

14. Install a ¹⁹⁄₆₄ in. dia. drill in chuck. Set drill press speed to a low speed suitable for aluminum. Feed drill slowly to obtain a good finish to holes.

15. Ream the choke shaft bores to a final size of ⁵⁄₁₆ in.. For best results use a piloted ⁵⁄₁₆ in. reamer.

16. Blow out all metal chips using compressed air. Thoroughly clean the carburetor body in a carburetor cleaner.

Carburetor Assembly

1. Install screws into the tapped holes that enter the choke shaft bores until the screws bottom lightly.

2. Coat the outside surface of choke shaft bushings with Loctite® from kit. Carefully press bushings into carburetor body using a smooth-jawed vice. Stop pressing when bushings bottom against screws.

For Model M8 (½ in. Carb.) — Make sure the bushing is pressed below the surface of the large choke shaft boss until the bushing bottoms against screw.

3. Allow Loctite® to "set" for 5-10 minutes then remove screws.

4. Install new choke shaft in bushings. Rotate shaft and check for binding.

NOTE: *If binding occurs, locate and correct the cause before proceeding. Use choke shaft to align bushings if necessary.*

5. Remove choke shaft and allow Loctite® to "set" for an additional 30 minutes before proceeding.

6. Wipe away all excess Loctite® from bushings and choke shaft.

7. Make sure the dust seal counterbore in carburetor is thoroughly clean and free of chips and burrs.

8. Install a throttle shaft (without throttle lever) into carburetor body to use as a pilot.

For Model M8 (½ in. Carb) — Use the old throttle shaft removed previously.

For Models M10, M12 (1 in. Carb.) — Use one of the remaining new throttle shafts from kit.

9. Coat the outside surface of throttle shaft bushing with Loctite® from kit. Slip bushing over shaft. Using installation tool from kit and vice, press bushing into counterbore until it bottoms in carburetor body.

10. Allow Loctite® to "set" for 5-10 minutes then remove throttle shaft.

11. Install new throttle shaft with lever into carburetor body. Rotate shaft and check for binding.

NOTE: *If binding occurs, locate cause and*

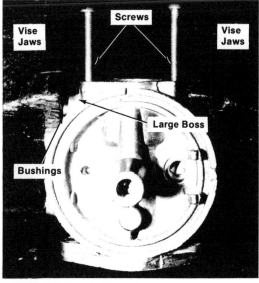

Installing choke shaft bushings

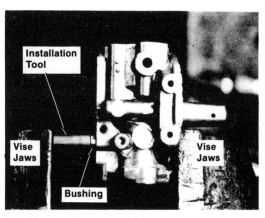

Installing throttle shaft bushings

Installing choke shaft

correct before proceeding. Use throttle shaft to align bushing if necessary.

12. Remove shaft and allow Loctite® to "set" for an additional 30 minutes before proceeding.

13. Wipe away all excess Loctite® from bushing and throttle shaft.

14. Install new detent spring and ball into carburetor body in the side opposite choke lever.

15. Compress detent ball and spring and insert choke shaft through bushings. Make sure the choke lever is on the correct side of carburetor body.

16. Install choke plate to choke shaft. Make sure marks are aligned and plate is positioned properly in bore. Apply Loctite® to threads of (2) #3-48x$\frac{7}{32}$ in. screws. Install screws so they are slightly loose.

17. Operate choke lever. Check for binding between choke plate and carburetor bore. Loosen screws and adjust plate as necessary; then tighten screws securely.

18. Install throttle shaft into carburetor with cutout portion of shaft facing out.

19. Install throttle plate to throttle shaft. Make sure marks are aligned and plate is positioned properly in bore. Apply Loctite® to threads of (2) #3-48x$\frac{7}{32}$ in. screws. Install screws so they are slightly loose.

20. Apply finger pressure to throttle shaft to keep it firmly seated against pivot in carburetor body. Rotate the throttle shaft until throttle plate fully closes the bore around its entire perimeter; then tighten screws.

21. Operate throttle lever and check for binding between throttle plate and carburetor bore. Loosen screws and adjust plate as necessary; then tighten screws securely.

22. Install the fuel inlet seal gasket and fuel inlet seat into carburetor body. Torque seat to 35-45 inch lbs.

23. Install the fuel inlet needle into inlet seat. Install Float and slide float pin through float hinge and float hinge towers on carburetor body.

24. Set Float Level: Invert carburetor so the float tab rests on the fuel inlet needle. There should be $\frac{11}{64}$ in. ± $\frac{1}{32}$ in. clearance between the machined surface of body and the free end of float. Behind the float tab with a small screwdriver to adjust.

25. Set float drop: Turn the carburetor over to its normal operating position and allow float to drop to its lowest level. The float drop should be limited to $1\frac{1}{32}$ in. between the machined surface of the body and the bottom of the free end of float. Bend the float tab with a small screwdriver to adjust.

26. Check float-to-float hinge tower clearance: Invert the carburetor so the float tab rests on the fuel inlet needle. Insert a 0.010 in. feeler gauge between float and float hinge towers. If the feeler gauge cannot be inserted, or there is interference between between the float and towers, file the towers to obtain the proper clearance.

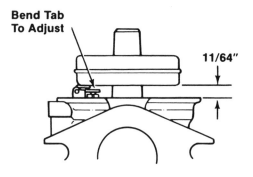

Inverted Carburetor

Setting float level

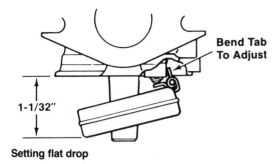

1-1/32"

Bend Tab To Adjust

Setting flat drop

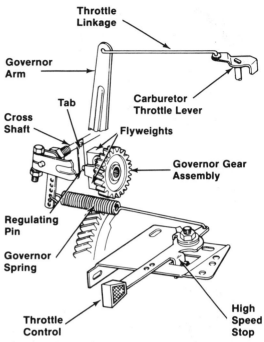

Centrifugal flyweight mechanical governor

(Labels: Throttle Linkage, Governor Arm, Tab, Cross Shaft, Carburetor Throttle Lever, Flyweights, Governor Gear Assembly, Regulating Pin, Governor Spring, Throttle Control, High Speed Stop)

27. Install the bowl gasket and baffle gasket. Position baffle gasket so the inner edge is against the float hinge towers.

28. Install the fuel bowl so it is centered on the baffle gasket. Make sure the baffle gasket and bowl are positioned properly to ensure a good seal.

29. Install the bowl retaining screw gasket and bowl retaining screw. Torque screw to 50-60 inch lbs.

30. Install the idle speed adjusting screw and spring. Install the idle fuel and main fuel adjusting needles and springs. Turn the adjusting needles clockwise until they bottom lightly.

   WARNING: *The ends of adjusting needles are tapered to critical dimensions. Damage to needles and seats will result if needles are forced.*

31. Reinstall the carburetor to the engine using a new gasket.

32. Adjust the carburetor as outlined under the "Adjustment" portion of this section.

Governor

Magnum engines are equipped with a centrifugal flyweight mechanical governor. It is designed to hold the engine speed constant under changing load conditions. The governor gear/flyweight mechanism is mounted within the crankcase and is driven off the gear on the camshaft.

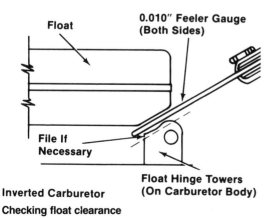

Float

0.010" Feeler Gauge (Both Sides)

File If Necessary

Float Hinge Towers (On Carburetor Body)

Inverted Carburetor

Checking float clearance

Centrifugal force acting on the rotating governor gear assembly causes the flyweights to move outward as speed increases and inward as speed decreases. As the flyweights move outward they force the regulating pin of the assembly to move outward. The regulating pin contacts the tab on the cross shaft, causing the shaft to rotate with changing speed. One end of the cross shaft protrudes through the side of the crankcase. Through external linkage attached to the cross shaft, the rotating action is transmitted to the throttle plate of carburetor.

When the engine is at rest and the throttle is in the "fast" position, the tension of the governor spring holds the throttle valve open. When the engine is operating (governor gear assembly is rotating), the force applied by the regulating pin against the cross shaft tends to close the throttle valve. The governor spring tension and the force applied by the regulating pin are in "equilibrium" during operation, holding the engine speed constant.

When a load is applied and the engine speed (and governor speed) decreases, the governor spring tension moves the governor arm to open the throttle plate wider. This admits more fuel and restores engine speed. (This action takes place very rapidly, so a reduction in speed is hardly noticed.) As the speed reaches the governed setting, the governor spring tension and the force applied by the regulating pin will again be in equilibrium. This maintains engine speed at a relatively constant level.

Governed speed may be at a fixed point as on constant speed applications, or variable as determined by a throttle control lever.

ADJUSTMENT

CAUTION: *The maximum allowable speed for these engines is 3600 RPM, no load. Never tamper with the governor setting to increase the maximum speed. Severe personal injury and damage to the engine or equipment can result if operated at speeds above maximum.*

Initial Adjustment

Make this initial adjustment whenever the governor arm is loosened or removed from cross shaft. Make sure the throttle linkage is connected to governor arm and throttle lever on carburetor to ensure proper setting.

1. Pull the governor arm away from the carburetor as far as it will go.

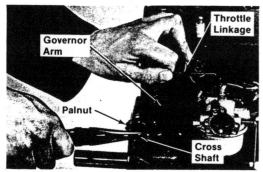

Initial governor adjustment

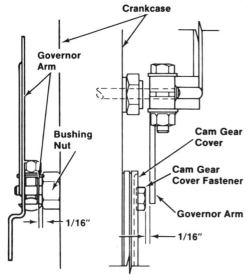

Model M8	Models M10, M12, M14, M16

Governor arm clearance

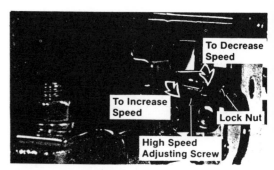

High speed adjusting screw—model M8

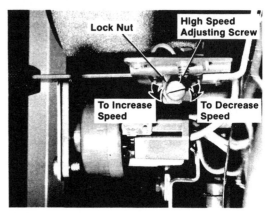

High speed adjusting screw—models M10, M12

2. Grasp the end of cross shaft with pliers and turn counterclockwise as far as it will go.

3. Tighten the pawlnut on governor arm to 15 inch lbs. torque.

NOTE: *On Model M8 — Make sure there is at least $\frac{1}{16}$ in. clearance between governor arm and cross shaft bushing nut prevent interference.*

On Models M10, M12 — Make sure there is at least $\frac{1}{16}$ in. clearance between governor arm and upper left cam gear cover fastener to prevent interference.

High Speed Adjustment

The maximum allowable speed is 3600 RPM, no load. The actual high speed setting depends on the application. Refer to the equipment manufacturer's instructions for specific high speed settings. Check the operating speed with a tachometer; do not exceed the maximum. To adjust high speed stop:

1. Loosen the lock nut on high speed adjusting screw.

2. Turn the adjusting screw in or out until desired speed is reached. Tighten the lock nut.

3. Recheck the speed with the tachometer; readjust if necessary.

Sensitivity Adjustment

Governor sensitivity is adjusted by repositioning the governor spring in the holes in governor arm. If set too sensitive, speed surging will occur with a change in load. If a big drop in speed occurs when normal load is applied, the governor should be set for greater sensitivity.

The standard spring position on Model M8 engines is in the third hole from the cross shaft. On Model M10, M12 engines, the standard position is in the sixth hole from the cross shaft. The position can vary, depending on the engine application. Therefore, make a note of (or mark) the spring position before removing it from the governor arm.

To increase sensitivity, increase the governor spring tension by moving the spring towards the cross shaft.

To decrease sensitivity, and allow broader control, decrease spring tension by moving the spring away from the cross shaft.

Engine-Mounted Throttle and Choke Controls

DISASSEMBLY AND ASSEMBLY

Model M8

1. Remove the governor spring (21) from throttle control lever (6) and governor arm. Remove the choke linkage (9) from choke control lever (8) and choke lever on carburetor. Remove the kill switch lead from kill switch (2).
2. Remove the hex cap screw (22), hex cap screws (5, 18), plain washers (4, 19), and spacers (3, 20). Remove the control assembly from handle bracket and engine crankcase.
3. Remove the wing nut (10), plain washer (11), choke control lever (8), wave washer (12), spacer (13), locking tab (14), wave washer (15), and throttle control lever (6) from control bracket (1).
4. Remove high speed adjusting screw (16, 17), and bowden wire clamps (7) as necessary.

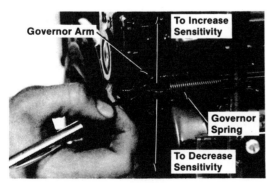

Governor sensitivity adjustment

To assemble:

1. Install high speed adjusting screw (16, 17), and bowden wire clamps (7) to control levers and bracket as necessary.
2. Install throttle control lever (6), wave washer (15), locking tab (14), spacer (13), wave washer (12), choke control lever (8), plain washer (11), and wing nut (10) to control bracket (1).
3. Install the control assembly to crankcase and handle bracket. Secure with the hex cap screw (22), spacers (3, 20), plain washers (4, 19), and hex cap screws (5, 18).
4. Install the choke linkage (9) to choke lever on carburetor and choke control lever (8). Install the governor spring (21) to governor arm and throttle control lever (6). Install the kill switch lead to kill switch (2).

Models M10, M12

1. Remove the governor spring (1) from throttle control lever (5) and governor arm. Remove the choke linkage (47) from linkage retaining bushing (43, 44) in choke shaft (45).
2. Remove the wiring connector from key switch (22). Remove the kill switch lead from kill switch (19).
3. Remove the self-tapping screw securing stabilizer bracket (16) to blower housing/bearing plate. Remove the hex cap screw (27), split lock washer (26), and spacer (21). Remove the hex cap screws securing cam gear cover and control panel bracket (23) to crankcase.
4. Remove key switch (22, 24, 25) from control panel bracket (23).
5. Remove the choke knob (32), pan head screws (31), internal tooth lock washers (30), and panel with decal (28, 29).
6. Remove the hex cap screws (17), plain washers (18), and choke shaft bracket (36) from control panel bracket (23).
7. Remove the choke shaft (45) with e-ring (37). Remove hex cap screws (33), plain washers (34), and bowden wire bracket (9).
8. Remove the slotted hex cap screws (42), split lock washers (41), and bowden wire bracket (38).
9. Remove the bowden wire clamps (39, 48), choke shaft bushings (35), and linkage retaining bushings (43, 46) as necessary.
10. Remove the hex cap screw (14) and throttle control bracket assembly (15) from control panel bracket (23).
11. Remove the hex cap screw (10), plain washer (11), and stabilizer bracket (16) from throttle control bracket (15).
12. Remove the hex lock nut (2), locking tab (3), plain washer (4), throttle control lever (5), and wave washer (9), from throttle control bracket (15).

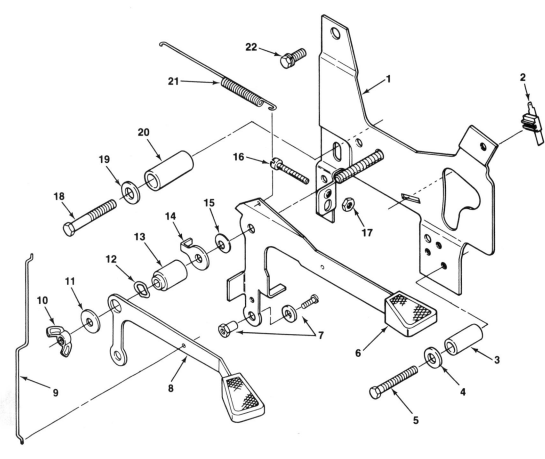

Index No.	Description	Index No.	Description
1	Control Bracket	12	Wave Washer
2	Kill Switch	13	11/16" Spacer
3	1" Spacer	14	Locking Tab
4	#10 Plain Washer	15	Wave Washer
5	#10-24x1-3/8" Hex Cap Screw	16	#8-32x1" Fillister Head Screw (High
6	Throttle Control Lever		Speed Adjusting Screw)
7	Bowden Wire Clamp	17	#8-32 Hex Nut (High Speed Adjusting
8	Choke Control Lever		Screw Lock Nut)
9	Choke Linkage	18	1/4-20x1-7/8" Hex Cap Screw
10	Wing Nut	19	1/4" Plain Washer
11	1/4" Plain Washer	20	1-7/32" Spacer
		21	Governor Spring
		22	1/4-20x1/2" Hex Cap Sems Screw

Engine mounted throttle and choke controls—model M8

13. Remove bowden wire clamp (13), linkage retaining bushing (6), high speed adjusting screw (8), and nut (7) as necessary.

To assemble:

1. Install the bowden wire clamp (13) to throttle control bracket (15).

2. Install the linkage retaining bushing (6), high speed adjusting screw (8), and nut (7) to throttle control lever (5).

3. Install the wave washer (9), throttle control lever (5), plain washer (4), locking tab (3), and hex lock nut (2) to throttle control bracket (15). Make sure the locking tab goes into the

hole in throttle control bracket. Torque hex lock nut to 15-25 inch lbs.

4. Install the stabilizer bracket (16), plain washer (11), and hex cap screw (10) to throttle control bracket.

5. Install the throttle control bracket assembly (15) and hex cap screw (14) to control panel bracket (23).

6. Install the linkage retaining bushings (43, 46) to choke shaft (45).

7. Install the choke shaft bushings (35) to choke shaft bracket (36).

8. Install the bowden bracket wire bracket

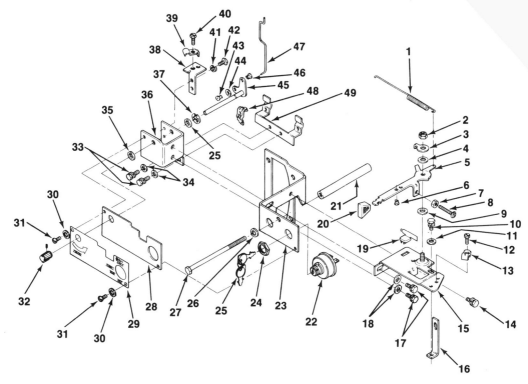

Engine mounted throttle and choke controls—models M10, M12

Index No.	Description
1	Governor Spring
2	1/4-20 Hex Lock Nut
3	Locking Tab
4	1/4" Plain Washer
5	Throttle Control Lever
6	Linkage Retaining Bushing (Black Plastic)
7	#10-24 Hex Nut (High Speed Adjusting Screw Lock Nut)
8	#10-24x3/8" Fillister Head Screw (High Speed Adjusting Screw)
9	1/4" Wave Washer
10	1/4-20x3/8" Hex Cap Sems Screw
11	1/4" Plain Washer
12	#10-24x3/8" Sltd. Hex Head Screw
13	Bowden Wire Clamp
14	1/4-20x3/8" Hex Cap Sems Screw
15	Throttle Control Bracket
16	Stabilizer Bracket
17	1/4-20x5/8" Hex Cap Sems Screw (2)
18	1/4" Plain Washer (2)
19	Kill Switch
20	Knob
21	4-1/2" Spacer
22	Keyswitch
23	Control Panel Bracket
24	Hex Nut
25	Keys
26	1/4" Split Lock Washer
27	1/4-20x5-1/16" Hex Cap Screw
28	Panel
29	Decal
30	#10 Internal Tooth Lock Washer (2)
31	#10-24x3/8" Pan Head Screw (2)
32	Choke Knob
33	#10-24x1/2" Hex Cap Sems Screw (2)
34	1/4" Plain Washer (2)
35	Choke Shaft Bushing (2)
36	Choke Shaft Bracket
37	E-Ring
38	Bowden Wire Bracket
39	Bowden Wire Clamp
40	#10-24x3/8" Sltd. Hex Head Screw
41	#10 Split Lock Washer (2)
42	#10-24x3/8" Sltd. Hex Head Screw (2)
43	Linkage Retaining Bushing (White Plastic)
44	3/16" Plain Washer
45	Choke Shaft
46	Linkage Retaining Bushing (Black Plastic)
47	Choke Linkage
48	Bowden Wire Clamp (2)
49	Bowden Wire Bracket

(38), split lock washers (41), and slotted hex cap screws (42) to choke shaft bracket (36).

9. Install the bowden wire bracket (49), plain washers (34), and hex cap screws (33) to choke shaft bracket (36).

10. Install choke shaft (45) with e-ring (37) into bushings (35). Install the choke shaft bracket assembly (35), plain washers (18), and hex cap screw (17) to control panel bracket (23).

11. Install the panel with decal (28, 29), inter-

s (30), and pan head
ke knob (32) to choke

22, 24, 25) to control

secure the control panel bracket (23) and
cam gear cover to crankcase using new gaskets
and the hex cap screws removed previously. Install the spacer (21), split lock washer (26), and
hex cap screw (27). Secure the stabilizer bracket (16) to blower housing/bearing plate with the
self-tapping screw removed previously.

14. Install the wiring connector to key switch
(22). Install the kill switch lead to kill switch
(19).

15. Install the choke linkage (47) to linkage
retaining bushing (43, 44) in choke shaft (45).
Install the governor spring (1) to throttle control lever (5) and governor arm.

RETRACTABLE STARTERS

CAUTION: *Retractable starters contain a
powerful, flat wire recoil spring that is under*

*tension. Don not remove the center screw
from starter until the spring tension is released. Removing the center screw before releasing spring tension, or improper starter
disassembly, can cause the sudden and potentially dangerous release of the spring.*

Always wear safety goggles when servicing
retractable starters — full face protection is
recommended.

To ensure personal safety and proper starter disassembly, the following procedures
must be followed carefully.

REMOVAL

Remove the five screws securing the starter
assembly to blower housing.

TO INSTALL STARTER

1. Install starter to blower housing using the
five mounting screws. Leave screws slightly
loose.

2. Pull the handle out approx. 8 to 10 in. until the pawls engage in the drive cup. Hold the
handle in this position and tighten the screws
securely.

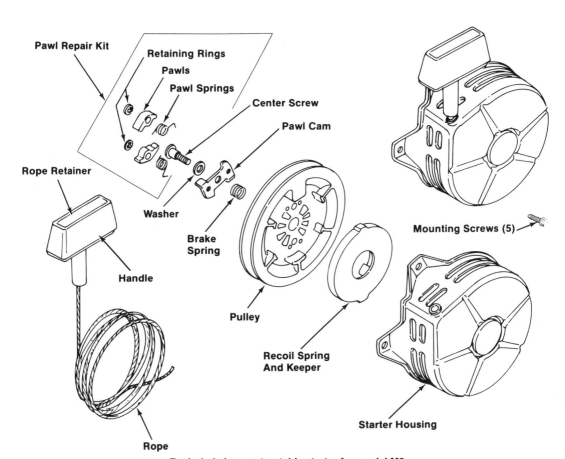

Exploded view—retractable starter for model M8

STARTER PAWLS (DOGS) REPLACEMENT

Model M8

NOTE: *Use pawl repair kit no. 41 757 02. This kit includes two starter pawls, two pawl springs, two retaining rings, and installation instructions.*

1. Remove the starter from engine.

CAUTION: *Do not remove the center screw of the starter when replacing pawls. Removal of the center screw can cause the sudden and potentially dangerous release of the recoil spring. It is not necessary to remove the center screw when making this repair.*

2. Carefully note the position of the pawls, pawl springs, and retaining rings before disassembly. (Components must be assembled correctly for proper operation.).

3. Remove the retaining rings, pawls, and pawl springs from pins on pulley.

4. Clean pins and lubricate them with any commercially available bearing grease.

5. Install new pawl springs, pawls, and retaining rings. When properly installed, the pawl springs will hold the pawls against the pawl cam.

CAUTION: *Make sure the retaining rings are securely seated in grooves of pins. Failure to seat the retaining rings can cause pawls to dislodge during operation.*

6. Pull rope to make sure pawls operate properly.

7. Install starter.

ROPE REPLACEMENT

The rope can be replaced without complete starter disassembly.

1. Remove the starter from engine.

2. Pull the rope out approx. 12 in. and tie a temporary (slip) knot in it to keep it from retracting into starter.

3. Remove the rope retainer from inside handle. Untie the knot and remove the retainer and handle.

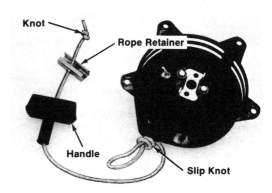

Removing handle

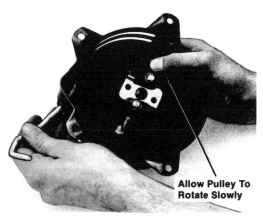

Releasing spring tension

4. Hold the pulley firmly with thumb and untie the slip knot. Allow the pulley to rotate slowly as the spring tension is released.

5. When all spring tension on the starter pulley is released, remove old rope from pulley.

6. Tie a single knot in one end of new rope.

7. Rotate the pulley counterclockwise (when viewed from pawl side of pulley) until the spring is tight. (Approx. 6 full turns of pulley).

8. Rotate the pulley clockwise until the rope pocket is aligned with the rope guide bushing housing.

NOTE: *Do not allow pulley/spring to unwind. Enlist the aid of a helper if necessary, or use a c-clamp to hold pulley in position.*

9. Insert the new rope into the rope pocket of pulley and through rope guide bushing in housing.

10. Tie a slip knot approx. 12 in. from the free end of rope. Hold pulley firmly with thumb and allow pulley to rotate slowly until the temporary knot reaches the rope guide bushing in housing.

11. Slip the handle and rope retainer onto rope. Tie a single knot at the end of rope and install rope retainer into handle.

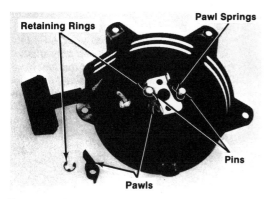

Starter pawls

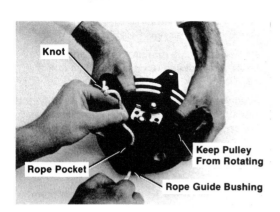

Installing rope

NOTE: *If the pulley and housing do not separate easily, the spring could be engaged with the pulley, or there is still tension on the spring. Return the pulley to the housing and repeat step 7 before separating the pulley and housing.*

10. Note the position of the spring and keeper assembly on the pulley. (The spring and keeper assembly must be correctly positioned on pulley for proper operation.) Remove the spring and keeper assembly from the pulley as a package.

CAUTION: *Do not remove the spring from the keeper. Severe personal injury could result from the sudden uncoiling of the spring.*

11. Remove the rope from the pulley. If necessary, remove the starter pawl components from pulley as instructed under "To Replace Starter Pawls".

Inspection And Service

1. Carefully inspect rope, starter pawls, housing, center screw, and other components for wear or damage.

2. Replace all worn or damaged components.

3. Do not attempt to rewind a spring that has come out to the keeper. Order and install a new spring and keeper assembly.

4. Clean all old grease and dirt from starter components. Generously lubricate the spring, and the center shaft of starter housing with any commercially available bearing grease.

M8 STARTER ASSEMBLY

1. Make sure spring is well lubricated with grease. Position the spring and keeper assembly to pulley (side opposite pawls). The outside spring tail must be positioned opposite the rope pocket.

2. Install the pulley with spring and keeper assembly into the starter housing. The pulley is in position when the center shaft is extending slightly above the face of the pulley. Do not rewind the pulley and recoil spring at this time.

12. Untie the slip knot in rope and pull the handle out until the rope is fully extended. Slowly retract the rope into the starter. If the spring has been properly tensioned, the rope will fully retract until the handle hits the housing.

M8 STARTER DISASSEMBLY

1. Remove the starter from engine.

CAUTION: *Do not remove the center screw from starter until the spring tension is released. Removing the center screw before releasing spring tension, or improper starter disassembly, can cause the sudden and potentially dangerous release of the spring. Follow these instructions carefully to ensure personal safety and proper starter disassembly. Make sure adequate face protection is worn by all persons in the area.*

2. Pull the rope out approx. 12 in. and tie a temporary (slip) knot in it to keep it from retracting into starter.

3. Remove the rope retainer from inside handle. Untie the knot and remove the rope retainer from inside handle. Untie the knot and remove the retainer and handle.

4. Hold the pulley firmly with thumb and untie the slip knot. Allow the pulley to rotate slowly as the spring tension is released.

5. When all spring tension on the pulley has been released, remove the rope from the pulley.

6. Remove the center screw, washer, pawl cam, and brake spring.

7. Rotate the pulley clockwise 2 full turns. This will ensure the pulley is disengaged from the spring.

8. Hold pulley into starter housing and invert starter so the pulley is away from your face, and away from others in the area.

9. Rotate the pulley slightly from side to side and carefully separate the pulley from the starter housing.

Installing pulley and spring into housing

3. Lubricate the brake spring sparingly with grease. Install the brake spring into the recess in center shaft of starter housing. (Make sure the threads in center shaft remain clean, dry, and free of grease or oil.).

4. Apply a small amount of Loctite® #271 to the threads of center screw. Install the center screw with washer and cam to the center shaft. Torque screw 65-75 inch lbs.

5. If necessary, install the pawl springs, pawls, and retaining rings to pins on starter pulley.

6. Tension the spring and install the rope and handle as instructed in steps 5 through 12 under "Rope Replacement".

7. Install the starter to engine.

MODELS M10, M12
STARTER DISASSEMBLY

1. Remove the starter from engine.

CAUTION: *Do not remove the center screw from starter until the spring tension is released. Removing the center screw before releasing spring tension, or improper starter disassembly, can cause the sudden and potentially dangerous release of the spring. Follow these instructions carefully to ensure personal safety and proper disassembly. Make sure adequate face protection is worn by all persons in the area.*

2. Pull the rope out approx. 12 in. and tie a temporary (slip knot) in it to keep it from retracting into starter.

3. Remove the rope retainer from inside han-

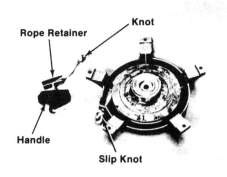

Removing handle

dle. Untie the knot and remove retainer and handle.

4. Rotate the pulley counterclockwise until the notch in pulley is next to the rope guide bushing.

5. Hold the pulley firmly to keep it from turning. Untie the slip knot and pull the rope through the bushing.

6. Place the rope into the notch in pulley. This will keep the rope from interfering with the starter housing leg reinforcements as the pulley is rotated (step 7).

7. Hold the housing and pulley with both hands. Release pressure on the pulley and allow it to rotate slowly as the spring tension is released. Be sure to keep the rope in the notch.

8. Make sure the spring tension is fully re-

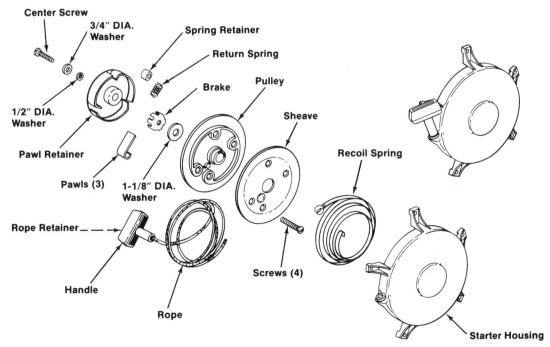

Exploded view—retractable starter for models M10, M12

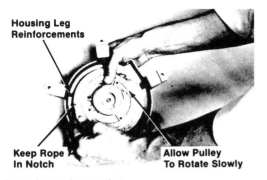

Releasing spring tension

Removing pulley from housing

leased. (The pulley should rotate easily in either direction.).

9. When all spring tension on the pulley is released, remove the center screw, ¾ in. DIA. washer, and ½ in. DIA. washer.

10. Carefully lift the pawl retainer from pulley.

CAUTION: *A small return spring and nylon spring retainer (spacer) are located under the pawl retainer. These parts are fragile and can easily be lost or damaged. If necessary, use a small screwdriver to loosen the spring retainer from the post on pulley. Replace the spring if it is broken, stretched, or shows other signs of damage.*

11. Remove the 1⅛ in. DIA. thrust washer, brake, return spring, nylon spring retainer, and pawls.

12. Rotate the pulley clockwise 2 full turns. There should be no resistance to this rotation. This will ensure the pulley is disengaged from the recoil spring.

13. Hold the pulley into the starter housing and invert starter so the pulley is away from your face and others in the area.

14. Rotate the pulley slightly from side to side and carefully separate the pulley from the starter housing.

If the pulley and housing do not separate easily, the spring could be engaged with the pulley,

or there is still tension on the spring. Return the pulley to the housing and repeat step 12 before separating the pulley and the housing.

15. Only if it necessary for the repair of starter, remove the spring from the starter housing as instructed under "To Replace Recoil Spring." Do not remove the spring unless it is absolutely necessary.

Inspection And Service

1. Carefully inspect the rope, starter pawls, housing, center screw, center shaft, spring, and other components for wear or damage.

2. Replace all worn or damaged components.

3. Carefully clean all oil, grease and dirt from starter components. Lubricate the spring, center shaft, and certain other components as specified in these instructions with any commercially available bearing grease.

Rope Replacement

1. Disassemble starter as instructed in steps 2 through 14 under "Disassembly."

2. Remove the 4 Phillips head screws securing the pulley and sheave. Separate the pulley and sheave and remove the old rope.

3. Position the new rope in the notch in the pulley and around the rope lock post.

NOTE: *Rope of the incorrect diameter and/or type will not lock properly in the pulley.*

4. Install the sheave on the pulley and install the 4 Phillips head screws. Use care not to strip or cross-thread the threads in pulley.

5. Inspect the pulley to make sure the sheave is securely joined to the pulley. Pull firmly on the rope to make sure it is securely retained in the pulley.

Recoil Spring Replacement

CAUTION: *Do not attempt to pull or pry the recoil spring or the housing. Doing so can cause the sudden and potentially dangerous release of the spring from the housing. Follow these instructions carefully to ensure personal safety and proper spring*

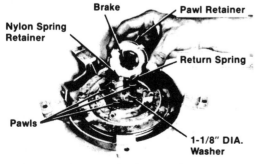

Removing pawl retainer, pawls, and related components

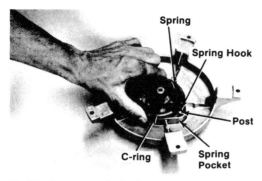

Spring
Spring Hook
Post
C-ring
Spring Pocket

Positioning new spring/c-ring

replacement. Make sure adequate face protection is worn throughout the following procedure.

1. Carefully note the position of the spring in the housing. The new spring must be installed in the proper position — it is possible to install it backwards in the housing.

2. Place the housing on a flat wooden surface with the recoil spring and center shaft down and away from you.

3. Grasp the housing by the top so that your fingers are protected. Do not wrap your fingers around the edge of the hosing.

4. Lift the housing and rap it firmly against the wooden surface. Repeat this procedure until the spring is released from the spring pocket in housing.

5. Discard the old spring.

CAUTION: *Do not attempt to rewind or reinstall a spring once it has been removed from the starter housing. Severe personal injury could result from the sudden uncoiling of the spring. Always order and install a new spring which is held in a specially designed "c-ring" spring retainer.*

6. Thoroughly clean the starter housing removing all old grease and dirt.

7. Carefully remove the masking tape surrounding the new spring/c-ring.

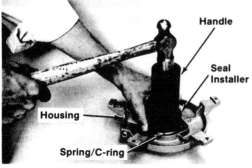

Handle
Seal Installer
Housing
Spring/C-ring

Installing spring under seal installer and handle

8. Position the spring/c-ring to the housing so the spring hook is over the post in the housing. make sure the spring is coiled in the correct direction.

9. Using Seal Installer #11791 and Handle #11795, or equivalent:

   a. Hook the spring hook over the post in housing.

   b. Make sure the spring/c-ring is centered over the spring pocket in housing.

   c. Drive the spring out of the c-ring and into the spring pocket using the seal installer and handle.

10. Make sure all of the spring coils are bottomed against ribs in spring pocket. Use the seal installer and handle to bottom the coils, as necessary.

11. Lubricate the spring moderately with wheel bearing before reassembling the starter.

STARTER ASSEMBLY

1. Install the recoil spring into the starter housing as instructed under "Recoil Spring."

2. Sparingly lubricate the center shaft of starter with wheel bearing grease.

3. Make sure the rope is in good condition. If necessary, replace the rope as instructed under "Rope Replacement."

Ready the pulley and rope for assembly by unwinding all of the rope from pulley. Place the rope into the notch in pulley. This will keep the rope from interfering with the starter housing leg reinforcements as the pulley is rotated later during reassembly.

4. Install the pulley onto the center shaft. If the pulley does not seat fully, it is resting on the inner spring coil. Rotate the pulley slightly from side to side while exerting slight downward pressure. This should move the inner spring coil out of the way and allow the pulley to drop into position.

The pulley is in position when the center shaft is flush with the face of the pulley. Do not wind the pulley and recoil spring at this time.

5. Install the starter pawls into the appropriate pockets in the pulley.

6. Sparingly lubricate the underside of the 1⅛ in. DIA. washer with grease and install it over the center shaft. Make sure the threads in center shaft remain clean, dry, and free of grease or oil.

7. Sparingly lubricate the insides of the "legs" of the brake spider with grease. Install the brake to the retainer.

8. Install the small return ring to the pawl retainer. Make sure it is positioned properly.

9. Position the pawl retainer and return spring next to the small post on pulley. Install the free loop of the return spring over the post. Install the nylon spring retainer over the post.

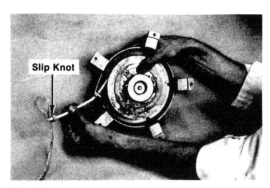

Winding rope onto pulley

10. Invert the pawl retainer over the pawls and center hub of pulley. Take great care not to damage or unhook the return spring. Make sure the pawls are positioned in the slots of pawl retainer.

11. As a test, rotate the pawl retainer slightly clockwise. Pressure from the return spring should be felt. In addition, the pawl retainer should return to its original position when released.

If no spring pressure is felt or the retainer does not return, the spring is damaged, unhooked, or improperly assembled. Repeat steps 8, 9, and 10 to correct the problem.

12. Sparingly lubricate the ½ in. DIA. washer and ¾ in. DIA. washer with grease. Install the ½ in. DIA. washer then the ¾ in. DIA. washer in the center of pawl retainer. Make sure the threads in center shaft remain clean, dry, and free of grease or oil.

13. Apply a small amount of Loctite® #271 to the threads of center screw. Install the center screw to center shaft. Torque screw to 55-70 inch lbs.

14. Rotate the pulley counterclockwise (when viewed from the pawl side of pulley) until the spring is tight. (Approx. 4 full turns of pulley.) Make sure the fully extended rope is held in the notch in pulley to prevent interference with the housing leg reinforcements.

15. Rotate the pulley clockwise until the notch is aligned with the rope guide bushing of housing.

NOTE: *Do not allow the pulley/spring to unwind. Enlist the aid of a helper, or use a c-clamp to hold pulley in position.*

16. Insert the free end of rope through rope guide bushing. Tie a temporary (slip) knot approx. 12 in. from the free end of rope.

17. Hold the pulley firmly with thumbs and allow the pulley to rotate slowly until the slip knot reaches the rope guide bushing of housing.

18. Slip the handle and rope retainer onto rope. Tie a single knot at the end of rope and install rope retainer into handle.

19. Untie the slip knot and pull the handle out until the rope is fully extended. Slowly retract the rope into the starter. If the spring has been properly tensioned, the rope will fully retract until the handle hits the housing.

ELECTRONIC MAGNETO IGNITION SYSTEM

This engine is equipped with a state-of-the-art electronic magneto ignition system. This system consists of the following components:

- A magnet assembly, which is PERMANENTLY affixed to the flywheel.
- An electronic magneto ignition module, which is mounted to the engine bearing plate.

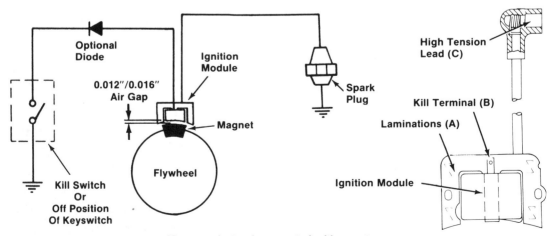

Magnum electronic magneto ignition system

- A kill switch or key switch which stops the engine by grounding the ignition module.

Operation

As the flywheel rotates and the magnet assembly moves past the ignition module, a low voltage is induced in the primary windings of the module. When the primary voltage is precisely at its peak, the module induces a high voltage in its necessary windings. This high voltage creates a spark at the tip of the spark plug, igniting the fuel-air mixture in the combustion chamber. The timing of the spark is automatically controlled by the module. Therefore, no ignition timing adjustments are necessary or possible with this system.

WARNING: *Do not connect 12 volts to the ignition system or to any wire connected to the ignition module.*

The ignition system operates independently of the battery, starting charging, and other auxiliary electrical systems. Connecting 12 volts to the ignition module can cause the module to burn out. This type of damage is not covered by the engine warranty.

A break-before-make type key switch is required to prevent damage to the ignition module.

Ignition Module

REMOVAL

1. Remove the high-tension lead and kill lead from slots in air baffle. Remove the kill lead from kill terminal of module.
2. Remove the hex cap screws, plain washers, module, and air baffle.
3. Separate the module and air baffle.

INSTALLATION

1. Install the module, plain washers, and hex cap screws. Move the modules as far from flywheel/magnet as possible – tighten the screws slightly.
2. Insert a 0.018 in. flat feeler gauge (or shim stock) between the magnet and module.
3. Loosen the hex cap screws so the magnet pulls module down. Tighten the screws to 32 inch lbs.
4. Remove the feeler gauge or shim stock. Due to the pull of the magnet, the bearing plate will flex lightly. The magnet-to-module air gap should be within the range of 0.012-0.016 in..
5. Rotate the flywheel back and forth; check to make sure the magnet does not strike the module. Check gap with feeler gauge and readjust if necessary.
6. Install the air baffle over module. Install the kill lead to terminal of module. Install high-tension lead and kill lead to slots in baffle.

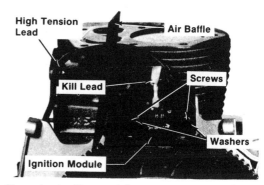

Removing ignition module

Kill Lead With Optional Diode

An optional in-line diode is installed in the kill lead of some Magnum engines. This diode protects the module from burning out, in the event voltage is applied to the kill lead.

The diode is rated such that failure (and subsequent module burn out) is highly unlikely. In the event a module with a diode protected kill lead does burn out, the diode should be tested.

DIODE TEST

Use an ohmmeter (or continuity tester) to test the diode.

1. Disconnect the kill lead terminals from the kill switch and ignition module.
2. Place the meter leads (or tester leads) across the kill lead. In one direction, the resistance should be infinity ohms (open circuit – no continuity). Reverse the test leads; some resistance should be measured (closed circuit – continuity).
3. If the resistance is infinity ohms in both directions (no continuity), the kill lead or diode is open.
4. Cut the protective tubing to expose the leads of diode. Perform the resistance (or continuity) test in step 2 to the diode leads. This will confirm if the lead or the diode is at fault.

Ignition system tester

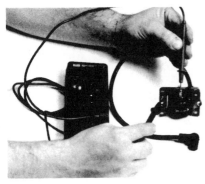

Testing module primary

Testing module secondary

5. If the resistance is 0 ohms in both directions (continuity), the diode is shorted.

KILL LEAD/DIODE REPLACEMENT

When servicing the kill lead, the entire lead can be replaced or, just the portion containing the diode. Refer to the appropriate Parts Manual for lead part numbers.

Replacing the entire lead usually requires removing the bearing plate (refer to the "Disassembly and Reassembly" sections). Use the following procedure to replace just the portion of lead with diode.

1. Cut off the diode portion of kill lead approximately 4¾ in. from terminal.
2. Strip ¼ in. of insulation from kill lead.
3. Crimp the "insulating" connector of replacement diode/lead assembly to kill lead.

Spark Plug

Engine misfire or starting problems are often caused by a spark plug in poor condition or with improper gap settings.

SERVICE

Every 100 operating hours remove the spark plug, check its condition, and reset gap or replace with new plug as necessary.

1. Before removing the spark plug, clean the area around the base of plug to keep dirt and debris out of the engine.
2. Remove the plug and check its condition. Replace the plug if it is worn or if reuse is questionable.
   * Original Equipment
     RCJ-8 — On Model M8
     RH-10 — On Models M10 and M12
   CAUTION: *CAUTION: Do not clean the spark plug in a machine using abrasive grit. Some grit could remain in spark plug and enter the engine causing extensive wear and damage.*
3. Check the gap using a wire feeler gauge. Adjust gap to 0.025 in. by carefully bending the ground electrode.
4. Reinstall the spark plug into cylinder head. Torque plug to 18-22 ft. lbs.

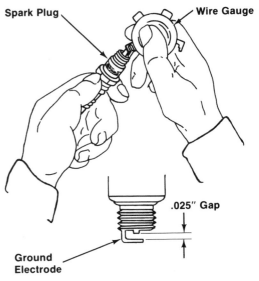

Servicing spark plug

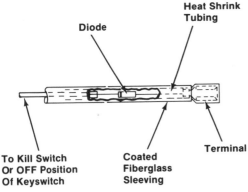

Kill lead with in-line diode

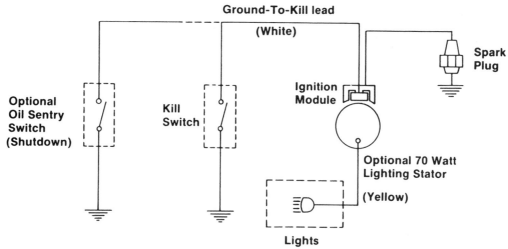

Wiring diagram—manual start engines/70 watt lighting

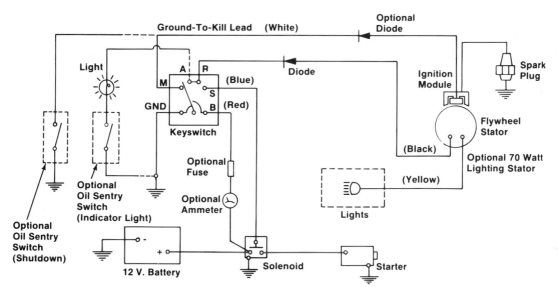

Wiring diagram—electric start engines/1.25 amp or 3 amp unregulated battery charging system/7 watt lighting

INSPECTION

Inspect the spark plug as soon as is removed from the cylinder head. The deposits on the tip are an indication of the general condition of piston rings, valves, and carburetor.

BATTERY

Batteries are supplied by the equipment manufacturer. A 12-volt battery with a rating of at least 32 amp. hr.; 250 is recommended. Re-fer to the equipment manufacturer's instructions for specific information.

BATTERY TEST

If the battery charge is not sufficient to crank the engine, recharge the battery.

CAUTION: *Do not attempt to jump start the engine with another battery. Starting the engine with batteries larger than those recommended can burn out the starter motor.*

Test the battery voltage by connecting D.C. voltmeter across the battery terminals — crank the engine. If the battery drops below 9 volts

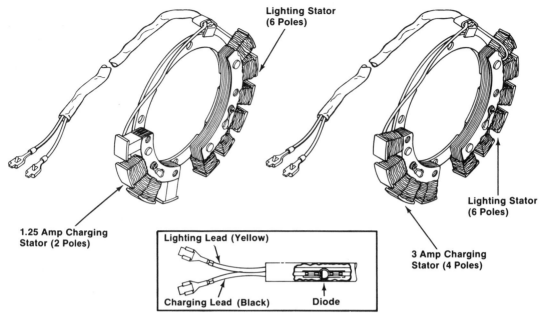

1.25 amp or 3 amp stator/70 watt lighting stator

while cranking, the battery is discharged or faulty.

BATTERY CHARGING

CAUTION: *Batteries contain sulphuric acid. To prevent acid burns, avoid contact with skin, eyes, and clothing.*

Batteries produce explosive hydrogen gas while being charged. Charge the battery in well ventilated areas. Keep cigarettes, sparks, open flame, and other sources of ignition away from the battery at all times.

To prevent accidental shorting and the resulting sparks, remove all jewelry when servicing the battery.

When disconnecting battery cables, always disconnect the negative (-) (ground) cable first. When connecting battery cables, always connect the negative cable last.

Before disconnecting the negative (-) ground cable, make sure all switches are OFF. If ON, a spark will occur at the ground cable terminal which could cause an explosion if hydrogen gas or gasoline vapors are present.

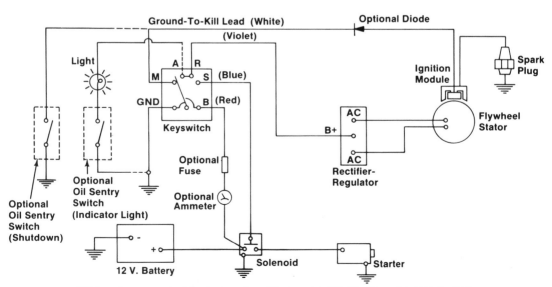

Wiring diagram—electric start engines/15 amp regulated battery charging system

Keep batteries and acid out of the reach of children.

BATTERY MAINTENANCE

1. Regularly check the level of electrolyte. Add distilled water as necessary to maintain the recommended level.

WARNING: *Do not overfill the battery. Poor performance or early failure due to loss of electrolyte will result.*

2. Keep the cables, terminals, and external surfaces of battery clean. A build-up of corrosive acid or grime on the external surfaces can self- discharge the battery. Self-discharging happens rapidly when moisture is present.

3. Wash the cables, terminals, and external surfaces with a baking soda and water solution. Rinse thoroughly with clean water.

WARNING: *Do not allow the baking soda solution to enter the cells as this will destroy the electrolyte.*

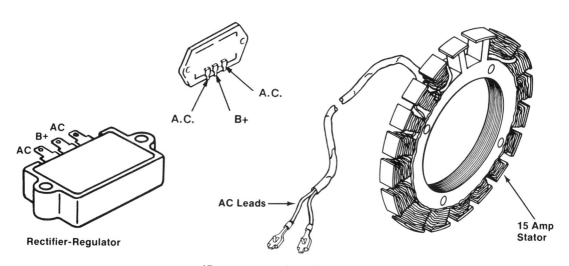

15 amp stator and rectifier-regulator

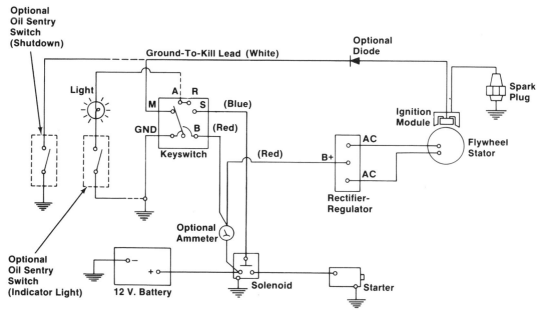

Wiring diagram—electric start engines/25 amp regulated battery charging system

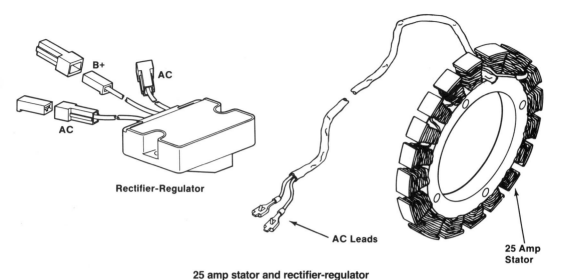

25 amp stator and rectifier-regulator

KEY SWITCH

A key switch is used on Magnum engines equipped with instrument panels. It is a three position (OFF, RUN, START), break-before-make type switch.

Testing

Test the switch for continuity using an ohmmeter or continuity test light. For each switch position, continuity should be present across the terminals listed in the table below.

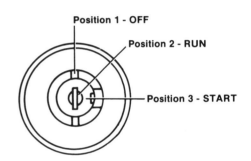

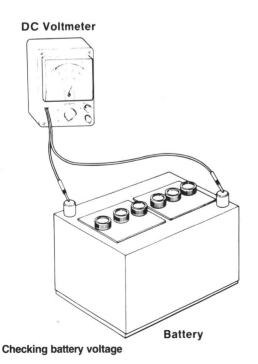

Checking battery voltage

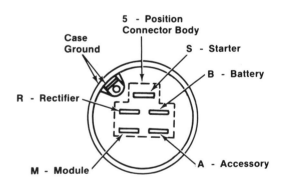

Key switch

SOLENOID

A solenoid is used on electric start engines equipped with an instrument panel or key switch. The solenoid is an electrically-actuated normally open switch designed for heavy current loads.

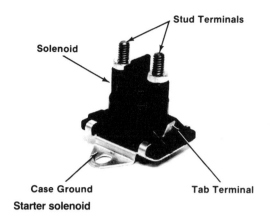

Starter solenoid

The solenoid is used to switch the heavy current required by the starter using the key switch (designed for low current loads).

TESTING

1. Connect an ohmmeter or continuity tester across the stud terminals of solenoid.

2. Apply 12 volts DC across the tab terminal and case ground of solenoid and observe ohmmeter or tester.

NOTE: *Apply positive (+) of voltage supply to tab terminal; negative (-) to case ground.*

3. The ohmmeter or tester should indicate continuity as long as voltage is applied. If there is no continuity, the solenoid is probably faulty and should be replaced.

4. Measure the resistance of the coil in the solenoid using an ohmmeter. Connect one meter lead to the case ground and one lead to the tab terminal.

• If the resistance is 5.2-6.3 ohms, the coil is OK.

• If the resistance is low or 0 ohms, the coil is shorted. Replace the solenoid.

• If the resistance is infinity ohms, the coil is open. Replace solenoid.

ELECTRIC STARTER

This is a permanent magnet, bendix-drive electric starter.

Operation

When power is applied to the starter, the armature rotates. As the armature rotates, the drive pinion moves out on the splined drive shaft into mesh with the flywheel ring gear. When the pinion reaches the end of the drive shaft, it rotates the flywheel cranking the engine.

When the engine starts, the flywheel rotates faster than the armature and drive pinion. This moves the drive pinion out of mesh with the ring gear and into the retracted position. When power is removed from the starter, the armature stops rotating and the pinion is held in the retracted position by the anti-drift spring.

WARNING: *Do not crank the engine continuously for more than 10 seconds at a time. If the engine does not start, allow a 60 second cooldown period between starting attempts. Failure to follow these guidelines can burn out the starter motor.*

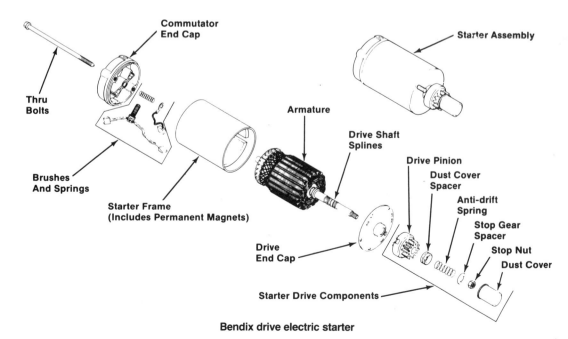

Bendix drive electric starter

If the engine develops sufficient speed to disengage the starter but does not keep running (a "false start"), the engine rotation must be allowed to come to a complete stop before attempting to restart the engine. If the starter is engaged while the flywheel is rotating, the starter pinion and flywheel ring gear may clash. This can damage the starter.

If the starter does not crank the engine, shut off the starter immediately. Do not make further attempts to start the engine until the condition is corrected. Do not jump start using another battery. Using batteries larger than those recommended can burn out the starter motor.

Do not drop the starter or strike the starter frame. Doing so can damage the ceramic permanent magnets.

Starter

REMOVAL AND INSTALLATION

Refer to the "Engine Disassembly and Reassembly" sections for starter removal and installation procedures.

NOTE: *When the through bolts are removed from the bearing plate and starter, the drive end cap and commutator end cap can separate from the starter frame.*

To prevent the starter from becoming completely disassembled, make sure the end caps are taped and held securely against starter frame when removing the through bolts. Reinstall the through bolts and temporarily secure with ¼-20 hex nuts to keep starter assembled.

STARTER DRIVE SERVICE

Every 500 operating hours or annually (whichever occurs first), clean and lubricate the drive splines of the starter. If the drive pinion is badly worn, or has chipped or broken teeth, it must be replaced.

It is not necessary to disassemble the starter to service the drive components. Service the drive as follows:

1. Hold the drive pinion in a vice with soft jaws when removing and installing the stop nut. The armature will rotate with the nut only until the drive pinion stops against internal spacers.

NOTE: *Do not overtighten the vice as this can distort the drive pinion.*

2. Remove the dust cover, stop nut, stop gear spacer, anti-drift spring, dust cover spacer, and drive pinion.

3. Clean the drive shaft splines with solvent. Dry the splines thoroughly.

4. Apply a small amount of Loctite® No. 271 to stop nut threads.

5. Reinstall the drive pinion, dust cover spacer, anti-drift spring, stop gear spacer, and stop

nut. Torque stop nut to 160 inch lbs. Install the dust cover.

DISASSEMBLY

1. Remove the dust cover, stop nut, stop gear spacer, anti-drift spring, dust cover spacer, and drive pinion. Refer to "Starter Drive Service."

2. Remove the temporary nuts and through bolts.

3. Remove the drive end cap and thrust washer.

4. Remove the commutator end cap with brushes and springs.

5. Remove the armature from inside the starter frame.

6. Install the brush springs and brushes into the pockets in brush holder. Make sure the chamfered sides of brushes are away from the springs.

NOTE: *Use a brush holder tool to keep the brushes in the pockets. A brush holder tool can easily be made from a thin sheet metal.*

Commutator Service

Clean the commutator with a coarse, lint free cloth. Do not use emery cloth. If the commutator is badly worn or grooved, turn down on a lathe, or replace the armature.

ASSEMBLY

1. Insert the armature into the starter frame. Make sure the magnets are closer to the drive shaft end of armature. The magnets will hold the armature inside the frame.

2. Install the thrust washer and drive end cap. Make sure the match marks on end cap and frame are aligned.

3. Install the brush holder tool to keep the brushes in the pockets of commutator end cap.

4. Install the commutator end cap to armature and starter frame. Firmly hold the drive end cap and commutator end cap to the starter frame. Remove the brush holder tool.

5. Make sure the match marks on end cap are aligned. Install the through bolts and temporary nuts to keep the starter assembled.

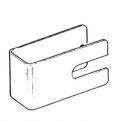

Sheet Metal Brush Holder Tool

Brush holder tool

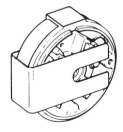

Brush Holder Tool Installed Over Brushes And End Cap

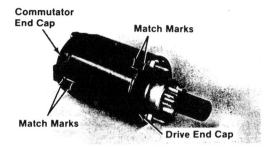

Starter assembly match marks

6. Install the drive pinion, dust cover spacer, anti-drifting spring, stop gear spacer, stop nut, and dust cover. Refer to "Starter Drive Service."

OIL SENTRY OIL LEVEL MONITOR

Operation

Some engines are equipped with optional Oil Sentry system. Oil Sentry uses a float switch in the oil pan to detect a low engine oil level. On stationary or unattended applications (pumps, generators, etc.) the float switch can be used to ground the ignition module to stop the engine. On vehicular applications (garden tractors, mowers, etc.) and those equipped with a battery or electric start, the float switch can be used to activate a "low oil" warning light.

The following instructions will enable switch removal, installation, and testing without removing the oil pan. Follow these instructions carefully to prevent damage to the switch.

Float Switch

REMOVAL

1. Make sure the engine/equipment is resting on a level surface.
2. Remove the oil drain plug and drain oil from crankcase.
3. Disconnect float switch leads.
4. Using a $9/16$ in. open end wrench, turn switch counterclockwise ¼ TURN to loosen.

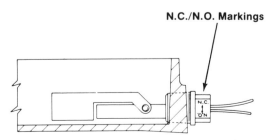

Float switch removal

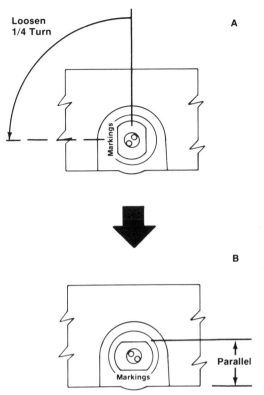

Float switch removal

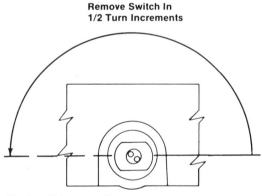

Float switch removal

STOP turning switch when flat surface on float switch is in a horizontal position. (Flat surface parallel with base of oil pan and N.C./N.O. markings down.).

5. Turn the switch counterclockwise in ½ TURN INCREMENTS using a smooth, continuous action. Pause briefly between increments and keep the flat surface of float switch in a horizontal position (parallel with base of oil pan).

WARNING: *To prevent damage to the float switch, and to enable you to "feel" if the float*

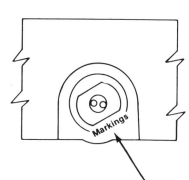

Do Not Pause Rotation Of Switch With N.C./N.O. Markings In This Position

Float switch removal

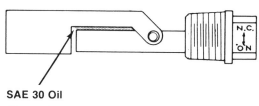

SAE 30 Oil

Float switch removal

from the location in oil pan where switch will be installed.

WARNING: *To prevent damage to the float switch, and to enable you to "feel" if the float strikes the oil pan, INSTALL THE SWITCH BY HAND as long as it is loose enough for you to do so.*

4. Apply Loctite® No. 592 Teflon® sealant (or equivalent) to the entire thread area of switch.

5. Apply a thick film of clean SAE 30 oil to the float and switch body as shown.

6. Hold the switch with the flat surface in a vertical position. (N.C./N.O. markings to the left.) Insert the switch into the oil pan and turn the switch ¼ turn. STOP turning the switch when the flat surface on switch is in a horizontal position. Flat surface parallel with base of oil pan and N.C./N.O. markings up.).

7. Turn the switch clockwise in ½ TURN INCREMENTS using a smooth continuous action. Pause briefly between increments and keep the flat surface of switch in a horizontal position (parallel with base of oil pan.).

NOTE: *Several ½ turn increments may be required until the threads on switch engage in oil pan.*

strikes the oil pan, REMOVE THE SWITCH BY HAND as soon as it is loose enough for you to do so.

When turning the float switch, use a smooth, continuous action for the ENTIRE ½ turn increment. Pausing the rotation of the switch in the position shown will cause the float to strike the oil pan. If the float does not strike the oil pan, STOP turning the switch, then use the following procedure.

a. Turn the switch clockwise until the flat surface is in a vertical position as shown. (N.C./N.O. markings on left.) This will allow to float to return against the switch body.

b. Turn the switch counterclockwise ¼ TURN. STOP turning switch when flat surface is in a horizontal position. (Flat surface parallel with base of oil pan and N.C./N.O. markings down.).

c. Turn the switch counterclockwise in ½ TURN INCREMENTS as instructed in step 5 above.

INSTALLATION

1. Make sure the engine/equipment is resting on a level surface.

2. Remove the oil drain plug and drain oil from crankcase.

3. When adding this switch as an accessory, remove and discard the ½ in. NPSF pipe plug

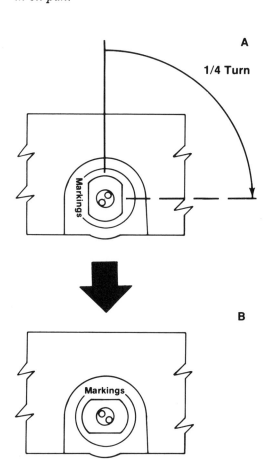

A

1/4 Turn

B

Float switch installation

**Install Switch In
1/2 Turn Increments**

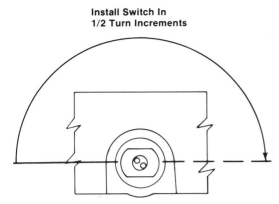

Float switch installation

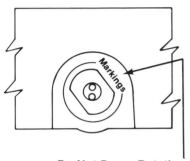

**Do Not Pause Rotation
Of Switch With N.C./N.O.
Markings In This Position**

Float switch installation

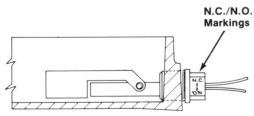

**N.C./N.O.
Markings**

Float switch installation

Pausing the rotation of the switch in the position shown will cause the float to strike the oil pan.

If the float does strike the oil pan, STOP turning the switch, then use the following procedure.

a. Turn the switch counterclockwise until the flat surface is in a vertical position, (N.C./N.O. markings on left.) This will allow the float to return against the switch body.

b. Turn the switch clockwise ¼ turn. STOP turning switch when flat surface is in a horizontal position. (Flat surface parallel

with base of oil pan and N.C./N.O. markings up.).

c. Turn the switch clockwise in ½ turn increments as instructed in step 7 above.

8. Turn in the switch approximately five (5) to six (6) full turns to obtain the proper position. Use a $\frac{9}{16}$ in. open end wrench to tighten the switch. The "N.C." markings on switch will be at the top when the switch is positioned properly.

FLOAT SWITCH TEST

Test switch for continuity by placing a ohmmeter of continuity test light across leads.

● Switch Position A: No Continuity (switch open)

● Switch Position B: Continuity (switch closed)

Perform the following tests to ensure that the float switch is positioned and working properly before connecting the leads.

NOTE: *These tests apply to engines equipped with a standard oil pan and dipstick. Special oil pan and/or dipstick arrangements can give inaccurate test results.*

1. Connect a continuity test light across float switch leads. The light should be "on".

2. Install oil drain plug and refill crankcase with oil. The light should be "off" after oil is above the "L" mark on the dipstick.

3. If the float switch fails this test:

a. Make sure the switch is in the proper position with the "N.C." markings at the top.

b. If switch is positioned properly, drain oil and remove switch (see "Float Switch Removal"). If the float is not attached to the switch body, the oil pan must be removed.

c. replace a faulty or broken switch with a new one. (See "Float Switch Installation".)

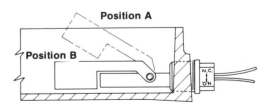

Position A

Position B

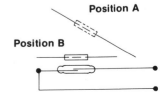

Position A

Position B

Float switch test

OPERATIONAL TEST

Reconnect the leads and perform the following test.

1. Make sure the oil level is up to , but not over "F" mark on dipstick.

2. Start the engine. If the switch is wired as a low oil level shutdown, the engine should start. If the switch is wired to activate a low oil warning light, the light should be "off."

3. Stop the engine. Drain the oil until the oil level is below the "L" mark on dipstick. If properly wired, the engine will not start or the light will be "on".

4. If the test results of steps 2 and 3 are not as indicated, check for improper wiring and/or improper float installation.

AUTOMATIC COMPRESSION RELEASE

All Magnum single cylinder engines are equipped with Automatic Compression Release (ACR). The ACR mechanism lowers compression at cranking speeds to make starting easier.

OPERATION

The ACR mechanism consists of two flyweights and a spring attached to the gear on camshaft. When the engine is rotating at low cranking speeds (600 RPM or lower) the flyweights are held by the spring in the position shown.

In this position, the tab on the larger flyweight protrudes above the exhaust cam lobe. This lifts the exhaust valve off of its seat during the first part of the compression stroke. The reduced compression results in an effective compression ratio of about 2:1 during cranking.

After the engine speed increases to about 600 RPM, centrifugal force moves the flyweights to the position shown. In this position the tab on the larger flyweight drops into the recess in the exhaust cam lobe. When in recess, the tab has no effect on the exhaust valve and the engine operates at full compression and full power.

When the engine is stopped, the spring returns the flyweights to the position shown, ready for the next start.

INSPECTION AND SERVICE

1. Check exhaust valve to tappet clearance and adjust as necessary to specification.

2. Remove cylinder head and turn the crankshaft clockwise by hand and observe the exhaust valve carefully. When the piston is approx. ⅔ of the way up the cylinder during the compression stroke, the exhaust valve should lift off the seat slightly. If the exhaust valve

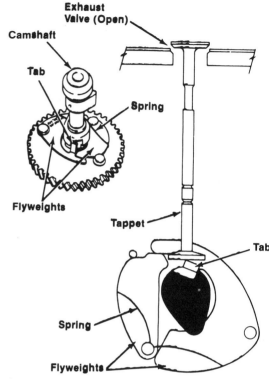

Automatic compression release (acr)—starting position

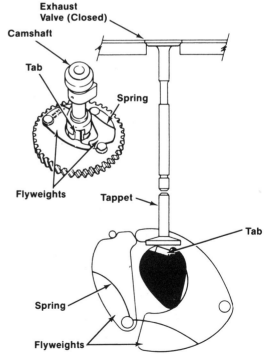

Automatic compression release (acr)—running position

does not lift, the ACR spring may be unhooked or broken. To service the spring, remove the oil pan and rehook the spring or replace it. The camshaft does not have to be removed.

The flyweights are not serviceable. If they are stuck or worn excessively, the camshaft must be replaced.

WARNING: *The tab on the flyweights is hardened and is not adjustable. Do not attempt to bend the tab — it will break and a new camshaft will be required.*

ENGINE MECHANICAL SERVICE

COMPRESSION TESTING

Because of the ACR mechanism, it is difficult to obtain an accurate compression reading.

To check the condition of the combustion chamber, and related mechanisms, physical inspection and a crankcase vacuum test are recommended.

M8 DISASSEMBLY

CAUTION: *Before servicing the engine or equipment, always remove the spark plug lead to prevent the engine from starting accidentally. Ground the lead to prevent sparks that could cause fires.*

The following sequence is suggested for complete engine disassembly. This procedure may have to be varied slightly to accommodate options or special equipment.

Clean all parts thoroughly as the engine is disassembled. Only clean parts can be accurately inspected and gauged for wear or damage. There are many commercially available cleaners that quickly remove grease, oil, and grime from engine parts. When such a cleaner is used, follow the manufacturer's instructions carefully. Make sure all traces of the cleaner are removed before the engine is reassembled and placed in operation — even small amounts of

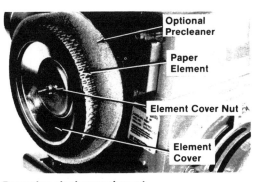

Removing air cleaner element

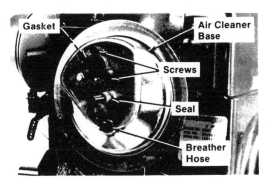

Removing air cleaner base

these cleaners quickly break down the lubricating properties of engine oil.

1. Disconnect the spark plug.
2. Drain the oil.
3. Remove the wing nut and air cleaner cover.
4. Remove the precleaner (if so equipped), element cover nut, element cover, paper element, and seal.
5. Remove the screws, air cleaner base, gasket, and breather hose.
6. Remove cap screws, muffler, gasket, and heat shield.
7. Remove the hex cap screws and rectifier-regulator.
8. Remove the connector from rectifier-regulator.

CAUTION: *Gasoline may be present in carburetor and fuel system. Gasoline is extremely flammable, and its vapors can explode if ignited. Keep cigarettes, sparks, open flames, and other sources of ignition away from the engine. Wipe up spilled fuel immediately.*

9. Remove the wing nut, plain washer, choke lever, and choke linkage. (Reinstall choke lever, plain washer, and wing nut after removing linkage.).
10. Close the fuel shut-off valve at fuel tank (if so equipped) or drain fuel from tank.

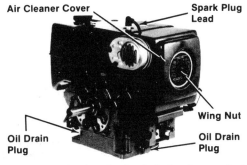

Remving spark plug lead, oil drain plug, and air cleaner cover

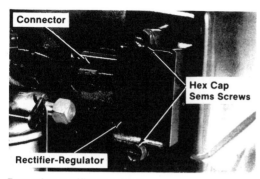

Removing rectifier-regulator

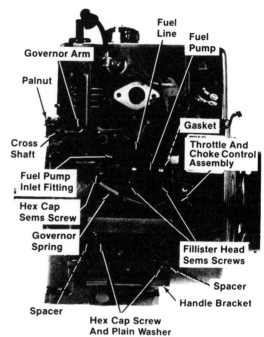

Removing fuel pump, external governor components, and throttle and choke controls

11. Loosen the hose clamp, and remove fuel line at carburetor.

12. Remove the slotted hex cap screws, carburetor, throttle linkage, and gasket.

CAUTION: *Gasoline may be present in fuel pump and fuel system. Gasoline is extremely flammable, and its vapors can explode if ignited. Keep cigarettes, sparks, open flames, and other sources of ignition away from engine. Wipe up spilled fuel immediately.*

13. Disconnect the fuel line from fuel pump inlet fitting.

14. Remove the fillister head screws, plain washer, fuel pump, and gasket.

15. Note the position of the governor spring in governor arm.

16. Loosen the pawlnut and remove governor arm from cross shaft. Remove the governor spring.

NOTE: *Loosening pawlnut or removing governor arm will disrupt governor to cross shaft adjustment. Readjustment will be required upon reassembly.*

17. Remove the hex cap screw, hex cap screws, plain washers, and spacers.

18. Remove the throttle and choke control assembly from handle bracket and engine crankcase.

19. Disconnect the lead from engine kill switch (if so equipped).

20. With retractable starters, remove the screws and starter assembly.

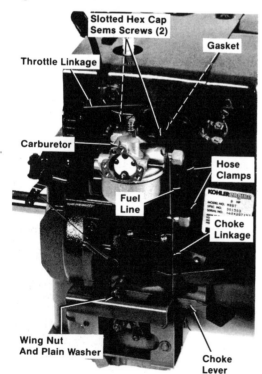

Removing choke linkage, throttle linkage, and carburetor

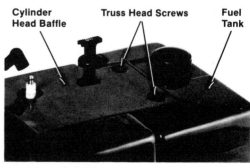

Removing fuel tank

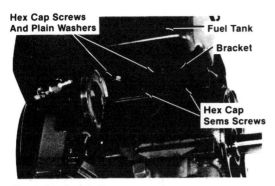

Removing fuel tank

Removing fuel tank bracket from crankcase

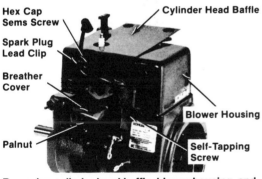

Removing cylinder head baffle, blower housing, and breather cover

21. With electric starters:

a. Remove the lead from stud terminal of electric starter.

b. Remove the pawlnut, lain washer, and hex cap screw from starter tail brace.

c. Place masking tape across the commutator end cap and frame.

d. Remove the bottom through bolt, plain washer, self-tapping screw, and starter tail brace.

e. Hold the commutator end cap against frame, and carefully remove top through bolt. Remove starter from bearing plate.

NOTE: *The starter may become disassembled if the end caps are not taped or held against the frame.*

f. Reinstall the through bolts and two ¼-20 hex nuts to keep starter assembled during remaining engine disassembly.

g. Remove the leads from solenoid. Remove the pawlnuts, screws, and solenoid from bracket.

CAUTION: *Gasoline may be present in fuel tank and fuel system. Gasoline is extremely flammable, and its vapors can explode if ignited. Keep cigarettes, sparks, open flames, and other sources of ignition away from engine. Wipe up spilled fuel immediately.*

22. Remove the fuel line from tank outlet fitting.

23. Remove the hex cap screws, truss head screws, and fuel tank with bracket.

24. Remove the hex cap screws, plain washers, and bracket from fuel tank, if necessary.

25. Remove the hex cap screws, split lock washers, and bracket from crankcase, if necessary.

26. Remove the hex cap screw, spark plug lead clip, plain washer, self-tapping screw, and cylinder head baffle.

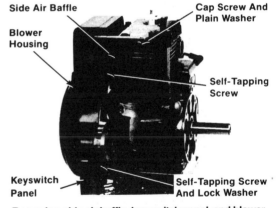

Removing side air baffle, key switch panel, and blower housing

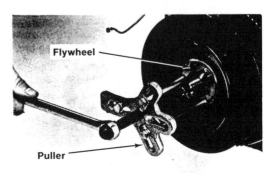

Removing flywheel using a puller

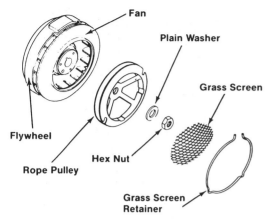

Removing grass screen, rope pulley, and flywheel—rope start models

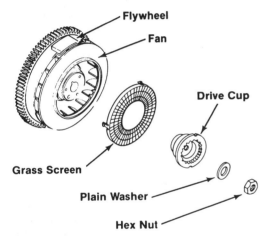

Removing drive cup, grass screen, and flywheel—retractable start models

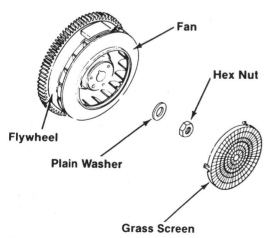

Removing grass screen and flywheel—electric start models

27. Remove the self-tapping screws, hex cap screw, plain washer, side air baffle, key switch panel (if so equipped), and blower housing.

28. Remove the pawlnut and breather cover with filter.

29. Remove the seal, gasket, breather plate, gasket, and stud (if necessary).

30. Remove the spark plug, hex cap screws, plain washers, bracket, cylinder head, and gasket.

31. Remove the hex cap screws, plain washers, ignition module, and air baffle.

32. Remove the high-tension lead and kill lead from slots in baffle. Separate the ignition module and air baffle, if necessary.

CAUTION: *Always use the flywheel strap wrench to hold flywheel when loosening or tightening flywheel and fan retaining fasteners. Do not use any type of bar or wedge between fins of cooling fan, as the fins could become cracked or damaged.*

Always use a puller to remove flywheel from crankshaft. Do not strike the crankshaft or flywheel, as these parts could become cracked or damaged.

33. With rope start models:

a. Remove the grass screen retainer and grass screen.

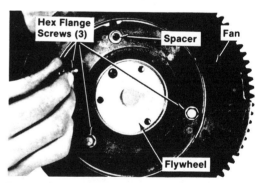

Removing fan from flywheel

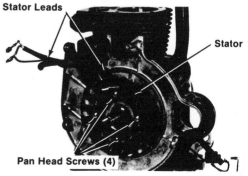

Removing stator

b. Hold the flywheel with strap wrench and loosen hex nut. Remove the hex nut, plain washer, and drive cup.

c. Remove the grass screen from fan.

34. With electric start models:

a. Remove the grass screen from fan.

b. Hold the flywheel with strap wrench and loosen hex nut. Remove the hex and plain washer.

35. Remove the flywheel from crankshaft using a puller.

36. Remove the hex flange screws, spacers and fan.

CAUTION: *Do not attempt to remove the ignition magnet from flywheel. Loosening or removing the magnet mounting screws could cause the magnet to come off during engine operation and be thrown from the engine causing severe injury. Replace the flywheel if magnet is damaged.*

37. Remove the connector body from stator leads.

38. Remove the pan head screws and stator.

39. Rotate the crankshaft until piston is at top dead center of compression stroke (both valves closed and piston flush with top of bore).

40. Compress the valve springs with a valve spring compressor and remove keepers.

41. Remove the valve spring compressor, then remove the valves, intake valve spring retainer, exhaust valve rotator, and valve springs.

NOTE: *Some models use a valve rotator on both valves.*

42. Remove the hex cap screws and solenoid bracket from starter side of oil pan.

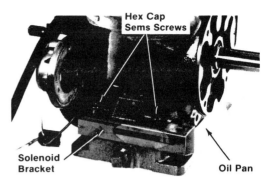

Removing solenoid bracket and oil pan

Removing handle bracket and oil pan

WARNING: *Make sure the piston is at top dead center in bore to prevent damage to oil dipper on connecting rod.*

43. Remove the hex nuts, split lock washers, plain washers, and handle bracket from studs on carburetor side of oil pan. Remove the oil pan and gasket from crankcase.

44. Remove the hex nuts and connecting rod cap.

NOTE: *If a carbon ridge is present at top of bore, use a ridge reamer tool to remove it before attempting to remove piston.*

45. Carefully push the connecting rod and piston out top of bore.

46. Remove the retainer and wrist pin. Separate the piston from connecting rod.

47. Remove the top and center compression rings using a ring expander tool.

48. Remove oil control ring rails, then remove rails spacer.

NOTE: *To make reassembly easier, mark the positions of the fuel line and wiring harness before removing the bearing plate. Mark the locations where they exit from between the crankcase and bearing plate, on both the carburetor and starter sides.*

49. Remove the hex cap screws securing bearing plate to crankcase.

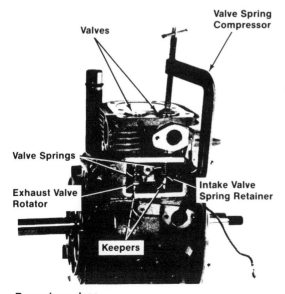

Removing valves

50. Remove the bearing plate from crankshaft using a puller.

NOTE: *The front bearing may remain either in the bearing plate or on the crankshaft, when the bearing plate is removed.*

51. Press the crankshaft out of crankcase from PTO side.

NOTE: *If the repair does not require separating the bearing plate from the crankshaft, the crankshaft and bearing plate can be pressed out as an assembly.*

52. Drive the camshaft pin (and cup plug on bearing plate side) out of crankcase from PTO side.

53. Remove the camshaft pin, camshaft, and shims (on bearing plate side of camshaft).

54. Mark the tappets as being intake or exhaust. Remove the tappets from crankcase.

NOTE: *The intake valve tappet is closest to the bearing plate side of crankcase. The exhaust valve tappet is closest to the PTO side of crankcase.*

55. Remove the stop pin, copper washer, and governor gear.

56. Remove the bushing nut and plain washer. Remove the cross shaft from inside crankcase.

57. Remove the oil seals from crankcase and bearing plate.

Removing connecting rod and piston

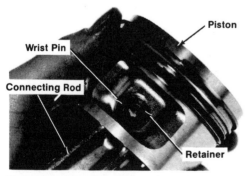

Removing piston from connecting rod

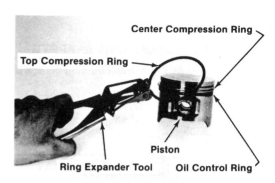

Removing piston rings

58. Press the bearings out of bearing plate and crankcase.

NOTE: *If bearings have remained on the crankshaft, remove using a puller.*

M10, M12 DISASSEMBLY

CAUTION: *Before servicing the engine or equipment, always remove the spark plug lead to prevent the engine fro starting accidentally. Ground the lead to prevent sparks that could cause fires.*

The following sequence is suggested for complete engine disassembly. This procedure may have to be varied slightly to accommodate options or special equipment.

Clean all parts thoroughly as the engine is disassembled. Only clean parts can be accurately inspected and gauged for wear or damage. There are many commercially available cleaners that quickly remove grease, oil, and grime from engine parts. When such a cleaner is used, follow the manufacturer's instructions carefully. Make sure all traces of the cleaner are removed before the engine is reassembled and placed in operation — even small amounts of these cleaners quickly break down the lubricating properties of engine oil.

1. Disconnect the spark plug.

Removing spark plug lead, oil drain plug, air cleaner cover, and muffler

2. Drain the oil.

3. Remove the wing nut and air cleaner cover.

4. Remove the precleaner, element cover nut, element cover, paper element, and seal.

5. Remove the three screws, air cleaner base, gasket, and breather hose.

6. Remove the muffler and threaded exhaust pipe.

7. Remove two screws and the rectifier-regulator.

8. Remove the electrical connector from the rectifier-regulator.

CAUTION: *Gasoline may be present in carburetor and fuel system. Gasoline is extremely flammable, and its vapors can explode if ignited. Keep cigarettes, sparks, open flames, and other sources of ignition away from the engine. Wipe up spilled fuel immediately.*

9. Remove the throttle linkage from the nylon inserts in governor arm and carburetor throttle lever. Remove the choke linkage from the nylon insert in the choke control lever, then from the carburetor choke lever.

10. Close the fuel shut-off valve at fuel tank (if so equipped) or drain fuel from tank.

11. Loosen the hose clamp and remove fuel line from the carburetor inlet.

Removing rectifier-regulator

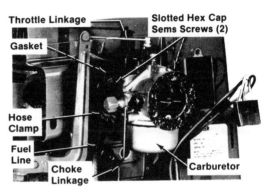

Removing choke linkage, throttle linkage, and carburetor

12. Remove two slotted hex cap screws, the carburetor, and gasket.

13. Note the position of the governor spring in governor arm.

14. Loosen pawlnut and remove governor arm from cross shaft.

NOTE: *Loosening pawlnut or removing governor arm will disrupt governor arm to cross shaft adjustment. Readjustment will be required upon reassembly.*

15. Remove the governor spring from the governor arm.

16. Remove the electrical connector from the back of key switch.

17. Remove the hex cap screw, plain washer, and spacer. Remove the self-tapping screw securing the bracket to blower housing/bearing plate. Remove four hex cap screws, cam gear cover, gasket, throttle and choke control assembly, and gasket.

18. Remove pawlnut, breather cover, and gasket.

19. Remove the filter, seal, reed stop, reed, breather plate, gasket, and stud.

20. Disconnect the fuel line from the fuel pump inlet fitting.

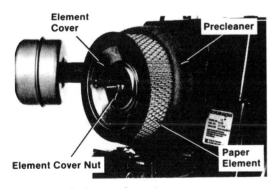

Removing air cleaner element

Removing air cleaner base

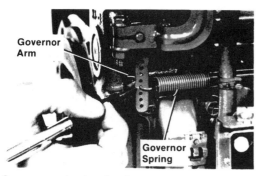

Governor spring location in governor arm

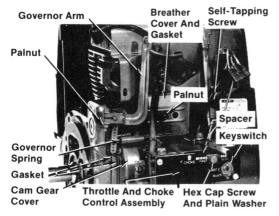

Removing external governor components, and throttle and choke controls

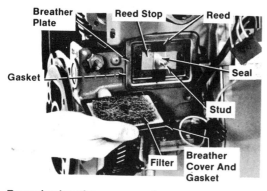

Removing breather components

21. Remove the fillister head screws, plain washers, fuel pump, and gasket.

22. Remove five screws and the starter assembly.

CAUTION: *Gasoline may be present in fuel tank and fuel system. Gasoline is extremely flammable, and its vapors can explode if ignited. Keep cigarettes, sparks, and open flames, and other sources of ignition away from engine. Wipe up spilled fuel immediately.*

23. Disconnect leads from starter and solenoid.

24. Remove the self-tapping screws and solenoid from the fuel tank lower bracket.

25. Remove the fuel line from tank outlet fitting.

26. Remove the self-tapping screw securing starter tail brace to fuel tank bracket and remove the two acorn nuts and washers at the top of fuel tank.

27. Remove two hex cap screws and fuel tank with bracket.

28. Remove pawlnuts, fuel tank lower bracket, and isolation mounts from fuel tank, if necessary.

29. Remove the dipstick, fillister head screws, oil fill/dipstick tube, and gasket.

30. Place across the commutator end cap and starter frame.

31. Remove the self-tapping screw, bottom through bolt, and starter tail brace.

32. Hold the commutator end cap against frame and carefully remove top through bolt. Remove starter from bearing plate.

CAUTION: *The starter may become disassembled if end caps are not taped or held against frame.*

33. Reinstall through bolts and two (2) ¼-20 hex nuts to keep starter assembled during remaining engine disassembly.

Removing fuel pump

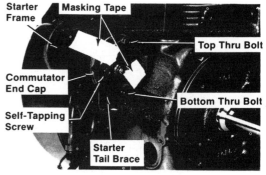

Removing starter tail brace and starter

Removing starter

40. Remove the spark plug lead and kill lead from the slots in the baffle. Separate the ignition module and air baffle, if necessary.

CAUTION: *Always use a flywheel strap wrench to hold the flywheel when loosening or tightening flywheel and fan retaining fasteners. Do not use any type of bar or wedge between fins of cooling fan, as the fins could become cracked or damaged. Always use a puller to remove flywheel from crankshaft. Do not strike the crankshaft or flywheel, as these parts could become cracked or damaged.*

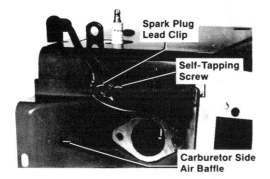
Removing carburetor side air baffle

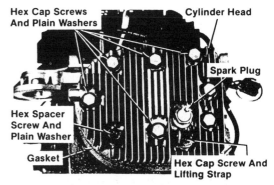
Removing spark plug and cylinder head

34. Remove the hex cap screw, plain washer, spark plug lead clip, and carburetor side air baffle.

35. Remove the hex cap screw, plain washer, self-tapping screw, and starter side air baffle.

36. Remove the truss head screw and cylinder head baffle.

37. Remove the remaining self-tapping screws and the blower housing.

38. Remove the spark plug, hex cap screws, lifting strap, hex spacer screw, plain washers, cylinder head, and gasket.

39. Remove the hex cap screws, plain washers, ignition module, and air baffle.

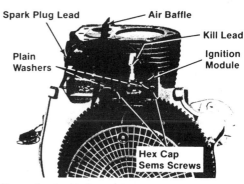
Removing ignition module and air baffle

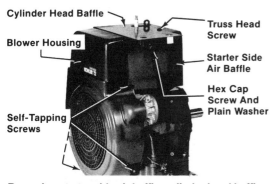
Removing starter side air baffle, cylinder head baffle and blower housing

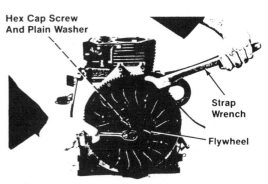
Removing flywheel fastener

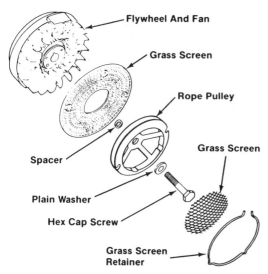

Removing grass screen, rope pulley, and flywheel—rope start models

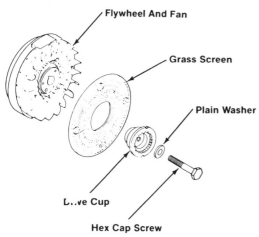

Removing grass screen, drive cup, and flywheel—retractable start models

b. Hold the flywheel with a strap wrench and loosen hex cap screw securing flywheel to crankshaft. Remove the hex cap screw and plain washer.

44. Remove the flywheel from the crankshaft using a puller.

45. Remove the hex cap screws, fan, and spacers, if necessary.

CAUTION: *Do not attempt to remove ignition magnet from flywheel. Loosening or removing magnet mounting screws could cause the magnet to come off during engine operation and be thrown from the engine causing severe injury. Replace the flywheel if magnet is damaged.*

46. Remove the connector body from the stator leads. Remove the self-tapping screw and stator lead clip from bearing plate.

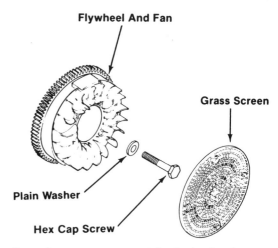

Removing grass screen and flywheel—electric start models

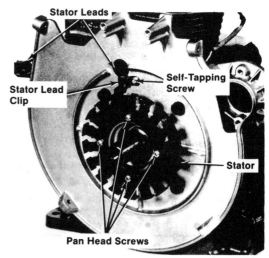

Removing stator

41. With rope start models:

a. Remove the grass screen retainer and wire mesh grass screen from rope pulley.

b. Hold the flywheel with a strap wrench and loosen the hex cap screw. Remove the hex cap screw, plain washer, rope pulley, and spacer. Remove the nylon grass screen from the fan.

42. With retractable start models:

a. Hold the flywheel with a strap wrench and loosen hex cap screw securing flywheel to crankshaft. Remove the hex cap screw, plain washer, and drive cup.

b. Remove the grass screen from the fan.

43. With electric start models:

a. Remove the grass screen from the fan.

Removing valves

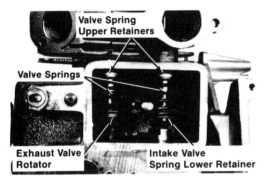

Removing valves

Removing oil pan

47. Remove the pan head screws and stator.

48. Rotate the crankshaft until the piston is at top dead center of compression stroke (both valves closed and piston flush with top of bore).

49. Compress the valve springs with a valve spring compressor and remove the keepers.

50. Remove the valve spring compressor, then remove the valves, intake valve spring lower retainer, exhaust valve rotator, valve springs, and valve spring upper retainers.

NOTE: *Some models use a valve rotator on both valves.*

51. Remove the hex cap screws, oil pan, and gasket.

WARNING: *Make sure the piston is at top dead center in bore to prevent damage to oil dipper on connecting rod.*

52. Remove the hex nuts and connecting rod cap.

NOTE: *If a carbon ridge is present at top of bore, use a ridge reamer tool to remove it before attempting to remove piston.*

53. Carefully push the connecting rod and piston out top of bore.

54. Remove the retainer and wrist pin. Separate the piston from the connecting rod.

55. Remove the top and center compression rings and the oil control ring spacer using a ring expander tool.

NOTE: *To make reassembly easier, mark the positions of the fuel line and wiring harness before removing the bearing plate. Mark the locations where they exit from between the crankcase and bearing plate, on both the carburetor and starter sides.*

56. Remove the hex cap screws securing the bearing plate to crankcase.

57. Remove the bearing plate from the crankshaft using a puller.

NOTE: *The front bearing may remain either in the bearing plate or on the crankshaft when the bearing plate is removed.*

58. Press the crankshaft out of the crankcase from the PTO side.

NOTE: *If the repair does not require separating the bearing plate from the crankshaft, the crankshaft and bearing plate can be pressed out as an assembly.*

59. Drive the camshaft pin (and cup plug on bearing plate side) out of the crankcase from the PTO side.

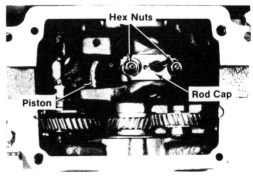

Removing connecting rod and piston

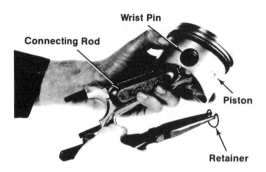

Removing piston from connecting rod

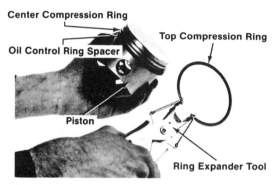

Removing piston rings

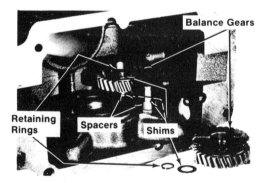

Removing balance gears

60. Remove the camshaft pin, camshaft, and shim(s) (on bearing plate side of camshaft).

61. Mark the tappets as being either intake or exhaust. Remove the tappets from the crankcase.

NOTE: *The intake valve tappet is closest to the bearing plate side of crankcase. The exhaust valve tappet is closest to the PTO side of crankcase.*

62. Remove the retaining rings, shims, balance gears with needle bearings, shims, and spacers.

63. Remove the stop pin, copper washer, governor gear, and thrust washer.

64. remove bushing nut and sleeve. Remove cross shaft from inside crankcase.

65. Remove the oil seals from the crankcase and bearing plate.

66. Press the bearings out of the bearing plate and crankcase.

NOTE: *If the bearings have remained on the crankshaft, remove bearing by using a puller.*

INSPECTION AND REPAIR/CONDITIONING

All parts should be thoroughly cleaned — dirty parts cannot be accurately gauged or inspected properly for wear or damage. There are many commercially available cleaners that quickly remove grease, oil and grime accumulation from engine parts. If such a cleaner is used, follow the manufacturer's instructions carefully, and make sure that all of the cleaner is removed before the engine is reassembled and placed in operation. Even small amounts of these cleaners quickly break down the lubricating properties of engine oils.

Flywheel Inspection

Inspect the flywheel for cracks, and the flywheel keyway for damage. Replace flywheel if cracked. replace the flywheel, the crankshaft, and the key if flywheel key is sheared or the keyway damaged.

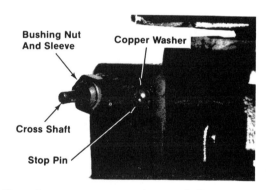

Removing governor gear and cross shaft

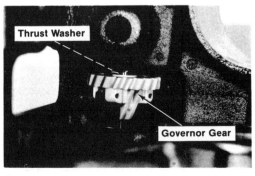

Removing governor gear and cross shaft

Inspect ring gear for cracks or damage. Kohler no longer provides ring gears as a serviceable part. Replace flywheel if the ring gear is damaged.

Cylinder Head Inspection

Blocked cooling fins often cause localized "hot spots" which can result in a "blown" cylinder head gasket. If the gasket fails, high temperature gases can burn away portions of the aluminum alloy head. A cylinder head in this condition must be replaced.

If the cylinder head appears in good condition, use a block of wood or plastic scraper to scrape away carbon deposits. Be careful not to nick or scratch the aluminum, especially in gasket seating area.

The cylinder head should also be checked for flatness. Use a feeler gauge and a surface plate or a piece of plate glass to make this check. Cylinder head flatness should not vary more than 0.003 in.; if it does, replace the cylinder head.

NOTE: *Measure cylinder head flatness between each cap screw hole.*

In cases where the head is warped or burned, it will also be necessary to replace the head screws. The high temperatures that warped or burned the head could have made the screws ductile which will cause them to stretch when tightened.

Cylinder Block Inspection and Reconditioning

Check all gasket surfaces to make sure they are free of gasket fragments. gasket surfaces must also be free of deep scratches or nicks.

Scoring of the Cylinder Wall: Unburned fuel, in severe cases, can cause scuffing and scoring of the cylinder wall. As raw fuel seeps down the cylinder wall, it washes the necessary lubricating oils off the piston and cylinder wall so that the piston rings make metal to metal contact with the wall. Scoring of the cylinder wall can also be caused by localized hot spots resulting from blocked cooling fins or from inadequate or contaminated lubrication.

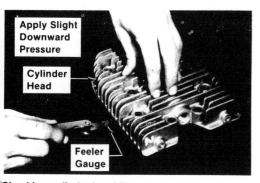

Apply Slight Downward Pressure

Cylinder Head

Feeler Gauge

Checking cylinder head flatness

Measuring cylinder bore

If the cylinder bore is badly scored, excessively worn, tapered, or out of round, resizing is necessary. Use an inside micrometer to determine amount of wear (see Specifications, Tolerances, And Special Torque Values, then select the next suitable oversize of either 0.003 in., 0.010 in. or 0.030 in.. Resizing to one of these oversizes will allow usage of the available oversize piston and ring assemblies. Initially, resize using a boring bar, then use the following procedures for honing the cylinder:

HONING

While most commercially available cylinder hones can be used with either portable drills or drill presses, the use of a low speed drill press is preferred as it facilitates more accurate alignment of the bore in relation to the crankshaft crossbore. Honing is best accomplished at a drill speed of about 250 RPM and 60 strokes per minute. After installing coarse stones in hone, proceed as follows:

1. Lower hone into bore and after centering, adjust so that stones are in contact with the cylinder wall. Use of a commercial cutting-cooling agent is recommended.

2. With the lower edge of each stone positioned even with the lowest edge of the bore, start drill and honing process. Move hone up and down while resizing to prevent formation of cutting ridges. Check size frequently.

NOTE: *Keep in mind the temperatures caused by honing may cause inaccurate measurements. Make sure the block is cool when measuring.*

3. When bore is within 0.0025 in. of desired size, remove coarse stones and replace with burnishing stones. Continue with burnishing stones until within 0.0005 in. of desired size and then use finish stones (220-280 grit) and polish to final size. A cross hatch should be observed if honing is done correctly. The cross hatch should intersect at approximately 23-33 degrees off the horizontal. Too flat an angle could cause the rings to skip and wear exces-

sively, too high an angle will result in high oil consumption.

4. After resizing, check the bore for roundness, taper, and size. Use an inside micrometer, telescoping gauge, or bore gauge to take measurements. The measurements should be taken at three locations in the cylinder — at the top, middle, and bottom. Two measurements should be taken (perpendicular to each other) at each of the three locations.

5. Thoroughly clean cylinder wall with soap and hot water. Use a scrub brush to remove all traces of boring/honing debris. Dry thoroughly and apply a light coat of SAE 10 oil to prevent rust.

Measuring Piston-to-Bore Clearance

Before installing the piston into the cylinder bore, it is necessary that the clearance be accurately checked. This step is often overlooked, and if the clearances are not within specifications, generally engine failure will result.

NOTE: *Do not use a feeler gauge to measure piston-to-bore clearance — it will yield inaccurate measurements. Use a micrometer.*

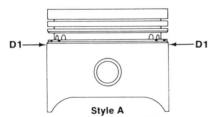

Style A—Measure piston diameter (D1) perpendicular to piston pin just below the oil ring groove.

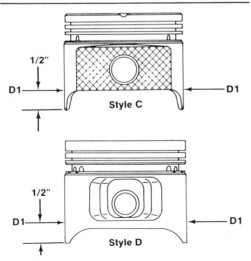

Styles C and D—Measure piston diameter (D1) perpendicular to piston pin at 1/2″ above the bottom of the skirt.

Measuring piston diameter

The following procedures should be used to accurately measure the piston to bore clearance.

1. Use a micrometer and measure the diameter of the piston.

2. Use an inside micrometer, telescoping gauge, or bore gauge and measure the cylinder bore. Take the measurement approximately 2½ in. below the top of the bore and perpendicular to the piston pin.

3. Piston-to-bore clearance is the difference between the bore and the piston diameter (step 2 minus step 1). Clearance should be: 0.007-0.010 in. (style A piston), 0.003-0.005 in. (style C piston), 0.0034-0.0051 in. (style D piston).

Valve Inspection and Service

Carefully inspect valve mechanism parts. Inspect valve springs and related hardware for excessive wear or distortion. Valve spring free height should be at approximately the dimension given in the chart below. Check valves and valve seat area or inserts for evidence of deep pitting, cracks or distortion. Check clearance of valve stems in guides.

Hard starting, or loss of power accompanied by high fuel consumption may be symptoms of faulty valves. Although these symptoms could also be be attributed to worn rings, remove and check valves first. After removal, clean valve head, face and stem with power wire brush and then carefully inspect for defects such as warped valve head, excessive corrosion or worn stem end. Replace valves found to be in bad condition. A normal valve and valves in bad condition are shown in the accompanying illustrations.

Valve Guides

If a valve guide is worn beyond specifications, it will not guide the valve in a straight line. This may result in a burnt valve face or seat, loss of compression, and excessive oil consumption.

To check valve guide to stem clearance, thoroughly clean the valve guide and, using a split-ball gauge, measure the inside diameter. Then, using an outside micrometer, measure the diameter of the valve stem at several points on the stem where it moves in the valve guide. Use the largest stem diameter to calculate the clearance. If the clearance exceeds 0.006 on intake or 0.008 on exhaust valves, determine whether the valve stem or the guide is responsible for the excessive clearance.

NOTE: *The exhaust valves on these engines have a slightly tapered valve stem to help prevent sticking. Because of the taper, the valve stem must be measured in two places to determine if valve stem is worn. If the valve stem*

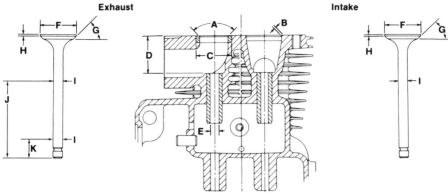

Exhaust   Intake

	Dimension	M8		M10, M12, M14		M16	
		Intake	Exhaust	Intake	Exhaust	Intake	Exhaust
A	Seat Angle	89°	89°	89°	89°	89°	89°
B	Seat Width	.037/.045	.037/.045	.037/.045	.037/.045	.037/.045	.037/.045
C	Insert O. D.	—	1.2525/1.2535	—	1.2525/1.2535	1.5035/1.5045	1.5035/1.5045
D	Guide Depth	1.281	1.312	1.996*	1.996*	1.996*	1.996*
E	Guide I.D.	.312/.313	.312/.313	.312/.313	.312/.313	.312/.313	.312/.313
F	Valve Head Diameter	1.380/1.370	1.130/1.120	1.380/1.370	1.130/1.120	1.380/1.370	1.380/1.370
G	Valve Face Angle	45°	45°	45°	45°	45°	45°
H	Valve Margin (Min.)	.031	.031	.031	.031	.031	.031
I	Valve Stem Dia.	.3103/.3110	—	.3103/.3110	—	.3103/.3110	—
	Valve Stem Dia. @ J	—	.3074/.3081	—	.3074/.3081	—	.3074/.3081
	Valve Stem Dia. @ K	—	.3084/.3091	—	.3084/.3091	—	.3084/.3091
J	(I) Measurement Location	—	2.530	—	3.060	—	3.060
K	(I) Measurement Location	—	.535	—	.835	—	.835

*Approximate. Should be flush with top of valve guide counterbore.

Valve details

diameter is within specifications, replace the valve guide.

VALVE GUIDE REPLACEMENT

The valve guides are a tight press fit in the cylinder block. A valve guide removal tool is recommended to remove the guides (refer to "Special Tools" section). To remove valve guide, proceed as follows:

1. Install $^5/_{16}$-18 NC nut on coarse threaded end of 2½ in. long stud (M8) or 3½ in. long stud (M10, M12).

2. Insert other end of stud through valve guide bore and install $^5/_{16}$-24 NF nut. Tighten both nuts securely.

NOTE: *Valve guide must be held firmly by the stud assembly so that all side hammer force will act on the guide.*

3. Assemble the valve guide removal adapter to the stud and then the slide hammer to the adapter.

4. use the slide hammer to pull the guide out.

To Install:

1. Make sure valve guide bore is clean and free of nicks or burrs.

2. Using valve guide driver (refer to "Special Tools" section), align and then press guide in until valve guide driver bottoms on valve guide counterbore.

3. Valve guides are often slightly compressed during insertion. Use a piloted reamer and then a finishing reamer to resize the guide bore to 0.3125 in..

Valve Seat Inserts

The intake valve seat is usually machined into the cylinder block, however, certain applications may specify a hard alloy insert. The exhaust valve seat is a replaceable alloy insert. If the seat becomes badly pitted, cracked, or distorted, the insert must be replaced.

The insert is a tight press fit in the cylinder block. A valve seat removal tool is recommended for this job (refer to "Special Tools" section). Since insert removal causes loss of metal in the insert bore area, use only service replacement inserts, which are slightly larger to provide proper retention in the cylinder block. Make sure new insert is properly started and pressed into bore to prevent cocking of the insert.

a.

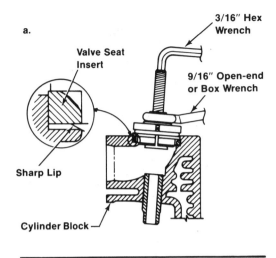

b.

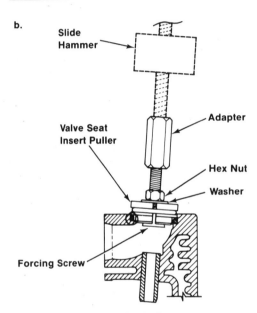

Pulling valve seat insert (typical)

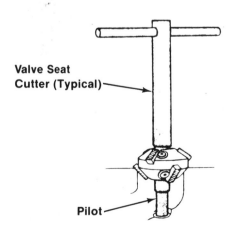

Standard valve seat cutter

VALVE SEAT INSERT REPLACEMENT

1. Install valve seat puller on forcing screw and lightly secure with washer and nut.

2. Center the puller assembly on valve seat insert.

3. Hold forcing screw with a hex wrench to prevent turning and slowly tighten nut.

NOTE: *Make sure sharp lip on puller (see insert) engages in joint between bottom of valve seat insert and cylinder block counterbore, all the way around.*

4. Continue to tighten nut until puller is tight against valve seat insert.

5. Assemble adapter to valve seat puller forcing screw and slide hammer to adapter.

6. Use slide hammer to remove valve seat insert.

To install:

1. Make sure valve seat insert bore is clean and free of nicks or burrs.

2. Align valve seat insert in counterbore and using valve seat installer and driver (refer to ''Special Tools'' section), press seat until bottomed.

3. Use a standard valve seat cutter and cut seat to dimensions shown.

Reground or new valves must be lapped in to provide proper fit. Use a hand valve grinder with suction cup for final lapping. Lightly coat valve face with ''fine'' grade of grinding compound, then rotate valve on seat with grinder. Continue grinding until smooth surface is obtained on seat and on valve face. Thoroughly clean cylinder block in soap and hot water to remove all traces of grinding compound. After

| Model | End Gap | |
	New	Used
M8	.007/.017	.007/.027
M10 M12 M14 M16	.010/.020	.010/.030

Measuring piston ring end gap

drying cylinder block apply a light coating of SAE 10 oil to prevent rusting.

Piston and Rings

Three different styles of pistons are currently being used in Kohler Magnum engines.

Style "A" pistons were used in M8 engines prior to serial number 1601300012 and are used in all M10, M12 engines. The style "A" pistons can be identified by its full skirt and by its lack of an installation direction identifier on its crown (a new piston can be installed facing in either direction).

The Style "D" piston has been used in M8 engines from serial number 1601300012 on up. It can be identified by its partial skirt and rectangular recessed area around the piston pin bore. In addition, it has an installation direction identifier, Fly, which is stamped into the top of the piston. The style D piston is to be installed with the arrow of the Fly mark pointing towards the flywheel.

Measuring piston ring side clearance

INSPECTION

Scuffing and scoring of piston and cylinder wall occurs when internal temperatures approach the melting point of the piston. Temperatures high enough to do this are created by friction, which is usually attributed to improper lubrication, and/or overheating of the engine.

Style A

1. Oil Control Ring - (Bottom Groove): Install the expander spring, spacer (use a piston ring installation tool), and rails.

2. Compression Ring - (Center Groove): Install the expander spring and then the ring (use a piston ring installation tool). Make sure "pip" mark on ring is up.

3. Compression Ring - (Top Groove): Install the chrome compression ring (use a piston ring installation tool). Make sure "pip" mark on ring is up.

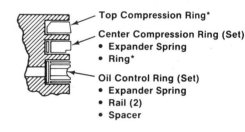

Top Compression Ring*

Center Compression Ring (Set)
• Expander Spring
• Ring*

Oil Control Ring (Set)
• Expander Spring
• Rail (2)
• Spacer

Style C

1. Oil Control Ring - (Bottom Groove): Install the expander spring, spacer (use a piston ring installation tool), and rails.

2. Compression Ring - (Center Groove): Install the expander, ring (use a piston ring installation tool), and rail. Make sure "pip" mark on ring is up.

3. Compression Ring - (Top Groove): Install the chrome compression ring (use a piston ring installation tool). Make sure "pip" mark on ring is up.

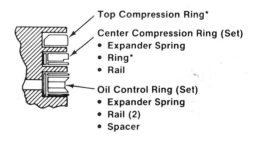

Top Compression Ring*

Center Compression Ring (Set)
• Expander Spring
• Ring*
• Rail

Oil Control Ring (Set)
• Expander Spring
• Rail (2)
• Spacer

Style D

1. Oil Control Ring - (Bottom Groove): Install the expander and rails. Make sure the ends of expander are not overlapped.

2. Compression Ring - (Center Groove): Install the beveled ring using a piston ring installation tool. Make sure the "pip" mark is up and PINK dykem stripe is to the left of end gap.

3. Compression Ring - (Top Groove): Install the top ring using a piston ring installation tool. Make sure the "pip" mark is up and BLUE dykem stripe is to the left of end gap.

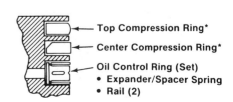

Top Compression Ring*

Center Compression Ring*

Oil Control Ring (Set)
• Expander/Spacer Spring
• Rail (2)

*Install with "pip" mark *facing up.*

Piston ring installation

Normally, very little wear takes place in the piston boss-piston pin area. If the original piston and connecting rod can be reused after new rings are installed, the original pin can also be reused but new piston pin retainers are required. The piston pin is included as part of the piston assembly — if the pin boss in piston, or the pin are worn or damaged, a new piston assembly is required.

Ring failure is usually indicted by excessive oil consumption and blue exhaust smoke. When rings fail, oil is allowed to enter the combustion chamber where it is burned along with the fuel. High oil consumption can also occur when the piston ring end cap gap is incorrect because the ring cannot properly conform to the cylinder wall under this condition. Oil control is also lost when ring gaps are not staggered during installation.

When cylinder temperatures get too high, lacquer and varnish collect on piston causing rings to stick which results in rapid wear. A worn ring usually takes on a shiny or bright appearance. Scratches on rings and piston are caused by abrasive material such as carbon, dirt, or pieces of hard metal.

Detonation damage occurs when a portion of the fuel charge ignites spontaneously from heat and pressure shortly after ignition. This creates two flame fronts which meet and explode to create extreme hammering pressures on a specific area of the piston. Detonation generally occurs from using fuels with too low of an octane rating.

Preignition or ignition of the fuel charge before the timed spark can cause damage similar to detonation. Preigniton damage is often more quickly burned right through the piston dome. Preignition is caused by a hot spot in the combustion chamber from its sources such as: Glowing carbon deposits, blocked fins, improperly seated valves or wrong spark plug.

Standard and 0.10″ undersize connecting rods

Service

Magnum service replacement pistons are available in STD bore size, and in 0.003 in., 0.010 in., 0.020 in., and 0.030 in. oversizes. Replacement pistons include new piston ring sets and new piston pins.

Service replacement piston rings sets are also available separately for STD/.003 in. (same ring set for both sizes), 0.010 in., 0.020 in. and 0.030 in. oversized pistons. Always use new piston rings when installing pistons. Never reuse old rings.

The cylinder bore must be deglazed before service ring sets are used.

Some important points to remember when servicing piston rings:

1. If the cylinder block does not need reboring and if the old piston is within wear limits and free of score or scuff marks, the old piston may be reused.

2. Remove old rings and clean up grooves. Never reuse old rings.

3. Before installing new rings on piston, place top two rings, each in turn, in its running area in cylinder bore and check end cap.

4. After installing the new compression (top and middle) rings on piston, check piston-to-ring side clearance. Maximum recommended side clearance is 0.006 in.. If side clearance is greater than 0.006 in., a new piston must be used.

PISTON RINGS

Rings must be installed correctly. Ring installation instructions are usually included with new ring sets. Follow instructions carefully. Use a piston ring expander to install rings. Install the bottom (oil control) ring first and the top compression ring last.

Posi-Lock Connecting Rods

Posi-Lock connecting rods are used in all Magnum engines. On model M8 engines with the style D pistons, the connecting rods have a

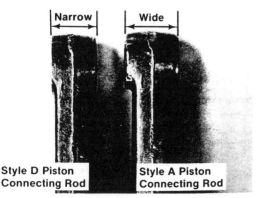

Magnum M8 posi-lock connecting rods

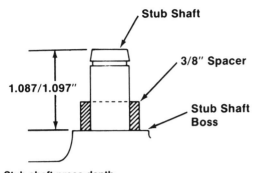

Stub Shaft

3/8" Spacer

1.087/1.097"

Stub Shaft Boss

Stub shaft press depth

narrower piston pin end than on the earlier (style A) Posi-Lock connecting rods. Therefore, the Posi-Lock connecting rods used with the stlye D pistons are not interchangeable with the Posi-Lock connecting rods used with style A pistons.

INSPECTION AND SERVICE

Check bearing area (big end) for excessive wear, score marks, running and side clearances. Replace rod and cap if scored or excessively worn.

Service replacement connecting rods are available in STD crankpin size and 0.010 undersize. The 0.010 in. undersize rod can be identified by the drilled hole located in the lower end of the rod shank. Always refer to the appropriate parts information to ensure the correct replacements are used.

Balance Gears and Stub Shafts

Most M10 and M12 Magnum engines are equipped with a balance gear system. M8 Magnum engines do not have balance gears.

The system consists of two gears and spacers (used to control end play) mounted on stub shafts which are pressed into the crankcase. The gears and spacers are held on the shafts with snap-ring retainers. The gears are timed with and driven by the engine crankshaft.

INSPECTION AND REPAIR

Use a micrometer and measure the stub shaft diameter. If the diameter is less than 0.4996 in., replace the stub shaft. use an arbor press to push old shaft out and new shaft in. Press the new shaft in until it is 1.087-1.097 in. from stub shaft boss.

Inspect the gears fro worn or chipped teeth and for worn needle bearings. Use an arbor press and driver to replace bearings, if required.

Governor Gear

INSPECTION

Inspect the governor gear teeth. Look for any evidence of worn, chipped or cracked teeth. If one or more of these problems is noted, replace the governor gear.

Camshaft and Crankshaft

INSPECTION AND SERVICE

Inspect the gear teeth on both the crankshaft and camshaft. If the teeth are badly worn, chipped or some are missing, replacement of the damaged components will be necessary.

Also, inspect the crankshaft bearings for scoring, grooving, etc. Do not replace bearings unless they show signs of damage or are out of running clearance specifications. If crankshaft turns easily and noiselessly, and there is no evidence of scoring, grooving, etc., on the races or bearing surfaces, the bearings can be reused.

Check crankshaft keyways. If worn or chipped, replacement of the crankshaft will be necessary. Also inspect the crankpin for score marks or metallic pickup. Slight score marks can be cleaned with crocus cloth soaked in oil. If wear limits, as stated in "Specifications, Tolerances And Special Torque Values", are exceeded, it will be necessary to either replace the crankshaft or regrind the crankpin to 0.010 in. undersize. If reground, a 0.010 in. undersize connecting rod (big end) must then be used to achieve proper running clearance. Measure the crankpin for size, taper and out-of-round.

NOTE: *If the crankpin is reground, visually check to insure that the fillet blends smoothly with the crankpin surface.*

MODEL M8 ASSEMBLY

The following sequence is suggested for complete engine reassembly. This procedure assumes that all components are new or have been reconditioned, and all component subassembly work has been completed. This procedure may have to be varied slightly to accommodate options or special equipment.

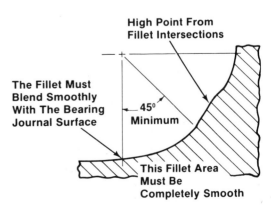

High Point From Fillet Intersections

The Fillet Must Blend Smoothly With The Bearing Journal Surface

45° Minimum

This Fillet Area Must Be Completely Smooth

Crankpin fillets

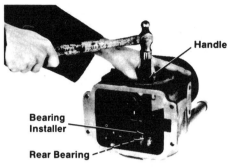

Installing rear bearing

Installing camshaft

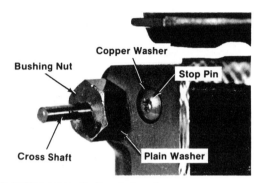

Installing cross shaft and stop pin

WARNING: *Make sure the engine is assembled using all specified torque valves, tightening sequences, and clearances. Failure to observe specifications could cause severe engine wear or damage.*

1. Install the rear bearing into crankcase using the #4747 handle and appropriate bearing installer. (Refer to the "Special Tools" section.) Make sure the bearing is bottomed fully, and straight and true in bore.

2. Install the cross shaft, plain washer, and bushing nut. Torque the bushing nut to 100-120 inch lbs.

3. Install the governor gear, copper washer, and stop pin.

4. Install the intake valve tappet and exhaust valve tappet into crankcase. (Intake valve tappet towards bearing plate side; exhaust valve tappet towards the PTO side of crankcase.).

5. Install the camshaft, one 0.010 in. shim spacer, and camshaft pin (from bearing late side). Do not drive the camshaft pin into final position at this time.

6. Measure camshaft end play between spacer and crankcase boss using a flat feeler gauge. Recommended camshaft end play is 0.005-0.010 in.. Add or subtract 0.005 in. and/or 0.010 in. shim spacers as necessary to obtain the proper end play.

7. Drive the camshaft pin into PTO side of crankcase until it is 0.275-0.285 in. from machined bearing plate gasket surface.

8. Apply Loctite® #290 (or equivalent) to the cup plug. Install the cup plug into bore in bearing plate mounting surface to a depth of 0.055-0.065 in..

9. Lubricate the rear crankshaft bearing surface. Insert the crankshaft through rear bearing.

NOTE: *If the crankshaft and bearing plate have not been separated, position the fuel line and wiring harness between the bearing plate and crankcase before pressing the crankshaft all the way in.*

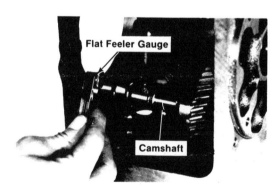

Measuring camshaft end play

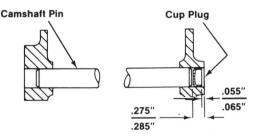

Installing camshaft pin and cup plug

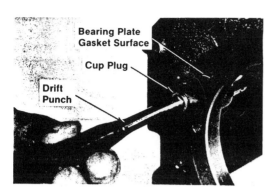

Installing cup plug

10. Align the timing mark on crankshaft with the timing mark on camshaft. Press crankshaft into rear bearing. Make sure the camshaft and crankshaft gears mesh and timing marks align while pressing.

11. Install the front bearing into bearing plate using the #4747 handle and appropriate bearing installer. (Refer to the "Special Tools" Section.) Make sure the bearing is bottomed fully, and straight and true inbore.

12. Position the fuel line and wiring harness (if so equipped) to crankcase.

13. Adjust the fuel line and wiring harness to their final positions just before securing the bearing plate to crankcase.

Aligning crankshaft and camgear

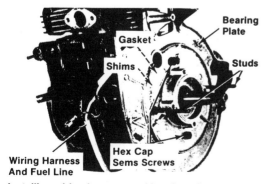

Installing wiring harness and bearing plate

14. Install ¼-20 studs into two bearing plate mounting holes. The studs ease locating and assembly of shims, gasket, and bearing plate.

15. Lubricate the bearing surface of crankshaft and bearing. Install the gasket, two or three 0.005 in. shims (as required), and bearing plate over studs.

NOTE: *Crankshaft end play is determined by the thickness of the gasket and shims between crankcase and bearing plate. Check the end play after bearing plate is installed.*

16. Install two hex cap screws and hand tighten. Remove the locating studs, and install remaining two hex cap screws and hand tighten.

17. Position the wiring harness and fuel line in their final positions as marked during disassembly.

18. Tighten the screws evenly, drawing bearing plate to crankcase. Torque the screws to 115 inch lbs.

19. Check the crankshaft end play between the inner bearing race and shoulder of crankshaft using a flat feeler gauge. Recommended total end play is 0.002-0.023 in. If measured end play is not within limits, remove the bearing plate and remove or install shims as necessary.

20. Slide the appropriate seal sleeves over crankshaft. (Refer to the "Special Tools" section.) Generously lubricate the lips of oil seals with light grease. Slide the oil seals over sleeves.

21. Use the #11795 handle and appropriate seal drivers, install oil seals to the following depths:
- Front oil Seal (Bearing Plate): $\frac{1}{32}$ in.
- Rear Oil Seal (Crankcase PTO End): ⅛ in.
- Tolerance on seal position: $+\frac{3}{64}$ in.; $-\frac{1}{64}$ in.

22a. On "Style A" Pistons: Install wrist pin and retainers.

22b. On "Style D" Pistons
  a. Orient the piston and connecting rod so the "Fly" symbol on piston and match marks

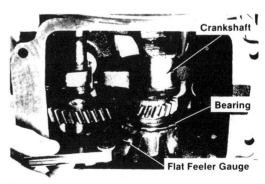

Measuring crankshaft end play

Installing oil seals using sleeve

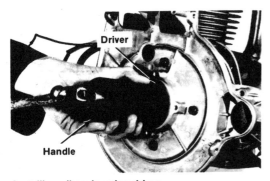

Installing oil seals using driver

on connecting rod are facing the same direction.

b. Install wrist pin and retainers.

WARNING: *Proper orientation of the piston/connecting rod inside engine is extremely important. Improper orientation may cause extensive wear or damage.*

23. Stagger the piston rings in grooves until end gaps are 120 degrees apart.

24. Lubricate the piston and rings with engine oil. Install a piston ring compressor around piston.

25. Orient the "Fly" mark and match marks on connecting rod towards the flywheel end of

crankshaft. Gently push the piston/connecting rod into bore — do not pound on piston.

26. Lubricate the crankshaft and connecting rod journal surfaces with engine oil. Install the connecting rod cap — make sure the match marks are aligned and the oil hole is towards camshaft.

27. Install the hex nuts and torque in increments as follows: New rod — 140 inch lbs.; Used/Reinstalled — 100 inch lbs.

CAUTION: *To prevent damage to connecting rod and engine, do not overtorque — loosen — and retorque the hex nuts on Posi-Lock connecting rods. Torque nuts, in increments, directly to the specified values.*

28. Rotate the crankshaft until piston is at top dead center in bore to protect dipper on connecting rod.

29. Install the gasket, oil pan, solenoid bracket, and hex cap screws to starter side of oil pan.

30. Install the handle bracket, plain washers, split lock washers and hex nuts to studs on carburetor side of oil pan.

31. Rotate the crankshaft until piston is at top dead center of compression stroke.

32. Install the valves and measure valve-to-tappet clearance using a flat feeler gauge.

NOTE: *Valve faces and seats must be lapped-in before checking/adjusting valve clearance.*

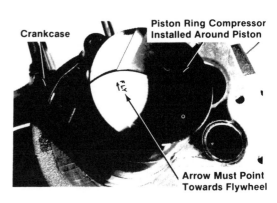

Installing pistons

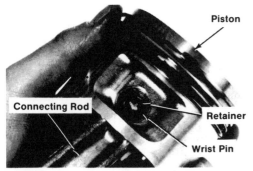

Installing piston to connecting rod (style "d" piston shown)

Installing connecting rod cap

Installing solenoid bracket and oil pan

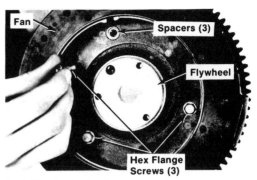

Installing fan to flywheel

33. Adjust valve-to-tappet clearance, as necessary. Intake Valve – 0.006-0.008 in.; Exhaust Valve – 0.017-0.019 in.

If clearance is too small, grind end of valve stems until correct clearance is obtained. Make sure stems are ground perfectly flat and smooth.

If clearance is too large, replace the valves and recheck clearance.

NOTE: *Large clearances can also be reduced by grinding the valves and/or valve seats. refer to the "Inspection And Repair/Reconditioning" section for valve specifications.*

34. Install the valve springs (close coils to top), intake valve spring retainer, exhaust valve rotator, and valves.

NOTE: *Some models use a valve rotator on both valves.*

35. Compress the springs using a valve spring compressor and install keepers.

36. Route the leads through hole in bearing plate. Install the stator and pan head screws.

CAUTION: *Damaging Crankshaft and Flywheel Could Cause Personal Injury!*

Using improper procedures to install the flywheel can crack or damage the crankshaft and/or flywheel. This not only causes extensive engine damage, but also is a serious

threat to the safety of persons nearby, since broken fragments can be thrown from the engine. Always observe and use the following precautions and procedures when installing the flywheel:

WARNING: *Before installing the flywheel, make sure the crankshaft taper and flywheel hub are clean, dry, and completely free of lubricants. The presence of lubricants can cause the flywheel to be overstressed and damaged when the cap screw is torqued to specification.*

Make sure square flywheel key is installed only in the flat area of keyway, not in the rounded area. The flywheel can become cracked or damaged if the key is installed in the rounded area of keyway.

Always use the flywheel strap wrench to hold flywheel when tightening flywheel fastener. Do not use any type of bar or wedge between the cooling fins or flywheel ring gear, as these parts could become cracked or damaged.

37. Install the spacers, fan and hex flange screws. Torque screws to 115 inch lbs.

38. Place the flywheel on crankshaft. Install the grass screen, and drive cup or rope start pulley as follows:

a. With Rope Start – Install rope pulley, plain washer, and hex nut (lubricate threads with oil). Hold Flywheel with strap wrench and torque hex nut to 85-90 ft. lbs. Install grass screen and grass screen retainer.

b. With Retractable Start – Install the grass screen to fan. Install the drive cup, plain washer, and hex nut (lubricate threads with oil). Hold the flywheel with strap wrench and torque hex nut to 85-90 ft. lbs. Install the grass screen to fan.

39. Install the module, plain washers, and hex cap screws. Move the module as far from flywheel/magnet as possible. Tighten the hex cap screws slightly.

40. Insert a 0.018 in. flat feeler gauge or shim stock between magnet and module. Loosen hex

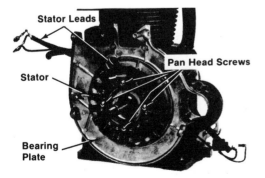

Installing stator

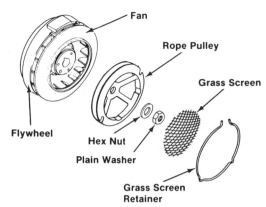

Installing flywheel, rope pulley, and grass screen—rope start models

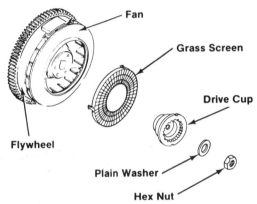

Installing flywheel, grass screen, and drive cup—retractable start models

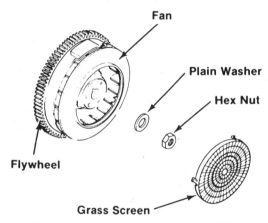

Installing flywheel and grass screen—electric start models

cap screws so magnet pulls module down. Tighten hex cap screws to 32 inch lbs. Remove feeler gauge or shim stock. Due to the pull of the magnet the bearing plate will flex slightly. The magnet-to-module air gap should be within the range of 0.012-0.016 in..

41. Rotate the flywheel back and forth; check to make sure magnet does not strike module. Check the gap with feeler gauge and readjust if necessary.

42. Install air baffle over module, Install the kill lead and high-tension lead into slots in baffle..

43. Install the gasket, cylinder head, bracket, plain washers, and hex cap screws.

44. Torque the hex cap screws (in increments) in the sequence shown to 15-20 ft. lbs.

45. Install the spark plug (.025 in. gap); torque to 18-22 ft. lbs.

46. Install the stud, gasket, breather plate, gasket, and seal. Make sure the small hole in breather plate is at the bottom.

47. Install the breather cover with filter, and pawlnut.

48. Install the blower housing, key switch panel (if so equipped), and self-tapping screws. Leave the screws slightly loose.

49. Install the side air baffle, self-tapping screw, plain washer, and hex cap screw. Leave the screws slightly loose.

50. Install the cylinder head baffle, plain washer, spark plug lead clip, hex cap screw, and self-tapping screw. Leave the screws slightly loose.

51. Tighten the screws securely when all pieces are in position.

Installing cylinder head and spark plug

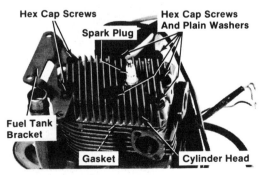

Installing air baffle to module

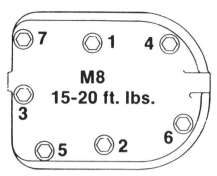

Cylinder head fastener torque sequence

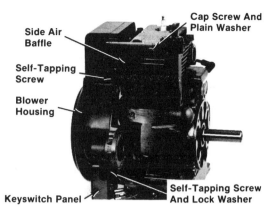

Installing blower housing, key switch panel, and side air baffle

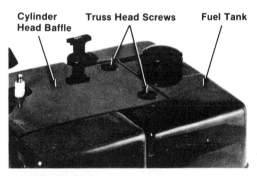

Installing fuel tank

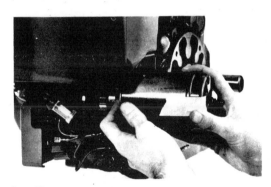

Installing starter

52. Install the bracket, split lock washers, and hex cap screws to crankcase.

53. Install the bracket, plain washers, and hex cap screws to fuel tank. Torque the hex cap screws to 90 inch lbs. maximum.

54. Install the fuel tank with bracket, truss head screws, and hex cap screws. Leave the screws loose until all pieces are in position. Torque the truss head screws to 90 inch lbs. maximum. Torque the hex cap screws to 70 inch lbs. maximum.

55. Install the fuel filter and fuel line to tank outlet.

56. Install the solenoid, screws, and pawlnuts to bracket. Install the leads to solenoid.

57. Remove the ¼-20 hex nuts and through bolts from electric starter.

WARNING: *Be sure to hold the commutator end cap and drive end against the starter frame to prevent the starter from becoming disassembled.*

58. Install the starter to bearing plate, and install the top through bolt. Leave the bolt slightly loose.

NOTE: *Route fuel line and wiring harness behind starter.*

59. Install the starter tail brace, self-tapping screws, plain washer, and bottom through bolt. Install the hex cap screws, plain washer, and pawlnut. Leave the screws slightly loose.

60. Tighten the starter through bolts and other hardware securely when all pieces are in position.

CAUTION: *Make sure the electric starter stud terminal is centered in the slot in tail brace. Electric arcing may occur if terminal is not centered or it touches the tail brace.*

Installing breather components

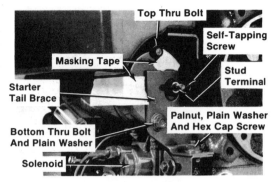

Installing starter and starter tail brace

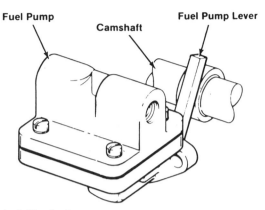

Installing fuel pump

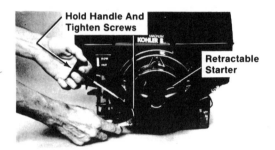

Installing retractable starter

70. Install the throttle linkage, gasket, carburetor, and slotted hex cap screws.

71. Remove the wing nut, plain washer, and choke control lever. Install choke linkage to choke control lever and carburetor choke lever. Reinstall choke control lever, plain washer, and wing nut.

72. Adjust the governor as instructed under "Governor Adjustment."

73. The governor cross shaft/governor arm must be adjusted every time the governor arm is loosened or removed from cross shaft.

61. Install the retractable starter and hex cap screws. Leave the screws slightly loose.

62. Pull the starter handle out 8-10 in. until pawls engage in the drive cup. Hold the handle in this position and tighten screws securely.

63. If the throttle and choke control lever assembly is equipped with a kill switch, install the kill lead from module to kill switch.

64. Install the throttle and choke control lever assembly to handle bracket and engine crankcase. Secure with the spacers, plain washers, hex cap screws, and hex cap screw.

65. Install the governor spring to throttle lever and governor arm. For proper engine operation, make sure the spring is installed in the correct position in governor arm.

66. Install the governor arm to cross shaft. Leave the pawlnut slightly loose as the governor arm and cross shaft will be adjusted after the carburetor and throttle linkage are installed.

67. Install the gasket, fuel pump, plain washers, and fillister head screws.

WARNING: *Make sure the fuel pump lever is positioned above the camshaft. Damage to the fuel pump, and subsequent severe damage could result if the lever is positioned below the canmshaft.*

68. Connect the fuel line (from tank) to fuel pump inlet fitting.

69. Install the fuel line and hose clamp.

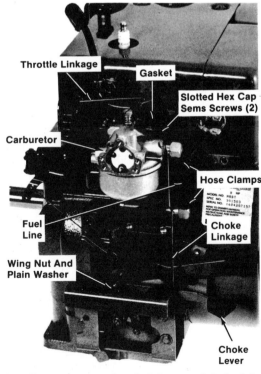

Installing carburetor, throttle linkage, and choke linkage

Governor arm/bushing clearance

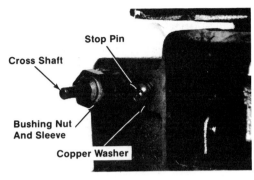

Installing governor gear and cross shaft

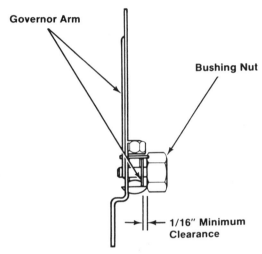

Governor arm/bushing clearance

a. Pull the governor arm away from the carburetor as far as it will go.

b. Grasp end of cross shaft with pliers and turn counterclockwise as far as it will go.

c. Torque the pawlnut on governor arm to 15 inch lbs.

NOTE: *Make sure there is at least $\frac{1}{16}$ in. clearance between governor arm and bushing in crankcase to prevent interference.*

74. Insert B+ lead into center position of connector. Install the stator leads/connector to rectifier-regulator.

75. Install the rectifier-regulator and hex cap scres.

76. Install the heat shield, gasket, muffler, and hex cap screws.

77. Install the breather hose, gasket, air cleaner base, and screws.

WARNING: *Make sure the breather hose seals tightly in air cleaner base and breather cover to prevent unfiltered air from entering engine.*

78. Install the seal, paper element, element cover, and element cover nut. Tighten nut to 50 inch lbs. torque.

79. If so equipped, install the foam precleaner (cleaned and oiled) over paper element.

80. Install air cleaner cover and wing nut. Tighten wing nut until it is snug. Do not overtighten.

PREPARE THE ENGINE FOR OPERATION

The engine is now completely reassembled. Before operating the engine, be sure to do the following:

● Make sure all hardware is tightened securely and oil drain plugs are installed.

● Fill the crankcase with the correct amount, weight, and type of oil.

● Fill the fuel tank with the proper type of gasoline and open fuel shut-off valve (if equipped).

● Adjust the carburetor main fuel needle, idle fuel needle, or idle speed adjusting screw as necessary. Refer to the "Fuel System And Governor" section.

● Make sure the maximum engine speed doe not exceed 3600 RPM. Adjust the high speed stop as necessary. Refer to the "Fuel System And Governor" section.

MODELS M10 and M12 ASSEMBLY

The following sequence is suggested for complete engine reassembly. This procedure assumes that all components are new or have been reconditioned, and all component subassembly work has been completed. This procedure may have to varied slightly to accommodate options or special equipment.

WARNING: *Make sure the engine is assembled using all specified torque values, tightening sequences, and clearances. Failure to observe specifications could cause severe engine wear or damage.*

1. Install the rear bearing into crankcase using the #4747 handle and appropriate bearing installer. (Refer to the "Special Tools" section).

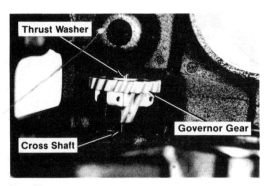

Installing governor gear and cross shaft

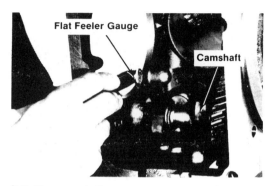

Installing camshaft

Make sure the bearing is bottomed fully, and is straight and true in bore.

2. Install the cross shaft, sleeve, and bushing nut. Torque bushing nut to 100-120 inch lb.

3. Install the thrust washer, governor gear, copper washer, and stop pin.

4. Install the intake valve tappet and exhaust valve tappet into crankcase. (Intake valve tappet towards bearing plate side; exhaust valve tappet towards PTO side of crankcase.).

5. Install the camshaft, one 0.010 in. shim spacer, and the camshaft pin (from bearing plate side). Do not drive the camshaft pin into its final position at this time.

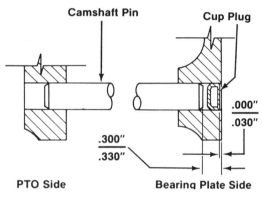

Installing camshaft pin and cup plug

Installing tappets

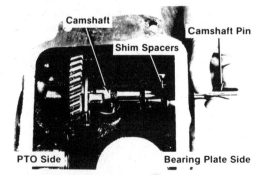

Measuring camshaft end play

6. Measure the camshaft end play between the spacer and crankcase boss using a flat feeler gauge. Recommended camshaft end play is 0.005-0.010 in.. Add or subtract 0.005 in. and/or 0.010 in. shim spacers as necessary to obtain the proper end play.

7. Drive the camshaft pin into the PTO side of crankcase until it is 0.300-0.330 in. from machined bearing plate gasket surface.

8. Apply Loctite® #290 (or equivalent) to cup plug. Install the cup plug into bore in bearing plate mounting surface. Plug should be FLUSH to 0.030 in. below mounting surface.

NOTE: *The balance gears must be timed to the crankshaft whenever the crankshaft is installed. Use a balance gear timing tool to simplify this procedure. If the balance gears must be timed without using the tool, do not install the lower balance gear (closest to oil pan) until after the crankshaft has been installed.*

9. On engines with balance gears: Install the ⅜ in. spacer, one 0.010 in. shim spacer, balance gear, one 0.020 in. shim spacer, and retaining ring (rounded edge towards balance gear).

Check end play with a flat feeler gauge. Recommended end play is 0.002-0.010 in.. If end play is not within range, install or remove 0.005

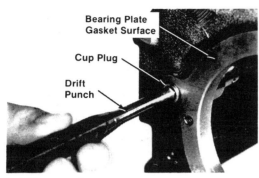

Installing cup plug

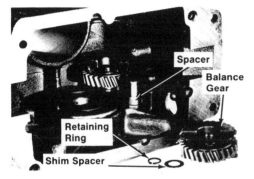

Installing balance gears

in. and 0.010 in. spacers, as necessary. Balance gear spacer kit, Kohler Part 47 755 01, contains enough ⅜ in., 0.005 in., 0.010 in., and 0.020 in. spacers to obtain correct end play for both balance gears.

10. On Engines Without Balance Gears:

a. Lubricate the crankshaft rear bearing surface. Insert the crankshaft through the rear bearing.

NOTE: *If the crankshaft and bearing plate have not been separated, position the fuel line and wiring harness between the bearing plate and crankcase before pressing the crankshaft all the way in.*

b. Align the primary timing mark on crankshaft with the timing mark on camshaft. Press the crankshaft into rear bearing. Make sure the camshaft and crankshaft gears mesh and that the timing marks remain aligned while pressing.

11. On Engines With Balance Gears:

METHOD 1 – WITH BALANCE GEAR TIMING TOOL

a. Align the primary timing marks of balance gears with the teeth on timing tool. Insert tool so it meshes with gears. Hold or clamp tool against oil pan gasket surface.

b. Lubricate the crankshaft rear bearing surface. Insert the PTO end of crankshaft through rear bearing. "Straddle" the prima-

ry and secondary timing marks on crankshaft over the rear bearing oil drain. Press the crankshaft into rear bearing until the crankgear is just above the camshaft gear but but not in mesh with it.

NOTE: *If the crankshaft and bearing plate have not been separated, position the fuel line and wiring harness between the bearing plate and crankcase before pressing the crankshaft all the way in.*

c. Remove the balance gear timing tool and align the primary timing mark on the crankshaft with the timing mark on the camshaft gear. Press the crankshaft all the way into the rear bearing. Make sure the camshaft and crankshaft gears mesh and that the timing marks align while pressing.

d. Check the timing of the crankshaft, camshaft, and balance gears:

• The primary timing mark on crankshaft should align with the secondary timing mark on lower balance gear.

• The primary timing mark on crankshaft should align with the timing mark on camshaft.

If the marks do not align, the timing is incorrect and must be corrected.

METHOD 2 – WITHOUT BALANCE GEAR TIMING TOOL

NOTE: *The lower balance gear should be installed after the crankshaft has been installed.*

a. Lubricate the crankshaft rear bearing surface. Insert the PTO end of crankshaft through rear bearing. Align the primary timing mark on crankshaft with the primary timing mark on upper balance gear. Press the crankshaft into rear bearing until the crankgear just starts to mesh (about ⅟₁₆ in.) with the center ring of balance gear teeth.

NOTE: *If the crankshaft and bearing plate have not been separated, position the fuel line and wiring harness between the bearing plate and crankcase before pressing the crankshaft all the way in.*

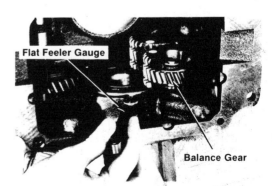

Measuring balance gear end play

Checking crankshaft and balance gear alignment

b. Align the primary timing mark on the crankshaft with the timing mark on the camshaft gear. Press the crankshaft all the way into the rear bearing. Make sure the camshaft and crankshaft gears mesh and that the timing marks align while pressing.

c. Position the crankshaft so it is about 15 degrees past BDC. Install ⅜ in. spacer, and one 0.010 in. shim spacer. Align the secondary timing mark on the lower balance gear with the secondary timing timing mark on the crankshaft. Install the lower balance gear on the stub shaft. If properly timed, the primary timing mark on the crankshaft will now be aligned with the secondary timing mark on the lower balance gear.

d. Install one (1) 0.020 in. shim spacer and retaining ring (rounded edge towards gear). Check end play of lower balance gear as instructed under "INSTALL BALANCE GEARS".

e. Check the timing of the crankshaft, camshaft, and balance gears:

• The primary mark on crankshaft should align with the primary timing mark on upper balance gear.

• The primary mark on crankshaft should align with the secondary timing mark on lower balance gear.

• The primary mark on crankshaft should align with the timing mark on camshaft.

If the marks do not align, the timing is incorrect and must be corrected.

12. Install the front bearing into the bearing plate using the #4747 handle and appropriate bearing installer. (Refer to the "Special Tools" Section). Make sure the bearing is bottomed fully, and straight and true in the bore.

13. Position the fuel line and wiring harness (if so equipped) to crankcase.

14. Adjust the fuel line and wiring harness to their final positions just before securing the bearing plate to the crankcase.

15. Install ⅜-16 studs into two of the bearing plate mounting holes. The studs ease locating

and assembly of shims, gasket, and bearing plate.

16. Lubricate the bearing surface of crankshaft and bearing. Install the gasket, two or three 0.005 in. shims (as required)*, and bearing plate over studs.

NOTE: *Crankshaft end play is determined by the thickness of the gasket and shims between crankcase and bearing plate. Check the end play after the bearing plate is installed.*

17. Install two hex cap screws and hand tighten. remove the locating studs, and install the remaining two hex cap screws and hand tighten.

18. Position the wiring harness and fuel line in their final positions as marked during disassembly.

19. Tighten the screws evenly, drawing bearing plate to crankcase. Torque screws to 35 ft. lbs.

20. Check crankshaft end play between the inner bearing race and shoulder of crankshaft using a flat feeler gauge. Recommended total end play is 0.003-0.020 in.. If measured end play is not within limits, remove the bearing plate and, remove or install shims as necessary.

21. Slide the appropriate seal sleeves over the crankshaft (refer to the "Special Tools" Section). Generously lubricate the lips of the oil seals with light grease. Slide the oil seals over the sleeves.

22. Use the #11795 handle and appropriate seal drivers to install the oil seals to the following depths:

• Front Oil Seal (Bearing Plate) − $\frac{1}{32}$ in.
• Rear Oil Seal (Crankcase PTO End) − ⅛ in.
• Tolerance on seal position − + $\frac{3}{64}$ in.; − $\frac{1}{64}$ in.

23a. With "Style A" Piston − Install wrist pin and retainers.

23b. With "Style C" Piston

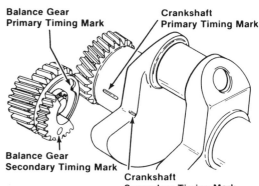

Balance Gear Primary Timing Mark   **Crankshaft Primary Timing Mark**

Balance Gear Secondary Timing Mark   **Crankshaft Secondary Timing Mark**

Timing marks on balance gear and crankshaft

WARNING: *Proper orientation of the piston to the connecting rod is extremely important. Improper orientation may cause extensive wear or damage.*

a. Orient piston and connecting rod so that the notch on piston and the match mark on connecting rod are facing the same direction.

b. Install wrist pin and retainers.

24. Stagger the piston rings in their grooves until end gaps are 120 degrees apart.

25. Lubricate the piston and rings with engine oil. Install the piston ring compressor around piston.

26. Orient the notch (on "Style C" piston) and match marks on connecting rod towards the flywheel end of crankshaft. Gently push the piston/connecting rod into bore — do not pound on piston.

27. Lubricate the crankshaft and connecting rod journal surfaces with engine oil. Install the connecting rod cap — make sure the match marks are aligned and the oil hole is towards the camshaft. Install hex nuts and torque in increments as follows: New rod — 260 inch lbs.; Used/Reinstalled Rod — 200 inch lbs.

WARNING: *To prevent damage to connecting rod and engine, do not overtorque — loosen — and retorque the hex nuts on Posi-Lock connecting rods. Torque nuts, in increments, directly to the specified value.*

28. Rotate the crankshaft until the piston is at top dead center in bore to protect the dipper on the connecting rod.

29. Install the gasket, oil pan, and hex cap screws. Tighten screws securely.

30. Rotate the crankshaft until piston is at top dead center of compression stroke.

31. Install the valves and measure the valve-to-tappet clearance using a flat feeler gauge. Valve-to-tappet cold clearance: Intake Valve — 0.008-0.010 in.; Exhaust valve — 0.017-0.019 in.

32. Adjust valve-to-tappet clearance, as necessary. Adjust valve-to-tappet clearance by turning the adjusting screw on tappets.

Adjusting valve-to-tappet clearance

33. Install the valve spring upper retainers, valve springs (close coils to top), intake valve spring lower retainer, exhaust valve rotator, and valves.

NOTE: *Some models use a valve rotator on both valves.*

34. Compress springs using a valve spring compressor and install keepers.

35. Route the leads through the hole in bearing plate. Install stator and pan head screws. Install stator lead clip and self-tapping screw.

36. insert stator leads into outer positions of connector body.

CAUTION: *Damaging Crankshaft and Flywheel Could Cause Personal Injury! Using improper procedures to install the flywheel can crack or damage the crankshaft and/or flywheel. This not only causes extensive engine damage, but also is a serious threat to the safety of persons nearby, since broken fragment could be thrown from the engine. Always observe and use the following precau-*

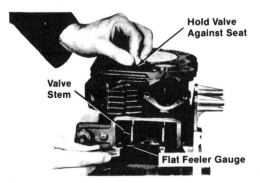

Measuring valve-to-tappet clearance

Hold Valve Against Seat

Valve Stem

Flat Feeler Gauge

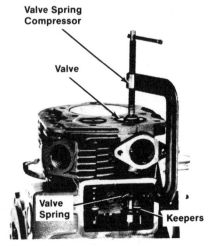

Installing valve keepers

Valve Spring Compressor

Valve

Valve Spring

Keepers

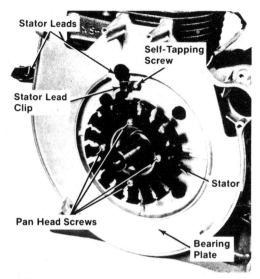

Installing stator

tions and procedures when installing the flywheel:

Before installing the flywheel, make sure the crankshaft taper and flywheel hub are clean, dry, and completely free of lubricants. the presence of lubricants can cause the flywheel to be overstressed and damaged when the cap screw is torqued to specification.

Always use a flywheel strap wrench to hold flywheel when tightening flywheel fastener. Do not use any type of bar or wedge between the cooling fins or flywheel ring gear, as these parts could become cracked or damaged.

37. install the spacers, fan and hex flange screws. Torque screws to 115 inch lbs.

38. Place the flywheel on the crankshaft. Install the grass screen, and drive cup or rope start pulley as follows:

a. With Rope Start – Install the nylon grass screen to the fan. Install the spacer, rope pulley, plain washer, and hex cap screw (lubricate threads with oil). Hold the flywheel with a strap wrench and torque hex cap screw to 40-45 ft. lbs. Install the grass screen to the fan.

b. With Retractable Start – Install the grass screen to the fan. Install the drive cup, plain washer, and hex cap screw (lubricate threads with oil). Hold the flywheel with a strap wrench and torque hex cap screw to 40-45 ft. lbs.

c. With Electric Start – Install the plain washer and hex cap screw (lubricate threads with oil). Hold the flywheel with a strap wrench and torque hex cap screw to 40-45 ft. lbs. Install the grass screen to the fan.

39. install the module, plain washers, and hex cap screws. Move the module as far from the flywheel/magnet as possible – tighten the hex cap screws slightly.

40. insert a 0.018 in. flat feeler gauge or shim stock betweem magnet and module. Loosen hex cap screws so magnet pulls module down. Tighten hex cap screws to 32 inch lbs. Remove feeler gauge or shim stock. Due to the pull of the magnet the bearing plate will flex slightly. The magnet to module air gap should be within the final range of 0.012-0.016 in..

41. Rotate the flywheel back and forth; check to make sure the magnet does not strike module. Check gap with a feeler gauge and readjust, if necessary.

42. Install the air baffle over the module. Install the kill lead and spark plug into the baffle.

43. Install the gasket, cylinder head, plain washers, hex spacer screw, lifting strap, and hex cap screws.

44. Torque the hex cap screws and hex spacer screw (in increments) in the sequence shown, to 25-30 ft. lbs.

45. Install the blower housing and two lower self-tapping screws. Leave the screws loose.

46. Install the cylinder head baffle and truss head screw. leave the screw loose.

47. Install the starter side air baffle, plain washer, hex cap screw, and self-tapping screw. Leave the screws loose.

48. Install the carburetor side air baffle, spark plug lead clip, plain washer, and hex cap screw. Leave the screw loose.

49. Tighten the screws securely when all pieces are in position.

50. Remove the ¼-20 hex nuts and through bolts from electric starter.

NOTE: *Be sure to hold the commutator end cap and drive end cap against the starter frame to prevent the starter from becoming disassembled.*

51. install the starter to bearing plate and install the through bolts. Tighten bottom through bolt hand tight, then tighten top through bolt securely.

NOTE: *Route fuel line and wiring harness behind starter.*

52. Remove the bottom through bolt after the top bolt has been tightened.

NOTE: *Install the starter tail brace, bottom through bolt, and starter solenoid after installing the fuel tank.*

53. If removed, install the isolation mounts to the fuel tank as follows:

a. Top of Tank: Install the threaded portion, ½ in. long, into the brass inserts in top of tank. Tighten isolation mounts hand tight.

b. Bottom of Tank: Install the threaded portion, ⅜ in. long, into the brass inserts in bottom of tank. Tighten isolation mounts hand tight.

54. Install bracket and pawlnuts to bottom isolation mounts. Tighten pawlnuts securely.

55. Insert the threaded portion of top isolation mounts through holes in cylinder head baffle. Install the plain washers and acorn nuts. Tighten the acorn nuts securely.

56. Install the plain washers and hex cap screws through bracket and into crankcase. Leave the screws slightly loose.

57. Adjust the position of the fuel tank until the top of tank is even with top of blower housing. Tighten hex cap screws securely.

58. Install the fuel filter and fuel line to tank outlet.

59. Install the starter tail brace, bottom through bolt, plain washer, and self-tapping screw. Tighten all screws securely when all pieces are in position.

60. Install the solenoid and self-tapping screws to fuel tank bracket. Install leads to solenoid and starter.

61. Install the gasket, oil fill/dipstick tube, fillister head screws, and dipstick.

62. Install the retractable starter and hex cap screws. Leave the screws slightly loose.

63. Pull the starter handle out 8-10 in. until the pawls engage in the drive cup. Hold the handle in this position and tighten screws securely.

64. Install the gasket, fuel pump, plain washers, and fillister head screws.
WARNING: *Make sure the fuel pump lever is positioned above the camshaft. Damage to the fuel pump, and subsequent severe engine damage could result if the lever is positioned below the camshaft. Torque the screws to 40-45 inch lbs.*

65. Connect the fuel line to fuel pump inlet fitting.

66. Install the stud, gasket, breather plate, reed, reed stop, seal, and filter.

67. Install the long leg of governor spring to throttle control lever.

68. Install the gasket, throttle and choke control assembly, gasket, cam gear cover, plain washer, hex cap screws, and self-tapping screw. Torque cam gear cover screws to 115 inch lbs. Install the spacer, plain washer, and hex cap screw.

69. Install the connector/wiring harness to back of key switch.

70. Install the governor spring to the governor arm. Install the governor arm to the cross shaft. Leave the pawlnut slightly loose as the governor arm and cross shaft will be adjusted after the carburetor and throttle linkage are installed.

71. Install the fuel line and hose clamps.

72. Install the gasket, carburetor, and slotted hex cap screws.

73. Install the throttle linkage into the nylon inserts in the governor arm and carburetor throttle lever.

74. Adjust the governor as instructed below.

75. Install the choke linkage to the carburetor choke lever, and then into the nylon insert in the choke control lever.

76. The governor cross shaft/governor arm must be adjusted every time the governor arm is loosened or removed from cross shaft.
   a. Pull the governor arm away from the carburetor as far as it will go.
   b. Grasp end of cross shaft with pliers and turn counterclockwise as far as it will go.
   c. Torque the pawlnut on governor arm to 15 inch lbs.
NOTE: *Make sure there is at least $1/16$ in. clearance between the governor arm and the upper-left cam gear cover fastener to prevent interference.*

77. Insert the B+ lead into the center position of connector. Install the stator leads/connector to the rectifier-regulator.

78. Install the rectifier-regulator and hex cap screws.

79. Install the threaded exhaust pipe and muffler.

80. Install the breather hose, gasket, air cleaner base, and screws.
WARNING: *Make sure that the breather hose seals tightly in the air cleaner base and the breather cover to prevent unfiltered air from entering the engine.*

81. Install the seal, paper element, element cover, and element cover nut. Torque the nut to 50 inch lbs.

82. If equipped, install the optional foam, precleaner (cleaned and oiled) over the paper element.

83. Install the air cleaner and wing nut. Tighten the wing nut until it is snug. Do not overtighten.

PREPARE THE ENGINE FOR OPERATION

The engine is now completely reassembled. Before operating the engine, be sure to do the following:
- Make sure all hardware is tightened securely and oil drain plugs are installed.
- Fill the crankcase with the correct amount, weight, and type of oil.
- Fill the fuel tank with the proper type of gasoline and open fuel shut-off valve (if equipped).
- Adjust the carburetor main fuel needle, idle fuel needle, or idle speed adjusting screw as necessary. Refer to the "Fuel System And Governor" section.
- Make sure the maximum engine speed does not exceed 3600 RPM. Adjust the high speed stop as necessary. Refer to the "Fuel System And Governor" section.

13

Tecumseh 4-Stroke
2 through 5 Hp

ENGINE IDENTIFICATION

Lauson 4 cycle engines are identified by a model number stamped on a nameplate. The nameplate is located on the crankcase of vertical shaft models and on the blower housing of horizontal shaft models.

A typical model number appears on the illustration showing the location of the nameplate for vertical crankshaft engines. This number is interpreted as follows:

- V — vertical shaft engine
- 60 — 6.0 horsepower
- 70360J — the specification number. The last three numbers (360) indicate that this particular engine is a variation on the basic model line.
- 2361J — serial number
- 2 — year of manufacture
- 361 — the calendar day of manufacture
- J — line and shift location at the factory.

MAINTENANCE

Air Cleaner Service

Service all the oil/foam polyurethane and oil bath air cleaner elements in the same manner as the Briggs and Stratton components. See Chapter Four.

The Tecumseh treated paper element type air cleaner consists of a pleated paper element encased in a metal housing and must be replaced as a unit. A flexible tubing and hose clamps connect the remotely mounted air filter to the carburetor.

Clean the element by lightly tapping it. Do not distort the case. When excessive carburetor adjustment or loss of power results, inspect the air filter to see if it is clogged. Replacing a severely restricted air filter should show an immediate performance improvement.

Check the oil level in the oil bath type air cleaners regularly to make sure the level is cor-

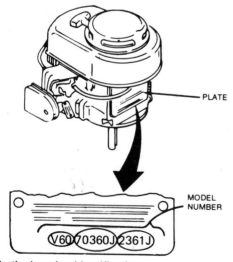

Vertical engine identification

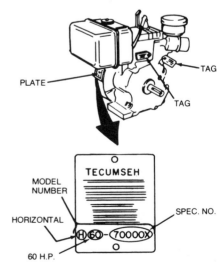

Horizontal engine identification

General Engine Specifications
Vertical Crankshaft Engines

Model	Bore & Stroke	Displacement	Horsepower
LAV25	2.3125 × 1.8438	7.75	2½
LAV30	2.3125 × 1.8438	7.75	3
TVS75	2.3125 × 1.8438	7.75	3
LV35	2.5000 × 1.8438	9.06	3½
LAV35	2.5000 × 1.8438	9.06	3½
TVS90	2.5000 × 1.8438	9.06	3½
LAV40	2.6250 × 1.9375	10.5	4
TVS105	2.6250 × 1.9375	10.5	4
V40, V40B	2.5000 × 2.2500	11.04	4
VH40	2.5000 × 2.2500	11.04	4
LAV50	2.812 × 1.9375	12.0	5
TVS120	2.812 × 1.9375	12.0	5
V50	2.625 × 2.2500	12.17	5
VH50	2.625 × 2.2500	12.17	5

General Engine Specifications
Horizontal Crankshaft Engines

Model	Bore & Stroke (in.)	Displacement (cu in.)	Horsepower
H25	2.3125 × 1.8438	7.75	2½
H30	2.3125 × 1.8438	7.75	3
H35	2.5000 × 1.8438	9.06	3½
H40	2.5000 × 2.2500	11.04	4
HH40	2.5000 × 2.2500	11.04	4
HS40	2.6250 × 1.9375	10.5	4
H50	2.6250 × 2.2500	12.17	5
HH50	2.6250 × 2.2500	12.17	5
HS50	2.8120 × 1.9375	12.0	5

rect. To add oil, unscrew the wingnut, pull off the filter element and add oil along the side of the filter until the level is correct. Use the same type and viscosity oil used in the engine.

If the filter is dirty, remove it and wash it in solvent. Also remove the filter bowl, drain the oil, and wash the filter in solvent. Refill the bowl with clean oil after putting it into position on the air horn.

A plain paper element is also used. It should be removed every 10 hours, or more often if the air is dusty. Tap or blow out the dirt from the inside with low pressure air. This type should be replaced at 50 hours. If clogged sooner, it may be washed in soap and water and rinsed by flushing from the inside until the water is clear. Blow dry with low pressure compressed air.

To service the KLEEN-AIRE system, remove

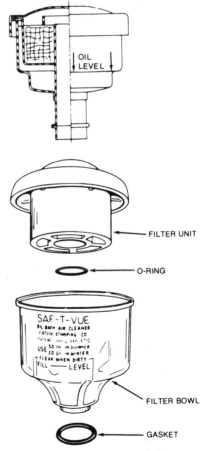

Exploded view of oil bath type air cleaner

the element, wash it in soap and mild detergent, pat dry, and then coat with oil. Squeeze the oil to distribute it evenly and remove the excess. Make sure all mounting surfaces are tight to prevent leakage.

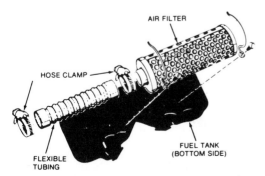

Treated paper element air cleaner (used on Craftsman engines)

Lubrication

OIL AND FUEL RECOMMENDATIONS

Use fresh (less than one month old) gasoline, of "Regular" grade. Unleaded fuel is preferred, but leaded fuel is acceptable.

Use oil having SG classification. Use these viscosities for aluminum engines:
- Summer − above 32°F (0°C): S.A.E. 30 (S.A.E. 10W-30 or 10W-40 are acceptable substitutes).
- Winter − Below 32°F (0°C): S.A.E. 5W-30 (S.A.E. 10W is an acceptable substitute). (Including Snow King Snow Blower Engines)
- Winter − Below 0°F (−18°C) only: S.A.E. 10W diluted with 10% kerosene is an acceptable substitute. (Including Snow King Snow Blower Engines)

Use these viscosities for cast iron engines:
- Summer − Above 32°F (0°C): S.A.E. 30
- Winter − Above 32°F (0°C): S.A.E. 10W

Tune-Up Specifications

The following basic specifications apply to all the engines covered in this section:
- Spark Plug Gap: 0.030 in. (0.76mm)
- Ignition Point Gap: 0.020 in. (0.50mm)
- Valve Clearance: 0.010 in. (0.25mm) for both intake and exhaust

For timing dimension, which varies from engine to engine, see the complete specifications at the rear of this section.

Spark Plug Service

Spark plugs should be removed, cleaned, and adjusted periodically. Check the electrode gap with a wire feeler gauge and adjust the gap. Replace the plugs if the electrodes are pitted and burned or the porcelain is cracked. Refer to the Tecumseh master parts manual for the correct replacement number. Apply a little graphite grease to the threads to prevent sticking. Be sure the cleaned plugs are free of all foreign material.

Breaker Points

ADJUSTMENT

1. Disconnect the fuel line from the carburetor.

2. Remove the mounting screws, fuel tank, and shroud to provide access to the flywheel.

3. Remove the flywheel with either a puller (over 3.5 hp) or by using a screwdriver to pry underneath the flywheel while tapping the top lightly with a soft hammer.

4. Remove the dust cover and gasket from the magneto and crank the engine over until the breaker points of the magneto are fully opened.

5. Check the condition of the points and replace them if they are burned or pitted.

6. Check the point gap with a feeler gauge. Adjust them, if necessary, as per the directions on the dust cover. Refer to the specifications chart at the end of this chapter for point gap.

REPLACEMENT

1. Gain access to the points and inspect them as described above. If the points are badly pitted, follow the remaining steps to replace them.

2. Remove the nuts that hold the electrical leads to the screw on the movable breaker point spring. Remove the movable breaker point from stud.

3. Remove the screw and stationary breaker point. Put a new stationary breaker point on the breaker plate; install the screw, but do not tighten. This point must be moved to make the proper air gap when the points are adjusted.

4. Position a new movable breaker point on the stud.

5. Adjust the breaker point gap with a flat feeler gauge and tighten the screw.

6. Check the new point contact pattern and remove all grease, finger-prints, and dirt from contact surfaces.

7. Adjust the timing as described below.

Ignition Timing

ADJUSTMENT

1. Remove the cylinder head bolts, and move the head (with gasket in place) so that the spark plug hole is centered over the piston.

2. Using a ruler (through the spark plug hole) or special plunger type tool, carefully turn the engine back and forth until the piston is at exactly Top Dead Center. Tighten the thumbscrew on the tool.

3. Find the timing dimension for your engine in the specifications at the rear of the manual. Then, back off the position of the piston until it is about halfway down in the bore. Lower the ruler (or loosen the thumbscrew and lower the plunger, if using the special tool) exactly the required amount (the amount of the timing dimension). Then, hold the ruler in place (or tighten the special tool thumbscrew) and, finally, carefully rotate the engine forward until the piston just touches the ruler or tool plunger.

4. Install a timing light or place a very thin piece of cellophane between the contact points. Loosen and rotate the stator just until the timing light shows a change in current flow or the cellophane pulls out of contact gap easily. Then, tighten stator bolts to specified torque.

5. Install the leads, point cover, flywheel, and shrouding.

SOLID STATE IGNITION SYSTEM CHECKOUT

The only on-engine check which can be made to determine whether the ignition system is working, is to separate the high tension lead from the spark plug and check for spark. If there is a spark, then the unit is all right and the spark plug should be replaced. No spark indicates that some other part needs replacing.

Check the individual components as follows:

• High Tension Lead: Inspect for cracks or indications of arcing. Replace the transformer if the condition of the lead is questionable.

• Low Tension Leads: Check all leads for shorts. Check the ignition cut-off lead to see that the unit is not grounded. Repair the leads, if possible, or replace them.

• Pulse Transformer: Replace and test for spark.

• Magneto: Replace and test for spark. Time the magneto by turning it counterclockwise as far as it will go and then tighten the retaining screws.

• Flywheel: Check the magnets for strength. With the flywheel off the engine, it should attract a screwdriver that is held 1 in. (25mm) from the magnetic surface on the inside of the flywheel. Be sure that the key locks the flywheel to the crankshaft.

Carburetor Mixture Adjustments

1. If the carburetor has been overhauled, or the engine won't start, make initial mixture screw adjustments as specified in the chart.

2. Start the engine and allow it to warm up to normal running temperature. With the engine running at maximum recommended rpm, loosen the main adjustment screw until engine rpm drops off, then tighten the screw until the

engine starts to cut out. Note the number of turns from one extreme to the other. Loosen the screw to a point midway between the extremes.

NOTE: *Some carburetors have fixed jets. If there is no main adjusting screw and receptacle, no adjustment is needed.*

3. After the main system is adjusted, move the speed control lever to the idle position and follow the same procedure for adjusting the idle system.

4. Test the engine by running it under a normal load. The engine should respond to load pickup immediately. An engine that "dies" is too lean. An engine which ran roughly before picking up the load is adjusted too rich.

Governor

ADJUSTMENT

Air Vane Type

1. Operate the engine with the governor adjusting lever or panel control set to the highest possible speed position and check the speed. If the speed is not within the recommended limits, the governed speed should be adjusted.

2. Loosen the locknut on the high speed limit adjusting screw and turn the adjusting screw out to increase the top engine speed.

Mechanical Type

1. Set the control lever to the idle position so that no spring tension affects the adjustment.

2. Loosen the screw so that the governor lever is loose in the clamp.

Chart of Initial Carburetor Adjustments

Adjustment	For Engines Built Prior to 1977	For Engines Built After 1977
Main Adjustment	V50-60-1¼ H50-60-1¼	Same
Idle Adjustment	V50-60-70-1 Turn H50-60-70-1 Turn	Same
Idle Speed (Top of Carburetor) Regulating screw	Back out screw, then turn in until screw just touches throttle lever and continue 1 turn more (if idle RPM is given set final idle speed with a tachometer)	

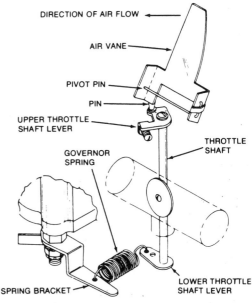

Schematic of the operation of an air vane governor

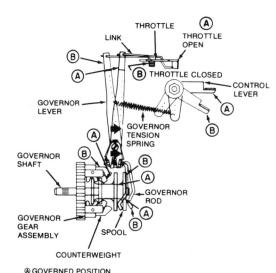

A GOVERNED POSITION
B NON-GOVERNED POSITION
◆ DIRECTION OF ADJUSTMENT—THIS SCHEMATIC

Schematic of mechanical governor operation

3. Rotate both the lever and the clamp to move the throttle to the full open position (away from the idle speed regulating screw).

4. Tighten the screw when no end-play exists in the direction of open throttle.

5. Move the throttle lever to the full speed setting and check to see that the control linkage opens the throttle.

Compression Check

1. Run the engine until warm to lubricate and seal the cylinder.

2. Remove the spark plug and install a compression gauge. Turn the engine over with the pull starter or electric starter.

3. Compression on new engines is 80 psi. If the reading is below 60 psi., repeat the test after removing the gauge and squirting about a teaspoonful of engine oil through the spark plug hole. If the compression improves temporarily following this, the problem is probably with the cylinder, piston, and rings. Otherwise, the valves require service.

FUEL SYSTEM

Carburetor

NOTE: *Four-cycle Tecumseh engines use float or diaphragm type carburetors.*

REMOVAL AND INSTALLATION

1. Drain the fuel tank. Remove the air cleaner and disconnect the carburetor fuel lines.

2. If necessary, remove any shrouding or control panels to provide access to carburetor.

3. Disconnect the choke or throttle control wires at the carburetor.

4. Remove the cap screws, or nuts and lockwashers that hold the carburetor to the engine; remove the carburetor.

5. Secure the carburetor on to engine.

6. Install the shrouding or control panels. Connect the choke and throttle control wires.

7. Position the control panel to carburetor. Connect the carburetor fuel lines.

8. Install the air cleaner.

9. Adjust the carburetor as described above.

GENERAL OVERHAUL INSTRUCTIONS

1. Carefully disassemble the carburetor removing all non-metallic parts, i.e.; gaskets, viton seats and needles, O-rings, fuel pump valves, etc.

NOTE: *Nylon check balls used in some diaphragm carburetor models may or may not be serviceable. Check to be sure of serviceability before attempting removal.*

2. Clean all metallic parts with solvent.

NOTE: *Nylon can be damaged if subjected to harsh cleaners for prolonged periods.*

3. The large O-rings sealing the fuel bowl to the carburetor body must be in good condition to prevent leakage. If the O-ring leaks, interfering with the atmospheric pressure in the float bowl, the engine will run rich. Foreign material can enter through the leaking area and cause blocking of the metering orifices. This O-ring should be replaced after the carburetor has been disassembled for repair. Lubricate the new O-ring with a small amount of oil to allow the fuel bowl to slide onto the O-ring properly. Hold the carburetor body in an inverted position and place the O-ring on the carburetor body and then position the fuel bowl.

4. The small O-rings used on the carburetor

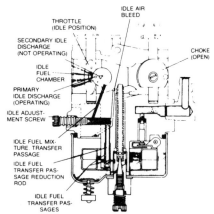

The idle operation of a float feed carburetor. The throttle plate closes, restricting the flow of fuel and air, forcing the engine to run on a reduced volume of fuel and air.

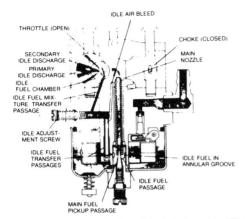

The choke position on a float feed carburetor. The closed choke plate restricts air, creating a richened mixture by drawing in a greater proportion of fuel.

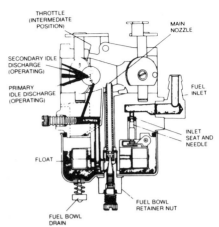

The intermediate operation of a float feed carburetor. The throttle plate "cracks" open to reduce the restriction and the engine runs on an increased volume of fuel and air.

adjustment screws must be in good condition or a leak will develop and cause improper adjustment of carburetor.

5. Check all adjusting screws for wear. The illustration shows a worn screw and a good screw. Replace screws that are worn.

6. Check the carburetor inlet needle and seat for wear, scoring, or other damage. Replace defective parts.

7. Check the carburetor float for dents, leaks, worn hinge or other damage.

8. Check the carburetor body for cracks, clogged passages, and worn bushings. Clean clogged air passages with clean, dry compressed air.

9. Check the diaphragms on diaphragm carburetors for cracks, punctures, distortion, or deterioration.

10. Check all shafts and pivot pins for wear on the bearing surfaces, distortion, or other damage.

NOTE: *Each time a carburetor is disassembled, it is good practice to install a repair kit.*

11. Where there is excessive vibration, a damper spring may be used to assist in holding the float against the inlet needle thus minimizing the flooding condition. Two types of springs are available; the float shaft (hinge pin) type and the inlet needle mounted type.

12. Float shaft spring positioning:

a. The spring is slipped over the shaft.

b. The rectangular shaped spring end is hooked onto the float tab.

c. The shorter angled spring end is placed onto the float bowl gasket support.

13. Note that on late model carburetors, the spring clip fastened to the inlet needle has been revised to provide a damping effect. The clip fastens to the needle and is hooked over the float tab.

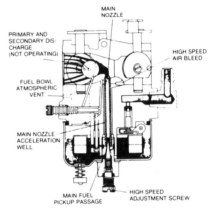

FUEL ■■
AIR
MIXTURE ■■

The high speed operation of a float feed carburetor. The air venturi replaces the throttle plate as the restricting device and the engine runs on its greatest volume of fuel and air.

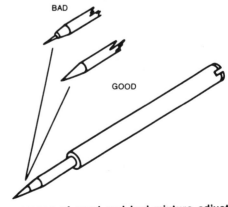

Appearance of good and bad mixture adjusting screws

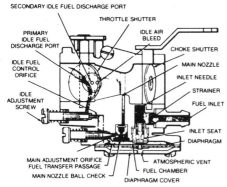

The choke position of the diaphragm carburetor. The closed choke plate restricts the amount of air, creating a richened mixture by drawing in a greater proportion of fuel.

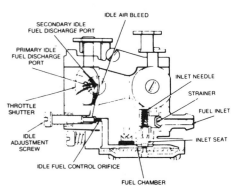

The intermediate operation of a diaphragm carburetor. The throttle plate "cracks" to decrease the restriction and the engine runs on an increased volume of fuel and air.

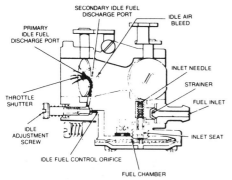

The idling operation of a diaphragm carburetor. The throttle plate closes, restricting the flow of fuel and air, forcing the engine to run on a reduced volume of fuel and air.

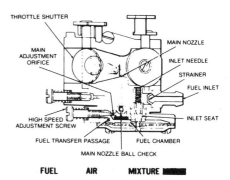

The high speed operation of a diaphragm carburetor. The air ventui replaces the throttle plate as the restricting device and the engine runs on its greatest volume of fuel and air.

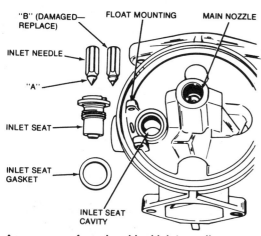

Appearance of good and bad inlet needles

FLOAT FEED CARBURETOR

Throttle

1. Examine the throttle lever and plate prior to disassembly. Replace any worn parts.

2. Remove the screw in the center of the throttle plate and pull out the throttle shaft lever assembly.

3. When reassembling, it is important that the lines on the throttle plate are facing out when in the closed position. Position the throttle plates with the two lines at 12 and 3 o'clock. The throttle shaft must be held in tight to the bottom bearing to prevent the throttle plate from riding on the throttle bore of the body which would cause excessive throttle plate wear and governor hunting.

Choke

Examine the choke lever and shaft at the bearing points and holes into which the linkage is fastened and replace any worn parts. The choke plate is inserted into the air horn of the carburetor in such a way that the flat surface of the choke is toward the fuel bowl.

Idle Adjusting Screw

Remove the idle screw from the carburetor body and examine the point for damage to the seating surface on the taper. If damaged, replace the idle adjusting needle. Tension is main-

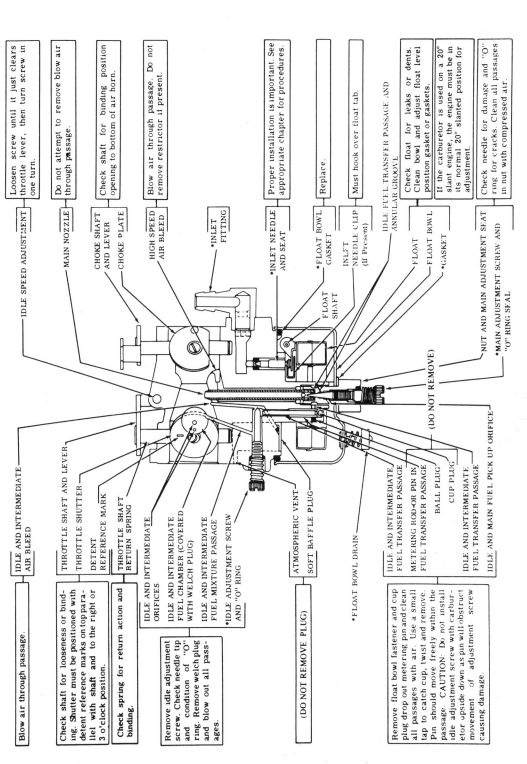

Service hints for float feed carburetors

Blow air through passage.

Check shaft for looseness or binding. Shutter must be positioned with detent reference marks on top parallel with shaft and to the right or 3 o'clock position.

Check spring for return action and binding.

Remove idle adjustment screw. Check needle tip and condition of "O" ring. Remove welch plug and blow out all passages.

(DO NOT REMOVE PLUG)

Remove float bowl fastener and cup plug drop out metering pin and clean all passages with air. Use a small tap to catch cup, twist and remove. Pin should move freely within the passage. CAUTION: Do not install idle adjustment screw with carburetor upside down as pin will obstruct movement of adjustment screw causing damage.

IDLE AND INTERMEDIATE AIR BLEED

THROTTLE SHAFT AND LEVER

THROTTLE SHUTTER

DETENT REFERENCE MARK

THROTTLE SHAFT RETURN SPRING

IDLE AND INTERMEDIATE ORIFICES

IDLE AND INTERMEDIATE FUEL CHAMBER (COVERED WITH WELCH PLUG)

IDLE AND INTERMEDIATE FUEL MIXTURE PASSAGE

*IDLE ADJUSTMENT SCREW AND "O" RING

ATMOSPHERIC VENT

SOFT BAFFLE PLUG

*FLOAT BOWL DRAIN

IDLE AND INTERMEDIATE FUEL TRANSFER PASSAGE

METERING ROD-OR PIN IN FUEL TRANSFER PASSAGE

BALL PLUG

CUP PLUG

IDLE AND INTERMEDIATE FUEL TRANSFER PASSAGE

IDLE AND MAIN FUEL PICK UP ORIFICE

(DO NOT REMOVE)

Loosen screw until it just clears throttle lever, then turn screw in one turn.

Do not attempt to remove blow air through passage.

Check shaft for binding position opening to bottom of air horn.

Blow air through passage. Do not remove restrictor if present.

IDLE SPEED ADJUSTMENT

MAIN NOZZLE

CHOKE SHAFT AND LEVER

CHOKE PLATE

HIGH SPEED AIR BLEED

*INLET FITTING

*INLET NEEDLE AND SEAT

FLOAT SHAFT

*FLOAT BOWL GASKET

INLET NEEDLE CLIP (If Present)

IDLE FUEL TRANSFER PASSAGE AND ANNULAR GROOVE

FLOAT

FLOAT BOWL

*GASKET

NUT AND MAIN ADJUSTMENT SEAT

*MAIN ADJUSTMENT SCREW AND "O" RING SEAL

Proper installation is important. See appropriate chapter for procedures.

Replace.

Must hook over float tab.

Check float for leaks or dents. Clean bowl and adjust float level position gasket or gaskets.

If the carburetor is used on a 20° slant engine, the engine must be in its normal 20° slanted position for adjustment.

Check needle for damage and "O" ring for cracks. Clean all passages in nut with compressed air.

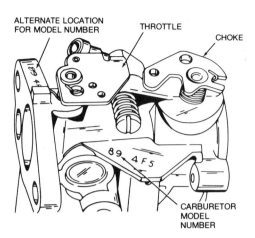

Float feed carburetor identification number

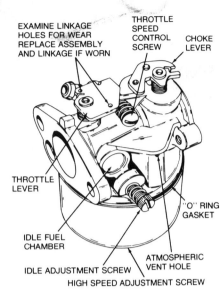

External view of a Tecumseh float type carburetor

tained on the screw with a coil spring and sealed with an O-ring. Examine and replace the O-ring if it is worn or damaged.

High Speed Adjusting Jet

Remove the screw and examine the taper. If the taper is damaged at the area where it seats, replace the screw and fuel bowl retainer nut as an assembly.

The fuel bowl retainer nut contains the seat for the screw. Examine the sealing O-ring on the high speed adjusting screw. Replace the O-ring if it indicates wear or cuts. During the reassembly of the high speed adjusting screw, position the coil spring on the adjusting screw, followed by the small brass washer and the O-ring seal.

Fuel Bowl

To remove the fuel bowl, remove the retaining nut and fiber washer. Replace the nut if it is cracked or worn.

The retaining nut contains the transfer passage through which fuel is delivered to the high speed and idle fuel system of the carburetor. It is the large hole next to the hex nut end of the fitting. If a problem occurs with the idle system of the carburetor, examine the small fuel passage in the annular groove in the retaining nut. This passage must be clean for the proper transfer of fuel into the idle metering system.

The fuel bowl should be examined for rust and dirt. Thoroughly clean it before installing it. If it is impossible to properly clean the fuel bowl, replace it.

Check the drain valve for leakage. Replace the rubber gasket on the inside of the drain valve if it leaks.

Examine the large O-ring that seals the fuel bowl to the carburetor body. If it is worn or

cracked, replace it with a new one, making sure the same type is used (square or round).

Float

1. Remove the float from the carburetor body by pulling out the float axle with a pair of needle nose pliers. The inlet needle will be lifted off the seat because it is attached to the float with an anchoring clip.

2. Examine the float for damage and holes. Check the float hinge for wear and replace it if worn.

3. The float level is checked by positioning a #4 drill bit across the rim between the center leg and the unmachined surface of the index pad, parallel to the float axle pin. If the index pad is machined, the float setting should be made with a #9 drill bit.

4. Remove the float to make an adjustment. Bend the tab on the float hinge to correct the float setting.

NOTE: *Direct compressed air in the opposite*

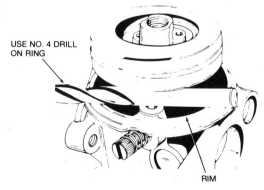

Adjusting the float level

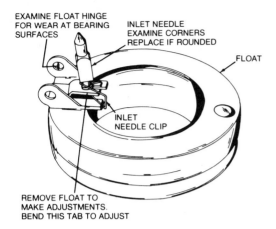

EXAMINE FLOAT HINGE FOR WEAR AT BEARING SURFACES

INLET NEEDLE EXAMINE CORNERS REPLACE IF ROUNDED

FLOAT

INLET NEEDLE CLIP

REMOVE FLOAT TO MAKE ADJUSTMENTS. BEND THIS TAB TO ADJUST

Float, inlet needle, and clip

direction of normal flow of air or fuel (reverse taper) to dislodge foreign matter.

Inlet Needle and Seat

1. The inlet needle sits on a rubber seat in the carburetor body instead of the usual metal fitting.

2. Remove it, place a few drops of heavy engine oil on the seat, and pry it out with a short piece of hooked wire.

3. The grooved side of the seat is inserted first. Lubricate the cavity with oil and use a flat faced punch to press the inlet seat into place.

4. Examine the inlet needle for wear and rounding off of the corners. If this condition does exist, replace the inlet needle.

Fuel Inlet Fitting

1. The inlet fitting is removed by twisting and pulling at the same time.

2. Use sealer when reinstalling the fitting. Insert the tip of the fitting into the carburetor body. Press the fitting in until the shoulder contacts the carburetor. Only use inlet fittings without screens.

Carburetor Body

1. Check the carburetor body for wear and damage.

2. If excessive dirt has accumulated in the atmospheric vent cavity, try cleaning it with carburetor solvent or compressed air. Remove the welch plug only as a last resort.

NOTE: *The carburetor body contains a pressed-in main nozzle tube at a specific depth and position within the venturi. Do not attempt to remove the main nozzle. Any change in nozzle positioning will adversely affect the metering quality and will require carburetor replacement.*

3. Clean the accelerating well around the main nozzle with compressed air and carburetor cleaning solvents.

4. The carburetor body contains two cup plugs, neither of which should be removed. A cup plug located near the inlet seat cavity, high up on the carburetor body, seals off the idle bleed. This is a straight passage drilled into the carburetor throat. Do not remove this plug. Another cup plug is located in the base where the fuel bowl nut seals the idle fuel passage. Do not remove this plug or the metering rod.

5. A small ball plug located on the side of the idle fuel passage seals this passage. Do not remove this ball plug.

6. The welch plug on the side of the carburetor body, just above the idle adjusting screw, seals the idle fuel chamber. This plug can be removed for cleaning of the idle fuel mixture passage and the primary and secondary idle fuel discharge ports. Do not use any tools that might change the size of the discharge ports, such as wire or pins.

Resilient Tip Needle

Replace the inlet needle. Do not attempt to remove or replace the seat in the carburetor body.

Viton Seat

Using a 10–24 or 10–32 tap, turn the tap into the brass seat fitting until it grasps the seat firmly. Clamp the tap shank into a vise and tap the carburetor body with a soft hammer until the seat slides out of the body.

To replace the viton seat, position the replacement over the receptical with the soft rubber like seat toward the body. Use a flat punch and a small hammer to drive the seat into the body until it bottoms on the shoulder.

TECUMSEH AUTOMATIC NON-ADJUSTABLE FLOAT FEED CARBURETOR

This carburetor has neither a choke plate nor idle and main mixture adjusting screws. There is no running adjustment. The float adjustment

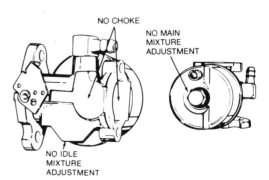

NO CHOKE

NO MAIN MIXTURE ADJUSTMENT

NO IDLE MIXTURE ADJUSTMENT

Auto-Magic carburetor

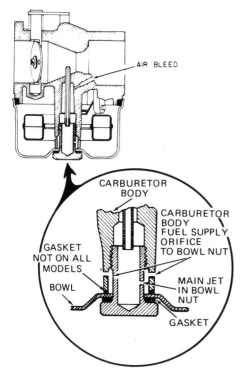

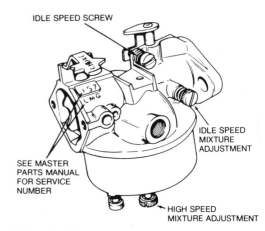

Walbro float feed carburetor

Variation on non-adjustable float feed carburetor

is the standard Tecumseh float setting of 0.210 in. (5.3mm).

Cleaning

Remove all non-metallic parts and clean them using a procedure similar to that for the other carburetors. Never use wires through any of the drilled holes. Do not remove the baffling welch plug unless it is certain there is a blockage under the plug. There are no blind passageways in this carburetor.

Some engines use a variation on the Automatic Nonadjustable carburetor which has a different bowl hold-on nut and main jet orifices. There are two main jet orifices and a deeper fuel reserve cavity, but service procedures are the same.

WALBRO AND TILLOTSON FLOAT FEED CARBURETORS

Procedures are similar to those for the Tecumseh float carburetor with the exceptions noted below.

Main Nozzle

The main nozzle in Wallbro carburetors is cross drilled after it is installed in the carburetor. Once removed, it cannot be reinstalled, since it is impossible to properly realign the cross drilled holes. Grooved service replacement main nozzles. are available which allow alignment of these holes.

Float Shaft Spring

Carefully position the float shaft spring on models so equipped. The spring dampens float action when properly assembled. Use needlenosed pliers to hook the end of the spring over the float hinge and then insert the pin as far as possible before lifting the spring from the hinge into position. Leaving the spring out or improper installation will cause unbalanced float action and result in a touchy adjustment.

Float Adjustment

1. To check the float adjustment, invert the assembled float carburetor body. Check the clearance between the body and the float, opposite the hinge. Clearance should be $\frac{1}{8}$ in. $\pm$ $\frac{1}{64}$ in. (3mm $\pm$ 0.4mm).

2. To adjust the float level, remove the float shaft and float. Bend the lip of the float tang to correct the measurement.

3. Assemble the parts and recheck the adjustment.

TILLOTSON E FLOAT FEED TYPE CARBURETOR

The following adjustments are different for this carburetor.

Running Adjustment

1. Start the engine and allow it to warm up to operating temperatures. Make sure the choke is fully opened after the engine is warmed up.

2. Run the engine at a constant speed while slowly turning the main adjustment screw in until the engine begins to lose speed; then slowly back it out about $\frac{1}{8}$–$\frac{1}{4}$ of a turn until maximum speed and power is obtained (4000 rpm). This is the correct power adjustment.

3. Close the throttle and cause the engine to idle slightly faster than normal by turning the idle speed regulating screw in. Then turn the

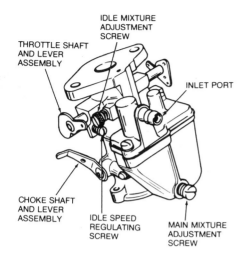

Tillotson Model E float carburetor

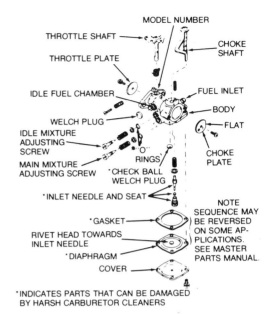

*INDICATES PARTS THAT CAN BE DAMAGED BY HARSH CARBURETOR CLEANERS

Exploded view of a Tecumseh diaphragm carburetor

idle adjustment speed screw in until the engine begins to lose speed; then turn it back ¼–½ of a turn until the engine idles smoothly. Adjust the idle speed regulating screw until the desired idling speed is acquired.

4. Alternately open and close the throttle a few times for an acceleration test. If stalling occurs at idle speeds, repeat the adjustment procedures to get the proper idle speed.

Float Level Adjustment

1. Remove the carburetor float bowl cover and float mechanism assembly.

2. Remove the float bowl cover gasket and, with the complete assembly in an upside down position and the float lever tang resting on the seated inlet needle, a measurement of $1\frac{5}{64}$ in. (27.4mm) should be maintained from the free end flat rim, or edge of the cover, to the toe of the float. Measurement can be checked with a standard straight rule or depth gauge.

3. If it is necessary to raise or lower the float lever setting, remove the float lever pin and the float, then carefully bend the float lever tang up or down as required to obtain the correct measurement.

DIAPHRAGM CARBURETORS

Diaphragm carburetors have a rubber-like diaphragm that is exposed to crankcase pressure on one side and to atmospheric pressure on the other side. As the crakcase pressure decreases, the diaphragm moves against the inlet needle allowing the inlet needle to move from its seat which permits fuel to flow through the inlet valve to maintain the correct fuel level in the fuel chamber.

An advantage of this type of system over the float system, is that the engine can be operated in any position.

NOTE: *In rebuilding, use carburetor cleaner* *only on metal parts, except for the main nozzle in the main body.*

Throttle Plate

Install the throttle plate with the short line that is stamped in the plate toward the top of the carburetor, parallel with the throttle shaft, and facing out when the throttle is closed.

Choke Plate

Install the choke plate with the flat side of the choke toward the fuel inlet side of the carburetor. The mark faces in and is parallel to the choke shaft.

Idle Mixture Adjustment Screw

There is a neoprene O-ring on the needle. Never soak the O-ring in carburetor solvent. Idle and main mixture screws vary in size and design, so make sure that you have the correct replacement.

Idle Fuel Chamber

The welch plug can be removed if the carburetor is extremely dirty.

Diaphragms

Diaphragms are serviced and replaced by removing the four retaining screws from the cover. With the cover removed, the diaphragm and gasket may be serviced. Never soak the diaphragm in carburetor solvent. Replace the diaphragm if it is cracked or torn. Be sure there are no wrinkles in the diaphragm when it is replaced. The diaphragm rivet head is always placed facing the inlet needle valve.

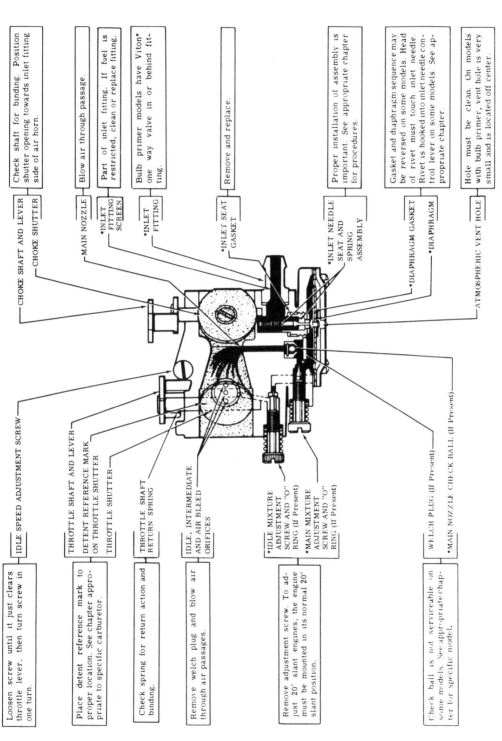

CHOKE SHAFT AND LEVER

Check shaft for binding. Position shutter opening towards inlet fitting side of air horn.

CHOKE SHUTTER

MAIN NOZZLE

Blow air through passage.

*INLET FITTING SCREEN

Part of inlet fitting. If fuel is restricted, clean or replace fitting.

*INLET FITTING

Bulb primer models have Viton* one way valve in or behind fitting.

*INLET SEAT GASKET

Remove and replace.

*INLET NEEDLE SEAT AND SPRING ASSEMBLY

Proper installation of assembly is important. See appropriate chapter for procedures.

*DIAPHRAGM GASKET

*DIAPHRAGM

Gasket and diaphragm sequence may be reversed on some models. Head of rivet must touch inlet needle. Rivet is hooked into inlet needle control lever on some models. See appropriate chapter.

ATMOSPHERIC VENT HOLE

Hole must be clean. On models with bulb primer, vent hole is very small and is located off center.

IDLE SPEED ADJUSTMENT SCREW

Loosen screw until it just clears throttle lever, then turn screw in one turn.

THROTTLE SHAFT AND LEVER

Place detent reference mark to proper location. See chapter appropriate to specific carburetor.

DETENT REFERENCE MARK ON THROTTLE SHUTTER

THROTTLE SHUTTER

THROTTLE SHAFT RETURN SPRING

Check spring for return action and binding.

IDLE, INTERMEDIATE AND AIR BLEED ORIFICES

Remove welch plug and blow air through air passages.

*IDLE MIXTURE ADJUSTMENT SCREW AND "O" RING (If Present)

*MAIN MIXTURE ADJUSTMENT SCREW AND "O" RING (If Present)

Remove adjustment screw. To adjust 20° slant engines, the engine must be mounted in its normal 20° slant position.

WELCH PLUG (If Present)

Check ball is not serviceable on some models. See appropriate chapter for specific model.

*MAIN NOZZLE CHECK BALL (If Present)

* NON METALLIC ITEMS - CAN BE DAMAGED BY HARSH CARBURETOR CLEANERS

Service hints for the diaphragm carburetors

Inlet Needle and Seat

The inlet seat is removed by using either a slotted screwdriver (early type) or a $9/32$ in. socket. The inlet needle is spring loaded, so be careful when removing it.

Fuel Inlet Fitting

All of the diaphragm carburetors have an integral strainer in the inlet fitting. To clean it, either reverse flush it or use compressed air after removing the inlet needle and seat. If the strainer is lacquered or otherwise unable to be cleaned, replace the fitting.

CRAFTSMAN FUEL SYSTEMS

Changes In Late Model Carburetors

The newest Craftsman carburetors incorporate the following changes:

a. The cable form of control is replaced by a control knob.

b. The fuel pickup is longer and has a collar machined into it which must be installed tight against the carburetor body.

c. The fuel pickup screen is pressed onto the ends of the fill tubes on both models, but the measured depth has changed.

d. The cross-drilled passages have been eliminated, as has the O-ring on the body. There are no cup plugs.

e. The fuel tank and reservoir tube have been revised-the reservoir tube being larger.

DISASSEMBLY AND SERVICE

1. Remove the air cleaner assembly and remove the four screws on the top of the carburetor body to separate the fuel tank from the carburetor.

2. Remove the O-ring from between the carburetor and the fuel tank. Examine it for cracks and damage and replace it if necessary.

3. Carefully remove the reservoir tube from the fuel tank. Observe the end of the tube that rested on the bottom of the fuel tank. It should be slotted.

4. Remove the control valve by turning the valve clockwise until the flange is clear of the retaining boss. Pull the valve straight out and examine the O-ring seal for damage or wear. If possible, use a new O-ring when reassembling.

5. Examine the fuel pick up tube. There are no valves or ball checks that may become inoperative. These parts can normally be cleaned with carburetor solvent. If it is found that the passage cannot be cleared, the fuel pick up tubes can be replaced. Carefully remove the old ones so as not to enlarge the opening in the carburetor body. If the pickup tube and screen must be replaced, follow the directions shown

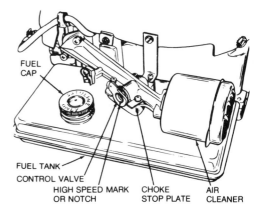

FUEL CAP

FUEL TANK
CONTROL VALVE
HIGH SPEED MARK
OR NOTCH
CHOKE
STOP PLATE
AIR
CLEANER

Craftsman fuel tank mounted carburetor

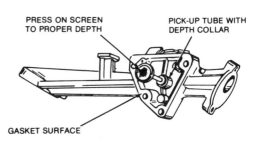

PRESS ON SCREEN
TO PROPER DEPTH
PICK-UP TUBE WITH
DEPTH COLLAR

GASKET SURFACE

LATE MODEL

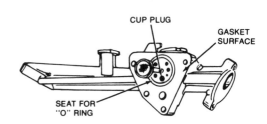

CUP PLUG
GASKET
SURFACE

SEAT FOR
"O" RING

EARLY MODEL

Details of pick-up tube used on revised Craftsman carburetor

in the illustration for the type of carburetor (early or late model) on which you are working.

6. Assemble the carburetor in reverse order of disassembly. Use new O-rings and gaskets. When assembling reservoir tube, hold the carburetor upside down and place the reservoir tube over the pickup tube with the slotted end up. Make sure the intake manifold gasket is correctly positioned-it can be assembled blocking the intake passage partially.

Adjustments

1. Move the carburetor control valve to the high speed position. The mark on the face of the valve should be in alignment with the retaining boss on the carburetor body.

2. Move the operator's control on the equipment to the high speed position.

3. Insert the bowden wire into the hole of the

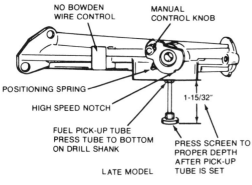

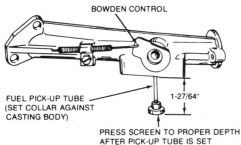

Details of manual control knob and several other changes incorporated in new Craftsman carburetors

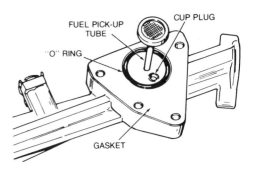

Positioning of the reservoir tube in the fuel tank

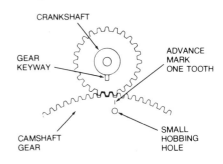

FOR CRAFTSMAN CARBURETOR ONLY—
AND ONLY IF ENGINE HAS NO INTERNAL
FLYWEIGHT GOVERNOR

Timing an engine with the Craftsman fuel tank mounted carburetor

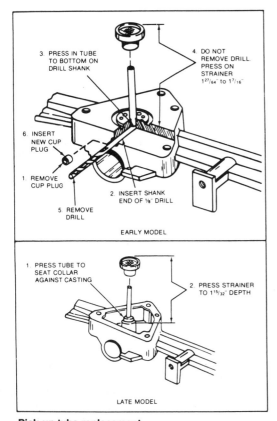

Pick-up tube replacement

control valve. Clamp the bowden wire sheath to the carburetor body.

NOTE: *If the engine was disassembled and the camshaft removed, be sure that the timing marks on the camshaft gear and the keyway in the crankshaft gear are aligned when reinserting the camshaft. Then lift the camshaft enough to advance the camshaft gear timing mark to the right (clockwise) ONE tooth, as viewed from the power take-off end of the crankshaft.*

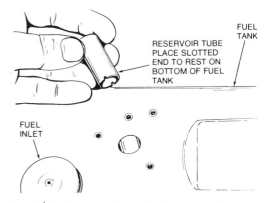

The fuel pick-up tube and O-ring on the early model Craftsman carburetor

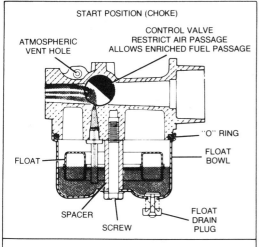

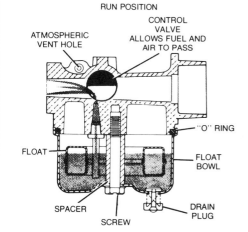

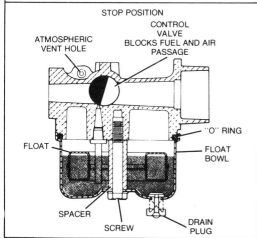

Start, run and stop throttle positions of a Craftsman float type carburetor

CRAFTSMAN FLOAT TYPE CARBURETORS

Craftsman float type carburetors are serviced in the smae manner as the other Tecumseh float type carburetors. The throttle control

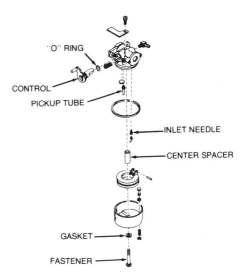

Exploded view of the Craftsman float type carburetor

valve has three positions: stop, run, and start.

When the control valve is removed, replace the O-ring. If the engine runs sluggishly, consider the possibility of a leaky O-ring.

To remove the fuel pickup tube, clamp the tube in a vise and then twist the carburetor body. Check the small jet in the air horn while the tube is out. In replacement, position the tube squarely and then press in on the collar until the collar seats.

In assembly, install the gasket and bolt through the bowl, position the centering spacer onto the bolt, and then attach the parts to the carburetor body.

The camshaft timing mark must be advanced one tooth in relation to crankshaft gear timing mark, as shown in the illustration above. However, when this type carburetor is used with a float bowl reservoir and variable governor adjustment, time it as for other Tecumseh engines — with the camshaft and crankshaft timing marks aligned.

Governor

The mechanical governor is located inside the mounting flange. See engine disassembly instructions, below. To disassemble the governor, see the illustration, and: remove the retaining ring, pull off the spool, remove the second retaining ring, and then pull off the gear assembly and retainer washer.

Check for wear on all moving surfaces, but especially gear teeth, the inside diameter of the gear where it rides on the shaft, and the flyweights where they work against the spool.

If the governor shaft must be replaced, it should be started into the boss with a few taps using a soft hammer, and then pressed in with a

Shaft Installed Dimension/ Engine Model Chart

Engine Model	"A" Exposed Shaft Length (see figure)
LAV30-50 H25-35 HS40-50	$1^{5}/_{16}$"
V50	$1^{19}/_{32}$"
H50 HH40	$1^{7}/_{16}$"

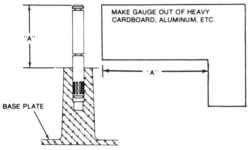

Measuring governor shaft installed dimension

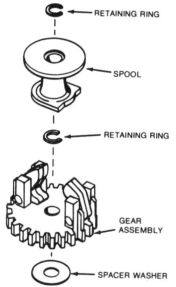

Exploded view of standard mechanical governor

press or vise. The shaft can be installed by positioning a wooden block on top and tapping the upper surface of the block, but the use of a vise or press is much preferred.

The shaft must be pressed in until just the required length is exposed, as measured from the top of the shaft boss to the upper end of the shaft. See the chart.

The governor is installed in reverse of the removal procedure. Connect the linkage and then adjust as described in the Tune-Up section.

ENGINE OVERHAUL

Timing Gears

Correctly matched camshaft gear and crankshaft gear timing marks are necessary for the engine to perform properly.

On all camshafts the timing mark is located in line with the cneter of the hobbing hole (small hole in the face of the gear). If no line is visible, use the cneter of the hobbing hole to align with the crankshaft gear marked tooth.

On crankshafts where the gear is held on by a key, the timing mark is the tooth in line with the keyway.

On crankshafts where the gear is pressed onto the crankshaft, a tooth is bevelled to serve as the timing mark.

On engines with a ball bearing on the power take-off end of the crankshaft, look for a bevelled tooth which serves as the crankshaft gear timing mark.

If the engine uses a Craftsman type carburetor, the camshaft timing mark must be advanced clockwise one tooth ahead of the match-

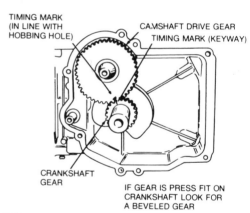

Timing marks

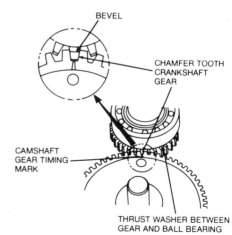

Timing marks

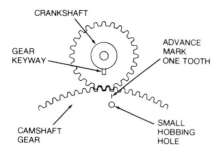

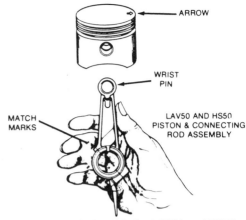

Piston-to-rod relationship for LAV50 and HS50 engines

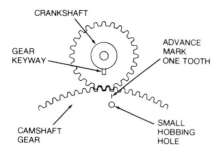

Timing marks

ing timing mark on the crankshaft, the exception being the Craftsman variable governed fuel systems.

NOTE: *If one of the timing gears, either the crankshaft gear or the camshaft gear, is damaged and has to be replaced, both gears should be replaced.*

Crankshaft

INSPECTION

Inspect the crankshaft for worn or crossed threads that can't be redressed; worn, scratched, or damaged bearing surfaces; misalignments; flats on the bearing surfaces. Replace the shaft if any of these problems are in evidence — do not try to straighten a bent shaft.

In replacement, be sure to lubricate the bearing surfaces and use oil seal protectors. If the camshaft gear requires replacement, replace the crankshaft gear, also.

LAV35–LAV50 and H35–HS50 crankshafts have a press fit gear. If the camshaft gear requires replacement on these engines, the crankshaft must be replaced, as the gear connot be replaced separately.

Pistons

When removing the pistons, clean the carbon from the upper cylinder bore and head. The piston and pin must be replaced in matched pairs.

A ridge reamer must be used to remove the ridge at the top of the cylinder bore on some engines.

Clean the carbon from the piston ring groove. A broken ring can be used for this operation.

Some engines have oversize pistons which can be identified by the oversize engraved on the piston top.

There is a definite piston-to-connecting rod-to-crankshaft arrangement which must be maintained when assembling these parts. If the piston is assembled in the bore 180° out of position, it will cause immediate binding of the parts.

Piston Rings

Always replace the piston rings in sets. Ring gaps must be staggered. When using new rings, wipe the cylinder wall with fine emery cloth to deglaze the wall. Make sure the cylinder wall is thoroughly cleaned after deglazing. Check the ring gap by placing the ring squarely in the center of the area in which the rings travel and measuring the gap with a feeler gauge. Do not spread the rings too wide when assembling them to the pistons. Use a ring leader to install the rings on the piston.

The top compression ring has an inside

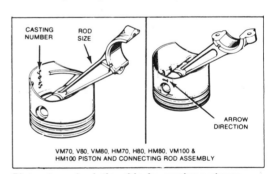

Piston-to-rod relationship for engines shown

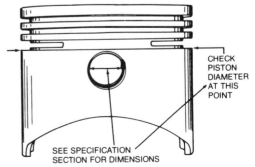

Check piston dimensions

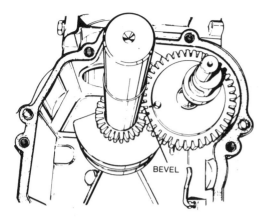

Timing marks for the LAV40 and HS40 engines

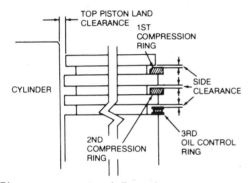

Ring arrangement and dimensions

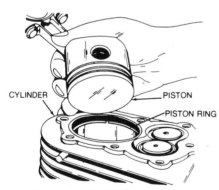

Squaring the ring in the bore

Checking the ring gap

chamfer. This chamfer must go UP. If the second ring has a chamfer, it must also face UP. If there is a notch on the outside diameter of the ring, it must face DOWN.

Check the ring gap on the old ring to determine if the ring should be replaced. Check the ring gap on the new ring to determine if the cylinder should be rebored to take oversize parts.

NOTE: *Make sure that the ring gap is measured with the ring fitted squarely in the worn part of the cylinder where the ring usually rides up and down on the piston.*

Connecting Rods

Be sure that the match marks align when assembling the connecting rods to the crankshaft. Use new self-locking nuts. Whenever locking tabs are included, be sure that the tabs lock the nuts securely. NEVER try to straighten a bent crankshaft or connecting rod. Replace them if necessary. When replacing either the piston, rod, crankshaft, or camshaft, liberally lubricate all bearings with engine oil before assembly.

The following engines have offset connecting rods: LAV40, LAV50, HS40, HS50. The LAV40, LAV50, HS40, HS50 engines have the caps fitted from opposite to the camshaft side of the engine.

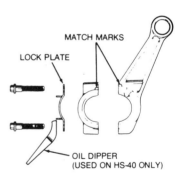

Connecting rod assembly for the LAV40 and HS40 engine

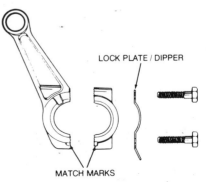

Connecting rod assembly for the V70, V80, H70 and H80 engines

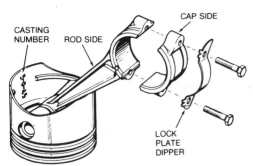

Connecting rod and piston assembly for the V80 and H80 engines

On engine with Durlock rod bolts, torque the bolts as follows:
- LAV25–50, H25, 35, HS40–50, 110 inch lbs.
- V50, H50, VH50, HH50, 150 inch lbs.

NOTE: *Early type caps can be distorted if the cap is not held to the crankpin while threading the bolts tight. Undue force should not be used.*

Later rods have serrations which prevent distortion during tightening. They also have match marks which must face out when assembling the rod. On the LAV50 and the HS50 engines, the piston must be fitted to the rod with the arrow on the top of the piston pointing to the right and the match marks on the rod facing you when the piston is pinned to the rod.

Camshaft

Before removing the camshaft, align the timing marks to relieve the pressure on the valve lifters, on most engines.

In installation, align the gears for this type of camshaft as they were right before removal. After installation, turn the crankshaft gear clockwise in order to check for proper alignment of timing marks.

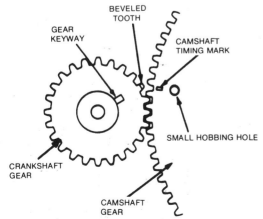

Alignment of timing marks for camshaft removal on VM80 and VM100 engines

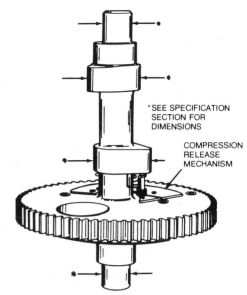

Check the dimensions of the camshaft

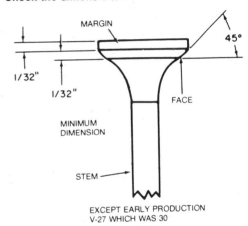

Dimensions of the valve face

Clean the camshaft in solvent, then blow the oil passages dry with compressed air. Replace the camshaft if it shows wear of evidence of scoring. Check the cam dimensions against those in the chart.

If the engine has a mechanical fuel pump, it may have to be removed to properly reinstall the camshaft. If the engine is equipped with the Insta-matic Ezee-Start Compression Release, and any of the parts have to be replaced due to wear or damage, the entire camshaft must be replaced. Be sure that the oil pump (if so equipped) barrel chamber is toward the fillet of the camshaft gear when assembled.

NOTE: *If a damaged gear is replaced, the crankshaft gear should also be replaced.*

Valve Springs

The valve springs should be replaced whenever an engine is overhauled. Check the free length of the springs. Comparing one spring with the other can be a quick check to notice any differences. If a difference is noticed, carefully measure the free length, compression length, and strength of each spring. See the specifications chart at the end of this section.

Some valve springs use dampening coils — coils that are wound closer together than most of the coils of the spring. Where these are present, the spring must be mounted so the dampening coils are on the stationary (upper) end of the spring.

Valve Lifters

The stems of the valves serve as the lifters. On the 4 hp light frame models, the lifter stems are of different lengths. Because this engine is a cross port model, the shorter intake valve lifter goes nearest the mounting flange.

The valve lifters are identical on standard port engines. However once a wear pattern is established, they should not be interchanged.

Valve Grinding and Replacement

Valves and valve seats can be removed and reground with a minimum of engine disassembly.

Remove the valves as follows:

1. Raise the lower valve spring caps while holding the valve heads tightly against the valve seat to remove the valve spring retaining pin. This is best achieved by using a valve spring compressor. Remove the valves, springs, and caps from the crankcase.

2. Clean all parts with a solvent and remove all carbon from the valves.

3. Replace distorted or damaged valves. If the valves are in usable condition, grind the valve faces in a valve refacing maching and to the angle given in the specifications chart at the end of this section. Replace the valves if the faces are ground to less than $\frac{1}{32}$ in. (0.8mm).

4. Whenever new or reground valves are installed, lap in the valves with lapping compound to insure an air-tight fit.

NOTE: *There are valves available with oversize stems.*

5. Valve grinding changes the valve lifter clearance. After grinding the valves check the valve lifter clearance as follows:

    a. Rotate the crankshaft until the piston is set at the TDC position of the compression stroke.

    b. Insert the valves in their guides and hold the valves firmly on their seats.

    c. Check for a clearance of 0.010 in. (0.25mm) between each valve stem and valve lifter with a feeler gauge.

    d. Grind the valve stem in a valve resur-

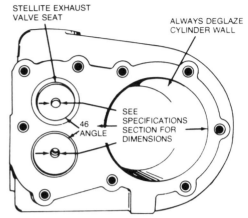

Check the dimensions of the valve seats, guides, and the cylinder

facing machine set to grind a perfectly square face with the proper clearance.

6. Install valves as follows on Early Models:

    a. Position the valve spring and upper and lower valve spring caps under the valve guides for the valve to be installed.

    b. Install the valves in the guides, making sure that the valve marked **EX** is inserted in the exhaust port. The valve stem must pass through the valve spring and the valve spring caps.

    c. Insert the blade of a screwdriver under the lower valve spring cap and pry the spring up.

    d. Insert the valve pin through the hole in the valve stem with a long nosed pliers. Make sure the valve pin is properly seated under the lower valve spring cap.

Install the valves as follows on Later Models:

    a. Position the valve caps and spring in the valve compartment.

    b. Install the valves in guides with the valve marked **EX** in exhaust port. The valve stem must pass through the upper valve cap and spring. The lower cap should sit around the valve lifter exposed end.

    c. Compress the valve spring so that the shank is exposed. DO NOT TRY TO LIFT THE LOWER CAP WITH THE SPRING.

    d. Lift the lower valve cap over the valve stem shank and center the cap in the smaller diameter hole.

    e. Release the valve spring tension to lock the cap in place.

REBORING THE CYLINDER

1. First, decide whether to rebore for 0.010 in. (0.25mm) or 0.020 in. (0.50mm).

2. Use any standard commercial hone of

ROUGH REAMING WORN ALUMINUM BEARING (MAGNETO SIDE) FOR ALUMINUM BEARING ONLY

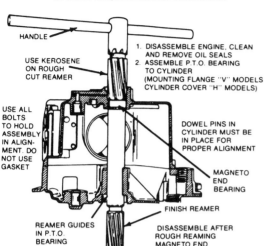

HANDLE

USE KEROSENE ON ROUGH CUT REAMER

USE ALL BOLTS TO HOLD ASSEMBLY IN ALIGN-MENT. DO NOT USE GASKET

1. DISASSEMBLE ENGINE, CLEAN AND REMOVE OIL SEALS
2. ASSEMBLE P.T.O. BEARING TO CYLINDER (MOUNTING FLANGE "V" MODELS CYLINDER COVER "H" MODELS)

DOWEL PINS IN CYLINDER MUST BE IN PLACE FOR PROPER ALIGNMENT

MAGNETO END BEARING

FINISH REAMER

REAMER GUIDES IN P.T.O. BEARING

DISASSEMBLE AFTER ROUGH REAMING MAGNETO END

FINISH REAMING NEW MAGNETO BUSHING

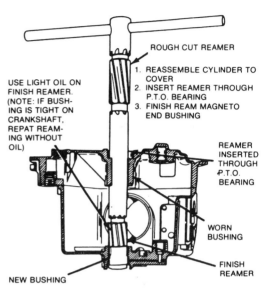

ROUGH CUT REAMER

USE LIGHT OIL ON FINISH REAMER. (NOTE: IF BUSH-ING IS TIGHT ON CRANKSHAFT, REPAT REAM-ING WITHOUT OIL)

1. REASSEMBLE CYLINDER TO COVER
2. INSERT REAMER THROUGH P.T.O. BEARING
3. FINISH REAM MAGNETO END BUSHING

REAMER INSERTED THROUGH P.T.O. BEARING

WORN BUSHING

NEW BUSHING

FINISH REAMER

WORN BUSHING REMOVAL (MAGNETO END) FOR BRONZE BUSHING ONLY

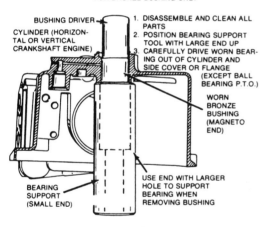

BUSHING DRIVER

CYLINDER (HORIZON-TAL OR VERTICAL CRANKSHAFT ENGINE)

1. DISASSEMBLE AND CLEAN ALL PARTS
2. POSITION BEARING SUPPORT TOOL WITH LARGE END UP
3. CAREFULLY DRIVE WORN BEAR-ING OUT OF CYLINDER AND SIDE COVER OR FLANGE (EXCEPT BALL BEARING P.T.O.)

WORN BRONZE BUSHING (MAGNETO END)

BEARING SUPPORT (SMALL END)

USE END WITH LARGER HOLE TO SUPPORT BEARING WHEN REMOVING BUSHING

ROUGH REAMING WORN ALUMINUM BEARING (P.T.O. END) FOR ALUMINUM BEARING ONLY

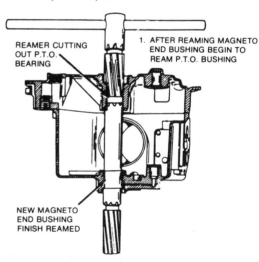

REAMER CUTTING OUT P.T.O. BEARING

1. AFTER REAMING MAGNETO END BUSHING BEGIN TO REAM P.T.O. BUSHING

NEW MAGNETO END BUSHING FINISH REAMED

INSTALLING NEW BRONZE BUSHING (MAGNETO SIDE)

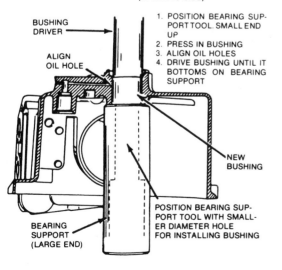

BUSHING DRIVER

ALIGN OIL HOLE

1. POSITION BEARING SUP-PORT TOOL. SMALL END UP
2. PRESS IN BUSHING
3. ALIGN OIL HOLES
4. DRIVE BUSHING UNTIL IT BOTTOMS ON BEARING SUPPORT

NEW BUSHING

BEARING SUPPORT (LARGE END)

POSITION BEARING SUP-PORT TOOL WITH SMALL-ER DIAMETER HOLE FOR INSTALLING BUSHING

WORN BUSHING REMOVAL (P.T.O. END) FOR BRONZE BUSHING ONLY

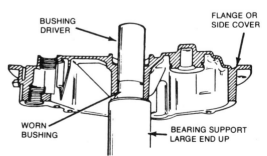

BUSHING DRIVER

FLANGE OR SIDE COVER

WORN BUSHING

BEARING SUPPORT LARGE END UP

INSTALLING BRONZE BUSHING P.T.O. END

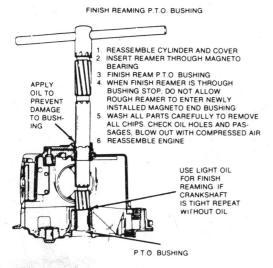

BUSHING DRIVER

BUSHING

1. DISASSEMBLE
2. POSITION BEARING SUPPORT TOOL
3. PRESS IN BUSHING
4. ALIGN OIL HOLE
5. DRIVE BUSHING UNTIL IT BOTTOMS ON BEARING SUPPORT

FLANGE OR SIDE COVER

ALIGN OIL HOLES AND SLOTS

BEARING SUPPORT SMALL END UP

FINISH REAMING P.T.O. BUSHING

APPLY OIL TO PREVENT DAMAGE TO BUSHING

1. REASSEMBLE CYLINDER AND COVER
2. INSERT REAMER THROUGH MAGNETO BEARING
3. FINISH REAM P.T.O. BUSHING
4. WHEN FINISH REAMER IS THROUGH BUSHING STOP, DO NOT ALLOW ROUGH REAMER TO ENTER NEWLY INSTALLED MAGNETO END BUSHING
5. WASH ALL PARTS CAREFULLY TO REMOVE ALL CHIPS. CHECK OIL HOLES AND PASSAGES, BLOW OUT WITH COMPRESSED AIR
6. REASSEMBLE ENGINE

USE LIGHT OIL FOR FINISH REAMING. IF CRANKSHAFT IS TIGHT REPEAT WITHOUT OIL

P.T.O. BUSHING

suitable size. Chuck the hone in the drill press with the spindle speed of about 600 rpm.

3. Start with coarse stones and center the cylinder under the press spindle. Lower the hone so the lower end of the stones contact the lowest point in the cylinder bore.

4. Rotate the adjusting nut so that the stones touch the cylinder wall and then begin honing at the bottom of the cylinder. Move the hone up and down at a rate of 50 strokes a minute to avoid cutting ridges in the cylinder wall. Every fourth or fifth stroke, move the hone far enough to extend the stones 1 in. (25mm) beyond the top and bottom of the cylinder bore.

5. Check the bore size and straightness every thirty or forty strokes. If the stones collect metal, clean them with a wire brush each time the hone is removed.

6. Hone with coarse stones until the cylinder bore is within 0.002 in. (0.05mm) of the desired finish size. Replace the coarse stones with burnishing stones and continue until the bore is to within 0.0005 in. (0.0127mm) of the desired size.

7. Remove the burnishing stones and install

finishing stones to polish the cylinder to the final size.

8. Clean the cylinder with solvent and dry it thoroughly.

9. Replace the piston and piston rings with the correct oversize parts.

REBORING VALVE GUIDES

The valve guides are permanently installed in the cylinder. However, if the guides wear, they can be rebored to accommodate a $\frac{1}{32}$ in. (0.8mm) oversize valve stem. Rebore the valve guides in the following manner:

1. Ream the valve guides with a standard straight shanked hand reamer or a low speed drill press. Refer to the specifications chart at the end of this section for the correct valve stem guide diameter.

2. Redrill the upper and lower valve spring caps to accommodate the oversize valve stem.

3. Reassemble the engine, installing valves with the correct oversize stems in the valve guides.

REGRINDING VALVE SEATS

The valve seats need regrinding only if they are pitted or scored. If there are no pits or scores, lapping in the valves will provide a proper valve seat. Valve seats are not replaceable. Regrind the valve seats as follows:

1. Use a grinding stone or a reseater set to provide the proper angle and seal face dimensions.

2. If the seat is over $\frac{3}{32}$ in. (2.4mm) wide after grinding, use a 15° stone or cutter to narrow the face to the proper dimensions.

3. Inspect the seats to make sure that the cutter or stone has been held squarely to the valve seat and that the same dimension has been held around the entire circumference of the seat.

4. Lap the valves to the reground seats.

Torquing the Cylinder Head

Torque the cylinder head to 200 inch lbs. in 4 equal stages of 50 inch lbs. Follow the sequence shown in the appropriate illustration for each tightening stage.

Bearing Service
LIGHTWEIGHT ALUMINUM BEARING REPLACEMENT

The aluminum bearing must be cut out using the rough cut reamer and the procedures shown in steps 1A and 4A. Follow illustrated steps 1A, 2, 3, 4A, 5 and 6 to install bronze bushings in place of the aluminum bearings.

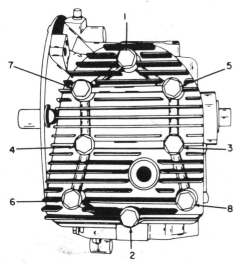

Cylinder head tightening sequence for all engines except 8 hp models

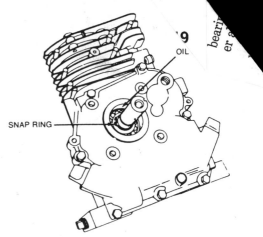

On H20-HS50 H.P. horizontal crankshaft engines, remove the oil seal and snap ring to remove the cylinder cover

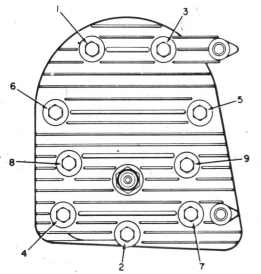

Cylinder head tightening sequence for 8 hp models

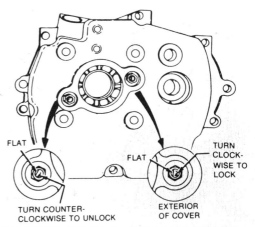

H40-HM100 H.P. horizontal crankshaft engines —locking and unlocking the bearing from outside

LONG LIFE AND CAST IRON ENGINES WITHOUT BALL BEARINGS

The worn bronze bushing must be driven out before the new bushing can be installed. Follow illustrated steps 1B, 2, 3, 4B, 5 and 6, to replace the main bearings on these units.

LONG LIFE AND CAST IRON ENGINES WITH BALL BEARING ON THE P.T.O. (POWER TAKE-OFF) SIDE OF THE CRANKSHAFT

The side cover containing the ball bearing must be removed and a substitute cover with either a new bronze bushing or aluminum bearing must be used instead. Follow illustrated steps 1B, 2 and 3 only.

SPECIAL TOOLS

The task of main bearing replacement is made easier by using one of two Tecumseh main bearing tool kits. Kit 670161 is used to replace main bearings on the lightweight engines except HS, LAV40 and 50 models. Kit 670165 is used to replace main bearings on the medium weight engines except HS, LAV40 and 50 models.

GENERAL NOTES ON BUSHING REPLACEMENT

1. Your fingers and all parts must be kept very clean when replacing bushings.
2. On splash lubricated horizontal engines, the oil hole in the bushing is to be lined up with the oil hole that leads into the slot in the original bearing.
3. In the event it is necessary to replace the mounting flange or cylinder cover, the magneto end bearing must be rebushed. The P.T.O.

g should also be rebushed to assure prop-
alignment.

4. Oil should be used to finish-ream the
bushings. In the event the crankshaft does not
rotate freely repeat the finish-reaming operation without oil.

5. Kerosene should be used as a cutting lubricant while rough-reaming.

6. Be sure that the dowel pins are in the cylinder block when assembling the mounting
flange or cylinder cover. Use all bolts to hold the
assembly together.

7. Remove the reamer by rotating it in the
same direction as it is turned during the reaming operation. DO NOT TURN THE REAMER
BACKWARDS.

BALL BEARING SERVICE – H20 THROUGH HS50 H.P. HORIZONTAL CRANKSHAFT ENGINES

1. Remove the crankshaft P.T.O. end oil seal.
Drive an awl or similar tool into the metal seal
body and pry out.

2. Use snap ring pliers to remove the snap
ring.

3. Reassembly is in reverse order. Secure the
cylinder cover, install the snap ring and oil seal.
Protect the oil seal to prevent damage during
installation.

BALL BEARING SERVICE – H40, 50 HORIZONTAL CRANKSHAFT ENGINES

1. Prior to attempting removal of the cylinder cover, observe the area around the crankshaft P.T.O. oil seal. Compare it with the illustration, and if there are bearing locks, follow instructions below:

a. Remove the locking nuts using the proper socket wrench. Note fiber washer located
under nut; this must be reinstalled. Lift side
cover from cylinder after removing the side
cover bolts.

b. Install the bearing retainer bolts, fiber
washer and locking nuts in the proper sequence in the cover.

2. Also note the following points:

a. On some engines, a locking type retainer bolt is used. To release the bolt, merely
loosen the locking nut and turn the retainer
bolt counterclockwise to the unlocked position with needle nose pliers to permit the side
cover to be removed. Note that the flats on
the retainer bolts must be turned so they face
the crankshaft to be relocked upon installation. Don't force them! Torque the locking
nuts only to 15–22 inch lbs.

b. The ball bearing used in horizontal
crankshaft engines has a restricted fit. The
bearing is heated and put onto the cold crankshaft. As the bearing cools it grasps the

crankshaft tightly and must be removed cold.
Remove the ball bearing with a bearing splitter (separator) and a puller. The bearing may
be heated by placing it into a container with a
sufficient amount of oil to cover the bearing.
The bearing should not rest on the bottom of
the container. Suspend the bearing on a wire
or set the bearing onto a spacer block of wood
or wire mesh. Heat the oil and bearing carefully until the oil smokes, quickly remove the
bearing and slide it onto the crankshaft.

c. The bearing must seat tightly against
the thrust washer which in turn rests tightly
against the crankshaft gear.

d. When a ball bearing is used it is not possible to see the keyway in the crankshaft gear
which is normally used for timing. Because of
this, one tooth of the crankshaft gear is
chamfered. This chamfered tooth of the
crankshaft gear is positioned opposite the
timing mark on the camshaft gear. The use of
a ball bearing requires the removal of the
crankshaft when it is necessary to remove the
camshaft. When replacing the crankshaft
and camshaft, mate the timing marks and insert it into the cylinder block as an assembly.

LUBRICATION

Barrel and Plunger Oil Pump System

This system is driven by an eccentric on the
camshaft. Oil is drawn through the hollow camshaft from the oil sump on its intake stroke.
The passage from the sump through the camshaft is aligned with the pump opening. As the
camshaft continues rotation (pressure stroke),
the plunger force the oil out. The other port in
the camshaft is aligned with the pump, and directs oil out of the top of the camshaft.

At the top of the camshaft, oil is forced
through a crankshaft passage to the top main
bearing groove which is aligned with the drilled
crankshaft passage. Oil is directed through this
passage to the crankshaft connecting rod journal and then spills from the connecting rod to

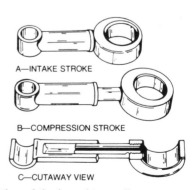

A—INTAKE STROKE

B—COMPRESSION STROKE

C—CUTAWAY VIEW

Operation of the barrel type oil pump

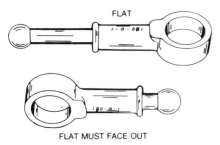

Installation of the barrel type oil pump

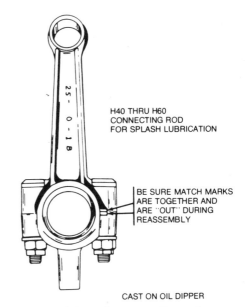

Splash type lubrication connecting rod

lubricate the cylinder walls. Splash is used to lubricate the other parts of the engine.

A pressure relief port in the crank case relieves excessive pressures when the oil viscosity is extremely heavy due to cold temperatures, or when the system is plugged or damaged. Normal pressure is 7 psi.

SERVICE

Remove the mounting flange or the cylinder cover, whichever is applicable. Remove the barrel and plunger assembly and separate the parts.

Clean the pump parts in solvent and inspect the pump plunger and barrel for rough spots or wear. If the pump plunger is scored or worn, replace the entire pump.

Before reassembling the pump parts, lubricate all of the parts in engine oil. Manually operate the pump to make sure the plunger slides freely in the barrel.

Lubricate all the parts and position the barrel on the camshaft eccentric. If the oil pump has a chamfer only on one side, that side must be placed toward the camshaft gear. The flat goes away from the gear, thus out to work against the flange oil pickup hole.

Install the mounting flange. Be sure the plunger ball seats in the recess in the flange before fastening it to the cylinder.

Spray Mist Lubrication

Late model LAV40, LAV30, and LAV35 engines have a spray mist lubrication system. This system is the same as the barrel and plunger oil pump system except that (1) the pressure relief port is changed to a calibrated spray mist orifice and (2) the crankshaft is not rifle-drilled from the top main to the crank pin. Lubrication is sprayed to the narrow rod cap area through the spray mist hole.

Splash Lubrication

Some engines utilize the splash type lubrication system. The oil dipper, on some engines, is cast onto the lower connecting rod bearing cap. It is important that the proper parts are used to ensure the longest engine life.

Gear Type Oil Pump System

The gear type lubrication pump is a crankshaft driven, positive displacement pump. It pumps oil from the oil sump in the engine base to the camshaft, through the drilled camshaft passage to the top main bearing, through the drilled crankshaft, to the connecting rod journal on the crankshaft.

Spillage from the connecting rod lubricates the cylinder walls and normal splash lubricates the other internal working parts. There is a pressure relief valve in the system.

SERVICE

Disassemble the pump as follows: remove the screws, lockwashers, cover, gear, and displacement member.

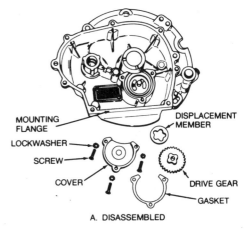

Disassembled view of the gear type lubrication system

Wash all of the parts in solvent. Inspect the oil pump ddive gear and displacement member for worn or broken teeth, scoring, or other damage. Inspect the shaft hole in the drive gear for wear. Replace the entire pump if cracks, wear, or scoring is evident.

To replace the oil pump, position the oil pump displacement member and oil pump gear on the shaft, then flood all the parts with oil for priming during the initial starting of the engine.

The gasket provides clearance for the drive gear. With a feeler gauge, determine the clearance between the cover and the oil pump gear. The clearance desired is 0.006–0.007 in. (0.15–0.18mm). Use gaskets, which are available in a variety of sizes, to obtain the correct clearance. Position the oil pump cover and secure it with the screws and lockwashers.

Cross Reference for Vertical Crankshaft Engines

Size	Model	Column
2½ HP	LAV25	1
3HP	LAV30	1
	TVS75	1
3½ HP	LV35	2
	LAV35	2
	TVS90	2
4 HP	LAV40	3
	TVS105	3
	V40 thru V40B	7
	VH40	7
10.0 CI	ECV100	4
	TNT100	14
10.5 CI	ECV105	5
11.0 CI	ECV110	12
5 HP	LAV50	6
	TVS120	6
	V50	9
	VH50	9
12.0 CI	ECV120	13
	TNT120	15

Cross Reference Chart for Horizontal Crankshaft Engines

Size	Model	Column
2½ HP	H25	1
3 HP	H30	1
3½ HP	H35	2
9.0 CI	ECH90	2
4 HP	H40	7
	HH40	7
	HS40	3
5 HP	H50	9
	HH50	9
	HS50	6

Craftsman Engines Cross Reference Chart

Craftsman Engine Models	See Column	Craftsman Engine Models	See Column	Craftsman Engine Models	See Column
143.50040	7	143.151012–143.153032	1	143.171212–143.173042	1
143.50045		143.154012–143.154142	2	143.174012–143.174292	2
		143.155012–143.155062	9	143.175012–143.175072	9
143.131022–143.131102	1	143.156022		143.177012–143.177072	7
143.135012–143.135112	9	143.157012–143.157032	7		
143.137012	7			143.181042–143.183042	1
143.137032		143.161012–143.163062	1	143.184012–143.184212	2
		143.164012–143.164202	2	143.184232–143.184252	4
143.141012–143.143032	1	143.165012–143.165052	9	143.184262–143.184402	2
143.145012–143.145072	9	143.167012–143.167042	7	143.185012–143.185052	9
143.146022				143.186062	
143.146022		143.171012–143.171172	1	143.187022–143.187102	3
143.147012–143.147032	7	143.171202	2		

Craftsman Engines Cross Reference Chart (cont.)

Craftsman Engine Models	See Column	Craftsman Engine Models	See Column	Craftsman Engine Models	See Column
143.191012–143.191052	1	143.224432	4	143.254302	2
143.194012–143.194052	2	143.225012	13	143.254312	
143.194062	4	143.225022		143.254322	4
143.194072–143.194092	2	143.225032–143.225052	9	143.254332	2
143.194102	4	143.225062	13	143.254342	4
143.194112–143.194142	2	143.225072		143.254352	
143.195012	9	143.225082–143.225102	9	143.254362	2
143.195022		143.227012–143.227072	12	143.254372	4
143.197012	3			143.254382	
143.197022	5	143.233012	1	143.254392	2
143.197032		143.233032		143.254402	4
143.197042–143.197072	3	143.233042		143.254412	
143.197082	5	143.234022–143.234052	2	143.254432	2
		143.234062–143.234092	4	143.254442	4
143.201032–143.203012	1	143.234102–143.234162	2	143.254452	2
143.204022	4	143.234192		143.254462	4
143.204032–143.204052	2	143.234202		143.254472	2
143.204062	4	143.234212–143.234232	4	143.254482	
143.204072–143.204092	2	143.234242–143.234262	2	143.254492	4
143.204102	4	143.235012	13	143.254502–143.254532	2
143.204132		143.235022		143.255012–143.255112	6
143.204142–143.204192	2	143.235032	6	143.257012–143.257072	3
143.204202	4	143.235042	13		
143.205022	9	143.235052		143.264012–143.264042	2
143.207012–143.207052	3	143.235062	9	143.264052–143.264082	4
143.207062	5	143.235072	6	143.264092	2
143.207072	3	143.237012	12	143.264102	4
143.207082	5	143.237022		143.264232–143.264342	2
		143.237032	5	143.264352–143.264372	4
143.213012–143.213042	1	143.237042	3	143.264382	2
143.214012–143.214032	2			143.264392–143.264412	4
143.214042–143.214072	4	143.244032	2	143.264422	2
143.214082–143.214252	2	143.244042	4	143.264432–143.264482	4
143.214262–143.214282	4	143.244052		143.264492	2
143.214292	2	143.244062		143.264502	
143.214302		143.244072–143.244112	2	143.264512	4
143.214312	4	143.244122–143.244142	4	143.264522	2
143.214322		143.244202	2	143.264542	
143.214332	2	143.244212	4	143.264562–143.264672	4
143.214342		143.244222	2	143.264682	2
143.214352	4	143.244232		143.265012–143.265192	6
143.216042–143.216062	3	143.244242	4	143.267012–143.267042	3
143.217012–143.217032	5	143.244252	4		
143.217042–143.217072	3	143.244262–143.244282	2	143.274022–143.274072	4
143.217092	5	143.244292–143.244332	4	143.274092–143.274132	2
143.217102	3	143.245012	6	143.274142	4
		143.245042	9	143.274152	
143.223012–143.223052	1	143.245052–143.245072	13	143.274162–143.274182	2
143.224012	2	132.245082		143.274192–143.274242	4
143.224022		143.245092	6	143.274252	2
143.224032	4	143.245102–143.245132	13	143.274262	4
143.224062	2	143.245142	6	143.274272–143.274322	2
143.224072	4	143.245152		143.274402–143.274482	4
143.224092–143.224132	2	143.245162	13	143.275012–143.275052	6
143.224142	1	143.245172	6	143.276022	4
143.224162–143.224222	2	143.245182		143.277012	3
143.224232	4	143.245192	13	143.277022	
143.224242					
143.224252–143.224282	2	143.254012–143.254052	2	143.284012	2
143.224292	4	143.254062	4	143.284022	1
143.224302		143.254072–143.254122	2	143.284032	2
143.224312–143.224342	2	143.254142–143.254192	4	143.284042	4
143.224352	4	143.254212	2	143.284052	2
143.224362		143.254222		143.284062	
143.224372–143.224422	2	143.254232–143.254292	4	143.284072	4

Craftsman Engines Cross Reference Chart (cont.)

Craftsman Engine Models	See Column
143.284082	2
143.284092	
143.284102	4
143.284112	2
143.284142	
143.284152	
143.284162	
143.284182	
143.284212	4
143.284312	2
143.284322	
143.284332	4
143.284342	
143.284352	
143.284382	4
143.284402	2
143.284412	
143.284442	4
143.284362	
143.284392	2
143.284482	
143.284452	4
143.284472	
143.285012	6
143.285022	
143.285032	
143.521081	9
143.525021	9
143.526011	
143.531052	1
143.531082	
143.531122	
143.531132	
143.531142	2
143.531152	1
143.531172	
143.531182	
143.534012–143.534072	2
143.535012–143.535062	9
143.537012	7
143.541012	1
143.541042–143.541062	1
143.541112–143.541152	1
143.541172–143.541202	1
143.541222	1
143.541282–143.541302	1
143.544012–143.544042	2

Craftsman Engine Models	See Column
143.545012–143.545042	9
143.547012–143.547032	7
143.551012	1
143.551032	
143.551052–143.551192	1
143.554012–143.554082	2
143.555012–143.555052	9
143.557012–143.557082	7
143.565022	9
143.566212	9
143.567012–143.567042	7
143.571002–143.571122	1
143.571152	2
143.571162	1
143.571172	
143.574022–143.574102	2
143.575012–143.575042	9
143.581002–143.581102	1
143.584012–143.584142	2
143.585012–143.585042	9
143.587012–143.587042	3
143.591012–143.591142	1
143.594022–143.594082	2
143.594092	2
143.594102	
143.595012	9
143.595042	
143.597012–143.597032	3
143.601022–143.601062	1
143.604012	2
143.604022	4
143.604032	2
143.604042	
143.604052	4
143.604062	2
143.604072	
143.605012	9
143.605022	
143.605052	
143.607012–143.607032	3
143.607042–143.607062	3
143.611012–143.611112	1
143.614012–143.614032	4
143.614042	2
143.614052	4

Craftsman Engine Models	See Column
143.614062–143.614162	2
143.615012–143.615092	9
143.617012–143.617182	3
143.621012–143.621092	1
143.624012–143.624112	2
143.625012–143.625132	9
143.627012–143.627042	3
143.631012–143.631092	1
143.634012	2
143.634032	
143.635012	9
143.635022	
143.635032	6
143.635052	9
143.637012	3
143.641012–143.641062	1
143.641072	2
143.644012–143.644082	2
143.645012–143.645032	6
143.647012–143.647062	3
143.651012–143.651072	1
143.654022–143.654322	2
143.655012	6
143.655032	
143.657012–143.657052	3
143.661012–143.661062	1
143.664012–143.664332	2
143.665012–143.665082	6
143.667012	3
143.667022	
143.667032	6
143.667042–143.667082	3
143.674012	2
143.675012	6
143.675022	
143.675032	9
143.675042	6
143.677012	3
143.677022	
143.686072	9
143.687012	3
143.694126	4
143.694132	2

Torque Specifications

Model/Part	Inch Pounds	Ft. Pounds
Cylinder Head Bolts	160–200	13–16
Connecting Rod Bolts	65–75	5.5–6
TVS75, 90 & 105, 2.5 thru 4 H.P. (Durlok Rod Bolts) 4–5 H.P. Small Frame	95–110 80–95	7.9–9.1 6.6–7.9
ECH90, ECV100, TNT100	75–80	6.2–6.7

TVS120, 5 H.P. Small Frame
(Durlok Rod Bolts)
   5–6 H.P. Medium Frame
   5–6 H.P. Medium Frame (Durlok Rod Bolts)
	110–130
	86–110
	130–150
		9.1–10.8
		7.1–9.1
		10.8–12.5

ECV105, ECV110, ECV120, TNT120
   7, 8 & 10 Medium Frame
   7, 8 & 10 Medium Frame (Durlok Rod Bolts)
	80–95
	106–130
	150–170
		6.6–7.9
		8.8–10.8
		12.5–14.1

Cylinder Cover or Flange-to-Cylinder	65–110	5.5–9
Cylinder Cover 5–7 H.P. Medium Frame, H Models	100–140	8.3–11.6
Flywheel Nut	360–396	30–33
Spark Plug	180–360	15–30
Magneto Stator to Cylinder	40–90	3.3–7.5
Starter to Blower Housing or Cylinder	40–60	3.5–5
Housing Baffle to Cylinder	48–72	4–6
Breather Cover (Top Mount ECV)	40–50	3.3–4.1
Breather Cover	20–26	1.7–2.1
Intake Pipe to Cylinder	72–96	6–8
Carburetor to Intake Pipe	48–72	4–6
Air Cleaner to Carburetor (Plastic)	8–12	1
Tank Plate to Bracket (Plastic)	100–144	9–12
Tank to Housing	45–65	3.7–5

Muffler Bolts to Cylinder
   1–5 H.P. Small Frame
   4–5 H.P. Medium Frame
	30–45
	90–150
		2.5–3.5
		8–12

6:1 Gear Reduction Cover to Housing	100–144	8.5–12
Gear Reduction Cover to Housing	65–110	5–9
Oil Drain Plug $1/8 - 27$	35–50	1.1–4.1
$1/4 - 18$	65–85	4.5–7
$3/8 - 18$	80–100	6.6–9
$5/8 - 18$	90–150	7.5–12.5
$1/2 - 14$	80–100	6.6–9

Ball Bearing Retainer 2.5
   2.5–5 H.P. Small frame
   5–10 H.P. Medium frame
	45–60
	15–22
		3.7–5
		1.5

Craftsman Exclusive Fuel System to Cylinder	72–96	6–8
Electric Starter-to-Cylinder	50–60	4–5

Engine Specifications

Reference Column	1	2	3	4	5	6	7	8	9	10	11	12
Displacement	7.75	9.06	10.5	10.0	10.5	12.0	11.04	12.17	11.5	12.0	10.0	12.0
Stroke	1$^{27}/_{32}$"	1$^{27}/_{32}$"	1$^{15}/_{16}$"	1$^{27}/_{32}$"	1$^{15}/_{16}$"	1$^{15}/_{16}$"	2$^1/_4$"	2$^1/_4$"	1$^{15}/_{16}$"	1$^{15}/_{16}$"	1$^{27}/_{32}$"	1$^{15}/_{16}$"
Bore	2.3125 2.3135	2.5000 2.5010	2.625 2.626	2.625 2.626	2.625 2.626	2.812 2.813	2.5000 2.5010	2.625 2.626	2.750 2.751	2.812 2.813	2.625 2.626	2.812 2.813
Timing Dimension Before Top Dead Center for Vertical Engines	V.060 .070	V.065	V.035	.035	.035	V.040 .060	V.050	H.050	V.035	V.035	V.035	V.035
Timing Dimension Before Top Dead Center for Horizontal Engines	H.060 .070	H.030 .040	H.035			H.055	H.050	H.050				
Point Setting	.020	.020	.020	.020	.020	.020	.020	.020	.020	.020	.020	.020
Spark Plug Gap	.030	.030	.030	.030	.030	.030	.030	.030	.030	.030	.030	.030
Valve Clearance	.010 Both	.010 Both	.010 Both	.010 Both	.010 Both	.010 Both	.010 Both	.010 Both	.010 Both	.010 Both	.010 Both	.010 Both
Valve Seat Angle	46°	46°	46°	46°	46°	46°	46°	46°	46°	46°	46°	46°
Valve Spring Free Length	1.135"	1.135"	1.135"	1.135"	1.135"	1.135"	1.562"	1.462"	1.135"	1.135"	1.135"	1.135"
Valve Guides Over-Size Dimensions	.2805 .2815	.2805 .2815	.2805 .2815	.2805 .2815	.2807 .2817	In. .280 Ex. .278	.3432 .3442	.343 .344	.2805 .2815	.2805 .2815	.2805 .2815	.2805 .2815
Valve Seat Width	.035 .045	.035 .045	.035 .045	.035 .045	.035 .045	.035 .045	.042 .052	.042 .052	.035 .045	.035 .045	.035 .045	.035 .045
Crankshaft End Play	.005 .027	.005 .027	.005 .027	.005 .027	.005 .027	.005 .027	.005 .027	.005 .027	.005 .027	.005 .027	.005 .027	.005 .027
Crankpin Journal Diameter	.8610 .8615	.8610 .8615	.9995 1.0000	.8610 .8615	.9995 1.0000	.9995 1.0000	1.0615 1.0620	1.0615 1.0620	.9995 1.0000	.9995 1.0000	.8610 .8615	.9995 1.0000
Cylinder Main Bearing Dia.	.8755 .8760	.8755 .8760	1.0005 1.0010	.8755 .8760	1.0005 1.0010	1.0005 1.0010	1.0005 1.0010	1.0005 1.0010	1.0005 1.0010	1.0005 1.0010	.8755 .8760	1.0005 1.0010

Measurement												
Cylinder Cover Main Bearing Dia.	.8755 / .8760	.8755 / .8760	1.0005 / 1.0010	.8755 / .8760	1.2010 / 1.2020	1.0005 / 1.0010	1.0005 / 1.0010	1.0005 / 1.0010	1.0005 / 1.0010	1.0005 / 1.0010	.8755 / .8760	1.0005 / 1.0010
Conn. Rod. Dia. Crank Bearing	.8620 / .8625	.8620 / .8625	1.0005 / 1.0010	.8620 / .8625	1.0005 / 1.0010	1.0005 / 1.0010	1.0630 / 1.0635	1.0630 / 1.0635	1.0005 / 1.0010	1.0005 / 1.0010	.8620 / .8625	.8620 / .8625
Piston Diameter	2.3090 / 2.3095	2.4950 / 2.4955	2.6200 / 2.6205	2.6200 / 2.6205	2.604 / 2.608	2.8070 / 2.8075	2.492 / 2.4945	2.6210 / 2.6215	2.7450 / 2.7455	2.8070 / 2.8075	2.6200 / 2.6205	2.8070 / 2.8075
Piston Pin Diameter	.5629 / .5631	.5629 / .5631	.5629 / .5631	.5629 / .5631	.5631 / .5635	.5629 / .5631	.6248 / .6250	.6248 / .6250	.5629 / .5631	.5629 / .5631	.5629 / .5631	.5629 / .5631
Width of Comp. Ring Groove	.0955 / .0977	.0955 / .0975	.0925 / .0935	.0955 / .0975	.0955 / .0975	.0955 / .0975	.0955 / .0975	.0955 / .0975	.0795 / .0815	.0955 / .0975	.0955 / .0975	.0955 / .0975
Width of Oil Ring Grooves	.125 / .127	.125 / .127	.156 / .158	.156 / .158	.156 / .158	.156 / .158	.156 / .158	.156 / .158	.1565 / .1585	.1565 / .1585	.1565 / .1585	.1565 / .1585
Side Clearance of Ring Groove (Top) Comp.	.002 / .005		.002 / .004	.002 / .005	.002 / .005	.003 / .004	.002 / .003	.002 / .004	.002 / .004	.003 / .004	.003 / .0045	.0028 / .0039
(Bot.) Oil	.002 / .005	.002 / .003	.001 / .004	.001 / .004	.001 / .004	.002 / .003	.002 / .003	.002 / .004	.001 / .002	.001 / .002	.0010 / .0030	.0018 / .0038
Ring End Gap	.007 / .020	.007 / .020	.007 / .020	.007 / .020	.007 / .020	.007 / .020	.007 / .020	.007 / .020	.007 / .020	.007 / .020	.007 / .020	.007 / .020
Top Piston Land Clearance	.0015 / .0145	.015 / .018	.0165 / .0215	.017 / .022	.017 / .022	.017 / .022	.015 / .018	.017 / .020	.024 / .027	.018 / .021	.017 / .022	.017 / .022
Piston Skirt Clearance	.0025 / .0040	.0045 / .0060	.0045 / .0060	.0045 / .0060	.0050 / .0065	.0045 / .0060	.0055 / .0070	.0035 / .0050	.0045 / .0060	.0045 / .0060	.0045 / .0060	.0045 / .0060
Camshaft Bearing Dia.	.4975 / .4980	.4975 / .4980	.4975 / .4980	.4975 / .4980	.505 / .513	.4975 / .4980	.6230 / .6235	.6230 / .6235	.4975 / .4980	.4975 / .4980	.4975 / .4980	.4975 / .4980
Dia. of Crankshaft Mag. Main Brg.	.8735 / .8740	.8735 / .8740	.9985 / .9990	.8735 / .8740	.9985 / .9990	.9985 / .9990	.9985 / .9990	.9985 / .9990	.9990 / .9995	.9990 / .9995	.8735 / .8740	.9985 / .9990
Dia. of Crankshaft P.T.O. Main Brg.	.8735 / .8740	.8735 / .8740	.9985 / .9990	.8735 / .8740	.9985 / .9990	.9985 / .9990	.9985 / .9990	.9985 / .9990	.9985 / .9990	.9985 / .9990	.8735 / .8740	.9985 / .9990

A. For VM80 & HM80 engines only - Displacement is 19.41"

B. For VM80 & HM80 engines only - Bore is 3.125" (3⅛"). 3.126"

Note C. For VM80 & HM80 engines only - Piston Diameter is 3.1205" 3.1195"

14
Tecumseh 4-Stroke
6 through 12 Hp

ENGINE IDENTIFICATION

Lauson 4 cycle engines are identified by a model number stamped on a nameplate. The nameplate is located on the crankcase of vertical shaft models and on the blower housing of horizontal shaft models.

A typical model number appears on the illustration showing the location of the nameplate for vertical crankshaft engines. This number is interpreted as follows:

- V — vertical shaft engine
- 60 — 6.0 horsepower
- 70360J — the specification number. The last three numbers (360) indicate that this particular engine is a variation on the basic model line.
- 2361J — serial number
- 2 — year of manufacture
- 361 — the calendar day of manufacture
- J — line and shift location at the factory

MAINTENANCE

Air Cleaner Service

Service all the oil/foam polyurethane and oil bath air cleaner elements in the same manner as the Briggs and Stratton components. See Chapter Four.

The Tecumseh treated paper element type air cleaner consists of a pleated paper element encased in a metal housing and must be replaced as a unit. A flexible tubing and hose clamps connect the remotely mounted air filter to the carburetor.

Clean the element by lightly tapping it. Do not distort the case. When excessive carburetor adjustment or loss of power results, inspect the air filter to see if it is clogged. Replacing a severely restricted air filter should show an immediate performance improvement.

Check the oil level in the oil bath type air cleaners regularly to make sure the level is cor-

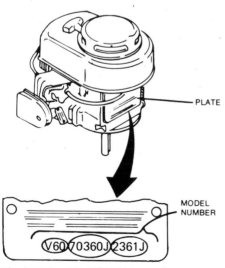

Vertical engine identification

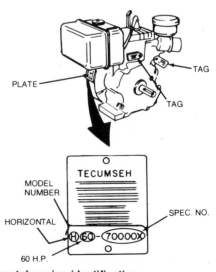

Horizontal engine identification

General Engine Specifications
Vertical Crankshaft Engines

Model	Bore & Stroke	Displacement	Horsepower
V60	2.625 × 2.5000	13.53	6
VH60	2.625 × 2.5000	13.53	6
V70	2.750 × 2.5313	15.0	7
VH70	2.750 × 2.5313	15.0	7
VM70	2.750 × 2.5313	15.0	7
V80	3.062 × 2.5313	18.65	8
VM80	3.125 × 2.5313	19.41	8
VM100	3.187 × 2.5313	17.16	8
ECV100	2.625 × 1.8438	10.0	—
TNT100	2.625 × 1.8434	20.2	—
ECV105	2.625 × 1.9375	10.5	—
ECV110	2.750 × 1.9375	11.5	—
ECV120	2.812 × 1.9375	12.0	—
TNT120	2.812 × 1.9375	12.0	—

General Engine Specifications
Horizontal Crankshaft Engines

Model	Bore & Stroke (in.)	Displacement (cu in.)	Horsepower
H60	2.6250 × 2.5000	13.53	6
HH60	2.6250 × 2.5000	13.53	6
H70	2.7500 × 2.5313	15.0	7
HH70	2.7500 × 2.5313	15.0	7
HM70	2.9375 × 2.5313	17.16	7
H80	3.0620 × 2.5313	18.65	8
HM80	3.0620 × 2.5313	18.65	8
HM100	3.1870 × 2.5313	20.2	10
ECH90	2.5000 × 1.8438	9.06	—

pat dry, and then coat with oil. squeeze the oil to distribute it evenly and remove the excess. Make sure all mounting surfaces are tight to prevent leakage.

rect. To add oil, unscrew the wingnut, pull off the filter element and add oil along the side of the filter until the level is correct. Use the same type and viscosity oil used in the engine.

If the filter is dirty, remove it and wash it in solvent. Also remove the filter bowl, drain the oil, and wash the filter in solvent. Refill the bowl with clean oil after putting it into position on the air horn.

A plain paper element is also used. It should be removed every 10 hours, or more often if the air is dusty. Tap or blow out the dirt form the inside with low pressure air. This type should be replaced at 50 hours. If clogged sooner, it may be washed in soap and water and rinsed by flushing from the inside until the water is clear. Blow dry with low pressure compressed air.

To service the KLEEN-AIRE system, move the element, wash it in soap and mild detergent,

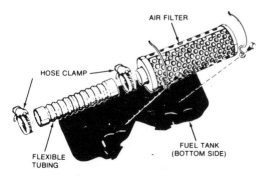

Treated paper element air cleaner (used on Craftsman engines)

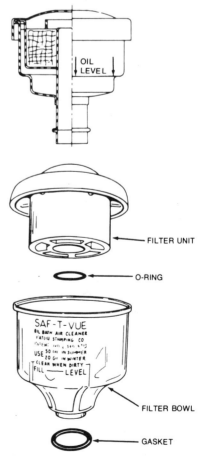

Exploded view of oil bath type air cleaner

Lubrication

OIL AND FUEL RECOMMENDATIONS

Use fresh (less than one month old) gasoline, of "Regular" grade. Unleaded fuel is preferred, but leader fuel is acceptable.

Use oil having SG classification. Use these viscosities for aluminum engines:
- Summer – above 32°F (0°C): S.A.E. 30 (S.A.E. 10W-30 or 10W-40 are acceptable substitutes)
- Winter – Below 32°F (0°C): S.A.E. 5W-30 (S.A.E. 10W is an acceptable substitute). (Including Snow King Snow Blower Engines)
- Winter – Below 0°F (−18°C) only: S.A.E. 10W diluted with 10% kerosene is an acceptable substitute. (Including Snow King Snow Blower Engines)

Use these viscosities for cast iron engines:
- Summer – Above 32°F (0°C): S.A.E. 30
- Winter – Above 32°F (0°C): S.A.E. 10W

Tune-Up Specifications

The follow basic specifications apply to all the engines covered in this section:
- Spark Plug Gap: 0.030 in. (0.76mm)
- Ignition Point Gap: 0.020 in. (0.50mm)
- Valve Clearance: 0.010 in. (0.25mm) for both intake and exhaust.

For timing dimension, which varies from engine to engine, see the complete specifications at the rear of this section.

Spark Plug Service

Spark plugs should be removed, cleaned, and adjusted periodically. Check the electrode gap with a wire feeler gauge and adjust the gap. Replace the plugs if the electrodes are pitted and burned or the porcelain is cracked. Refer to the Tecumseh master parts manual for the correct replacement number. Apply a little graphite grease to the threads to prevent sticking. Be sure the cleaned plugs are free of all foreign material.

Breaker Points

ADJUSTMENT

1. Disconnect the fuel line from the carburetor.
2. Remove the mounting screws, fuel tank, and shroud to provide access to the flywheel.
3. Remove the flywheel with either a puller (over 3.5 hp) or by using a screwdriver to pry underneath the flywheel while tapping the top lightly with a soft hammer.
4. Remove the dust cover and gasket from the magneto and crank the engine over until the breaker points of the magneto are fully opened.

5. Check the condition of the points and replace them if they are burned or pitted.
6. Check the point gap with a feeler gauge. Adjust them, if necessary, as per the directions on the dust cover. Refer to the specifications chart at the end of this chapter for point gap.

REPLACEMENT

1. Gain access to the points and inspect them as described above. If the points are badly pitted, follow the remaining steps to replace them.
2. Remove the nuts that hold the electrical leads to the screw on the movable breaker point spring. Remove the movable breaker point from stud.
3. Remove the screw and stationary breaker point. Put a new stationary breaker point on the breaker plate; install the screw, but do not tighten. This point must be moved to make the proper air gap when the points are adjusted.
4. Position a new movable breaker point on the stud.
5. Adjust the breaker point gap with a flat feeler gauge and tighten the screw.
6. Check the new point contact pattern and remove all grease, finger-prints, and dirt from contact surfaces.
7. Adjust the timing as described below.

Ignition Timing

ADJUSTMENT

1. Remove the cylinder head bolts, and move the head (with gasket in place) so that the spark plug hole is centered over the piston.
2. Using a ruler (through the spark plug hole) or special plunger type tool, carefully turn the engine back and forth until the piston is at exactly Top Dead Center. Tighten the thumbscrew on the tool.
3. Find the timing dimension for your engine in the specifications at the rear of the manual. Then, back off the position of the piston until it is about halfway down in the bore. Lower the ruler (or loosen the thumbscrew and lower the plunger, if using the special tool) exactly the required amount (the amount of the timing dimension). Then, hold the ruler in place (or tighten the special tool thumbscrew) and, finally carefully rotate the engine forward until the piston just touches the ruler or tool plunger.
4. Install a timing light or place a very thin piece of cellophane between the contact points. Loosen and rotate the stator just until the timing light shows a change in current flow or the cellophane pulls out of contact gap easily. Then, tighten stator bolts to specified torque.
5. Install the leads, point cover, flywheel, and shrouding.

SOLID STATE IGNITION SYSTEM CHECKOUT

The only on-engine check which can be made to determine whether the ignition system is working, is to separate the high tension lead from the spark plug and check for spark. If there is a spark, then the unit is allright and the spark plug should be replaced. No spark indicates that some other part needs replacing.

Check the individual components as follows:

• High Tension Lead: Inspect for cracks or indications of arcing. Replace the transformer if the condition of the lead is questionable.

• Low Tension Leads: Check all leads for shorts. Check the ignition cut-off lead to see that the unit is not grounded. Repair the leads, if possible, or replace them.

• Pulse Transformer: Replace and test for spark.

• Magneto: Replace and test for spark. Time the magneto by turning it counterclockwise as far as it will go and then tighten the retaining screws.

• Flywheel: Check the magnets for strength. With the flywheel off the engine, it should attract a screwdriver that is held 1 in. (25mm) from the magnetic surface on the inside of the flywheel. Be sure that the key locks the flywheel to the crankshaft.

Carburetor Mixture Adjustments

1. If the carburetor has been overhauled, or the engine won't start, make initial mixture screw adjustments as specified in the chart.

2. Start the engine and allow it to warm up to normal running temperature. With the engine running at maximum recommended rpm, loosen the main adjustment screw until engine rpm drops off, then tighten the screw until the engine starts to cut out. Note the number of turns from one extreme to the other. Loosen the screw to a point midway between the extremes.

NOTE: *Some carburetors have fixed jets. If there is no main adjusting screw and receptacle, no adjustment is needed.*

3. After the main system is adjusted, move the speed control lever to the idle position and follow the same procedure for adjusting the idle system.

4. Test the engine by running it under a normal load. The engine should respond to load pickup immediately. An engine that "dies" is too lean. An engine which ran roughly before picking up the load is adjusted too rich.

Governor

ADJUSTMENT

Air Vane Type

1. Operate the engine with the governor adjusting lever or panel control set to the highest possible speed position and check the speed. If the speed is not within the recommended limits, the governed speed should be adjusted.

2. Loosen the locknut on the high speed limit adjusting screw and turn the adjusting screw out to increase the top engine speed.

Chart of Initial Carburetor Adjustments

Adjustment	For Engines Built Prior to 1977	For Engines Built After 1977
Main Adjustment Up to 7 HP	V-60-70-1¼ H-60-70-1¼	Same
Main Adjustment VM70-80-100 & HM70-80-100	1¼	1½
Idle Adjustment Up to 7 HP	V-60-70-1 Turn H-60-70-1 Turn	Same
Idle Adjustment VM70-80-100 & HM70-80-100	1½	1¼
Idle Speed (Top of Carburetor) Regulating screw	Back out screw, then turn in until screw just touches throttle lever and continue 1 turn more (if idle RPM is given set final idle speed with a tachometer)	

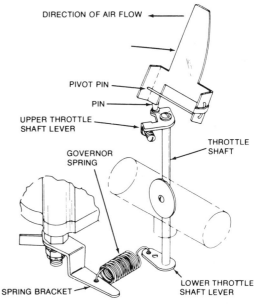

Schematic of the operation of an air vane governor

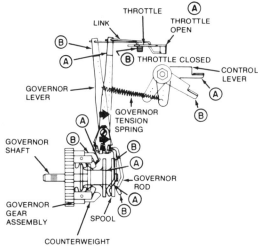

Schematic of mechanical governor operation

Ⓐ GOVERNED POSITION
Ⓝ NON-GOVERNED POSITION
◆ DIRECTION OF ADJUSTMENT—THIS SCHEMATIC

Mechanical Type

1. Set the control lever to the idle position so that no spring tension affects the adjustment.
2. Loosen the screw so that the governor lever is loose in the clamp.
3. Rotate both the lever and the clamp to move the throttle to the full open position (away from the idle speed regulating screw).
4. Tighten the screw when no end-play exists in the direction of open throttle.
5. Move the throttle lever to the full speed setting and check to see that the control linkage opens the throttle.

Compression Check

1. Run the engine until warm to lubricate and seal the cylinder.
2. Remove the spark plug and install a compression gauge. Turn the engine over with the pull starter or electric starter.
3. Compression on new engines is 80 psi. If the reading is below 60 psi., repeat the test after removing the gauge and squirting about a teaspoonful of engine oil through the spark plug hole. If the compression improves temporarily following this, the problem is probably with the cylinder, piston, and rings. Otherwise, the valves require service.

FUEL SYSTEM

Carburetor

NOTE: *Four-cycle Tecumseh engines use float or diaphragm type carburetors.*

REMOVAL AND INSTALLATION

1. Drain the fuel tank. Remove the air cleaner and disconnect the carburetor fuel lines.
2. If necessary, remove any shrouding or control panels to provide access to carburetor.
3. Disconnect the choke or throttle control wires at the carburetor.
4. Remove the cap screws, or nuts and lockwashers that hold the carburetor to the engine; remove the carburetor.
5. Secure the carburetor on to engine.
6. Install the shrouding or control panels. Connect the choke and throttle control wires.
7. Position the control panel to carburetor. Connect the carburetor fuel lines.
8. Install the air cleaner.
9. Adjust the carburetor as described above.

GENERAL OVERHAUL INSTRUCTIONS

1. Carefully disassemble the carburetor removing all non-metallic parts, i.e.; gaskets, viton seats and needles, O-rings, fuel pump valves, etc.
   NOTE: *Nylon check balls used in some diaphragm carburetor models may or may not be serviceable. Check to be sure of serviceability before attempting removal.*
2. Clean all metallic parts with solvent.
   NOTE: *Nylon can be damaged if subjected to harsh cleaners for prolonged periods.*
3. The large O-rings sealing the fuel bowl to the carburetor body must be in good condition to prevent leakage. If the O-ring leaks, interfering with the atmospheric pressure in the float bowl, the engine will run rich. Foreign material can enter through the leaking area and cause blocking of the metering orifices. This O-ring should be replaced after the carburetor has been disassembled for repair. Lubricate the new O-ring with a small amount of oil to allow the fuel bowl to slide onto the O-ring properly. Hold the carburetor body in an inverted position and place the O-ring on the carburetor body and then position the fuel bowl.
4. The small O-rings used on the carburetor adjustment screws must be in good condition or a leak will develop and cause improper adjustment of carburetor.
5. Check all adjusting screws for wear. The illustration shows a worn screw and a good screw. Replace screws that are worn.
6. Check the carburetor inlet needle and seat for wear, scoring, or other damage. Replace defective parts.
7. Check the carburetor float for dents, leaks, worn hinge or other damage.
8. Check the carburetor body for cracks, clogged passages, and worn bushings. Clean clogged air passages with clean, dry compressed air.

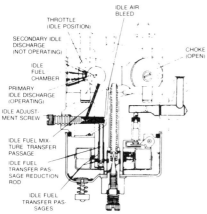

The idle operation of a float feed carburetor. The throttle plate closes, restricting the flow of fuel and air, forcing the engine to run on a reduced volume of fuel and air.

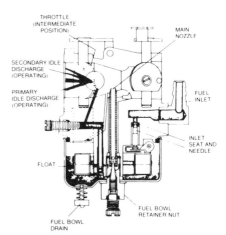

The intermediate operation of a float feed carburetor. The throttle plate "cracks" open to reduce the restriction and the engine runs on an increased volume of fuel and air.

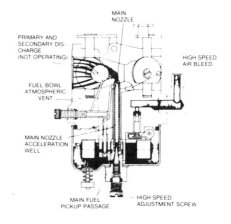

FUEL ■■■
AIR
MIXTURE ■■■

The high speed operation of a float feed carburetor. The air venturi replaces the throttle plate as the restricting device and the engine runs on its greatest volume of fuel and air.

9. Check the diaphragms on diaphragm carburetors for cracks, punctures, distortion, or deterioration.

10. Check all shafts and pivot pins for wear on the bearing surfaces, distortion, or other damage.

NOTE: *Each time a carburetor is disassembled, it is good practice to install a repair kit.*

11. Where there is excessive vibration, a damper spring may be used to assist in holding the float against the inlet needle thus minimizing the flooding condition. Two types of springs are available; the float shaft (hinge pin) type and the inlet needle mounted type.

12. Float shaft spring positioning:

a. The spring is slipped over the shaft.

b. The rectangular shaped spring end is hooked onto the float tab.

c. The shorter angled spring end is placed onto the float bowl gasket support.

13. Note that on late model carburetors, the spring clip fastened to the inlet needle has been revised to provide a damping effect. The clip fastens to the needle and is hooked over the float tab.

FLOAT FEED CARBURETOR

Note the following points when rebuilding these carburetors.

Throttle

1. Examine the throttle lever and plate prior to disassembly. Replace any worn parts.

2. Remove the screw in the center of the throttle plate and pull out the throttle shaft lever assembly.

3. When reassembling, it is important that the lines on the throttle plate are facing out when in the closed position. Position the throttle plates with the two lines at 12 and 3 o'clock.

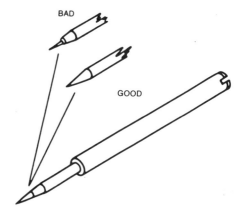

BAD

GOOD

Appearance of good and bad mixture adjusting screws

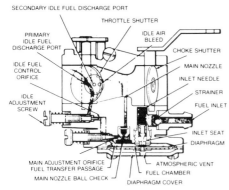

The choke position of the diaphragm carburetor. The closed choke plate restricts the amount of air, creating a richened mixture by drawing in a greater proportion of fuel.

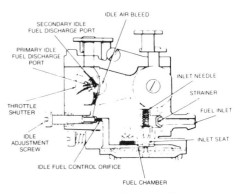

The intermediate operation of a diaphragm carburetor. The throttle plate "cracks" to decrease the restriction and the engine runs on an increased volume of fuel and air.

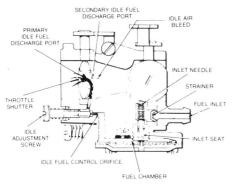

The idling operation of a diaphragm carburetor. The throttle plate closes, restricting the flow of fuel and air, forcing the engine to run on a reduced volume of fuel and air.

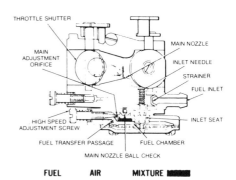

FUEL　　AIR　　MIXTURE ▓▓▓▓

The high speed operation of a diaphragm carburetor. The air ventui replaces the throttle plate as the restricting device and the engine runs on its greatest volume of fuel and air.

The throttle shaft must be held in tight to the bottom bearing to prevent the throttle plate from riding on the throttle bore of the body which would cause excessive throttle plate wear and governor hunting.

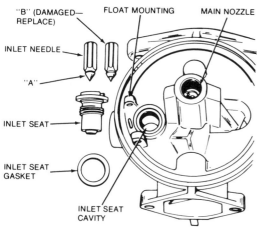

Appearance of good and bad inlet needles

Choke

Examine the choke lever and shaft at the bearing points and holes into which the linkage is fastened and replace any worn parts. The choke plate is inserted into the air horn of the carburetor in such a way that the flat surface of the choke is toward the fuel bowl.

Idle Adjusting Screw

Remove the idle screw from the carburetor body and examine the point for damage to the seating surface on the taper. If damaged, replace the idle adjusting needle. Tension is maintained on the screw with a coil spring and sealed with an O-ring. Examine and replace the O-ring if it is worn or damaged.

High Speed Adjusting Jet

Remove the screw and examine the taper. If the taper is damaged at the area where it seats, replace the screw and fuel bowl retainer nut as an assembly.

The fuel bowl retainer nut contains the seat for the screw. Examine the sealing O-ring on the

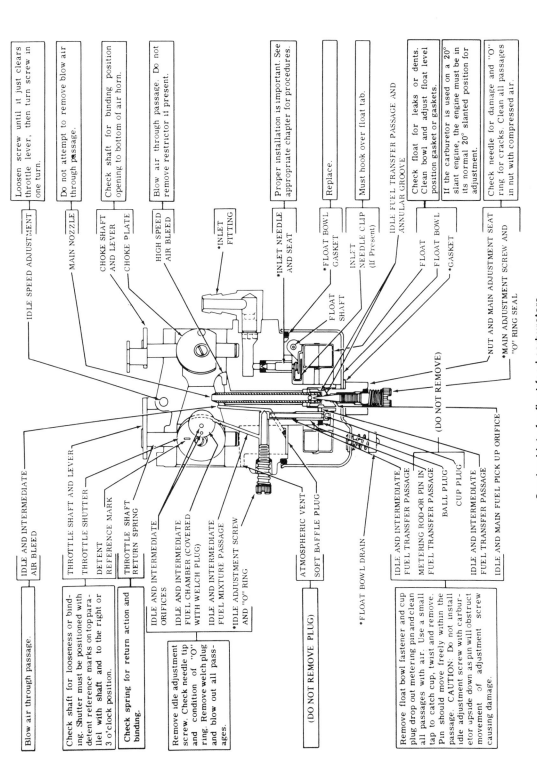

Loosen screw until it just clears throttle lever, then turn screw in one turn.

— IDLE SPEED ADJUSTMENT

Do not attempt to remove blow air through passage.

— MAIN NOZZLE

Check shaft for binding position opening to bottom of air horn.

— CHOKE SHAFT AND LEVER

— CHOKE PLATE

Blow air through passage. Do not remove restrictor if present.

— HIGH SPEED AIR BLEED

— *INLET FITTING

Proper installation is important. See appropriate chapter for procedures.

— *INLET NEEDLE AND SEAT

— FLOAT SHAFT

Replace.

— *FLOAT BOWL GASKET

Must hook over float tab.

— INLET NEEDLE CLIP (If Present)

— IDLE FUEL TRANSFER PASSAGE AND ANNULAR GROOVE

Check float for leaks or dents. Clean bowl and adjust float level position gasket or gaskets.

— FLOAT

— FLOAT BOWL

If the carburetor is used on a 20° slant engine, the engine must be in its normal 20° slanted position for adjustment.

— *GASKET

— (DO NOT REMOVE)

Check needle for damage and "O" ring for cracks. Clean all passages in nut with compressed air.

— NUT AND MAIN ADJUSTMENT SEAT

— *MAIN ADJUSTMENT SCREW AND "O" RING SEAL

Blow air through passage.

— IDLE AND INTERMEDIATE AIR BLEED

Check shaft for looseness or binding. Shutter must be positioned with detent reference marks on top parallel with shaft and to the right or 3 o'clock position.

— THROTTLE SHAFT AND LEVER

— THROTTLE SHUTTER

— DETENT REFERENCE MARK

Check spring for return action and binding.

— THROTTLE SHAFT RETURN SPRING

— IDLE AND INTERMEDIATE ORIFICES

Remove idle adjustment screw. Check needle tip and condition of "O" ring. Remove welch plug and blow out all passages.

— IDLE AND INTERMEDIATE FUEL CHAMBER (COVERED WITH WELCH PLUG)

— IDLE AND INTERMEDIATE FUEL MIXTURE PASSAGE

— *IDLE ADJUSTMENT SCREW AND "O" RING

— ATMOSPHERIC VENT

— SOFT BAFFLE PLUG

(DO NOT REMOVE PLUG)

— *FLOAT BOWL DRAIN

Remove float bowl fastener and cup plug drop out metering pin and clean all passages with air. Use a small tap to catch cup, twist and remove. Pin should move freely within the passage. CAUTION: Do not install idle adjustment screw with carburetor upside down as pin will obstruct movement of adjustment screw causing damage.

— IDLE AND INTERMEDIATE FUEL TRANSFER PASSAGE

— METERING ROD OR PIN IN FUEL TRANSFER PASSAGE

— BALL PLUG

— CUP PLUG

— IDLE AND INTERMEDIATE FUEL TRANSFER PASSAGE

— IDLE AND MAIN FUEL PICK UP ORIFICE

Service hints for float feed carburetors

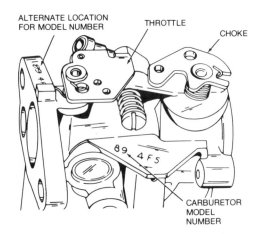

Float feed carburetor identification number

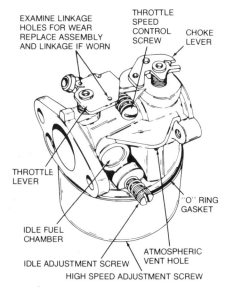

External view of a Tecumseh float type carburetor

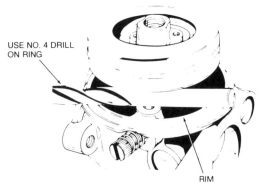

Adjusting the float level

The fuel bowl should be examined for rust and dirt. Thoroughly clean it before installing it. If it is impossible to properly clean the fuel bowl, replace it.

Check the drain valve for leakage. Replace the rubber gasket on the inside of the drain valve if it leaks.

Examine the large O-ring that seals the fuel bowl to the carburetor body. If it is worn or cracked, replace it with a new one, making sure the same type is used (square or round).

Float

1. Remove the float from the carburetor body by pulling out the float axle with a pair of needle nose pliers. The inlet needle will be lifted off the seat because it is attached to the float with an anchoring clip.

2. Examine the float for damage and holes. Check the float hinge for wear and replace it if worn.

3. The float level is checked by positioning a #4 drill bit across the rim between the center leg and the unmachined surface of the index pad, parallel to the float axle pin. If the index pad is machined, the float setting should be made with a #9 drill bit.

4. Remove the float to make an adjustment. Bend the tab on the float hinge to correct the float setting.

NOTE: *Direct compressed air in the opposite direction of normal flow of air or fuel (reverse taper) to dislodge foreign matter.*

Inlet Needle and Seat

1. The inlet needle sits on a rubber seat in the carburetor body instead of the usual metal fitting.

2. Remove it, place a few drops of heavy engine oil on the seat, and pry it out with a short piece of hooked wire.

3. The grooved side of the seat is inserted first. Lubricate the cavity with oil and use a flat faced punch to press the inlet seat into place.

4. Examine the inlet needle for wear and

high speed adjusting screw. Replace the O-ring if it indicates wear or cuts. During the reassembly of the high speed adjusting screw, position the coil spring on the adjusting screw, followed by the small brass washer and the O-ring seal.

Fuel Bowl

To remove the fuel bowl, remove the retaining nut and fiber washer. Replace the nut if it is cracked or worn.

The retaining nut contains the transfer passage through which fuel is delivered to the high speed and idle fuel system of the carburetor. It is the large hole next to the hex nut end of the fitting. If a problem occurs with the idle system of the carburetor, examine the small fuel passage in the annular groove in the retaining nut. This passage must be clean for the proper transfer of fuel into the idle metering system.

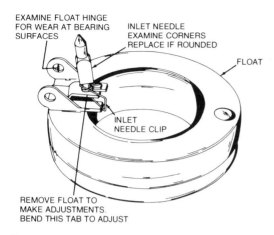

EXAMINE FLOAT HINGE
FOR WEAR AT BEARING
SURFACES

INLET NEEDLE
EXAMINE CORNERS
REPLACE IF ROUNDED

FLOAT

INLET
NEEDLE CLIP

REMOVE FLOAT TO
MAKE ADJUSTMENTS.
BEND THIS TAB TO ADJUST

Float, inlet needle, and clip

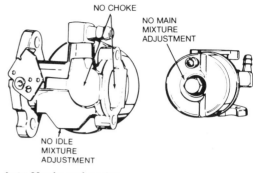

NO CHOKE

NO MAIN
MIXTURE
ADJUSTMENT

NO IDLE
MIXTURE
ADJUSTMENT

Auto-Magic carburetor

rounding off of the corners. If this condition does exist, replace the inlet needle.

Fuel Inlet Fitting

1. The inlet fitting is removed by twisting and pulling at the same time.

2. Use sealer when reinstalling the fitting. Insert the tip of the fitting into the carburetor body. Press the fitting in until the shoulder contacts the carburetor. Only use inlet fittings without screens.

Carburetor Body

1. Check the carburetor body for wear and damage.

2. If excessive dirt has accumulated in the atmospheric vent cavity, try cleaning it with carburetor solvent or compressed air. Remove the welch plug only as a last resort.

NOTE: *The carburetor body contains a pressed-in main nozzle tube at a specific depth and position within the venturi. Do not attempt to remove the main nozzle. Any change in nozzle positioning will adversely affect the metering quality and will require carburetor replacement.*

3. Clean the acclerating well around the main nozzle with compressed air and carburetor cleaning solvents.

4. The carburetor body contains two cup plugs, neither of which should be removed. A cup plug located near the inlet seat cavity, high up on the carburetor body, seals off the idle bleed. This is a straight passage drilled into the carburetor throat. Do not remove this plug. Another cup plug is located in the base where the fuel bowl nut seals the idle fuel passage. Do not remove this plug or the metering rod.

5. A small ball plug located on the side of the idle fuel passage seals this passage. Do not remove this ball plug.

6. The welch plug on the side of the carbure-tor body, just above the idle adjusting screw, seals the idle fuel chamber. This plug can be removed for cleaning of the idle fuel mixture passage and the primary and secondary idle fuel discharge ports. Do not use any tools that might change the size of the discharge ports, such as wire or pins.

Resilient Tip Needle

Replace the inlet needle. do not attempt to remove or replace the seat in the carburetor body.

Viton Seat

Using a 10–24 or 10–32 tap, turn the tap into the brass seat fitting until it grasps the seat firmly. Clamp the tap shank into a vise and tap the carburetor body with a soft hammer until the seat slides out of the body.

To replace the viton seat, position the replacement over the receptical with the soft rubber like seat toward the body. Use a flat punch and a small hammer to drive the seat into the body until it bottoms on the shoulder.

TECUMSEH AUTOMATIC NON-ADJUSTABLE FLOAT FEED CARBURETOR

This carburetor has neither a choke plate nor idle and main mixture adjusting screws. There is no running adjustment. The float adjustment is the standard Tecumseh float setting of #4 drill bit.

Cleaning

Remove all non-metallic parts and clean them using a procedure similar to that for the other carburetors. Never use wires through any of the drilled holes. Do not remove the baffling welch plug unless it is certain there is a blockage under the plug. There are no blind passageways in this carburetor.

Some engines use a variation on the Automatic Nonadjustable carburetor which has a different bowl hold-on nut and main jet orifices. There are two main jet orifices and a deeper fuel reserve cavity, but service procedures are the same.

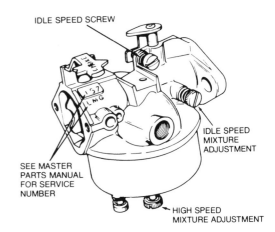

Walbro float feed carburetor

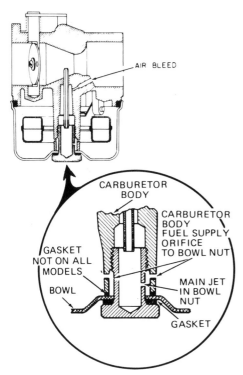

Variation on non-adjustable float feed carburetor

WALBRO AND TILLOTSON FLOAT FEED CARBURETORS

Procedures are similar to those for the Tecumseh float carburetor with the exceptions noted below.

Main Nozzle

The main nozzle in Wallbro carburetors is cross drilled after it is installed in the carburetor. Once removed, it cannot be reinstalled, since it is impossible to properly realign the cross drilled holes. Grooved service replacement main nozzles are available which allow alignment of these holes.

Float Shaft Spring

Carefully position the float shaft spring on models so equipped. The spring dampens float action when properly assembled. Use needlenosed pliers to hook the end of the spring over the float hinge and then insert the pin as far as possible before lifting the spring from the hinge into position. Leaving the spring out or improper installation will cause unbalanced float action and result in a touchy adjustment.

Float Adjustment

1. To check the float adjustment, invert the assembled float carburetor body. Check the

clearance between the body and the float, opposite the hinge. Clearance should be $\frac{1}{8}$ in. $\pm$ $\frac{1}{64}$ in. (3mm $\pm$ 0.4mm).

2. To adjust the float level, remove the float shaft and float. Bend the lip of the float tang to correct the measurement.

3. Assemble the parts and recheck the adjustment.

TILLOTSON E FLOAT FEED TYPE CARBURETOR

The following adjustments are different for this carburetor.

Running Adjustment

1. Start the engine and allow it to warm up to operating temperatures. Make sure the choke is fully opened after the engine is warmed up.

2. Run the engine at a constant speed while slowly turning the main adjustment screw in until the engine begins to lose speed; then slow-

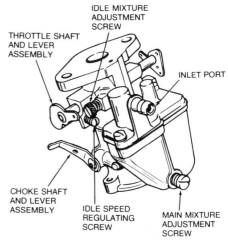

Tillotson Model E float carburetor

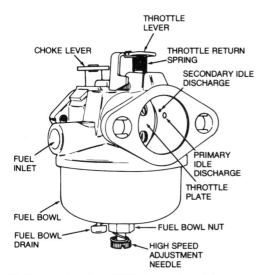

Walbro Carburetor #631635—engine side

ly back it out about ⅛–¼ of a turn until maximum speed and power is obtained (4000 rpm). This is the correct power adjustment.

3. Close the throttle and cause the engine to idle slightly faster than normal by turning the idle speed regulating screw in. Then turn the idle adjustment speed screw in until the engine begins to lose speed; then turn it back ¼–½ of a turn until the engine idles smoothly. Adjust the idle speed regulating screw until the desired idling speed is acquired.

4. Alternately open and close the throttle a few times for an acceleration test. If stalling occurs at idle speeds, repeat the adjustment procedures to get the proper idle speed.

Float Level Adjustment

1. Remove the carburetor float bowl cover and float mechanism assembly.

2. Remove the float bowl cover gasket and, with the complete assembly in an upside down position and the float lever tang resting on the seated inlet needle, a measurement of ¹⁵⁄₆₄ in. (6mm) should be maintained from the free end flat rim, or edge of the cover, to the toe of the float. Measurement can be checked with a standard straight rule or depth gauge.

3. If it is necessary to raise or lower the float lever setting, remove the float lever pin and the float, then carefully bend the float lever tang up or down as required to obtain the correct measurement.

WALBRO CARBURETORS FOR V80, VM80, H80, AND HM80 ENGINES

Adjustment

The following initial carburetor adjustments are to be used to start the engine. For proper carburetion adjustment, the atmospheric vent

must be open. Examine and clean it if necessary.

1. Idle adjustment — 1¼ turn from its seat.
2. High speed adjustment — 1½ turn form its seat.
3. Throttle stop screw — 1 turn after contacting the throttle lever.

After the engine reaches normal operating temperature, make the final adjustments for best idle and high speed within the following ranges. Recommended speeds: Idle: 1800–2300 rpm. High speed: 3450–3750 rpm.

Rebuilding Notes

1. The throttle plate is installed with the lettering (if present) facing outward when closed. The throttle plate is installed on the throttle level with the lever in the closed position if there is binding after the plate is in position, loosen the throttle plate and reposition it.

2. Before removing the fuel bowl nut, remove the high speed adjusting needle. Use a ⁷⁄₁₆ in. (11mm) box wrench or socket to remove the fuel bowl nut. When replacing the fuel bowl

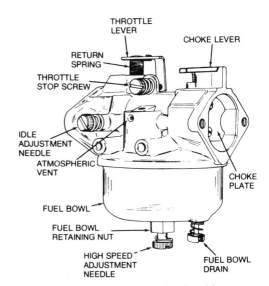

Walbro Carburetor #631635—intake side

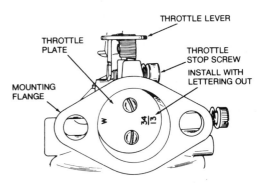

Installation of the throttle plate

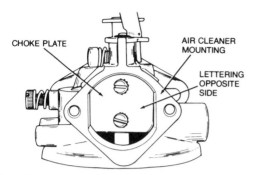

Installation of the choke plate

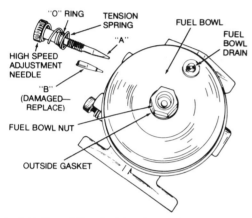

Installation of the fuel bowl and the high speed adjustment needle

nut, be sure to position the fiber gasket under the nut and tighten it securely.

3. Examine the high speed needle tip and, if it appears to be worn, replace it. When the high speed jet is replaced, the main nozzle, which includes the jet seat, should also be replaced. The original main nozzle cannot be used. There are special replacement nozzles available.

4. The inlet needle valve is replaceable if it appears to be worn. The inlet valve seat is also replaceable and should be replaced if the needle valve is replaced.

Float Adjustment

1. The Float setting for this carburetor is $5/64$–$7/64$ in. (2.0–2.8mm).

2. The float is set in the traditional manner, at the opposite end of the float from the float hinge and needle valve.

3. Bend the adjusting tab to adjust the float level.

DIAPHRAGM CARBURETORS

Diaphragm carburetors have a rubber-like diaphragm that is exposed to crankcase pressure on one side and to atmospheric pressure on the other side. As the crankcase pressure decreases, the diaphragm moves against the inlet needle

allowing the inlet needle to move from its seat which permits fuel to flow through the inlet valve to maintain the correct fuel level in the fuel chamber.

An advantage of this type of system over the float system, is that the engine can be operated in any position.

NOTE: *In rebuilding, use carburetor cleaner only on metal parts, except for the main nozzle in the main body.*

Throttle Plate

Install the throttle plate with the short line that is stamped in the plate toward the top of the carburetor, parallel with the throttle shaft, and facing out when the throttle is closed.

Choke Plate

Install the choke plate with the flat side of the choke toward the fuel inlet side of the carburetor. The mark faces in and is parallel to the choke shaft.

Idle Mixture Adjustment Screw

There is a neoprene O-ring on the needle. Never soak the O-ring in carburetor solvent. Idle and main mixture screws vary in size and design, so make sure that you have the correct replacement.

Idle Fuel Chamber

The welch plug can be removed if the carburetor is extremely dirty.

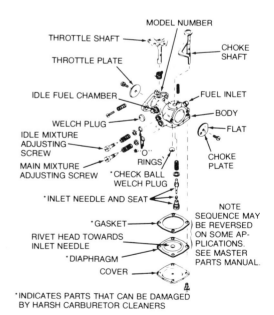

Exploded view of a Tecumseh diaphragm carburetor

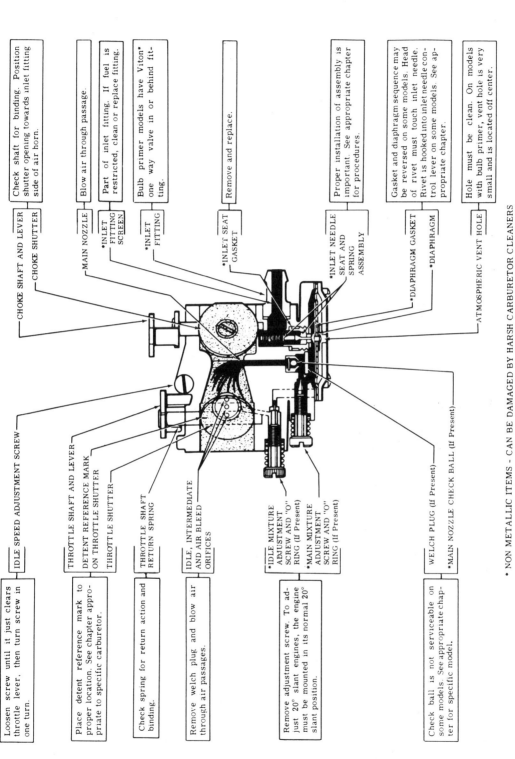

CHECK SHAFT AND LEVER — Check shaft for binding. Position shutter opening towards inlet fitting side of air horn.

CHOKE SHUTTER

MAIN NOZZLE — Blow air through passage.

*INLET FITTING SCREEN — Part of inlet fitting. If fuel is restricted, clean or replace fitting.

INLET FITTING — Bulb primer models have Viton one way valve in or behind fitting.

*INLET SEAT GASKET — Remove and replace.

*INLET NEEDLE SEAT AND SPRING ASSEMBLY — Proper installation of assembly is important. See appropriate chapter for procedures.

*DIAPHRAGM GASKET — Gasket and diaphragm sequence may be reversed on some models. Head of rivet must touch inlet needle. Rivet is hooked into inlet needle control lever on some models. See appropriate chapter.

*DIAPHRAGM

ATMOSPHERIC VENT HOLE — Hole must be clean. On models with bulb primer, vent hole is very small and is located off center.

IDLE SPEED ADJUSTMENT SCREW — Loosen screw until it just clears throttle lever, then turn screw in one turn.

THROTTLE SHAFT AND LEVER

DETENT REFERENCE MARK ON THROTTLE SHUTTER — Place detent reference mark to proper location. See chapter appropriate to specific carburetor.

THROTTLE SHUTTER

THROTTLE SHAFT RETURN SPRING — Check spring for return action and binding.

IDLE, INTERMEDIATE AND AIR BLEED ORIFICES — Remove welch plug and blow air through air passages.

*IDLE MIXTURE ADJUSTMENT SCREW AND "O" RING (If Present)
*MAIN MIXTURE ADJUSTMENT SCREW AND "O" RING (If Present) — Remove adjustment screw. To adjust 20° slant engines, the engine must be mounted in its normal 20° slant position.

WELCH PLUG (If Present) — Check ball is not serviceable on some models. See appropriate chapter for specific model.

*MAIN NOZZLE CHECK BALL (If Present)

* NON METALLIC ITEMS - CAN BE DAMAGED BY HARSH CARBURETOR CLEANERS

Service hints for the diaphragm carburetors

Diaphragms

Diaphragms are serviced and replaced by removing the four retaining screws from the cover. With the cover removed, the diaphragm and gasket may be serviced. Never soak the diaphragm in carburetor solvent. Replace the diaphragm if it is cracked or torn. Be sure there are no wrinkles in the diaphragm when it is replaced. The diaphragm rivet head is always placed facing the inlet needle valve.

Inlet Needle and Seat

The inlet seat is removed by using either a slotted screwdriver (early type) or a $9/32$ in. socket. The inlet needle is spring loaded, so be careful when removing it.

Fuel Inlet Fitting

All of the diaphragm carburetors have an integral strainer in the inlet fitting. To clean it, either reverse flush it or use compressed air after removing the inlet needle and seat. If the strainer is lacquered or otherwise unable to be cleaned, replace the fitting.

CRAFTSMAN FUEL SYSTEMS

Changes in Late Model Carburetors

The newest Craftsman carburetors incorporate the following changes:

a. The cable form of control is replaced by a control knob.

b. The fuel pickup is longer and has a collar machined into it which must be installed tight against the carburetor body.

c. The fuel pickup screen is pressed onto the ends of the fill tubes on both models, but the measured depth has changed.

d. The cross-drilled passages have been eliminated, as has the O-ring on the body. There are no cup plugs.

e. The fuel tank and reservoir tube have been revised — the reservoir tube being larger.

Disassembly and Service

1. Remove the air cleaner assembly and remove the four screws on the top of the carburetor body to separate the fuel tank from the carburetor.

2. Remove the O-ring from between the carburetor and the fuel tank. Examine it for cracks and damage and replace it if necessary.

3. Carefully remove the reservoir tube from the fuel tank. Observe the end of the tube that rested on the bottom of the fuel tank. It should be slotted.

4. Remove the control valve by turning the valve clockwise until the flange is clear of the retaining boss. Pull the valve straight out and

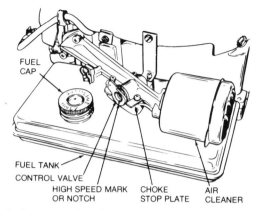

FUEL CAP

FUEL TANK
CONTROL VALVE
HIGH SPEED MARK OR NOTCH
CHOKE STOP PLATE
AIR CLEANER

Craftsman fuel tank mounted carburetor

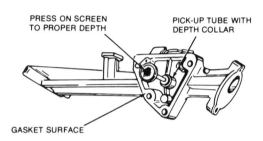

PRESS ON SCREEN TO PROPER DEPTH
PICK-UP TUBE WITH DEPTH COLLAR
GASKET SURFACE

LATE MODEL

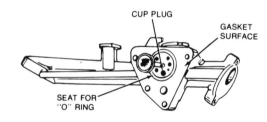

CUP PLUG
GASKET SURFACE
SEAT FOR "O" RING

EARLY MODEL

Details of pick-up tube used on revised Craftsman carburetor

examine the O-ring seal for damage or wear. If possible, use a new O-ring when reassembling.

5. Examine the fuel pick up tube. There are no valves or ball checks that may become in-operative. These parts can normally be cleaned with carburetor solvent. If it is found that the passage cannot be cleared, the fuel pick up tubes can be replaced. Carefully remove the old ones so as not to enlarge the opening in the carburetor body. If the pickup tube and screen must be replaced, follow the directions shown in the illustration for the type of carburetor (early or late model) on which you are working.

6. Assemble the carburetor in reverse order of disassembly. Use new O-rings and gaskets. When assembling reservoir tube, hold the carburetor upside down and place the reservoir tube over the pickup tube with the slotted end up. Make sure the intake manifold gasket is

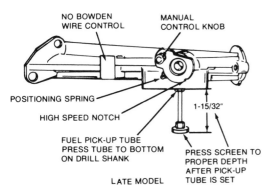

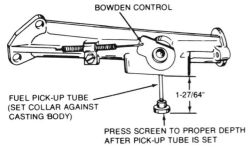

Details of manual control knob and several other changes incorporated in new Craftsman carburetors

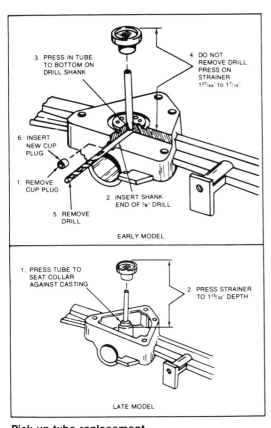

Pick-up tube replacement

correctly positioned — it can be assembled blocking the intake passage partially.

Adjustments

1. Move the carburetor control valve to the high speed position. The mark on the face of the valve should be in alignment with the retaining boss on the carburetor body.

2. Move the operator's control on the equipment to the high speed position.

3. Insert the bowden wire into the hole of the control valve. Clamp the bowden wire sheath to the carburetor body.

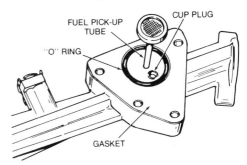

Positioning of the reservoir tube in the fuel tank

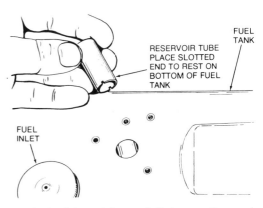

The fuel pick-up tube and O-ring on the early model Craftsman carburetor

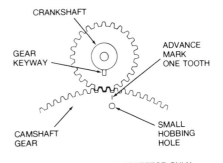

Timing an engine with the Craftsman fuel tank mounted carburetor

NOTE: *If the engine was disassembled and the camshaft removed, be sure that the timing marks on the camshaft gear and the keyway in the crankshaft gear are aligned when reinserting the camshaft. Then lift the camshaft enough to advance the camshaft gear timing mark to the right (clockwise) ONE tooth, as viewed from the power take-off end of the crankshaft.*

CRAFTSMAN FLOAT TYPE CARBURETORS

Craftsman float type carburetors are serviced in the same manner as the other Tecumseh float type carburetors. The throttle control valve has three positions: stop, run, and start.

When the control valve is removed, replace the O-ring. If the engine runs sluggishly, consider the possibility of a leaky O-ring.

To remove the fuel pickup tube, clamp the tube in a vise and then twist the carburetor body. Check the small jet in the air horn while the tube is out. In replacement, position the tube squarely and then press in on the collar until the collar seats.

In assembly, install the gasket and bolt through the bowl, position the centering spacer onto the bolt, and then attach the parts to the carburetor body.

The camshaft timing mark must be advanced one tooth in relation to crankshaft gear timing mark, as shown in the illustration above. However, when this type carburetor is used with a float bowl reservoir and variable governor adjustment, time it as for other Tecumseh engines — with the camshaft and crankshaft timing marks aligned.

Governor

The mechanical governor is located inside the mounting flange. See engine disassembly instructions, below. To disassemble the governor, see the illustration, and: remove the retaining ring, pull off the spool, remove the second retaining ring, and then pull off the gear assembly and retainer washer.

Check for wear on all moving surfaces, but especially gear teeth, the inside diameter of the gear where it rides on the shaft, and the flyweights where they work against the spool.

If the governor shaft must be replaced, it should be started into the boss with a few taps using a soft hammer, and then pressed in with a press or vise. The shaft can be installed by positioning a wooden block on top and tapping the upper surface of the block, but the use of a vise or press is much preferred.

The shaft must be pressed in until just the required length is exposed, as measured from the

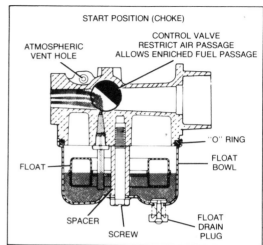

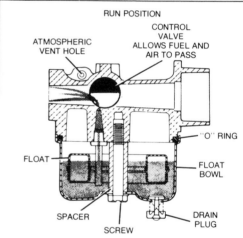

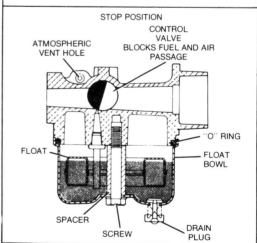

Start, run and stop throttle positions of a Craftsman float type carburetor

top of the shaft boss to the upper end of the shaft. See the chart.

The governor is installed in reverse of the removal procedure. Connect the linkage and then adjust as described in the Tune-Up section.

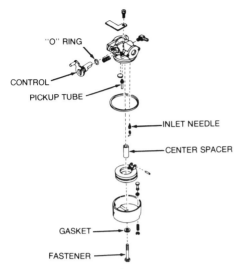

"O" RING

CONTROL

PICKUP TUBE

INLET NEEDLE

CENTER SPACER

GASKET

FASTENER

Exploded view of the Craftsman float type carburetor

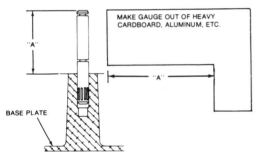

MAKE GAUGE OUT OF HEAVY CARDBOARD, ALUMINUM, ETC.

"A"

"A"

BASE PLATE

Measuring governor shaft installed dimension

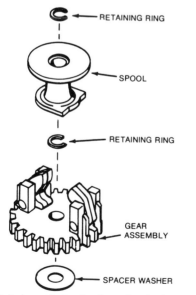

RETAINING RING

SPOOL

RETAINING RING

GEAR ASSEMBLY

SPACER WASHER

Exploded view of standard mechanical governor

Shaft Installed Dimension/ Engine Model Chart

Engine Model	"A" Exposed Shaft Length (see figure)
TNT100-120 ECV100-105-110-120 ECH90 TVS75-90-105-120	$1^{5}/_{16}''$
V60 VM70-80-100	$1^{19}/_{32}''$
H60 HH60-70	$1^{7}/_{16}''$
HM70-80-100	$1^{13}/_{32}''$

ENGINE OVERHAUL

Timing Gears

Correctly matched camshaft gear and crankshaft gear timing marks are necessary for the engine to perform properly.

On all camshafts the timing mark is located in line with the center of the hobbing hole (small hole in the face of the gear). If no line is visible, use the center of the hobbing hole to align with the crankshaft gear marked tooth.

On crankshafts where the gear is held on by a key, the timing mark is the tooth in line with the keyway.

On crankshafts where the gear is pressed onto the crankshaft, a tooth is bevelled to serve as the timing mark.

On engines with a ball bearing on the power take-off end of the crankshaft, look for a bevelled tooth which serves as the crankshaft gear timing mark.

If the engine uses a Craftsman type carburetor, the camshaft timing mark must be advanced clockwise one tooth ahead of the matching timing mark on the crankshaft, the excep-

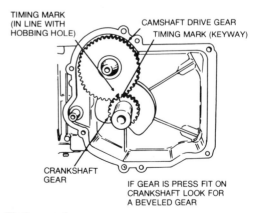

TIMING MARK (IN LINE WITH HOBBING HOLE)

CAMSHAFT DRIVE GEAR

TIMING MARK (KEYWAY)

CRANKSHAFT GEAR

IF GEAR IS PRESS FIT ON CRANKSHAFT LOOK FOR A BEVELED GEAR

Timing marks

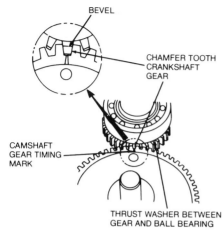

Timing marks

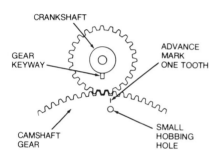

CRAFTSMAN CARBURETOR ONLY

Timing marks

tion being the Craftsman variable governed fuel systems.

NOTE: *If one of the timing gears, either the crankshaft gear or the camshaft gear, is damaged and has to be replaced, both gears should be replaced.*

Crankshaft

INSPECTION

Inspect the crankshaft for worn or crossed threads that can't be redressed; worn, scratched, or damaged bearing surfaces; misalignments; flats on the bearing surfaces. Replace the shaft if any of these problems are in evidence — do not try to straighten a bent shaft.

In replacement, be sure to lubricate the bearing surfaces and use oil seal protectors. If the camshaft gear requires replacement, replace the crankshaft gear, also.

Pistons

When removing the pistons, clean the carbon from the upper cylinder bore and head. The piston and pin must be replaced in matched pairs.

A ridge reamer must be used to remove the ridge at the top of the cylinder bore on some engines.

Clean the carbon from the piston ring groove. A broken ring can be used for this operation.

Some engines have oversize pistons which can be identified by the oversize engraved on the piston top.

There is a definite piston-to-connecting rod-to-crankshaft arrangement which must be maintained when assembling these parts. If the piston is assembled in the bore 180° out of position, it will cause immediate binding of the parts.

Piston Rings

Always replace the piston rings in sets. Ring gaps must be staggered. When using new rings, wipe the cylinder wall with fine emery cloth to deglaze the wall. Make sure the cylinder wall is thoroughly cleaned after deglazing. Check the ring gap by placing the ring squarely in the center of the area in which the rings travel and measuring the gap with a feeler gauge. Do not spread the rings too wide when assembling them to the pistons. Use a ring leader to install the rings on the piston.

The top compression ring has an inside chamfer. This chamfer must go UP. If the second ring has a chamfer, it must also face UP. If there is a notch on the outside diameter of the ring, it must face DOWN.

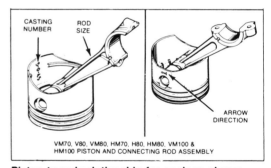

VM70, V80, VM80, HM70, H80, HM80, VM100 & HM100 PISTON AND CONNECTING ROD ASSEMBLY

Piston-to-rod relationship for engines shown

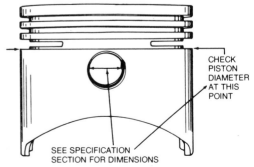

Check piston dimensions

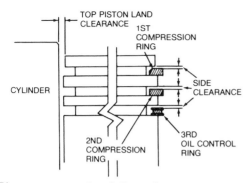

Ring arrangement and dimensions

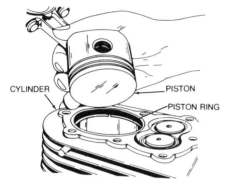

Squaring the ring in the bore

Checking the ring gap

Check the ring gap on the old ring to determine if the ring should be replaced. Check the ring gap on the new ring to determine if the cylinder should be rebored to take oversize parts.

NOTE: *Make sure that the ring gap is measured with the ring fitted squarely in the worn part of the cylinder where the ring usually rides up and down on the piston.*

Connecting Rods

Be sure that the match marks align when assembling the connecting rods to the crankshaft. Use new self-locking nuts. Whenever locking tabs are included, be sure that the tabs lock the nuts securely. NEVER try to straighten a bent crankshaft or connecting rod. Replace them if

necessary. When replacing either the piston, rod, crankshaft, or camshaft, liberally lubricate all bearings with engine oil before assembly.

The following engines have offset connecting rods: V70, VH70, VM70, V80, VM80, H70, HH70, HM70, H80, HM80. ECV105, ECV110, ECM120, and TNT120 engines have the caps fitted from opposite to the camshaft side of the engine. The following engines have the cap fitted from the camshaft side: V70, VH70, VM70, V80, VM80, H70, HH70, HM70, H80, HM80, VM100 and HM100.

On H70, HH70, HM70, H80, HM80, V70, VH70, VM70, V80, VM80, VM100 and HM100 engines, a dipper is stamped into the lockplate. Use a new lockplate whenever the rod cap is removed.

On engine with Durlock rod bolts, torque the bolt as follows:

• TVS75, 90, 105, 120, ECH90, TNT100, 120, ECV100, 105, 110 and 120–110 inch lbs.

• V60–80, H60–80, VH60–70, HH60–70, VM70–100 and HM70–100–150 inch lbs.

NOTE: *Early type caps can be distorted if the cap is not held to the crank pin while threading the bolts tight. Undue force should not be used.*

Later rods have serrations which prevent distortion during tightening. They also have match marks which must face out when assem-

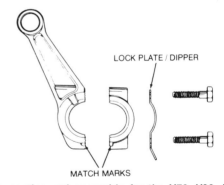

Connecting rod assembly for the V70, V80, H70 and H80 engines

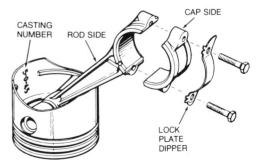

Connecting rod and piston assembly for the V80 and H80 engines

bling the rod. On the V80 and H80 engines, the piston and rod must fit so that the number inside the casting is on the rod side of the rod/cap combination.

Camshaft

Before removing the camshaft, align the timing marks to relieve the pressure on the valve lifters, on most engines.

On VM80 and VM100 engines, while the basic timing is the same, the crankshaft must be rotated so that the timing mark is located 3 teeth further counterclockwise (referring to crankshaft gear rotation). This clears the camshaft of the compression release mechanism for easier removal.

In installation, align the gears for this type of camshaft as they were right before removal. Af-

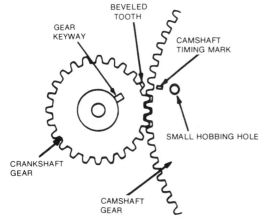

Alignment of timing marks for camshaft removal on VM80 and VM100 engines

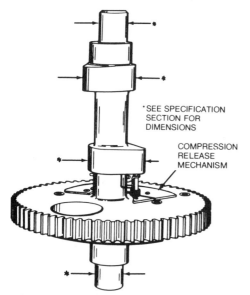

Check the dimensions of the camshaft

ter installation, turn the crankshaft gear clockwise in order to check for proper alignment of timing marks.

Clean the camshaft in solvent, then blow the oil passages dry with compressed air. Replace the camshaft if it shows wear of evidence of scoring. Check the cam dimensions against those in the chart.

If the engine has a mechanical fuel pump, it may have to be removed to properly reinstall the camshaft. If the engine is equipped with the Insta-matic Ezee-Start Compression Release, and any of the parts have to be replaced due to wear or damage, the entire camshaft must be replaced. Be sure that the oil pump (if so equipped) barrel chamber is toward the fillet of the camshaft gear when assembled.

NOTE: *If a damaged gear is replaced, the crankshaft gear should also be replaced.*

Valve Springs

The valve springs should be replaced whenever an engine is overhauled. Check the free length of the springs. Comparing one spring with the other can be a quick check to notice any difference. If a difference is noticed, carefully measure the free length, compression length, and strength of each spring. See the specifications chart at the end of this section.

Some valve springs use dampening coils that are wound closer together than most of the coils of the spring. Where these are present, the spring must be mounted so the dampening coils are on the stationary (upper) end of the spring.

Valve Lifters

The stems of the valves serve as the lifters. On the 4 hp light frame models, the lifter stems are of different lengths. Because this engine is a cross port model, the shorter intake valve lifter goes nearest the mounting flange.

The valve lifters are identical on standard port engines. However once a wear pattern is established, they should not be interchanged.

Valve Grinding and Replacement

Valves and valve seats can be removed and reground with a minimum of engine disassembly.

Remove the valves as follows:

1. Raise the lower valve spring caps while holding the valve heads tightly against the valve seat to remove the valve spring retaining pin. This is best achieved by using a valve spring compressor. Remove the valves, springs, and caps from the crankcase.

2. Clean all parts with a solvent and remove all carbon from the valves.

3. Replace distorted or damaged valves. If the valves are in usable condition, grind the valve faces in a valve refacing machine and to

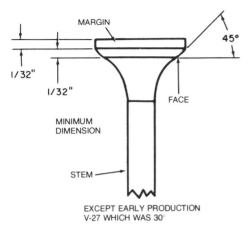

Dimensions of the valve face

the angle given in the specifications chart at the end of this section. Replace the valves if the faces are ground to less than $\frac{1}{32}$ in. (0.8mm).

4. Whenever new or reground valves are installed, lap in the valves with lapping compound to insure an air-tight fit.

NOTE: *There are valves available with oversize stems.*

5. Valve grinding changes the valve lifter clearance. After grinding the valves check the valve lifter clearance as follows:

a. Rotate the crankshaft until the piston is set at the TDC position of the compression stroke.

b. Insert the valves in their guides and hold the valves firmly on their seats.

c. Check for a clearance of 0.010 in. (0.25mm) between each valve stem and valve lifter with a feeler gauge.

d. Grind the valve stem in a valve resurfacing machine set to grind a perfectly square face with the proper clearance.

6. Install valves as follows on Early Models:

a. Position the valve spring and upper and lower valve spring caps under the valve guides for the valve to be installed.

b. Install the valves in the guides, making sure that the valve marked **EX** is inserted in the exhaust port. The valve stem must pass through the valve spring and the valve spring caps.

c. Insert the blade of a screwdriver under the lower valve spring cap and pry the spring up.

d. Insert the valve pin through the hole in the valve stem with a long nosed pliers. Make sure the valve pin is properly seated under the lower valve spring cap.

Install the valves as follows on Later Models:

a. Position the valve caps and spring in the valve compartment.

b. Install the valves in guides with the valve marked **EX** in exhaust port. The valve stem must pass through the upper valve cap and spring. The lower cap should sit around the valve lifter exposed end.

c. Compress the valve spring so that the shank is exposed. DO NOT TRY TO LIFT THE LOWER CAP WITH THE SPRING.

d. Lift the lower valve cap over the valve stem shank and center the cap in the smaller diameter hole.

e. Release the valve spring tension to lock the cap in place.

REBORING THE CYLINDER

1. First, decide whether to rebore for 0.010 in. (0.25mm) or 0.020 in. (0.50mm).

2. Use any standard commercial hone of suitable size. Chuck the hone in the drill press with the spindle speed of about 600 rpm.

3. Start with coarse stones and center the cylinder under the press spindle. Lower the hone so the lower end of the stones contact the lowest point in the cylinder bore.

4. Rotate the adjusting nut so that the stones touch the cylinder wall and then begin honing at the bottom of the cylinder. Move the hone up and down at a rate of 50 strokes a minute to avoid cutting ridges in the cylinder wall. Every fourth or fifth stroke, move the hone far enough to extend the stones 1 in. (25mm) beyond the top and bottom of the cylinder bore.

5. Check the bore size and straightness every thirty or forty strokes. If the stones collect metal, clean them with a wire brush each time the hone is removed.

6. Hone with coarse stones until the cylinder bore is within 0.002 in. (0.05mm) of the desired finish size. Replace the coarse stones with burnishing stones and continue until the bore is to

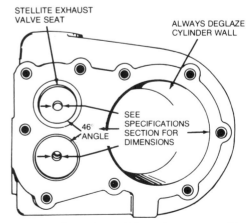

Check the dimensions of the valve seats, guides, and the cylinder

within 0.0005 in. (0.0127mm) of the desired size.

7. Remove the burnishing stones and install finishing stones to polish the cylinder to the final size.

8. Clean the cylinder with solvent and dry it thoroughly.

9. Replace the piston and piston rings with the correct oversize parts.

REBORING VALVE GUIDES

The valve guides are permanently installed in the cylinder. However if the guides wear, they can be rebored to accommodate a $\frac{1}{32}$ in. (0.8mm) oversize valve stem. Rebore the valve guides in the following manner:

1. Ream the valve guides with a standard straight shanked hand reamer or a low speed drill press. Refer to the specifications chart at the end of this section for the correct valve stem guide diameter.

2. Redrill the upper and lower valve spring caps to accommodate the oversize valve stem.

3. Reassemble the engine, installing valves with the correct oversize stems in the valve guides.

REGRINDING VALVE SEATS

The valve seats need regrinding only if they are pitted or scored. If there are no pits or scores, lapping in the valves will provide a proper valve seat. Valve seats are not replaceable. Regrind the valve seats as follows:

1. Use a grinding stone or a reseater set to provide the proper angle and seal face dimensions.

2. If the seat is over $\frac{3}{64}$ in. (1.2mm) wide after grinding, use a 15° stone or cutter to narrow the face to the proper dimensions.

3. Inspect the seats to make sure that the cutter or stone has been held squarely to the valve seat and that the same dimension has been held around the entire circumference of the seat.

4. Lap the valves to the reground seats.

Torquing Cylinder Head

Torque the cylinder head to 200 inch lbs. in 4 equal stages of 50 inch lbs. Follow the sequence shown in the appropriate illustration for each tightening stage.

Bearing Service

LIGHTWEIGHT ALUMINUM BEARING REPLACEMENT

The aluminum bearing must be cut out using the rough cut reamer and the procedures shown in steps 1A and 4A. Follow illustrated

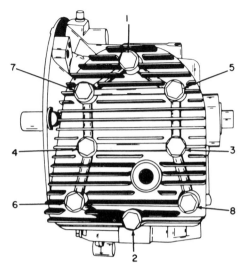

Cylinder head tightening sequence for all engines except 8 hp models

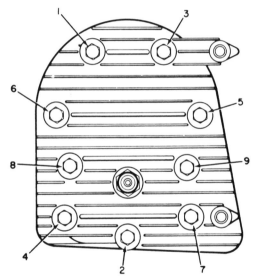

Cylinder head tightening sequence for 8 hp models

steps 1A, 2, 3, 4A, 5 and 6 to install bronze bushings in place of the aluminum bearings.

LONG LIFE AND CAST IRON ENGINES WITHOUT BALL BEARINGS

The worn bronze bushing must be driven out before the new bushing can be installed. Follow illustrated steps 1B, 2, 3, 4B, 5 and 6, to replace the main bearings on these units.

LONG LIFE AND CAST IRON ENGINES WITH BALL BEARING ON THE P.T.O. (POWER TAKE-OFF) SIDE OF THE CRANKSHAFT

The side cover containing the ball bearing must be removed and a substitute cover with ei-

ROUGH REAMING WORN ALUMINUM BEARING
(MAGNETO SIDE) FOR ALUMINUM BEARING ONLY

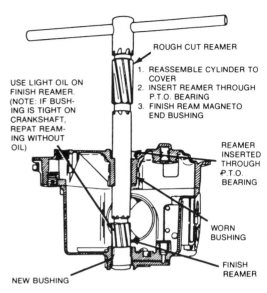

HANDLE

USE KEROSENE
ON ROUGH
CUT REAMER

1. DISASSEMBLE ENGINE, CLEAN
   AND REMOVE OIL SEALS
2. ASSEMBLE P.T.O. BEARING
   TO CYLINDER
   (MOUNTING FLANGE "V" MODELS
   CYLINDER COVER "H" MODELS)

USE ALL
BOLTS
TO HOLD
ASSEMBLY
IN ALIGN-
MENT. DO
NOT USE
GASKET

DOWEL PINS IN
CYLINDER MUST BE
IN PLACE FOR
PROPER ALIGNMENT

MAGNETO
END
BEARING

REAMER GUIDES
IN P.T.O.
BEARING

FINISH REAMER

DISASSEMBLE AFTER
ROUGH REAMING
MAGNETO END

FINISH REAMING NEW MAGNETO BUSHING

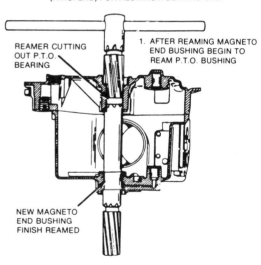

ROUGH CUT REAMER

USE LIGHT OIL ON
FINISH REAMER.
(NOTE: IF BUSH-
ING IS TIGHT ON
CRANKSHAFT,
REPAT REAM-
ING WITHOUT
OIL)

1. REASSEMBLE CYLINDER TO
   COVER
2. INSERT REAMER THROUGH
   P.T.O. BEARING
3. FINISH REAM MAGNETO
   END BUSHING

REAMER
INSERTED
THROUGH
P.T.O.
BEARING

WORN
BUSHING

FINISH
REAMER

NEW BUSHING

WORN BUSHING REMOVAL (MAGNETO END)
FOR BRONZE BUSHING ONLY

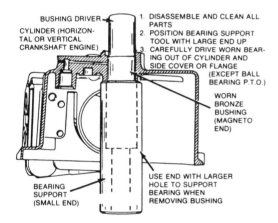

BUSHING DRIVER

CYLINDER (HORIZON-
TAL OR VERTICAL
CRANKSHAFT ENGINE)

1. DISASSEMBLE AND CLEAN ALL
   PARTS
2. POSITION BEARING SUPPORT
   TOOL WITH LARGE END UP
3. CAREFULLY DRIVE WORN BEAR-
   ING OUT OF CYLINDER AND
   SIDE COVER OR FLANGE
   (EXCEPT BALL
   BEARING P.T.O.)

WORN
BRONZE
BUSHING
(MAGNETO
END)

BEARING
SUPPORT
(SMALL END)

USE END WITH LARGER
HOLE TO SUPPORT
BEARING WHEN
REMOVING BUSHING

ROUGH REAMING WORN ALUMINUM BEARING
(P.T.O. END) FOR ALUMINUM BEARING ONLY

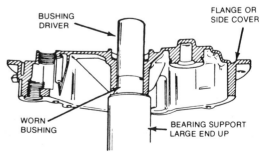

REAMER CUTTING
OUT P.T.O.
BEARING

1. AFTER REAMING MAGNETO
   END BUSHING BEGIN TO
   REAM P.T.O. BUSHING

NEW MAGNETO
END BUSHING
FINISH REAMED

INSTALLING NEW BRONZE BUSHING
(MAGNETO SIDE)

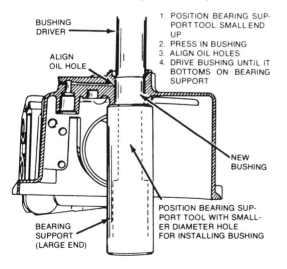

BUSHING
DRIVER

ALIGN
OIL HOLE

1. POSITION BEARING SUP-
   PORT TOOL. SMALL END
   UP
2. PRESS IN BUSHING
3. ALIGN OIL HOLES
4. DRIVE BUSHING UNTIL IT
   BOTTOMS ON BEARING
   SUPPORT

NEW
BUSHING

BEARING
SUPPORT
(LARGE END)

POSITION BEARING SUP-
PORT TOOL WITH SMALL-
ER DIAMETER HOLE
FOR INSTALLING BUSHING

WORN BUSHING REMOVAL (P.T.O. END)
FOR BRONZE BUSHING ONLY

BUSHING
DRIVER

FLANGE OR
SIDE COVER

WORN
BUSHING

BEARING SUPPORT
LARGE END UP

INSTALLING BRONZE BUSHING P.T.O. END

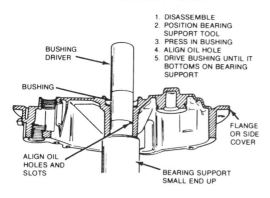

1. DISASSEMBLE
2. POSITION BEARING SUPPORT TOOL
3. PRESS IN BUSHING
4. ALIGN OIL HOLE
5. DRIVE BUSHING UNTIL IT BOTTOMS ON BEARING SUPPORT

BUSHING DRIVER

BUSHING

ALIGN OIL HOLES AND SLOTS

FLANGE OR SIDE COVER

BEARING SUPPORT SMALL END UP

FINISH REAMING P.T.O. BUSHING

APPLY OIL TO PREVENT DAMAGE TO BUSH- ING

1. REASSEMBLE CYLINDER AND COVER
2. INSERT REAMER THROUGH MAGNETO BEARING
3. FINISH REAM P.T.O. BUSHING
4. WHEN FINISH REAMER IS THROUGH BUSHING STOP, DO NOT ALLOW ROUGH REAMER TO ENTER NEWLY INSTALLED MAGNETO END BUSHING
5. WASH ALL PARTS CAREFULLY TO REMOVE ALL CHIPS. CHECK OIL HOLES AND PAS- SAGES, BLOW OUT WITH COMPRESSED AIR
6. REASSEMBLE ENGINE

USE LIGHT OIL FOR FINISH REAMING. IF CRANKSHAFT IS TIGHT REPEAT WITHOUT OIL

P.T.O. BUSHING

ther a new bronze bushing or aluminum bearing must be used instead. Follow illustrated steps 1B, 2 and 3 only.

SPECIAL TOOLS

The task of main bearing replacement is made easier by using one of two Tecumseh main bearing tool kits. Kit 670161 is used to replace main bearings on the lightweight engines except HS models. Kit 670165 is used to replace main bearings on the medium weight engines except HS models.

GENERAL NOTES ON BUSHING REPLACEMENT

1. Your fingers and all parts must be kept very clean when replacing bushings.
2. On splash lubricated horizontal engines, the oil hole in the bushing is to be lined up with the oil hole that leads into the slot in the original bearing.
3. In the event it is necessary to replace the mounting flange or cylinder cover, the magneto end bearing must be rebushed. The P.T.O.

bearing should also be rebushed to assure proper alignment.

4. Oil should be used to finish-ream the bushings. In the event the crankshaft does not rotate freely repeat the finish-reaming operation without oil.

5. Kerosene should be used as a cutting lubricant while rough-reaming.

6. Be sure that the dowel pins are in the cylinder block when assembling the mounting flange or cylinder cover. Use all bolts to hold the assembly together.

7. Remove the reamer by rotating it in the same direction as it is turned during the reaming operation. DO NOT TURN THE REAMER BACKWARDS.

REMOVAL AND INSTALLATION OF CRANK-SHAFT BUSHING FOR 8 AND 10 HORSE-POWER ENGINES

The illustrations show the mounting flange for a vertical engine. Procedures also apply to the cylinder cover for a horizontal engine. Use tool No. 670247 removal end and arbor press to press bushing from P.T.O. bearing end. Note the position of oil slots in the bushing which must align with the oil slots in the mounting flange.

To install, insert a new bushing on the installation end of tool No. 670247. Position the slots so they properly align with the oil slots in the cover and press the bushing in with an arbor press.

After the new bushing is installed, use a light coating of oil and finish reaming with reamer, part No. 670248 (handle 690160). Assemble the P.T.O. mounting flange to the cylinder. Use all bolts with dowel pins to hold the assembly in alignment. Insert the tool through the bushing and cylinder crankshaft magneto end bearing as shown. Rotate the cutting edge clockwise in the P.T.O. bushing. Remove the tool in the same direction of rotation. Do not allow the cutting edge of reamer to touch the magneto end of the cylinder.

BALL BEARING SERVICE H60 THROUGH HM100 H.P. HORIZONTAL CRANKSHAFT ENGINES

1. Prior to attempting removal of the cylinder cover, observe the area around the crankshaft P.T.O. oil seal. Compare it with the illustration, and if there are bearing locks, follow instructions below:

   a. Remove the locking nuts using the proper socket wrench. Note fiber washer located under nut: this must be reinstalled. Lift side cover from cylinder after removing the side cover bolts.

   b. Install the bearing retainer bolts, fiber

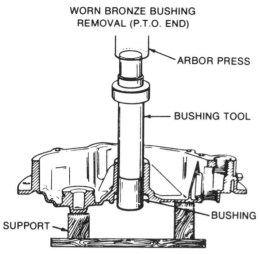

Bushing removal (8 and 10 horsepower engines)

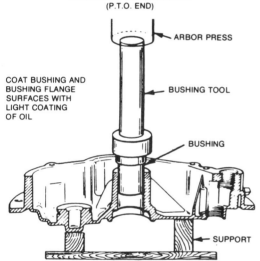

Bushing installation (8 and 10 horsepower engines)

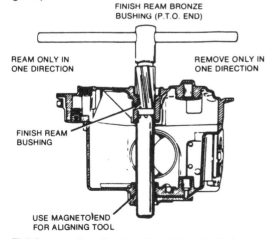

Finish—reaming the bushing (8 and 10 horsepower engines)

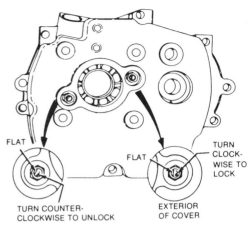

H60-HM100 H.P. horizontal crankshaft engines —locking and unlocking the bearing from outside

washer and locking nuts in the proper sequence in the cover.

2. Also note the following points:

a. On some engines, a locking type retainer bolt is used. To release the bolt, merely loosen the locking nut and turn the retainer bolt counterclockwise to the unlocked position with needle nose pliers to permit the side cover to be removed. Note that the flats on the retainer bolts must be turned so they face the crankshaft to be relocked upon installation. Don't force them! Torque the locking nuts only to 15–22 inch lbs.

b. The ball bearing used in horizontal crankshaft engines has a restricted fit. The bearing is heated and put onto the cold crankshaft. As the bearing cools it grasps the crankshaft tightly and must be removed cold. Remove the ball bearing with a bearing splitter (separator) and a puller. The bearing may be heated by placing it into a container with a sufficient amount of oil to cover the bearing. The bearing should not rest on the bottom of the container. Suspend the bearing on a wire or set the bearing onto a spacer block of wood or wire mesh. Heat the oil and bearing carefully until the oil smokes, quickly remove the bearing and slide it onto the crankshaft.

c. The bearing must seat tightly against the thrust washer which in turn rests tightly against the crankshaft gear.

d. When a ball bearing is used it is not possible to see the keyway in the crankshaft gear which is normally used for timing. Because of this, one tooth of the crankshaft gear is chamfered. This chamfered tooth of the crankshaft gear is positioned opposite the timing mark on the camshaft gear. The use of a ball bearing requires the removal of the crankshaft when it is necessary to remove the camshaft. When replacing the crankshaft and camshaft, mate the timing marks and insert it into the cylinder block as an assembly.

Barrel and Plunger Oil Pump System

This system is driven by an eccentric on the camshaft. Oil is drawn through the hollow camshaft from the oil sump on its intake stroke. The passage from the sump through the camshaft is aligned with the pump opening. As the camshaft continues rotation (pressure stroke), the plunger force the oil out. The other port in the camshaft is aligned with the pump, and directs oil out of the top of the camshaft.

At the top of the camshaft, oil is forced through a crankshaft passage to the top main bearing groove which is aligned with the drilled crankshaft passage. Oil is directed through this passage to the crankshaft connecting rod journal and then spills from the connecting rod to lubricate the cylinder walls. Splash is used to lubricate the other parts of the engine.

A pressure relief port in the crankcase relieves excessive pressures when the oil viscosity is extremely heavy due to cold temperatures, or when the system is plugged or damaged. Normal pressure is 7 psi.

SERVICE

Remove the mounting flange or the cylinder cover, whichever is applicable. Remove the barrel and plunger assembly and separate the parts.

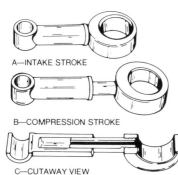

A—INTAKE STROKE

B—COMPRESSION STROKE

C—CUTAWAY VIEW

Operation of the barrel type oil pump

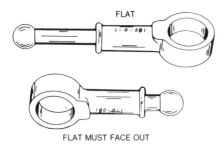

FLAT

FLAT MUST FACE OUT

Installation of the barrel type oil pump

Clean the pump parts in solvent and inspect the pump plunger and barrel for rough spots or wear. If the pump plunger is scored or worn, replace the entire pump.

Before reassembling the pump parts, lubricate all of the parts in engine oil. Manually operate the pump to make sure the plunger slides freely in the barrel.

Lubricate all the parts and position the barrel on the camshaft eccentric. If the oil pump has a chamfer only on one side, that side must be placed toward the camshaft gear. The flat goes away from the gear, thus out to work against the flange oil pickup hole.

Install the mounting flange. Be sure the plunger ball seats in the recess in the flange before fastening it to the cylinder.

Splash Lubrication

Some engines utilize the splash type lubrication system. The oil dipper, on some engines, is cast onto the lower connecting rod bearing cap. It is important that the proper parts are used to ensure the longest engine life.

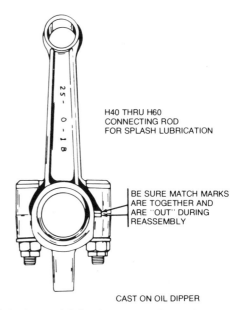

H40 THRU H60
CONNECTING ROD
FOR SPLASH LUBRICATION

BE SURE MATCH MARKS
ARE TOGETHER AND
ARE "OUT" DURING
REASSEMBLY

CAST ON OIL DIPPER

Splash type lubrication connecting rod

Gear Type Oil Pump System

The gear type lubrication pump is a crankshaft driven, positive displacement pump. It pumps oil from the oil sump in the engine base to the camshaft, through the drilled camshaft passage to the top main bearing, through the drilled crankshaft, to the connecting rod journal on the crankshaft.

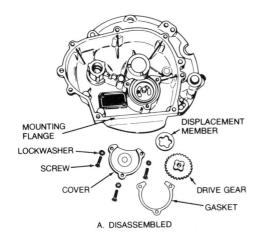

MOUNTING
FLANGE

DISPLACEMENT
MEMBER

LOCKWASHER

SCREW

COVER

DRIVE GEAR

GASKET

A. DISASSEMBLED

Disassembled view of the gear type lubrication system

Spillage from the connecting rod lubricates the cylinder walls and normal splash lubricates the other internal working parts. There is a pressure relief valve in the system.

SERVICE

Disassemble the pump as follows: remove the screws, lockwashers, cover, gear, and displacement member.

Wash all of the parts in solvent. Inspect the oil pump drive gear and displacement member for worn or broken teeth, scoring, or other damage. Inspect the shaft hole in the drive gear for wear. Replace the entire pump if cracks, wear, or scoring is evident.

To replace the oil pump, position the oil pump displacement member and oil pump gear on the shaft, then flood all the parts with oil for priming during the initial starting of the engine.

The gasket provides clearance for the drive gear. With a feeler gauge, determine the clearance between the cover and the oil pump gear. The clearance desired is 0.006–0.007 in. (0.15–0.18mm). Use gaskets, which are available in a variety of sizes, to obtain the correct clearance. Position the oil pump cover and secure it with the screws of lockwashers.

Craftsman Engines Cross Reference Chart

Craftsman Engine Models	See Column	Craftsman Engine Models	See Column	Craftsman Engine Models	See Column
143.50040	7	143.196042–143.196072	10	143.224022	
143.50045		143.196082	8	143.224032	4
				143.224062	2
143.131022–143.131102	1	143.197012	3	143.224072	4
143.135012–143.135112	9	143.197022	5	143.224092–143.224132	2
143.136012–143.136052	8	143.197032		143.224142	1
143.137012	7	143.197042–143.197072	3	143.224162–143.224222	2
143.137032		143.197082	5	143.224232	4
				143.224242	
143.141012–143.143032	1	143.201032–143.203012	1	143.224252–143.224282	2
143.145012–143.145072	9	143.204022	4	143.224292	4
143.146012	8	143.204032–143.204052	2	143.224302	
143.146022		143.204062	4	143.224312–143.224342	2
143.147012–143.147032	7	143.204072–143.204092	2	143.224352	4
		143.204102	4	143.224362	
143.151012–143.153032	1	143.204132		143.224372–143.224422	2
143.154012–143.154142	2	143.204142–143.204192	2	143.224432	4
143.155012–143.155062	9	143.204202	4	143.225012	13
143.156012	8	143.205022	9	143.225022	
143.156022		143.206012	8	143.225032–143.225052	9
143.157012–143.157032	7	143.206022	10	143.225062	13
		143.206032	8	143.225072	
143.161012–143.163062	1	143.207012–143.207052	3	143.225082–143.225102	9
143.164012–143.164202	2	143.207062	5	143.226012	8
143.165012–143.165052	9	143.207072	3	143.226032	
143.166012–143.166052	8	143.207082	5	143.226072	10
143.167012–143.167042	7			143.226082	
		143.213012–143.213042	1	143.226092–143.226122	11
143.171012–143.171172	1	143.214012–143.214032	2	143.226131–143.226182	8
143.171202	2	143.214042–143.214072	4	143.226192	11
143.171212–143.173042	1	143.214082–143.214252	2	143.226202	10
143.174012–143.174292	2	143.214262–143.214282	4	143.226212	
143.175012–143.175072	9	143.214292	2	143.226222–143.226262	8
143.176012–143.176092	8	143.214302		143.226272	10
143.177012–143.177072	7	143.214312	4	143.226282	
		143.214322		143.226292	11
143.181042–143.183042	1	143.214332	2	143.226302	10
143.184012–143.184212	2	143.214342		143.226312	11
143.184232–143.184252	4	143.214352	4	143.226322	8
143.184262–143.184402	2	143.216012–143.216032	10	143.226332	
143.185012–143.185052	9	143.216042–143.216062	3	143.226342	10
143.186012	8	143.216072–143.216092	10	143.226352	11
143.186022–143.186042	10	143.216122	8	143.227012–143.227072	12
143.186052	8	143.216132	11		
143.186062		143.216142	8	143.233012	1
143.186072–143.186112	10	143.216152	11	143.233032	
143.186122	8	143.216162		143.233042	
143.187022–143.187102	3	143.216172		143.234022–143.234052	2
		143.216182	8	143.234062–143.234092	4
143.191012–143.191052	1	143.217012–143.217032	5	143.234102–143.234162	2
143.194012–143.194052	2	143.217042–143.217072	3	143.234192	
143.194062	4	143.217092	5	143.234202	
143.194072–143.194092	2	143.217102	3	143.234212–143.234232	4
143.194102	4			143.234242–143.234262	2
143.194112–143.194142	2	143.223012–143.223052	1	143.235012	13
143.195012	9	143.224012	2		
143.195022					
143.196012–143.196032	8				

Craftsman Engines Cross Reference Chart (cont.)

Craftsman Engine Models	See Column	Craftsman Engine Models	See Column	Craftsman Engine Models	See Column
143.235022		143.246242	10	143.264422	2
143.235032	6	143.246252	11	143.264432-143.264482	4
143.235042	13	143.246262	10	143.264492	2
143.235052		143.246272-143.247292	11	143.264502	
143.235062	9	143.246302	10	143.264512	4
143.235072	6	143.246312		143.264522	2
143.236012	8	143.246322	11	143.264542	
143.236022-143.236042	11	143.246332		143.264562-143.264672	4
143.236052	8	143.246342	10	143.264682	2
143.236062	11	143.246352	8	143.265012-143.265192	6
143.236072		143.246362	16	143.266012	11
143.236082	8	143.246382		143.266022	
143.236092	10	143.246392	8	143.266032	8
143.236102	8			143.266042	10
143.236112		143.254012-143.254052	2	143.266052	
143.236122	10	143.254062	4	143.266062	8
143.236132	8	143.254072-143.254122	2	143.266082	
143.236142	11	143.254142-143.254192	4	143.266092-143.266132	10
143.236152	8	143.254212	2	143.266142-143.266242	11
143.237012	12	143.254222		143.266252	8
143.237022		143.254232-143.254292	4	143.266262	11
143.237032	5	143.254302	2	143.266272-143.266302	10
143.237042	3	143.254312		143.266312	11
		143.254322	4	143.266322	
143.244032	2	143.254332	2	143.266332	10
143.244042	4	143.254342	4	143.266342	11
143.244052		143.254352		143.266352	10
143.244062		143.254362	2	143.266362	11
143.244072-143.244112	2	143.254372	4	143.266372-143.266412	8
143.244122-143.244142	4	143.254382		143.266422	11
143.244202	2	143.254392	2	143.266432-143.266452	8
143.244212	4	143.254402	4	143.266462	16
143.244222	2	143.254412		143.266472	
143.244232		143.254432	2	143.266482	11
143.244242	4	143.254442	4	143.267012-143.267042	3
143.244252	4	143.254452	2		
143.244262-143.244282	2	143.254462	4	143.274022-143.274072	4
143.244292-143.244332	4	143.254472	2	143.274092-143.274132	2
143.245012	6	143.254482		143.274142	4
143.245042	9	143.254492	4	143.274152	
143.245052-143.245072	13	143.254502-143.254532	2	143.274162-143.274182	2
143.245082		143.255012-143.255112	6	143.274192-143.274242	4
143.245092	6	143.256012	11	143.274252	2
143.245102-143.245132	13	143.256022	8	143.274262	4
143.245142	6	143.256032	10	143.274272-143.274322	2
143.245152		143.256042	11	143.274402-143.274482	4
143.245162	13	143.256052	8	143.275012-143.275052	6
143.245172	6	143.256062	11	143.276022	4
143.245182		143.256072		143.276032	11
143.245192	13	143.256082	8	143.276042	
143.246012	8	143.256092		143.276052	16
143.246022	11	143.256102	10	143.276062-143.276162	11
143.246032		143.256112	11	143.276182	8
143.246042	8	143.256122	8	143.276192	10
143.246052-143.246072	10	143.256132	10	143.276202	8
143.246082	11	143.257012-143.257072	3	143.276222	10
143.246092				143.276242	11
143.246102	10	143.264012-143.264042	2	143.276252	8
143.246112		143.264052-143.264082	4	143.276262	11
143.246122	11	143.264092	2	143.276272	11
143.246132	10	143.264102	4	143.276282	10
143.246142		143.264232-143.264342	2	143.276292	11
143.246152-143.246212	11	143.264352-143.264372	4	143.276302	11
143.246222	10	143.264382	2	143.276322-143.276342	10
143.246232	11	143.264392-143.264412	4	143.276352	11

Craftsman Engines Cross Reference Chart (cont.)

Craftsman Engine Models	See Column	Craftsman Engine Models	See Column	Craftsman Engine Models	See Column
143.276362	16	143.531052	1	143.596022	
143.276372–143.276392	10	143.531082		143.596042	8
143.276402	16	143.531122		143.596052	10
143.276412	8	143.531132		143.596072–143.596122	8
143.276422	10	143.531142	2	143.597012–143.597032	3
143.276432–143.276472	11	143.531152	1		
143.276482	16	143.531172		143.601022–143.601062	1
143.277012	3	143.531182		143.604012	2
143.277022		143.534012–143.534072	2	143.604022	4
		143.535012–143.535062	9	143.604032	2
143.284012	2	143.536012–143.536062	8	143.604042	
143.284022	1	143.537012	7	143.604052	4
143.284032	2			143.604062	2
143.284042	4	143.541012	1	143.604072	
143.284052	2	143.541042–143.541062	1	143.605012	9
143.284062		143.541112–143.541152	1	143.605022	
143.284072	4	143.541172–143.541202	1	143.605052	
143.284082	2	143.541222	1	143.606012–143.606052	10
143.284092		143.541282–143.541302	1	143.606092	8
143.284102	4	143.544012–143.544042	2	143.606102	10
143.284112	2	143.545012–143.545042	9	143.607012–143.607032	3
143.284142		143.546012–143.546022	8	143.607042–143.607062	3
143.284152		143.547012–143.547032	7		
143.284162				143.611012–143.611112	1
143.284182		143.551012	1	143.614012–143.614032	4
143.284212	4	143.551032		143.614042	2
143.284312	2	143.551052–143.551192	1	143.614052	4
143.284322		143.554012–143.554082	2	143.614062–143.614162	2
143.284332	4	143.555012–143.555052	9	143.615012–143.615092	9
143.284342		143.556012–143.556282	8	143.616012	10
143.284352		143.557012–143.557082	7	143.616022–143.616112	8
143.284372	16			143.616122	10
143.284382	4	143.565022	9	143.616132	8
143.284402	2	143.566002–143.566202	8	143.616142	
143.284412		143.566212	9	143.617012–143.617182	3
143.284432	2	143.566222–143.566252	8		
143.284362		143.567012–143.567042	7	143.621012–143.621092	1
143.284392	2			143.624012–143.624112	2
143.284442		143.571002–143.571122	1	143.625012–143.625132	9
143.284482		143.571152	2	143.626012	10
143.284452	4	143.571162	1	143.626022	8
143.284472		143.571172		143.626032	10
143.285012	6	143.574022–143.574102	2	143.626042	8
143.285022		143.575012–143.575042	9	143.626052–143.626122	10
143.285032		143.576002–143.576202	8	143.626132	8
143.286102	16			143.626142	10
143.286022	17	143.581002–143.581102	1	143.626152	
143.286032	10	143.584012–143.584142	2	143.626162	8
143.286072–143.286092	11	143.585012–143.585042	9	143.626172	10
143.286112		143.586012–143.586042	8	143.626182	8
143.286122		143.586052–143.586062	10	143.626192	10
143.286132	10	143.586072–143.586082	8	143.626202	8
143.286142	11	143.586112–143.586142	10	143.626212	10
143.286152		143.586152	8	143.626222–143.626262	8
143.286162		143.586162	10	143.626282	11
143.286172		143.586172–143.586242	8	143.626292	10
		143.586252	10	143.626302	8
143.505010	8	143.586262–143.586282	8	143.626312	10
143.505011		143.587012–143.587042	3	143.626322	
143.521081	9			143.627012–143.627042	3
143.525021	9	143.591012–143.591142	1		
143.526011		143.594022–143.594082	2	143.631012–143.631092	1
143.526021	8	143.594092	2	143.634012	2
143.526031	8	143.594102		143.634032	
		143.595012	9	143.635012	9
		143.595042		143.635022	
		143.596012	10		

Craftsman Engines Cross Reference Chart (cont.)

Craftsman Engine Models	See Column	Craftsman Engine Models	See Column	Craftsman Engine Models	See Column
143.635032	6	143.656202	8	143.674012	2
143.635052	9	143.656212	11	143.675012	6
143.636012	11	143.656222		143.675022	
143.636022		143.656232	10	143.675032	9
143.636032	10	143.656242	11	143.675042	6
143.636042	11	143.656252	8	143.676012	11
143.636052	8	143.656262	10	143.676022	
143.636062	10	143.656272		143.676032	10
143.636072	11	143.656282	11	143.676042	11
143.637012	3	143.657012–143.657052	3	143.676052	
				143.676062	16
143.641012–143.641062	1	143.661012–143.661062	1	143.676072	
143.641072	2	143.664012–143.664332	2	143.676102	10
143.644012–143.644082	2	143.665012–143.665082	6	143.676112	8
143.645012–143.645032	6	143.666012	10	143.676122	10
143.646012–143.646032	10	143.666022		143.676132	8
143.646042	11	143.666032	11	143.676142	11
143.646052		143.666042–143.666072	10	143.676152	16
143.646072–143.646102	10	143.666082	11	143.676162	
143.646112	8	143.666092		143.676172	10
143.646122	10	143.666102–143.666142	8	143.676182	11
143.646132		143.666152	11	143.676192	10
143.646142	11	143.666162		143.676202	11
143.646152	10	143.666172	8	143.676212	16
143.646162	11	143.666202		143.676222	11
143.646172	10	143.666222	10	143.676232	8
143.646182		143.666232	11	143.676242	8
143.646192	8	143.666242	8	143.676252	11
143.646202	10	143.666252	10	143.676262	16
143.646212–143.646232	11	143.666272	8	143.677012	3
143.647012–143.647062	3	143.666282	10	143.677022	
		143.666292	8		
143.651012–143.651072	1	143.666302	10	143.686012	17
143.654022–143.654322	2	143.666312		143.686022	
143.655012	6	143.666322	11	143.686032	11
143.655032		143.666332	16	143.686042	
143.656012–143.656052	8	143.666342	10	143.686052	
143.656062	10	143.666352	11	143.686062	10
143.656082	11	143.666362	16	143.686072	9
143.656092	8	143.666372	8	143.687012	3
143.656102	10	143.666382	10		
143.656112	8	143.667012	3	143.694126	4
143.656122–143.656152	10	143.667022		143.694132	2
143.656162–143.656182	8	143.667032	6	143.694134	11
143.656192	10	143.667042–143.667082	3		

Torque Specifications

Model/Part	Inch Pounds	Ft. Pounds
Cylinder Head Bolts	160–200	13–16
Connecting Rod Bolts	65–75	5.5–6
ECH90, ECV100, TNT100	75–80	6.2–6.7

TVS120, 5 H.P. Small Frame
(Durlok Rod Bolts)
  6 H.P. Medium Frame
  6 H.P. Medium Frame (Durlok Rod Bolts)
	110–130
	86–110
	130–150
		9.1–10.8
		7.1–9.1
		10.8–12.5

ECV105, ECV110, ECV120, TNT120
  7, 8 & 10 Medium Frame
  7, 8 & 10 Medium Frame (Durlok Rod Bolts)
	80–95
	106–130
	150–170
		6.6–7.9
		8.8–10.8
		12.5–14.1

Cylinder Cover or Flange-to-Cylinder	65–110	5.5–9
Cylinder Cover 6–7 H.P. Medium Frame, H Models	100–140	8.3–11.6
Flywheel Nut	360–396	30–33
Spark Plug	180–360	15–30
Magneto Stator to Cylinder	40–90	3.3–7.5
Starter to Blower Housing or Cylinder	40–60	3.5–5
Housing Baffle to Cylinder	48–72	4–6
Breather Cover (Top Mount ECV)	40–50	3.3–4.1
Breather Cover	20–26	1.7–2.1
Intake Pipe to Cylinder	72–96	6–8
Carburetor to Intake Pipe	48–72	4–6
Air Cleaner to Carburetor (Plastic)	8–12	1
Tank Plate to Bracket (Plastic)	100–144	9–12
Tank to Housing	45–65	3.7–5

Muffler Bolts to Cylinder
  1–5 H.P. Small Frame
  4–5 H.P. Medium Frame
	30–45
	90–150
		2.5–3.5
		8–12

6:1 Gear Reduction Cover to Housing	100–144	8.5–12
Gear Reduction Cover to Housing	65–110	5–9
Oil Drain Plug 1/8—27	35–50	1.1–4.1
1/4—18	65–85	4.5–7
3/8—18	80–100	6.6–9
5/8—18	90–150	7.5–12.5
1/2–14	80–100	6.6–9

Ball Bearing Retainer 2.5
  2.5–5 H.P. Small Frame
  5–10 H.P. Medium Frame
	45–60
	15–22
		3.7–5
		1.5

Craftsman Exclusive Fuel System to Cylinder	72–96	6–8
Electric Starter-to-Cylinder	50–60	4–5

Cross Reference for Vertical Crankshaft Engines

Size	Model	Column
6 HP	V60	8
	VH60	8
7 HP	V70	10
	VH70	10
	VM70	17
8 HP	V80	11
	VM80	11
10 HP	VM100	16

Cross Reference Chart for Horizontal Crankshaft Engines

Size	Model	Column
6 HP	H60	8
	HH60	8
7 HP	H70	10
	HH70	10
	HM70	17
8 HP	H80	11
	HM80	11
10 HP	HM100	16

Engine Specifications

Reference Column	1	2	3	4	5	6	7	8	9
Displacement	7.75	9.06	10.5	10.0	10.5	12.0	11.04	13.53	12.17
Stroke	$1^{27}/_{32}''$	$1^{27}/_{32}''$	$1^{15}/_{16}''$	$1^{27}/_{32}''$	$1^{15}/_{16}''$	$1^{15}/_{16}''$	$2^{1}/_{4}''$	$2^{1}/_{2}''$	$2^{1}/_{4}''$
Bore	2.3125 2.3135	2.5000 2.5010	2.625 2.626	2.625 2.626	2.625 2.626	2.812 2.813	2.5000 2.5010	2.625 2.626	2.625 2.626
Timing Dimension Before Top Dead Center for Vertical Engines	V.060 .070	V.065	V.035	.035	.035	V.040 .060	V.050	V.050	H.050
Timing Dimension Before Top Dead Center for Horizontal Engines	H.060 .070	H.030 .040	H.035			H.055	H.050	H.050	H.050
Point Setting	.020	.020	.020	.020	.020	.020	.020	.020	.020
Spark Plug Gap	.030	.030	.030	.030	.030	.030	.030	.030	.030
Valve Clearance	.010 Both	.010 Both	.010 Both	.010 Both	.010 Both	.010 Both	.010 Both	.010 Both	.010 Both
Valve Seat Angle	46°	46°	46°	46°	46°	46°	46°	46°	46°
Valve Spring Free Length	1.135″	1.135″	1.135″	1.135″	1.135″	1.135″	1.562″	1.462″	1.462″
Valve Guides Over-Size Dimensions	.2805 .2815	.2805 .2815	.2805 .2815	.2805 .2815	.2807 .2817	In. .280 Ex. .278	.3432 .3442	.3432 .3442	.343 .344
Valve Seat Width	.035 .045	.035 .045	.035 .045	.035 .045	.035 .045	.035 .045	.042 .052	.042 .052	.042 .052
Crankshaft End Play	.005 .027	.005 .027	.005 .027	.005 .027	.005 .027	.005 .027	.005 .027	.005 .027	.005 .027
Crankpin Journal Diameter	.8610 .8615	.8610 .8615	.9995 1.0000	.8610 .8615	.9995 1.0000	.9995 1.0000	1.0615 1.0620	1.0615 1.0620	1.0615 1.0620
Cylinder Main Bearing Dia.	.8755 .8760	.8755 .8760	1.0005 1.0010	.8755 .8760	1.0005 1.0010	1.0005 1.0010	1.0005 1.0010	1.0005 1.0010	1.0005 1.0010
Cylinder Cover Main Bearing Dia.	.8755 .8760	.8755 .8760	1.0005 1.0010	.8755 .8760	1.2010 1.2020	1.0005 1.0010	1.0005 1.0010	1.0005 1.0010	1.0005 1.0010
Conn. Rod. Dia. Crank Bearing	.8620 .8625	.8620 .8625	1.0005 1.0010	.8620 .8625	1.0005 1.0010	1.0005 1.0010	1.0630 1.0635	1.0630 1.0635	1.0630 1.0635
Piston Diameter	2.3090 2.3095	2.4950 2.4955	2.6200 2.6205	2.6200 2.6205	2.604 2.608	2.8070 2.8075	2.492 2.4945	2.6210 2.6215	2.6210 2.6215
Piston Pin Diameter	.5629 .5631	.5629 .5631	.5629 .5631	.5629 .5631	.5631 .5635	.5629 .5631	.6248 .6250	.6248 .6250	.6248 .6250
Width of Comp. Ring Groove	.0955 .0977	.0955 .0975	.0925 .0935	.0955 .0975	.0955 .0975	.0955 .0975	.0955 .0975	.0955 .0975	.0955 .0975
Width of Oil Ring Groove	.125 .127	.125 .127	.156 .158	.156 .158	.156 .158	.156 .158	.156 .158	.156 .158	.156 .158

Side Clearance of Ring Groove		1	2	3	4	5	6	7	8	9
	(Top) Comp.	.002 .005	.002 .003	.002 .004	.002 .005	.002 .005	.003 .004	.002 .003	.002 .004	.002 .004
	(Bot.) Oil			.001 .004	.001 .004	.001 .004	.002 .003		.002 .004	.002 .004

Reference Column	1	2	3	4	5	6	7	8	9
Ring End Gap	.007 .020	.007 .020	.007 .020	.007 .020	.007 .020	.007 .020	.007 .020	.007 .020	.007 .020
Top Piston Land Clearance	.0015 .0145	.015 .018	.0165 .0215	.017 .022	.017 .022	.017 .022	.015 .018	.017 .020	.017 .020
Piston Skirt Clearance	.0025 .0040	.0045 .0060	.0045 .0060	.0045 .0060	.0050 .0065	.0045 .0060	.0055 .0070	.0035 .0050	.0035 .0050
Camshaft Bearing Dia.	.4975 .4980	.4975 .4980	.4975 .4980	.4975 .4980	.505 .513	.4975 .4980	.6230 .6235	.6230 .6235	.6230 .6235
Dia. of Crankshaft Mag. Main Brg.	.8735 .8740	.8735 .8740	.9985 .9990	.8735 .8740	.9985 .9990	.9985 .9990	.9985 .9990	.9985 .9990	.9985 .9990
Dia. of Crankshaft P.T.O. Main Brg.	.8735 .8740	.8735 .8740	.9985 .9990	.8735 .8740	.9985 .9990	.9985 .9990	.9985 .9990	.9985 .9990	.9985 .9990

A. For VM80 & HM80 engines only—Displacement is 19.41″
B. For VM80 & HM80 engines only—Bore is 3.125″/3.126″ (3⅛″).
C. For VM80 & HM80 engines only—Piston Diameter is 3.1205″/3.1195″.

Engine Specifications (cont.)

Reference Column		10	11	12	13	14	15	16	17
Displacement		15.0	18.65 See Note A	11.5	12.0	10.0	12.0	20.2	17.16
Stroke		$2^{17}/_{32}''$	$2^{17}/_{32}''$ See Note B	$1^{15}/_{16}''$	$1^{15}/_{16}''$	$1^{27}/_{32}''$	$1^{15}/_{16}''$	$2^{17}/_{32}''$	$2^{17}/_{32}''$
Bore		2.750 2.751	3.062 3.063	2.750 2.751	2.812 2.813	2.625 2.626	2.812 2.813	3.187 3.188	2.9375 2.9385
Timing Dimension Before Top Dead Center for Vertical Engines		V.050	V.070	V.035	V.035	V.035	V.035	V.070	V.070
Timing Dimension Before Top Dead Center for Horizontal Engines		H.050	H.070					H.070	H.070
Point Setting		.020	.020	.020	.020	.020	.020	.020	.020
Spark Plug Gap		.030	.030	.030	.030	.030	.030	.030	.030
Valve Clearance		.010 Both	.010 Both	.010 Both	.010 Both	.010 Both	.010 Both	.010 Both	.010 Both
Valve Seat Angle		46°	46°	46°	46°	46°	46°	46°	46°
Valve Spring Free Length		1.462″	1.462″	1.135″	1.135″	1.135″	1.135″	1.462″	1.462″
Valve Guides Over-Size Dimensions		.3432 .3442	.3432 .3442	.2805 .2815	.2805 .2815	.2805 .2815	.2805 .2815	.3432 .3442	.3432 .3442
Valve Seat Width		.042 .052	.042 .052	.035 .045	.035 .045	.035 .045	.035 .045	.042 .052	.042 .052
Crankshaft End Play		.005 .027	.005 .027	.005 .027	.005 .027	.005 .027	.005 .027	.005 .027	.005 .027
Crankpin Journal Diameter		1.1865 1.1870	1.1865 1.1870	.9995 1.0000	.9995 1.0000	.8610 .8615	.9995 1.0000	1.1865 1.1870	1.1865 1.1870
Cylinder Main Bearing Dia.		1.0005 1.0010	1.0005 1.0010	1.0005 1.0010	1.0005 1.0010	.8755 .8760	1.0005 1.0010	1.0005 1.0010	1.0005 1.0010
Cylinder Cover Main Bearing Dia.		1.0005 1.0010	1.1890 1.1895	1.0005 1.0010	1.0005 1.0010	.8755 .8760	1.0005 1.0010	1.1890 1.1895	1.1890 1.1895
Conn. Rod. Dia. Crank Bearing		1.1880 1.1885	1.1880 1.1855	1.0005 1.0010	1.0005 1.0010	.8620 .8625	1.0005 1.0010	1.1880 1.1885	1.1880 1.1885
Piston Diameter		2.7450 2.7455	3.0575 3.0585 See Note C	2.7450 2.7455	2.8070 2.8075	2.6200 2.6205	2.8070 2.8075	3.1817 3.1842	2.9325 2.9335
Piston Pin Diameter		.6248 .6250	.6248 .6250	.5629 .5631	.5629 .5631	.5629 .5631	.5629 .5631	.6248 .6250	.6248 .6250
Width of Comp. Ring Groove		.0795 .0805	.0955 .0975	.0795 .0815	.0955 .0975	.0955 .0975	.0955 .0975	.0955 .0975	.0975 .0955
Width of Oil Ring Groove		.188 .189	.188 .190	.1565 .1585	.1565 .1585	.1565 .1585	.1565 .1585	.188 .190	.188 .190
Side Clearance of Ring Groove	(Top) Comp.	.002 .003	.003 .004	.002 .004	.003 .004	.003 .0045	.0028 .0039	.0020 .0050	.0028 .0051
	(Bot.) Oil	.001 .003	.002 .003	.001 .002	.001 .002	.0010 .0030	.0018 .0038	.001 .004	.0018 .0029
Ring End Gap		.007 .020	.007 .020	.007 .020	.007 .020	.007 .020	.007 .020	.007 .020	.007 .020
Top Piston Land Clearance		.023 .028	.031 .034	.024 .027	.018 .021	.017 .022	.017 .022	.029 .034	.030 .035
Piston Skirt Clearance		.0045 .0060	.0035 .0055	.0045 .0060	.0045 .0060	.0045 .0060	.0045 .0060	.0028 .0063	.004 .006
Camshaft Bearing Dia.		.6230 .6235	.6230 .6235	.4975 .4980	.4975 .4980	.4975 .4980	.4975 .4980	.6230 .6235	.6230 .6235
Dia. of Crankshaft Mag. Main Brg.		.9985 .9990	.9985 .9990	.9990 .9995	.9990 .9995	.8735 .8740	.9985 .9990	.9985 .9990	.9985 .9990
Dia. of Crankshaft P.T.O. Main Brg.		.9985 .9990	1.1870 1.1875	.9985 .9990	.9985 .9990	.8735 .8740	.9985 .9990	1.1870 1.1875	1.1870 1.1875

15
Tecumseh 2-Stroke
2 through 5 Hp

ENGINE IDENTIFICATION

The identification taps may be located at a variety of places on the engine. The type number is the most important number since it must be included with any correspondence about a particular engine.

Early engines listed the type number as a suffix of the serial number. For example on number 123456789 P 234, 234 is the type number. In the number 123456789 H 104–02B; 104–02B is the type number. In either case the type number is important.

If you use short block to repair the engine, be sure that you transfer the serial number and type number tag to the new short block.

On the newer engines, reference is sometimes made to the model number. The model number tells the number of cylinders, the design (vertical or horizontal) and the cubic inch displacement.

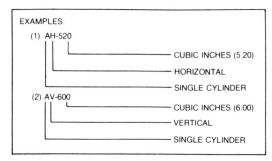

Model number interpretation

MAINTENANCE

Air Cleaners

The instructions below detail the procedures involved in cleaning the various types of elements. See the illustrations for exploded views to aid disassembly and assembly.

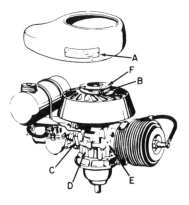

A. NAMEPLATE ON AIR SHROUD	D. STAMPED ON CRANKCASE
B. MODEL & TYPE NUMBER PLATE	E. STAMPED ON CYLINDER FLANGE
C. METAL TAG ON CRANKCASE	F. STAMPED ON STARTER PULLEY

Location of identification numbers on 2 cycle engines

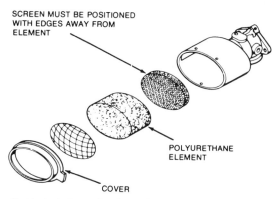

SCREEN MUST BE POSITIONED WITH EDGES AWAY FROM ELEMENT

POLYURETHANE ELEMENT

COVER

Exploded view of polyurethane air cleaner

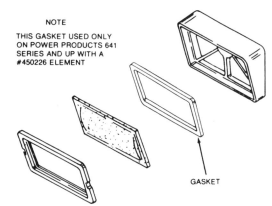

NOTE

THIS GASKET USED ONLY ON POWER PRODUCTS 641 SERIES AND UP WITH A #450226 ELEMENT

GASKET

Exploded view of felt type air cleaner

POLYURETHANE AIR CLEANER

1. Wash the element in a solvent or detergent and water solution by squeezing similar to a sponge.

2. Clean the air cleaner housing and cover with the same solution. Dry thoroughly.

3. Dry the element by squeezing or with compressed air if available.

4. Apply a generous quantity of oil to the element sides and open ends. Squeeze vigorously to distribute oil and to remove excess oil.

ALUMINUM FOIL AIR CLEANER

1. Dip the aluminum foil filter in solvent. Flush out all dirt particles.

2. Shake out the filter thoroughly to remove all solvent, then dip the filter element in oil. Allow the oil to drain from the filter. Clean the screens and filter body.

NOTE: *The concave screen and retainer cover or ring are not used on later models. They are replaced with a clip which rolls into the groove in the lip of the body.*

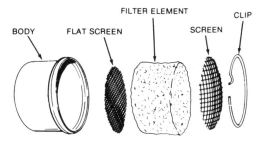

FILTER ELEMENT

CLIP

BODY   FLAT SCREEN   SCREEN

Exploded view of aluminum foil type air cleaner

FELT TYPE AIR CLEANERS

1. To clean felt air cleaners, merely blow compressed air through the element in the reverse direction to normal air flow. Felt elements may also be washed in nonflammable solvents or soapy water. Blow dry with compressed air.

NOTE: *Power Products type numbers 641 and up, use a gasket between the element and the base. The gasket is used only with this element; earlier versions did not have a gasket.*

FIBER ELEMENT AIR CLEANER

1. Remove the filter and place the cover in a normal position on the filter. With the filter element down to semi-seal it, blow compressed air through the cover hole to reverse air flow, forcing dirt particles out.

2. Clean the cover mounting bracket with a damp cloth.

DRY PAPER AIR CLEANER

1. Tap the element on a workbench or any solid object to dislodge larger particles of dirt.

2. Wash the element in soap and water. Rinse from the inside until it is thoroughly flushed and the water coming through is free of soap.

3. Allow the element to dry completely or use low pressure compressed air blown from the inside to speed the process.

4. Inspect the element for cracks or holes, and replace if necessary.

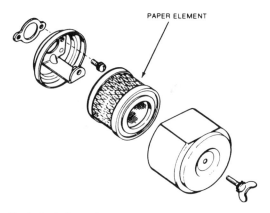

PAPER ELEMENT

Exploded view of paper element type air cleaner

Lubrication

OIL AND FUEL RECOMMENDATIONS

Power Products 2 cycle engines are mist-lubricated by oil mixed with the gasoline. For the best performance, use regular grade, leaded fuel, with 2 cycle or outboard oil rated SAE 30 or SAE 40. Regular grade unleaded fuel is an acceptable substitute. The terms 2 cycle or outboard are used by various manufacturers to designate oil they have designed for use in 2 cycle engines. Multiple weight oil such as all season 10W–30, are not recommended.

If you have to mix the gas and oil when the temperature is below 35°F (1.6°C), heat up the oil first, then mix it with the gas. Oil will not mix with gas when the temperature is approaching freezing. However, if you use oil that has been warmed first it will not be affected by low temperatures.

The proportion of oil to fuel is absolutely critical to two-stroke operation. If too little oil is used, overheating and damage to engine parts will occur (this can even result from running the engine too lean). If excessive oil is used, spark plug fouling, smoke in the exhaust, and even misfire can occur. Mix carefully and precisely. Follow Power Products recommendations for your particular engine, and disregard fuel container labels.

Fuel/oil mix must be clean and fresh. Fuel deteriorates enough to form troublesome gum and varnish after more than a month. Dirt in the fuel can cause clogging of carburetor passages and even engine wear.

Tune-Up Specifications

All spark plugs are gapped at 0.035 in. (0.90mm). Because of the great number of individual models of Power Products engines that exist, an individual chart of Tune-Up specifications is impractical. Refer to the charts at the end of this section for breaker point gap and timing dimension specifications.

Spark Plugs

Spark plugs should be removed and cleaned of deposits frequently, especially in two-stroke engines because they burn the lubricating oil right with the fuel. Carefully inspect the plug for severely eroded electrodes or a cracked insulator, and replace the plug if either condition exists or if deposits cannot be adequately removed. Set the gap to 0.035 in. (0.90mm) with a wire type feeler gauge, and install the plug, torquing it to 18–22 ft. lbs.

Make sure to replace the plug with one of the same type and heat range. If the plug is fouled, poor quality or old fuel, a rich mixture, or the wrong fuel/oil mix may be at fault. Also, make sure the engine's exhaust ports are not clogged.

Breaker Points

REMOVAL AND INSTALLATION

1. First remove the flywheel as described below:

a. Remove the screws, engine shroud, and starter. Determine the direction of rotation of the flywheel nut by looking at the threads. Then, place a box wrench on the nut and tap with a soft hammer in the proper direction.

b. The flywheel is removed with a special puller or a special knock off tool. The knock off tool must not be used on 660, 670, or 1500 ball bearing models. To use the knock off tool, screw it onto the crankshaft until it is within $1/16$ in. (1.6mm) of the flywheel. Hold the flywheel firmly and rap the top of the puller sharply with a hammer to jar it loose. Pull the flywheel off.

c. If a puller is being used, the flywheel will have three cored holes into which a set of self-tapping screws are turned. The handle which operates the bolt at the center of the puller's collar is then turned to pull the flywheel off the crankshaft. If this is not adequate to do the job, heat the center of the alloy flywheel with a butane torch to expand it before turning the puller handle.

2. Remove the nuts that hold the electrical leads to the screw on the movable breaker point spring. Remove the movable breaker point from the stud.

3. Remove the screw and stationary breaker point. Put a new stationary breaker point on breaker plate; install the screw, but do not tighten it fully.

4. Position a new movable breaker point on the post.

5. Check that the new points contact each other properly and remove all grease, fingerprints, and dirt from the points.

ADJUSTMENT

1. If necessary (as when checking the gap of old points), loosen the screw which mounts the stationary breaker contact. Rotate the crankshaft until the contact cam follower rests right on the highest point of the cam.

2. Using a flat feeler gauge of the dimension shown under "point gap" in the charts at the rear of this section, check the dimension of the gap and, if incorrect, move the breaker base in the appropriate direction by wedging a screwdriver between the dimples on the base plate and the notch in the breaker plate. When gap is correct, tighten the screw. Recheck the gap and, if necessary, reset it.

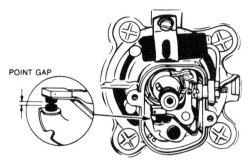

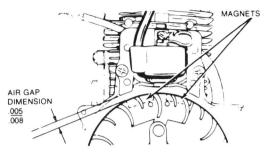

Adjusting point gap

Adjusting magneto armature air gap. Note magnets on flywheel

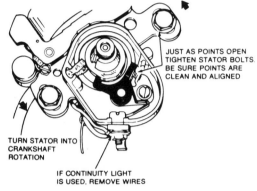

JUST AS POINTS OPEN
TIGHTEN STATOR BOLTS.
BE SURE POINTS ARE
CLEAN AND ALIGNED

TURN STATOR INTO
CRANKSHAFT
ROTATION

IF CONTINUITY LIGHT
IS USED, REMOVE WIRES

Adjusting ignition timing

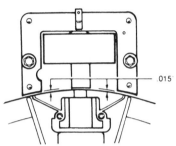

Adjusting magneto armature air gap. Note wider gap

Adjusting Ignition Timing

1. Remove the spark plug and install a special timing tool or thin ruler. With the tool lockscrew loose or the ruler riding on the piston, rotate the crankshaft back and forth to find Top Dead Center. Tighten the tool lockscrew or use a straightedge across the cylinder head, if you're using a ruler, to measure Top Center. Look up the timing dimension in the specifications at the back of this section.

2. Turn the crankshaft backwards so the piston descends. Then, reset the position of the special tool downward the amount of the dimension and tighten the lockscrew, or move the ruler down that amount.

3. Very carefully bring the piston upward by turning the crankshaft until the top of the piston just touches the tool or ruler.

4. Install a piece of cellophane between the contact surfaces. Loosen the ignition stator lockscrews and turn the stator until the cellophane is clamped tightly between the contact surfaces. Turn the stator until the cellophane can just be pulled out (as contacts start to open), and then tighten the stator lockscrews.

Magneto Armature Air Gap

There are two types of magnetos. Compare appearance of your engine with each illustration to determine whether it looks like the type which employs a gap of 0.005–0.008 in. (0.13–0.20mm) or the type with a gap of 0.015 in. (0.38mm).

1. Loosen the two screws which hold the laminations and coil to the block. Turn the flywheel around so the magnets line up directly with the ends of the laminations. Pull the laminations/coil assembly upward.

2. Insert a gap gauge of 0.005–0.008 in. (0.13–0.20mm) between the flywheel and laminations on either side. On units with a gap of 0.015 in. (0.38mm), use two of the above numbered parts or a 0.015 in. (0.38mm) gauge. Allow the attraction of the magnets to pull the coil/laminations assembly toward the flywheel.

3. On the magneto type with a 0.005–0.008 in. (0.13–0.20mm) dimension, use Loctite® Grade A on the screws and torque to 35–45 inch lbs. On the other type magneto, torque the screws to 20–30 inch lbs. Recheck the gap and readjust, if necessary.

Mixture Adjustment

1. If the engine will not start or the carburetor has recently been disassembled, both idle and main mixture screws may be turned in very gently until they just bottom, and then turned out exactly one turn. In this case, back out the idle speed screw until throttle is free, then turn screw in until it just contacts the throttle. Turn it one turn more exactly.

2. Allow the engine to warm up to normal running temperature. With the engine running

at maximum recommended rpm, loosen the main metering screw until the engine rolls, then tighten the screw until the engine starts to cut out. Note the number of turns from one extreme to the other. Loosen the screw to a point midway between the extremes.

3. Set the throttle to idle speed and repeat Step 2 for that adjusting screw.

NOTE: *Some carburetors do not have a main mixture adjustment. Others employ a drilled mixture screw which provides about the right mixture when fully screwed in. In some weather conditions, operation may be improved by setting this screw just slightly off the seat for smoother running.*

Governor Adjustments

POWER TAKEOFF END MECHANICAL GOVERNOR

1. To adjust the governor, remove the outboard bearing housing. Use a $3/32$ in. allen wrench to loosen the set screw.

2. Squeeze the top and bottom governor rings, fully compressing the governor spring.

3. Hold the upper arm of the bell crank parallel to the crankshaft and insert a $3/32$ in. allen

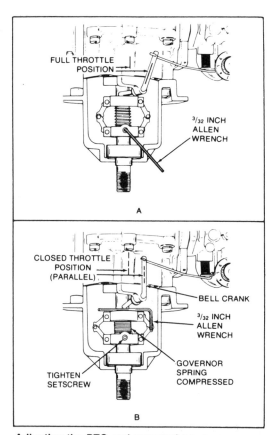

Adjusting the PTO end mounted governor

wrench between the upper ring and the bell crank.

4. Slide the governor assembly onto the crankshaft so that the allen wrench just touches the bell crank.

5. Tighten the set screw to secure the governor to the crankshaft.

6. Install the bearing adapter, mount the engine, and check the engine speed with a tachometer. It should be about 3200–3400 rpm.

NOTE: *Never attempt to adjust the governor by bending the bellcrank or the link.*

7. If the speed is not correct, readjust the governor by moving the assembly toward the crankcase to increase speed, and away from the crankcase to decreased speed.

MECHANICAL FLYWHEEL TYPE GOVERNOR ADJUSTMENT

As engine speed increases, the links are thrown outward, compressing the link springs. The links apply a thrust against the slide ring, moving it upward and compressing the governor spring. As the slide ring moves away from the thrust block of the bellcrank assembly, the throttle spring causes the thrust block to maintain engagement and close the throttle slightly.

As the throttle closes and engine speed decreases, force on the slide ring decreases so that it moves downward, pivots the bellcrank outward to overcome the force of the throttle spring, and opens the throttle to speed up the engine. In this manner, the operating speed of the engine is stabilized to the adjusted governor setting.

1. To adjust the governor, loosen the bracket screw and slide the governor bellcrank assembly toward or away from the flywheel. Move the bellcrank toward the flywheel to increase speed and away from the flywheel to decrease speed.

2. Tighten the screw to secure the bracket.

3. Make minor speed adjustments by bending the throttle link at the bend in the center of the link.

NOTE: *Do not lubricate the governor assem-*

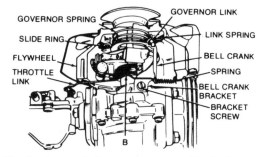

Flywheel mounted governor assembly (cutaway view)

bly or the governor bellcrank assembly of fly-wheel mounted governors.

ADJUSTING 2-CYCLE AIR VANE GOVERNORS

1. Loosen the self-locking nut that holds the governor spring bracket to the engine crankcase.

2. Adjust the spring bracket to increase or decrease the governor spring tension. Increasing spring tension increases speed and decreasing spring tension decreases speed.

3. After adjusting, the spring bracket should not be closer than $\frac{1}{16}$ in. (1.6mm) to the crankcase.

4. Tighten the self-locking nut.

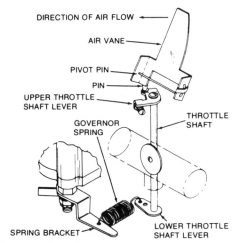

Diagram of an air vane governor

FUEL SYSTEM

Carburetor

REMOVAL AND INSTALLATION

1. Remove the air cleaner. Drain the fuel tank. Disconnect the carburetor fuel lines.

2. If necessary, remove any shrouding or control panels to gain access to the carburetor.

3. Disconnect the choke or throttle control wires at the carburetor.

4. Remove the cap screws, or nuts and lockwashers and remove the carburetor from the engine.

5. To install, reverse the removal procedure, using new gaskets.

OVERHAUL

Tecumseh two-and four-stroke engines employ a common series of carburetors. Refer to the Four-Stroke Tecumseh Engine section for specific carburetor overhaul procedures.

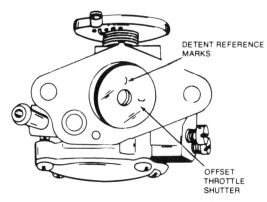

Position detent reference marks of throttle shutter as shown

Idle Governor

SERVICE

1. Remove the shutter fastener and allow the shutter to drop out of the air horn.

2. Note location of the spring end in the disc-shaped throttle lever. The spring should be placed into the same hole during reassembly.

3. Remove the retainer clip and lift out the throttle shaft.

4. Replace all worn parts and reassemble in reverse order.

NOTE: *Note the position of the throttle shutter, as shown. The reference marks must be positioned as shown when shutter is installed.*

Fuel Pump

SERVICE

Float Type Carburetor With Integral Pump

1. If the engine runs, but roughly, make both carburetor mixture adjustments.

2. Make sure the fuel supply is adequate and the tank is in the proper position.

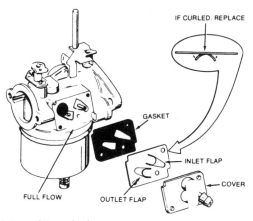

Integral type fuel pump

3. Make sure the fuel tank valve is open.

4. Make sure the pick-up tube is not cracked.

5. Remove the carburetor and make sure the pulsation passage is properly aligned.

6. Check for air leaks at the gasket surface.

7. Remove the cover and check the condition of the inlet and outlet flaps—if curled, replace the flap leaf.

ENGINE OVERHAUL

Disassembly

SPLIT CRANKCASE ENGINES

1. Remove the shroud and fuel tank if so equipped.

2. Remove the flywheel and the ignition stator.

3. Remove the carburetor and governor linkage. Carefully note the position of the carburetor wire links and springs for reinstallation.

4. Lift off the reed plate and gasket if present and inspect them. They should not bend away from the sealing surface plate more than 0.010 in. (0.25mm).

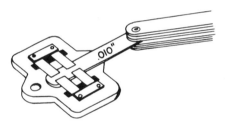

Checking the reed valve clearance

5. Remove the spark plug and inspect it.

6. Remove the muffler. Be sure that the muffler and the exhaust ports are not clogged with carbon. Clean them if necessary.

7. Remove the transfer port cover and check for a good seal.

8. Remove the cylinder head, if so equipped. NOTE: *Some models utilize a locking compound on the cylinder head screws. Removing the screws on such engines can be difficult. This is especially true with screws having slotted head for a straight screwdriver blade. The screws can be removed if heat is applied to the head of the screw with an electric soldering iron.*

9. On engines having a governor mounted on the power take-off end of the crankshaft, remove the screws that hold the outboard bearing housing to the crankcase. Clean the PTO end of the crankshaft and remove the outboard bearing housing and bearing. Loosen the set screw that holds the governor assembly to the crankshaft, slide the entire governor assembly from

the crankshaft. Remove the screw that holds the governor bellcrank bracket to the crankcase. Remove the governor bellcrank and bracket.

10. Make match marks on the cylinder and crankcase. Remove the four nuts and lockwashers that hold the cylinder to the crankcase.

11. Remove the cylinder by pulling it straight out from the crankcase.

12. To separate the two crankcase halves, remove all of the screws that hold the crankcase halves together.

13. With the crankcase in a vertical position, grasp the top half of the crankcase and hold it firmly. Strike the top end of the crankcase with a rawhide mallet, while holding the assembly over a bench to prevent damage to parts when they fall. The top half of the crankcase should separate from the remaining assembly.

14. Invert the assembly and repeat the procedure to remove the other casting half from crankcase on ball bearing units.

15. Each time the crankshaft is removed from the crankcase, seals at the end of the crankcase should be replaced. To replace the seals, use a screwdriver or an ice pick to remove the seal retainers and remove and discard the old seals. Install the seals in the bores of the crankcase halves. The seals must be inserted into the bearing well with the channel groove toward the internal side of the crankcase. Retain the seal with the retainer. Seat the retainer spring into the spring groove.

UNIBLOCK ENGINES

1. Remove the shroud and fuel tank. Note the condition of the air vane governor, if so equipped.

2. Remove the starter cap and flywheel nut, noting the position of the belleville washer.

3. Remove the flywheel—see "Breaker Points Removal and Installation," above.

4. Remove the head. Save the old head gasket for use when replacing the piston, but procure a new gasket for use in final assembly.

5. Remove the cylinder block cover plate to gain access to the connecting rod bolts.

6. Note the location of the connecting rod match marks for reassembly.

7. Remove the piston. Remove the ridge first, if necessary, with a ridge reamer. Push the piston and connecting rod through the top of cylinder.

8. Remove the crankshaft from the cylinder block assembly. On engines with crankshaft ball bearings:

   a. Remove the four shroud base screws and tap the shroud base so the base and crankshaft can be removed together.

   b. To remove bearing with crankshaft

from base: USE SAFETY GLASSES AND HEAT RESISTANT GLOVES. Using a propane torch, heat the area on the base around the outside of the bearing until there is enough expansion to remove the base from the bearing on the crankshaft. Now remove and discard the seal retainer ring, seal retainer and seal.

c. To remove the bearing race, remove the retainer ring on the crankshaft with snap ring pliers, and with the use of a bearing splitter or arbor press, remove the ball bearing.

CAUTION: *Support the crankshaft's top counterweight to prevent bending. Also, bearing is to be pressed on via the inner race only.*
On other engines:

When equipped with a sleeve or needle bearing, use a seal protector and lift the crankshaft out of the cylinder. Be careful not to lose the bearing needles.

When equipped with a ball bearing, use a mallet to strike the crankshaft on the P.T.O. end while holding the block in your hand.

9. In assembly, bear the following points in mind:

a. Use a ring compressor to install piston. Be careful not to allow the rings to catch on the recess for the head gasket. Use the old head gasket to take up the space in the recess. Do not force the piston into the cylinder, or damage to rings or piston could occur.

b. To install the ball bearing on the crankshaft, slide the bearing on the crankshaft and fit it on the shaft by tapping using a mallet and tool, part number 670258 or press the ball bearing on the crankshaft with an arbor press. Install the retainer ring.

c. To install the crankshaft with a ball bearing, heat the shroud base to expand the bearing seat and drop the ball bearing into the seat of the base shroud. Allow it to cool. Install a new seal retainer ring, seal retainer, and seal.

10. After the shroud base and flywheel are back in place, adjust the air gap between the coil core and flywheel as described above under "Magnet Air Gap Adjustment."

Connecting Rod Service

1. For engines using solid bronze or aluminum connecting rods, remove the two self-locking cap screws which hold the connecting rod to the crankshaft and remove the rod cap. Note the match marks on the connecting rod and cap. These marks must be reinstalled in the same position to the crankshaft.

2. Engines using steel connecting rods are equipped with needle bearings at both crankshaft and piston pin end. Remove the two set

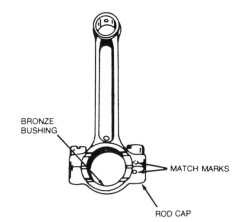

Connecting rod match marks

screws that hold the connecting rod and cap to the crankshaft, taking care not to lose the needle bearings during removal.

3. Needle bearings at the piston pin end of steel rods are caged and can be pressed out as an assembly if damaged.

4. Check the connecting rod for cracks or distortion. Check the bearing surfaces for scoring or wear. Bearing diameters should be within the limits indicated in the table of specifications located at the end of this section.

5. There are two basic arrangements of needles supplied with the connecting rod crankshaft bearing: split rows of needles and a single row of needles. Service needles are supplied with a beeswax coating. The beeswax holds the needles in position.

6. To install the needle bearings, first make sure that the crankshaft bearing journal and the connecting rod are free from oil and dirt.

7. Place the needle bearings with the beeswax onto a cool metallic surface to stiffen the beeswax. Body temperature will melt the wax, so avoid handling.

8. Remove the paper backing on the bearings and wrap the needles around the crankshaft journal. The beeswax will hold the needles onto the journal. Position the needles uniformly onto the crankpin.

NOTE: *When installing the split row of needles, wrap each row of needles around the journal and try to seal them together with gentle but firm pressure to keep the bearings from unwinding.*

9. Place the connecting rod onto the journal, position the rod cap, and secure it with the capscrews. Tighten the screw to the proper specifications.

10. Force solvent (lacquer thinner) into the needles just installed to remove the beeswax, then force 30W oil into the needles for proper lubrication.

Piston and Rings Service

1. Clean all carbon from the piston and ring grooves.
2. Check the piston for scoring or other damage.
3. Check the fit of the piston in the cylinder bore. Move the piston from side-to-side to check clearance. If the clearance is not greater than 0.0003 in. (0.0076mm) and the cylinder is not scored or damaged, then the piston need not be replaced.
4. Check the piston ring side clearance to make sure it is within the limits recommended.
5. Check the piston rings for wear by inserting them into the cylinder about ½ in. (13mm) from the top of the cylinder. Check at various places to make sure that the gap between the ends of the ring does not exceed the dimensions recommended in the specifications table at the end of this section. Bore wear can be checked in the same way, except that a new ring is used to measure the end gap.
6. If replacement rings have a beveled or chamfered edge, install them with the bevel up toward the top of the piston. Not all engines use beveled rings. The two rings installed on the piston are identical.
7. When installed, the offset piston used on the AV600 and the AV520 engines must have the **V** stamped in the piston head (some have hash marks) facing toward the right as the engine is viewed from the top or piston side of the engine.

NOTE: *Some AV520 and AV600 engines do not have offset pistons. Only offset pistons will have the "V" or the hash marks on the piston head. Domed pistons must be installed so that the slope of the piston is toward the exhaust port.*

A. SPLIT ROWS OF NEEDLE BEARINGS

B. SINGLE ROW OF NEEDLE BEARINGS

Needle bearing arrangement. Double rows of bearings are placed with the tapered edges facing out

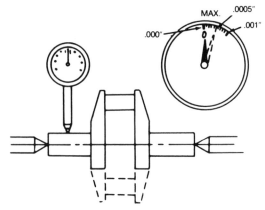

Checking the crankshaft for out-of-roundness

Crankshaft Service

1. Use a micrometer to check the bearing journals for out-of-roundness. The main bearing journals should not be more than 0.0005 in. (0.0127mm) out-of-round. Connecting rod journals should not be more than 0.001 in. (0.025mm) out-of-round. Replace a crankshaft that is not within these limits.

NOTE: *Do not attempt to regrind the crankshaft since undersize parts are not available.*

2. Check the tapered portion of the crankshaft (magneto end), keyways, and threads. Damaged threads may be restored with a thread die. If the taper of the shaft is rusty, it indicates that the engine has been operating with a loose flywheel. Clean the rust off the taper and check for wear. If the taper or keyway is worn, replace the crankshaft.
3. Check all of the bearing journal diameters. They should be within the limits indicated in the specifications table at the end of this section.
4. Check the crankshaft for bends by placing it between two pivot points. Position the dial indicator feeler on the crankshaft bearing surface and rotate the shaft. The crankshaft should not be more than 0.002–0.004 in. (0.05–0.10mm) out-of-round.

Bearing Service

1. Do not remove the bearings unless they are worn or noisy. Check the operation of the bearings by rotating the bearing cones with your fingers to check for roughness, binding, or any other signs of unsatisfactory operation. If the bearings do not operate smoothly, remove them.
2. To remove the bearings from the crankcase, the crankcase must be heated. Use a hot plate to heat the crankcase to no more than 400°F (204°C). Place a ⅛ in. (3mm) steel plate

over the hot plate to prevent overheating. At this temperature, the bearings should drop out with a little tapping of the crankcase.

3. The replacement bearing is left at room temperature and dropped into the heated crankcase. Make sure that the new bearing is seated to the maximum depth of the cavity.

NOTE: *Do not use an open flame to heat the crankcase halves and do not heat the crankcase halves to more than 400°F (204°C). Uneven heating with an open flame or excessive temperature will distort the case.*

4. The needle bearings will fall out of the bearing cage with very little urging. Needles can be reinstalled easily by using a small amount of all-purpose grease to hold the bearings in place.

5. Cage bearings are removed and replaced in the same manner as ball bearings.

6. Sleeve bearings cannot be replaced. Both crankcase halves must be discarded if a bearing is worn excessively.

Assembly

1. The gasket surface where the crankcase halves join must be thoroughly clean before reassembly. Do not buff or use a file or any other abrasive that might damage the mating surfaces.

NOTE: *Crankcase halves are matched. If one needs to be replaced, then both must be replaced.*

2. Place the PTO half of the crankcase onto the PTO end of the crankshaft. Use seal protectors where necessary.

3. Apply a thin coating of sealing compound to the contact surface of one of the crankcase halves.

4. Position one crankcase half on the other. The fit should be such that some pressure is required to bring the two halves together. If this is not the case, either the crankcase halves and/or the crankshaft must be replaced.

5. Secure the halves with the screws provided, tightening the screws alternately and evenly. Before tightening the screws, check the union of the crankcase halves on the cylinder mounting side. The halves should be flat and smooth at the union to provide a good mounting face for the cylinder. If necessary, realign the halves before tightening the screws.

6. The sleeve tool should be placed into the crankcase bore from the direction opposite the crankshaft. Insert the tapered end of the crankshaft through the half of the crankcase to which the magneto stator is mounted. Remove the seal tools after installing the crankcase halves.

7. Stagger the ring ends on the piston and check for the correct positioning on domed piston models.

8. Place the cylinder gasket on the crankcase end.

9. Place the piston into the cylinder using the chamfer provided on the bottom edge of the cylinder to compress the rings.

10. Secure the cylinder to the crankcase assembly.

Type Number-to-Letter Cross Reference Chart

Type No.	Column Letter	Type No.	Column Letter	Type No.	Column Letter
1 thru 44	A	611	F	1001	D
46 thru 68	B	614–01 thru 614–04	E	1002 thru 1002D	G
69 thru 77	D	614–05 thru 614–06A	F	1003	C
78 thru 80	C	615–01 thru 615–01A	E	1004 thru 1004A	H
81 thru 83	D	615–04	F	1005 thru 1005A	C
84 thru 85	C	615–05 thru 615–10A	E	1006	H
86 thru 87	B	615–11 thru 615–18	F	1007 thru 1008B	C
89	C	615–19 thru 615–27A	E	1009 thru 1010B	G
91	D	615–28	F	1011 thru 1019E	H
93	D	615–29 thru 615–39	E	1020	G
94 thru 98	H	616–01 thru 616–11	E	1021	C
99	C	616–12 and 616–14	F	1022 thru 1022C	D
		616–16 thru 616–40	E	1023 thru 1026A	H
201 thru 208	A	617A thru 617–01	E	1027 thru 1027B	C
209 thru 244	B	617–02 thru 617–03A	F	1028 thru 1030C	H
245	D	617–04 thru 617–04A	E	1031B thru 1031C	G
246 thru 248	B	617–05 thru 617–05A	F	1032	C
249 thru 251	D	617–06	E	1033 thru 1033F	G
252	B	618 thru 618–16	E	1034 thru 1034G	H
253 thru 255	D	618–17	F	1035 thru 1036	C
256 thru 261	B	618–18	E	1037 thru 1039C	D
262 thru 265A	D	619 thru 619–03	E	1040 thru 1041A	D
266 thru 267	B	621 thru 621–11	E	1042 thru 1042C	G
268 thru 272	D	621 thru 621–12A	F	1042D thru 1042E	H
273 thru 275	B	621–13 thru 621–15	E	1042F	G
276	D	622 thru 622–07	E	1042G and 1042H	H
277 thru 279	B	623 and 623A	E	1042I thru 1043B	G
280 thru 281	D	623–01	F	1043C thru 1043F	H
282	B	623–02 thru 623–33E	E	1043G thru 1044E	G
283 thru 284	D	623–34	F	1045 thru 1045F	B
285 thru 286	B	623–35 and 623–36	E	1046 thru 1051B	H
287	D	624 thru 630–09	J	1052	G
288 thru 291B	B	632–02A	K	1053 thru 1054C	H
292 thru 294	D	632–04 and 632–05A	K	1055 thru 1056B	G
295 thru 296	B	633 thru 634–09	J	1057	H
297	F	635A and B	K	1058 thru 1058A	G
298 thru 299	B	635–03B	K	1059	D
		635–04B	K	1060 thru 1060C	H
301 thru 375		635–06A thru 635–10	K	1061 and 1062	C
These are twin		636 thru 636–11	J	1063A thru 1063C	H
cylinder units –		637 thru 637–16	J	1064	G
out of production		638 thru 638–100	F	1065 thru 1067C	D
401 thru 402	L	639	M	1068 and 1068A	G
403	M	640	O	1069	H
404 thru 406B	L	641	K	1070 thru 1070B	C
407 thru 407C	M	642	I	1071 thru 1075D	H
408 thru 410B	L	643	J	1076 thru 1084	H
411 thru 411B	M	650	N	1085 and 1085A	G
412 thru 423	L	670	H	1086 thru 1140A	H
424 thru 427	M				
				1141 thru 1142	G
501 thru 509A	E	701 thru 701–1C	G	1143 thru 1145	H
		701–2 thru 701–2D	H	1146 thru 1149A	I
601 thru 601–01	F	701–3 thru 701–3C	G	1149A thru 1153B	H
602 thru 602–02B	F	701–4 thru 701–4C	H	1158 thru 1159	G
603A thru 603–23	E	701–5 thru 701–5C	G	1160 thru 1161A	I
604 thru 604–25	E	701–6 thru 701–6C	H	1162 and 1162A	G
605 thru 605–18	E	701–7 thru 701–7C	G	1163 thru 1163A	H
606 thru 606–05B	E	701–8 thru 701–11	H	1165 thru 1168A	G
606–06 thru 606–07	F	701–12 thru 701–13A	G	1169 thru 1174	H
606–08 thru 606–13	E	701–14 thru 701–17	H	1175 and 1175A	I
608 thru 608–C	E	701–18 thru 701–19	G	1176 thru 1177A	H
610–A thru 610–14	E	701–19A	H	1179 thru 1179A	I
610–15 thru 610–16	F	701–20 thru 701–22A	G	1180 thru 1181	G
610–19 thru 610–20	E	701–24	H	1182 and 1182A	I

Type Number-to-Letter Cross Reference Chart (cont.)

Type No.	Column Letter	Type No.	Column Letter	Type No.	Column Letter
1183 thru 1185	G	1345	J	1441	P
1186A thru 1186C	J	1348 and 1348A	G	1442 thru 1442B	G
1187 thru 1192	G	1350 thru 1350C	I	1443	I
1192A thru 1196B	J			1444 and 1444A	G
1197 thru 1197A	G	1550A	P	1445	I
1198 and 1198A	H			1446 and 1446A	A
1199 and 1199A	J	1351 thru 1351B	K	1447	G
		1352 thru 1352B	I	1448 thru 1450	F
1206 thru 1208B	J	1353	K	1450A thru 1450B	F
1210 thru 1215C	K	1354 thru 1355A	I	1450C thru 1450E	F
1216 thru 1216A	H	1356 and 1356B	K	1453	K
1217 thru 1220A	J	1357 thru 1358	I	1454 and 1454A	A
1221	H	1359 thru 1362B	K	1455 thru 1456	K
1222 thru 1223	J	1363 thru 1369A	G	1459	G
1224 thru 1225A	H	1372 thru 1375A	G	1460 thru 1460F	A
1226 thru 1227B	K	1376 and 1376A	J	1461	K
1228 thru 1229A	J	1377 thru 1378	K	1462	A
1230 thru 1231	H	1379 thru 1379A	H	1463	K
1232	G	1380 thru 1380B	K	1464 thru 1464B	L
1233 thru 1237B	K	1381	G	1465	A
1238 thru 1238C	H	1382	H	1466 thru 1466A	F
1239 thru 1243	J	1383 thru 1383B	K	1467 thru 1468	K
1244 thru 1245A	K	1384 thru 1385	G	1471 thru 1471B	E
1246 thru 1247	J	1386	I	1472 thru 1472C	L
1248	H	1387 thru 1388	K	1473 thru 1473B	A
1249 thru 1251A	J	1389	G	1474	L
1252 thru 1254A	K	1390 thru 1390B	H	1475 thru 1476	A
1255	J	1391	K	1477	G
1256 thru 1262B	K	1392	J	1478	J
1263	J	1393	G	1479	G
1264 thru 1265E	K	1394 thru 1395A	P	1482 and 1482A	F
1266 thru 1267	G	1396	K	1483	F
1269 thru 1270D	K	1397	H	1484 thru 1484D	A
1271 thru 1271B	G	1398 thru 1399	K	1485	G
1272 thru 1275	K			1486	D
1276	H	1400	K	1487	J
1277 thru 1279D	K	1401 thru 1401F	F	1488 thru 1488D	A
1280	J	1402 and 1402B	G	1489 thru 1490B	C
1283 thru 1284D	K	1403A and 1403B	K	1491	L
1286 thru 1286A	H	1404 and 1404A	K	1493 and 1493A	G
1287	K	1405 thru 1406A	H	1494 and 1495A	B
1288	J	1407 thru 1408	K	1496	G
1289 thru 1289A	G	1409A	J	1497	A
1290 thru 1293A	K	1410 thru 1412A	I	1498	E
1294 thru 1295	J	1413 thru 1416	I	1499	F
1296 thru 1298	K	1417 and 1417A	K		
		1418 and 1418A	P	1500	E
1300 thru 1303	K	1419 and 1419A	K	1501A thru 1501E	A
1304 thru 1307	J	1420 and 1420A	H	1503 thru 1503D	L
1308 thru 1316A	K	1421 and 1421A	K	1506 thru 1507	F
1317 thru 1317B	J	1422 thru 1423	P	1508	G
1318 thru 1320B	K	1424	K	1509	C
1321 thru 1322	J	1425	G	1510	L
1323	K	1426 thru 1426B	P	1511	C
1325	G	1427 and 1427A	H	1512 and 1512A	B
1326 thru 1326F	K	1428 thru 1429A	P	1513	L
1327 thru 1327B	H	1430A	G	1515 thru 1516C	C
1328B and 1328C	K	1431	P	1517	E
1329	J	1432 and 1432A	G	1518	D
1330	H	1433	K	1519 thru 1521	A
1331	J	1434 thru 1435A	P	1522	L
1332	J	1436 and 1436A	I	1523	A
1333	I	1437	J	1524	B
1334	I	1439	I	1527	C
1343 thru 1344A	H	1440 thru 1440D	A	1528	A

Type Number-to-Letter Cross Reference Chart (cont.)

Type No.	Column Letter	Type No.	Column Letter	Type No.	Column Letter
1529A and 1529B	C	2045 thru 2046B	F	40069 thru 40075	N
1530 thru 1530B	A	2047 thru 2048	D		
1531 thru 1535B	C	2049 thru 2049A	F		
1536	L	2050 thru 2050A	D	710101 thru 710116	E
1537	A	2051 thru 2052A	D	710124 thru 710130	E
1538 thru 1541A	L	2053 thru 2055	F	710131 thru 710137	E
1542	E	2056	D	710138 thru 710149	E
1543 thru 1546	A	2057	F	710154	M
1547	C	2058 thru 2058B	D	710201 thru 710209	E
1549	C	2059 thru 2063	F	710210 thru 710218	E
		2064 thru 2064A	D	710219 thru 710227	E
S–1801 thru 1822	F	2065	F	710228	M
1823 and 1824	E	2066	D	710150	G
		2067 thru 2071B	F	710151	H
2001 thru 2003	B			710155	L
2004 thru 2006	D	2200 thru 2201A	D	710157	H
2007 thru 2007B	B	2202 thru 2204	E	710229	H
2008 thru 2008B	D	2205 thru 2205A	D	710230	N
2009	B	2206 thru 2206A	G	710234	N
2010 thru 2011	D	2207	D		
2012	F	2208	G		
2013 thru 2014	B	2768	C	200.183112	F
2015 thru 2018	D			200.18322	F
2020	F			200.193132	F
2021	D	40001 thru 40028	N	200.193142	F
2022 thru 2022B	F	40029 thru 40032C	O	200.193152	G
2023 thru 2026	D	40033	N	200.193162	G
2027	B	40034 thru 40045A	O	200.203172	H
2028 thru 2029	D	40046	N	200.203182	H
2030 thru 2031	B	40047 thru 40052	O	200.203192	H
2032 thru 2033A	D	40053 thru 40054A	N	200.213112	H
2034 thru 2035C	F	40056 thru 40060B	O	200.213122	H
2036 thru 2037	B	40061 thru 40062B	N	200.503111	F
2038	F	40063 thru 40064	O	200.583111	F
2039 thru 2044	C	40065 thru 40066	N	200.593121	F
		40067 thru 40068	O	200.613111	F

Specifications for 2 Cycle Engines with Split Crankcases

	A	B	C	D	E	F	G	H
Bore	1.500 1.5005	1.6253 1.6258	1.7503 1.7508	1.7503 1.7508	2.000	2.000	2.000	2.000
Stroke	1.375	1.50	1.50	1.50	1.50	1.50	1.50	1.50
Displacement Cubic Inches	2.43	3.10	3.60	3.60	4.70	4.70	4.70	4.70
Point Gap	.020	.020	.020	.020	.020	.020	.015	.015
Timing B.T.D.C. Before Top Dead Center	1/16" or .0625	5/32" or .1562	5/32" or .1562	1/4" or .250	5/32" or .1562	5/32" or .1562	5/32"	1/4" or .250 11/64" for "super"
Spark Plug Gap	.030	.030	.030	.030	.030	.030	.030	.030
Piston Ring End Gap	.003 .008	.005 .010	.005 .010	.005 .010	.006 .011	.006 .011	.006 .011	.006 .011
Piston Diameter	1.4966 1.4969	1.6216 1.6219	1.7461 1.7464	1.7461 1.7464	1.9948 1.9951	1.9948 1.9951	1.9948 1.9951	1.9949 1.9955
Piston Ring Groove Width	.095 .096	.095 .096	.095 .096	.095 .096	.095 .096	.095 .096	.095 .096	.095 .096
Piston Ring Width	.093 .0935	.093 .0935	.093 .0935	.093 .0935	.093 .0935	.093 .0935	.093 .0935	.093 .0935
Piston Pin Diameter	.3750 .3751	.3750 .3751	.3750 .3751	.3750 .3751	.3750 .3751	.3750 .3751	.3750 .3751	Early .3750 .3761 Late .4997 .4999
Connecting Rod Diameter Crank Bearing	.6869 .6874	.6869 .6874	.6869 .6874	.6986 .6989 w/o needles	.6869 .6874	.6869 .6874	.6869 .6874	.6935 .6939 w/o needles
Crankshaft Rod Needle Diameter				.0653 .0655				.0653 .0655
Crank Pin Journal Diameter	.6860 .6865	.6860 .6865	.6860 .6865	.5615 .5618	.6860 .6865	.6860 .6865	.6860 .6865	.5615 .5618
Crankshaft P.T.O. Side Main Brg. Dia.	.6689 .6693	.6689 .6693	.6690 .6694	.6689 .6693	.9995 1.0000	.6689 .6693	.9995 1.0000	.9995 1.0000
Crankshaft Magneto Side Main Brg. Dia.	.6689 .6693	.6689 .6693	.6689 .6693	.6690 .6694	.7495 .7500	.6689 .6693	.7495 .7500	.7495 .7500
Crankshaft End Play	.003 .008	.003 .008	.003 .008	.003 .008	.009 .022	.009 .022	.009 .022	.009 .022

Specifications for 2 Cycle Engines with Split Crankcases (cont.)

I	J	K	L	M	N	O	P	
2.000	2.000	2.093 2.094	2.2505 2.2510	2.2505 2.2510	2.5030 2.5035	2.5030 2.5035	2.000	Bore
1.50	1.625	1.63	2.00	2.00	1.625	1.680	1.50	Stroke
4.70	5.10	5.80	8.00	8.00	7.98	8.25	4.70	Displacement Cubic Inches
.015	.020	.015	.020	.020	.020	.020	.015	Point Gap
$11/64''$ or .175	$11/64''$ or .175	$3/32''$ or .095	$1/8''$ or .125	$3/32''$ or .095	$11/64''$ or .175	$11/64''$ or .175	.90	Timing B.T.D.C. Before Top Dead Center
.035	.030	.030	.030	.030	.030	.030	.035	Spark Plug Gap
.006 .011	.006 .011	.006 .011	.007 .015	.007 .015	.005 .013	.005 .013	.006 .011	Piston Ring End Gap
1.9948 1.9951	1.9951 1.9948	2.0880 2.0883	2.2460 2.2463	2.2460 2.2463	2.4960 2.4963	2.4960 2.4963	1.9948 1.9951	Piston Diameter
.095 .096	.095 .096	T.0655 .0665 L.0645 .0655	.095 .096	.095 .096	T.0655 .0665 L.0645 .0655	T.0655 .0665 L.0645 .0655	.095 .096	Piston Ring Groove Width
.093 .0935	.093 .0935	.0615 .0625	.093 .0935	.093 .0935	.0615 .0625	.0615 .0625	.093 .0935	Piston Ring Width
.4997 .4999	.3750 .3751	.4997 .4999	.5000 .5001	.3000 .5001	.4997 .4999	.4997 .4999	.4997 .4999	Piston Pin Diameter
.6941 .6944	.6869 .6874	.9407 .9412	1.000 1.0004	1.000 1.0004	.9407 .9412	.9407 .9412	.6941 .6944	Connecting Rod Diameter Crank Bearing
.0653 .0655		.0943 .0945	.0943 .0945	.0943 .0945	.0943 .0945	.0943 .0945	.0653 .0655	Crankshaft Rod Needle Diameter
.6860 .6865	.6860	.7499 .7502	.8096 .8099	.8096 .8099	.7499 .7502	.7499 .7502	.6860 .6865	Crank Pin Journal Diameter
.9995 1.0000	.9995 1.0000	.6990 .6994	.9839 .9842	.9839 .9842	.7871 .7875	.7871 .7875	.9995 1.0000	Crankshaft P.T.O. Side Main Brg. Dia.
.7495 .7500	.7495 .7500	.6990 .6994	.9839 .9842	.9839 .9842	.7498 .7501	.7498 .7501	.7495 .7500	Crankshaft Magneto Side Main Brg. Dia.
.009 .022	.009 .022	.003 .008	.003 .008	.003 .008	.008 .013	.008 .013	.009 .022	Crankshaft End Play

Uniblock Cross Reference Chart

Type No.	Column No.	Type No.	Column No.	Type No.	Column No.
Vertical Crankshaft Engines		**Horizontal Crankshaft Engines**		**Horizontal Crankshaft Engines**	
638 thru 638–100	6	1401 thru 1401F	16	1508	7
		1401G, H	17	1509	3
642–01, A	9A	1401J	27	1510	12
642–02, A, B, C, D	9A	1402 and 1402B	7	1511	3
642–02E, F	9B	1425	7	1512 and 1512A	2
642–03, A, B	9A	1430A	7	1513	12
642–04, A, B, C	9A	1432 and 1432A	7	1515 thru 1516C	3
642–05, A, B	9A	1440 thru 1440D	1	1517	5
642–06, A	9A	1442 thru 1442B	7	1518	4
642–07, A, B	9A	1444 and 1444A	7	1519 thru 1521	1
		1448 thru 1450	16	1522	12
642–07C	9B	1450A thru 1450B	16	1523	1
642–08	9B	1450C thru 1450E	16	1524	2
642–08A, B	9A	1450F	17	1525A	16
642–09 thru 642–14	9A	1454 and 1454A	1	1527	3
642–13A, 14A, 14B	9B	1459	7	1528	1
642–15 thru 642–22	9B	1460 thru 1460F	1	1529A and 1520B	3
642–24 thru 642–30	9C	1462	1	1530 thru 1530B	1
		1464 thru 1464B	12	1531	3
670–01 thru 670–101	8	1465	1	1534A	17
		1466 thru 1466A	16	1535B	3
200–183112	6	1471 thru 1471B	5	1536	12
200–183122	6	1472 thru 1472C	12	1537	1
200–193132	6	1473 thru 1473B	1	1538 thru 1541A	12
200–193142	6	1474	12	1542	5
200–193152	7	1475 thru 1476	1	1543 thru 1546	1
200–193162	7	1479	7	1517	3
200–203172	8	1482 and 1482A	16	1519	3
200–203182	8	1483	16	1551	16
200–203192	8	1484 thru 1484D	3	1552	20
200–213112	8	1485	7	1553	16
200–213122	8	1486	4	1554 and 1554A	3
200–243112	8	1488 thru 1488D	1	1555 and 1556	16
200–283012	8	1489 thru 1490B	3	1561	19
		1491	12	1572	2
		1493 and 1493A	7	1573	3
		1494 and 1495A	2	1574 thru 1577	23
		1496	7	1575	24
		1497	1	1578	25
		1498	5	1581 thru 1582A	23
		1499	16	1583 thru 1595	26
		1500	5	200–503111	16
		1501A thru 1501E	1	200–583111	16
		1503 thru 1503D	12	200–593121	16
		1506	16	200–613111	16
		1506B	17	200–672102	26
		1507	16	200–682102	26

Torque Specifications for 2-Cycle Engines

Application	Torque	Application	Torque
Carburetor and Reed Plates		Cylinder head to cylinder (635 type engine)	45–50 in. pounds
Carburetor to crankcase, Carburetor to adapter, or Carburetor adapter to crankcase	70–75 in. pounds	Cable clip and transfer port cover to cylinder	25–30 in. pounds
Carburetor to snow blowers cover	30–35 in. pounds	Cable clip to cylinder Stop lever to cylinder	25–30 in. pounds
Carburetor outlet fitting	40 in. pounds	Spark plug	18–22 ft. pounds
Reed and cover plates 639 type engines	50–60 in. pounds with Loctite, type A	Transfer cover cross port engines	25–30 in. pounds
Reed to plate 635 type engines	12–18 in. pounds	**Crankshaft and Connecting Rods**	
Crankcase and Cylinder		Aluminum and bronze rods to rod cap	40–50 in. pounds
Crankcase to crankcase cover	23–30 in. pounds	Steel rod to rod cap	70–80 in. pounds
Crankcase to crankcase cover screws	35–40 in. pounds	Flywheel nut on tapered end of crankshaft: Aluminum hub on iron or steel shaft.	18–25 ft. pounds
Mounting cylinder or carburetor to crankcase studs	50 in. pounds	Steel hub flywheel on iron shaft	18–25 ft. pounds
Base to crankcase	240–250 in. pounds	Steel hub flywheel on steel shaft	30 ft. pounds
Cylinder to crankcase nuts	70–75 in. pounds	**Governor and Bell Crank Parts**	
In cylinder	100–110 in. pounds	Power take-off end governor lower ring to crankshaft setscrew	30–35 in. pounds
Spark plug stop lever and head shroud to head	50–60 in. pounds	Bell crank bracket to crankcase	20–25 in. pounds
Cylinder head to cylinder	30–40 in. pounds	Governor cover to crankcase	50–60 in. pounds
Cylinder head to cylinder	50–60 in. pounds 80–90 in. pounds		

Specifications Chart

	1	2	3	4	5	6	7	8	9A	9B	9C	12
Bore	2.093 2.094	2.093 2.094	2.093 2.094	2.093 2.094	2.093 2.094	2.093 2.094	2.093 2.094	2.093 2.094	2.093 2.094	2.093 2.094	2.093 2.094	2.093 2.094
Stroke	1.250	1.410	1.410	1.410	1.410	1.500	1.500	1.500	1.500	1.500	1.500	1.410
Cu. In. Displacement	4.40	4.80	4.80	4.80	4.80	5.20	5.20	5.20	5.20	5.20	5.20	4.80
Point Gap	.017	.017	.017	.017	.017	.018	.017	.020	.018	.020	.020	.017
Timing B.T.D.C.	.122"	.100"	.135"	.100"	.135"	.100"	.185"	.070"	.110"	.085" See Note 1	.078" See Note 2	.135"
Spark Plug Gap	.035	.035	.035	.035	.035	.035	.035	.035	.035	.035	.035	.035
Piston Ring End Gap	.007 .017	.007 .017	.006 .011	.006 .014	.006 .011	.006 .014	.007 .017	.006 .016	.007 .017	.006 .016	.006 .016	.007 .017
Piston Diameter	2.0080 2.0870	2.0880 2.0870	2.0885 2.0875	2.0885 2.0875	2.0885 2.0875	2.0880 2.0870	2.0880 2.0870	2.0880 2.0870	2.0880 2.0870	2.0880 2.0820	2.0880 2.0870	2.0880 2.0870
Piston Ring Groove Width (Top)	.0655 .0665	.0655 .0665	.0655 .0665	.0975 .0985	.0655 .0665	.0975 .0985	.0655 .0665	.0655 .0665	.0655 .0665	.0655 .0665	.0655 .0665	.0655 .0665
Piston Ring Groove Width (Bot.)	.0645 .0655	.0645 .0655	.0645 .0655	.0955 .0965	.0645 .0655	.0955 .0965	.0645 .0655	.0645 .0655	.0645 .0655	.0645 .0655	.0645 .0655	.0645 .0655
Piston Ring Width	.0625 .0615	.0625 .0615	.0625 .0615	.0925 .0935	.0625 .0615	.0925 .0935	.0625 .0615	.0625 .0615	.0625 .0615	.0625 .0615	.0625 .0615	.0625 .0615

Piston Pin Diameter	.4999 .4997	.4999 .4997	.4999 .4997	.3750 .3751	.4999 .4997	.4999 .4997	.3750 .3751	.4999 .4997	.4999 .4997	.4999 .4997
Connecting Rod Diameter Crank Bearing	—	—	.6886 .6879 Dowels	—	—	1.0053 1.0023 Liner Dia.	—	1.0053 1.0023 Liner Dia.	1.0053 1.0023 Liner Dia.	1.0053 1.0023 Liner Dia.
Crankshaft Rod Needle Dia.	.0655 .0653	.0655 .0653	—	.0655 .0653	—	.0781 .0780	—	.0781 .0780	.0781 .0780	.0655 .0653
Crank Pin Journal Diameter	.5621 .5614	.5621 .5614	.6865 .6857	.5618 .5611	.6865 .6857	.8450 .8442	.6865 .6857	.8450 .8442	.8450 .8442	.5618 .5611
Crankshaft P.T.O. Side Main Brg. Dia.	.6695 .6691	.6695 .6691	.6695 .6691	.6694 .6690	.8750 .8745	1.0003 .9998	.8750 .8745	1.0003 .9998	1.0003 .9998	.6694 .6690
Crankshaft Magneto Side Main Brg. Dia.	.6695 .6691	.6695 .6691	.6695 .6691	.6694 .6690	.7500 .7495	.7503 .7498	.7500 .7495	.7503 .7498	.6695 .6691	.6695 .6691
Crankshaft End Play	None	None	None	None	.003 .016	.003 .016	.003 .016	.003 .016	None	None

NOTE 1: 642-08 14A, 14B B.T.D.C. = .110"
642-16D, 19A, 20A, 21 22 B.T.D.C. = .078"
NOTE 2: 642-24, 26, 29 B.T.D.C. = .085"
643-2a, 25, 26 B.T.D.C. = .085"
NOTE 3: 643-13 B.T.D.C. = .095"
NOTE 4: 643-03A, 05A, 13, 14 = .020"

Specifications Chart

	14	16	17	19	20	23	24	25	26	27
Bore	2.093 2.094	2.093 2.094	2.093 2.094	2.093 2.094	2.093 2.094	2.093 2.094	2.093 2.094	2.093 2.094	2.093 2.094	2.093 2.094
Stroke	1.500	1.500	1.500	1.410	1.250	1.500	1.410	1.410	1.500	1.500
Cu. In. Displacement	5.20	5.20	5.20	4.80	4.40	5.20	4.80	4.80	5.20	5.20
Point Gap	.018	.017	.017	.017	.017	.017	.017	.020	.020	.017
Timing B.T.D.C.	.100″	.110″	.110″	.100″	.122″	.110″	.135″	Fixed	.062″	.100″
Spark Plug Gap	.035	.035	.035	.035	.035	.035	.035	.035	.035	.035
Piston Ring End Gap	.006 .014	.006 .016	.006 .016	.007 .017	.007 .017	.006 .016	.007 .017	.007 .017	.006 .016	.006 .016
Piston Diameter	2.0880 2.0870	2.0885 2.0875	2.0890 2.0880	2.0880 2.0870	2.0880 2.0870	2.0880 2.0870	2.0880 2.0870	2.0880 2.0870	2.0880 2.0870	2.0885 2.0875
Piston Ring Groove Width (Top)	.0975 .0985	.0645 .0655	.0645 .0655	.0655 .0665	.0655 .0665	.0655 .0665	.0655 .0665	.0655 .0665	.0655 .0665	.0655 .0665
Piston Ring Groove Width (Bot.)	.0955 .0965	.0645 .0655	.0645 .0655	.0645 .0655	.0645 .0655	.0645 .0655	.0645 .0655	.0645 .0655	.0645 .0655	.0645 .0655

Piston Ring Width	.0925 / .0935	.0625 / .0615	.0625 / .0615	.0625 / .0615	.0625 / .0615	.0625 / .0615	.0625 / .0615	.0625 / .0615	.0625 / .0615
Piston Pin Diameter	.3750 / .3751	.4999 / .4997	.4999 / .4997	.4999 / .4997	.4999 / .4997	.4999 / .4997	.4999 / .4997	.4999 / .4997	.4999 / .4997
Connecting Rod Diameter Crank Bearing	—	—	—	.8534 / .8504 Liner Dia.	—	—	—	.8534 / .8504 Liner Dia.	.8919 / .8924
Crankshaft Rod Needle Dia.	—	—	.0655 / .0653	.0781 / .0780	.0655 / .0653	.0655 / .0653	.0655 / .0653	.0781 / .0780	.0781 / .0780
Crank Pin Journal Diameter	.6868 / .6857	.6865 / .6857	.5621 / .5614	.6927 / .6919	.5618 / .5611	.5621 / .5614	.5621 / .5614	.6927 / .6919	.6927 / .6922
Crankshaft P.T.O. Side Main Brg. Dia.	.6695 / .6691	1.0003 / .9998	.6695 / .6691	.6695 / .6691	.6695 / .6691	.6695 / .6691	.6695 / .6691	.7503 / .7498	.6695 / .6691
Crankshaft Magneto Side Main Brg. Dia.	.7500 / .7495	.7500 / .7495	.6695 / .6691	.6695 / .6691	.6695 / .6691	.6695 / .6691	.6695 / .6691	.6695 / .6691	.7503 / .7498
Crankshaft End Play	.003 / .016	None	None	None	None	None	None	None	.003 / .016

A. on Engines prior to 660-24: 7505, 7198

16
Tecumseh 2-Stroke
6 through 12 Hp

ENGINE IDENTIFICATION

The identification tags may be located at a variety of places on the engine. The type number is the most important number since it must be included with any correspondence about a particular engine.

Early engines listed the type number as a suffix of the serial number. For example on number 123456789 P 234, 234 is the type number. In the number 123456789 H 104–02B; 104–02B is the type number. In either case the type number is important.

If you use short block to repair the engine, be sure that you transfer the serial number and type number tag to the new short block.

On the newer engines, reference is sometimes made to the model number. The model number tells the number of cylinders, the design (vertical or horizontal) and the cubic inch displacement.

GENERAL ENGINE SPECIFICATIONS

A detailed listing of the great number of Power Products two-stroke engine models is provided in the Type No./Column No. cross reference chart at the back of this section.

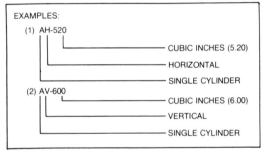

EXAMPLES:

(1) AH-520
CUBIC INCHES (5.20)
HORIZONTAL
SINGLE CYLINDER

(2) AV-600
CUBIC INCHES (6.00)
VERTICAL
SINGLE CYLINDER

Model number interpretation

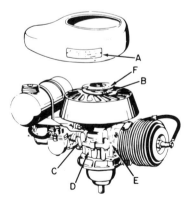

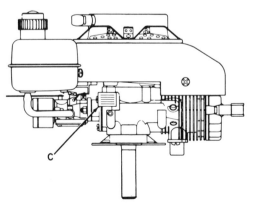

A. NAMEPLATE ON AIR SHROUD
B. MODEL & TYPE NUMBER PLATE
C. METAL TAG ON CRANKCASE
D. STAMPED ON CRANKCASE
E. STAMPED ON CYLINDER FLANGE
F. STAMPED ON STARTER PULLEY

Location of identification numbers on 2 cycle engines

MAINTENANCE

Air Cleaners

The instructions below detail the procedures involved in cleaning the various types of elements. See the illustrations for exploded views to aid disassembly and assembly.

POLYURETHANE AIR CLEANER

1. Wash the element in a solvent or detergent and water solution by squeezing similar to a sponge.
2. Clean the air cleaner housing and cover with the same solution. Dry thoroughly.
3. Dry the element by squeezing or with compressed air if available.
4. Apply a generous quantity of oil to the element sides and open ends. Squeeze vigorously to distribute oil and to remove excess oil.

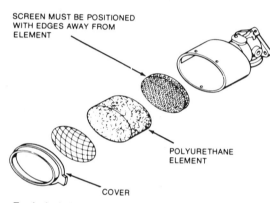

SCREEN MUST BE POSITIONED WITH EDGES AWAY FROM ELEMENT

POLYURETHANE ELEMENT

COVER

Exploded view of polyurethane air cleaner

ALUMINUM FOIL AIR CLEANER

1. Dip the aluminum foil filter in solvent. Flush out all dirt particles.
2. Shake out the filter thoroughly to remove all solvent, then dip the filter element in oil. Allow the oil to drain from the filter. Clean the screens and filter body.
NOTE: *The concave screen and retainer cover or ring are not used on later models. They are replaced with a clip which rolls into the groove in the lip of the body.*

FELT TYPE AIR CLEANERS

1. To clean felt air cleaners, merely blow compressed air through the element in the reverse direction to normal air flow. Felt elements may also be washed in non-flammable solvents or soapy water. Blow dry with compressed air.
NOTE: *Power Products type numbers 641 and up, use a gasket between the element and the base. The gasket is used only with this element; earlier versions did not have a gasket.*

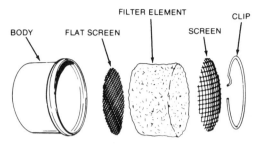

FILTER ELEMENT · CLIP · BODY · FLAT SCREEN · SCREEN

Exploded view of aluminum foil type air cleaner

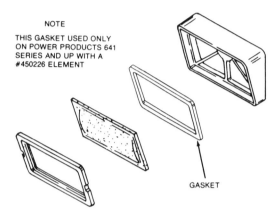

NOTE

THIS GASKET USED ONLY ON POWER PRODUCTS 641 SERIES AND UP WITH A #450226 ELEMENT

GASKET

Exploded view of felt type air cleaner

FIBER ELEMENT AIR CLEANER

1. Remove the filter and place the cover in a normal position on the filter. With the filter element down to semi-seal it, blow compressed air through the cover hole to reverse air flow, forcing dirt particles out.
2. Clean the cover mounting bracket with a damp cloth.

DRY PAPER AIR CLEANER

1. Tap the element on a workbench or any solid object to dislodge larger particles of dirt.
2. Wash the element in soap and water. Rinse from the inside until it is thoroughly

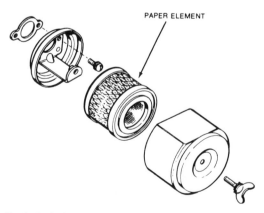

PAPER ELEMENT

Exploded view of paper element type air cleaner

flushed and the water coming through is free of soap.

3. Allow the element to dry completely or use low pressure compressed air blown from the inside to speed the process.

4. Inspect the element for cracks or holes, and replace if necessary.

Lubrication

OIL AND FUEL RECOMMENDATIONS

Power Products 2 cycle engines are mist-lubricated by oil mixed with the gasoline. For the best performance, use regular grade, leaded fuel, with 2 cycle or outboard oil rated SAE 30 or SAE 40. Regular grade unleaded fuel is an acceptable substitute. The terms 2 cycle or outboard are used by various manufacturers to designate oil they have designed for use in 2 cycle engines. Multiple weight oil such as all season 10W–30, are not recommended.

If you have to mix the gas and oil when the temperature is below 35°F (1.6°C), heat up the oil first, then mix it with the gas. Oil will not mix with gas when the temperature is approaching freezing. However, if you use oil that has been warmed first it will not be affected by low temperatures.

The proportion of oil to fuel is absolutely critical to two-stroke operation. If too little oil is used, overheating and damage to engine parts will occur (this can even result from running the engine too lean). If excessive oil is used, spark plug fouling, smoke in the exhaust, and even misfire can occur. Mix carefully and precisely. Follow Power Products recommendations for your particular engine, and disregard fuel container labels.

Fuel/oil mix must be clean and fresh. Fuel deteriorates enough to form troublesome gum and varnish after more than a month. Dirt in the fuel can cause clogging of carburetor passages and even engine wear.

Tune-Up Specifications

All spark plugs are gapped at 0.035 in. (0.90mm). Because of the great number of individual models of Power Products engines that exist, an individual chart of Tune-Up specifications is impractical. Refer to the charts at the end of this section for breaker point gap and timing dimension specifications.

Spark Plugs

Spark plugs should be removed and cleaned of deposits frequently, especially in two-stroke engines because they burn the lubricating oil right with the fuel. Carefully inspect the plug for severely eroded electrodes or a cracked insu-

lator, and replace the plug if either condition exists or if deposits cannot be adequately removed. Set the gap to 0.035 in. (0.90mm) with a wire type feeler gauge, and install the plug, torquing it to 18–22 ft. lbs.

Make sure to replace the plug with one of the same type and heat range. If the plug is fouled, poor quality or old fuel, a rich mixture, or the wrong fuel/oil mix may be at fault. Also, make sure the engine's exhaust ports are not clogged.

Breaker Points

REMOVAL AND INSTALLATION

1. First remove the flywheel as described below:

    a. Remove the screws, engine shroud, and starter. Determine the direction of rotation of the flywheel nut by looking at the threads. Then, place a box wrench on the nut and tap with a soft hammer in the proper direction.

    b. The flywheel is removed with a special puller or a special knock off tool. The knock off tool must not be used on 660, 670, or 1500 ball bearing models. To use the knock off tool, screw it onto the crankshaft until it is within $\frac{1}{16}$ in. (1.6mm) of the flywheel. Hold the flywheel firmly and rap the top of the puller sharply with a hammer to jar it loose. Pull the flywheel off.

    c. If a puller is being used, the flywheel will have three cored holes into which a set of self-tapping screws are turned. The handle which operates the bolt at the center of the puller's collar is then turned to pull the flywheel off the crankshaft. If this is not adequate to do the job, heat the center of the alloy flywheel with a butane torch to expand it before turning the puller handle.

2. Remove the nuts that hold the electrical leads to the screw on the movable breaker point spring. Remove the movable breaker point from the stud.

3. Remove the screw and stationary breaker point. Put a new stationary breaker point on breaker plate; install the screw, but do not tighten it fully.

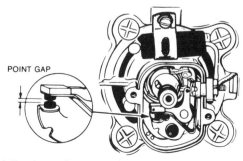

Adjusting point gap

4. Position a new movable breaker point on the post.

5. Check that the new points contact each other properly and remove all grease, fingerprints, and dirt from the points.

ADJUSTMENT

1. If necessary (as when checking the gap of old points), loosen the screw which mounts the stationary breaker contact. Rotate the crankshaft until the contact cam follower rests right on the highest point of the cam.

2. Using a flat feeler gauge of the dimension shown under "Point Gap" in the charts at the rear of this section, check the dimension of the gap and, if incorrect, move the breaker base in the appropriate direction by wedging a screwdriver between the dimples on the base plate and the notch in the breaker plate. When gap is correct, tighten the screw. Recheck the gap and, if necessary, reset it.

Adjusting Ignition Timing

1. Remove the spark plug and install a special timing tool or thin ruler. With the tool lockscrew loose or the ruler riding on the piston, rotate the crankshaft back and forth to find Top Dead Center. Tighten the tool lockscrew or use a straightedge across the cylinder head, if you're using a ruler, to measure Top Center. Look up the timing dimension in the specifications at the back of this section.

2. Turn the crankshaft backwards so the piston descends. Then, reset the position of the special tool downward the amount of the dimension and tighten the lockscrew, or move the ruler down that amount.

3. Very carefully bring the piston upward by turning the crankshaft until the top of the piston just touches the tool or ruler.

4. Install a piece of cellophane between the contact surfaces. Loosen the ignition stator lockscrews and turn the stator until the cellophane is clamped tightly between the contact surfaces. Turn the stator until the cellophane can just be pulled out (as contacts start to open), and then tighten the stator lockscrews.

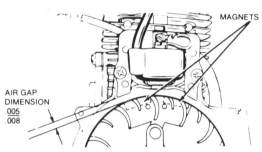

Adjusting magneto armature air gap. Note magnets on flywheel

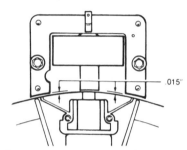

Adjusting magneto armature air gap. Note wider gap

Magneto Armature Air Gap

There are two types of magnetos. Compare appearance of your engine with each illustration to determine whether it looks like the type which employs a gap of 0.005–0.008 in. (0.13–0.20mm) or the type with a gap of 0.015 in. (0.38mm).

1. Loosen the two screws which hold the laminations and coil to the block. Turn the flywheel around so the magnets line up directly with the ends of the laminations. Pull the laminations/coil assembly upward.

2. Insert a 0.005–0.008 in. (0.13–0.20mm) gauge between the flywheel and laminations on either side. On units with a gap of 0.015 in. (0.38mm), use two of the above numbered parts or a 0.015 in. (0.38mm) gauge. Allow the attraction of the magnets to pull the coil/laminations assembly toward the flywheel.

3. On the magneto type with a 0.005–0.008 in. (0.13–0.20mm) dimension, use Loctite Grade A on the screws and torque to 35–45 inch lbs. On the other type magneto, torque the screws to 20–30 inch lbs. Recheck the gap and readjust, if necessary.

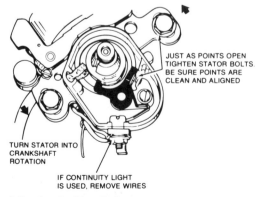

Adjusting ignition timing

Mixture Adjustment

1. If the engine will not start or the carburetor has recently been disassembled, both idle and main mixture screws may be turned in very gently until they just bottom, and then turned out exactly one turn. In this case, back out the idle speed screw until throttle is free, then turn screw in until it just contacts the throttle. Turn it one turn more exactly.

2. Allow the engine to warm up to normal running temperature. With the engine running at maximum recommended rpm, loosen the main metering screw until the engine rolls, then tighten the screw until the engine starts to cut out. Note the number of turns from one extreme to the other. Loosen the screw to a point midway between the extremes.

3. Set the throttle to idle speed and repeat Step 2 for that adjusting screw.

NOTE: *Some carburetors do not have a main mixture adjustment. Others employ a drilled mixture screw which provides about the right mixture when fully screwed in. In some weather conditions, operation may be improved by setting this screw just slightly off the seat for smoother running.*

Governor Adjustments

POWER TAKEOFF AND MECHANICAL GOVERNOR

1. To adjust the governor, remove the outboard bearing housing. Use a $^3/_{32}$ in. allen wrench to loosen the set screw.

2. Squeeze the top and bottom governor rings, fully compressing the governor spring.

3. Hold the upper arm of the bell crank parallel to the crankshaft and insert a $^3/_{32}$ in. allen wrench between the upper ring and the bell crank.

4. Slide the governor assembly onto the crankshaft so that the allen wrench just touches the bell crank.

5. Tighten the set screw to secure the governor to the crankshaft.

6. Install the bearing adapter, mount the engine, and check the engine speed with a tachometer. It should be about 3200–3400 rpm.

NOTE: *Never attempt to adjust the governor by bending the bellcrank or the link.*

7. If the speed is not correct, readjust the governor by moving the assembly toward the crankcase to increase speed, and away from the crankcase to decreased speed.

MECHANICAL FLYWHEEL TYPE GOVERNOR ADJUSTMENT

As engine speed increases, the links are thrown outward, compressing the link springs.

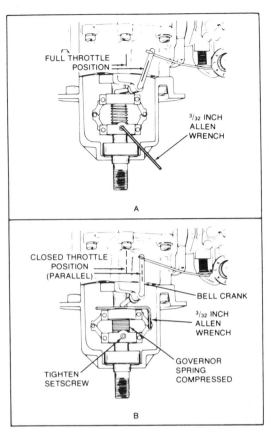

Adjusting the PTO end mounted governor

The links apply a thrust against the slide ring, moving it upward and compressing the governor spring. As the slide ring moves away from the thrust block of the bellcrank assembly, the throttle spring causes the thrust block to maintain engagement and close the throttle slightly.

As the throttle closes and engine speed decreases, force on the slide ring decreases so that it moves downward, pivots the bellcrank outward to overcome the force of the throttle spring, and opens the throttle to speed up the engine. In this manner, the operating speed of the engine is stabilized to the adjusted governor setting.

1. To adjust the governor, loosen the bracket screw and slide the governor bellcrank assembly toward or away from the flywheel. Move the bellcrank toward the flywheel to increase speed and away from the flywheel to decrease speed.

2. Tighten the screw to secure the bracket.

3. Make minor speed adjustments by bending the throttle link at the bend in the center of the link.

NOTE: *Do not lubricate the governor assembly or the governor bellcrank assembly of flywheel mounted governors.*

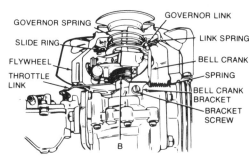

Flywheel mounted governor assembly (cutaway view)

ADJUSTING 2 CYCLE AIR VANE GOVERNORS

1. Loosen the self-locking nut that holds the governor spring bracket to the engine crankcase.
2. Adjust the spring bracket to increase or decrease the governor spring tension. Increasing spring tension increases speed and decreasing spring tension decreases speed.
3. After adjusting, the spring bracket should not be closer than $\frac{1}{16}$ in. (1.6mm) to the crankcase.
4. Tighten the self-locking nut.

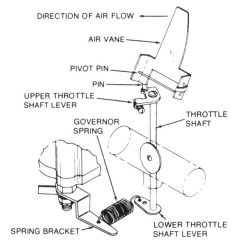

Diagram of an air vane governor

FUEL SYSTEM

Carburetor

REMOVAL AND INSTALLATION

1. Remove the air cleaner. Drain the fuel tank. Disconnect the carburetor fuel lines.
2. If necessary, remove any shrouding or control panels to gain access to the carburetor.
3. Disconnect the choke or throttle control wires at the carburetor.
4. Remove the cap screws, or nuts and lock-

washers and remove the carburetor from the engine.
5. To install, reverse the removal procedure, using new gaskets.

OVERHAUL

Tecumseh two-and four-stroke engines employ a common series of carburetors. Refer to the Four-Stroke Tecumseh Engine section for specific carburetor overhaul procedures.

Idle Governor

SERVICE

1. Remove the shutter fastener and allow the shutter to drop out of the air horn.
2. Note location of the spring end in the disc-shaped throttle lever. The spring should be placed into the same hole during reassembly.
3. Remove the retainer clip and lift out the throttle shaft.
4. Replace all worn parts and reassemble in reverse order.

NOTE: *Note the position of the throttle shutter, as shown. The reference marks must be positioned as shown when shutter is installed.*

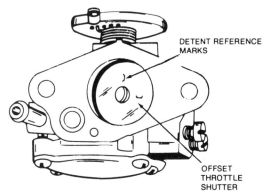

Position detent reference marks of throttle shutter as shown

Fuel Pump

SERVICE

Float Type Carburetor With Integral Pump

1. If the engine runs, but roughly, make both carburetor mixture adjustments.
2. Make sure the fuel supply is adequate and the tank is in the proper position.
3. Make sure the fuel tank is open.
4. Make sure the pick-up tube is not cracked.
5. Remove the carburetor and make sure the pulsation passage is properly aligned.
6. Check for air leaks at the gasket surface.
7. Remove the cover and check the condition

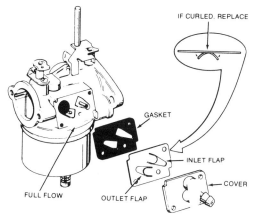

Integral type fuel pump

of inlet and outlet flaps-if curled, replace the flap leaf.

ENGINE OVERHAUL

Disassembly

SPLIT CRANKCASE ENGINES

1. Remove the shroud and fuel tank if so equipped.

2. Remove the flywheel and the ignition stator.

3. Remove the carburetor and governor linkage. Carefully note the position of the carburetor wire links and springs for reinstallation.

4. Lift off the reed plate and gasket if present and inspect them. They should not bend away from the sealing surface plate more than 0.010 in. (0.25mm).

5. Remove the spark plug and inspect it.

6. Remove the muffler. Be sure that the muffler and the exhaust ports are not clogged with carbon. Clean them if necessary.

7. Remove the transfer port cover and check for a good seal.

8. Remove the cylinder head, if so equipped. NOTE: *Some models utilize a locking compound on the cylinder head screws. Removing the screws on such engines can be difficult. This is especially true with screws hav-*

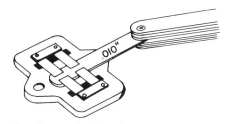

Checking the reed valve clearance

ing slotted head for a straight screwdriver blade. The screws can be removed if heat is applied to the head of the screw with an electric soldering iron.

9. On engines having a governor mounted on the power take-off end of the crankshaft, remove the screws that hold the outboard bearing housing to the crankcase. Clean the PTO end of the crankshaft and remove the outboard bearing housing and bearing. Loosen the set screw that holds the governor assembly to the crankshaft, slide the entire governor assembly from the crankshaft. Remove the screw that holds the governor bellcrank bracket to the crankcase. Remove the governor bellcrank and bracket.

10. Make match marks on the cylinder and crankcase. Remove the four nuts and lockwashers that hold the cylinder to the crankcase.

11. Remove the cylinder by pulling it straight out from the crankcase.

12. To separate the two crankcase halves, remove all of the screws that hold the crankcase halves together.

13. With the crankcase in a vertical position, grasp the top half of the crankcase and hold it firmly. Strike the top end of the crankcase with a rawhide mallet, while holding the assembly over a bench to prevent damage to parts when they fall. The top half of the crankcase should separate from the remaining assembly.

14. Invert the assembly and repeat the procedure to remove the other casting half from the crankcase on ball bearing units.

15. Each time the crankshaft is removed from the crankcase, seals at the end of the crankcase should be replaced. To replace the seals, use a screwdriver or an ice pick to remove the seal retainers and remove and discard the old seals. Install the seals in the bores of the crankcase halves. The seals must be inserted into the bearing well with the channel groove toward the internal side of the crankcase. Retain the seal with the retainer. Seat the retainer spring into the spring groove.

UNIBLOCK ENGINES

1. Remove the shroud and fuel tank. Note the condition of the air vane governor, if so equipped.

2. Remove the starter cap and flywheel nut, noting the position of the belleville washer.

3. Remove the flywheel – see "Breaker Points Removal and Installation," above.

4. Remove the head. Save the old head gasket for use when replacing the piston, but procure a new gasket for use in final assembly.

5. Remove the cylinder block cover plate to gain access to the connecting rod bolts.

6. Note the location of the connecting rod match marks for reassembly.

7. Remove the piston. Remove the ridge first, if necessary, with a ridge reamer. Push the piston and connecting rod through the top of cylinder.

8. Remove the crankshaft from the cylinder block assembly. On engines with crankshaft ball bearings:

a. Remove the four shroud base screws and tap the shroud base so the base and crankshaft can be removed together.

b. To remove bearing with crankshaft from base: USE SAFETY GLASSES AND HEAT RESISTANT GLOVES! Using a propane torch, heat the area on the base around the outside of the bearing until there is enough expansion to remove the base from the bearing on the crankshaft. Now remove and discard the seal retainer ring, seal retainer and seal.

c. To remove the bearing race, remove the retainer ring on the crankshaft with snap ring pliers, and with the use of a bearing splitter or arbor press, remove the ball bearing.

CAUTION: *Support the crankshaft's top counterweight to prevent bending. Also, bearing is to be pressed on via the inner race only.*
On other engines:

When equipped with a sleeve or needle bearing, use a seal protector and lift the crankshaft out of the cylinder. Be careful not to lose the bearing needles.

When equipped with a ball bearing, use a mallet to strike the crankshaft on the P.T.O. end while holding the block in your hand.

9. In assembly, bear the following points in mind:

a. Use a ring compressor to install piston. Be careful not to allow the rings to catch on the recess for the head gasket. Use the old head gasket to take up the space in the recess. Do not force the piston into the cylinder, or damage to rings or piston could occur.

b. To install the ball bearing on the crankshaft, slide the bearing on the crankshaft and fit it on the shaft by tapping using a mallet and tool, part number 670258 or press the ball bearing on the crankshaft with an arbor press. Install the retainer ring.

c. To install the crankshaft with a ball bearing, heat the shroud base to expand the bearing seat and drop the ball bearing into the seat of the base shroud. Allow it to cool. Install a new seal retainer ring, seal retainer, and seal.

10. After the shroud base and flywheel are back in place, adjust the air gap between the coil core and flywheel as described above under "Magnet Air Gap Adjustment."

Connecting Rod Service

1. For engines using solid bronze or aluminum connecting rods, remove the two self-locking cap screws which hold the connecting rod to the crankshaft and remove the rod cap. Note the match marks on the connecting rod and cap. These marks must be reinstalled in the same position to the crankshaft.

2. Engines using steel connecting rods are equipped with needle bearings at both crankshaft and piston pin end. Remove the two set screws that hold the connecting rod and cap to the crankshaft, taking care not to lose the needle bearings during removal.

3. Needle bearings at the piston pin end of steel rods are caged and can be pressed out as an assembly if damaged.

4. Check the connecting rod for cracks or distortion. Check the bearing surfaces for scoring or wear. bearing diameters should be within the limits indicated in the table of specifications located at the end of this section.

5. There are two basic arrangements of needles supplied with the connecting rod crankshaft bearing: split rows of needles and a single row of needles. Service needles are supplied with a beeswax coating. The beeswax holds the needles in position.

6. To install the needle bearings, first make sure that the crankshaft bearing journal and the connecting rod are free from oil and dirt.

7. Place the needle bearings with the beeswax onto a cool metallic surface to stiffen the beeswax. Body temperature will melt the wax, so avoid handling.

8. Remove the paper backing on the bearings and wrap the needles around the crankshaft journal. The beeswax will hold the needles onto

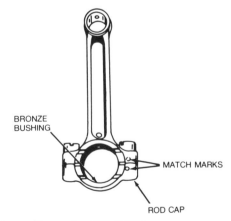

BRONZE BUSHING

MATCH MARKS

ROD CAP

Connecting rod match marks

the journal. Position the needles uniformly onto the crankpin.

NOTE: *When installing the split row of needles, wrap each row of needles around the journal and try to seal them together with gentle but firm pressure to keep the bearings from unwinding.*

9. Place the connecting rod onto the journal, position the rod cap, and secure it with the capscrews. Tighten the screw to the proper specifications.

10. Force solvent (lacquer thinner) into the needles just installed to remove the beeswax, then force 30W oil into the needles for proper lubrication.

Piston and Rings Service

1. Clean all carbon from the piston and ring grooves.

2. Check the piston for scoring or other damage.

3. Check the fit of the piston in the cylinder bore. Move the piston from side-to-side to check clearance. If the clearance is not greater than 0.003 in. (0.076mm) and the cylinder is not scored or damaged, then the piston need not be replaced.

4. Check the piston ring side clearance to make sure it is within the limits recommended.

5. Check the piston rings for wear by inserting them into the cylinder about ½ in. (13mm) from the top of the cylinder. Check at various places to make sure that the gap between the ends of the ring does not exceed the dimensions recommended in the specifications table at the end of this section. Bore wear can be checked in the same way, except that a new ring is used to measure the end gap.

6. If replacement rings have a bevelled or chamfered edge, install them with the bevel up toward the top of the piston. Not all engines use bevelled rings. The two rings installed on the piston are identical.

7. When installed, the offset piston used on the AV600 and the AV520 engines must have the **V** stamped in the piston head (some have hash marks) facing toward the right as the engine is viewed from the top or piston side of the engine.

NOTE: *Some AV520 and AV600 engines do not have offset pistons. Only offset pistons will have the* **V** *or the hash marks on the piston head. Domed pistons must be installed so that the slope of the piston is toward the exhaust port.*

Crankshaft Service

1. Use a micrometer to check the bearing journals for out-of-roundness. The main bearing journals should not be more than 0.0005 in. (0.0127mm) out-of-round. Connecting rod journals should not be more than 0.001 in. (0.025mm) out-of-round. Replace a crankshaft that is not within these limits.

NOTE: *Do not attempt to regrind the crankshaft since undersize parts are not available.*

2. Check the tapered portion of the crankshaft (magneto end), keyways, and threads. Damaged threads may be restored with a thread die. If the taper of the shaft is rusty, it indicates that the engine has been operating with a loose flywheel. Clean the rust off the taper and check for wear. If the taper or keyway is worn, replace the crankshaft.

3. Check all of the bearing journal diameters. They should be within the limits indicated in the specifications table at the end of this section.

A. SPLIT ROWS OF NEEDLE BEARINGS

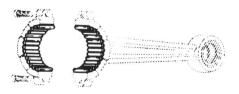

B. SINGLE ROW OF NEEDLE BEARINGS

Needle bearing arrangement. Double rows of bearings are placed with the tapered edges facing out

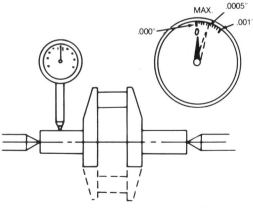

Checking the crankshaft for out-of-roundness

4. Check the crankshaft for bends by placing it between two pivot points. Position the dial indicator feeler on the crankshaft bearing surface and rotate the shaft. The crankshaft should not be more than 0.002–0.004 in. (0.05–0.10mm) out-of-round.

Bearing Service

1. Do not remove the bearings unless they are worn or noisy. Check the operation of the bearings by rotating the bearing cones with your fingers to check for roughness, binding, or any other signs of unsatisfactory operation. If the bearings do not operate smoothly, remove them.

2. To remove the bearings from the crankcase, the crankcase must be heated. Use a hot plate to heat the crankcase to no more than 400°F (204°C). Place a ⅛ in. (3mm) steel plate over the hot plate to prevent overheating. At this temperature, the bearings should drop out with a little tapping of the crankcase.

3. The replacement bearing is left at room temperature and dropped into the heated crankcase. Make sure that the new bearing is seated to the maximum depth of the cavity.

NOTE: *Do not use an open flame to heat the crankcase halves and do not heat the crankcase halves to more than 400°F (204°C). Uneven heating with an open flame or excessive temperature will distort the case.*

4. The needle bearings will fall out of the bearing cage with very little urging. Needles can be reinstalled easily by using a small amount of all-purpose grease to hold the bearings in place.

5. Cage bearings are removed and replaced in the same manner as ball bearings.

6. Sleeve bearings cannot be replaced. Both crankcase halves must be discarded if a bearing is worn excessively.

Assembly

1. The gasket surface where the crankcase halves join must be thoroughly clean before reassembly. Do not buff or use a file or any other abrasive that might damage the mating surfaces.

NOTE: *Crankcase halves are matched. If one needs to be replaced, then both must be replaced.*

2. Place the PTO half of the crankcase onto the PTO end of the crankshaft. Use seal protectors where necessary.

3. Apply a thin coating of sealing compound to the contact surface of one of the crankcase halves.

4. Position one crankcase half on the other. The fit should be such that some pressure is required to bring the two halves together. If this is not the case, either the crankcase halves and/or the crankshaft must be replaced.

5. Secure the halves with the screws provided, tightening the screws alternately and evenly. Before tightening the screws, check the union of the crankcase halves on the cylinder mounting side. The halves should be flat and smooth at the union to provide a good mounting face for the cylinder. If necessary, realign the halves before tightening the screws.

6. The sleeve tool should be placed into the crankcase bore from the direction opposite the crankshaft. Insert the tapered end of the crankshaft through the half of the crankcase to which the magneto stator is mounted. Remove the seal tools after installing the crankcase halves.

7. Stagger the ring ends on the piston and check for the correct positioning on domed piston models.

8. Place the cylinder gasket on the crankcase end.

9. Place the piston into the cylinder using the chamfer provided on the bottom edge of the cylinder to compress the rings.

10. Secure the cylinder to the crankcase assembly.

Type Number-to-Letter Cross Reference Chart

Type No.	Column Letter	Type No.	Column Letter	Type No.	Column Letter
1 thru 44	A	611	F	1001	D
46 thru 68	B	614–01 thru 614–04	E	1002 thru 1002D	G
69 thru 77	D	614–05 thru 614–06A	F	1003	C
78 thru 80	C	615–01 thru 615–01A	E	1004 thru 1004A	H
81 thru 83	D	615–04	F	1005 thru 1005A	C
84 thru 85	C	615–05 thru 615–10A	E	1006	H
86 thru 87	B	615–11 thru 615–18	F	1007 thru 1008B	C
89	C	615–19 thru 615–27A	E	1009 thrù 1010B	G
91	D	615–28	F	1011 thru 1019E	H
93	D	615–29 thru 615–39	E	1020	G
94 thru 98	H	616–01 thru 616–11	E	1021	C
99	C	616–12 and 616–14	F	1022 thru 1022C	D
		616–16 thru 616–40	E	1023 thru 1026A	H
201 thru 208	A	617A thru 617–01	E	1027 thru 1027B	C
209 thru 244	B	617–02 thru 617–03A	F	1028 thru 1030C	H
245	D	617–04 thru 617–04A	E	1031B thru 1031C	G
246 thru 248	B	617–05 thru 617–05A	F	1032	C
249 thru 251	D	617–06	E	1033 thru 1033F	G
252	B	618 thru 618–16	E	1034 thru 1034G	H
253 thru 255	D	618–17	F	1035 thru 1036	C
256 thru 261	B	618–18	E	1037 thru 1039C	D
262 thru 265A	D	619 thru 619–03	E	1040 thru 1041A	D
266 thru 267	B	621 thru 621–11	E	1042 thru 1042C	G
268 thru 272	D	621 thru 621–12A	F	1042D thru 1042E	H
273 thru 275	B	621–13 thru 621–15	E	1042F	G
276	D	622 thru 622–07	E	1042G and 1042H	H
277 thru 279	B	623 and 623A	E	1042I thru 1043B	G
280 thru 281	D	623–01	F	1043C thru 1043F	H
282	B	623–02 thru 623–33E	E	1043G thru 1044E	G
283 thru 284	D	623–34	F	1045 thru 1045F	B
285 thru 286	B	623–35 and 623–36	E	1046 thru 1051B	H
287	D	624 thru 630–09	J	1052	G
288 thru 291B	B	632–02A	K	1053 thru 1054C	H
292 thru 294	D	632–04 and 632–05A	K	1055 thru 1056B	G
295 thru 296	B	633 thru 634–09	J	1057	H
297	F	635A and B	K	1058 thru 1058A	G
298 thru 299	B	635–03B	K	1059	D
		635–04B	K	1060 thru 1060C	H
301 thru 375		635–06A thru 635–10	K	1061 and 1062	C
These are twin		636 thru 636–11	J	1063A thru 1063C	H
cylinder units—		637 thru 637–16	J	1064	G
out of production		638 thru 638–100	F	1065 thru 1067C	D
401 thru 402	L	639	M	1068 and 1068A	G
403	M	640	O	1069	H
404 thru 406B	L	641	K	1070 thru 1070B	C
407 thru 407C	M	642	I	1071 thru 1075D	H
408 thru 410B	L	643	J	1076 thru 1084	H
411 thru 411B	M	650	N	1085 and 1085A	G
412 thru 423	L	670	H	1086 thru 1140A	H
424 thru 427	M				
				1141 thru 1142	G
501 thru 509A	E	701 thru 701–1C	G	1143 thru 1145	H
		701–2 thru 701–2D	H	1146 thru 1149A	I
601 thru 601–01	F	701–3 thru 701–3C	G	1149A thru 1153B	H
602 thru 602–02B	F	701–4 thru 701–4C	H	1158 thru 1159	G
603A thru 603–23	E	701–5 thru 701–5C	G	1160 thru 1161A	I
604 thru 604–25	E	701–6 thru 701–6C	H	1162 and 1162A	G
605 thru 605–18	E	701–7 thru 701–7C	G	1163 thru 1163A	H
606 thru 606–05B	E	701–8 thru 701–11	H	1165 thru 1168A	G
606–06 thru 606–07	F	701–12 thru 701–13A	G	1169 thru 1174	H
606–08 thru 606–13	E	701–14 thru 701–17	H	1175 and 1175A	I
608 thru 608–C	E	701–18 thru 701–19	G	1176 thru 1177A	H
610–A thru 610–14	E	701–19A	H	1179 thru 1179A	I
610–15 thru 610–16	F	701–20 thru 701–22A	G	1180 thru 1181	G
610–19 thru 610–20	E	701–24	H	1182 and 1182A	I

Type Number-to-Letter Cross Reference Chart (cont.)

Type No.	Column Letter	Type No.	Column Letter	Type No.	Column Letter
1183 thru 1185	G	1345	J	1441	P
1186A thru 1186C	J	1348 and 1348A	G	1442 thru 1442B	G
1187 thru 1192	G	1350 thru 1350C	I	1443	I
1192A thru 1196B	J			1444 and 1444A	G
1197 thru 1197A	G	1550A	P	1445	I
1198 and 1198A	H			1446 and 1446A	A
1199 and 1199A	J	1351 thru 1351B	K	1447	G
		1352 thru 1352B	I	1448 thru 1450	F
1206 thru 1208B	J	1353	K	1450A thru 1450B	F
1210 thru 1215C	K	1354 thru 1355A	I	1450C thru 1450E	F
1216 thru 1216A	H	1356 and 1356B	K	1453	K
1217 thru 1220A	J	1357 thru 1358	I	1454 and 1454A	A
1221	H	1359 thru 1362B	K	1455 thru 1456	K
1222 thru 1223	J	1363 thru 1369A	G	1459	G
1224 thru 1225A	H	1372 thru 1375A	G	1460 thru 1460F	A
1226 thru 1227B	K	1376 and 1376A	J	1461	K
1228 thru 1229A	J	1377 thru 1378	K	1462	A
1230 thru 1231	H	1379 thru 1379A	H	1463	K
1232	G	1380 thru 1380B	K	1464 thru 1464B	L
1233 thru 1237B	K	1381	G	1465	A
1238 thru 1238C	H	1382	H	1466 thru 1466A	F
1239 thru 1243	J	1383 thru 1383B	K	1467 thru 1468	K
1244 thru 1245A	K	1384 thru 1385	G	1471 thru 1471B	E
1246 thru 1247	J	1386	I	1472 thru 1472C	L
1248	H	1387 thru 1388	K	1473 thru 1473B	A
1249 thru 1251A	J	1389	G	1474	L
1252 thru 1254A	K	1390 thru 1390B	H	1475 thru 1476	A
1255	J	1391	K	1477	G
1256 thru 1262B	K	1392	J	1478	J
1263	J	1393	G	1479	G
1264 thru 1265E	K	1394 thru 1395A	P	1482 and 1482A	F
1266 thru 1267	G	1396	K	1483	F
1269 thru 1270D	K	1397	H	1484 thru 1484D	A
1271 thru 1271B	G	1398 thru 1399	K	1485	G
1272 thru 1275	K			1486	D
1276	H	1400	K	1487	J
1277 thru 1279D	K	1401 thru 1401F	F	1488 thru 1488D	A
1280	J	1402 and 1402B	G	1489 thru 1490B	C
1283 thru 1284D	K	1403A and 1403B	K	1491	L
1286 thru 1286A	H	1404 and 1404A	K	1493 and 1493A	G
1287	K	1405 thru 1406A	H	1494 and 1495A	B
1288	J	1407 thru 1408	K	1496	G
1289 thru 1289A	G	1409A	J	1497	A
1290 thru 1293A	K	1410 thru 1412A	I	1498	E
1294 thru 1295	J	1413 thru 1416	I	1499	F
1296 thru 1298	K	1417 and 1417A	K		
		1418 and 1418A	P	1500	E
1300 thru 1303	K	1419 and 1419A	K	1501A thru 1501E	A
1304 thru 1307	J	1420 and 1420A	H	1503 thru 1503D	L
1308 thru 1316A	K	1421 and 1421A	K	1506 thru 1507	F
1317 thru 1317B	J	1422 thru 1423	P	1508	G
1318 thru 1320B	K	1424	K	1509	C
1321 thru 1322	J	1425	G	1510	L
1323	K	1426 thru 1426B	P	1511	C
1325	G	1427 and 1427A	H	1512 and 1512A	B
1326 thru 1326F	K	1428 thru 1429A	P	1513	L
1327 thru 1327B	H	1430A	G	1515 thru 1516C	C
1328B and 1328C	K	1431	P	1517	E
1329	J	1432 and 1432A	G	1518	D
1330	H	1433	K	1519 thru 1521	A
1331	J	1434 thru 1435A	P	1522	L
1332	J	1436 and 1436A	I	1523	A
1333	I	1437	J	1524	B
1334	I	1439	I	1527	C
1343 thru 1344A	H	1440 thru 1440D	A	1528	A

Type Number-to-Letter Cross Reference Chart (cont.)

Type No.	Column Letter	Type No.	Column Letter	Type No.	Column Letter
1529A and 1529B	C	2045 thru 2046B	F	40069 thru 40075	N
1530 thru 1530B	A	2047 thru 2048	D		
1531 thru 1535B	C	2049 thru 2049A	F	710101 thru 710116	E
1536	L	2050 thru 2050A	D	710124 thru 710130	E
1537	A	2051 thru 2052A	D	710131 thru 710137	E
1538 thru 1541A	L	2053 thru 2055	F	710138 thru 710149	E
1542	E	2056	D	710154	M
1543 thru 1546	A	2057	F	710201 thru 710209	E
1547	C	2058 thru 2058B	D	710210 thru 710218	E
1549	C	2059 thru 2063	F	710219 thru 710227	E
		2064 thru 2064A	D	710228	M
S–1801 thru 1822	F	2065	F	710150	G
1823 and 1824	E	2066	D	710151	H
		2067 thru 2071B	F	710155	L
2001 thru 2003	B			710157	H
2004 thru 2006	D	2200 thru 2201A	D	710229	H
2007 thru 2007B	B	2202 thru 2204	E	710230	N
2008 thru 2008B	D	2205 thru 2205A	D	710234	N
2009	B	2206 thru 2206A	G		
2010 thru 2011	D	2207	D		
2012	F	2208	G	200.183112	F
2013 thru 2014	B	2768	C	200.18322	F
2015 thru 2018	D			200.193132	F
2020	F	40001 thru 40028	N	200.193142	F
2021	D	40029 thru 40032C	O	200.193152	G
2022 thru 2022B	F	40033	N	200.193162	G
2023 thru 2026	D	40034 thru 40045A	O	200.203172	H
2027	B	40046	N	200.203182	H
2028 thru 2029	D	40047 thru 40052	O	200.203192	H
2030 thru 2031	B	40053 thru 40054A	N	200.213112	H
2032 thru 2033A	D	40056 thru 40060B	O	200.213122	H
2034 thru 2035C	F	40061 thru 40062B	N	200.503111	F
2036 thru 2037	B	40063 thru 40064	O	200.583111	F
2038	F	40065 thru 40066	N	200.593121	F
2039 thru 2044	C	40067 thru 40068	O	200.613111	F

Uniblock Cross Reference Chart

Type No.	Column No.	Type No.	Column No.	Type No.	Column No.
Vertical Crankshaft Engines		**Horizontal Crankshaft Engines**		**Horizontal Crankshaft Engines**	
638 thru 638–100	6	1398 thru 1399	11	1509	3
639 thru 639–13A	13			1510	12
		1400	11	1511	3
		1401 thru 1401F	16	1512 and 1512A	2
		1401G, H	17	1513	12
640–02 thru 640–06B	21	1401J	27	1515 thru 1516C	3
640–07 thru 640–18	22	1402 and 1402B	7	1517	5
641 thru 641–14	11	1425	7	1518	4
642–01, A	9A	1430A	7	1519 thru 1521	1
642–02, A, B, C, D	9A	1432 and 1432A	7	1522	12
642–02E, F	9B	1440 thru 1440D	1	1523	1
642–03, A, B	9A	1442 thru 1442B	7	1524	2
642–04, A, B, C	9A	1444 and 1444A	7	1525A	16
642–05, A, B	9A	1448 thru 1450	16	1527	3
642–06, A	9A	1450A thru 1450B	16	1528	1
642–07, A, B	9A	1450C thru 1450E	16	1529A and 1520B	3
		1450F	17	1530 thru 1530B	1
642–07C	9B	1454 and 1454A	1	1531	3
642–08	9B	1459	7	1534A	17
642–08A, B	9A	1460 thru 1460F	1	1535B	3
642–09 thru 642–14	9A	1462	1	1536	12
642–13A, 14A, 14B	9B	1464 thru 1464B	12	1537	1
642–15 thru 642–22	9B	1465	1	1538 thru 1541A	12
642–24 thru 642–30	9C	1466 thru 1466A	16	1542	5
643–01, A, 03, A	10A	1471 thru 1471B	5	1543 thru 1546	1
643–03B, C	10B	1472 thru 1472C	12	1517	3
643–04, 05A	10A	1473 thru 1473B	1	1519	3
643–05B	10B	1474	12	1550A	15
643–13, 14	10A	1475 thru 1476	1	1551	16
643–14A, B, C	10B	1479	7	1552	20
643–15	10A	1482 and 1482A	16	1553	16
643–15A thru 643–28	10B	1483	16	1554 and 1554A	3
		1484 thru 1484D	3	1555 and 1556	16
		1485	7	1557 thru 1560	15
650	14	1486	4	1561	19
660–11 thru 660–32	18	1488 thru 1488D	1	1562 thru 1571	15
670–01 thru 670–101	8	1489 thru 1490B	3	1572	2
		1491	12	1573	3
200–183112	6	1493 and 1493A	7	1574 thru 1577	23
200–183122	6	1494 and 1495A	2	1575	24
200–193132	6	1496	7	1578	25
200–193142	6	1497	1	1581 thru 1582A	23
200–193152	7	1498	5	1583 thru 1595	26
200–193162	7	1499	16		
200–203172	8	1500	5		
200–203182	8	1501A thru 1501E	1	200–503111	16
200–203192	8	1503 thru 1503D	12	200–583111	16
200–213112	8	1506	16	200–593121	16
200–213122	8	1506B	17	200–613111	16
200–243112	8	1507	16	200–672102	26
200–283012	8	1508	7	200–682102	26

Specifications for 2 Cycle Engines with Split Crankcases

	A	B	C	D	E	F	G	H
Bore	1.500 1.5005	1.6253 1.6258	1.7503 1.7508	1.7503 1.7508	2.000	2.000	2.000	2.000
Stroke	1.375	1.50	1.50	1.50	1.50	1.50	1.50	1.50
Displacement Cubic Inches	2.43	3.10	3.60	3.60	4.70	4.70	4.70	4.70
Point Gap	.020	.020	.020	.020	.020	.020	.015	.015
Timing B.T.D.C. Before Top Dead Center	$1/16''$ or .0625	$5/32''$ or .1562	$5/32''$ or .1562	$1/4''$ or .250	$5/32''$ or .1562	$5/32''$ or .1562	$5/32''$	$1/4''$ or .250 $11/64''$ for "super"
Spark Plug Gap	.030	.030	.030	.030	.030	.030	.030	.030
Piston Ring End Gap	.003 .008	.005 .010	.005 .010	.005 .010	.006 .011	.006 .011	.006 .011	.006 .011
Piston Diameter	1.4966 1.4969	1.6216 1.6219	1.7461 1.7464	1.7461 1.7464	1.9948 1.9951	1.9948 1.9951	1.9948 1.9951	1.9949 1.9955
Piston Ring Groove Width	.095 .096	.095 .096	.095 .096	.095 .096	.095 .096	.095 .096	.095 .096	.095 .096
Piston Ring Width	.093 .0935	.093 .0935	.093 .0935	.093 .0935	.093 .0935	.093 .0935	.093 .0935	.093 .0935
Piston Pin Diameter	.3750 .3751	.3750 .3751	.3750 .3751	.3750 .3751	.3750 .3751	.3750 .3751	.3750 .3751	Early .3750 .3761 Late .4997 .4999
Connecting Rod Diameter Crank Bearing	.6869 .6874	.6869 .6874	.6869 .6874	.6986 .6989 w/o needles	.6869 .6874	.6869 .6874	.6869 .6874	.6935 .6939 w/o needles
Crankshaft Rod Needle Diameter				.0653 .0655				.0653 .0655
Crank Pin Journal Diameter	.6860 .6865	.6860 .6865	.6860 .6865	.5615 .5618	.6860 .6865	.6860 .6865	.6860 .6865	.5615 .5618
Crankshaft P.T.O. Side Main Brg. Dia.	.6689 .6693	.6689 .6693	.6690 .6694	.6689 .6693	.9995 1.0000	.6689 .6693	.9995 1.0000	.9995 1.0000
Crankshaft Magneto Side Main Brg. Dia.	.6689 .6693	.6689 .6693	.6689 .6693	.6690 .6694	.7495 .7500	.6689 .6693	.7495 .7500	.7495 .7500
Crankshaft End Play	.003 .008	.003 .008	.003 .008	.003 .008	.009 .022	.009 .022	.009 .022	.009 .022

Specifications for 2 Cycle Engines with Split Crankcases (cont.)

I	J	K	L	M	N	O	P	
2.000	2.000	2.093 2.094	2.2505 2.2510	2.2505 2.2510	2.5030 2.5035	2.5030 2.5035	2.000	Bore
1.50	1.625	1.63	2.00	2.00	1.625	1.680	1.50	Stroke
4.70	5.10	5.80	8.00	8.00	7.98	8.25	4.70	Displacement Cubic Inches
.015	.020	.015	.020	.020	.020	.020	.015	Point Gap
$^{11}/_{64}$" or .175	$^{11}/_{64}$" or .175	$^{3}/_{32}$" or .095	$^{1}/_{8}$" or .125	$^{3}/_{32}$" or .095	$^{11}/_{64}$" or .175	$^{11}/_{64}$" or .175	.90	Timing B.T.D.C. Before Top Dead Center
.035	.030	.030	.030	.030	.030	.030	.035	Spark Plug Gap
.006 .011	.006 .011	.006 .011	.007 .015	.007 .015	.005 .013	.005 .013	.006 .011	Piston Ring End Gap
1.9948 1.9951	1.9951 1.9948	2.0880 2.0883	2.2460 2.2463	2.2460 2.2463	2.4960 2.4963	2.4960 2.4963	1.9948 1.9951	Piston Diameter
.095 .096	.095 .096	T.0655 .0665 L.0645 .0655	.095 .096	.095 .096	T.0655 .0665 L.0645 .0655	T.0655 .0665 L.0645 .0655	.095 .096	Piston Ring Groove Width
.093 .0935	.093 .0935	.0615 .0625	.093 .0935	.093 .0935	.0615 .0625	.0615 .0625	.093 .0935	Piston Ring Width
.4997 .4999	.3750 .3751	.4997 .4999	.5000 .5001	.3000 .5001	.4997 .4999	.4997 .4999	.4997 .4999	Piston Pin Diameter
.6941 .6944	.6869 .6874	.9407 .9412	1.000 1.0004	1.000 1.0004	.9407 .9412	.9407 .9412	.6941 .6944	Connecting Rod Diameter Crank Bearing
.0653 .0655		.0943 .0945	.0943 .0945	.0943 .0945	.0943 .0945	.0943 .0945	.0653 .0655	Crankshaft Rod Needle Diameter
.6860 .6865	.6860	.7499 .7502	.8096 .8099	.8096 .8099	.7499 .7502	.7499 .7502	.6860 .6865	Crank Pin Journal Diameter
.9995 1.0000	.9995 1.0000	.6990 .6994	.9839 .9842	.9839 .9842	.7871 .7875	.7871 .7875	.9995 1.0000	Crankshaft P.T.O. Side Main Brg. Dia.
.7495 .7500	.7495 .7500	.6990 .6994	.9839 .9842	.9839 .9842	.7498 .7501	.7498 .7501	.7495 .7500	Crankshaft Magneto Side Main Brg. Dia.
.009 .022	.009 .022	.003 .008	.003 .008	.003 .008	.008 .013	.008 .013	.009 .022	Crankshaft End Play

Torque Specifications for 2-Cycle Engines

Application	Torque	Application	Torque
Carburetor and Reed Plates		Cylinder head to cylinder (635 type engine)	45–50 in. pounds
Carburetor to crankcase, Carburetor to adapter, or Carburetor adapter to crankcase	70–75 in. pounds	Cable clip and transfer port cover to cylinder	25–30 in. pounds
Carburetor to snow blowers cover	30–35 in. pounds	Cable clip to cylinder Stop lever to cylinder	25–30 in. pounds
Carburetor outlet fitting	40 in. pounds	Spark plug	18–22 ft. pounds
Reed and cover plates 639 type engines	50–60 in. pounds with Loctite, type A	Transfer cover cross port engines	25–30 in. pounds
Reed to plate 635 type engines	12–18 in. pounds	**Crankshaft and Connecting Rods**	
Crankcase and Cylinder		Aluminum and bronze rods to rod cap	40–50 in. pounds
Crankcase to crankcase cover	23–30 in. pounds	Steel rod to rod cap	70–80 in. pounds
Crankcase to crankcase cover screws	35–40 in. pounds	Flywheel nut on tapered end of crankshaft: Aluminum hub on iron or steel shaft.	18–25 ft. pounds
Mounting cylinder or carburetor to crankcase studs	50 in. pounds	Steel hub flywheel on iron shaft	18–25 ft. pounds
Base to crankcase	240–250 in. pounds	Steel hub flywheel on steel shaft	30 ft. pounds
Cylinder to crankcase nuts	70–75 in. pounds	**Governor and Bell Crank Parts**	
In cylinder	100–110 in. pounds	Power take-off end governor lower ring to crankshaft setscrew	30–35 in. pounds
Spark plug stop lever and head shroud to head	50–60 in. pounds	Bell crank bracket to crankcase	20–25 in. pounds
Cylinder head to cylinder	30–40 in. pounds	Governor cover to crankcase	50–60 in. pounds
Cylinder head to cylinder	50–60 in. pounds 80–90 in. pounds		

Specifications Chart

	1	2	3	4	5	6	7	8	9A	9B	9C	12
Bore	2.093 2.094	2.093 2.094	2.093 2.094	2.093 2.094	2.093 2.094	2.093 2.094	2.093 2.094	2.093 2.094	2.093 2.094	2.093 2.094	2.093 2.094	2.093 2.094
Stroke	1.250	1.410	1.410	1.410	1.410	1.500	1.500	1.500	1.500	1.500	1.500	1.410
Cu. In. Displacement	4.40	4.80	4.80	4.80	4.80	5.20	5.20	5.20	5.20	5.20	5.20	4.80
Point Gap	.017	.017	.017	.017	.017	.018	.017	.020	.018	.020	.020	.017
Timing B.T.D.C.	.122"	.100"	.135"	.100"	.135"	.100"	.185"	.070"	.110"	.085" See Note 1	.078" See Note 2	.135"
Spark Plug Gap	.035	.035	.035	.035	.035	.035	.035	.035	.035	.035	.035	.035
Piston Ring End Gap	.007 .017	.007 .017	.006 .011	.006 .014	.006 .011	.006 .014	.007 .017	.006 .016	.007 .017	.006 .016	.006 .016	.007 .017
Piston Diameter	2.0080 2.0870	2.0880 2.0870	2.0885 2.0875	2.0885 2.0875	2.0885 2.0875	2.0880 2.0870	2.0880 2.0870	2.0880 2.0870	2.0880 2.0870	2.0880 2.0820	2.0880 2.0870	2.0880 2.0870
Piston Ring Groove Width (Top)	.0655 .0665	.0655 .0665	.0655 .0665	.0975 .0985	.0655 .0665	.0975 .0985	.0655 .0665	.0655 .0665	.0655 .0665	.0655 .0665	.0655 .0665	.0655 .0665
(Bot.)	.0645 .0655	.0645 .0655	.0645 .0655	.0955 .0965	.0645 .0655	.0955 .0965	.0645 .0655	.0645 .0655	.0645 .0655	.0645 .0655	.0645 .0655	.0645 .0655
Piston Ring Width	.0625 .0615	.0625 .0615	.0625 .0615	.0925 .0935	.0625 .0615	.0925 .0935	.0625 .0615	.0625 .0615	.0625 .0615	.0625 .0615	.0625 .0615	.0625 .0615

Parameter												
Piston Pin Diameter	.4999 / .4997	.4999 / .4997	.4999 / .4997	.3750 / .3751	.4999 / .4997	.3750 / .3751	.4999 / .4997	.4999 / .4997	.4999 / .4997	.4999 / .4997	.4999 / .4997	.4999 / .4997
Connecting Rod Diameter Crank Bearing	—	—	—	.6886 / .6879 Dowels	—	—	—	1.0053 / 1.0023 Liner Dia.	—	1.0053 / 1.0023 Liner Dia.	1.0053 / 1.0023 Liner Dia	—
Crankshaft Rod Needle Dia.	.0655 / .0653	.0655 / .0653	.0655 / .0653	—	.0655 / .0653	—	.0655 / .0653	.0781 / .0780	—	.0781 / .0780	.0781 / .0780	.0655 / .0653
Crank Pin Journal Diameter	.5618 / .5611	.5621 / .5614	.5621 / .5614	.6865 / .6857	.5618 / .5611	.6865 / .6857	.5618 / .5611	.8450 / .8442	.6865 / .6857	.8450 / .8442	.8450 / .8442	.5621 / .5614
Crankshaft P.T.O. Side Main Brg. Dia.	.6695 / .6691	.6695 / .6691	.6695 / .6691	.6695 / .6691	.6695 / .6691	.8750 / .8745	.6694 / .6690	1.0003 / .9998	.8750 / .8745	1.0003 / .9998	1.0003 / .9998	.6695 / .6691
Crankshaft Magneto Side Main Brg. Dia.	.6695 / .6691	.6695 / .6691	.6695 / .6691	.6695 / .6691	.6695 / .6691	.7500 / .7495	.6694 / .6690	.6695 / .6691	.7500 / .7495	.7503 / .7498	.6695 / .6691	.6695 / .6691
Crankshaft End Play	None	None	None	None	None	.003 / .016	None	None	.003 / .016	.003 / .016	None	None

NOTE 1: 642-08 14A, 14B B.T.D.C. = .110"
         642-16D, 19A, 20A, 21 22 B.T.D.C. = .078"

NOTE 2: 642-24, 26, 29 B.T.D.C. = .085"
         643-2a, 25, 26 B.T.D.C. = .085"

NOTE 3: 643-13 B.T.D.C. = .095"

NOTE 4: 643-03A, 05A, 13, 14 = .020"

Specifications Chart

	14	16	17	19	20	23	24	25	26	27
Bore	2.093 2.094	2.093 2.094	2.093 2.094	2.093 2.094	2.093 2.094	2.093 2.094	2.093 2.094	2.093 2.094	2.093 2.094	2.093 2.094
Stroke	1.500	1.500	1.500	1.410	1.250	1.500	1.410	1.410	1.500	1.500
Cu. In. Displacement	5.20	5.20	5.20	4.80	4.40	5.20	4.80	4.80	5.20	5.20
Point Gap	.018	.017	.017	.017	.017	.017	.017	.020	.020	.017
Timing B.T.D.C.	.100"	.110"	.110"	.100"	.122"	.110"	.135"	Fixed	.062"	.100"
Spark Plug Gap	.035	.035	.035	.035	.035	.035	.035	.035	.035	.035
Piston Ring End Gap	.006 .014	.006 .016	.006 .016	.007 .017	.007 .017	.006 .016	.007 .017	.007 .017	.006 .016	.006 .016
Piston Diameter	2.0880 2.0870	2.0885 2.0875	2.0890 2.0880	2.0880 2.0870	2.0880 2.0870	2.0880 2.0870	2.0880 2.0870	2.0880 2.0870	2.0880 2.0870	2.0885 2.0875
Piston Ring Groove Width (Top)	.0975 .0985	.0645 .0655	.0645 .0655	.0655 .0665	.0655 .0665	.0655 .0665	.0655 .0665	.0655 .0665	.0655 .0665	.0655 .0665
Piston Ring Groove Width (Bot.)	.0955 .0965	.0645 .0655	.0645 .0655	.0645 .0655	.0645 .0655	.0645 .0655	.0645 .0655	.0645 .0655	.0645 .0655	.0645 .0655

	1	2	3	4	5	6	7	8	9	10
Piston Ring Width	.0625 / .0615	.0625 / .0615	.0625 / .0615	.0625 / .0615	.0625 / .0615	.0625 / .0615	.0625 / .0615	.0625 / .0615	.0625 / .0615	.0925 / .0935
Piston Pin Diameter	.4999 / .4997	.4999 / .4997	.4999 / .4997	.4999 / .4997	.4999 / .4997	.4999 / .4997	.4999 / .4997	.4999 / .4997	.3750 / .3751	.3750 / .3751
Connecting Rod Diameter Crank Bearing	.8919 / .8924	.8534 / .8504 Liner Dia.	—	—	.8534 / .8504 Liner Dia.	—	—	—	—	—
Crankshaft Rod Needle Dia.	.0781 / .0780	.0781 / .0780	.0655 / .0653	.0655 / .0653	.0781 / .0780	.0655 / .0653	.0655 / .0653	.0655 / .0653	—	—
Crank Pin Journal Diameter	.6927 / .6922	.6927 / .6919	.5621 / .5614	.5621 / .5614	.6927 / .6919	.5618 / .5611	.5621 / .5614	.5621 / .5614	.6865 / .6857	.6868 / .6857
Crankshaft P.T.O. Side Main Brg. Dia.	.6695 / .6691	.7503 / .7498	.6695 / .6691	.6695 / .6691	.6695 / .6691	.6695 / .6691	.6695 / .6691	.6695 / .6691	1.0003 / .9998	.8750 / .8745
Crankshaft Magneto Side Main Brg. Dia.	.7503 / .7498	.6695 / .6691	.6695 / .6691	.6695 / .6691	.7503 / .7498	.6695 / .6691	.6695 / .6691	.6695 / .6691	.7500 / .7495	.7500 / .7495
Crankshaft End Play	.003 / .016	None	None	None	None	None	None	None	None	.003 / .016

A. on Engines prior to 660-24: 7505, 7198

17
Tecumseh Vector

CARBURETION

Proper carburetor function is dependent on clean fresh fuel and a well maintained air cleaner system. Most causes of carburetion problems are directly related to stale fuel and dirt ingestion. Inspection of the carburetor for dirt wear and fuel deposits should always be done before servicing the carburetor.

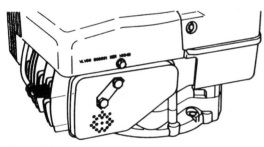

Engine identification

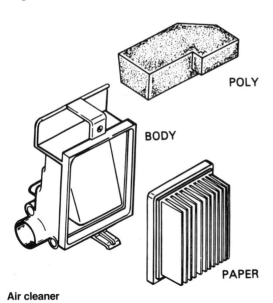

POLY

BODY

PAPER

Air cleaner

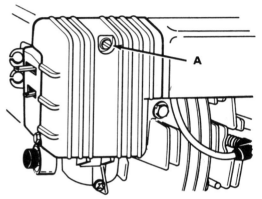

A

Cover screw

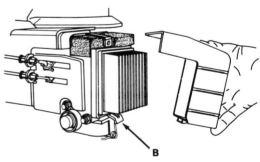

B

Press tab

Carburetor Identification

Tecumesh carburetors are identified by a model number and date code stamped on the carburetor as shown. When servicing carburetors, use the engine model number or the model number on the carburetor to find repair parts.

The Vector carburetor is a float feed, non-adjustable carburetor, with a 1 piece extruded aluminum body. The float bowl, float, nozzle, and venturi are nonmetallic, eliminating the corrosion and varnishing problems associated with

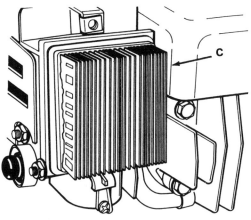

Filter

similar metallic parts. Common service areas of the carburetor are contained in the fuel bowl. These areas are the float, needle, seat and main nozzle. All of these parts can be serviced without removing the carburetor body from the engine.

FLOAT BOWL SERVICE

1. Disconnect and plug the fuel line.
2. Remove the bowl drain screw.
3. Remove the float bowl by snapping the bale spring towards the throttle end of the carburetor.

NOTE: *If a screwdriver or similar tool is used to aid in the bail removal, care must be taken not to permanently bend the retainer.*

4. Pull out the main nozzle and spring. Inspect the man nozzle for deposits. Be sure to check the cross holes on the body of the nozzle

and the main jet orifice in the bottom of the nozzle. Use compressed air or monofiliment fishing line to remove any deposits ion the main jet or cross holes. Replace the O-ring if damaged.

5. The float is held in the float bowl by the float pin which is pressed into tabs on the top of the float support towers. To remove the float:

a. Insert a screwdriver into the rectangular hole in the float at the hinge.

b. Carefully pry the hinge shaft out of the tabs in the float bowl.

c. Carefully lift the float out of the float bowl and inspect for damage or deposits.

d. Clean the idle passageway with compressed air, or probe with tag wire.

NOTE: *The inlet needle is attached to the float and shield also be inspected for damage or deposits.*

6. The inlet seal can be removed with a small

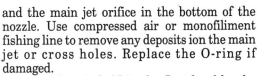

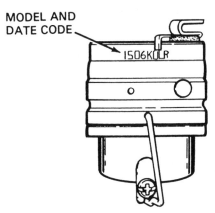

Carburetor identification

Ref. No.	Part Name
1	Carburetor Body
2	Throttle Shaft and Lever Assembly
3	Dust Seal (throttle)
4	Throttle Shutter
5	Throttle shutter screw
6	Float Bowl
7	Float Pin
8	Float
9	Gasket, Float bowl to body
10	Inlet Needle & Seat Assy.
11	Bowl Drain Assy.
12	Tube, Main Nozzle
13	"O" Ring, Main nozzle tube
14	Spring, Main nozzle tube
15	Retainer, Float bowl
16	Welch Plug, Idle mixing well

Carburetor exploded view

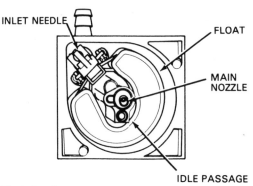

INLET NEEDLE

FLOAT

MAIN NOZZLE

IDLE PASSAGE

Float chamber

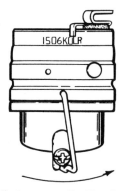

ISO6KULR

Swing bale clip to remove float bowl

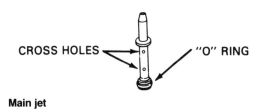

CROSS HOLES → "O" RING

Main jet

wire hook or forced out with compressed air. Inspect the float bowl and main nozzle area for sediment and deposits. Use a mild carburetor cleaner to loosen and remove deposits and sediment.

7. Install a new inlet seat into the float bowl. The grooved side of the inlet seat goes into the float bowl first. Place a drop of oil on the seat and press it in with a flat punch until it seats. Do not scratch the inlet bore.

8. Slide the inlet needle drops into the fuel inlet.

9. Snap the float shaft into the tabs in the float bowl. It is not necessary to adjust the float height even if the float has been replaced.

10. Drop the main nozzle spring into the main nozzle well in the float bowl. Put a small amount of oil on the main nozzle O-ring and

push the nozzle into the main nozzle well, O-ring end first.

11. Place a new gasket on top of the float bowl (the gasket will only fit onto the float bowl one way.) Hold the float bowl to the carburetor body and snap the retainer into position. Reinstall the bowl drain screw, do not overtighten, reattach the fuel line.

NOTE: *Bowl service is all that is normally required for routine carburetor maintenance.*

CARBURETOR OVERHAUL

To rebuild the carburetor body it is necessary to remove the carburetor from the engine.

1. Remove the speed control plate.
2. Remove the air cleaner body from the carburetor body.
3. Disconnect and plug the fuel line.
4. Remove the carburetor mounting studs.
5. Remove the governor link.
6. Drain the carburetor float bowl.
7. Disassemble the float bowl (see Bowl Service).

NOTE: *Before disassembling the carburetor body, check the throttle shaft and body for ex-*

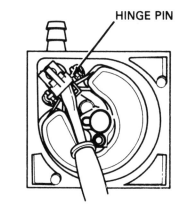

HINGE PIN

Main jet installation

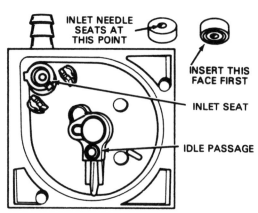

INLET NEEDLE SEATS AT THIS POINT

INSERT THIS FACE FIRST

INLET SEAT

IDLE PASSAGE

Inlet needle seat installation

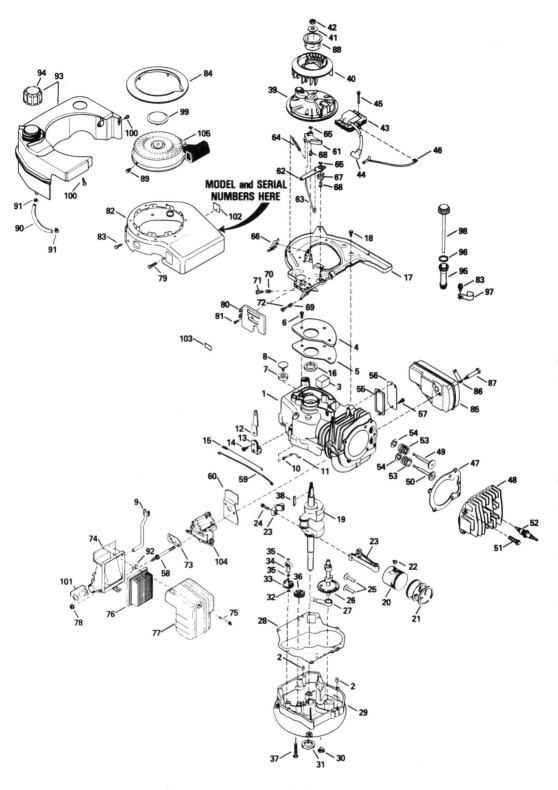

MODEL and SERIAL
NUMBERS HERE

Engine exploded view

Ref. No.	Part Name	Ref. No.	Part Name
1	Cylinder Assy.	54	Cap, Valve spring
2	Pin, Dowel	55	Gasket, Valve cover
3	Element, Breather	56	Cover, Valve spring box
4	Cover, Breather	57	Screw, Hex hd. Sems, 10-24 x 1/2
5	Gasket, Breather cover	58	Stud, Carburetor mounting
6	Screw, Hex washer hd., thread forming, 10-24 x 1/2	59	Link, Governor
		60	Spacer, Carburetor mounting
7	Body, Breather valve	61	Lever Assy., Brake
8	Valve, Breather check	62	Lever, Brake control
9	Breather Tube	63	Link, Brake control lever
10	Washer, Flat	64	Spring, Brake
11	Rod, Governor	65	Ring, Retaining
12	Lever, Governor	66	Terminal
13	Clamp, Governor lever	67	Spring, Brake control lever
14	Screw, Hex washer hd., 8-32 x 5/16	68	Bushing, Brake control lever & brake lever
15	Spring, Governor extension	69	Spring, Compression
16	Seal, Oil	70	Spring, Compression
17	Baffle, Blower housing (Incl. No. 195)	71	Screw, Fil. hd., 5-40 x 7/16
18	Screw, Hex washer hd. taptite, 1/4-20 x 5/8	72	Screw, Fil. hd., 6-32 x 21/32
		73	Gasket, Carburetor to air cleaner
19	Crankshaft Assy.	74	Body, Air cleaner (Incl. Nos. 239, 299 & 350)
20	Piston & Pin Assy.	75	Screw, Fil hd. Sems, 10-32 x 2-3/32
21	Ring Set, Piston	76	Filter, Air cleaner (Paper)
22	Ring, Piston pin retaining	77	Cover, Air cleaner
23	Rod Assy., Connecting	78	Nut, Lock, 1/4-20
24	Bolt, Connecting rod	79	Screw, Hex washer hd., taptite, 1/4-20 x 11/16
25	Lifter, Valve	80	Plate, Control Assy. cover
26	Camshaft Assy.	81	Screw, Hex washer hd., taptite, 8-32 x 1/2
27	Pump Assy., Oil	82	Housing, Blower
28	Gasket, Mounting Flange	83	Screw, Hex washer hd. taptite, 1/4-20 x 1/2
29	Flange, Mounting	84	Ring, Starter
30	Plug, Oil drain	85	Muffler
31	Seal, Oil	86	Plate, Muffler locking
32	Washer, Flat	87	Screw, Hex hd. shoulder, 5/16-18 x 2-11/32
33	Gear Assy., Governor	88	Cup, Starter
34	Spool, Governor	89	Screw, Hex washer hd., 8-32 x 21/64
35	Ring, Retaining	90	Line, Fuel
36	Gear, Idler	91	Clamp, Fuel line
37	Screw, Hex washer hd., 1/4-20 x 1-9/16	92	Clip, "U" Type Nut, 10-32
38	Key, Flywheel	93	Tank Assy., Fuel
39	Flywheel	94	Cap, Fuel
40	Fan, Flywheel	95	Tube, Oil fill
41	Washer, Belleville	96	"O" Ring
42	Nut, Flywheel	97	Clip, Fill tube
43	Solid State Assy.	98	Dipstick, Oil
44	Cover, Spark plug	99	Plug, Starter
45	Screw, Hex washer hd. Sems, 10-24 x 1	100	Screw, Hex washer hd. 10-32 x 35/64
46	Wire Assy., Ground	101	Primer
47	Gasket, Cylinder head	102	Decal, Instruction
48	Head, Cylinder	103	Decal, Primer
49	Valve, Exhaust	104	Carburetor
50	Valve, Intake	105	Starter, Rewind
51	Screw, Hex flange hd., 5/16-18 x 1-1/2		
52	Spark Plug (Champion RJ-19LM or equivalent)		
53	Spring, Valve		

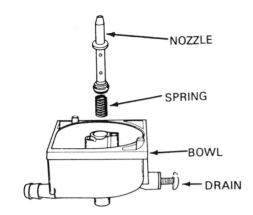

Float adjustment

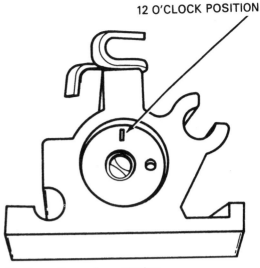

Shutter scribe mark positioning

cessive wear. Remove the shutter screw and discard. Inspect the shutter for damage; discard if damaged.

Cleaning

To properly clean the carburetor body, the welch plugs should be removed to expose drilled passages. To remove welch plug, sharpen a small chisel to a sharp wedge point. Drive the chisel into the welch plug, push down on chisel and pry plug out of position.

After the welch plug is removed from the carburetor it can be soaked in a commercial carburetor cleaner no longer than 30 minutes. Be sure to follow the directions on the container.

After the carburetor has been soaked, all passages mat be probed with monofilament fishing line and compressed air to open plugged or restricted passages.

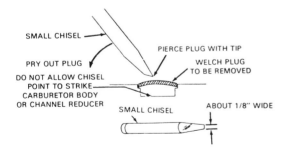

Welch plug removal

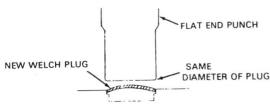

Welch plug installation

Assembly

1. Install a new welch plug over the idle fuel chamber with the raised portion up. Use a punch equal to the size of the plug, to fasten the plug. Do not dent or drive the center of the plug below the top surface of the carburetor.

2. Install the throttle and shutter (use a new shutter screw and dust seal). The scribe mark on the shutter must be in the 12 o'clock position.

NOTE: *If the scribe mark is out of position the shutter may stick.*

3. To rebuild the Float Bowl, refer to the previous section on float bowl service.

4. Install the carburetor to the engine using a new gasket. The primer passage in the air cleaner body should be cleaned before it is reinstalled over the carburetor.

PRIMER BULB SERVICE

1. Grasp the primer bulb with a needle nose pliers and roll the pliers along the air cleaner body.

2. After removing the primer bulb, the retaining ring must be removed. Use a screwdriver to carefully pry the retainer out of the air cleaner body. Do not reuse old bulb or retainer.

3. Press the new bulb and retainer into position using a deep reach socket.

CAUTION: *Wear safety glasses or goggles when removing retainer.*

4. After the primer bulb is removed, clean the primer passages thoroughly.

5. Install air cleaner body over the carburetor using a new gasket.

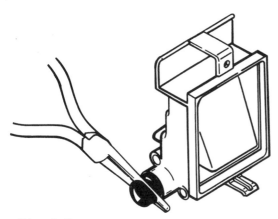

Primer bulb removal

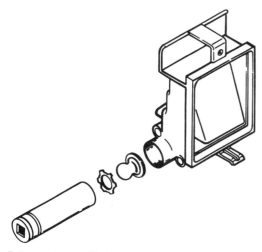

Primer bulb installation

GOVERNORS AND LINKAGE

All Tecumseh 4-cycle engines of recent manufactures are equipped with mechanical type governors. As the speed of an engine increases, centrifugal force moves the weights outward, lifting up the governor spool which contacts the governor shaft; this in turn closes the throttle. As engine speed decreases, the weights are pulled inward by the spring which opens the throttle. Thus, the engine speed controls the throttle opening and maintains a certain governed speed.

The governor gear on the Vector engine is driven by the crankshaft through an idler gear.

The idler gear is captured in the mounting flange by both the crankshaft gear and the governor gear.

The governor and idler shafts are pressed

into the flange or cover to a specific dimension and is serviced as an assembly.

LINKAGE INSTALLATION

The solid link is always connected from the throttle lever on the carburetor to the lower hole on the governor lever. The shorter bend has to be toward the governor. The governor extension spring is connected with the spring and hooked into the upper hole of the governor lever and the extension end hooked through the speed control lever. To remove the governor spring, carefully twist the extension end counterclockwise to unhook the extension spring at the speed control lever. Do not bend or distort governor extension spring.

GOVERNOR ADJUSTMENT

1. With engine stopped, loosen the screw holding the governor clamp and lever.

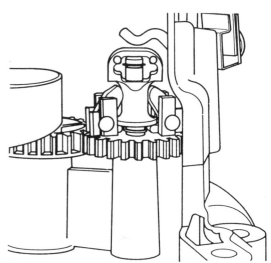

Governor assembly

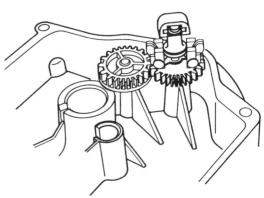

The idler gear is held by the crankshaft gear and governor gear

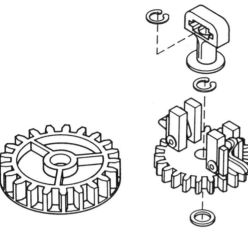

Governor gear components

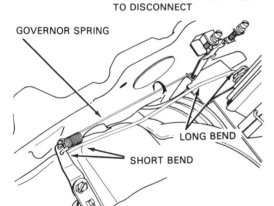

TWIST COUNTERCLOCKWISE
TO DISCONNECT

GOVERNOR SPRING

LONG BEND

SHORT BEND

Governor adjustment

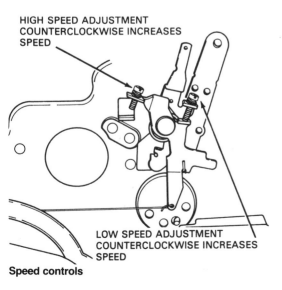

HIGH SPEED ADJUSTMENT
COUNTERCLOCKWISE INCREASES
SPEED

LOW SPEED ADJUSTMENT
COUNTERCLOCKWISE INCREASES
SPEED

Speed controls

2. Turn the clamp clockwise, then push governor lever connected to the throttle to a full wide open position.

3. Hold the lever and clamp in this position and tighten the screw.

SPEED CONTROLS

The Vector engine has an adjustable speed control. Never exceed the manufacturer's recommended speeds.

REWIND STARTER

DISASSEMBLY

1. After removing the rewind from the engine blower housing, release the tension on the rewind spring.

2. Place a ¾ in. deep reach socket inside the retainer pawl. Set the rewind on a bench, supported on the socket.

3. Using a ⁵⁄₁₆ in. roll punch, drive out the center pin.

4. All components that are in need of service should be replaced.

NOTE: *Care must be used when handling the pulley because the rewind spring and cover is held by the bosses in the pulley.*

ASSEMBLY

1. Reverse the above listed keeping in mind that the starter dogs with the dog springs must snap back to the center of the pulley.

2. Always replace the center pin with a new pin upon reassembly. Also place the two new plastic washers between the center lag and retainer pawl. Disacard old plastic washer. The new plastic washers will be provided along with the new center pin.

3. Check retainer pawl. It is worn, bent or damaged in any manner replace upon reassembly.

4. Tap the new center pin in until it is within ⅛ in. of the top of the starter.

NOTE: *Driving the center pin in too far will cause the retainer pawl to bend and the starter dogs will not engage starter cup.*

ELECTRIC STARTERS

REMOVAL

1. Remove face plate, air cleaner assembly and gas tank.

2. Compress plastic grommet and pull it out of the blower housing.

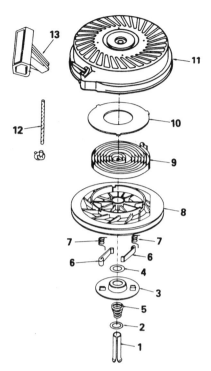

Ref. No.	Part Name
	Starter, Rewind
1	Pin, Spring (Incl. No. 4)
2	Washer
3	Retainer
4	Washer
5	Spring, Brake
6	Dog, Starter
7	Spring, Dog
8	Pulley
9	Spring, Rewind
10	Cover, Spring
11	Housing Assy., Starter
12	Rope, Starter (Length 98" & 9/64" dia.)
13	Handle, Starter

Rewind starter—exploded view

3. Slide the wire through slot, being careful not to cut the wire insulation.

4. Remove blower housing, remove flywheel (see flywheel section) and inspect ring gear for wear or damage. Replace if necessary (see flywheel section).

5. Remove nuts on both sides of pinion. Drop starter out of back plate and remove ground wire.

DRIVE ASSEMBLY SERVICE

Pinion gear parts should be checked for damage or wear. If the gear does not engage or slips, it should be washed in solvent (rubber parts cleaned with soap and water) to remove dirt and grease, and dried thoroughly. If damaged replace parts.

Remove, inspect and replace as necessary. Assembly is the reverse of disassembly.

NOTE: *For ease of assembly, assemble armature into brush end frame first. Place a small amount of light grease such as Lubriplate® between the drive nut and helix on armature shaft. DO NOT apply lubricant to pinion driver.*

BRUSHES INSPECTION

Before removing armature, check brushes for wear. Make sure brushes are not worn to the point where brush wire bottoms out in the slot of brush holder. Brush springs must have enough strength to keep tension on the brushes and hold them against the commutator. If brushes are in need if change, replace the entire end cap assembly.

ARMATURE CHECK

If commutator bars are glazed or dirty, they can be turned down in a lather. While rotating, hold a strip of 00 sandpaper lightly on the commutator, moving it back and forth. Do not use emery cloth. Recut grooves between commutator bars to depth equal to the width of the insulators.

Using a continuity tester to make certain no continuity exists between the commutator (copper) and the iron of the armature, rotate armature and check out all commutator bars.

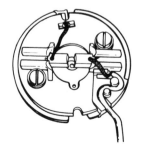

MAIN JET

END CAP
AND BRUSHES
(ASSEMBLY)

Starter brushes

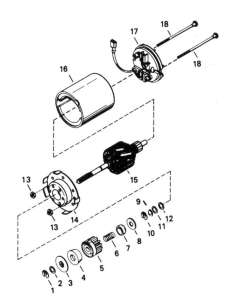

1. Retainer ring
2. Dust washer
3. Drive nut
4. Pinion driver
5. Gear
6. Anti-drift spring
7. Spring retainer (spring collapses into retainer)
8. Cup washer (cup washer cupped over retainer spring)
9. Washer (metal)
10. Retainer ring
11. Thrust washer (metal)
12 Washer (plastic)
13. Lock nuts
14. Cap assembly drive end
15. Armature
16. Housing
17. Cap assembly commutator end
18. Bolts

Electric starter—exploded view

The armature can be thoroughly checked with a growler if available.

STARTER ASSEMBLY

1. Attach the ground wire prior to assembling the electric starter to the baffle.

2. Attach the black ground wire to the electric starter through bolt so that the wire extends between the two adjacent end cap prongs.

3. Place the starter into the black plate with the ground wire bolt away from the carburetor.

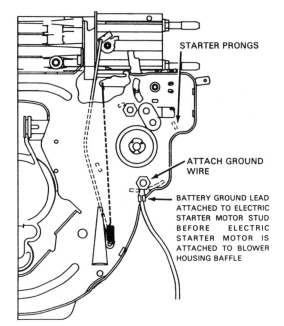

STARTER PRONGS

ATTACH GROUND WIRE

BATTERY GROUND LEAD ATTACHED TO ELECTRIC STARTER MOTOR STUD BEFORE ELECTRIC STARTER MOTOR IS ATTACHED TO BLOWER HOUSING BAFFLE

Ground wire attachment

Note that the throttle linkage is routed around starter while the governor spring is routed through the end cap springs.

4. Tighten nuts on starter bolts.

5. Place blower housing on engine and slide wires through slot making sure not to cut insulation.

6. Press plastic grommet into hole.

7. Reassemble gas tank, air cleaner assembly and face plate.

FLYWHEELS

The Vector engine uses one of two types of flywheels. The first type is a cast iron high inertia flywheel. This type of flywheel will have a pressed on ring gear if the engine is equipped with an electric starter. The other is an aluminum type.

REMOVAL

1. Disconnect the battery from the engine before servicing.

2. Remove the ignition module,

3. Remove the brake pressure from the flywheel.

4. To remove the flywheel nut, use a flywheel strap wrench to hold the flywheel, while turning the flywheel nut counterclockwise.

5. Lift the starter cup and fan off of the flywheel. (Aluminum flywheel only).

6. Remove the flywheel using a flywheel puller or knock-off tool.

NOTE: *On engines with cored holes (not tapped) use flywheel puller Part No. 670306.*

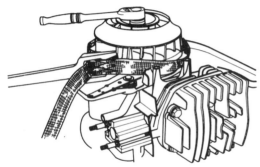

Flywheel nut removal

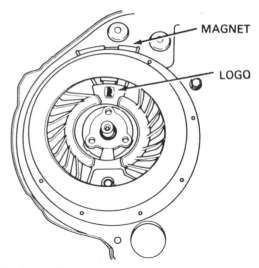

Fan installation

7. Screw a knock-off tool down until it touches the flywheel, then back off 1 turn. Using a large screwdriver, pry upward under the flywheel (side opposite the brake) and tap sharply and squarely on the knock-off tool to break the flywheel loose. If necessary rotate flywheel a half turn and repeat until it loosens.

NOTE: *Do not attempt to remove flywheel using a jaw type puller on the outer diameter of the flywheel or flywheel breakage will occur.*

Never use a pry bar with any type of curve on the end. Breather cover damage can result.

INSTALLATION

1. Inspect brake pad to be free of dirt, oil or grease. If pad is contaminated, or less than 0.060 in. at the narrowest point, replace. See Flywheel brake section for procedure.
2. Compress brake lever.
3. Install flywheel key.
4. Install flywheel.

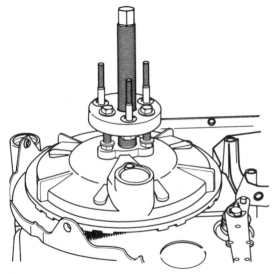

Flywheel removal

5. Install the fan onto the flywheel so the Tecumseh logo on the fan is on the magnet side of the flywheel.
6. Place starter cup into position and torque nut to specification. Use a strap wrench to hold the flywheel.

Flywheel Brake System
OPERATION

Use of the blade brake clutch in conjunction with either a top or side mounted recoil starter or 2 volt electric starter. The blade stops within three seconds after the operator lets go of the blade control bail at the operator position and the engine continues to run. Starter rope handle is on the engine.

Use of a recoil starter (top or side mounted) with the rope handle on the engine as opposed to within 24 inches of the operator position. This method is acceptable if the mower deck passes the 360 degree foot probe test. A specified foot probe must not contact the blade when applied completely around the entire blade housing. This alternative can be used with engine mounted brake systems and typical bail controls. The blade stops within three seconds after the operator lets go of the blade control bail at the operator position and the engine is stopped.

The Brake Starter Mechanism may be used with either of two options for starting:
1. Manual Rope Start
2. 12 Volt Starter System

Each system requires the operator to start unit behind mower handle in operator zone area. The electric start system also provides a charging system for battery recharge when engine is running.

TO STOP THE ENGINE In the stop position the brake pad is applied to the inside edge of the flywheel; at the same time the ignition system is grounded out.

TO START THE ENGINE In order to restart the engine, the control must be applied. This action pulls the brake pad away from the inside edge of the flywheel and opens the ignition ground switch.

On electric start systems the starter is energized to start the engine.

On non-electric start systems, recoil started rope must be pulled to start engine.

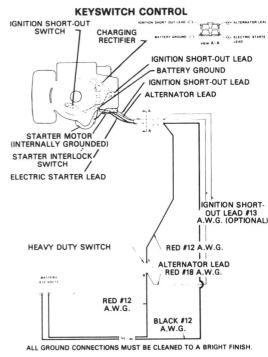

KEYSWITCH CONTROL

ALL GROUND CONNECTIONS MUST BE CLEANED TO A BRIGHT FINISH.

Electric start system wiring

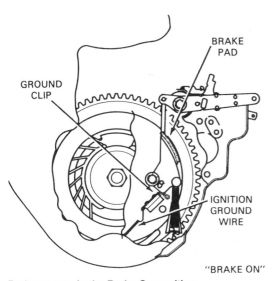

Brake system in the Brake On position

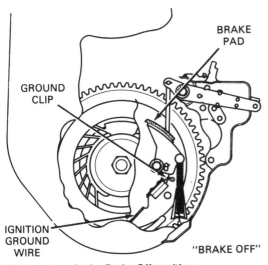

Brake system in the Brake Off position

BRAKE PAD REPLACEMENT

1. If equipped with electric starter, locate wire routing through blower housing. Compress the grommet and pull out of the blower housing. Carefully slide wires through the slot. DO NOT cut the wire insulation on the blower housing.
2. Remove flywheel.
3. Remove pad lever E-clip. Lift pad lever, and unhook spring and link.
4. Attach link to pad lever install pad lever and E-clip.
5. Attach spring to lever first. Use a needle nose pliers to hook the spring into the baffle.
   NOTE: *It is important to attach the pad lever spring with the short hook on the pad lever and the long hook to the blower housing baffle.*

BRAKE CONTROL LEVER REPLACEMENT

1. Mark hole that spring is installed into baffle.
2. Remove E-clip from brake lever shaft.
3. Lift brake control lever and unhook link. Replace with new lever and reassemble in reverse order.
4. Replacement springs must be the same size and color.
5. Be sure control lever spring is in proper hole in blower housing baffle before reassembly.

NOTE: *When removing the brake lever with a reverse pull brake, the pad lever must be removed to unhook the brake link from the brake lever.*

Control Switch

The brake lever must close the switch before the starter can be engaged. Disconnect battery from circuit before making check.

Engines equipped with an electric starter have a control switch which is attached to the brake lever. The brake lever must close the switch before the starter can be engaged.

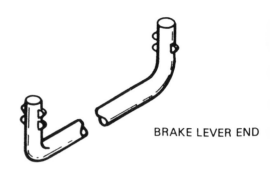

BRAKE LEVER END

PAD LEVER END

Control link attachment

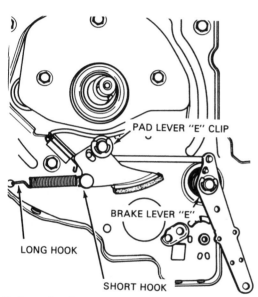

PAD LEVER "E" CLIP

BRAKE LEVER "E"

LONG HOOK

SHORT HOOK

Brake pad replacement

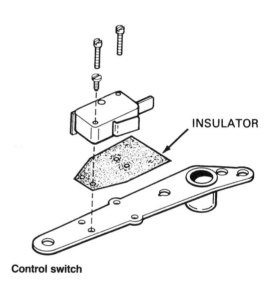

INSULATOR

Control switch

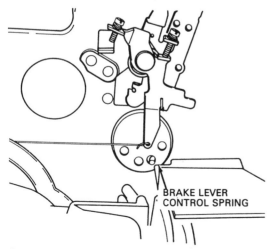

BRAKE LEVER CONTROL SPRING

Brake control lever replacement

CHECKING THE CONTROL SWITCH

1. Disconnect the battery from the circuit. Use a continuity light or meter to check control switch operation.
2. Disconnect the wire harness at the engine.
3. Attach one continuity light lead to the electric starter lead.
4. Attach the other continuity light lead to the battery ground lead. With leads attached, press the control switch lever and the continuity light should go on, if not replace switch.

SWITCH REPLACEMENT

1. Carefully grind off the heads of rivets, remove the rivets from the back side of brake lever.
2. Use the self-tapping screw to make threads in the lever, install the switch to the brake lever in the proper position and secure the switch to the lever with the machine screws. Be careful, over-tightening of the screws could break the switch.

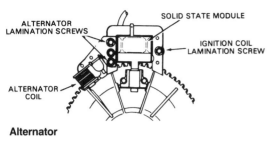

Alternator

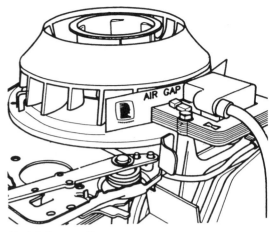

Model air gap adjustment

ALTERNATOR

The 350 Milliamp charging system consists of a single alternator coil mounted to one side of the solid state module.

Do not operate engine with charging system disconnected. Damage to diode may occur.

CHECKING THE SYSTEM

Connect voltmeter at the battery (should read battery voltage). The battery MUST BE IN CIRCUIT for test to perform properly. next, start engine-voltage should read higher than when engine is off. If there is a change upward in voltage, the charging system is working. If there is no change in voltage, the alternator should be replaced. Set volt/ohmmeter to 0-20 volt D.C. scale for test.

IGNITION SYSTEM

Tecumseh's solid state capacitor discharge ignition (CDI) is an all electronic ignition sys-

tem and is encapsulated in epoxy for protection against dirt and moisture.

As the magnets in the flywheel rotate past the charge coil, electrical energy is produced in the module. This energy is transferred to a capacitor where it is stored until it is needed to fire the spark plug.

The magnet continues rotating past a trigger coil where a low voltage signal is produced and closes an electronic switch (SCR).

The energy which was stored in the capacitor is now transferred through the switch (SCR) to a transformer where the voltage is increased form 200 volts to 25,000 volts. This voltage is transferred by means of the high tension lead to th spark plug, where it arcs across the electrode of the spark plug and ignited the fuel-air mixture.

Spark Plug
SERVICE

Spark plugs should be replaced periodically. Check electrode gap with wire feeler gauge and adjust gap. Replace if electrode is pitted, burned or the porcelain is cracked. Be sure cleaned plugs are free of all foreign material. Use a spark plug tester to check for spark.

If spark plug fouls frequently, check for the following condition:
1. Incorrect spark plug
2. Poor grade gasoline
3. Breather plugged
4. Oil level too high
5. Engine using excessive oil
6. Clogged air cleaner

NOTE: *The module has two holes on the one leg of the lamination, to secure the 350 milliamp charging system.*

The proper air gap setting between magnets and the laminations on CDI systems is 0.0125

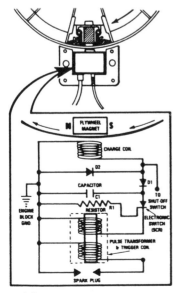

Ignition module

in. Place a 0.0125 in. gauge between the magnets and laminations and tighten mounting screws to a torque of 30-40 inch pounds. Recheck gap setting to make certain there is proper clearance between the magnets and laminations.

NOTE: *Due to variations betweem pole shoes, air gap may vary from 0.005-0.020 in. when flywheel is rotated. There is no further timing adjustement on external laminations systems.*

PISTON, RINGS AND CONNECTING ROD

Piston

Before removing piston, clean any carbon from the top of the cylinder bore to prevent ring breakage when removing the piston. Push the

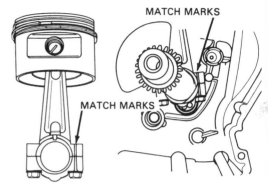

Connecting rod matchmarks

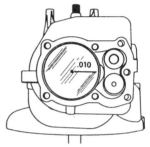

Oversize piston identification

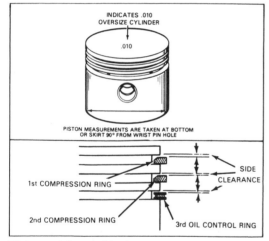

Piston and ring positioning

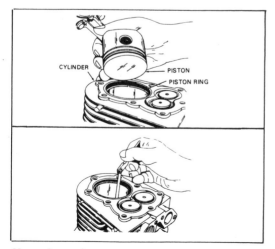

Measuring end gap

rod and piston out through the top of the cylinder.

Oversize pistons are identified by the size imprinted on the piston as shown. Check the piston for wear by measuring at the bottom of the skirt 90 degrees from the wrist pin hole. Clean the carbon from the piston ring grooves, install new rings and measure side clearance.

Replace rings in sets and always stagger ring gaps. When installing new rings, deglaze cylinder wall, using a commercially available deglazing tool.

Use a ring expander to remove and replace rings. Do not spread the rings too wide or breakage will result.

Both compression rings will have a chamfer on the inside edge. The rings must be installed with the chamfer up.

To check ring end gap, place ring squarely in center of ring travel area. Using the piston to push the ring down into the cylinder at least one inch.

Check ring gap on new ring to determine if cylinder should be rebored to take oversize parts.

Connecting Rods

Match marked on connecting rods must always align and must face outward toward the mechanic when installed in an engine.

A new piston can be installed on to the connecting rod in either direction. It is necessary to replace the connecting rod be sure to mark the calve side of the piston.

Install the piston to the connecting rod so that the piston will be in the same position when reinstalled in the engine.

The connecting rod bolts use fine threads to insure torque retention. For the proper torque specification see the table of specifications.

CYLINDERS AND CYLINDER HEADS

Cylinder
INSPECTION

Check cylinder for dirty, broken or cracked fins, worn or scored bearings or scored cylinder bore surface, and warped head mounting surfaces.

The cylinder must be replaced if the cylinder head mounting surface is warped extensively.

If cylinder bore is worn more tan 0.005 in. oversize, out-of-round or scored, it should be replaced or rebored to 0.010 in. or 0.020 in. oversize. In some cases engines are built with an oversize cylinder; in these instances, they are identified with the oversize value imprinted in the cylinder as pictured.

REBORING CYLINDER

To rebore cylinder use a commercial hone of suitable size chucked in a drill press with a spindle speed of approximately 600 R.P.M.

Start with coarse stones and center cylinder under press spindle. Lower them so lower end of stones contacts lowest point in cylinder bore.

Rotate adjusting nut so that stones touch cylinder wall and begin honing at bottom of cylinder. Move hone up or down at rate of 50 strokes per minute to avoid cutting ridges in cylinder wall. Every fourth or fifth stroke, move hone far enough to extend the stones one inch beyond top and bottom of cylinder bore.

Check bore every thirty or forty strokes for size and straightness. If stones collect metal, clean with a wire brush each time hone is removed.

Hone with coarse stones until cylinder bore is within 0.002 inch of desired finish size. Replace coarse stones with burnishing stones and continue until bore is to within 0.0005 inch of desired size.

Remove burnishing stones and install finishing stones to polish cylinder to final size.

Clean cylinder with soap and water, and dry thoroughly.

Replace piston and piston rings with correct oversize parts.

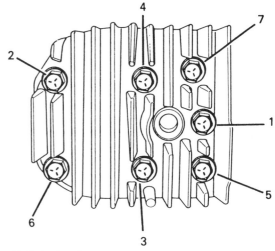

Cylinder head torque sequence

Cylinder Head

Check cylinder heads for warpage by placing on a flat surface. If warped extensively, replace head. Always replace head gasket and torque head bolts in 50 inch lbs. increments in the numbered sequence to a torque of 180-220 inch lbs.

CRANKSHAFT

Crankshaft
INSPECTION

Inspect crankshaft for worn, scratched or damaged bearing surfaces, out-of-round or flat spots on the journal area, or a bent P.T.O. end.

NOTE: *Never try to straighten a bent crankshaft.*

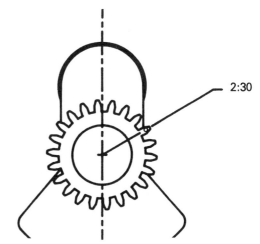

Camshaft timing mark at the 2:30 position

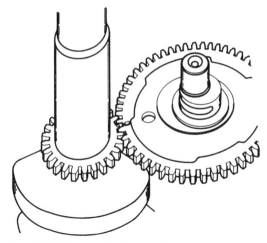

Camshaft timing mark alignment

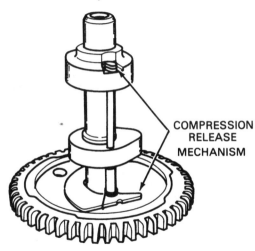

COMPRESSION
RELEASE
MECHANISM

Compression release mechanism

When installing a crankshaft, lubricate all bearing surfaces and use oil seal protector part no. 670327 or equivalent

CRANKSHAFT TIMING MARK

The crankshaft has a pressed on timing gear. This gear has a small dimple punched on one side of the teeth on this gear. This dimple is a timing mark. With the crankpin at top dead center, the timing mark should be in the 2:30 position.

The camshaft has an aligning mark in line with the timing hole on the camshaft gear. Line this mark up with the dimple on the crankshaft gear.

Timing marks on crankshaft gear and camshaft gear must be aligned for proper valve timing.

CAMSHAFT

REMOVAL

Align timing marks to relieve train pressure. Lift out camshaft.

The camshaft has a mechanical compression release mechanism. A pin which runs through both cam lobes extends past the exhaust lobe and lifts the valve to relieve compression for easier starting. When the engine starts, centrifugal force moves the flyweights outward, moving the pin below the lobe, allowing full compression. The compression release mechanism is non-serviceable (replace camshaft assembly. if damaged or worn.)

LUBRICATION SYSTEM

All Tecumesh Vector engines use a positive displacement plunger oil pump to pump oil from the crankcase, up through the camshaft to a passage in the breather box to the top of the crankshaft main bearing, and ultra balance bearings.

Oil is pressure sprayed out of a small hole between the crankshaft and ultra-balance bearing, to lubricate the connecting rod journal area. If a heavy leakage is noted from the breather cover check for plugged mist hole.

NOTE: *Not all Vector engines are equipped with ultra-balance.*

Oil Pump

An eccentric on the camshaft works the plunger in the barrel back and forth, forcing oil up the center of the camshaft. A ball on the end of the plunger locates in a recess in the flange

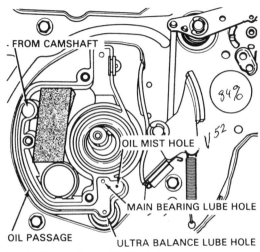

FROM CAMSHAFT

OIL MIST HOLE

MAIN BEARING LUBE HOLE

OIL PASSAGE

ULTRA BALANCE LUBE HOLE

Lubrication system with Ultraballance

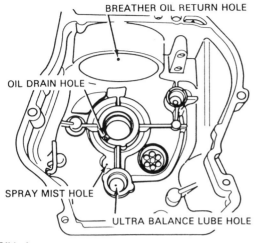

Oil holes

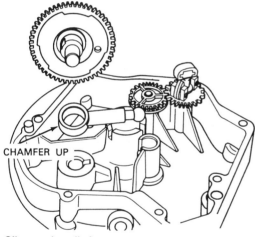

Oil pump installation

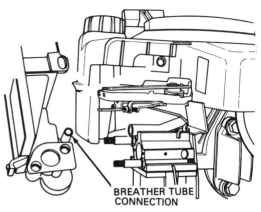

Breather tube installation

cover. When installing oil pump. make certain the chamfered side of the pump faces the camshaft, and the plunger ball seats in the recess of the flange cover.

The Vector engine has a top mounted integral breather.

The breather compartment is located under the flywheel. A check valve allows excess crankcase pressure to be vented through the element and out the breather tube. The breather tube is connected to the air cleaner body. When reassembling the breather, DO NOT pinch the filter element under the breather cover or leak may occur.

Condensed oil vapors are returned to the crankcase by means of the oil return hole. The oil return hole is opened and closed in the cylinder by the piston.

The breather filter element can be cleaned using solvent.

When reinstalling the check valve, apply oil

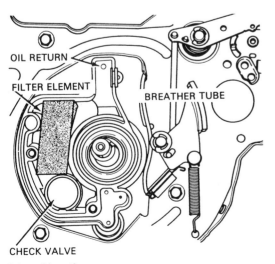

Integral breather

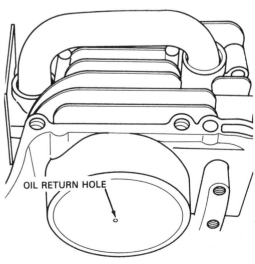

Oil return hole location

to aid in assembly. A new breather valve body can be pressed into the block to replace a damaged breather valve body.

VALVES, LIFTERS, SPRING & VALVE SEATS

Valves

Valves must be in good condition, properly sealing and the proper gap must be maintained for full power, easy starting and efficient operation.

VALVE REMOVAL

1. To remove valves, raise the lower valve spring caps, while holding the valve head tightly against the seat.
2. Move the lower cap, so it will slip off the end of the valve.
3. Clean all parts and remove carbon from valve heads and stems. If valves are is usable condition, grind the valve faces to a 45 degree angle. Replace valves if they are damaged, distorted or if the margin is ground to less than $\frac{1}{32}$ in.

Valve Seats

Valve seats are not replaceable. If they are burned or pitted, they can be reground using a grinding stone or valve reseater. Seats are ground at an angle of 46 degrees, to a width of $\frac{3}{64}$ in.

The recommended procedure to properly cut a valve seat is to use the Neway Cutting System, which consists of three different degree-cutters.

1. Use the 60 degree cutter to clean and narrow the seat from the bottom toward the center.
2. Use the 31 degree cutter to clean and narrow the seat from the top toward the center.

Valves are not identical. Make sure the valve marked **EX** or **X** is installed in the exhaust

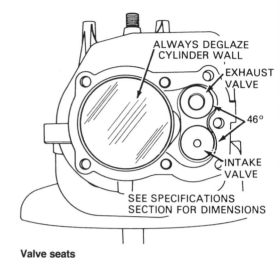

Valve seats

valve location, and the valve marked **I** is installed in the intake valve location. If the valves are unmarked, the nonmagnetic valve is installed in the exhaust valve location.

VALVE ADJUSTMENT

Clearance between the valve stem and lifter must be set to the recommended specifications when the engine is cold. Check these clearances with the piston T.D.C. on the compression stroke. Grind end of valve stem with a valve grinder, or use a **V** block to hold the valve square on grinding wheel, grinding to the proper 0.008 in. clearance.

VALVE INSTALLATION

1. Position valve caps and spring in the valve compartment.
2. Install valves in guides with valve marked **I** in the intake port. The valve stem must pass through the spring. The valve spring cap should sit around the valve lifter exposed end.
3. Use a valve spring compressor to compress the valve spring. Position the valve spring cap onto the valve stem and release valve spring tension to lock cap in place.

VALVE LIFTERS

It is a good practice not to interchange lifters, even though they are identical, once a wear pattern has been established.

OVERSIZE VALVE GUIDES

Valve guides are permanently installed in the cylinder. If they become worn excessively, they can be reamed oversized to accommodate a $\frac{1}{32}$ in. oversize valve stem.

Ream guides with a straight shanked reamer or low speed drill press. Refer to Table of Specifications to determine correct oversize dimen-

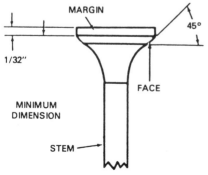

Valve dimensions

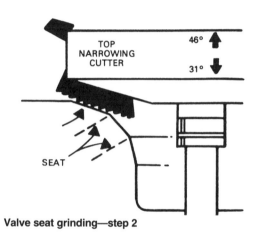

Valve seat grinding—step 1

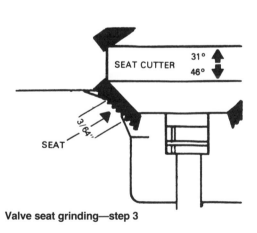

Valve seat grinding—step 2

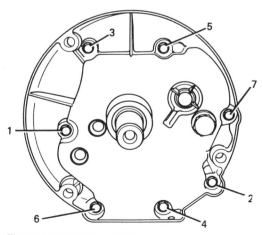

Valve seat grinding—step 3

sion. Reamers are available through your Tecumseh parts suppliers. See Tool Section for correct part numbers.

Redrill the valve spring cap, to accommodate the oversize valve stems.

After oversizing valve guides - the seats must be recut to align with the valve guides.

OIL SEAL AND MOUNTING FLANGE

Oil Seal

SERVICE

1. Drain oil from crankcase. If the crankshaft end is rusty or pitted, polish the crankshaft with emery cloth so it will not damage the bearings when the cover is removed.

2. Remove mounting bolts and slide seal protector-driver tool, Part No 670327 or equivalent, into the oil seal. If necessary, tap edge of flange or cover lightly with a soft hammer to remove cover.

3. Clean and inspect the cover for wear and scoring of bearings. Inspect crankshaft bearings. Replace any worn or damaged parts.

4. If crankshaft is out of engine, remove old oil seal by tapping them out with a screwdriver or punch from the inside, To remove a seal with

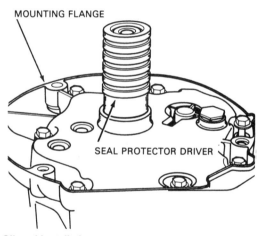

Oil seal installation

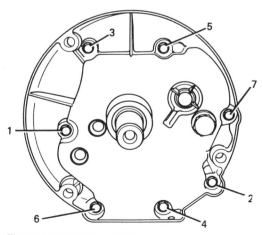

Flange bolt torque sequence

the crankshaft in the engine, insert a screwdriver between the seal and the crankshaft and pry the seal out.

5. Lubricate the outside of the new oil seal with oil prior to installation.

6. Use seal driver-protector tool Part No. 670327, or euqivalent. Place oil seal over the driver-protector and place over crankshaft, driving it into position using universal driver No. 670272. The seal will automatically be driven into the proper depth.

7. Torque flange bolts in numerical order as shown in illustration.

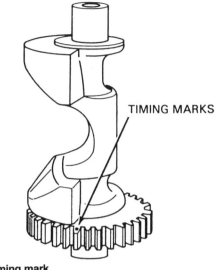

Timing mark

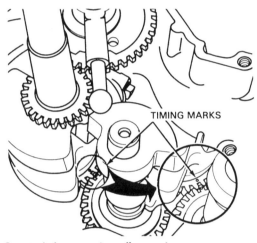

Counterbalance system alignment

ULTRA-BALANCE

The single shaft counterbalance is driven by a gear on the crankshaft, to counteract the imbalance caused by the counterweights on the crankshaft.

To correctly align the counterbalance system, rotate the piston to 90 past TDC and insert the single-shaft counterbalance into its boss in the crankcase with the punch mark on the gear in alignment with the crankshaft punch mark.

VECTOR SPECIFICATIONS

	VLV4	VLV5
Displacement	11.19	12.56
Stroke	2.047	2.047
Bore	2.6390	2.7960
	2.6380	2.7950
Air Gap Dimension	.0125	.0125
Spark plug gap	.030	.030
Valve Clearance	.008	
	.008	
Valve Seat Angle	46°	46°
Valve Seat Width	.035	.035
	.045	.045
Valve Guide Oversize Dia.	.2807	.2807
	.2817	.2817
Crankshaft End Play	.005	.005
	.027	.027
Crankpin Journel Dia.	1.0235	1.0235
	1.0230	1.0230
Crankshaft Magneto Main Brg. Dia	1.0242	1.0242
	1.0237	1.0237
Crankshaft P.T.O. Main Brg. Dia	1.0242	1.0242
	1.0237	1.0237
Camshaft Bearing Dia.	.4980	.4980
	.4975	.4975
Conn. Rod Dia. Crank Brg.	1.0246	1.0246
	1.0240	1.0240
Piston Diameter	2.6340	2.7910
	2.6330	2.7900
Ring Groove Side Clearance 1st & 2nd Comp.	.002	.002
	.005	.005
Side Clearance (Bot.) Oil	.0005	.0005
	.0035	.0035
Piston Skirt Clearance	.004	.004
	.006	.006
Ring End Gap	.007	.007
	.020	.020
Cylinder Main Brg. Dia	1.0262	1.0262
	1.0257	1.0257
Cylinder Cover/Flange Main Bearing Diameter	1.0262	1.0262
	1.0257	1.0257

VECTOR TORQUE SPECIFICATIONS

	Inch-Lbs.
Governor Rod Clamp to Lever	7-12
Breather Cover	40-50
Valve Box Cover	25-35
Connecting Rod	95-110
Cylinder Head	180-220
Mounting Flange or Cylinder Cover	100-130
Housing Baffle to Cylinder	80-120
Solid State Ignition to Cylinder	30-50
Alternating Coil Assembly to Lamination	25-35
Flywheel Nut	400-440
Housing to Baffle	35-45
Carburetor Stud to Cylinder	50-75
A/C Hex Nut to Stud	35-45
Control Face Plate to Baffle	30-40
Starter - Top Mounting	20-30
Electric Starter to Baffle	10-15
5/8-18 Plug (Hex Flange)	90-150
Plastic Tank to Housing	12-20
Threaded Fill Tube (Plastic)	45-65
Large Diameter Oil Fill Plug	Hand Tight
Muffler Mounting (Shoulder Screw)	100-165
A/C Body & Housing to Baffle	35-45
Conduit Clip Screw	5-15
Muffler Deflector	10-25

18
Wisconsin

ENGINE IDENTIFICATION

There is a Wisconsin name plate attached to the blower housing of the engine on which is stamped the model number, serial number, and specification number along with the size and rpm rating. The model, serial, and specification number must be given when obtaining replacement parts for any of the engines. Make certain that the identification plate remains with the engine on which it was originally installed.

MAINTENANCE

Air Cleaner Service
DRY ELEMENT TYPE

If the unit is operated in a very dusty atmosphere, remove the element by unscrewing the wingnut and removing the cover. Shake out accumulated dirt (do not tap) once each day. Under normal operating conditions, the most frequent service required is a weekly washing of the element. Rinse the element under cold water and then dip repeatedly into a solution of mild, non-sudsing detergent and warm water. Rinse in cold water and allow to dry overnight. Avoid freezing temperatures until the element is dry.

After five washings, or one year of service, whichever comes first, replace the element.

OIL BATH TYPE
All Series Except ACN and BKN

If the engine is run in a very dusty atmosphere, service the cleaner daily according to the instructions printed on the unit.

Ordinarily, remove the wingnut and pull off the cover and filter element and wash it in solvent. Drain oil from the filter bowl and clean it with a clean rag. Fill the filter bowl with engine oil to the line, and reassemble the unit. Install the wing nut.

ACN and BKN

The air cleaner must be serviced frequently: weekly in a clean atmosphere, and as often as daily in a dusty atmosphere. Ordinary service consists of snapping off the spring bail and re-

Wisconsin name plate

General Engine Specifications

Model	Bore & Stroke (in.)	Displacement (cu. in.)	Horsepower @ RPM
S-7D	3 x 2⅝	18.6	7.25 @ 3600
S-8D	3⅛ x 2⅝	20.2	8.25 @ 3600
TR-10D	3⅛ x 2⅝	20.2	—
TRA-10D	3⅛ x 2⅞	22.05	10.1 @ 3600
TRA-12D	3½ x 2⅞	27.66	12.0 @ 3600
ALN	2⅝ x 2¾	14.9	6.0 @ 3600
BKN	2⅞ x 2¾	17.8	7.0 @ 3600
AEN	3 x 3¼	23.0	9.2 @ 3600
AENL	3 x 3¼	23.0	9.2 @ 3600
AENS	3 x 3¼	23.0	9.2 @ 3600

Special type oil bath air cleaner used on series ACN and BKN

Dry type air cleaner

Crankcase Capacity Chart

S-7D, S-8D, TR-10D, TRA-10D, TRA-12D	1 qt.
AEN, AENL, AENS	3 pts.
ACN, BKN	2 pts.
Clutch Unit Housing—ACN, BKN	½ pt.
Reduction Unit Housing—ACN, BKN	1 pt.

service and may be left on the engine. However, if extreme conditions have made it dusty, remove it from the engine bracket and wash it in solvent.

Lubrication

OIL AND FUEL RECOMMENDATIONS

Oils of grade SG may be used in Wisconsin engines. Viscosity recommendations are as follows:
- Above 40°F (4°C) − SAE 30
- 15°F to 40°F (−9°C to +4°C) − SAE 20–20W
- 0°F to 15°F (−18°C to −9°C) − SAE 10W
- Below 0°F (−18°C) − SAE 5W–20

Fuel should be regular grade of 90 octane or above. Fuel should be of known quality to provide adequate protection against gum formation, and adequate assurance that it will be free of moisture and sediment. Remember that fuel of too low an octane rating may cause engine knock and severe damage.

Check the oil level every 8 hours and replenish. Check more frequently when the engine is

Oil bath type air cleaner

moving the bowl from the bottom of the unit for service. Clean out the cup and baffle, and then refill with about 4 fl.oz. (118mL) of engine oil.

The filter element does not ordinarily need

Tune-Up Specifications

Model	Plug Type	Plug Gap (in.)	Point Gap (in.)	Idle Speed
S-7D	AC-C86, Champion D-16J	.030	.020	①
S-8D	AC-C86, Champion D-16J	.030	.020	①
TR-10D	AC-C86, Champion D-16J	.030	.020	②
TRA-10D	AC-C86, Champion D-16J	.030	.020	②
TRA-12D	AC-C86, Champion D-16J	.030	.020	②
ACN	AC-C86, Champion D-16J	.030	.020 ③	④
BKN	AC-C86, Champion D-16J	.030	.020 ③	④
AEN	AC-C86, Champion D-16J	.030	.020 ③	④
AENL	AC-C86, Champion D-16J	.030	.020 ③ ₁	④
AENS	AC-C86, Champion D-16J	.030	.020 ③	④

① Throttle screw 2 turns open, or lowest smooth speed
② Throttle screw 1¼ turns open, or lowest smooth speed
③ Applies to battery ignition—with magneto, point gap is .015
④ Lowest smooth speed

new. Drain the old oil and replace it every 50 operating hours. Always change the oil when the engine is hot, by removing the crankcase drain plug. Fill crankcase to the level of the filler plug hole.

Spark Plugs

The outside of the plug, the electrodes and insulator on the underside should be kept clean. As often as significant deposits form, remove the plug and wire brush deposits away. Set the spark plug gap by bending the side electrode to get a gap of 0.030 in. (0.76mm), as measured by a wire type feeler gauge. Clean the threads on the plug and in the cylinder head before installing the plug. Use a new gasket, and torque to 25–30 ft. lbs. If the plug has deposits than cannot be removed, or if the electrodes are badly burned or there is evidence of cracking of the insulator, either inside or outside, replace the plug.

Breaker Points

REMOVAL AND INSTALLATION

1. Remove the breaker box cover.
2. Disconnect the terminal strip by loosening the screw and pulling it off the contact set.
3. Remove the point attaching screws and remove the contact set.
4. To install, first position the points, noting that on some types a prong located on the underside of the contact set must fit into a hole in the breaker box. Install the mounting screw or screws just tightly enough to hold the contacts in place.

5. Set the gap and time the engine as described in the procedures below.

SETTING BREAKER GAP

1. If necessary, loosen the breaker mounting screws so the point gap can be changed. Turn the engine flywheel back and forth until the contacts are as far apart as they can be.
2. Place the screwdriver in the adjusting slot and slide a flat feeler gauge of the proper dimension (see tune-up chart) between the contacts.
3. Adjust the gap with the screwdriver until the gauge has a very slight pull when sliding straight through the point gap.
4. On AEN, AENL, AENS, ACN, and BKN, tighten the contact mounting screw. Then, recheck the gap. Reset if necessary. On these engines, timing need not be reset after contact gap

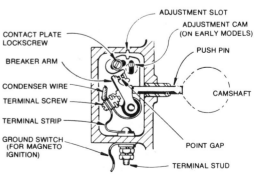

Locations of breaker points, lockscrew, and terminal strip in a typical breaker box adjustment unless the magneto or timer position has been disturbed.

5. On all other engines, leave the contact mounting screw(s) only slightly tight, and proceed to the engine timing procedure below.

Ignition Timing Adjustment

S–7D, S–8D, TR–10D, TRA–10D and TRA–12D

1. Remove the breaker box cover. Disconnect the coil primary wire at the bottom of the breaker box.

2. Line up the flywheel timing mark and the pointer with the engine on compression stroke. The timing mark on the flywheel can be seen through the opening on the right side of the flywheel shroud. The engine is on the compression stroke if the breaker arm push pin is moving as the timing marks approach alignment.

3. Connect a self powered test lamp or timing light between an engine ground and the terminal stud on the bottom of the breaker box. If necessary, slightly loosen the contact set mounting screw so the gap can easily be changed.

4. Close the points slowly with a screwdriver in the adjusting slot, just until the light goes out. Tighten the mounting screw.

5. Turn the flywheel counterclockwise until the light goes on, and then rotate it slowly forward and stop just as light goes out. At this point, the timing marks should be lined up. If necessary, readjust the gap slightly. Widen the gap if the light goes out too early; narrow the gap if the light goes out too soon.

6. Install the breaker cover and reconnect the primary wire to the terminal stud.

AEN, AENL, AENS, ACN AND BKN WITH MAGNETO

1. The magneto need not be timed unless it is removed from the engine. On ACN and BKN engines, take off the shroud and remove the timing inspection hole plug. On AEN, AENL and AENS engines, simply remove the plug, which is located near the magneto mounting. Remove the spark plug. Then, turn the engine over until the piston is coming up on compression stroke (air will be expelled from the spark plug hole) and the **D/C** and **X** marked vane on the flywheel lines up with the mark on the vertical centerline of the cooling shroud. On AEN, AENL and AENS engines, remove the plug from the hole in the shroud to see the flywheel marks.

2. When installing the magneto on ACN and BKN engines, mesh the magneto and camshaft gears so the two timing marks line up. They are visible through the inspection hole located to

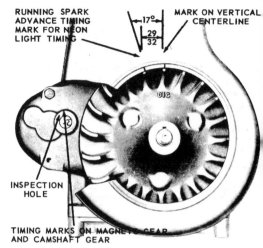

Magneto timing marks for ACN, BKN engines

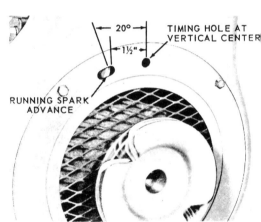

Flywheel timing marks can be seen by removing the plug in the fan shroud on AEN, AENL, and AENS engines

the left side of the flywheel. On AEN, AENL and AENS engines, mesh the magneto gears so that the **X** marked gear tooth is visible through the inspection hole.

3. Timing may be checked by slowly rotating the engine past the point where the flywheel **D/C** and **X** marked vanes pass the vertical centerline mark. The impulse coupling will snap when the marks are lined up, if the timing is correct.

AEN, AENL, AENS, ACN AND BKN ENGINES WITH BATTERY IGNITION

1. Set the engine flywheel at the position described in Step 1 of the procedure above, in the same way.

2. If the timer unit has been removed from the engine, turn the timer cam counterclock-

wise, using the gear on the back of the unit, until the points just begin to open (you will feel increased friction). Then, mount the timer to the engine.

3. Loosen the clamp lever screw which keeps the unit from rotating. On ACN and BKN engines, turn the timing unit clockwise $3/64$ in. (1.2mm) as measured on the circumference of the timer body, to get 2° of spark advance. On AEN, AENL and AENS engines, rotate the unit clockwise $1/8$ in. (3mm) to get 5° of advance.

4. Mark the timing marks with chalk, install the spark plug, and connect a timing light.

5. Start the engine and run it at 1800 rpm or higher, as measured with a tach. On ACN and BKN engines, turn the unit as required to align the flywheel mark and the running advance timing mark, located on the shroud to the left (counterclockwise) of the centerline mark. On AEN, AENL and AENS engines, rotate the unit as necessary to align the marked vane of the flywheel with the running advance timing hole in the shroud. Tighten the clamp screw.

Carburetor Mixture Adjustments

1. If the engine seems to be running very poorly due to improper fuel/air mixture, or if it will not start, make the following preliminary settings. Make the settings by turning the mixture screw in until it seats only very gently, then outward the required number of turns:

• S-7D, S-8D — Turn main jet adjustment out 1–1¼ turns.
• AEN, AENL, AENS — Turn main jet adjustment out 1¼ turns.
• ACN, BKB — Turn main jet adjustment out 1¼ turns.
• TRA-12D, TRA-10D, TR-10D — Turn main jet open 1¼ turns, idle jet open 1 turn.

2. After making preliminary settings, run the engine until hot and check acceleration. If engine stumbles, open the main jet ¼ turn at a time until response is smooth.

3. Slow the engine down to idle speed and adjust idle mixture screw in or out for the smoothest idle.

Governor Adjustment

S–7D, S–8D, TR–10D, TRA–10D AND TRA–12D

1. Loosen the governor lever clamp screw so that the fulcrum shaft can be turned independently of the governor lever and the lever moves to full throttle position. Then, turn the shaft counterclockwise until the internal governor vane stops against the flywheel thrust pin.

2. Tighten the clamp screw. See "Speed Adjustment" below.

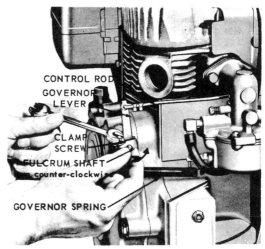

Making S-7D and S-8D governor adjustment

ACN, BKN, AENL, AEN AND AENS

1. Disconnect the rod at the governor lever. Move the rod as far as possible toward the carburetor.

2. Move the governor lever as far as possible in the same direction.

3. Hold both parts in this position and turn the rod in or out of the swivel block until the hole in the lever indexes with the end of the rod. On ACN and BKN engines, turn the rod two more turns inward. Install the rod in the lever and install the cotter pin. See "Speed Adjustment" below.

SPEED ADJUSTMENT

The governor lever is provided with a number of holes so that the engine can be operated at different speeds. If the governor spring has been removed from the hole, or if the speed range of the engine is to be changed, the proper hole in the lever must first be selected, and the adjusting screw must then be turned for fine adjustment.

1. Run the engine until hot, and connect a tachometer. Open the throttle control and install the governor spring into each of the holes in the lever to get as close as possible to the desired rpm (holes further away from the fulcrum of the lever give more speed). Once you've found the hole nearest the desired speed, note which hole you are using.

2. Loosen the locknut, disconnect the spring, and turn the screw for more tension to increase speed, or for less tension to decrease it.

Compression Check

No precise method of checking compression is required. However, on engines without compression release, compression may be checked by spinning the engine in the normal direction of rotation and checking for a substantial increase in resistance when the piston begins coming up on the compression stroke.

Generally, when compression is poor, the engine requires disassembly and major work. However, compression can be low because a long period without operation has permitted oil to drain off the cylinder walls. If this is suspected, remove the spark plug and squirt a small quantity of engine oil into the combustion chamber to seal it.

FUEL SYSTEM

Carburetor

DISASSEMBLY AND REASSEMBLY

NOTE: *See item below for inspection and cleaning procedure.*

Zenith 87 and Wisconsin L–51

1. Remove the three bowl assembly screws (37 & 38) and lockwashers (36) and separate fuel bowl (30) from throttle body (9).

2. Remove the main jet adjustment (34) and fiber washer (33), using a $^9/_{16}$ in. open end wrench.

3. Remove the main jet (32) and fiber washer (31), using Zenith Tool No. C161–83 main jet wrench or equivalent.

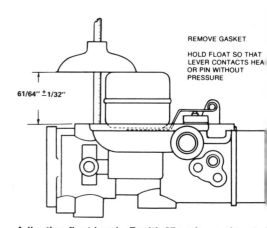

REMOVE GASKET

HOLD FLOAT SO THAT LEVER CONTACTS HEA OR PIN WITHOUT PRESSURE

61/64" ±1/32"

Adjusting float level—Zenith 87 series carburetor

4. Remove the idle jet (29), using a smal screwdriver.

5. Remove the bowl drain plug (35).

6. Remove the float axle (26) by pressing against the end with the blade of a screwdriver

7. Remove the float (27).

8. Remove the fuel valve needle (25), with your fingers.

9. Remove the fuel bowl to throttle body gas ket (28).

10. Remove the main discharge jet (23), using a small screwdriver.

11. Remove the fuel valve seat (25) and fiber washer (24), using Zenith Tool No. C161–85 or equivalent.

12. Remove the idle adjusting needle (11) and spring (10).

13. Install the fuel valve seat (25) and fiber washer (24), using Zenith Tool No. C161–85 or equivalent.

14. Install the main discharge jet (23), using a small screwdriver.

15. Install fuel valve needle (25) in seat (25) followed by float (27). Insert tapered end of float axle (26) into float bracket on side opposite slot and push through the other side. Press float axle (26) into slotted side until the axle is centered in bracket.

16. Check position of float assembly for correct measurement to obtain proper fuel leve using a depth gauge.

NOTE: *Do not bend, twist, or apply pressure on the float body. With bowl cover assembly in an inverted position, viewed from free end of float, the float body must be centered and a right angles to the machined surface. The float setting is measured from the machined surface (no gasket) of float bowl cover to top side of float body at highest point. This mea surement should be $^{61}/_{64}$ in. ± $^1/_{32}$ in (24.2mm ± 0.8mm). To increase or decrease distance between float body and machined*

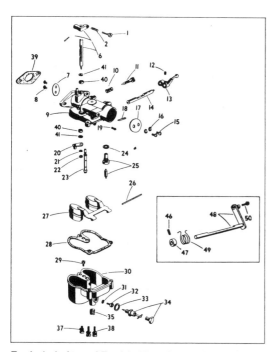

Exploded view of Zenith 87 series carburetor

surface use long nosed pliers and bend lever close to float body. Replace with new float if position is off more than $\frac{1}{16}$ in. (1.6mm).

17. Install throttle body to fuel bowl assembly gasket (29) on machined surface of throttle body (9).

18. Install the idle adjusting needle (11) and spring (10).

19. Install the main jet (32) and fiber washer (31), using Zenith Tool No. C161–83 main jet wrench or equivalent.

20. Install the main jet adjusting needle assembly (34) and fiber washer (33), using a $\frac{9}{16}$ in. open end wrench.

21. Install the idle jet (29), using a small screwdriver.

22. Install the bowl drain plug (35).

23. Install the three bowl assembly screws (38) and lockwashers (36) through the fuel bowl and into the throttle body and draw down firmly and evenly.

Zenith 72Y6

1. Remove the three assembly screws (2) that hold the bowl cover to the bowl.

2. Separate the bowl cover assembly (1) from the bowl assembly.

3. Remove the float axle (13) and float (12).

4. Remove the bowl cover gasket (16).

5. Remove the fuel valve needle and seat (15) with the gasket (14). Remove the fuel valve seat. Use tool C161–85 or equivalent.

6. Remove the idle adjusting screw needle (3) and spring (4).

7. Remove the throttle stop screw (5) and spring (6).

8. Hold the bowl cover inverted with the mounting flange to your right. Note that the closed throttle plate slopes down and away from you and that there is a mark stamped on the high side of the throttle plate. It is important that upon reassembly this same relationship is retained.

9. Hold the throttle shaft in the closed position, remove the throttle plate screw and lockwasher (11) and throttle plate (10).

10. Remove the throttle shaft and lever (9).

11. With a screwdriver, or similar tool, remove the throttle shaft dust seal retainer (8) and rubber shaft seal (7).

12. Remove the venturi (17) and idle tube (18) by inverting bowl cover.

NOTE: *Do not attempt to remove the main discharge jet. This part is pressed in and is not a serviceable item.*

13. Remove the lower main jet plug if a plug is used or remove the main jet adjustment (20) and gasket (21). Then remove the main jet (22). Use tool C161–83 or equivalent.

14. Hold the bowl (19) in a vertical position

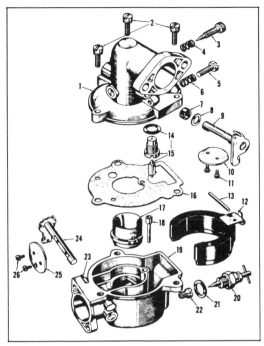

Exploded view of Zenith 72Y6 carburetor

with the air intake and bottom of bowl next to you and note that the closed choke plate slopes down and away. Observe the marking on the choke plate. It is important that upon reassembly, this same relationship is retained.

15. Remove the choke plate screws and lockwashers (26), choke plate (25), shaft and lever (24).

NOTE: *During cleaning, do not soak the float in solvent.*

16. Hold the bowl (19) vertically (with air intake upward), and insert the choke shaft and lever with the lever pointing downward.

17. Install the choke plate (25) with the letter **Z** toward the bottom of bowl.

18. Start, but do not tighten both the choke plate screw and the lockwasher (26).

19. Center the choke plate in the air intake bore by lightly tapping the choke plate on the high side. Hold it in this position with a finger and tighten the choke plate screws.

20. Install the main jet (22) using tool C161–83 or equivalent.

NOTE: *Before installing the main jet (20) and gasket (21), turn the adjusting needle several turns to the left (counterclockwise) to avoid damage to the main jet orifice during assembly.*

21. Install the main jet plug with a new fiber washer (21).

22. Hold the bowl in the operating position and install the idle jet (18), tube end down.

23. Install the venturi with the key at the lower edge of the venturi, in the matching slot at the choke valve side of the bowl.

24. Assemble a new rubber dust seal (7) against the throttle shaft bearing, with the lips of the seal toward the outside.

25. Install and stake the seal retainer washer (8).

26. Assemble the throttle shaft and lever (9) with the wide open stop lug (narrow lug) on shaft lever in contact with the stop on the casting when the shaft is in the wide open throttle position.

27. Hold the bowl cover inverted, with the mounting flange toward your right.

28. Install the throttle plate (10) with the mark stamped on the throttle plate on the high side of the plate and toward you.

29. Start, but do not tighten both throttle plate screw and lockwasher (11).

30. Gently tap the high side of the throttle plate to center the plate. Hold in this position with a finger and tighten the throttle plate screws.

31. Install the throttle stop screw (5) and spring (6).

32. Install the idle adjusting needle (3) and spring (4).

33. Install the fuel valve seat (15) with a fiber washer (14). Use tool C161–85 or equivalent.

34. Assemble the fuel valve needle and bowl cover gasket (16).

35. Carefully examine the float assembly (12) for evidence of wear or damage. This type of float is not adjustable and wear in any part of the fuel valve and float hinge assembly will raise the fuel level.

36. Install the float and float axle pin (13). Insert the bowl cover and check the float in the closed position. The float setting will be within limits if the float is parallel to the gasket seating surfaces of the bowl cover. Any necessary float correction should be made by replacing worn parts. DO NOT attempt to bend the float bracket.

37. Attach the bowl cover assembly (1) to the bowl using the three assembly screws (2).

Zenith 68–7

Use the detailed exploded view to guide you in disassembling and reassembling the carburetor. Clean and inspect all parts as described in the section below. When the float has been reassembled to the throttle body, invert the throttle body and support the float so that the lever contacts the head of the float pin without pressure. Measure from the surface of the casting (without gasket) to the top surface of the float (which is the bottom surface during normal operation). The distance should be $^{15}/_{32}$ in. $\pm$ $^{1}/_{32}$ in. (12mm

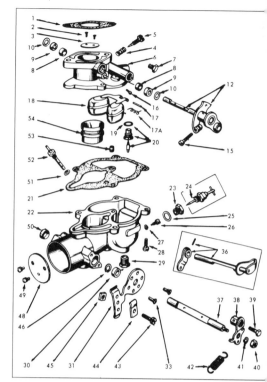

Exploded view of Zenith 68-7 carburetor

$\pm$ 0.8mm). If distance is incorrect, bend the float lever close to the float body with long nose pliers.

CLEANING AND INSPECTION

1. Clean all of the metal parts in a suitable solvent, removing all carbon deposits from the throttle bore and idle discharge passages. To ensure that all dirt is removed, blow compressed air through all passages in the throttle body and fuel bowl in the reverse direction from normal flow.

NOTE: *Never use wire or a drill to clean jet orifices or idle port openings.*

2. Check the float and make sure that it is not soaked with gasoline. Also check for wear on the float hinge and where the float contacts the inlet needle. Replace the float if any of the above conditions exist.

3. Inspect the main jet adjustment needle and the idle adjusting needle tapered ends to make sure that they are smooth and not grooved from being seated too hard. If there is a groove around the end of the taper, or if it is pitted, replace the needle.

4. Check the fuel inlet valve and seat for wear or damage. Replace the entire assembly as a unit if it doesn't look like new.

5. All gaskets, seals, retainers, and rubber O-rings must be replaced every time the carbure-

tor is overhauled, with the possible exception of the rubber O-rings which can be retained if they are in good condition.

6. Make preliminary adjustments of the main and idle jet adjusting needles before re-mounting the carburetor on the engine.

Fuel Pump

These instructions refer to overhaul of the LP–62 Series fuel pumps used on some Wisconsin engines. The pump requires rebuilding sometime after 500 hours of operation.

1. Disconnect the fuel lines and, if so equipped, remove the fuel strainer.

2. Scribe a mark across the two halves of the body. Use this mark to positively indicate fuel line inlet and outlet positions. Then, remove the fuel head-to-bracket screws (12), and re-move the fuel head (10).

3. Turn the fuel head over, note the positions of the valve assemblies, and then discard them. Clean the fuel head thoroughly in kerosene us-ing a fine wire brush.

4. Hold the head with the diaphragm surface upward, and evenly press in new valve gaskets. Carefully press in new valve assemblies evenly and without any distortion. Make sure each as-

sembly faces in the proper direction — they are check valves.

5. Remove the rocker arm spring (11) from the lower diaphragm section by inserting a screwdriver between coils and prying it out.

6. Hold the mounting bracket (9) in your left hand with the rocker arm toward you and your thumbnail on the end of the link (8). Compress the diaphragm spring (3) by placing the heel of your other hand on the diaphragm (2), and then rotate your hand 90° clockwise to unhook the diaphragm from the link. Remove the diaphragm.

7. Clean the mounting bracket in the same way you cleaned the fuel head.

8. Install the new diaphragm spring onto the bracket (9). Reconnect the new diaphragm to the link by reversing the removal procedure (Step 6). Replace the rocker arm spring (11).

9. Mount the completed mounting bracket assembly (9) onto the engine, using a new gasket (13).

10. Crank the engine over until the dia-phragm is laying flat on the mounting bracket. Remount the fuel head (10) with match marks aligned, tightening the screws only three turns. Crank the engine over until the diaphragm is pulled down to its lowest position. Fully tighten screws.

11. Remount the strainer (if so equipped) and install fuel lines to proper connections.

Governor

The governor consists of hardened parts which are only slightly stressed, so repair is rarely necessary. If parts must be replaced, however, the following procedure is useful in reassembling these heavily sprung parts:

Slip the spacer onto the camshaft first. Then, separate the flyweights far enough to permit the thrust sleeve to pass between them. Slide the thrust sleeve back so the flyweights will be

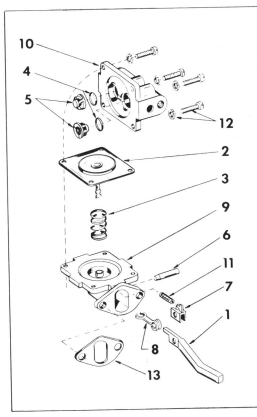

Fuel pump—exploded view

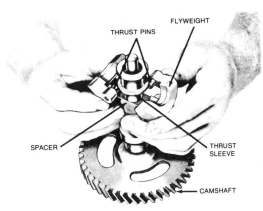

Assembling the governor

closed down between the two flanges of the thrust sleeve.

ENGINE OVERHAUL

The disassembly, inspection, and assembly of each component of the engine is discussed separately, because many times it is not necessary to disassemble the entire engine. The order in which the disassembly procedures are given may be changed to suit the job.

Whenever the engine is either partially or completely disassembled, all of the parts removed should be thoroughly cleaned. Be sure to use new gaskets when reassembling the engine and to lubricate all bearings.

If the engine is to be completely overhauled, remove the engine from the machinery it drives or operates and remove any accessories. If an external component is to be removed, or a minor adjustment made, it may not be necessary to remove the engine from the equipment it powers.

Fuel Tank

Close the fuel tank outlet valve and remove the fuel line. Unscrew the nuts or bolts that retain the tank to the cylinder head bolts and crankcase. The tank and bracket may then be removed as a complete unit. Replace the tank in reverse order, torquing cylinder head in sequence.

Air Cleaner and Carburetor

Unscrew the wing nut and remove the air cleaner. Remove the breather line at the inspection cover, the throttle rod clip at the governor lever, and the fuel line. Unscrew the bolts which hold the carburetor bracket and manifold to the engine and remove the carburetor and air cleaner bracket and the manifold as one. Replace in reverse order.

Starter Sheave and Flywheel Shroud

Remove the starter sheave by removing the three screws and washers which retain it to the flywheel. Remove the top cover and the cylinder side shroud. Disconnect the governor spring and remove the four screws that hold the flywheel shroud to the back plate. The entire flywheel shroud may now be removed. The back plate can be removed, if necessary, only after the flywheel is removed. Reassemble in the reverse order. Apply a ¼ in. (6mm) long bead of #271 Loctite® to the thread ends of the capscrews for mounting the sheet metal starter sheave. Use plain washers and lockwashers in

place of the rubber washers used previously and torque to 9–10 ft. lbs.

Rope Starter Sheave

Loosen and remove the rope starter sheave by installing a wrench on the hexagonal hub of the sheave and striking a sharp blow in the proper direction. Install in reverse order.

Air Shroud

Remove the cylinder head capscrews and, in cases where so equipped, the crankcase cap screws, and remove the air shroud. Usually, the fuel tank must be removed to remove this shroud, and in some cases, common mounting bolts may be used.

Cylinder Head

Remove the spark plug and unscrew the five cap screws that attach the cylinder head. Remove the cylinder head and gasket. Clean the carbon from the combustion chamber and all dirt from the cooling fins. Use a new gasket when installing the head. If screws of different lengths are used, judge their locations in reassembly from the lengths of the bosses on the head.

LARGE INSIDE RADIUS
TOWARD INLET VALVE

Removal and installation of the cylinder head and gasket

Torque the bolts precisely according to instructions below:
- ACN and BKN — Torque bolts to 14–18 ft. lbs.
- TR–10D, TRA–10D, TRA–12D, S–7D and S–8D — torque to 10 ft. lbs. all around; then to 14 ft. lbs; and finally to 18 ft. lbs.
- AEN, AENL and AENS — Coat screw threads with a mixture of oil and graphite and torque to 32 ft. lbs.

Valves and Valve Seat Inserts

Remove the valve inspection cover which is also the breather assembly. Use a valve spring compressor to compress the valve springs. On TR and TRA Model engines, be careful not to damage the breather reed in the valve spring compartment in compressing valve springs. Remove the valve spring retainers, the compressor, and the valve springs; take the valve out from the top of the cylinder block. Clean all carbon deposits from the valves, seats, ports, and guides. Inspect the condition of the valves, stems, guides, and seats, looking for burned, pitted, scored, or warped surfaces.

The exhaust valve and seat are made of Stellite®. A valve rotator is used on the exhaust valve only. Clean the valve rotator and make sure that it operates properly.

Both intake and exhaust valves have removable seat inserts on AEN, AENL and AENS models. On all other models, only the exhaust seat insert is replaceable. Valve seats are removed by means of a special puller. After the new seats are installed, they should be ground to the proper angle.

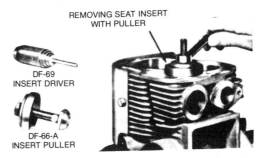

REMOVING SEAT INSERT WITH PULLER

DF-69 INSERT DRIVER

DF-66-A INSERT PULLER

Removal and installation of the valve seat inserts using special tools

Before grinding the seats or valves, check the valve-to-guide clearance. The illustration shows specifications for TR, TRA and S series engines. For AEN, AENL, AENS and ACH, stem-to-guide clearance is 0.003–0.005 in. (0.076–0.127mm) initially, and the limit is 0.007 in. (0.178mm). Valve and seat angles are 45° for these engines, also. Try replacing the valve to get the proper clearance. If clearance is still excessive, the guides can be pressed out and new ones installed (pressed in). A special tool, Wisconsin DF–72 driver or equivalent is required in installation of new guides. The guide must go in with the internal chamfer downward (towards the camshaft). All guides are pressed in with the top surface flush with the guide boss except for exhaust valve guides on TR and TRA series engines. On these models, the exhaust guide must extend $1/32$ in. (0.8mm) above the guide boss.

On TR and TRA series engines only, valve guides must be reamed to the dimensions shown in the illustration after they have been pressed into the guide bosses.

The valves should be ground (machined) at an authorized Wisconsin engine service outlet or other qualified machine shop to the specifications shown in the illustration. Then, they must be lapped, using a valve grinding compound by turning them back and forth from above with light downward pressure. Check the effectiveness of the lapping process by putting a dye such as "Prussian Blue" or a similar product on the valve sealing surface and seating the valve. The dye will show the pattern of the effective contact between valve and seat on the seat. The pattern shown must be a wide, uniform ring.

Finally, clean the valves and block with soap and water, rinse and wipe thoroughly, and then apply a coating of light oil to the cylinder walls to prevent rust.

Valve tappet clearance must be checked before the springs and keepers are reassembled

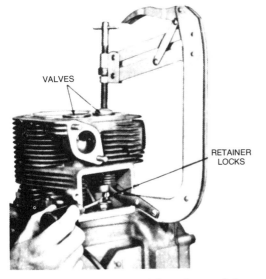

VALVES

RETAINER LOCKS

Removal and installation of the valves, retainers, and springs

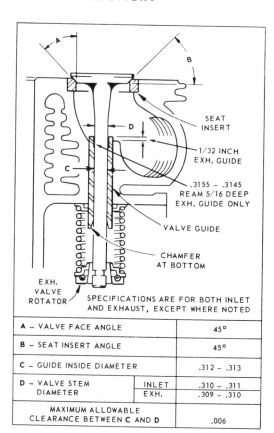

A – VALVE FACE ANGLE		45°	
B – SEAT INSERT ANGLE		45°	
C – GUIDE INSIDE DIAMETER		.312 – .313	
D – VALVE STEM DIAMETER	INLET	.310 – .311	
	EXH.	.309 – .310	
MAXIMUM ALLOWABLE CLEARANCE BETWEEN C AND D		.006	

Valve and guide measurements for TR and TRA and S-7 and S-8 Series engines

except on engines with adjustable tappets. Install the valves into the guides and seat them. Turn the camshaft as necessary until the cam for the valve to be checked points downward (the tappet is at the lowest possible position). If the engine uses a compression release, make sure the tappet is not riding on the compression release spoiler cam. Check the clearance between the head of the valve stem and the tappet. Clearance should be:

	Intake	Exhaust
TR and TRA Series Engines:	.006	.015
AEN, AENL, AENS Series Engines:	.008	.016
S-7D, S-8D Engines:	.006	.012
ACN, BKN Engines:	.008	.014

On engines with adjustable tappets, loosen the locknut with an open end wrench and turn the adjusting nut with another open end wrench until the gauge fits between the tappet and valve stem and can be pulled between the two with a slight amount of effort. On engines with plain tappets, if the clearance is smaller than specification, so that gauge cannot be inserted without lifting the valve off the seat, remove the valve and grind a small amount off the end of the stem. Recheck the clearance until it is adequate. Make sure the stem end is ground absolutely flat (parallel to the valve face) and that all grinding chips, etc. are removed from the valve stem before installation.

Assemble the springs, spring and spring seats or rotators, compress the springs, and install the retainer locks. Make sure the springs are seated properly in the locator cups. If they are not properly seated, they could cock to one side and cause the valve to stick.

Flywheel

ALL TR, TRA AND S ENGINES

If the flywheel is to be removed, loosen the retaining nut before the gear cover on the opposite end is removed.

NOTE: *Do not try to loosen the flywheel after the gear cover is removed. Do not strike the crankshaft when it is not supported by the gear cover.*

To remove the flywheel, first straighten the tab of the washer under the flywheel retaining nut. Place the correct size wrench on the flywheel retaining nut and strike the wrench sharply with a hammer to loosen the nut. Do not remove the nut completely, just unscrew it until it is flush with the end of the crankshaft. Turn the crankshaft until the keyway is at 10 o'clock. Pry outward on the flywheel with the outer end of the prybar at the 10 o'clock position on the flywheel. At the same time strike the end of the crankshaft with a soft hammer. This will loosen the flywheel from the tapered end of the crankshaft. Loosen the flywheel, but do not remove it at this point. It is necessary for the flywheel to remain on the crankshaft and support it while the gear cover and connecting rod are removed. Remove the flywheel only after the piston and connecting rod are removed.

When reassembling the engine, install the flywheel after the crankshaft is installed. Make sure that the woodruff key is in place before positioning the flywheel onto the crankshaft. Do not drive the flywheel onto the crankshaft by striking it with a hammer. Place a small length of pipe against the hub of the flywheel and tap the end of the pipe with a soft hammer until the flywheel is seated on the crankshaft taper. Assemble the washer and nut to the crankshaft with the tab of the washer inserted into the keyway of the flywheel. Tighten the nut only enough to hold the flywheel in place. Only after the crankshaft endplay has been adjusted is the flywheel nut to be tightened by sharply striking the wrench with a soft hammer. Bend the tab of the washer up against the nut.

AENL, AEN, AENS, ACN AND BKN ENGINES

1. Remove the four air intake screen mounting screws, and remove the screen.

2. Pull outward on the flywheel air fins, and gently tap on the end of the crankshaft with a soft hammer (do not use an ordinary, hard hammer) until the flywheel slides off the crankshaft taper.

3. To install the flywheel, first put the crankshaft key into position in the crankshaft keyway. Then, line up the keyway in the flywheel with the key, and slide the flywheel into position on the crankshaft taper. Finally, position a piece of pipe around the crankshaft and against the hub of the flywheel and strike the end of it sharply with the hammer.

Gear Cover

TR, TRA AND S ENGINES

To remove the gear cover, unscrew the cover cap screws and remove the governor lever. Tap the two dowel pins lightly from the crankcase side to break the cover loose from the crankcase.

NOTE: *A steel ball for the end thrust of the camshaft will most likely fall out when the cover is removed. Remove the spring from the end of the camshaft so it won't be lost.*

To reassemble the gear cover to the engine, position the spring into the end of the camshaft and mount the governor flyweight assembly.

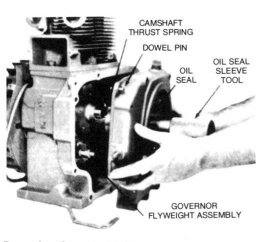

Removing the gear cover

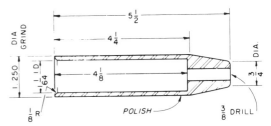

SLEEVE FOR ASSEMBLING GEAR COVER WITH OIL SEAL, ON TO CRANKSHAFT.

Dimensions of a suitable oil seal installation sleeve

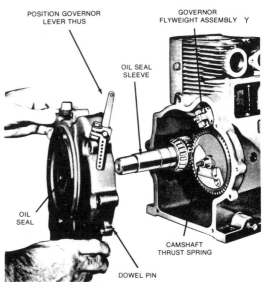

Positioning governor lever during gear cover installation

Lubricate the bearings, gears and tappets. Tap the dowel pins into the crankcase until they protrude about 1/8 in. (3mm) from the mounting flange face. Place a finger full of grease into the hole in the cover to retain the camshaft spring and ball in place. Lubricate the lip of the oil seal with engine oil. Lubricate the gear cover face with a light film of oil to hold the gasket in place. The best means of getting the oil seal onto the crankshaft is to make a tapered installation sleeve such as that shown in the illustration. If such a sleeve is available, or you can make one, install it onto the crankshaft.

Position the governor lever as shown in the illustration. Then, gently locate the cover around the crankshaft. If the seal sleeve is being used, it can simply be pushed into position. If a seal sleeve is not available, press the cover into position very carefully. It may be necessary to hold the crankshaft still and very gently rotate the cover back and forth in order to get it over the crankshaft sealing surface without damaging the seal.

Finally, remove the seal sleeve (if used) and torque the cover capscrews to 8 ft. lbs. Tap the dowel pins into place.

Connecting Rod, Piston and Piston Rings

TR, TRA AND S SERIES ENGINES

Unscrew the two cap bolts which hold the connecting rod cap to the connecting rod. The oil dipper will come off with the cap screws. Tap the ends of the bolts to loosen the connecting rod cap.

Remove all deposits from the cylinder that might hinder the removal of the piston. This is done with a ridge reamer.

Turn the crankshaft until the piston is at the top of the cylinder and push the connecting rod and piston assembly up and out of the engine.

The piston skirt is elliptical in shape. When measuring the piston-to-cylinder wall clearance, you must take the measurement at the bottom of the piston skirt thrust face. The thrust faces of the piston skirt are located at a 90° angle from the piston pin hole axis.

Install the piston rings so that the rings gaps are 90° apart around the circumference of the piston. A ring expander tool should be used to remove and install piston rings. If the tool is not available, the rings can be installed by placing

PISTON TO CYLINDER AT PISTON SKIRT THRUST FACES		.004 to .0045"
PISTON RING GAP		.010 to .020"
PISTON RING SIDE CLEARANCE IN GROOVES	TOP RING	.002 to .0035"
	2nd RING	.001 to .0025"
	OIL RING	.002 to .0035"
CONNECTING ROD TO CRANK PIN	DIAMETER	.0015 to .0005"
	SIDE	.009 to .016"
PISTON PIN TO CONNECTING ROD		.0002 to .0008"
PISTON PIN TO PISTON		.0000 to .0008" tight

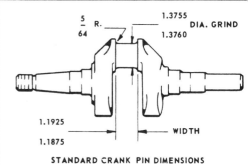

STANDARD CRANK PIN DIMENSIONS

Specifications for S series and TR and TRA engines except piston-to-cylinder specification for TRA-12D; that figure is .0025–.003 in

the open end of the ring into the appropriate groove and working the ring down over the piston. Install the bottom oil control ring first, the scraper ring second and the compression ring last. Be careful not to bend or distort the rings in any way. A notch mark or the word **top** will be stamped on each ring so as to identify which side of the ring should face the top of the piston. Before installing the piston assembly into the cylinder, oil the rings, cylinder wall, rod bearings, wrist pin and the piston itself. Use a ring compressor to install the piston assembly into the cylinder bore.

The piston and rod are mounted with the arrows on the connecting rod bolt boss and on th

Removing the piston and connecting rod assembly

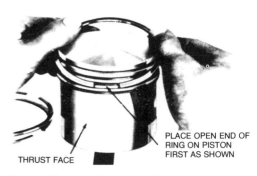

PLACE OPEN END OF RING ON PISTON FIRST AS SHOWN

THRUST FACE

Assembling a piston ring to the piston

ARROW
TOWARD OPEN END
OF CRANKCASE

Install the connecting rod and piston assembly with cast arrow facing open end of crankcase

CYLINDER BORE		3.0005 to 2.9995
PISTON TO CYLINDER AT PISTON SKIRT (THRUST FACE)	CAM-GROUND	SPLIT-SKIRT
	.003 to .0035"	.0045 to .005"
PISTON RING GAP		.010 to .022"
PISTON RING SIDE CLEARANCE IN GROOVES	TOP RING	.002 to .0035"
	2nd, 3rd RING	.001 to .0025"
	OIL RING	.0025 to .004"
PISTON PIN TO CONNECTING ROD BUSHING		.0005 to .0011"
PISTON PIN TO PISTON		.0000 to .0008" tight
CONNECTING ROD TO CRANK PIN – SIDE CLEARANCE		.009 to .018"
CONNECTING ROD **SHELL BEARING** TO CRANK PIN DIA. (VERTICAL)		.0011 to .0030"
CONNECTING ROD **BABBITT** BEARING TO CRANK PIN		.0007 to .0020"

Standard Crank Pin Dimensions $\frac{1}{8}$ R. 1.1260 / 1.1255 DIA. 1.255 / 1.250

Piston, ring, and connecting rod specifications for AEN, AENL, and AENS engines

cap matched up and facing toward the open end of the crankcase. The oil hole in the dipper, which is integral with the cap, will be toward the camshaft side of the engine.

If the cylinder is worn more than 0.005 in. (0.127mm) beyond the standard size, you should have it reground at an authorized Wisconsin shop or other reputable machine shop. It might be wise to consult with the machinist as to whether or not the rings should be replaced with a set of chromium rings. Rotate the crankshaft until it is at the bottom of its stroke. Tap the piston down so that the connecting rod seats onto the crankpin. Tighten the cap screws to 18–22 ft. lbs.

AEN, AENL, AENS, ACN AND BKN ENGINES

Drain the oil from the crankcase, and then place the engine on its side. Remove the base capscrews and washers, and remove the base and gasket. On AEN, AENL and AENS, remove the two capscrews which hold the oil pump to the crankcase and remove it.

Use a ½ in. socket wrench to remove the hex locknuts from the rod bolts. If there are lockwasher tabs, these must be straightened first. Tap the ends of the rod bolts lightly to free the cap, and remove it.

Use a ridge reamer to remove all carbon deposits from the cylinder wall above the piston. Turn the crankshaft until the piston is at the top of the cylinder. Push the rod and piston out through the top of the cylinder from below.

NOTE: *Do not let the rod bolts come in contact with the crankpin!*

AEN, AENL and AENS engines were originally furnished with babbit cast connecting rod bearings. The shell bearing type rods are now used, and these are interchangeable with the older type rod for service replacement. In reassembling shell bearings, make sure the locating lug for both bearing halves are on the same side of the rod — the side on which numbers are stamped. Fit the bearings according to the specifications shown.

In installing rings, use an expander, or, if none is available, install the rings open end first. Be careful to open the ring only far enough to get in onto the piston. Install the rings so the gaps are 90° apart. Go from bottom to top. Make sure the oil scraper ring is mounted as shown, with the scraper edge down, or severe oil pumping will result.

If the cylinder is worn more than 0.005 in. (0.127mm) beyond the standard size, you should have it reground at a Wisconsin authorized shop or other reputable machine shop. It might be wise to consult with the machinist on whether or not the rings should be replaced with a set of chromium rings.

On the AENL engine, if the split skirt type piston originally used is to be re-used, be sure to install it with the split toward the manifold side of the engine. In the case of cam ground pistons used on AEN, AENL and AENS engines, install the piston with the wide section of the skirt (wide thrust face) toward the fuel tank. Piston-to-cylinder clearance is measured at the center of the thrust face, at the bottom of the skirt.

When installing the piston into the cylinder, oil the rings, piston pin, rod bearings and cylinder wall. Use a ring compressor to hold the rings compressed while sliding the piston into the cylinder. On AEN, AENL and AENS engines, the numbers stamped on the rod and cap must be on the same side and the oil hole in the cap must face toward the oil pump.

On ACN and BKN engines, the arrow cast onto the connecting rod bolt boss must face toward the take-off end of the crankcase and the oil hole in the rod must face the camshaft.

The rod cap must be installed with the cast arrow lining up with the arrow on the rod.

Turn the crankshaft to Bottom Center position, and insert the piston into the cylinder, using a ring compressor until after the rings enter cylinder. Tap the piston down (with the rod hanging straight down) until the rod contacts the crankpin. Install the cap in the proper position as described above, and install the bolts and nuts (use new nuts on AEN, AENL and AENS). Torque to 14-20 ft. lbs. on ACN and BKN engines, 18-20 ft. lbs on AEN, AENL and AENS engines. Fold the lockwasher tabs over hex head and bolt boss, if so equipped.

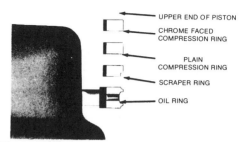

Piston ring locations for AEN, AENL, AENS, ACN engines. Note position in which oil scraper ring is mounted

Install the oil pump on AEN, AENL and AENS engines. Install the engine base using a new gasket. Torque the bolts to 6-8 ft. lbs. on ACN and BKN engines, and to 7-9 ft. lbs. on AEN, AENL and AENS engines.

Camshaft and Valve Tappets
S, TR AND TRA SERIES ENGINES

When removing the camshaft, turn the engine over on its side and push the tappets away from the camshaft so that they will clear the camshaft lobes when the camshaft is removed. the valves must be removed for this operation. After the camshaft is removed, mark the tappets as to location and then remove the valve tappets and inspect them for wear. The tappet stem diameter must be 0.309-0.310 in. (7.848-7.874mm), and the clearance in the guide hole must be 0.002-0.006 in. (0.05-0.15mm).

Install tappets into their original guide holes before installing the camshaft. Install the camshaft with the timing mark on the camshaft

PISTON TO CYLINDER	**MODEL ACN**	
	Up to 3000 R.P.M.	.005 to .0055"
AT	3000 R.P.M. & above	.006 to .0065"
	MODEL BKN	
PISTON SKIRT	Up to 3000 R.P.M.	.0055 to .006"
	3000 R.P.M. & above	.006 to .0065"
PISTON RING GAP		.012 to .022"
PISTON RING SIDE CLEARANCE IN GROOVES	TOP RING	.002 to .0035"
	2nd, 3rd RING	.001 to .0025"
	OIL RING	.0025 to .004"
CONNECTING ROD TO CRANK PIN – SIDE CLEARANCE		.009 to .016"
CONNECTING ROD **SHELL BEARING** TO CRANK PIN DIA. (VERTICAL)		.0009 to .0032"
CONNECTING ROD **BABBITT** BEARING TO CRANK PIN		.0007 to .002"
PISTON PIN TO CONNECTING ROD		.0001 to .0007"
PISTON PIN TO PISTON		.0000 to .0008" tight

Piston, ring, and connecting rod specifications for ACN and BKN engines

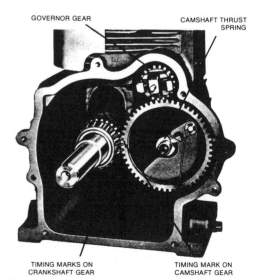

Aligning crankshaft gear and camshaft gear timing marks, S, TR and TRA engines

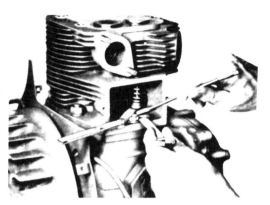

Adjusting valve tappet clearance

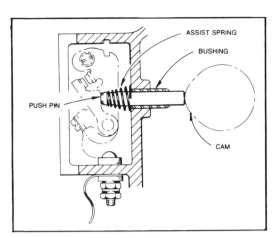

Breaker push pin and bushing

gear located between the two marked teeth on the crankshaft gear. Put the camshaft thrust spring into the end of the camshaft before installing the gear cover. Adjust or check the valve tappet clearance as described above.

ACN, BKN, AEN, AENL AND AENS ENGINES

To remove the camshaft, first raise the tappets until they clear the cam lobes. Pry out the expansion plug from the flywheel end of the crankcase. With a drift punch, drive out the camshaft pin from the flywheel end of the crankcase until it emerges from the opposite end of the crankcase. The camshaft should drop down inside the crankcase, with the expansion plug emerging in front of the camshaft pin.

On installation, align the timing marks as shown. Use new expansion plugs and make sure to drive in the camshaft support pin from the takeoff end of the crankcase.

Breaker Push Pin and Bushing
TR, TRA AND S SERIES ENGINES

Remove the breaker arm push pin and inspect it for wear. Replace parts as necessary. If

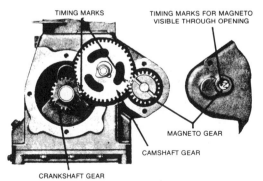

Aligning crankshaft, camshaft, and magneto timing marks, ACN, BKN, AEN, AENL, and AENS engines

you're replacing the pin, install the assist spring, small end toward the groove in the tapered end, from the plain end. The pin goes into the guide hole with the plain end toward the camshaft. If there is excessive clearance between pin and bushing, replace the bushing and then ream it to an inside diameter of 0.2785–0.2790 in. (7.074–7.086mm). Bushings are pressed in. Loctite® may be used to fasten them in place if there is excessive clearance between outside of the bushing and the crankcase.

Crankshaft
TR, TRA AND S SERIES ENGINES

The crankshaft is removed after the gear cover has been removed, the connecting rod disconnected and raised up out of the way. Remove the flywheel nut, flywheel, and the woodruff key. The crankshaft may now be pulled out of the open end of the crankcase. When reinstalling the crankshaft, mount the flywheel after the crankshaft is inserted into the crankcase. The flywheel supports the crankshaft while the connecting rod is attached. The flywheel nut is tightened only enough to hold the flywheel during end-play adjustment.

Stator Plate and End-Play Adjustment

The end-play of the crankshaft is adjusted by the application of various size gaskets behind the stator plate, which doubles in function as the front bearing support and an adaptor for the magneto coil. The stator plate should not be removed from the crankcase unless it has to be replaced.

To remove the stator plate, remove the four retaining screws and tap the plate from the inside until it falls off. Reassemble the stator

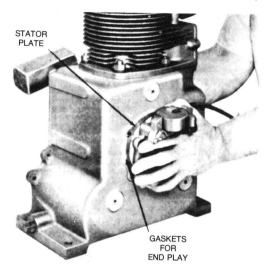

STATOR PLATE

GASKETS FOR END PLAY

Removal and installation of the stator plate

plate to the crankcase using new gaskets with the same total thickness as those originally installed. The stator plate mounting screws are to be torqued 8 ft. lbs. on all S, TR, and TRA series engines except the TRA–12D engine; tighten them on TRA–12D engines to 20–22 ft. lbs. End play is checked after the crankshaft, gear cover, and flywheel are mounted. End play is 0.002–0.005 in. (0.05–0.13mm) on S–7D and S–8D engines, and 0.001–0.004 (0.025–0.100mm) on TR–10D, TRA–10D, and TRA–12D.

Crankshaft end-play is measured with a dial indicator mounted on the PTO side of the crankshaft and a lever prying behind the flywheel. If new crankshaft roller bearings have been installed, they must be properly seated by tapping the ends of the crankshaft with a lead hammer before measuring the crankshaft end-play.

Crankshaft and End-Play

Remove the four main bearing plate capscrews at the power takeoff end. Pry off the plate and pull the crankshaft out.

On installation, use the same thickness of gaskets initially, and torque the mounting bolts to 10–12 ft. lbs. on ACN and BKN engines, and 20–22 ft. lbs. on AEN, AENL and AENS engines. Check the end play as described at the end of the section above. It should be 0.001–0.003 in. (0.025–0.076mm) on AEN, AENL and AENS engines, and 0.002–0.005 in. (0.05–0.13mm) on ACN and BKN engines. Change the gasket thicknesses in order to correct improper end play.

Make sure to align the punch mark on the front face of the crankshaft between two marked teeth of the camshaft gear.

Oil Pump

ACN AND BKN ENGINES

Drain the crankcase, place the engine on its side, and remove the engine base. Carefully note the order of disassembly of the check balls, springs, and other parts.

When assembling the pump, tap the check ball at the bottom of the pump very lightly with a punch and hammer to seat it. After the pump is assembled, fill the engine base with oil and work the pump plunger up and down with a screwdriver in order to check the pump's operation and fill the oil trough. Use a new base gasket and torque the bolts to 6–8 ft. lbs.

AEN, AENL AND AENS ENGINES

Remove the engine base by draining oil placing engine on its side, and then removing the capscrews and washers. Remove the two oil pump mounting capscrews and remove the oil pump. The main pump plunger, springs, and check balls come out the top, once the pump is away from the drive pushrod. The plug on the side of the discharge tube is removed to gain access to the discharge check ball and spring. Wash all parts in a good solvent.

New plunger-to-bore clearance is 0.003–0.005 in. (0.076–0.127mm). The limit is 0.008 in. (0.20mm). The pump should be replaced if the clearance is greater than the limit. Inspect the check ball seat in the bottom of the pump cylinder for wear, pitting, or dirt. Clean or replace the pump as necessary.

On reassembly:

1. Drop the intake check ball into the bottom of the pump cylinder and tap it very lightly in order to seat it. Insert the retainer, spring, and plunger into the bore. Install the discharge check ball and spring into the discharge tube.

2. Fill the engine base and put the oil pump into position. Operate the plunger with your

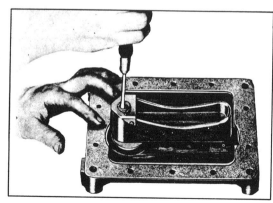

Priming ACN and BKN oil pump

finger to prime the pump and check operation. Install the oil pump mounting bolts.

3. Make sure the oil pump pushrod makes good contact with the plunger and the strainer screen is in good condition and properly mounted.

4. Install the engine base, using a new gasket. Torque the mounting bolts to 7–9 ft. lbs.

Break-In

An overhauled engine should be operated at 1600–1800 rpm with no load for one-half hour.

It should be operated at normal operating rpm, but still without load, for an additional four hours.

Valve Seat and Face Angle	Valve-to-Guide Clearance	
	Inlet	Exhaust
45°	0.001–0.003	0.003–0.005

Valve and guide measurements for BKN and all AE series engines.

19

Wisconsin Robin
2 through 12 Hp

IDENTIFICATION

There is an identification plate attached to the upper blower housing which lists the engine model on the left and individual engine serial number on the right. Both of these should be used when requesting parts. The engine models are EY25W and EY27W.

General Engine Specifications

Model	Bore & Stroke (in.)	Displacement (cu in.)	Horsepower @ RPM
EY25W	2.83 x 2.44	15.40	6.5 @ 3,600
EY27W	2.91 x 2.44	16.26	7.5 @ 3,600

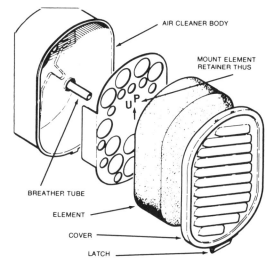

Exploded view of air cleaner

MAINTENANCE

Air Cleaner
SERVICE

The air cleaner should be serviced every 50 hours in normal operation, more often (daily) if the air is dusty.

First disassemble the unit as follows:

1. Remove the air cleaner cover, element and element retainer.

2. Disconnect the breather tube from the inspection cover.

3. Remove the two capscrews and remove the air cleaner body and gasket from the carburetor.

4. Wipe all metal parts clean. Wash the element only in either kerosene, or water and a liquid detergent. Do not wash in any other solvents.

5. Wrap the element in a cloth and squeeze it dry.

6. Pour engine oil into the filter until it is saturated, and then squeeze out the excess.

7. Reassemble in reversal of above. Make sure element retainer is installed with arrow up.

Lubrication
OIL AND FUEL RECOMMENDATIONS
Oil

Use only SG oils of the viscosity shown in the chart for both normal operation and break-in. See chart for crankcase capacities.

Fuel

Use only regular grade gasoline with an octane rating of 90 or above. Use only a reputable brand of fuel, and make sure it is free of both dirt and water. Note that low octane fuel may cause the engine to detonate and result in severe damage. Do not use gasoline that is more than one month old.

Oil Viscosity Chart

Season or Temperature	Grade of Oil*
Spring, Summer or Autumn (+120°F to +40°F)	SAE 30
Winter (+40°F to +15°F) (Below +15°F)	SAE 20 SAE 10W-30

*Use oils classified as Service MS or SD

	Crankcase Capacity	
Model		Capacity (pts.)
EY25W, EY27W		1.6

Spark Plug

The spark plug should be checked frequently for fouling, widened or otherwise improper gap, or more serious problems such as eroded electrodes or a cracked insulator. Clean carbon deposits from the electrodes with a wire brush, and set the gap to 0.020–0.025 in. (0.50–0.60mm) with a wire type feeler gauge. Bend only the side electrode. If electrodes are severely eroded so that the side electrode has lost its sharp, rectangular cross-section or the center electrode is very short, or if there are any cracks in the insulator, the spark plug should be replaced.

Always check the plug gap before installation, even if the plug is new. Install the plug with a new gasket and torque it to 24–27 ft. lbs.

Breaker Points

REMOVAL AND INSTALLATION

1. Remove the three mounting screws and remove the starter pulley. Install a 14mm socket wrench onto the flywheel nut and tap the wrench sharply with a soft hammer. If you have a wheel puller, remove the nut. Otherwise, un-

screw it until it is flush with the end of the crankshaft.

2. Remove the flywheel with a wheel puller or as follows:

3. Place a large screwdriver between the crankcase and the flywheel. The screwdriver must be in line with the keyway. While wedging the flywheel outward with the screwdriver, strike the outer end of the flywheel nut with a soft (brass, wood or plastic) hammer. This will bring the flywheel off the crankshaft taper.

4. Take off the point cover by removing mounting screws and pulling it off. Unscrew the terminal nut connecting condenser and coil wires to the contact set, and disconnect the wires. Remove the contact lockscrew, and remove the contacts.

5. Position the pin contacts on the crankcase, install the lockscrew, and tighten it just slightly.

6. Adjust the contact gap and time the engine as described below.

SETTING POINT GAP AND IGNITION TIMING

1. If necessary, remove the flywheel and point cover as described in Steps 1–4 above. Loosen the contact lockscrew.

2. Turn the engine over until the contact cam follower is at the very peak of the cam. Using a flat 0.014 feeler gauge, slide the points back and forth via the adjusting knob until the gauge just slides between the contact surfaces. Tighten the contact lockscrew. Recheck gap and, if necessary, reset it.

3. Connect a timing light between the coil primary ground. Align the **M** timing mark on the rim of the flywheel with the **D** mark on the lower left side of the crankcase by rotating the flywheel. See illustration.

4. Turn the flywheel counterclockwise slowly until the light either goes on or goes off, depending on the type. Turn it very slowly clockwise just until the light reacts again. If the timing marks are aligned, timing is correct. If the **M** mark is below the **D** mark (the **D** is on the

Tune-Up Specifications

Model	Plug Type	Plug Gap (in.)	Point Gap (in.)	Ignition Timing (deg Before Top Center)
EY25W	①	.020–.025	.014	23
EY27W	①	.020–.025	.014	23

① 14 mm. Champion L86,
    AC 44F
    NGK B6HS

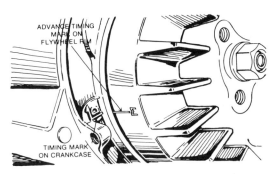

Aligning ignition timing marks

crankcase), the breaker gap is too large; if the **M** is above the **D**, the breaker gap is too small. Reset the contact gap as necessary. If timing is off about 2° or ⅛ in. (3mm) of flywheel rotation, the gap must be changed about 0.001 in. (0.025mm).

5. Reset the contact gap and recheck timing until timing is correct.

6. Remove the timing light and install the timing cover and flywheel. In installing the flywheel, slide it into place with key and keyway aligned, and then install retaining nut and tighten it just until lockwasher collapses. Finally, put a wrench on the nut and tap it lightly once or twice, or torque the nut to 44–47 ft. lbs. with a torque wrench.

Magneto Service

1. If the engine is hard to start or runs erratically, first service the spark plug. If this does not cure the problem, remove the flywheel and check for loose or broken ignition wires. Inspect the points. See "Breaker Point Removal and Installation," above. Repair the wires or replace the points and condenser. Set the point gap and timing, as required.

2. Check the spark by removing the plug and grounding it against the engine block with the high tension wire connected. Then, spin the engine. If the spark is erratic or weak, remove the ignition coil by removing the flywheel, feeding the high tension wire through the grommet in the wall of the cylinder block, disconnecting the primary wire, and removing the mounting screws and coil. Replace the coil in reverse of the above.

Governor

If the governor lever has been loosened or removed, perform the governor lever adjustment. Otherwise, skip to "Speed Regulation," below.

GOVERNOR LEVER ADJUSTMENT

1. Mount the governor lever with the clamp screw just slightly loose.

2. Install both the control rod and spring which connect the governor lever and the throttle lever. Mount the control lever assembly onto the crankcase but do not tighten the wingnut.

3. Connect the governor spring between the holes of both governor lever and control lever as shown in the illustration below.

4. Turn the control lever counterclockwise until the throttle in the carburetor is fully open. Lock the lever in this position by tightening the wingnut.

5. With the clamp screw loose so the governor shaft will turn independently of the governor lever, turn the governor shaft (use a screw-

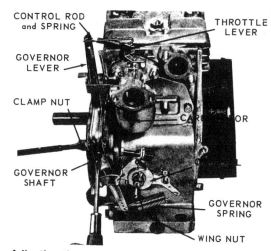

Adjusting the governor lever

driver in the groove in the end of the shaft) until you can feel the internal vane stop against the flywheel thrust sleeve (this is as far as the shaft can be turned without excessive force). Tighten the lever clamp nut.

SPEED REGULATION

1. Remove the load from the engine, and run it until it is hot.

2. Install the governor spring hooked to holes **1** and **B** as shown above.

3. Loosen the control lever wing nut so that the lever is free to move. Loosen the locknut on the adjusting screw. Find the desired no-load speed on the chart above that corresponds with the speed at which you want the engine to run when fully loaded.

4. Hold the control lever down so the adjusting screw is against the crankcase stop.

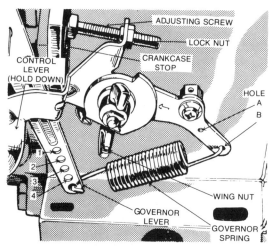

Adjusting governor speed

Governor No-Load/Load RPM Chart

Load RPM	No Load RPM		Spring Holes	
	EY25W	EY27W	EY25W	EY27W
1800	2330	2210	1-B	1-B
2000	2445	2375	1-B	1-B
2200	2595	2500	1-B	1-B
2400	2745	2660	1-B	1-B
2600	2900	2850	1-B	1-B
2800	3065	3020	1-B	1-B
3000	3230	3210	1-B	1-B
3200	3400	3385	1-B	1-B
3400	3580	3590	1-B	1-B
3600	3765	3760	1-B	1-B

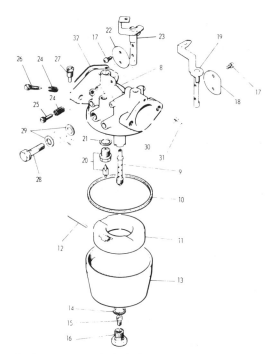

Carburetor—exploded view

5. Turn the adjusting screw in or out until the required no-load speed is obtained. Tighten the adjusting screw locknut.

6. if the engine is to operate at a fixed speed, tighten the control lever wingnut.

Carburetor

OVERHAUL

1. Using the illustration as a guide, remove the choke phillips head screws (17), and then take out the choke valve and shaft (18 and 19).

2. Remove the choke shaft retainer spring and ball (30 and 31) to prevent their being lost.

3. Remove the throttle plate phillips head screws (17) and take out the choke valve and shaft (18 and 19), being careful not to damage the edges of the throttle valve.

4. Remove the throttle stop screw and spring (14 and 25).

5. Remove the main jet holder (16) and then take off the float bowl (13).

6. Remove the main jet from the (15) jet holder.

7. Remove the main nozzle (9) from the carburetor body.

8. Remove the idle jet (27) using an appropriate tool to prevent damage to it.

9. Remove the float pin (12), float (11), and needle vale (20).

10. Inspect the float. Replace it if dented, fuel has leaked in, or if the float hinge pin or the tab that limits float travel is worn.

11. Clean all parts thoroughly in a solvent such as Bendix Metalclene or Speeclene, rinse in a cleaning solvent, and blow out all passages with low pressure compressed air in the reverse direction of normal flow. Make sure all carbon deposits have been removed from the throttle bore and idle discharge holes.

NOTE: *Never use a drill or wire to clean jets!*

12. Reassemble, keeping the following points in mind:

a. Replace the needle valve and seat with a matched valve and seat (as included in a repair kit).

b. Install the new idle jet and adjusting screw which are included in the repair kit. Make sure the idle jet is tightened firmly.

c. Install the new main jet, tighten securely, and then install the main jet holder and torque to 5.5 ft. lbs.

d. When assembling the choke, make sure the flat on the choke valve faces the main air jet.

ENGINE OVERHAUL

Tools

To overhaul this engine, which uses metric fasteners, you should have the following tools:

- 10mm thin wall socket
- 10mm standard socket
- 10mm deep socket
- 12mm, 14mm and 18mm standard sockets.
- 10mm, 12mm, and 14mm open end wrenches.

In addition, various special pullers, a valve spring compressor, and a valve set cutter are required. See the illustration. Wisconsin-Robin part numbers are provided for your use in ordering the tools either from them or from a tool manufacturer who makes equivalent tools which are cross-referenced.

The tools and Wisconsin-Robin part numbers are listed below:

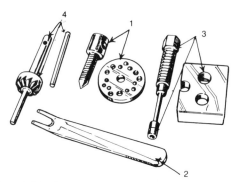

Special tools

Reference Number	Part Number	Part Name
1.	EYY790-350	Flywheel Puller
	EY016508500	Bolt, 8 x 50 mm (3 required)
2.	EYY790-282	Valve Spring Compressor
3.	EYY790-524	Valve Guide Puller
4.	EYH640-118	Seat Cutter (45°)

Engine Overhaul

Engine disassembly instructions are provided below, in proper sequence. Reassembly is primarily a simple reversal of disassembly. Notes on the extra procedures to be performed as the engine is put back together are included with the disassembly instructions for each part of the engine.

FUEL TANK

1. Disconnect the fuel line at the carburetor. Note that in reassembly, it is advisable to use a new fuel line.
2. Remove the fuel tank from the bracket.
3. Remove the tank bracket from the cylinder head.
4. In reassembly, wash the element per "Air Cleaner Service" instructions above, and correctly mount the element retainer as illustrated there.

FLYWHEEL SHROUD

1. Disconnect the coil primary wire from the stop button wire.
2. Remove the flywheel shroud from the cylinder case, and the baffle from the head.
3. Remove the baffle from the cylinder block.

AIR CLEANER

1. Remove the air cleaner cover, element and element retainer.
2. Disconnect the breather tube from the inspection cover.
3. Remove the two capscrews and remove the air cleaner body and gasket from the carburetor.

MUFFLER

Remove the two hex nuts and remove the muffler and gasket from cylinder case.

GOVERNOR LEVER AND CARBURETOR

1. Disconnect the governor spring from the lever and speed control assembly.
2. Remove the governor lever from the shaft, and, at the same time, disconnect the rod and spring from the lever and carburetor.
3. Remove the tow nuts and lockwashers, and remove the carburetor, insulating plate and gaskets from the cylinder case.
4. If necessary, the speed control assembly can be removed from the side of the crankcase by removing the wing nut and clip.
5. In reassembly, refer to "Governor Adjustment" above.

STARTING PULLEY AND FLYWHEEL

1. To remove the starting pulley, first remove the three mounting screws.
2. Place a 14mm socket wrench on the flywheel nut and give the wrench a sharp blow with a soft hammer. Remove the nut, spring washer and pulley.
3. Attach puller to flywheel—turn center bolt clockwise until flywheel becomes loose enough to be removed. If puller is not available, screw flywheel nut flush with end of crankshaft to protect shaft threads from being damaged. Place the end of a large screwdriver between the crankcase and flywheel in line with the keyway. Then, strike the end of the flywheel nut with a babbitt or other soft hammer and at the same time wedge outward with the screwdriver.
4. Disconnect the high tension cable from the spark plug, and slip the cable along with the rubber grommet through the hole, to the inside of the crankcase. Then remove the ignition coil along with the attached high tension cable by taking out the two mounting screws, and disconnecting the breaker assembly wire.

5. Remove the contact breaker and condenser by removing the point cover, and removing mounting screws from the cylinder case. Slip the coil primary wire along with the grommet through the hole in the side of the crankcase.

6. In reassembly, refer to "Setting Point Gap and Timing."

7. Securely tighten the flywheel nut after the timing is finalized, but first be sure the woodruff key is in position on the shaft. Do not drive the flywheel onto the taper of the crankshaft and do not overtighten the flywheel nut. Simply turn the nut until the lockwasher collapses. Then, tighten it by placing a wrench on the nut and giving the handle of the wrench 1 or 2 sharp blows with a soft hammer. If a torque wrench is available, tighten to 44–47 ft. lbs.

CYLINDER HEAD AND SPARK PLUG

1. Remove the spark plug from the cylinder head.

2. Loosen the mounting nuts and remove the cylinder head along with the gasket.

3. Clean the carbon from the combustion chamber and the dirt from among the cooling fins. Check the cylinder head mounting face for distortion. If warpage is evident, replace head.

4. In reassembly, use a new cylinder head gasket and spark plug. Torque the head nuts to 22 ft. lbs. Leave the spark plug out temporarily, for each in turning engine over for the remainder of assembly and for timing adjustments. When installing the spark plug, tighten it 24–27 ft. lbs. torque.

INTAKE AND EXHAUST VALVES

1. Remove the valve inspection cover, breather plate and gaskets from the cylindercase.

2. Lift the valve springs, by means of a compressor tool EYY790–282 or equivalent and remove the retainer locks with long nose pliers. Release the compressor tool and remove the intake valve and exhaust valve along with their respective spring and retainer. A standard Automotive type valve lifter can be used for removing valves, but is not practical for reassembly.

CAUTION: *Do not damage the gasket surface of the tappet chamber with the compressor tool.*

3. Clean carbon and gum deposits from the valves, seats, ports and guides.

4. In reassembly, replace valves that are badly burned, pitted or warped.

5. Correct the valve seat by using a 45° seat cutter tool No. EYH640–118 or equivalent as illustrated. The finished seat width should be 0.047–0.059 in. (1.2–1.5mm) – maximum usable width is 0.098 in. (2.5mm).

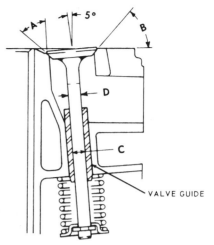

A – VALVE FACE ANGLE	45°
B – SEAT ANGLE	45°
C – GUIDE INSIDE DIAMETER	0.2756 to 0.2770"
D – VALVE STEM DIAMETER	0.273 to 0.274"
MAXIMUM ALLOWABLE CLEARANCE BETWEEN C AND D	0.006"

Valve Specifications

CAUTION: *Do not use an electric power driven grinding wheel to correct the valve seats.*

6. Valve guides should be replaced when the valve stem clearance becomes excessive. Use a valve guide puller tool EYY790–324 or equivalent. See illustration. Draw the valve guides out and press new guides in using the same puller tool. Refer to the illustration for clearance specifications and proper assembly.

7. After correcting the valve seats and replacing the valve guides, lap the valves in place until a uniform ring will show entirely around the face of the valve. Clean the valves, and wash the block thoroughly with a hot solution of soap and water. Wipe the cylinder walls with clean, lint free rags and light engine oil. Do not assemble the valve springs until the tappet clearance has been checked. See "Tappet Adjustment" below.

TAPPET ADJUSTMENT

With the tappet in its lowest position, hold valve down and insert a feeler gauge between the valve and tappet stem. The clearance for both intake and exhaust, with the engine cold is 0.006–0.008 in. (0.15–0.20mm).

Valve Specifications

If the clearance is less than it should be, grind the end of valve stem a very little at a time and remeasure. Stems must be ground square and flat.

If the clearance is too large, sink the valve seat with seat cutter tool.

After obtaining the correct clearance, assemble the valve springs and retainers, and secure them in place with the retainer locks. Check the operation of the valves by turning the crankshaft over by hand and remeasure the tappet clearance.

GEAR COVER AND CRANKSHAFT REMOVAL

1. Place a rag under the engine to absorb the remaining oil. Remove the gear cover mounting screws.

2. With a soft hammer, tap at even intervals around the outer surface of the gear cover until it breaks free of the crankcase face. Break the cover free carefully, so as to avoid damaging the oil seal.

3. Inspect the adjusting collar, oil seal, governor shaft and yoke. Replace any parts that are damaged or excessively worn.

4. Remove the flywheel woodruff key.

5. Pull the crankshaft out from open end of crankcase and take care not to damage the oil seal. If necessary, loosen shaft by tapping lightly at the flywheel end with a soft hammer.

NOTE: *The "Gear Cover and Crankshaft Installation" procedure is located with camshaft, connecting rod, and piston service, since that is the normal sequence of doing overhaul work.*

CAMSHAFT, TAPPETS AND TIMING MARKS

1. To prevent the tappets from falling out and becoming damaged when the camshaft is removed, turn the crankcase over on its side as shown. Push the tappets inward to clear the cam lobes, and remove the camshaft.

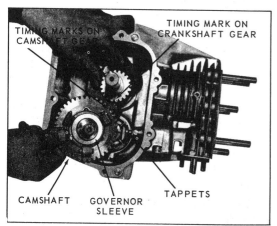

Postion in which engine should be placed while removing camshaft

2. Withdraw the tappets and mark them for identification with the hole from which they were removed.

3. In reassembly, put the tappets back in their corresponding guide hole. This will eliminate unnecessary valve stem grinding for obtaining correct tappet clearance.

4. Mount governor sleeve on end of camshaft by holding the shaft in a vertical position with the flyweights hanging down. Align the groove in the flange with the pin in the gear face and install the sleeve on shaft so that its flange fits in the groove between the heavy end and the thrust tabs of all three flyweights. Mount camshaft assembly in crankcase.

5. The timing marks on the camshaft gear and crankshaft gear must be matched up. Mount the camshaft so that the marked tooth on crankshaft gear is between the two marked teeth of the camshaft gear, see the illustration. If the valve timing is off, the engine will not function properly or may not run at all.

CONNECTING ROD AND PISTON

Disassembly

1. Straighten out the bent tabs of the lock plate and remove the bolts from the connecting rod.

2. Remove lock plate, oil dipper and connecting rod cap.

3. Scrape off all carbon deposits that might interfere with the removal of the piston from the upper end of the cylinder. Use a ridge reamer.

4. Turn the crankshaft until the piston is at top, then push the connecting rod and piston assembly upward and out through the top of the cylinder.

5. Remove the piston from connecting rod by taking out one of the snap rings and then removing the piston pin. A new snap ring should be used in reassembly.

Reassembly

1. Use a ring expander tool to prevent the ring from becoming distorted or broken when installing on the piston.

2. If an expander tool is not available, install the rings by placing the open end of the ring on the first land of the piston. Spread the ring only far enough to slip it over the piston and into the correct groove, being careful not to distort the ring.

3. With the expander tool, assemble the bottom ring first and work upward, installing the top ring last.

4. Mount the scraper ring with the scraper edge down, otherwise oil pumping and excessive oil consumption will result. Refer to the illustration for correct placement of rings.

5. Measure the diameter of the piston in the

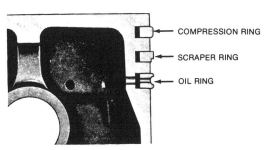

Location and positioning of rings

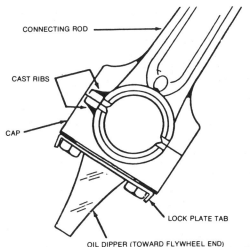

OIL DIPPER (TOWARD FLYWHEEL END)
MOUNT TOWARD GEAR COVER IF OPERATING
TILT IS TOWARD TAKE-OFF END.

Connecting rod and oil dipper assembly

center of the thrust faces at the bottom of the piston skirt, as illustrated.

6. Measure the cylinder bore and inspect it for out-of-round and taper. If the cylinder is scored or worn more than 0.005 in. (0.127mm) over standard size, it should be rebored and fitted with an oversize piston and rings. Refer to the chart for the clearance between the piston and cylinder. Size, clearance and wear limits are given in more detail at the end of this chapter.

7. When installing the piston in the cylinder, oil the piston, rings, wrist pin, rod bearings and cylinder wall before assembly. Stagger the piston ring gaps 90° apart around the piston. Use a piston ring compressor.

8. Turn the crankshaft to the bottom of the stroke and tap the piston down until the rod contacts the crankpin. Mount the connecting rod cap so that the cast rib between the face of rod and bolt boss matches up with the cast rib on the connecting rod. Assemble oil dipper to cap. The dipper should be toward the gear cover end of the connecting rod cap if engine is operated on a tilt toward the take off end. Mount the dipper toward the flywheel end if it's tilted in that direction or with a no tilt operation.

Install a new rod bolt lock plate. Mount the connecting rod bolts and tighten to 14.5–18.0 ft. lbs.

Check for free movement of the connection rod by turning the crankshaft over slowly. If

PISTON TO CYLINDER AT PISTON SKIRT THRUST FACE		EY18W	EY25W	EY27W
		.0016 .0032"	.0024 .0039"	.0028 .0052"
CONNECTING ROD TO CRANK PIN	DIA.	.0021 .0031"	.0016 .0026"	.0016 .0026"
	SIDE	.008 .0235"	.004 .012"	.004 .012"
PISTON PIN TO CONNECTING ROD		.0004 .0012"	.0006 .0014"	.0006 .0014"
D - CRANKSHAFT PIN DIAMETER		1.0210 1.0215"	1.1003 1.1008"	1.1003 1.1008"
W - CRANKSHAFT PIN WIDTH		.9846 .9882"	1.0630 1.0669"	1.0630 1.0669"
PISTON RING GAP		.002 .010"	.002 .010"	.008 .016"
PISTON RINGS – SIDE CLEARANCE IN GROOVES		.0004 .0030"	.0004 .0030"	.0004 .0022"
PISTON PIN TO PISTON		.00035" tight to .00039" loose		

STANDARD CRANK PIN DIMENSIONS

Piston, ring, and rod clearance specifications

satisfactory, bend the tabs on the lock plate against the hex head flat of the connecting rod bolts.

GEAR COVER AND CRANKSHAFT INSTALLATION

1. In reassembly, inspect the crankcase oil seal and main bearing for possible replacement.

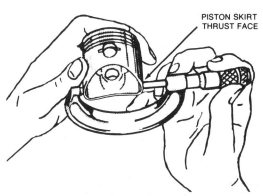

Measure piston diameter as shown

Mount the crankshaft with extreme care so as not to damage the lips of the oil seal. Use an oil seal sleeve if available.

2. End Play is regulated by means of the adjusting collar at the gear end of the crankshaft. This should be set immediately before mounting the gear cover as explained below.

NOTE: *Crankshaft End Play is regulated by the length of the adjusting collar. The end play should be 0.001–0.009 in. (0.025–0.230mm), engine cold. The adjusting collar is located between the crankshaft gear and main bearing at the take-off end of the engine. Replacement of the collar is seldom necessary unless the crankshaft or gear cover is replaced. To determine what length adjusting collar to use, refer to the illustration and steps below.*

1. With the gear cover removed, tap the end of the crankshaft slightly to insure that the shaft is shouldered against the front end main bearing.

2. Use a depth micrometer and measure the distance between the machined surface of crankcase face and end of crank gear — dimension **A**.

3. Measure the distance between the machined surface of gear cover and end of main bearing — dimension **B**.

4. The compressed thickness of gear cover gasket is 0.007 in. (0.18mm) — dimension **C**.

5. Select an adjusting collar that is 0.001–0.009 in. (0.025–0.230mm) less than the total length of **A, B,** and **C** from the chart.

6. Apply oil to the bearing surfaces, gear train and tappets. Also lubricate the lips of the

Adjusting Collar Dimension Chart

Model	Collar Length	Part Number
EY25W	.740 to .748″	EY25W2112a
EY27W	.748 to .756″	EY25W2112b
	.756 to .764″	EY25W2112c

oil seal and add a light film of oil on the gear cover face to hold the gasket in place.

7. Mount the adjusting collar to the crankshaft with the recess toward the crank gear.

8. Assemble the gear cover, being sure that the governor yoke is in a downward position, and be extremely careful not to damage the lips of the oil seal. If available, mount on oil seal sleeve on the crankshaft to prevent damage to the oil seal lips.

CAUTION: *Be sure the timing marks on the crankshaft and camshaft gear remain correctly mated when the end of the camshaft is fitted into the bearing hole of the gear cover.*

9. Tap the gear cover in place with a soft hammer, remove the oil seal sleeve and tighten the gear cover capscrews to 13 ft. lbs. torque.

10. Tap the end of the crankshaft with a soft hammer so that the crankshaft will shoulder against the main bearing at the flywheel end.

11. Tap the crankshaft in the opposite direction (from flywheel end) to seat the adjusting collar against the main bearing at the takeoff end.

12. Attach a dial indicator to one of the $5/16$–24 tapped holes on the face of the crankcase with the indicator plunger resting against the end of the crankshaft and set the dial at 0.

13. Wedge a screwdriver between the flywheel and the crankcase. The movement of the flywheel away from the engine block will register as end play on the indicator dial.

14. If end play is not within the limits of 0.007–0.009 in. (0.025–0.230mm), use the reading from the indicator dial to determine the new length adjusting collar to use. Replace the collar with one of the proper dimension, if necessary.

FINAL CHECKOUT AND BREAK-IN

After the major moving parts are assembled, turn the engine over using the starter pulley. Make sure it turns without unusual resistance. Check the basic ignition adjustments (point gap and timing), and make preliminary carburetor and governor adjustments. Refill the crankcase and fuel tank.

Break the engine in by running it as specified on the chart below, proceeding from top to bottom. Check the engine frequently for leaks, and make final carburetor and governor adjustments during the sequence.

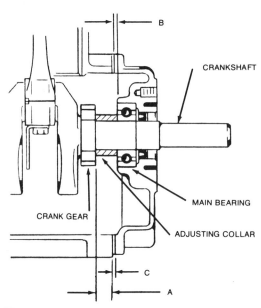

Measuring points for dimensions critical to crankshaft end play adjustment

Break-in Sequence

Load			Speed	Time
No load			2500 rpm	10 minutes
No load			3000 rpm	10 minutes
No load			3600 rpm	10 minutes
1.75 hp	2.5 hp	2.65 hp	3600 rpm	30 minutes
3.5 hp	5.0 hp	5.3 hp	3600 rpm	60 minutes

Torque Specifications
All figures in ft. lbs.

	Model EY25W	Model EY27W
Cylinder head nuts	24.5 to 27	†
Connecting rod bolts	14.5 to 18	†
Flywheel nut	*	*
Spark plug	*	*
Gear cover screws	*	*

Clearances and Wear Limits

Description	Model EY25W		Model EY27W	
	Tol	Limit	Tol	Limit
Flatness of cylinder head	.002	.006	†	†
Cylinder bore	2.8346 2.8354	2.841	2.9134 2.9141	2.9197
Bore-out of round	*	*	*	*
Cylindricity (taper)	*	*	*	*
Valve seat width	*	*	*	*
Valve guide bore	*	*	*	*
Piston diameter at skirt thrust faces (standard size)	2.8315 2.8323	2.8285	2.9090 2.9105	2.9072
Piston to cylinder clearance at skirt thrust faces	.0024 to .0039	.009	.0028 to .0052	.009
Ring groove width (top and 2nd ring)	*	*	.0787 .0797	.0852
Ring groove width (oil ring)	*	*	*	*
Ring width (top and 2nd ring)	*	*	.0776 .0783	.0741
Ring width (oil ring)	*	*	*	*
Piston rings—side clearance in groove	*	*	.0004 .0022	.006
Ring gap (at cylinder skirt)	*	*	.008 .016	.040
Pin hole in piston	.6297 .6301	.6311	†	†
Piston pin diameter	.6297 .6300	.6287	†	†
Piston pin to piston fit	*	*	*	*
Connecting rod (crank pin end)	1.1024 1.1029	1.104	†	†
Crank pin diameter	1.1003 1.1008	1.0983	†	†
Connecting rod to crank pin clearance	.0016 to .0026	.005	†	†
Connecting rod side clearance	.004 .012	.039	†	†

Clearances and Wear Limits (cont.)

Description	Model EY25W		Model EY27W	
	Tol	Limit	Tol	Limit
Connecting rod (piston pin end)	.6306 .6311	.6345	†	†
Piston pin to connecting rod clearance	.0006 to .0014	.0032	†	†
Con. rod—large and small bore alignment (parallel)	*	*	*	*
Con. rod—large and small bore centers	4.3307	4.3366	†	†
Crank pin—out of round	—	*	—	*
Cylindricity (taper)	—	*	—	*
Crank pin—parallel	—	*	—	*
Crankshaft journal diameter (take-off end)	1.1805 1.1809	1.1785	†	†
Crankshaft journal (flywheel end)	1.1806 1.1810	1.179	†	†
Crankshaft end play	*	—	*	—
Camshaft (cam rise)	*	*	*	*
Camshaft (journal diameter)	*	*	*	*
Valve spring (free height)	*	*	*	*
Valve spring (squareness)	—	*	—	*
Valve stem diameter	*	*	*	*
Valve stem clearance to guide	*	*	*	*
Valve stem—lock-pl. to groove clearance	*	*	*	*
Valve—length from groove to stem end	*	*	*	*
Valve—tappet clearance	*	*	*	*
Tappet—length	2.004	1.994	†	†
Tappet—stem to guide clearance	*	*	*	*
Ignition timing	*	—	*	—
Breaker contact opening	*	—	*	—
Spark plug gap	*	—	*	—
Spark plug	14 mm, Champ. L86, AC 44F, NGK B6HS			

*Model EY18W dimensions and specifications apply to Models EY25W and EY27W
†Model EY25W dimensions and specifications apply to Model EY27W

Mechanic's Data

General Conversion Table

Multiply By	To Convert	To	
		LENGTH	
2.54	Inches	Centimeters	.3937
25.4	Inches	Millimeters	.03937
30.48	Feet	Centimeters	.0328
.304	Feet	Meters	3.28
.914	Yards	Meters	1.094
1.609	Miles	Kilometers	.621
		VOLUME	
.473	Pints	Liters	2.11
.946	Quarts	Liters	1.06
3.785	Gallons	Liters	.264
.016	Cubic inches	Liters	61.02
16.39	Cubic inches	Cubic cms.	.061
28.3	Cubic feet	Liters	.0353
		MASS (Weight)	
28.35	Ounces	Grams	.035
.4536	Pounds	Kilograms	2.20
—	**To obtain**	**From**	**Multiply by**

Multiply By	To Convert	To	
		AREA	
.645	Square inches	Square cms.	.155
.836	Square yds.	Square meters	1.196
		FORCE	
4.448	Pounds	Newtons	.225
.138	Ft./lbs.	Kilogram/meters	7.23
1.36	Ft./lbs.	Newton-meters	.737
.112	In./lbs.	Newton-meters	8.844
		PRESSURE	
.068	Psi	Atmospheres	14.7
6.89	Psi	Kilopascals	.145
		OTHER	
1.104	Horsepower (DIN)	Horsepower (SAE)	.9861
.746	Horsepower (SAE)	Kilowatts (KW)	1.34
1.60	Mph	Km/h	.625
.425	Mpg	Km/1	2.35
—	**To obtain**	**From**	**Multiply by**

Tap Drill Sizes

National Coarse or U.S.S.		
Screw & Tap Size	Threads Per Inch	Use Drill Number
No. 5	40	39
No. 6	32	36
No. 8	32	29
No. 10	24	25
No. 12	24	17
1/4	20	8
5/16	18	F
3/8	16	5/16
7/16	14	U
1/2	13	27/64
9/16	12	31/64
5/8	11	17/32
3/4	10	21/32
7/8	9	49/64

National Coarse or U.S.S.		
Screw & Tap Size	Threads Per Inch	Use Drill Number
1	8	7/8
1 1/8	7	63/64
1 1/4	7	1 7/64
1 1/2	6	1 11/32

National Fine or S.A.E.		
Screw & Tap Size	Threads Per Inch	Use Drill Number
No. 5	44	37
No. 6	40	33
No. 8	36	29
No. 10	32	21

National Fine or S.A.E.		
Screw & Tap Size	Threads Per Inch	Use Drill Number
No. 12	28	15
1/4	28	3
6/16	24	1
3/8	24	Q
7/16	20	W
1/2	20	29/64
9/16	18	33/64
5/8	18	37/64
3/4	16	11/16
7/8	14	13/16
1 1/8	12	1 3/64
1 1/4	12	1 11/64
1 1/2	12	1 27/64

Drill Sizes In Decimal Equivalents

Inch	Decimal	Wire	mm	Inch	Decimal	Wire	mm	Inch	Decimal	Wire & Letter	mm	Inch	Decimal	Letter	mm	Inch	Decimal	mm
1/64	.0156		.39		.0730	49			.1614		4.1		.2717		6.9		.4331	11.0
	.0157		.4		.0748		1.9		.1654		4.2		.2720	I		7/16	.4375	11.11
	.0160	78			.0760	48			.1660	19			.2756		7.0		.4528	11.5
	.0165		.42		.0768		1.95		.1673		4.25		.2770	J		29/64	.4531	11.51
	.0173		.44	5/64	.0781		1.98		.1693		4.3		.2795		7.1	15/32	.4688	11.90
	.0177		.45		.0785	47			.1695	18			.2810	K			.4724	12.0
	.0180	77			.0787		2.0	11/64	.1719		4.36	9/32	.2812		7.14	31/64	.4844	12.30
	.0181		.46		.0807		2.05		.1730	17			.2835		7.2		.4921	12.5
	.0189		.48		.0810	46			.1732		4.4		.2854		7.25	1/2	.5000	12.70
	.0197		.5		.0820	45			.1770	16			.2874		7.3		.5118	13.0
	.0200	76			.0827		2.1		.1772		4.5		.2900	L		33/64	.5156	13.09
	.0210	75			.0846		2.15		.1800	15			.2913		7.4	17/32	.5312	13.49
	.0217		.55		.0860	44			.1811		4.6		.2950	M			.5315	13.5
	.0225	74			.0866		2.2		.1820	14			.2953		7.5	35/64	.5469	13.89
	.0236		.6		.0886		2.25		.1850	13		19/64	.2969		7.54		.5512	14.0
	.0240	73			.0890	43			.1850		4.7		.2992		7.6	9/16	.5625	14.28
	.0250	72			.0906		2.3		.1870		4.75		.3020	N			.5709	14.5
	.0256		.65		.0925		2.35	3/16	.1875		4.76		.3031		7.7	37/64	.5781	14.68
	.0260	71			.0935	42			.1890		4.8		.3051		7.75		.5906	15.0
	.0276		.7	3/32	.0938		2.38		.1890	12			.3071		7.8	19/32	.5938	15.08
	.0280	70			.0945		2.4		.1910	11			.3110		7.9	39/64	.6094	15.47
	.0292	69			.0960	41			.1929		4.9	5/16	.3125		7.93		.6102	15.5
	.0295		.75		.0965		2.45		.1935	10			.3150		8.0	5/8	.6250	15.87
	.0310	68			.0980	40			.1960	9			.3160	O			.6299	16.0
1/32	.0312		.79		.0981		2.5		.1969		5.0		.3189		8.1	41/64	.6406	16.27
	.0315		.8		.0995	39			.1990	8			.3228		8.2		.6496	16.5
	.0320	67			.1015	38			.2008		5.1		.3230	P		21/32	.6562	16.66
	.0330	66			.1024		2.6		.2010	7			.3248		8.25		.6693	17.0
	.0335		.85		.1040	37		13/64	.2031		5.16	21/64	.3281		8.33	43/64	.6719	17.06
	.0350	65			.1063		2.7		.2040	6			.3307		8.4	11/16	.6875	17.46
	.0354		.9		.1065	36			.2047		5.2		.3320	Q			.6890	17.5
	.0360	64			.1083		2.75		.2055	5			.3346		8.5	45/64	.7031	17.85
	.0370	63		7/64	.1094		2.77		.2067		5.25		.3386		8.6		.7087	18.0
	.0374		.95		.1100	35			.2087		5.3		.3390	R		23/32	.7188	18.25
	.0380	62			.1102		2.8		.2090	4			.3425		8.7		.7283	18.5
	.0390	61			.1110	34			.2126		5.4	11/32	.3438		8.73	47/64	.7344	18.65
	.0394		1.0		.1130	33			.2130	3			.3445		8.75		.7480	19.0
	.0400	60			.1142		2.9		.2165		5.5		.3465		8.8	3/4	.7500	19.05
	.0410	59			.1160	32		7/32	2188		5.55		.3480	S		49/64	.7656	19.44
	.0413		1.05		.1181		3.0		.2205		5.6						.7677	19.5
	.0420	58			.1200	31			.2210	2			.3504		8.9	25/32	.7812	19.84
	.0430	57			.1220		3.1		.2244		5.7		.3543		9.0		.7874	20.0
	.0433		1.1	1/8	.1250		3.17		.2264		5.75		.3580	T		51/64	.7969	20.24
	.0453		1.15		.1260		3.2		.2280	1			.3583		9.1		.8071	20.5
	.0465	56			.1280		3.25		.2283		5.8	23/64	.3594		9.12	13/16	.8125	20.63
3/64	.0469		1.19		.1285	30			.2323		5.9		.3622		9.2		.8268	21.0
	.0472		1.2		.1299		3.3		.2340	A			.3642		9.25	53/64	.8281	21.03
	.0492		1.25		.1339		3.4	15/64	.2344		5.95		.3661		9.3	27/32	.8438	21.43
	.0512		1.3		.1360	29			.2362		6.0		.3680	U			.8465	21.5
	.0520	55			.1378		3.5		.2380	B			.3701		9.4	55/64	.8594	21.82
	.0531		1.35		.1405	28			.2402		6.1		.3740		9.5		.8661	22.0
	.0550	54		9/64	.1406		3.57		.2420	C		3/8	.3750		9.52	7/8	.8750	22.22
	.0551		1.4		.1417		3.6		.2441		6.2		.3770	V			.8858	22.5
	.0571		1.45		.1440	27			.2460	D			.3780		9.6	57/64	.8906	22.62
	.0591		1.5		.1457		3.7		.2461		6.25		.3819		9.7		.9055	23.0
	.0595	53			.1470	26			.2480		6.3		.3839		9.75	29/32	.9062	23.01
	.0610		1.55		.1476		3.75	1/4	.2500	E	6.35		.3858		9.8	59/64	.9219	23.41
1/16	.0625		1.59		.1495	25			.2520		6.		.3860	W			.9252	23.5
	.0630		1.6		.1496		3.8		.2559		6.5		.3898		9.9	15/16	.9375	23.81
	.0635	52			.1520	24			.2570	F		25/64	.3906		9.92		.9449	24.0
	.0650		1.65		.1535		3.9		.2598		6.6		.3937		10.0	61/64	.9531	24.2
	.0669		1.7		.1540	23			.2610	G			.3970	X			.9646	24.5
	.0670	51		5/32	.1562		3.96		.2638		6.7		.4040	Y		31/32	.9688	24.6
	.0689		1.75		.1570	22		17/64	.2656		6.74	13/32	.4062		10.31		.9843	25.0
	.0700	50			.1575		4.0		.2657		6.75		.4130	Z		63/64	.9844	25.0
	.0709		1.8		.1590	21			.2660	H			.4134		10.5	1	1.0000	25.4
	.0728		1.85		.1610	20			.2677		6.8	27/64	.4219		10.71			